The Routledge Companion to Ethnic Marketing

The globalization of marketing has brought about an interesting paradox: as the discipline becomes more global, the need to understand cultural differences becomes all the more crucial. This is the challenge in an increasingly international marketplace, and a problem that the world's most powerful businesses must solve. From this challenge has grown the exciting discipline of ethnic marketing, which seeks to understand the considerable opportunities and challenges presented by cultural and ethnic diversity in the marketplace.

To date, scholarship in the area has been lively but disparate. This volume brings together cutting-edge research on ethnic marketing from thought leaders across the world. Each chapter covers a key theme, reflecting the increasing diversity of the latest research, including models of culture change, parenting and socialization, responses to web and advertising, role of space and social innovation in ethnic marketing, ethnic consumer decision making, religiosity, differing attitudes to materialism, acculturation, targeting and ethical and public policy issues.

The result is a solid framework and a comprehensive reference point for consumer researchers, students and practitioners.

Ahmad Jamal is Senior Lecturer in Marketing and Strategy at Cardiff Business School, Cardiff University, UK.

Lisa Peñaloza is Professor of Marketing at KEDGE Business School, France.

Michel Laroche is the Royal Bank Distinguished Professor of Marketing at the John Molson School of Business, Concordia University, Canada.

Recent developments have created an unprecedented climate of ethnic, religious and cultural changes on a global scale. This situation provides new and exciting opportunities. But, the question for academics and businesses, of course, is how best to define, challenge and suggest new markets, products and services created by a diverse ethnic, religious and cultural landscape. This edited volume by Dr Ahmad Jamal, Professor Lisa Peñaloza and Professor Michel Laroche is a rich source of thought for everyone who wants to get deeper insights into this question. I highly recommend *The Routledge Companion to Ethnic Marketing* as a relevant read that also helps to generate a dialogue necessary to extend our understand of this important area even further.

Professor Adam Lindgreen, *Head of Marketing and Strategy, Cardiff Business School, Cardiff University, UK*

Judging a book on the effect it has on the reader's thought processes, *The Routledge Companion to Ethnic Marketing* must be classified as outstanding. Its engaging style and argument clarity makes it an invaluable resource for researchers and in the classroom.

Guilherme D. Pires, *PhD, Associate Professor of Marketing, Newcastle Business School, University of Newcastle, Australia*

A most ambitious and comprehensive book geared to master Marketing to culturally diverse groups in the US and internationally. I am delighted to see an effort that includes models of culture change, cultural segmentation, religion, materialism, ethnic youth, and advertising approaches, in one comprehensive piece. This book puts culture at the core of marketing.

Felipe Korzenny, *PhD, Founder, Center for Hispanic Marketing Communication, Florida State University, USA and co-author of* Hispanic Marketing: Connecting with the New Latino Consumer

The Routledge Companion to Ethnic Marketing

Edited by Ahmad Jamal,
Lisa Peñaloza and
Michel Laroche

Routledge
Taylor & Francis Group

LONDON AND NEW YORK

First published 2015 by Routledge

2 Park Square, Milton Park, Abingdon, Oxfordshire OX14 4RN
52 Vanderbilt Avenue, New York, NY 10017

Routledge is an imprint of the Taylor & Francis Group, an informa business

First issued in paperback 2019

British Library Cataloguing in Publication Data
A catalogue record for this book is available from the British Library

Library of Congress Cataloging in Publication Data
A catalog record for this book has been requested

ISBN: 978-0-415-64363-4 (hbk)
ISBN: 978-0-367-86742-3 (pbk)

Typeset in Bembo
by Swales & Willis Ltd, Exeter, Devon, UK

Contents

Contents

Figures

Tables

Contributors

Intekhab (Ian) Alam is Professor of Marketing in the School of Business, State University of New York at Geneseo. He received his PhD from the University of Southern Queensland in Australia, Masters of Business from the Queensland University of Technology, Australia and MBA from Aligarh Muslim University, India. He conducts research in the area of new service development and global marketing. His research has been published in the *Journal of the Academy of Marketing Science, Journal of Product Innovation Management, Industrial Marketing Management, Journal of Services Marketing, Asia Pacific Journal of Marketing and Logistics, Journal of Marketing Management, Journal of Services Research, Service Industries Journal, Journal of Global Marketing, Journal of Service Management, International Marketing Review, Journal of Business and Industrial Marketing, Qualitative Market Research, International Journal of Emerging Markets* and *Journal of International Marketing and Exporting*.

Boris Bartikowski is Professor of Marketing at KEDGE Business School in France. His research efforts centre on cultural issues in consumer behaviour, online consumer behaviour and survey research methodology. He was awarded a doctorate degree in marketing from the University of Aix-Marseille in France and the University of Augsburg in Germany. He can be reached at boris.bartikowski@kedgebs.com.

Hernan Casakin is Senior Lecturer in the School of Architecture, Ariel University. He had appointments as Research Fellow in the Department of Cognitive Sciences, Hamburg University, the Environmental Simulation Laboratory, Tel Aviv University and recently in the Faculty of Architecture, TUDelft, Delft University of Technology, Netherlands. His research interests include design cognition, design and culture, and environmental psychology.

Christopher A. Chávez is Assistant Professor in the School of Journalism and Communication at the University of Oregon and his research and teaching focus lies at the intersection of globalization, media and culture. He is co-editor of *Identity: Beyond Tradition and McWorld Neoliberalism* and his research has appeared in several anthologies and peer-reviewed journals. Prior to his doctoral research, he worked as an advertising executive at TBWA Chiat/Day, Goodby, Silverstein & Partners and Publicis & Hal Riney.

Joseph Cherian is Associate Professor of Marketing at the Graham School of Management, Saint Xavier University, Chicago. His interests include multicultural marketing and marketing strategy.

Mark Cleveland is the Dancap Private Equity Professor of Consumer Behavior, DAN Management and Organizational Studies, University of Western Ontario. He conducts research into several areas of marketing, with a special focus on cross-cultural consumer behaviour, globalization and culture, ethnic identity and acculturation, culture and decision-making, cosmopolitanism, materialism, international market segmentation, services marketing, green marketing, gift-giving, advertising, psychometrics and scale development, as well as branding and positioning. To date, he has published 26 articles in leading journals, a book and several book chapters. His articles have appeared in the *Journal of International Marketing, Journal of Business Research, International Marketing Review, Psychology & Marketing, Journal of Economic Psychology, International Journal of Advertising, International Journal of Intercultural Relations, Journal of Consumer Marketing, Journal of Strategic Marketing, Journal of Consumer Behavior, Canadian Journal of Administrative Sciences* and *Journal of International Consumer Marketing*. His research has been presented at 30 conferences spanning 5 continents. He has conducted research on consumers living in the Americas (Canada, the United States, Mexico and Chile), Europe (United Kingdom, Sweden, France, the Netherlands, Hungary and Greece) and Asia (India, Taiwan, China, Korea, Japan, Thailand, Iran, Lebanon and Turkey). He is also an associate editor for the *International Marketing Review* and an ad-hoc reviewer for numerous marketing journals.

Esi Abbam Elliot is Assistant Professor of Marketing at Suffolk University. Her research interests are creativity and culture, and emerging and subsistence markets. Recent articles appear in the *Journal of Business Research, Journal of Product Innovation Management* and *Journal of Macromarketing*.

Ayantunji Gbadamosi received his PhD in marketing from the University of Salford, UK. He is currently the Chair of the Research and Knowledge Exchange Committee at the Business School of the University of East London. His papers have been published in several internationally recognized refereed journals. He has co-edited two books and contributed chapters to several others. He is the author of the book entitled *Low-Income Consumer Behaviour* and he is listed in *Who is Who in the World*.

Elif Izberk-Bilgin is Associate Professor of Marketing at the University of Michigan-Dearborn. Her research focuses on consumer activism, religious ideology in the marketplace, Islamic marketing, branding and sociological aspects of consumerism in emerging countries. Her work has been published in *Journal of Consumer Research, Journal of Academy of Marketing Science* and *Consumption, Markets and Culture*. She is the recipient of the 2012 Sidney J. Levy Award for research.

Ahmad Jamal is Senior Lecturer in Marketing and Strategy at Cardiff Business School, Cardiff University, UK. He is a senior examiner at the Chartered Institute of Marketing (CIM) and his research interests include the interplay of culture, ethnicity and consumption, and applications of self-concept including service quality in marketing. His ethnographic work involving food consumption among the ethnic minorities and native British in Bradford is considered as one of the most pioneering studies ever conducted in the UK. His recent work investigates consumer responses to religious labels such as the halal logo, the role of acculturation in explaining susceptibility to interpersonal influences, Islamic marketing and Islamic financial consumption.

He is the co-author of a consumer behaviour text and has published widely in such journals as the *Journal of Business Research, European Journal of Marketing, Journal of Marketing Management, Advances in Consumer Research, Journal of Strategic Marketing, Journal of Consumer Behavior, British Food Journal, Journal of Retailing and Consumer Services, International Journal of Bank Marketing, Marketing Intelligence and Planning* and *International Review of Retail, Distribution and Consumer Research.* He has attended special conferences/seminars on culture, ethnicity and marketing as both a panelist and a keynote speaker.

Durriya H. Z. Khairullah is Professor of Marketing at the School of Business at St. Bonaventure University. She earned her Bachelor of Commerce degree from Bombay University, her MBA from St. Bonaventure University and her doctorate in Marketing from Syracuse University. She has authored and co-authored a number of scholarly papers published in refereed professional journals and conference proceedings. Her research interests include advertising, acculturation and cross-cultural research of ethnic consumers. She enjoys travel and is active in community service.

Zahid Y. Khairullah is Professor in the School of Business, St. Bonaventure University. He possesses a BTech degree from IIT, Bombay, an MS in Engineering and a PhD in Management Science from SUNY at Buffalo. He has a number of publications in scholarly journals and professional conference proceedings to his credit. He serves in leadership positions at St. Bonaventure, in professional organizations and in the community. He is the recipient of several awards for service and professional excellence.

Michel Laroche is the Royal Bank Distinguished Professor of Marketing at the John Molson School of Business, Concordia University, Montreal (Canada). He holds a PhD and MPh (Columbia), an MS Ing (Johns Hopkins) and a DSc honoris causa (Guelph). He is a Fellow of the Royal Society of Canada, American Psychological Association, Society for Marketing Advances, and Academy of Marketing Science. He received the 2000 Jacques-Rousseau Medal for the best multidisciplinary researcher in Canada. He has published more than 150 journal articles in the *Journal of Consumer Research, Journal of the Academy of Marketing Science, Journal of Retailing, Marketing Letters, Journal of Service Research, International Journal of Information Management* and *Journal of Advertising Research.* His publications, among others, include more than 145 papers in proceedings, 26 textbooks and several book chapters. His research interests include acculturation, consumer behaviour, online marketing, services marketing, neuromarketing and advertising. He is the Managing Editor of the *Journal of Business Research* and a Member of the Board of Governors of the Academy of Marketing Sciences.

Wei-Na Lee is the F. J. Heyne Centennial Professor in Communication and Professor of Advertising and Public Relations at the University of Texas, Austin. Her research examines the role of culture in persuasive communication. Her work has been published in various book chapters, conference proceedings and in the *Journal of Advertising, Journal of Advertising Research, Psychology & Marketing, Journal of Business Research* and *International Journal of Advertising,* among others. She co-edited the book *Diversity in Advertising* (2005, Lawrence Erlbaum). She is a former editor of the *Journal of Advertising.*

Andrew Lindridge is employed at The Open University where he undertakes a variety of consumer and social marketing research studies surrounding the areas of culture, discrimination, ethnicity, migration and poverty. His work has appeared in a variety of journals including *The European Journal of Marketing, Journal of Business Research* and *The Annals of Tourism.* He has presented at a variety of European and North American conferences, including the Association of Consumer Research, EMAC (European Marketing Association Conference) and Consumer Culture Theory. He is the Editor for *Qualitative Market Research: An International Journal* and Associate Editor for *The Journal of Marketing Management*.

Abid Mehmood is a Research Fellow at Sustainable Places Research Institute, Cardiff University. His research focuses on social innovation, entrepreneurship, urban and regional development, and environmental governance. Recent publications include *Planning for Climate Change* (2010, edited with S. Davoudi and J. Crawford) and *The International Handbook on Social Innovation* (2013, edited with F. Moulaert, D. MacCallum and A. Hamdouch).

Sonny Nwankwo developed his research specialism in consumerism under conditions of market failure. Through his research he seeks to extend the normative boundaries of marketing by focusing on diverse and often culture-specific challenges of economic behaviour and the power of individuals to make choices both as consumers and entrepreneurs. He is a director of the Noon Centre for Equality and Diversity in Business at the University of East London and a fellow of the Chartered Institute of Marketing.

Sanya Ojo is a seasoned consultant and a researcher/associate lecturer at the School of Business and Law of the University of East London, UK. He has a BA (Hons) in Economics with International Politics and an MSc in International Business Management. He has over 30 years' experience in entrepreneurship (national and transnational), which informs his research interest in ethnic and diaspora entrepreneurship, and has published papers in this area. His other research interests extend to international business strategy and management.

Lisa Peñaloza is Professor of Marketing, Department of Marketing and Consumer Relations, KEDGE Business School, Bordeaux, France. Her ethnicity-related research in the US includes the acculturation of Mexican immigrant consumers and that of the multicultural marketers who target them, and for Whites in the nation, the joint cultural production of ranchers and city-slickers, the normalization of credit, and elderly identity. Since moving to Europe she has joined colleagues examining Nigerian couples in the UK and British ex-pat couples in Toulouse, while continuing her work in Latin America, tracking the usage and effects of remittance funds in Mexican families and the structured efforts of the gaúcho movement in Southern Brazil as means of cultural and market development. She has published in such journals as the *Journal of Consumer Research, Journal of Marketing, Public Policy and Marketing, Consumption, Markets and Culture, Marketing Theory* and *International Journal of Sociology and Social Policy*; produced a documentary film, *Generaciones/Generations*, exploring consumption and marketing in the Mexican American community in South Texas (2005, 47 minutes); and written a play, *Dinner with Marx and Baudrillard*, set in a Turkish Mediterranean village where a group of friends who had been imprisoned as students for protesting the 1980 market reforms hotly contest the political potential of consumption activism. She is a former editor of *Consumption, Markets, Culture*, and co-editor of the textbook, *Cultural Marketing Management* with Toulouse and Visconti (Routledge).

Guilherme D. Pires is Associate Professor and Head of the Marketing Discipline and the DBA Program Director at the Newcastle Business School, Faculty of Business and Law, University of Newcastle, Australia. He was the Head of the Newcastle Graduate School of Business and a visiting scholar at various universities in Canada, Portugal and the USA. A Trustee for the Business & Economics Society International, he is Associate Editor of the *International Journal of*

Behavioural and Health Research and an editorial board member for several international scholarly journals.

Cecilia Ruvalcaba is a PhD Candidate in Marketing at the University of California, Irvine. Her research focuses on phenomena relating to market legitimacy, value cocreation and issues pertaining to the Hispanic market such as legitimacy, identity and social media. She is currently working on research that pertains to Hispanic small businesses and their use of social media.

Yasmin K. Sekhon gained her doctorate at the University of Birmingham, UK. Her research looked at consumption patterns of first and second-generation immigrants. Her areas of research include consumption of luxury brands, the meaning and significance of luxury across cultures as well as the study of materialism in cross-cultural settings. She has published in a number of academic journals such as *Consumption, Markets and Culture Journal*, *Academy of Marketing Review*, *Non-profit and Voluntary Sector Quarterly* and *International Journal of Market Research*, among others. She is also on the editorial board of the *International Journal of Market Research* and Associate Editor of the *Journal of Marketing Management*. She has been invited to give talks at a number of universities both nationally and internationally. She continues to develop her research on cross-cultural consumption, including luxury brand consumption as well as the influence of identity on consumption. Most recently she is investigating the role of luxury clothing in personal and social identity formation.

Ven Sriram is Professor of Marketing at the Merrick School of Business, University of Baltimore, USA. His Bachelor's degree in Economics is from Madras University and Master's in Management is from Bombay University, both in India. He earned his PhD from the University of Maryland, College Park in the US. He has been a Fulbright scholar in Nepal and Turkey, a Fulbright senior specialist in Russia and a visiting fellow at the Centre of International Studies at Cambridge University, UK. His research and consulting interests focus on issues relating to marketing, strategy, entrepreneurship and social enterprises in emerging markets. He has co-edited a book, *Drivers of Global Business Success*, and has published over 30 articles in leading academic and practitioner journals such as *Thunderbird International Business Review*, *Journal of Business Research* and *Omega*. His research has been presented at several national and international conferences. He has trained students, managers and executives in Nepal, Turkey, Argentina, Mexico, Ghana and Russia.

John Stanton is Associate Professor (Marketing) and Director of Academic Program (Economics and Finance) at the School of Business, University of Western Sydney, Australia. His current research interests include electronic and internet marketing, the interface of economics, accounting and marketing, and marketing implications of cultural diversity in Western societies, with a focus on ethnicity. He has consulted for a variety of private enterprises and for the Office of Multicultural Affairs, Australia.

Ivonne M. Torres is an associate professor in the Department of Marketing at New Mexico State University. Her current research interests lie in the areas of culture and persuasion and has been published in the *Journal of Advertising Research*, *Journal of Public Policy & Marketing*, *Journal of Services Marketing*, *Journal of Business Research*, *Journal of Current Issues and Research in Advertising*, *Journal of Internet Commerce*, *Journal of Business Ethics* and *Journal of Advertising*.

Alladi Venkatesh is a professor at University of California, Irvine. His research focuses on the networked home and technology adoption and diffusion. Recently he has been working on social media and its implications on user-centred theory and practice. He has published in the *Journal of Consumer Research* (Best Paper Award), *Journal of Marketing, Management Science, Journal of Marketing Management, Marketing Theory* and others. He is the founding co-editor of the journal *Consumption, Markets and Culture*.

Luca M. Visconti is Associate Professor of Marketing at ESCP Europe, Paris campus, and Professor at IFM (Institut Français de la Mode), Paris. He holds a PhD in Business Administration and Management from Università Bocconi, Milan. His research involves the consumption of market minorities (migrants, gays, elderly consumers, bottom-of-the-pyramid consumers) as well as the consumption of collective goods (public space and public health). His research has appeared in the *Journal of Consumer Research, Marketing Theory, Journal of Macromarketing, Journal of Consumer Behavior, Journal of Business Research, Journal of Consumer Culture, Journal of Advertising, Industrial Marketing Management* and *Consumption, Markets & Culture*. His latest edited book is *Marketing Management: A Cultural Perspective* (with L. Peñaloza and N. Toulouse).

Zhiyong Yang is Associate Professor of Marketing at the University of Texas at Arlington (UTA). His research focuses on peer influence and parental influence. Along the line of peer influence, he examines how the opinion from others affects individuals' new product adoption, product choice, donation and saving behaviour. In the perspective of parental influence, he centres primarily on the effect of parental style on consumer socialization across different countries and different ethnic groups. His work has appeared in the *Journal of Marketing, Journal of Consumer Research, Journal of the Academy of Marketing Science, Journal of Retailing, Journal of Service Research, Journal of Business Research, Journal of Public Policy & Marketing, Journal of Macromarketing* and *Journal of Personal Selling and Sales Management*. His research has been funded by Statistics Canada, Quebec government and UTA. He currently serves on the editorial review boards of the *Journal of Business Research* and *Journal of Consumer Marketing*.

Jinnie Jinyoung Yoo is an assistant professor in the Department of Global Business Track at Gachon University in Korea (Republic of). She received a PhD in Advertising at the University of Texas at Austin. Her primary area of research focuses on multicultural advertising, consumer psychology and global brand communication. Prior to her graduate degree, she worked as a brand marketing consultant in several Asian countries including Korea, Japan, China and other Southeast Asian countries.

Miguel A. Zúñiga is an assistant professor of Marketing at the School of Business and Management at Morgan State University. He holds a BBA (2006), an MBA (2007) and a PhD in Business Administration (2012) from New Mexico State University. His research interests include consumer vulnerability, ethnic identification, ethnic marketing, cross-cultural marketing, business ethics and cultural persuasion. His research has been published in the *Journal of Business Research, Journal of Public Policy & Marketing* and *Journal of Internet Commerce*.

Acknowledgements

Chapter 8

Authors would like to thank Nancy Bell of Microsoft Corporation (Mountain View, California) for sponsoring the project and the Orange County Hispanic Chamber of Commerce for their assistance in providing a list of small businesses and contacting them on our behalf. Our thanks also to the following MBA students who assisted in data collection and report summary: Mark Lee, Lee Morrison, Tatiane Perazzo, Sheila Rahnama and Tiffany Wilson.

Chapter 15

The authors would like to thank Mr. Jose Guerrero, Mr. Hector Duarte, Mr. Gabriel Villa, Mr. Roberto Ferreyra and other artists in Pilsen Mexican community who participated in the interviews for this study. We would also like to thank Mr. Hector Duarte and Mr. Gabriel Villa for allowing us to use their original artworks in this chapter.

Part I
Why ethnic marketing?

Introduction to ethnic marketing

*Ahmad Jamal, Lisa Peñaloza
and Michel Laroche*

Introduction

Growing population numbers, increasing purchasing power and a heightened sense of ethnic pride among ethnic minority consumers across the globe represent significant marketing opportunities (Jamal 2003; Peñaloza 2007). Cultural and ethnic diversity in the marketplace affects and shapes social institutions. As examples, many educational institutions have developed diversity offices to accommodate a multicultural student body and staff, while up-and-coming chefs and families and pop restaurateurs steadily incorporate ethnic foods into local cuisine. Ethnic diversity affects businesses by presenting opportunities in developing new markets for a variety of products and services, as well as challenges related to working with diverse workers and consumers.

The extent to which ethnic minority segments of a population integrate into a host society has been a major concern in the social sciences since their inception, especially during the last seven decades. There is a growing demand for marketing strategies and theories that incorporate ethnicity, ethnic identity and culture, and recent scholarly work has provided useful insights into ethnic consumers' responses to marketing efforts such as sales promotions, advertising and media, to name a few. Substantial work exists exploring the interplay of ethnicity, identity, consumption and marketing in focusing on major ethnic groups in North America and to some extent in the UK, Europe and Australia.

Ethnic marketing texts (e.g. Pires and Stanton in press) offer practical insights into the marketing opportunities arising out of cultural diversity. Other scholarly work discusses marketing strategies in a multi-ethnic environment (e.g. Cui 1997). A substantial body of work in marketing investigates the impact of migration and resettlement on the consumption experiences of immigrants (e.g. Hui, Kim, Laroche and Joy 1992). However, much of this work stands in isolation from each other. The current text aims to systematically link scholarly work published across different regions of the world, to outline a framework for ethnic marketing and to serve as a reference point for consumer researchers, doctoral students and practitioners including marketers and policy makers.

Ethnic marketing in a globalized market economy

Ethnic marketing is an emerging field, and specific texts on the subject like Pires and Stanton (in press) highlight the importance of understanding the unique needs of ethnic minority consumers and developing resonant marketing strategies that meet their preferences. In such a context, marketers need to be aware of key issues relevant to ethnic minority people, for example, ethnic identity and community as these impact consumption. Such work goes beyond early concerns limited to the location and socio-demographic characteristics of ethnic peoples and the extent to which they differ from ethnic mainstream consumers.

The contemporary global marketplace is characterized by the simultaneous occurrence of global integration and persistent ethnic, racial, religious and national difference (Cleveland, Laroche and Hallab 2013; Peñaloza and Gilly 1999). Worldwide immigration patterns and domestic growth rates of recent decades have contributed towards the creation of large ethnic minority subcultures across the Western world (Jamal 2003). Ethnic marketing public policies are highly contested in the USA and Canada as well as across Europe and Australia.

Regarding cultural diversity in the marketplace, it is important to appreciate how marketers and consumers are 'positioned within and traversing multiple cultural spheres' (Peñaloza and Gilly 1999, p. 84). Co-operation between marketers and consumers, and across subcultures of consumers, is a cornerstone of social and economic development (Gentry, Jun and Tansuhaj 1995). One way of enhancing such co-operation is to better understand how marketers, ethnic minority consumers and mainstream consumers interact with and adapt to one another. Such interactions and adaptations are complex and extend well beyond the segmentation and targeting efforts of firms; as cities, tribes and even nations use marketing techniques for their development (Comaroff and Comaroff 2009).

However, it remains true that some marketers retain narrow views of the workings of culture based on their own experience (Jamal 1997; Peñaloza 2007; Peñaloza and Gilly 1999). Whether it arises from a failure of imagination, a failure to reflect upon the cultural processes, interactions and changes in their own lives and businesses, or a failure to realize that they, too, live in an 'other culture' from the perspective of others, this blindness is both the cause and effect of marketers' tendency to impose their own perspectives on other consumers as well as workers. Traditional approaches to the study of ethnic minority consumer behaviour have been oriented primarily as attempts to gain control over such behaviour in order to influence and direct it. This instrumentalism, while beneficial in terms of short term strategy, has stymied longer term strategic considerations and understandings of the interweaving of ethnicity and market development.

The rise of global markets and Global Consumer Culture (GCC), the rapid diffusion of social media globally and significant changes in lifestyle, global travel patterns and rates of international migration and mobility present significant opportunities as well as challenges in ethnic marketing.

Culture change

The issue of cultural difference, interaction and change is at the heart of ethnic marketing research and practice. Building on the work of many researchers, including Askegaard, Arnould, Kjeldgaard (2005), Peñaloza (1994) and Wallendorf and Reilly (1983), Laroche and Jamal (this volume) provide an insightful analysis and discussion of models of cultural change. A common assumption in acculturation research in marketing is that, as a result of prolonged contact and mutual influences between two or more cultures, cultural changes take place and these changes occur at an individual and a group level.

However, in practice, substantial research focuses on changes that occur to a single cultural group, and in almost all cases this is an ethnic minority group. Further work is needed that incorporates multiple cultural groups at the same time and includes mainstream consumers. Moreover, substantial differences exist in the way the term 'acculturation' is conceptualized and applied in an ethnic marketing context. In most cases, acculturation is interpreted as one form of an adaptation to new cultural environment, and the paradigm of acculturation as adaption dominates current thinking and practice (e.g. Chirkov 2009). Laroche and Jamal build upon the work of Luedicke (2011) in calling for future research going beyond the bi-dimensional models of cultural change.

Recent models focused on identity (e.g. Askegaard *et al.* 2005) broadened acculturation to incorporate three sets of institutional acculturation forces and agents: the first is aligned with a heritage culture, the second is aligned with a receiving culture and the third is aligned with a GCC. The three agents and forces stand in a co-productive yet competing relation to each other as they inform the four identity positions of hyperculture, assimilation, integration and pendulum.

The models acknowledge fluid movement between identity positions and such movement can take various forms, as the ethnic minority consumers express and experience 'situational ethnicity' (Deshpandé, Hoyer and Donthu 1986), 'culture swapping' (Oswald 1999), an 'oscillating pendulum' (Askegaard *et al.* 2005) and 'frame switching' (Luna, Ringberg and Peracchio 2008). Thus, as highlighted by Laroche and Jamal (this volume), ethnic marketers need to note that there is considerable diversity within ethnic minority groups and that people may take on multiple identity positions over the course of their lives. As their sentiments and concerns alter in specific contexts, ethnic minority consumers re-interpret and redefine the boundaries of the groups within which they exist (Jamal 1997). Discursive outcomes such as assimilation, integration, rejection and deculturation, as described by Berry (1980) may manifest; however, rather than viewing these conditions separately or independently from each other, it is important to note their constant interplay.

As highlighted by Laroche and Jamal (this volume), there remains a need for ethnic marketing researchers to go beyond the current conceptualizations of identity formation, acculturation and intergroup relations in considering the co-existence of two or more cultures. The distinction between acculturation processes and identity positions as outcomes, while useful in demarcating the scope of particular investigations, results in limited understandings of ethnicity overall (Jamal 1997). The idea of an outcome, as the product of a prior process, can only assume substance if the frame of observation is frozen in time (e.g. Chapman 1995) or is generalized across multiple observations. All societies and market institutions are, in some sense, constantly in a process of cultural change, and such changes are usefully examined with attention to internal and external forces and elements. As experienced by ethnic minority consumers, such notions of change may be understood in terms of co-constructive and competing models of time, space, being, having and consuming (Askegaard *et al.* 2005).

Scholarly acculturation work often studies various domains of cultural change like food, dress and language choices, which represent important symbolic systems (Barth 1969, pp. 9–38). Much further work is needed in other symbolic areas such as fashion, media and music consumption. Food, dress and language choices symbolize the manner in which consumers view and define themselves and others as insiders and outsiders (Douglas 1975). The ethnographic study of immigrant consumption necessarily touches upon broader questions regarding the interplay of culture and consumption more generally in appreciating the complex nature of cultural change (Peñaloza 1994; Jamal 2003).

Since the 1960s, immigrants from Latin America, Asia, Africa, the Caribbean and the Middle East have settled in North America, Western Europe and Australia. There are tremendous differences in the level of development and infrastructure of these nations, as well as different standards of living for individual migrants and their families. While somewhat problematic in potentially overemphasizing differences between nations and underemphasizing similarities between them (Nakata 2009), classifying societies as individualist or collectivist continues to be a common practice in ethnic marketing research. Schwartz *et al.* (2010) attempts to understand the tensions between migrant groups and the societies that receive them in terms of differences in their values as approximated by characterizing the nations of the migrants and the hosts as collectivist or individualist.

Also in this volume, Yang explains how different social goals impact cultural change. Specifically, the author suggests that the socialization goal toward collectivism drives people in the Eastern culture of China to exhibit high-context communication patterns in comparison with the socialization goal towards individualism in the Western culture of the USA that brings about low-context styles of communication. Yang relates differences between the concept- and socially oriented parental styles to the susceptibility of adolescents to peer influence. Furthermore, the author notes differences in authoritative, authoritarian and permissive parental styles across the two cultures. Whereas people from the US consider authoritative parenting to be the most effective style for socialization, people from China report the authoritarian style to be the appropriate means of regulating children's behaviour. Research implications support Laroche *et al.* (2007) in considering acculturative consistency within generations as a relevant factor in understanding family decision-making processes among ethnic minority cultures, while ethnic marketing implications advise the need to use culturally relevant symbols such as authority figures and elders in marketing communications targeting Eastern cultures.

A phenomenon largely under-researched in ethnic marketing is category disturbance (Chapman and Jamal 1997). Cultural categories are theoretical concepts that are specific to each culture and are acted out in daily life. As Chapman (1992) observed, 'the meeting of different cultures is a sustained experience of classificatory disturbance' (p. 158). The social-anthropological literature is rich in detailing the moral importance that social groups attach to maintaining the integrity of their systems of classification (Evans-Pritchard 1956; Lienhardt 1961). Differences in social classification can generate perceptual barriers and impact social relations within multicultural environments (Jamal and Chapman 2000; Chapman and Jamal 1997). In the context of the coming together of multiple cultures with varying values and classificatory systems, acculturation can be understood by investigating the structure and direction of the classificatory features that impact consumption (Applebaum and Jordt 1996; McCracken 1986). A domain relevant to investigating such categories in consumption is the internet.

The internet has accelerated globalization processes (Angelides 1997), enabling marketers to better tailor their marketing communication programs by developing culturally congruent websites (Luna, Peracchio and de Juan 2002). In this context, Bartikowski (this volume) discusses ethnic minority consumers' responses to the web. Demographic factors, socio-economic status and generational differences within ethnic minority groups account for the digital divide between the mainstream and ethnic minority consumers. The author finds that ethnic minority consumers are adapting social media, mobile devices (e.g. smart phones) and mobile applications more quickly than their mainstream counterparts. The strength of cultural identification appears to play a dominant role in explaining how ethnic minorities respond to marketing communications. Bartikowski's recommendation to ethnic marketers is to make efforts to identify those who care about their ethnic identity and position their communications efforts accordingly. Ethnic marketers can improve the effectiveness of their marketing communication efforts by developing websites that are culturally congruent.

Here, there and everywhere: identity, space and ethnic entrepreneurship

In emphasizing the relational dimensions of ethnic identity, Tonkin, Chapman and McDonald (1989) note that 'a group or an individual has no one identity, but a variety (a potentially very large variety) of possibilities, that only incompletely or partially overlap in social time and social space' (p. 17). The term 'ethnic' can be used to describe any social group (be it a minority or a majority group) and the notions of ethnic identity and ethnicity exist in a context of oppositions and relativities (Tajfel 1981; Jamal 1997). Most of the prior work discusses ethnic minority consumers' identity positions in the context of meeting one's heritage and receiving cultures. Built into such conceptualizations is the notion of space involving a contrast between here (new country) and there (back home). The essays in this section detail how ethnic identity, space and entrepreneurial activities are intertwined.

Visconti (this volume) emphasizes how identities of ethnic and mainstream consumers confront each other in specific spaces that resonate with physical, geopolitical, cultural, social, ideological and political dimensions. His research extends previous research on ethnicity and acculturation that has addressed the role of space in the context of a contrast between original and destination countries by expanding upon spatial metaphors and thus elaborating the rich and varied multicultural nature of everyday experience. Visconti elaborates how ethnic minorities use local, regional and supranational articulations of physical space in creating more nuanced and richer ethnic identities; how they compare, reinforce and modify the ethnic stereotypes that others impose on them, and how they become part of a nation in using its social services and in contributing to its cultural life. In viewing acculturation phenomena from the lens of physical, cultural and social spaces, Visconti suggests new research directions in investigating the acculturating experiences of both ethnic minority and mainstream groups and in considering more comprehensive social exchanges involving multiple countries and contexts. By incorporating spatial metaphors, his work has helped advance ethnic marketing and transformative research and public policy.

Visconti's chapter, like many of the chapters in this book, builds upon previous studies that consider consumption to be a personal, social and material process that constitutes identity and serves as the terrain for cultural expression. Consumption itself becomes a space (Visconti, this volume) where ethnic consumers experience the joys and pleasures of cultural familiarities and the challenges and discomforts of differences. In ways parallel to theoretical understandings of interpretations and meanings in the consumption of physical goods (Douglas and Isherwood 1980), the essential feature of space appears to be consumers' capacity to make linguistic and poetic sense. Thus, space is very good for thinking through the contexts, meetings and identity and community constructions of multiple cultures. Space is both visible in the physical sense and invisible in the social, cultural and ideological sense as vital parts of culture and as the arena in which ethnicity and ethnic identity are forged and contested.

The steady rise in ethnic minority populations and their spending power provide significant entrepreneurial opportunities (Jamal 2005; Ram 1994). Previous work by Wamwara-Mbugua, Cornwell and Boller (2008) discusses the acculturation experiences of Kenyan immigrants using the metaphor of 'an entrenched African American subculture' within a U.S. majority culture. Jamal (2003) noted that small and medium sized ethnic minority enterprises, ethnic media, and religious and cultural centres act as acculturating agents facilitating ethnic identity formulation. Mehmood, Jamal and Sriram (this volume), contribute to this previous work by emphasizing the social innovations and economic and social contributions to ethnic community of ethnic entrepreneurs. These authors explain the importance of social capital in building and bridging economic relations and consider social innovation as an ethno-marketing strategy for social and economic development and prosperity. The growth of ethnic entrepreneurs moves in the opposite direction from the global consolidation of capital, and thus provides an important source of dynamism in ethnic communities. Their work echoes earlier work that considers ethnic minorities not only as consumers but also as producers (e.g. Peñaloza and Gilly 1999). Abid *et al.* call for benchmarking the socially innovative features of ethnic entrepreneurship for developing and implementing innovative ethnic marketing strategies.

Also exploring entrepreneurship, Ojo, Nwankwo and Gbadamosi (this volume) track tensions and movements in the UK ethnic marketing landscape, as transnational activities, cross-border flows and the diffusion of ethnic minority entrepreneurship into the mainstream marketplace blur the boundaries among various ethnic groups. Prior research has attributed the growth limits of extended family ethnic minority businesses to family size and trust. The authors suggest that things may change when the younger generation takes control of these businesses. They elaborate additional dimensions of family owned enterprises, including breaking out of ethnic enclaves, business positioning and the role of entrepreneurial, symbolic and cultural capital as well as trust in ethnic entrepreneurship. The authors provide implications for future research that contextualize and add more nuanced understandings to dynamics of trust among ethnic entrepreneurs.

In a related domain, Ruvalcaba and Venkatesh (this volume) investigate internet-technology adoption among Hispanic small businesses in the USA. Using an ethnoconsumerist and ethno-marketing approach to understanding the motivation and barriers to technology usage, they identify cultural factors such as the tendency to stay connected with the community, the need for personal interaction, the lack of trust towards internet technology and risk aversiveness. Their findings identify a culture-based preference among Hispanic entrepreneurs for having a physical space instead of a virtual one and stress the importance of developing, maintaining and nurturing interpersonal relations with Hispanic clients. The perception that patterns of social relations within the Hispanic community are at risk triggers potential users' reluctance to use internet technology. To overcome this reluctance, the authors suggest enhancing the overall value proposition of technology products so that it resonates with Hispanic businesses, and assisting and empowering Hispanic entrepreneurs to utilize the cultural/social capital of the community in their businesses.

Their work raises important lessons for ethnic marketers. For example, the ethnoconsumerist and ethno-marketing approaches can provide deeper insights into the cultural dynamics underpinning business practices. In researching ethnic business practices, it is important to make explicit social relationships of various kinds, such as the value of business practices in the family and the community and the organization of time and space. Further, ethnoconsumerist and ethno-marketing approaches assist market researchers in attending to the specific meanings and rituals in business culture and to the culturally constituted nature of market behaviour (McCracken 1986). Implicit in such an approach is an effort to understand the entirety of the business system as manifest in the lived practices, through which individuals attribute sense and meaning to artifacts and activities. Because efforts to understand a different culture are always partial (Clifford and Marcus 1986), researchers' pursuit of holistic analysis and cultural understanding is of tremendous value.

Globalization, religion and materialism

The rapid and widespread movement of people, capital, and products and services is impacting ethnic consumers across the globe. The integration of multiple heritage and receiving cultures with multiple consumer cultures globally in markets impacts ethnic minority identity formation and reformulation (Askegaard et al. 2005). Religion is a significant marker of ethnic identity in the global marketplace (e.g., Jamal & Sukor 2014). Recent ethnic consumer research suggests differences between ethnic minority consumers with high levels of religiosity as compared to those with low levels of religiosity (Jamal and Sharifuddin 2014), with implications regarding materialism (Cleveland and Chang 2009), cultural identity

(Lindridge 2005), consumption (Sood and Nasu 1995) and power in the marketplace (Jamal 1997). Izberk-Bilgin (this volume) examines the myriad ways in which transnational flows of people, capital, products and services, and ideas inform ethnicity and religion in people's consumption and connections to brands. She elaborates the conflation of ethnicity and religion in ethnic marketing research and explains the divergent trends towards and away from religion in consumption and markets. Distinguishing between consumer activism, ethnoreligious ideologies, faith-based markets and marketing, the author highlights the convergent efforts of consumers, religious organizations, cultural intermediaries and government in altering the importance of religion in consumption. Her findings are particularly significant given the ever larger numbers of migrant workers, tourists, expatriates, refugees and students who cross borders and, in the process of doing so, encounter and react to what they perceive to be cultural threats and opportunities, thus contributing to an already heightened global sense of the 'religiously other'. In closing, Izberk-Bilgin maps future research directions at the intersection of religion, identity and social relations in exploring how markets and consumption facilitate people's pursuit of personal meaning and spiritual transcendence.

Cleveland (this volume) provides a comprehensive account of the extent to which ethnicity combines with acculturation to advance materialistic values across different cultures and consumption contexts. The rise of global mass media; significant advancements in technology, including the widespread adoption of internet and social media; tourism; cosmopolitanism; English language usage as well as an openness to GCC all act as agents of change impacting ethnic minority consumers' predispositions to adapt to other cultures and traditions and gain a materialist orientation. Yet at the same time, divergent counter trends also gain momentum, such that ethnic minority consumers reassert ethnic and religious identities and consumption practices. Ethnic marketers face the challenge of employing themes associated with materialism such as achievement, success, abundance, status and glamour, while at the same time reinforcing ethnic and cultural identities. The author closes with a timely call for anthropological perspectives in research on materialism across cultures.

Marketing, market segmentation and targeting

Ethnic difference is a basic consideration in market segmentation and targeting. Zúñiga and Torres (this volume) analyze demographic and lifestyle features of Hispanics, African Americans and Asian Americans in the USA and point to distinctions in education, technology usage, health care, and economic and political activities through which the three groups experience and cope with the forces of acculturation. Hispanics tend to avoid pan-ethnic labels like Hispanic and instead use family origin to identify themselves. They tend to have positive perceptions of the US and view learning English as a pathway to success. Self-reported high levels of brand loyalty characterize them as a valuable market for companies. Political affiliation continues to strongly support Democratic political candidates as 71 per cent of Hispanics voted for Barack Obama in 2012. African American consumers continue to grow in numbers and economic power. Those who strongly identify with African culture prefer adverts featuring African American models and these models appear fairly prominently in TV and print advertising, especially in specialized media. Asian Americans represent a diverse group in terms of country of origin. Japanese Americans are more likely to attend to English language media than Chinese, Vietnamese and Korean Americans, who preference their native languages. Most Asians are brand loyal but look for high-quality brands at reasonable prices. The significant growth of ethnic diversity, combined with growing affluence and purchasing power, active political participation and engagement, and greater use of new technologies in the US offers substantial opportunities while challenges remain in targeting and segmenting various minority groups in the diverse nature of ethnic groups and their use and preference for different languages.

Sekhon (this volume) explores the links among ethnicity, identity and consumption in addressing the bicultural self and identity in the consumption decision making of ethnic minority consumers. While acknowledging generational differences, the author suggests that ethnic minority consumers tend to experience multiple and fluid identities, and that consumption patterns, acculturation levels and self-relevant experiences help explain identity formation. She argues that ethnic minority consumer decision making is a complex, diverse and nonlinear process impacted by globalization, transnationalism and interactivity in the marketplace. Sekhon's work is consistent with recent acculturation work in marketing that considers the impact of macro- and micro-level factors on identity formation and the construction of ethnicity in consumption decision making.

In another work in this volume, Alam laments the dearth of marketing efforts targeting religious minorities with financial services. The author makes a case for multinational banks to enter the niche ethnic area of Islamic banking and finance with specially targeted services, warning that ethnic minority customers tend to be quite analytical and critical and may have higher than normal expectations for financial service providers. He further advises bank marketers to engage with ethnic minority customers, particularly those with strong ties in respective communities, at the very early stages in developing and tailoring their services and then later in helping disseminate financial knowledge using their own expertise and social networks.

Also important is attending to the variation within subcultures. The study of consumers at subcultural levels poses valuable opportunities to better understand patterns of class, status and ethnicity. Lindridge (this volume) discusses the key problems underpinning traditional approaches to segmenting ethnic minority markets. He notes that early applications of market segmentation by marketers at the turn of the century encouraged assimilation, whereas later efforts from the 1970s onward emphasized the unique needs of ethnic groups in segmenting markets. He cites the example of Proctor and Gamble targeting promotions for its hugely popular Gain detergent brand to the African American and Latino market segments in the US. His analysis highlights problems in the use of segmentation criteria requiring minimal within-group differences and maximal between-group differences. His discussion elaborates the shortcomings of demographic, geographic, psychographic and behaviouristic measures and the strengths of acculturation measures in segmenting markets and targeting consumers based on ethnicity.

Elliot, Cherian and Casakin (this volume) present the case of transcultural consumers who seek to embrace diversity and move beyond the confines of their own cultures by attending cultural festivals and purchasing art. Such consumers view cultural artifacts as opportunities to adapt and transform their personal and collective selves and rework their multiple, nested and elective identities. The authors argue for an approach to marketing ethnicity that considers consumption as integral to the construction of a transcultural identity. Citing the case of ethnic artists as cultural producers and visitors to the neighbourhood festival as transcultural consumers, the authors make a strong case for marketers to develop strategies that are inclusive of multiple cultural groups. Such scholarly work is emblematic of the significant opportunities in marketing research investigating the role of agency and subjectivity in the production and consumption of ethnicity.

Advertising

Yoo and Lee (this volume) explore ethnic consumers' responses to multicultural advertising using a range of theories including identification (Kelman 1961), distinctiveness (McGuire 1984), in-group biasness (Brewer 1979), accommodation and polarized appraisal (Linville 1982) theories. Overall, those who reported strong sentiments about their ethnicity and identity tended to prefer advertisements that were congruent with their culture and behaviour and feature ethnically similar models. Furthermore, ethnic minority consumers appreciate adverts that show sensitivity to their culture, and demonstrate higher levels of trust for culturally sensitive advertising messages.

Chávez's (this volume) attention to the need for cultural reflexivity in advertising practice and research is a timely one. Unbalanced representations of ethnicity in the marketplace create challenges for advertisers, their clients, consumers and society. The author speaks of particular challenges related to misrepresentations, faulty assumptions, and personal and organizational interests between cultural producers, consumers and intermediaries. He elaborates on the cultural homogeneity that results from the increased institutional concentration in advertising agencies, client appeasements and the professional ambitions of advertising executives. Ethnic marketers' tendency to invest authority in cultural intermediaries, in this case advertising agencies, can be self-defeating when they devalue the very cultural knowledge and expertise they seek. It is important to recognize that cultural knowledge construction in advertising is an inter-subjective process incorporating various subjectivities with differences in power. Implications from this work point to subtle cultural, personal and organizational barriers inhibiting the performance of advertising professionals and the ability of brand managers to accept the expertise of the cultural intermediaries they hire to learn about ethnic consumers. Chávez recommends that advertisers and marketers reflect upon and overcome their organizational biases in producing, circulating and disseminating cultural knowledge about ethnic minority consumers.

Khairullah and Khairullah (this volume) find cultural differences in how ethnic consumers perceive advertisements. In six studies of Asian-Indian Americans originating from India the authors noted that these consumers are among the wealthiest and highly educated ethnic segment in the US and include diverse religious, cultural and regional backgrounds. Those with low levels of acculturation report a preference for advertisements with Indian models over those with American models, although such preferences decrease as level of acculturation increases. The authors conclude that level of acculturation can guide firms in segmenting and targeting Indian American consumers.

Ethical and public policy in ethnic marketing

Ethnic minorities are a visible part of consumer culture in major cosmopolitan cities around the globe, triggering the need to apply a policy of fairness and equal opportunity for everyone. Indeed, there exists significant opportunities for making inroads into ethnic minority market segments for those who integrate ethics into their marketing strategy. Pires and Stanton (this volume) provide a comprehensive overview of ethical concerns regarding the way ethnicity is approached and integrated into marketing practices, including the social exclusion and loss of self-esteem by ethnic minority consumers that result from marketers' failure to address specific cultural needs and wants. Reinforcement of stereotypes, incorrect ascriptions to communities and race-based discrimination are additional ethical issues arising in ethnic market targeting efforts, and these issues are rendered increasingly important and complex in contributing to a 'digital divide' in access to information technology globally. The authors conclude by developing a comprehensive ethical assessment framework for firms to implement ethical ethnic marketing efforts.

In closing the book, Peñaloza (this volume) builds upon several of the previous chapters in discussing contemporary opportunities and challenges in public policy. She points to a growing trend towards greater awareness and sensitivity of ethnicity as a valid part of society, not just in private life, and emphasizes that ethnic minority consumers actively co-create value in marketing exchanges as both consumers and producers. In contributing insights to public policy regarding ethnic marketing, she highlights the inherently social and relational nature of cultural identity and ethnicity and the different positioning of ethnic groups in terms of access to resources and power structures. Citing the discussion of social plurality and difference in the social sciences, she recommends that public policy workers suspend their belief in their ability to truly know another as the means of better attaining the goals of dialogic and more effective forms of communication. She further discusses the legacy of post-colonial relations for its role in developing markets across the globe, and points to the growing realization among ethnic consumers that market activity can be harnessed for community development and the need for unifying public policy that serves the national mandates of fair and equal treatment. Public policy, ethnic differences and the reproduction of unequal power in the marketplace remain at the top of the many issues requiring greater understanding. Recommendations for public policy development and implementation point to the importance of positioning ethnic groups, and not just individual members, as valuable entities in their own right, worthy of recognition and address as agents and to the necessity of treating ethnic groups and people as equal participants in relation to others in the marketplace and in society.

References

Angelides, M. C. (1997) 'Implementing the internet for business: A global marketing opportunity'. *International Journal of Information Management*, 17(6): 405–19.

Applebaum, K. and Jordt, I. (1996) 'Notes toward an application of McCracken's "Cultural Categories" for cross-cultural consumer research'. *Journal of Consumer Research*, 23(3): 204–18.

Askegaard, S., Arnould, E. J. and Kjeldgaard, D. (2005) 'Postassimilationist ethnic consumer research: Qualifications and extensions'. *Journal of Consumer Research*, 32(1): 160–70.

Barth, F. (1969) *Ethnic Groups and Boundaries*. Boston, MA: Little, Brown.

Berry, W. J. (1980) 'Acculturation as varieties of adaptation'. In *Acculturation: Theory, Models and Some New Findings*, edited by A. M. Padilla. Boulder, CO: Westview Press, pp. 9–46.

Brewer, M. B. (1979) 'In-group bias in the minimal intergroup situation: A cognitive-motivational analysis'. *Psychological Bulletin*, 86(2): 307–24.

Chapman, M. (1992) *The Celts: The Construction of a Myth*. London: Macmillan.

Chapman, M. (1995) 'Freezing the frame: Dress and ethnicity in Brittany and gaelic Scotland'. In *Dress and Ethnicity: Change Across Space and Time*, edited by J. B. Eicher. Oxford: Berg Publishers, pp. 7–29.

Chapman M. and Jamal, A. (1997) 'Acculturation: Cross cultural consumer perceptions and the symbolism of domestic life'. In *Advances in Consumer Research*, Volume 34, edited by M. Brucks and D. J. MacInnis. Provo, UT: Association for Consumer Research, pp. 138–144.

Chirkov, V. (2009) 'Critical psychology of acculturation: What do we study and how do we study it when we investigate acculturation?' *International Journal of Intercultural Relations*, 33: 94–105.

Cleveland, M. and Chang, W. (2009) 'Migration and materialism: The roles of ethnic identity, religiosity, and generation'. *Journal of Business Research*, 62(10): 963–71.

Cleveland, M., Laroche, M. and Hallab, R. (2013) 'Globalization, culture, religion and values: Comparing consumption patterns of Lebanese Muslims and Christians'. *Journal of Business Research*, 62: 963–71.

Clifford, J. and Marcus G. E. (1986) *Writing Culture: The Poetics and Politics of Ethnography*. California, CA: University of California Press.

Comaroff, J. and Comaroff, J. (2009) *Ethnicity, Inc.* Chicago, IL: University of Chicago Press.

Cui, G. (1997) 'Marketing Strategies in a Multicultural Ethnic Environment'. *Journal of Marketing Theory and Practice*, 5(1): 122–34.

Deshpandé, R., Hoyer, W. D. and Donthu, N. (1986) 'The intensity of ethnic affiliation: A study of the sociology of hispanic consumption'. *Journal of Consumer Research*, 13(2): 214–20.

Douglas, M. (1975) *Implicit Meanings: Essays in Anthropology*. London: Routledge.

Douglas, M. and Isherwood B. (1980) *The World of Goods: Towards an Anthropology of Consumption.* New York, NY: Harmondsworth.

Evans-Pritchard, E. (1956) *Nuer Religion.* Oxford: Clarendon.

Gentry, J. W., Jun S. and Tansuhaj P. (1995) 'Consumer acculturation processes and cultural conflict: How generalizable is a North American model for marketing globally?' *Journal of Business Research*, 32(2): 129–39.

Hui, M., Kim C., Laroche M. and Joy A. (1992) 'Acculturation as a multidimensional process: Empirical evidence and implications for consumer researchers'. In *AMA Winter Educators' Conference Proceedings: Marketing Theory and Applications*, Volume 3, edited by C. T. Allen and T. J. Madden. Chicago, IL: American Marketing Association, pp. 466–73.

Jamal, A. (1997) 'Acculturation and consumer behaviour'. Unpublished doctoral dissertation. University of Bradford, UK.

Jamal, A. (2003) 'Marketing in a multicultural world: The interplay of marketing, ethnicity and consumption'. *European Journal of Marketing*, 37(11/12): 1599–620.

Jamal, A. (2005) 'Playing to win: An exploratory study of marketing strategies of small ethnic retail entrepreneurs in the UK'. *Journal of Retailing and Consumer Services*, 12(1): 1–13.

Jamal, A. and Chapman, M. (2000) 'Acculturation and inter-ethnic consumer perceptions: Can you feel what we feel?' *Journal of Marketing Management*, 16(4): 365–91.

Jamal, A. and Sharifuddin, J. (2014) 'Perceived value and usefulness of halal labelling: Role of religion and culture'. *Journal of Business Research*, 68(5): 933–41.

Jamal, A. and Shukor, S. (2014) 'Antecedents and outcomes of interpersonal influences and the role of acculturation: The case of young British-Muslims'. *Journal of Business Research*, 67(3): 237–45.

Kelman, H. C. (1961) 'Processes of Opinion Change'. *Public Opinion Quarterly*, 25(1): 57–78.

Laroche, M., Yang, Z., Kim, C. and Richard, M-O. (2007) 'How culture matters in children's purchase influence: A multi-level investigation'. *Journal of the Academy of Marketing Science*, 35(1): 113–26.

Lienhardt, G. (1961) *Divinity and Experience.* Oxford: Oxford University Press.

Lindridge, A. (2005) 'Religiosity and the construction of a cultural-consumption identity'. *Journal of Consumer Marketing*, 22(3): 142–51.

Linville, P. W. (1982) 'The complexity–extremity effect and age-based stereotyping'. *Journal of Personality and Social Psychology*, 42(2): 193–211.

Luedicke, M. (2011) 'Consumer acculturation theory: (Crossing) conceptual boundaries'. *Consumption Markets & Culture*, 14(3): 223–44.

Luna, D., Peracchio, L. A. and de Juan, M. D. (2002) 'Cross-cultural and cognitive aspects of website navigation'. *Journal of the Academy of Marketing Science*, 30(4): 397–410.

Luna, D., Ringberg, T. and Peracchio, L. A. (2008) 'One individual, two identities: Frame switching among biculturals'. *Journal of Consumer Research*, 35(2): 279–93.

McCracken, G. (1986) 'Culture and consumption: A theoretical account of the structure and movement of cultural meaning of consumer goods'. *Journal of Consumer Research*, 13(June): 71–84.

McGuire, W. J. (1984) 'Search for the self: Going beyond self-esteem and the reactive self'. In *Personality and the Prediction of Behavior*, edited by R. A. Zucker, J. Aronoff and A. I. Rabin. New York, NY: Academic Press, pp. 73–120.

Nakata, C. (2009) *Beyond Hofstede: Culture Frameworks for Global Marketing and Management.* Chicago, IL: Palgrave Macmillan.

Oswald, R. L. (1999) 'Culture swapping: Consumption and the ethnogenesis of middle-class Haitian immigrants'. *Journal of Consumer Research*, 25(4): 303–18.

Peñaloza, L. N. (1994) 'Atravesando fronteras/border crossing: A critical ethnographic exploration of the consumer acculturation of Mexican immigrants'. *Journal of Consumer Research*, 21(1): 32–54.

Peñaloza, L. (2007) 'Research with ethnic communities'. In *The Handbook of Qualitative Research in Marketing*, edited by R. Belk. Cheltenham, UK: Edward Elgar, pp. 547–59.

Peñaloza, L. and Gilly, M. C. (1999) 'Marketer acculturation: The changer and the changed'. *Journal of Marketing*, 63(3): 84–104.

Pires, G. D., Stanton, P. J. and Stanton, J. (2005) *Ethnic Marketing: Accepting the Challenge of Cultural Diversity.* London: Thomson Learning.

Ram, M. (1994) 'Unravelling social networks in ethnic minority firms'. *International Small Business Journal*, 12(3): 42–53.

Schwartz, S. J., Unger, J. B., Zamboanga, B. L. and Szapocznik, J. (2010) 'Rethinking the concept of acculturation: Implications for theory and research'. *American Psychologist*, 65(4): 237–51.

Sood, J. and Nasu, Y. (1995) 'Religiosity and nationality: An exploratory study of their effect on consumer behavior in Japan and the United States'. *Journal of Business Research*, 34(1): 1–9.

Tajfel, H. (1981) *Human Groups and Social Categories: Studies in Social Psychology*. Cambridge, MA: Cambridge University Press.

Tonkin, E., Chapman, M. and McDonald, M. (eds) (1989) *History and Ethnicity*. London: Routledge.

Wallendorf, M. and Reilly M. (1983) 'Ethnic migration, assimilation, and consumption'. *Journal of Consumer Research*, 10(December): 292–302.

Wamwara-Mbugua, L. W., Cornwell, T. B. and Boller, G. (2008) 'Triple acculturation: The role of African Americans in the consumer acculturation of Kenyan immigrants'. *Journal of Business Research*, 61(2): 83–90.

Part II

Processes of ethnic cultural change, socialization and technology

2

Models of culture change

Michel Laroche and Ahmad Jamal

Introduction

Migration involves movements of people from one place to another and many Western countries have a long history of attracting immigrants from different parts of the world. The impact of migration and resettlement on the consumption experiences of immigrants has long been a matter of great interest to researchers (Hui, Joy, Kim and Laroche 1992) in various disciplines like anthropology, sociology, social psychology and consumer behaviour. The key question of how immigrants remain involved with their culture of origin (even after spending substantial amounts of time in their respective countries of destination) is an enduring one in multicultural environments like the USA, Canada, Australia and the UK. Different theoretical frameworks exist explaining the phenomena, and this chapter aims to review such frameworks and identify future research directions.

Models of culture change

Melting pot and assimilation

In its purest form, the melting pot ideology 'assumed that each ethnic group would blend into a national whole that was greater than the sum of the ethnic parts' (Crispino 1980, p. 6). Such ideology underpins the phenomenon of assimilation, which is 'the process of interpenetration and fusion in which persons and groups acquire the memories, sentiments and attitudes of other persons or groups and by sharing their experience and history, are incorporated with them in a common cultural life' (Park and Burgess 1921, p. 735, cited in Gordon 1964, p. 62).

From this definition, Gordon (1964) identified seven types of assimilation. First, cultural or behavioural assimilation happens when the immigrants change their patterns (including religious beliefs and observance) to those of the host society. Second, structural assimilation happens when the immigrants enter, at a large scale, cliques, clubs and institutions of the host society on a primary group level. Third, marital assimilation occurs when the immigrants have large scale intermarriages with members of the host society. Fourth, identical assimilation occurs when the immigrants develop a sense of people-hood or ethnicity based exclusively on the values of host society. Fifth, attitudinal receptional assimilation occurs when the immigrants do not encounter any prejudiced attitudes. Sixth, behavioural receptional assimilation occurs when the immigrants do not encounter any discriminatory behaviour. Finally, civic assimilation occurs when the immigrants do not have any conflict for value and power with members of the host society.

According to Gordon, acculturation referred only to what he described as *cultural or behavioural assimilation*. Hence 'acculturation' in this sense was presented as part of an overall phenomenon called 'assimilation'. Accordingly, acculturation was treated as a linear bipolar process, by which individuals within immigrant communities give up the attitudes, values and behaviours of their original culture when acquiring those of the host culture (Gordon 1964). This definition confounds acquisition of host-cultural traits with the loss of original-cultural traits (Kim, Laroche and Tomiuk 2001). From a theoretical viewpoint, this perspective fails to consider alternatives to assimilation such as integrated or bi-cultural identities (Dion and Dion 2001).

Furthermore, a substantial amount of research in the last five decades into immigrants and the way they behave, act and consume does not provide significant support for everyone in the immigrants' communities to assimilate in the way described by Gordon (1964). The assimilation approach is also criticized on the grounds that the it is 'uni-directional', with movement always towards replacement of old (country of origin) with new (country of destination) (see for example Hui *et al.* 1992; Padilla 1980). Rather than assimilating in its purest form and in its entirety, immigrants tend to engage in a more complex form of adaptation: (a) acquiring some skills and/or traits to function within a host culture and (b) retaining aspects of their culture of origin. The former has been referred to as *acculturation* and the latter as *ethnic identity* (Phinney 1990; 1992).

Acculturation

According to Redfield, Linton and Herskovits (1936), acculturation 'results when groups of individuals having different cultures come into continuous first-hand contact, with subsequent changes in the original cultural patterns of either or both groups' (p. 149). The Social Science Research Council defined acculturation as the 'culture change that is initiated by the conjunction of two or more autonomous cultural systems' (Palmer 1954, p. 974). Most definitions found in the literature have common denominators: (a) people from two cultural origins; (b) continuous contact of two groups and (c) adaptation of cultural dimensions by individuals in groups. While cultural change occurs as a result of any intercultural contact anywhere in the world (e.g. teenagers around the world adopting Western cultural values due to their exposure to Global Consumer Culture (GCC) and engagement with global social media), the cultural change (under the term 'acculturation') is often studied among individuals (e.g., immigrants, refugees, asylum seekers and sojourners such as international students) living in countries or regions other than they were born (Schwartz Unger, Zamboanga and Szapocznik 2010).

Within marketing, 'consumer acculturation' is the 'process through which people raised in one culture acquire consumption-related values, attitudes and customs of another culture, through direct or indirect contact' (Schiffman, Dillon and Ngumah 1981). Peñaloza (1994) identifies three steps in the consumer acculturation process: (1) *move*, where one immigrates to a new country; (2) *translate*, where one associates host culture's concepts with home culture's ones to comprehend the new environment; and (3) *adapt*, where one learns how to function in the new culture. These steps of the consumer acculturation process are identified in several contexts, i.e., Hispanics, Blacks, European immigrants in the United States and Canada, and Muslims in Europe (Palumbo and Teich 2004). However, they do not follow a linear trend, but a complex, dynamic, cyclic and irregular process by which immigrants experience foreclosure (i.e. acceptance without question), then move to a crisis before finally reaching moratorium (i.e. questioning and experimenting). Immigrants can go back and forth through these phases before achieving an identity (Steenkamp 2001).

Ethnic identity

For Phinney (1990) ethnic identity is: (a) based on context and meaningfulness in relation to a dominant culture; (b) fluid and malleable after immigration; (c) confounded with acculturation; (d) more salient after immigration; and (e) not specific to one ethnic group. In many conceptualizations, ethnic identity and acculturation are confounded. This is represented by a bipolar model of acculturation or changing ethnic identity (Phinney 1990; Phinney and Ong 2007; Laroche, Pons and Richard 2009). This model represents an *assimilationist* perspective where acquisitions of host-cultural traits are accompanied by some weakening of the original culture. In others, the two constructs are independent. However, a further flexible perspective provides a more complex representation of changing culture (Berry 1990; Keefe and Padilla 1987; Mendoza 1989; Phinney 1990; Laroche *et al.* 2009). Thus, highly acculturated people may exhibit high ethnic identity; and conversely, high ethnic identity people may show varying levels of acculturation. This perspective is related to *multiculturalism* and is a better theoretical base for the study of culture change (Berry 1990).

Situational nature of culture change

Acculturation is viewed as a multi-dimensional process. Researchers argue that the acquisition of new cultural traits and the weakening of traditional cultures vary from trait to trait (Hui, Joy, Kim and Laroche 1993; Keefe and Padilla 1987; Mendoza 1989). This *selective acculturation* explains the tendency of immigrants to adopt some *strategic traits* such as learning English to gain employment while maintaining native values and traditions (Keefe and Padilla 1987). Thus, processes like acculturation or ethnic identity are adaptive responses to structural situations (Yancey, Eriksen and Juliani 1976; Frideres and Goldenberg 1982). Bouchet (1995) provides support by arguing that ethnic identity is like a bricolage whereby one builds self-identity on the basis of heterogeneous elements taken from a diversity of cultural representations and practices. Stayman and Deshpandé (1989) argue that persons in multicultural societies have a set of ethnic and other identities that are differentially salient in different situations. Like mainstream consumers, immigrants may have multiple selves (Markus and Kunda 1986) and may engage in culture swapping (Jamal 2003; Oswald 1999). Stayman and Deshpandé (1989) gave the example of the salience of Irish ethnicity felt by an Irish American on St. Patrick's Day, and how it might affect the choice of a restaurant on that day compared to non-Irish holidays.

Hyperacculturation

Wallendorf and Reilly (1983) found that Mexican Americans, Anglo Americans and Mexicans living in Mexico all had different consumption patterns, with Mexican Americans consuming the most 'American-type' products. Thus, Mexican Americans over-assimilate to *prior* perceptions of American cultural styles and these conceptions of American lifestyles may originate from inferences drawn from the mass media (ibid.). Similar patterns are found among Korean Americans (Wei-Na and Koog-Hyang 1992) and Italian Americans (Celeste 2006).

According to *cultivation theory*, people are brought up in a mass-mediated environment (Gerbner, Gross, Morgan and Signorielli 1980) and immigrants to the United States – while learning its culture – rely more on material symbols and indirect exposure (e.g. through television) than on direct exposure and participation in related events (Wallendorf and Arnould 1988). Television viewing studies find that people with little direct social experiences more likely assume that these images of the host society are real (Conway Dato-on 2000). Thus, immigrants may become over-assimilated to the host culture, falsely accepting the consumption cues provided by the mass media. The notion of hyper-acculturation or over-acculturation may also apply to members of the host society who may experience cultural change following their exposure to immigrant cultural groups (Jamal 2003). For example, Jamal (1996) documents instances of over-acculturation among the native English in Bradford (UK) who consumed spicier and hotter Asian dishes than did the British Pakistanis in the same town.

Askegaard, Arnould and Kjeldgaard (2005) studying Greenlandic immigrants in four Danish cities found evidence in support of Greenlandic hyperculture. Immigrants idealized cultural possessions associated with Greenland and consumed hyped commercial elements as emblems of authentic culture—with their identities becoming more Greenlandic than the Greenlandic people. This hyperassimilated identity involving elements of cultural maintenance and authenticity represented a reverse of the hyperassimilated identity identified by Wallendorf and Reilly (1983) in a North American context (Askegaard *et al.* 2005). There are other examples where immigrants seek to become more ethnic than their counterparts in the host culture. For example, Jamal (1997) documents the case of British Pakistanis in Bradford (UK) who sought to experience Islamic and cultural identities in the UK more strongly than the Muslims in Pakistan.

Dimensions of culture change

The indicators of acculturation are classified into behavioural, attitudinal, linguistic, psychological and socio-economic dimensions (Olmedo, Martinez and Martinez 1978). They vary in types and numbers from one group to another and from one study to another. For any specific group, these dimensions are the salient features of identification (Christian, Gadfield, Giles and Taylor 1976). Some of the accepted indicators of cultural change are: (a) *language*, (b) *friendship networks*, (c) *religion*, (d) *participation in ethnic organizations*, (e) *food preferences*, (f) *ethnic celebrations*, and (g) *politics* (e.g. Driedger 1975; Phinney 1990; Rosenthal and Feldman 1992). Other indicators of culture change include music, dress and media consumption (e.g. Peñaloza 1994).

An exhaustive literature search on ethnic identity and acculturation shows that some dimensions appear with higher frequencies (Laroche, Kim, Tomiuk and Belisle 2005). Thus, a structure of ethnic acculturation or identity applicable to many but not all groups may include: (a) one or more *language-based* dimensions and (b) an *ethnic attachment* dimension. Various language-based factors emerge as dimensions for several ethnic groups (Aboud and Christian 1979; de la Garza, Newcomb and Myers 1995; Giles, Taylor, Lambert and Goodwin 1976). Most measures include language-based items in contexts, which include *media consumption/exposure* (e.g. Keefe and Padilla 1987) and *family* (e.g., Keefe and Padilla 1987; Valencia 1985). *Ethnic attachment* also emerge as an important dimension of ethnic identity (Keefe and Padilla 1987; Kwan and Sodowsky 1997; Phinney 1992).

Bi-dimensional models

Scholars state that when original and host-cultural identities are independent, the cultural adaptation process can be better understood (Berry 2005; 2009). Congruent with this viewpoint, studies of ethnic groups in the United States and Canada find that the adaptation process does not necessarily cause the loss of one's original ethnic identity (Lambert, Mermigis and Taylor 1986). There are six key bi-dimensional models: (1) Berry's model, (2) Mendoza and Martinez's model, (3) Laroche and colleagues' model, (4) Cleveland and Laroche's AGCC model, (5) Cleveland and colleagues' extended model and (6) Laroche and colleagues' non-linear model.

Berry's model

For Berry (1990), countries with official multiculturalism policies and acceptance of ethnic cultures and identities allow for high degrees of culture maintenance across generations of immigrants.

Berry (1980) states that change occurs along two independent dimensions: (1) the degree of *maintenance* of the original culture and (2) the degree of *conformity* to the attitudes and behaviours of the host culture. Dichotomizing these two dimensions provides four acculturation patterns (ibid.). Thus, adapting to the values, norms and traditions of the host society does not require or accompany a weakening cultural maintenance. Those who maintain their original identity while adopting traits of the host culture follow an *integrationist* route. Those who maintain their original culture while rejecting host-cultural traits adopt a *separatist* position. Those who abandon their ethnic identity in favour of host-cultural traits follow the *assimilation* route. Finally, those who neither maintain original cultural traits, nor adopt host cultural ones are *marginalized* or *decultured*. Research on Berry's (1980) conceptual framework (e.g., Kim, Laroche and Joy 1990; Laroche, Kim, Hui and Tomiuk 1998; Hui *et al.* 1992) found strong support for the integrationist – rather than the assimilationist – perspective. Integrated (or 'bi-cultural') consumers often experience high levels of self-esteem, confidence and pro-social behaviours (e.g. Chen, Benet-Martínez and Bond 2008) and are better able to adapt to cultural differences (Benet-Martínez and Haritatos 2005).

Berry (1990) stated that the acculturation process may operate unevenly, i.e. ethnic minority consumers may exhibit varying levels of acculturation while acting on different social and family roles (O'Guinn and Faber 1985). For Stayman and Deshpandé (1989) the degree of acculturation is context-specific, i.e. one may acquire aspects of the host culture when deemed appropriate (e.g. at work), and reject the same when they are no longer appropriate (Jun, Ball and Gentry 1993). Many ethnic minority consumers seek the 'best of both worlds', valuing both heritage and host cultures, expressing positive attitudes towards consumables emblematic of both cultural environments (Askegaard *et al.* 2005).

Mendoza and Martinez's model

Mendoza and Martinez (1981) suggested a different four-typology conceptualization of acculturation patterns: (1) *cultural resistance* (i.e. actively or passively resisting acquisitions of host-cultural norms and behaviours while maintaining traditional customs), (2) *cultural shift* (i.e. new host-cultural norms are substituted for traditional customs), (3) *cultural incorporation* (i.e. customs are adapted from both original and host cultures) and (4) *cultural transmutation* (i.e. a unique subcultural entity is developed from a modification or combination of both native and host-cultural norms). One key aspect of Mendoza and Martinez's framework is that ethnic groups may use one acculturation pattern for certain customs while using other patterns for others: 'immigrant individuals are generally multifaceted with respect to the various types and dimensions of acculturation' (Mendoza 1989, p. 374). Despite differences in terminologies, there are overlaps and similarities between models proposed by Mendoza and Martinez (1981) and Berry (1980).

Laroche and colleagues' (Chinese, French/English, Italian and Greek) models

Derived from the bi-dimensional perspective to the immigrant adaptation process, a growing number of researchers (e.g. Laroche, Kim, Hui and Joy 1996) took a different approach by measuring the two dimensions (i.e. acculturation and ethnic identity) separately. Acculturation is multi-dimensional (Rogler, Cortes and Malgady 1991), implying that the adaptation process likely occurs at different rates in different socio-cultural spheres such as at work or in the family. This can be significant in collectivist cultures such as China that emphasize solidarity to the group and greatly value family life. Most acculturation research focuses on adult immigrant consumers and Laroche, Yang, Kim and Chan's (2006) attempt in incorporating influences in the family represented a step in the right direction. Interactions among children and parents play a significant role in the resettlement process in a new cultural environment and in inter-generational discourse within immigrant families. Laroche, Yang, Kim and Richard (2007) introduced the concept of *family acculturative distance* and showed it led to differing patterns of family decision making.

Chinese family triadic acculturation

Research by Laroche *et al.* (2006) fills a void in family studies by the development and valida-tion of an empirical family triadic self-report instrument that examines the acculturation levels of Chinese immigrant families in North America. The Chinese Family Triadic Acculturation (CFTA) scale conceptualizes acculturation as part of the immigrant adaptation process with multi-dimensional measures, and enables researchers to assess attitudes and behaviours in a vari-ety of situations. Unlike previous studies, they developed and validated an acculturation measure through multiple-respondent, multiple-item data from fathers, mothers and children. The use of multiple respondents as multiple methods required a strict measure purification process in which both internal consistency and inter-group agreement had to be taken into account. Of the twenty-two initial items, the purification process produced nine items that probed three distinct facets of acculturation. The CFTA scale included three factors, namely *English-Chinese (E-C) identification and attachment, English language use at home* and *E-C social interaction.* This solution was confirmed by another study conducted by Kim, Laroche and Tomiuk (2004).

The test of the construct validity of the CFTA scale entailed applying confirmatory factor analysis to the data, regarding three dimensions of acculturation as 'traits', and the average scores from different respondents on the multiple-item measures as 'methods'. Analyses yielded con-sistent evidence of the convergent and discriminant validity of the triadic measures. Therefore, the CFTA scale was treated as a reliable instrument in assessing the relative acculturation levels incorporating views of all family members for Chinese immigrant families.

One issue that arose concerned acculturation measurement. Media consumption embed-ded in the category of *English language use* in the questionnaire (i.e. language use when reading newspapers/magazines and watching movies/videotapes) neither showed up as a distinct dimension of acculturation nor was it revealed as significant factor loadings in factor analyses. This finding was surprising since media exposure has been found to relate significantly to immigrants' acculturation (Lee and Tse 1994). According to Douglas and Macquin (1977), the differences in lifestyles of consumers from different countries may lead to different effective-ness for different media. Given the distinctness of Chinese ethnic groups, further studies should extend media exposure measures to the exposure of TV and radio programs to investigate its role in the acculturation assessment of family triads.

Overall, as an exploratory investigation of the CFTA scale, the results were encouraging. Although further research is required with a larger sample and revised measures of mass communication, findings propose that the CFTA scale may exhibit satisfactory validity and reliability, and that it shows promise as a useful tool for researchers working with Chinese immigrant families.

French/English acculturation

Studies by Laroche *et al.* (1996) revealed that French Canadian (FC) ethnic affiliation and acculturative tendency toward the English Canadian (EC) culture were two major dimensions underlying FC ethnic change brought on by continuous contacts with English Canadians. *FC ethnic affiliation*, as indicated by FC social interactions, FC family, FC self-identification and attachment to FC culture, in essence reflected FC individuals' psychological, social, as well as cultural identification with their ethnic origins. On the other hand, the *acculturative tendency* dimension, as indicated by EC social interactions, attachment to EC culture and attitude toward cultural exchange, reflected FC individuals' social and psychological affinity towards the EC culture.

Italian/Greek ethnic identity

Laroche *et al.* (2005) adopt a *general* perspective on ethnic identity rather than a *specific* one in that the structure of ethnic identity is applicable to at least two groups, such as the Greeks and the Italians in North America. Traditional Greek and Italian cultures appear to be heterogeneous when aspects of identity are considered. Each is defined by specific cultural practices and traditions, yet they exemplify strongly imbedded characteristics that are common and equally important to both groups. Specifically, Laroche *et al.* suggest that ethnic identity, in such a context, involves multiple dimensions, which include: (a) *ethnic language use with family members*, (b) *ethnic language media exposure* and (c) *ethnic attachment*. The three dimensions formed important aspects of Greek and Italian ethnic identities within multicultural Canada. Language issues are clearly relevant to Italian and Greek identities.

The extant literature provides support by suggesting that *ethnic language use with family members* is very important to Greek and Italian ethnic identity maintenance (Lambert, Mermigis, and Taylor 1986; Rotunno and McGoldrick 1982; Stycos 1948). Similar conclusions appear with respect to *ethnic language media exposure*. For instance, both the Italian and Greek communities in major metropolitan areas of Canada (e.g., Montreal and Toronto) have their own ethnic language newspapers, magazines and radio stations. Also, print media forms from the original country are numerous and readily available within their ethnic neighbourhoods. The importance of *ethnic attachment* is also clear with either group. For example, Ramirez (1989) discusses the emergence of Italian churches/parishes, issues related to the creation of Italian schools and the number of Italian grocery stores, clubs, cafés and community organizations. Moreover, Italian immigrants from the same area in Italy tend to intermarry and form residential clusters in cities. Similar patterns and findings appear for the Greeks (Chimbos and Agocs 1983; Kourvetaris 1971; Lambert, Mermigis and Taylor 1986).

Acculturation to the global consumer culture

The issue of culture change is relevant and applicable to consumers around the world. We live in a global world that is characterized by social and cultural interconnectedness, facilitated by advancements in technology and, more than ever, exposure and use of social media and global consumer culture. The unprecedented improvements in worldwide systems of transport and communication are speeding up the velocity of the diffusion of ideas, information, goods, capital and consumer culture. In the backdrop of such trends, Cleveland and Laroche (2007) examined the complex interaction and contextual nature of local and global cultural influences on consumer behaviour and, in doing so, developed and validated a scale for Acculturation to the Global Consumer Culture (AGCC), which considered 'how individuals acquire the knowledge, skills and behaviors that are characteristic of a nascent and deterritorialized global consumer culture (GCC)' (p. 59). Their study identified seven drivers of culture change: (1) exposure to and use of English, (2) exposure to global and foreign mass media, (3) exposure to marketing activities of multinational corporations, (4) social interactions (e.g. travel, migration and contacts with foreigners), (5) cosmopolitanism, (6) openness to and desire to participate in the GCC and (7) self-identification with the GCC. This scale has been successfully tested in several different countries (Cleveland 2006; Hallab 2009; Naghavi 2011; Sobol 2008).

Exposure to global and foreign mass media

The key assumption is that the greater the exposure to global and foreign mass media, the greater the AGCC will be. The wide use of electronic media allows consumers from around the world to watch the same television shows and movies, listen to the same music and read the same news (Cross and Smits 2005); thus they are exposed to the same messages and brands. Western media is the 'teacher from which Third World countries learn to assimilate' (Schiller 1976, cited in Roedl 2006, p. 3). It is natural to 'want what others have', especially the rich and famous portrayed in television programs (Douglas and Isherwood 1978). American television is present in many countries as an agent of popular culture. The American film industry dominates domestic and international markets, accounting for 58 per cent to 93 per cent of the Western-European markets (Hesmondhalgh 2002). Also, the mass media developed from one-way communication to two-way interactions between sender and receiver (Castells 2000) to more interactive social media, which is 'democratizing the spread of information' (Legrain 2002, p. 313). However, the uneven penetration of electronic media leads to an imbalance of cultural influences in the development of the GCC. This is clear through the Western nature of internet content, 75 per cent of which is written in English (Gilsdorf 2006).

Exposure to and use of English

The key assumption is that a greater exposure and use of English language facilitates the AGCC. English is the language of science (Tenbruck 1990), business, tourism and diplomacy (Huntington 1996), and the symbol of modernism and internationalism (Ray, Ryder and Scott 1994; Alden, Steenkamp and Batra 1999; Graddol 2000). Many consumers around the world learn to read and write English (as part of secondary and higher education) and are thus able to use the English language as a main tool for operating in most fields: internet, commerce, banking and travelling. Almost all global brands originate from Western countries and extensively use English on product packaging and other forms of marketing communications. While the preference for mother tongue and national language has an impact, greater appreciation and use of English language facilitates acquisition of consumption-related phenomena such as the GCC.

Exposure to marketing activities of multinational corporations

A greater exposure to marketing activities of global brands and multinationals also facilitates culture change. In addition to mass media and language, marketing activities cross borders and influence consumer behaviour worldwide, facilitating culture change. In using advertising marketers inform consumers about their products, but in doing so they diffuse cultural values through a 'meaning transfer' (McCracken 1986). Brands are associated with 'an image, a set of emotions, a way of life' and 'are about meaning, not product attributes' (Legrain 2002, pp. 121–3). We live in a world of 'global brands' (e.g., Coca-Cola, Nike, Apple, BMW), 'global logos' (e.g., Nike's 'swoosh', McDonald's 'golden arches'), 'global icons' (e.g., Michael Jordon, Paris Hilton, James Bond), 'global products' (e.g., cell phones, fast foods, jeans, sushi) and 'global campaigns' (e.g., McDonald's 'Loving It!', Nike's 'Just Do It!') – all diffusing traits of the GCC. Multinationals advertise their products through branding and celebrity/ movie endorsements (Tanner 2002). Coca-Cola portrays the consumption of its beverage as 'America's promise of peace, freedom, prosperity, democracy, and shopping' (Tanner 2002, p. 42). Endorsement strategies are used by companies such as Nike sponsored by Tiger Woods in the PGA golf tournaments, Rolex – the wristwatches of James Bond – and FedEx, which was promoted in various blockbuster movies such as *Cast Away* and *Spiderman*.

Social interactions

Culture change is also facilitated by social interactions occurring through business and leisure travel, international studies and migration. People bring in their cultural heritage, which they unconsciously diffuse into the mainstream population (Graddol 2000). In addition, the same people returning home 'act as walking displays for glittering consumer goods they bring back from their adopted cultures' (Ger and Belk 1996, p. 281). Social interactions, through direct and indirect contacts, facilitate the propagation of the GCC (Appadurai 1996). Tourism is the largest industry in the world (Firat 1995; Legrain 2002). Today, travel is a mainstream activity that has become less expensive, faster and accessible to all. Migration is considered as a common occurrence with 175 million people living outside their country of origin in 2000 (Doyle 2004). Lower travel costs, relaxing barriers, advances in information and communication technology, better opportunities abroad, and the widespread use of English encourage and facilitate migration (ibid.).

Cosmopolitanism

Cultures are territorially bound, and people belonging to transnational cultures are frequent travellers, interacting with people from all around the world to become a part of local social networks (Thompson and Tambyah 1999). These individuals are 'cosmopolitans' described as 'intellectuals who are at home in the cultures of other peoples as well as their own' (Konrad 1984, p. 209), as people who have the 'willingness to explore and experience the panoply of transcultural diversity' (Thompson and Tambyah 1999, p. 216), as individuals 'participating in many worlds without becoming part of them' (Thompson and Tambyah 1999, p. 220), as cultural gatekeepers 'deciding what gets in, and what will be kept out, ignored, explicitly rejected' (Hannerz 1990, p. 258), and as 'core agents of global cultural flow' (Cleveland 2006, p. 71). Cosmopolitans are distinct from tourists, who only visit different countries and act as spectators of, rather than participants in, the culture (Hannerz 1990). Cosmopolitans 'want to be able to sneak backstage rather than being confined to the front stage areas' (Hannerz 1990, p. 242). To be labelled as cosmopolitan, an individual needs to possess enough competencies and flexibility (i.e. 'cultural intelligence') to adequately experience world cultures. Cosmopolitanism has been related to educational attainment (Robertson and Zill 1997), high motivation predisposing to cosmopolitan consumption practices (Holt 1998, cited in Thompson and Tambyah 1999, p. 217), and frequent travelling (Santora 2006).

Technology and television programs provide the opportunity to experience diverse lifestyles and cultures without leaving their country, and thus to be cosmopolitan (Hannerz 1990). Cosmopolitans use consumption as a means to integrate into the diverse societies they encounter. First, it allows them to live like the locals do, by eating the same foods, wearing the same clothes, listening to the same music and enjoying the same leisure activities. Second, consumption provides the opportunity to establish a network of local friendships, which further facilitates integration into the mainstream culture (Thompson and Tambyah 1999).

Openness to and desire to participate in the global consumer culture

Globalization has created a single forum, where all members live their daily lives and pursue their goals in relative terms, comparing themselves with others (Robertson 1992). It is human nature to admire and envy the possessions of others. Researchers found that individuals who admire the lifestyles and consumption patterns of other countries are more prone to desire the ownership of such goods (Appadurai 1996; Alden, Steenkamp and Batra 1999; Batra *et al.* 2000). However, individuals do not usually emulate all aspects of a foreign culture, but rather as Cleveland (2006, p. 74) stated 'the acculturation to the global consumer culture is believed to be a selective, contextual and adaptive process'.

Also, one does not need to be cosmopolitan to desire to participate in the GCC. For example, the 'global youth' segment desires consumer goods promoted through global media (Alden, Steenkamp and Batra 1999). However they do not necessarily integrate themselves into different world societies. Ji and McNeal (2001) explained that the younger generations are 'less culture-bound and more open to Western lifestyles and accompanying products' (p. 80) than older ones. Schlegel (2000) stated that it is increasingly difficult to differentiate adolescents based on their nationality because their dress, hair styles, music and restaurants tend to be the same worldwide. They increasingly speak the same language, namely English. The author also stated two reasons to explain the transportability of the global youth culture: first, its elements are often banal and require little effort from the listener, viewer, eater and wearer (e.g. fast food); second, it propagates universal concepts such as love, sex, fashion, wealth and power, which relate to adolescents everywhere.

Self-identification with the global consumer culture

Greater self-identification with the GCC also facilitates culture change. This dimension refers to 'self-ascribed membership in or outright identification with some form of global consumer culture' (Cleveland 2006, p. 165). Consumers around the globe are exposed to foreign cultural elements through travel, mass media and global advertising. Thus, they are free to select how much they want to identify with some lifestyles and belief systems (Ogden, Ogden and Schau 2004), which affects their patterns of thinking and behaving. This freedom of choice is contingent on individual factors such as accessibility, income, education and exposure. An individual's self-identification to the GCC allows to go beyond the mere interest or desire to be part of a global segment and leads to behaving in accordance with the values of the GCC (i.e. actively seek to purchase international products and become a global consumer).

Cleveland and colleagues expanded model

Cleveland, Laroche, Pons and Kastoun (2009) propose a new typology of culture-change patterns, based on the relative influence of ethnic identity and acculturation from a consumption perspective. Expanding on the culture-change categorizations proposed by others (Mendoza and Martinez 1981; Berry 1980), they propose a classification scheme composed of seven distinct culture-change patterns, as summarized in Table 2.1.

As opposed to the absolute boundaries implied by the categorizations proposed by Mendoza and Martinez (1981) and Berry (1980), their conceptualization of culture-change patterns and subsequent consumption behaviour is more of a matter of degree. Researchers (e.g., Belk 1974; McGuire, McGuire, Child and Fujioka 1978; McCracken 1986; Stayman and Deshpandé 1989) share the view that an individual's level of felt ethnicity is, at least in part, situationally determined. This suggests a 'heterogeneic' (McGuire *et al.* 1978) or elastic conceptualization of ethnicity, in that 'particular contexts may determine which of a person's communal identities or loyalties are appropriate at a given time' (Paden 1967, as cited in Okamura 1981, p. 452). They propose that – depending on the particular context – (home-culture) ethnic identification and/or (host-culture) acculturation will play greater, lesser, or non-significant roles in predicting consumption behaviours. Under certain conditions, consumption is unrelated to the cultural variables (culture-change pattern 1), whereas in other cases, consumption may reflect a uni-dimensional process of culture change: assimilation (pattern 7). Consumption behaviour may also be a 'purely monocultural' occurrence (whereby either acculturation or ethnic identification is strongly predictive of consumption, patterns 2 and 6, respectively), a 'relatively monocultural' occurrence (wherein either acculturation or ethnic identification dominates consumption, patterns 3 and 5, respectively), or a bi-cultural occurrence (whereby consumption is a more or less balanced function of both acculturation and ethnic identification, pattern 4).

Table 2.1 A proposed typology of culture-change patterns, as a function of acculturation and ethnic identification

Culture-change pattern	Description, relationship to consumption behavior (CB)	Mendoza's (1989) typology*	Berry's (1980) typology
1. Deculturation	No relationship of acculturation (Acc) nor ethnic identification (Id) to consumption behavior (CB).		Marginalization
2. Pure Acculturation	Acc strongly predictive of CB, Id non-significant.		
3. Acculturation dominant	Both Acc and Id predictive of CB; the former with substantially greater magnitude.	} Cultural incorporation*	} Integration
4. Balanced	Both Acc and Id rather equally predictive of CB.		
5. Ethnic identification dominant	Both Acc and Id predictive of CB; the latter with substantially greater magnitude.		
6. Pure ethnic identification	Id strongly predictive of CB, Acc non-significant.	Cultural resistance	Separation
7. Assimilation	Unidimensional process of acculturation: CB *negatively* related to Acc.	Culture shift	Assimilation

Note
*Under certain consumption characteristics/circumstances, Mendoza's (1989) fourth categorization, cultural transmutation (i.e., 'an alteration of native and alternate cultural practices to create a unique subcultural entity,' p. 373) may be a more appropriate descriptor.

Nonlinear model of acculturation

Following a review of the literature on the empirically found correlations between acculturation and ethnic identification, Laroche *et al.* (1998) proposed that linguistic acculturation was nonlinearly related to ethnic identity. An empirical study was conducted to test this relationship using data gathered from multiple studies investigating four different ethnic groups over a period of seven years. The findings indicated that these two dimensions of ethnicity were related, and that the postulated function provided an excellent fit to the data. The findings suggested a new model of adaptation called the 'attraction-resistance model', in which the acculturating group would initially resist any loss of ethnic identity. Over time, this resistance would weaken with increased losses of identity associated in increasing acculturation. The proposed model was consistent with the opposing needs of Brewer's (1991) social self: need for assimilation and need for differentiation.

Moving beyond the bi-dimensional models of acculturation

Flannery, Reise and Yu (2001) proposed a three-dimensional model as an alternative to the unidimensional and the bi-dimensional ones. Their model includes the dimension of home (identity) and host (acculturation) orientations, to which they add a third dimension of *ethnogenesis*, defined as the creation of a new culture or ethnicity (e.g. Oswald 1999). The key assumption is that when acculturation phenomena overlap with ethnicity phenomena, a new sense of ethnicity is formed that goes beyond the typical distinction between home and host cultures. For example, being a Chinese American is more than the simple sum of 'being Chinese' and 'being American'. As examples, Flannery *et al.* cite Glazer and Moynihan's (1970) descriptions of Italian Americans living in New York City, whereby such immigrants experience a new culture and a new sense of being shaped by distinctive experiences of life in the US. This dimension of ethnogenesis might well be related to Mendoza's (1989) cultural transmutation change pattern as well as reflecting Laroche *et al.*'s (1998) attraction-resistance model.

Flannery *et al.*'s (2001) argument is particularly relevant to immigrants who, after immigration and having lived in the new cultural environment for a while, can relate and identify with what Wamwara-Mbugua, Cornwell and Boller (2008) call an 'entrenched' subculture. In many Western countries, worldwide-immigration patterns of recent decades led to the creation of noticeable ethnic minority subcultures. Interactions with ethnic enclaves generate ongoing processes of cultural consolidation pertaining to traditional elements of the heritage culture (e.g., moral imperatives about sex, marriage and kinship responsibilities) and cultural reformulation in adjusting to the wider society of the receiving community (Weinreich 2009). Entrenched subcultures act as an important source of social, cultural and economic capitals for ethnic minority entrepreneurial initiatives and activities (e.g. Jamal 2005) and even cause marketers to change and adapt to acculturation processes in the marketplace (e.g. Peñaloza and Gilly 1999).

Askegaard *et al.* (2005) identify and emphasize the key role of transnational consumer culture as a third acculturation factor in addition to heritage and host cultures. In the context of Greenlandic being and Danish having, the Greenlandic immigrant identity formation became persistently self-reflexive. Strong evidence emerged in support of participants reclaiming Greenlandic identity through consumption and the integration of Greenland and Denmark in a transnational consumer and communications economy providing additional inputs to Greenlandic identity formation in Denmark. High awareness of global cultural economy and engagement with the GCC fuelled a questioning of ethnic identity as both Greenlandic and Danish identities were refracted through experiences in other parts of the world.

Moreover, Askegaard *et al.* identify the *oscillating pendulum* as an identity position not reflected in the acculturation research incorporating the bi-dimensional models of acculturation. The *oscillating pendulum* reflects the notion that, while acculturating, an ethnic minority consumer can experience the alienations and attractions of both heritage and host cultures. For example, participants expressed a need to retreat from the perceived mechanistic strictures of the market-mediated Danish world through repeated physical border crossing, desiring unadulterated doses of idealized Greenlandic cuisine and sociality and experiences of being in an authentic Greenland. At the same time, they felt that while in Greenland they would miss their experiences of being in Denmark (e.g., more variety and choice while shopping or less family obligations).

Jamal and Chapman (2000) also document the positivity and negativity of experiencing the heritage and host cultures and the ambivalent nature of being and having in an acculturative context. Everyday acculturative experiences involving interactions and perceptions of heritage and host cultures, ethnic minority consumers continuously revisit identity positions. The process of construction and deconstruction of identity is a continuous one and is based on day-to-day apprehension of reality, including understanding and awareness of having and being in the heritage and host cultures and in the transnational consumer culture.

The identity positions taken by ethnic minority consumers reflect multiple and often conflicting ideological positions in a given context; such identity positions are not a matter of strategic choices to be taken but are fluid depending perhaps on situational factors, lifestyle stages (Askegaard *et al.* 2005; Jamal 2003) and developments in global consumer and transnational culture (Cleveland and Laroche 2007).

Directions for future research

In order to develop a better understanding of cultural change that occurs due to acculturation, Weinreich (2009) calls for an alternative perspective on acculturation and identity formation processes. In doing so, the author makes a case for exploring primordialist sentiments and situationalist perspectives on ethnicity. Primordial consumers adhere to an ethnicity as an unquestioned one and a given one that continues through the generations, whereas situationalist consumers often amend or change their ethnic allegiances and behaviour to suit historical and biographical exigencies. Identity formation, reformulation and maintenance by ethnic minority consumers occur in a socio-historical context. According to Weinreich, ethnic minority consumers are unable to relinquish their biographical history of successively made identifications with individuals throughout childhood and beyond, even after integrating into the mainstream society. While experiencing conflicts and tensions and attempting to resolve conflicted identifications, many may generate creative expressions of newly formulated identities (Weinreich 2009). However, further empirical research is needed to investigate the fundamental identity processes that occur prior to and after migration and that underpin acculturation experiences of ethnic minority consumers.

With the socio-historical context, intercultural relations, the compatibility (or incompatibility) in values, attitudes and religion between (or among) cultural groups, countries and nations are important considerations for understanding acculturating experiences of ethnic minority consumers. For example, Üstüner and Holt's (2007) study demonstrates how class-based domination can shape rural-to-urban migrants' acculturation to their new social setting. Özçağlar-Toulouse and Üstüner (2009) further argue that quite often the migration is from less developed, mostly colonized countries to more developed, mostly colonizing countries, and hence the historical tensions between the host and home countries and the stigmas associated with each other's cultures can also shape immigrants' collective memories and acculturation experiences. Ethnic identity processes are quite nuanced and generally without explicit conscious awareness (despite Berry's 2009 call to study consciously adopted acculturation strategies) and issues such as racism, intolerance of differences and xenophobia play an important role in identity formation of immigrants (e.g. Kosic, Mannetti and Sam 2005; Weinreich 2009)

There are calls to consider the resulting changes in both groups (the heritage and receiving groups) that emerge during the process of acculturation (Berry 2005; 2009). In this context, further research can investigate cultural transformations of places, communities and political and social systems due to acculturation encounters.

At the individual level, Berry (2005; 2009) calls for considering the psychological changes that individuals undergo and their eventual adaptation and adjustment to their new situations. Such calls are normally made in the context of meeting of two cultures or living successfully in two cultures (e.g. Berry 2005). Research on bi-cultural consumers provides support by suggesting that such consumers internalize two cultures and elements of both cultures influence their thoughts, feelings and behaviours (e.g. Luna, Ringberg and Peracchio 2008).

In reality, a person may internalize more than two cultures. In the context of ethnic minority consumers, one can find many examples whereby consumers speak more than two languages. For example, there are many British Pakistanis in the UK who speak Urdu, Punjabi, Pushto, Arabic and English who frequently navigate in-between and within multiple cultural spheres (Jamal 1997). While prior research explored the notions of culture swapping (Jamal 2003; Oswald 1999), frame switching (Luna *et al.* 2008) and oscillating pendulum (Askegaard *et al.* 2005), further research is needed to investigate the extent to which ethnic minority consumers internalize more than two cultures and the subsequent impacts of such internalization on cognitions, thoughts and behaviours. This is particularly significant given that a growing number of scholars (e.g. Visconti *et al.* 2014) identify cultural sojourning, cultural tourism, cosmopolitanism, global citizenship, pan-ethnicity and transnational ethnicity all having similar or differential effects on being and consuming in multicultural, global market economies. Such work can focus on exploring specific learning mechanisms, coping strategies (for adjusting and responding to new environments) and acculturating identities (various ways of being and having) in a multicultural context.

Askegaard (2010) points to the direction that ethnic identity can be seen as a confluence of cultural, social, temporal and contextual influences, and hence there is a need to focus on the mechanisms with which factors like gender, temporal evolution, in-group differences or generational factors operate in the identity formation of ethnic minorities. In this context, Chytkova and Özçağlar-Toulouse (2010) examine the relationship between immigrant women's gender roles and the power discourses in the society and advocate considering consumer acculturation as a network of power relations in the ethnic minority consumers' lived experiences. Similarly, Visconti (2010) identifies different levels of cultural visibility/invisibility in the consumption of second-generation ethnic minority consumers when moving back and forth in ethnic and local consumption. Moreover, Peñaloza (2010) promotes considering the temporality in the study of identity projects of ethnic minority consumers with particular focus on dissecting changes in consumers' identities over time, as impacted by intergroup relations and marketplace activities.

Such scholarly work has added valuable insights into the social, cultural and contextual aspects of consumer acculturation experiences. Future work can examine the dynamics involved in acculturation experiences and ethnic minority consumer identity projects involving different contexts (e.g. private vs. public consumption, family vs. communal consumption and market-based vs. non-market based) and different actors (e.g. family members, friends, teachers and work colleagues). While previous research considered identity formation and acculturation experiences of ethnic minority consumers in relation to specific categories (e.g. food, clothing and media consumption), further research is needed to cover other areas such as financial services, public utilities and services, education, career choices and technology products.

References

Aboud, F. E. and Christian, J. (1979) 'The early development of ethnic identity and attitudes'. In *Cross-Cultural Contributions To Psychology*, edited by L. Eckensberger, Y. Poortinga and W. J. Lonner. Lisse, Holland: Swets and Zeitlinger, pp. 47–60.

Alden, D. L., Steenkamp, J.-B. and Batra, R. (1999) 'Brand positioning through advertising in Asia, North America, and Europe: The role of Global Consumer Culture'. *Journal of Marketing* 63(1): 75–87.

Appadurai, A. (1996) *Modernity at Large: Cultural Dimensions of Globalization*. Minnesota, MN: University of Minnesota Press.

Askegaard, S. (2010) 'We are not all the same: New issues, confluence, and divergence in consumer acculturation studies'. *Special Session Summary: Advances in Consumer Research*, 37: 10–14.

Askegaard, S., Arnould, E. J. and Kjeldgaard, D. (2005) 'Postassimilationist ethnic consumer research: Qualifications and extensions'. *Journal of Consumer Research*, 32: 160–70.

Batra, R., Ramaswamy, V., Alden, D. L., Steenkamp, J. B. E. M. and Ramachander, S. (2000) 'Effects of brand local/non-local origin on consumer attitudes'. *Journal of Consumer Psychology*, 9(2): 83–95.

Belk, R. W. (1974) 'An exploratory assessment of ssituational effects in buyer behavior'. *Journal of Marketing Research*, 11(2): 156–63.

Benet-Martínez, V. and Haritatos, J. (2005) 'Bicultural Identity Integration (BII): Components and psychosocial antecedents'. *Journal of Personality*, 73: 1015–50.

Berry, J. W. (1980) 'Introduction to methodology'. In *Handbook of Cross-Cultural Psychology Methodology*, Volume 2, edited by H. C. Triandis and J. W. Berry. Boston, MA: Allyn and Bacon, Inc., pp. 1–28.

Berry, J. W. (1990) 'Psychology of acculturation'. In *Cross-Cultural Perspectives: Proceedings of the Nebraska Symposium on Motivation*, edited by J. J. Berman. Lincoln, NE: University of Nebraska Press, pp. 201–34.

Berry, J. W. (2005) 'Acculturation: Living successfully in two cultures'. *International Journal of Intercultural Relations*, 29(6): 697–712.

Berry, J. W. (2009) 'A critique of critical acculturation'. *International Journal of Intercultural Relations*, 33: 361–71.

Bouchet, D. (1995) 'Marketing and the redefinition of ethnicity'. In *Marketing in a Multicultural World*, edited by J. A. Costa and G. J. Bamossy. London: Sage Publications, pp. 68–104.

Brewer, M. B. (1991) 'The social self: On being the same and ddifferent at the same time'. *Personality and Social Psychology Bulletin*, 17(5): 475–82.

Castells, M. (2000) *The Rise of The Network Society*, Second edition. Oxford: Blackwell Publishers.

Celeste, P. (2006) 'L'Avventura continua', *The Italian American Magazine*.

Chen, S. X., Benet-Martínez, V. and Bond, M. H. (2008) 'Bicultural identity, bilingualism, and psychological adjustment in multicultural societies: Immigration-based and globalization-based acculturation'. *Journal of Personality*, 76: 803–38.

Chimbos, P. and Agocs, C. (1983) 'Kin and hometown networks as support systems for the immigration and settlement of Greek-Canadians'. *Canadian Ethnic Studies*, 15(2): 42–56.

Christian, J., Gadfield, N. J., Giles, H. and Taylor, D. M. (1976) 'The multidimensional and dynamic nature of ethnic identity'. *International Journal of Psychology*, 11(4): 281–91.

Chytkova, Z. and Özçağlar-Toulouse N. (2010) 'She, who has the spoon, has the power: Immigrant women's use of food to negotiate power relations'. *Advances in Consumer Research*, 37: 10–14.

Cleveland, M. (2006). 'The local, the global, and the Creole: Ethnic identification, acculturation to global consumer culture and consumptionscapes'. Doctoral dissertation. Concordia University, AAT NR23847.

Cleveland, M. and Laroche, M. (2007) 'Acculturation to the global consumer culture: Scale development and research paradigm'. *Journal of Business Research*, 60(3): 249–59.

Cleveland, M., Laroche, M., Pons, F. and Kastoun, R. (2009) 'Acculturation and consumption: Textures of cultural adaptation'. *International Journal of Intercultural Relations*, 33(3): 196–212.

Conway Dato-on, M. (2000) 'Cultural assimilation and consumption behaviors: A methodological investigation'. *Journal of Managerial Issues*, 12(4): 427–46.

Crispino, J. A. (1980) *The Assimilation of Ethnic Groups: The Italian Case*. New York, NY: Center for Migration Studies.

Cross, G. and Smits, G. (2005) 'Japan, the U.S. and the globalization of children's consumer culture'. *Journal of Social History*, 38(4): 873–90.

de la Garza, F. O. M., Newcomb, M. D. and Myers, H. F. (1995) 'A multidimensional measure of cultural identity for Latino and Latina adolescents'. In *Hispanic Psychology: Critical Issues in Theory and Research*. London: Sage Publications, pp. 26–42.

Dion, K. K. and Dion, K. L. (2001) 'Gender and cultural adaptation in immigrant families'. *Journal of Social Issues*, 57(3): 511–21.

Douglas, M. and Isherwood, B. (1978) *The World of Goods*. New York, NY: Basic Books.

Douglas, S. P. and Macquin, A. (1977) *The Use of Notions of Sociocultural Trends or Lifestyle Analysis in Media Selection*. Working Paper.

Doyle, M. W. (2004) 'The challenge of worldwide migration'. *Journal of International Affairs*, 57(2): 1–5.

Driedger, L. (1975) 'In search of cultural identity factors: A comparison of ethnic students'. *Canadian Review of Sociology and Anthropology*, 12(2): 150–62.

Firat, A. F. (1995) 'Consumer culture, or culture consumed?' In *Marketing in a Multicultural World*, edited by J. A. Costa, and G. J. Bamossy. Thousand Oaks, CA: Sage Publications, pp. 105–23.

Flannery, W. P., Reise, S. P. and Yu, J. (2001) 'An empirical comparison of acculturation models'. *Personality and Social Psychology Bulletin*, 27(8): 1035–45.

Frideres, J. S. and Goldenberg, S. (1982) 'Ethnic identity: Myth and reality in Western Canada'. *International Journal of Intercultural Relations*, 6(4): 137–51.

Ger, G. and Belk, R. W. (1996) 'I'd like to buy the world a Coke: Consumptionscapes of the "less affluent world"'. *Journal of Consumer Policy*, 19(3): 271–304.

Gerbner, G., Gross, L., Morgan, M. and Signorielli, N. (1980) 'The "mainstreaming" of America: Violence profile no. 11'. *Journal of Communication*, 30(1): 10–29.

Giles, H., Taylor, D. M., Lambert, W. E. and Goodwin, A. (1976) 'Dimensions of ethnic identity: An example from Northern Maine'. *Journal of Social Psychology*, 100(1): 11–19.

Gilsdorf, J. (2006) 'Standard Englishes and world Englishes: Living with a polymorph business language'. *Journal of Business Communication*, 39(3): 364–78.

Glazer, N. and Moynihan, D. P. (1970) *Beyond the Melting Pot: The Negroes, Puerto Ricans, Jews, Italians, and Irish of New York City*, Second edition. Cambridge, MA: The MIT Press.

Gordon, M. M. (1964) *Assimilation in American Life*. New York, NY: Oxford University Press.

Graddol, D. (2000) *The Future of English*. London: The British Council.

Hallab, R. (2009) 'Acculturation to the global consumer culture and ethnic identity: An empirical study in Lebanon'. Unpublished Thesis. Concordia University.

Hannerz, U. (1990) 'Cosmopolitans and locals in world culture'. *Theory, Culture, and Society*, 7(2/3): 237–51.

Hesmondhalgh, D. (2002) *The Culture Industries*. Thousand Oaks, CA: Sage Publications.

Hui, M. K., Joy, A., Kim, C. and Laroche, M. (1992) 'Acculturation as a determinant of consumer behavior: Conceptual and methodological issues'. In *AMA Winter Educators' Conference Proceedings*, Volume 3, edited by C. T. Allen and T. J. Madden. Chicago, IL: American Marketing Association, pp. 466–73.

Hui, M. K., Joy, A., Kim, C. and Laroche, M. (1993) 'Equivalence of lifestyle dimensions across four major subcultures in Canada'. *Journal of International Consumer Marketing*, 5(3): 15–36.

Huntington, S. P. (1996) 'The West: Unique, not universal'. *Foreign Affairs*, 75(6): 28–46.

Jamal, A. (1996) 'Acculturation: The symbolism of ethnic eating among contemporary British consumers'. *British Food Journal*, 98(10): 14–28.

Jamal, A. (1997) 'Acculturation and Consumer Behaviour'. Unpublished doctoral dissertation. University of Bradford, UK.

Jamal, A. (2003) 'Marketing in a multicultural world: The interplay of marketing, ethnicity and consumption'. *European Journal of Marketing*, 37(11/12): 1599–620.

Jamal, A. (2005) 'Playing to win: An explorative study of marketing strategies of small ethnic retail entrepreneurs in the UK'. *Journal of Retailing and Consumer Services*, 12: 1–13.

Jamal, A. and Chapman, M. (2000) 'Acculturation and inter-ethnic consumer perceptions: Can you feel what we feel?' *Journal of Marketing Management*, 16(4): 365–91.

Ji, M. F. and McNeal, J. U. (2001) 'How Chinese children's commercials differ from those of the United States: A content analysis'. *Journal of Advertising*, 30(3): 79–92.

Jun, S., Ball, D. A. and Gentry, J. W. (1993) 'Modes of Consumer Acculturation'. In *Advances in Consumer Research*, edited by L. McAlister and M. L. Rothschild. Provo, UT: Association for Consumer Research, pp. 76–82.

Keefe, S. E. and Padilla, A. M. (1987) *Chicano Ethnicity*. Albuquerque, NM: University of New Mexico Press.

Kim, C., Laroche, M. and Joy, A. (1990) 'An empirical study of the effects of ethnicity on consumption patterns in a bi-cultural environment'. In *Advances in Consumer Research*, Volume 17, edited by M. E. Goldberg, G. J. Gorn and R. W. Polley. Provo, UT: Association for Consumer Research, pp. 839–46.

Kim, C., Laroche, M. and Tomiuk, M. A. (2001) 'A measure of acculturation for Italian Canadians: Scale development and construct validation'. *International Journal of Intercultural Relations*, 25: 607–37.

Kim, C., Laroche, M. and Tomiuk, M. A. (2004) 'The Chinese in Canada: A study in ethnic change with emphasis on gender roles'. *Journal of Social Psychology*, 144(1): 5–29.

Konrad, G. (1984) *Antipolitics*. San Diego and New York, NY: Harcourt Brace Jovanovich.

Kosic, A., Mannetti, L. and Sam, D. L. (2005) 'The role of majority attitudes towards out-group in the perception of the acculturation strategies of immigrants'. *International Journal of Intercultural Relations*, 29: 273–88.

Kourvetaris, G. (1971) 'Patterns of intergenerational subculture and intermarriage of the Greeks in the United States'. *International Journal of Sociology and the Family*, 7(4): 395–407.

Kwan, K.-L. K. and Sodowsky, G. R. (1997) 'Internal and external ethnic identity and their correlates: A study of Chinese American immigrants'. *Journal of Multicultural Counseling and Development*, 25: 51–67.

Lambert, W. E., Mermigis, L. and Taylor, D. M. (1986) 'Greek Canadians' attitudes towards own group and other ethnic groups: A test of the multiculturalism hypothesis'. *Canadian Journal of Behavioral Science*, 18(1): 35–51.

Laroche, M., Kim, C., Hui, M. K. and Joy, A. (1996) 'An empirical study of multidimensional ethnic change: The case of French Canadians in Quebec'. *Journal of Cross-Cultural Psychology*, 27(1): 114–31.

Laroche, M., Kim, C., Hui, M. K. and Tomiuk, M. A. (1998) 'Test of a nonlinear relationship between linguistic acculturation and ethnic identification'. *Journal of Cross-Cultural Psychology*, 29(3): 418–33.

Laroche, M., Kim, C., Tomiuk, M. A. and Belisle, D. (2005) 'Similarities in Italian and Greek multidimensional ethnic identity: Some implications for food consumption'. *Canadian Journal of Administrative Sciences*, 21(4): 143–67.

Laroche, M., Pons, F. and Richard, M.-O. (2009) 'The role of language in ethnic identity measurement: A multitrait-multimethod approach to construct validation'. *Journal of Social Psychology*, 149(4): 513–40.

Laroche, M., Yang, Z., Kim, C. and Chan, C. (2006) 'A family level measure of acculturation for Chinese immigrants'. In *Marketing and Multicultural Diversity*, edited by C. P. Rao. Burlington, VT: Ashgate Publishing, pp. 154–66.

Laroche, M., Yang, Z., Kim, C. and Richard, M. O. (2007) 'How culture matters in children's purchase influence: A multi-level investigation'. *Journal of the Academy of Marketing Science*, 35(1): 113–26.

Lee, W.-N. and Tse, D. K. (1994) 'Changing media consumption in a new home: Acculturation patterns among Hong Kong immigrants to Canada'. *Journal of Advertising*, 23(1): 57–68.

Lee, W.-N. and Um, K.-H. R. (1992) 'Ethnicity and consumer product evaluation: A cross-cultural comparison of Korean immigrants and Americans'. In *Advances in Consumer Research*, Volume 19, edited by J. F. Sherry, Jr. and B. Sternthal. Provo, UT: Association for Consumer Research, pp. 429–36.

Legrain, P. (2002) *Open World: The Truth about Globalization*. London: Abacus.

Luna, D., Ringberg, T. and Peracchio, L. A. (2008) 'One individual, two identities: Frame switching among biculturals'. *Journal of Consumer Research*, 35: 279–93.

Markus, H. and Kunda, Z. (1986) 'Stability and malleability of the self-concept'. *Journal of Personality and Social Psychology*, 51(4): 858–66.

McCracken, G. (1986) 'Culture and consumption: A theoretical account of the structure and movement of cultural meaning of consumer goods'. *Journal of Consumer Research*, 13(June): 71–84.

McGuire, W. J., McGuire, C. V., Child, P. and Fujioka, T. A. (1978) 'Salience of ethnicity in the spontaneous self-concept as a function of one's ethnic distinctiveness in the social environment'. *Journal of Personality and Social Psychology*, 36: 511–20.

Mendoza, R. H. (1989) 'An empirical scale to measure type and degree of acculturation in Mexican-American adolescents and adults'. *Journal of Cross-Cultural Psychology*, 20(4): 372–85.

Mendoza, R. H. and Martinez Jr., J. L. (1981) 'The measurement of acculturation'. In *Explorations in Chicano Psychology*, edited by A. Baron Jr. New York, NY: Praeger, pp. 71–82.

Naghavi, P. (2011) 'Acculturation to the global consumer culture and ethnic identity: An empirical study in Iran'. Unpublished Thesis. Concordia University.

O'Guinn T. C. and Faber, R. J. (1985) 'New perspectives on acculturation: The relationship of general and role specific acculturation with Hispanics' consumer attitudes'. In *Advances in Consumer Research*, Volume 12, edited by E. Hirschman and Morris Holbrook. Provo, UT: Association for Consumer Research, pp. 113–17.

Ogden, D. T., Ogden, J. and Schau, H. J. (2004) 'Exploring the impact of culture and acculturation on consumer purchase decisions: Toward a microcultural perspective'. *Academy of Marketing Science Review*, 8: 1–26.

Okamura, J. Y. (1981) 'Situational Ethnicity'. *Ethnic and Racial Studies*, 4(4): 452–65.

Olmedo, E. L., Martinez Jr., J. L. and Martinez, S. (1978) 'Measure of acculturation for Chicano adolescents'. *Psychological Reports*, 42: 159–70.

Oswald, R. L. (1999) 'Culture swapping: Consumption and the ethnogenesis of middle-class Haitian immigrants'. *Journal of Consumer Research*, 25: 303–18.

Özçağlar-Toulouse, N. and Üstüner, T. (2009) 'How do historical relationships between the host and home countries shape the immigrants' consumer acculturation processes?' In *Advances in Consumer Research*, Volume 36, edited by A. L. McGill and S. Shavitt. Duluth, MN: Association for Consumer Research, pp. 16–19.

Padilla, M. A. ed. (1980) *Acculturation: Theory, Models and Some New Findings*. Boulder, CO: Westview Press.

Palmer, G. (1954) *Labor Mobility in Six Cities: A Report on the Survey Patterns and Factors in Labor Mobility, 1940–1950*. New York, NY: Social Sciences Research Council.

Palumbo, F. A. and Teich, I. (2004) 'Market segmentation based on level of acculturation'. *Marketing Intelligence and Planning*, 22(4): 472–84.

Peñaloza, L. N. (1994) 'Atravesando fronteras/border crossing: A critical ethnographic exploration of the consumer acculturation of Mexican immigrants'. *Journal of Consumer Research*, 21(1): 32–54.

Peñaloza, L. N. (2010) 'Deciphering the socio-temporal dimensions of consumer identity development: A cultural genealogy'. *Advances in Consumer Research*, Volume 37, pp. 10–14.

Peñaloza, L. and Gilly, M. C. (1999) 'Marketer acculturation: The changer and the changed'. *Journal of Marketing*, 63: 84–104.

Phinney, J. S. (1990) 'Ethnic identity in adolescents and adults: Review of research'. *Psychological Bulletin*, 108(3): 499–514.

Phinney, J. S. (1992) 'The multigroup ethnic identity measure: A new scale for use with diverse groups'. *Journal of Adolescent Research*, 7(2): 156–76.

Phinney, J. S. (2006) 'Ethnic identity exploration in emerging adulthood'. In *Coming of Age in the 21st Century: The Lives and Contexts of Emerging Adults*, edited by A. Jeffrey and J. L. Tanner. Washington, DC: American Psychology Association, pp. 117–34.

Phinney, J. S. and Ong, A. D. (2007) 'Conceptualization and measurements of ethnic identity: Current status and future directions'. *Journal of Counseling Psychology*, 54(3): 271–81.

Ramirez, B. (1989) *The Italians in Canada*. Canada's Ethnic Groups Series: Booklet No. 14. Ottawa: Canadian Historical Association.

Ray, N. M., Ryder, M. E. and Scott, S. V. (1994) 'Toward an understanding of the use of foreign words in print advertising'. In *Globalization of Consumer Markets: Structures and Strategies*, edited by S. Hassan and E. Kaynak. New York, NY: International Business Press, pp. 7–62.

Redfield, R., Linton, R. and Herskovits, M. (1936) 'Memorandum on the study of acculturation'. *American Anthropologist*, 38(1): 149–52.

Robertson, J. P. and Zill, N. (1997) 'Matters of culture'. *American Demographics*, 19(9): 48–52.

Roedl, S. (2006) 'Mickey and mini: The global flow of cultural products'. *Journal of Language for International Business*, 17(1): 1–14.

Rogler, L. H., Cortes, D. E. and Malgady, R. G. (1991) 'Acculturation and mental health status among Hispanics: Convergence and new direction for research'. *American Psychologist*, 46(6): 585–97.

Rosenthal, D. A. and Feldman, S. S. (1992) 'The nature and stability of ethnic identity in Chinese youth: Effects of length of residence in two cultural contexts'. *Journal of Cross-Cultural Psychology*, 23(2): 214–227.

Rotunno, M. and McGoldrick, M. (1982) 'Italian families'. In *Ethnicity and Family Therapy*, edited by M. McGoldrick, J. Giordano and N. Garcia-Preto. Guildford: Guilford Press, pp. 340–63.

Santora, J. C. (2006) 'Crossing the digital divide: Do all global citizens have their passports?' *Academy of Management Perspectives*, 20(4): 118–19.

Schiffman, L. G., Dillon, W. R. and Ngumah, F. E. (1981) 'The influence of subcultural and personality factors on consumer acculturation'. *Journal of International Business Studies*, 12(2): 137–44.

Schlegel, A. (2000) 'The global spread of adolescent culture'. In *Negotiating Adolescence in Times of Social Change*, edited by L. J. Crockett, and R. K. Silberbeinsen. Cambridge, MA: Cambridge University Press, pp. 71–88.

Schwartz, S. J., Unger, J. B., Zamboanga, B. L. and Szapocznik, J. (2010) 'Rethinking the concept of acculturation: Implications for theory and research'. *American Psychologist*, 65(4): 237–51.

Sobol, K. (2008) 'The "Global Consumer Culture": An empirical study in The Netherlands'. Unpublished Thesis. Concordia University.

Stayman, D. M. and Deshpandé, R. (1989) 'Situational Ethnicity and Consumer Behavior'. *Journal of Consumer Research*, 16(3): 361–71.

Steenkamp, J.-B. E. (2001) 'The role of national culture in international marketing research'. *International Marketing Review*, 18(1): 30–42.

Stycos, J. M. (1948) 'The Spartan Greeks of Bridgetown'. *Common Ground*, 8: 61–70.

Tanner F., M. (2002) '"Federal Expression": Casting a brand and branding in *Cast Away*'. Master dissertation. University of Guelph, AAT MQ71814.

Tenbruck, F. H. (1990) 'The dream of a secular ecumene: The meaning and limits of policies of development'. In *Global Culture: Nationalism, Globalization, and Modernity*, edited by M. Featherstone. London, Newbury Park and New Delhi: Sage Publications, pp. 311–28.

Thompson, C. J. and Tambyah, S. K. (1999) 'Trying to be cosmopolitan'. *Journal of Consumer Research*, 26(3): 214–41.

Üstüner, T. and Holt, D. B. (2007) 'Dominated consumer acculturation: The social construction of poor migrant women's consumer identity projects in a Turkish squatter'. *Journal of Consumer Research*, 34(1): 41–56.

Valencia, H. (1985) 'Hispanic values and cultural research'. *Journal of the Academy of Marketing Science*, 17(1): 23–8.

Visconti, L. M. (2010) 'Cross generation: Cultural (in)visibility in the consumption of second generations'. *Advances in Consumer Research*, Volume 37, pp. 10–14.

Visconti, L. M., Jafari, A., Batat, W., Broeckerhoffd, A., Dedeoglue, A. O., Demangeotf, C., Kipnis, E., Lindridge, A., Peñaloza, L., Pullig, C., Regany, F., Ustundaglik, E. and Weinberger, M. F. (2014) 'Consumer ethnicity three decades after: A TCR agenda'. *Journal of Marketing Management*, 30(17–18): 1882–922.

Wallendorf, M. and Arnould, E. J. (1988) '"My favorite things": A cross-cultural inquiry into object attachment, possessiveness, and social linkage'. *Journal of Consumer Research*, 14(4): 531–47.

Wallendorf, M. and Reilly, M. D. (1983) 'Ethnic migration, assimilation and consumption'. *Journal of Consumer Research*, 10(3): 292–302.

Wamwara-Mbugua, L. W., Cornwell, T. B. and Boller, G. (2008) 'Triple acculturation: The role of African Americans in the consumer acculturation of Kenyan immigrants'. *Journal of Business Research*, 61(2): 83–90.

Weinreich, P. (2009) '"Enculturation", not "acculturation": Conceptualising and assessing identity processes in migrant communities'. *International Journal of Intercultural Relations*, 33: 124–39.

Yancey, W., Ericksen, E. and Juliani, R. (1976) 'Emergent ethnicity: A review and reformulation'. *American Sociological Review*, 41(3): 391–403.

3

Ethnic youth

Parental style and consumer socialization

Zhiyong Yang

Introduction

A substantial portion of the U.S. population consists of immigrants and all the indications are that the segment is growing in numbers. According to the 2010 Census, 37.9 per cent of the American population consisted of non-European ethnic groups; this proportion is expected to be at 48 per cent in 2030 (United States Census Bureau 2012). On the contrary, the non-immigrant population is expected to have a lower growth rate of 4 per cent to 12 per cent over the same period. With the steady rise in immigrant population and subsequent diversity in the marketplace, particularly in North America and across Europe and Australia, the topic of cultural influences on immigrants' consumption behaviour is attracting increasing attention (e.g., Forehand and Deshpandé 2001; Forehand, Deshpandé and Reed 2002; Laroche, Yang, Kim, and Richard 2007).

Traditionally, prior research has examined ethnic consumption, primarily focusing on adults and largely ignoring children (Laroche *et al.* 2007). A move towards understanding how rising immigration levels and subsequent cultural adaptation impact ethnic minority children's consumption attitudes and behaviours is particularly warranted because ethnic children now account for approximately 21.8 per cent of the American school-aged children (Humes, Jones and Ramirez 2010). Not only are children themselves important customers, but also their influence on family purchase decisions is steadily increasing (Caruana and Vassallo 2003). American children in the 1990s had three times the disposable income than they had in the 1980s, spending approximately an average of $23.4 billion each year (McNeal 1999). In addition to their direct spending, the American children's influence in family purchases increased from $5 billion in the 1960s to about $188 billion in 1997. Corresponding to this trend, every year over $1 billion is spent on media advertising to children through youth-oriented marketing channels that include television advertising, in-school marketing, the internet, product placements, kids clubs and toys/products (Austin and Reed 1999; Story and French 2004).

Acknowledging the important role of children as consumers, marketing researchers have paid serious attention to the topic of consumer socialization, which is broadly defined as the processes through which children accumulate consumption-related skills, knowledge and attitudes (Ward 1974). These processes encompass various socialization agent–learner relationships and modes of learning. One aspect of consumer socialization that has attracted considerable research concerns parental style, which is defined as 'a constellation of attitudes toward the child that are communicated to the child and that, taken together, create an emotional climate in which the parent's behaviors are expressed' (Darling and Steinberg 1993, p. 488). This chapter provides a comprehensive overview of the extent to which parental style affects consumer socialization in the Western and Eastern countries. Building upon the cross-cultural literature, the chapter further elaborates on how processes of culture change (e.g., cultural adaptation) among ethnic minority groups may affect such a socialization process. The chapter also outlines future research avenues in this relatively untapped domain.

Differences in socialization across cultures

Consumer socialization, as a profile of social realities, is an inherently cultural process (Laroche *et al.* 2007). Socialization processes and outcomes may differ due to distinct socialization goals followed by people in a given society. Socialization goal differences are manifested through several dimensions, including collectivism–individualism, power distance, uncertainty avoidance and sex-role orientation (Hofstede 1983). The socialization goal in mainstream Western cultures (e.g. the US, Canada and UK) is to develop an individual sense of identity and self-sufficiency away from family members (Triandis 1995). With this foundation, children are considered well-prepared to advance to adulthood and make decisions for themselves with less reference to family expectations. Even in the presence of family expectations, a sense of honour and integrity is attached to those who are able to follow their own initiatives and achieve their personal goals. By contrast, the socialization tasks in mainstream Far Eastern cultures (e.g., China, Korea and Japan) are to: 1) help children learn to control individualistic acts and to reduce unique individual characteristics; 2) develop collectivistic ideology and co-operative skills and behaviour including obedience, conformity and interdependence; 3) become an integral part of the larger group and make contributions to the achievement and welfare at collective societal level (Chen 2000; Triandis 1995).

The differences in socialization goals in Eastern and Western culture significantly impact marketing practices. For example, the socialization goal towards collectivism drives Eastern cultures to exhibit high-context communication patterns, whereas the Westerns prefer low-context styles due to their socialization goal towards individualism. This explains why advertisements in the West are vested in the explicit code, whereas Eastern adverts are often implicit and indirect (Gao, Ting-Toomey and Gudykunst 1996). More recently, Yang, Kim, Laroche, and Lee (2014) find that the Eastern and the Western consumers differ in other consumption-related patterns. For example, the Eastern adolescents are less susceptible to peer influence than their Western counterparts, suggesting that marketers should place a relatively stronger emphasis on targeting parents for children's merchandize in the East than in the West. Also, Eastern parents tend to be less concept-oriented and more socio-oriented than the Western parents, indicating that Eastern parents are less likely to engage in an open exchange of ideas with their children and to allow them to exercise much decision influence. Therefore, it would behove marketers to direct marketing communication more towards parents when launching children products in the Eastern countries (Yang *et al.* 2014).

Effect of parental style on socialization in Western cultures

Parental style plays a critical role as a transition belt to pass normative values and socialization goals of society from one generation to another (Yang and Laroche 2011). From an early age, parents provide their children with information about cultural priorities and parental expectations (LeVine *et al.* 1994). Through extended interaction with their parents, children internalize these inputs, slowly building up the desired cultural orientations (Yang and Laroche 2011).

In family socialization research, the most widely used approach in studying parenting style is Baumrind's (1971) authoritative-authoritarian-permissive typology, which was developed in the context of the United States. This tripartite model was later reconceptualized by Maccoby and Martin (1983) to reflect two specific underlying dimensions: *demandingness* refers to the extent to which parents show control, maturity demands and supervision in their parenting, and *responsiveness* refers to the extent to which parents show affective warmth, acceptance and involvement (Aunola, Stattin and Nurmim 2000; Maccoby and Martin 1983). The combined effects of these two dimensions yield a four-fold classification of parenting style.

Authoritative parents (both demanding and responsive) are warm and supportive, but also exert firm control. They value children's autonomy but at the same time expect disciplined conformity (Yang *et al.* 2014). Authoritarian parents (demanding but not responsive), on the other hand, maintain high levels of control over their children and limit children's autonomy. They judge and evaluate children's conduct by a set of standards endorsed by higher authority figures. They strictly enforce rules, favour children's unquestionable obedience and punish willful behaviour (Baumrind 1968; Carlson and Grossbart 1988). Permissive parents (responsive but not demanding) view children as having adult rights but few responsibilities (Baumrind 1978). These parents show emotional warmth and support and avoid confrontations, allowing their children to do what they want. Last, neglectful parents (neither demanding nor responsive) provide no structure and little or no monitoring of children's behaviour. They see children as having few rights or responsibilities that require parenting attention (Carlson and Grossbart 1988). Therefore, they do not support or encourage their children's self-regulation or impose control on their child's behaviour (Maccoby and Martin 1983; Baumrind 1991).

Socialization research has extensively used this typology for examining the role of parental style in explaining children's adjustment with respect to a wide array of developmental factors. Many of these studies have found authoritative parenting to be the most effective style for a variety of positive outcomes, such as pro-social development, psychological competence, school achievement and self-esteem (Lamborn, Mounts, Steinberg and Dornbusch 1991). In contrast, authoritarian parental style has been associated with decreased or more negative child outcomes such as increased internalized distress, problem behaviour and drug use, and poorer self-esteem (Lamborn *et al.* 1991). Substantial research has focused on investigating the effectiveness of parenting styles on childrens' or young adults' academic achievement. Findings suggest that a positive relationship exists between authoritative parenting style and high academic achievement (Steinberg, Lamborn, Darling, Mounts and Dornbusch 1994; Steinberg, Lamborn, Dornbusch and Darling 1992) and that a negative relationship exists between authoritarian parenting and low academic achievement (Steinberg 2001). Such research studies were primarily conducted in the United States involving middle class White American parents and their children.

In the context of consumer socialization, however, there is a paucity of research on the role of parenting style in children's consumer behaviour. Among the rare exceptions, Rose (1999) reports that the indulgent parenting style fosters greater purchase participation and influence by children in family purchase decisions than the authoritarian style. More recently, Yang *et al.* (2014) find that authoritarian parents are more socio-oriented than authoritative, permissive and neglectful parents, whereas authoritative and permissive parents are more concept-oriented than authoritarian and neglectful parents. Furthermore, adolescents with authoritative and permissive parents are more likely to use bilateral influence strategies (e.g., reasoning, bargaining) than those with authoritarian parents, while those with neglectful parents more likely use unilateral influence strategies (e.g., playing on emotions, stubborn persuasion) than those with other parental styles. These findings are generally in line with the socialization goals that these parental styles intend to transfer. From a managerial standpoint, a better understanding of the potential impact of parental styles on consumer socialization process is important to marketers. Parental styles are meaningful segmentation variables (Rose 1999). Knowing about the strategies children use to persuade their parents and the communication patterns in each segment helps marketers design adverts that best reflect their target consumers' communication style. For example, Yang *et al.* (2014) reveal that authoritative parents tend to promote a more open parent–child communication and allow their children greater consumption autonomy and influence in family purchases. As a result, if a marketer of teenagers' educational products wants to target the authoritative parental segment, it would be effective to direct marketing communication to both the child and the parents in view of the two-way, concept-oriented communication that is likely to be prevalent in authoritative families (ibid.).

Effect of parental style on socialization in Eastern cultures

Consistent with collectivistic socialization goals, the primary concerns in Eastern societies consist of getting along with others (i.e., group harmony), conforming to the group (i.e., family and society) and being well behaved (Chao 1996; Triandis 1995). Self-directed willingness and individual interests are subordinated to those of the collective, and individual behaviours that may threaten the group functioning are discouraged or even prohibited (Ho 1986; Triandis 1995). Accordingly, Eastern socialization and formal education systems stress discipline, morality, ethics and collectivism (Yang and Laroche 2011).

The general social orientation of the Eastern culture towards collectivism has great impact on parenting styles (Triandis 1995). It has long been found that Eastern parents tend to use a more authoritarian parenting style that discourages children's independence, creativity, assertiveness and individuality in order to foster conformity and interdependence in favour of the goals and interests of the family (Kagitcibasi 1996). As a result, Eastern parents are high in parental control and restrictiveness (Chao and Sue 1996; Ho 1986; Yang, Schaninger and Laroche 2013) and use more physical punishment and yelling at their children than middle class American parents (Kelley and Tseng 1992). Since the Eastern cultures 'legitimatize' parents' role as 'trainers' as well as their use of more power-assertive forms of discipline, authoritarian parenting does not seem to have as much negative impact on Eastern children's well-being as that on Western children's (Yang *et al.* 2014).

These findings provide a rich foundation for consumer researchers to understand cultural differences in some important socialization outcomes, for example susceptibility to peer influence among adolescents. Worldwide, adolescents are the most vulnerable (compared with older adults or younger children) to the opinions of their peers, such as their friends, activity partners and co-workers (Yang, Schaninger, and Laroche 2013). Marketing practitioners recognize the importance of peer influence when targeting adolescent consumers and spending huge amounts of money every year on advertising in youth-oriented channels, including television advertising, in-school marketing, product placements and children's clubs (Austin and Reed 1999). In international marketing, the conventional wisdom would suggest that, when targeting adolescent consumers, one should allocate larger budgets for interpersonal communications in collectivist cultures than in individualist ones, because Eastern children are often encouraged to sacrifice personal goals for the sake of having good relationships with others, whereas their Western counterparts are socialized to be independent from an early age (Triandis 1995). However, this is not the right strategy according to Yang and associates (Yang 2008; Yang and Laroche 2011). In their pioneering work, Yang and Laroche (2011) show that in individualist cultures, parental responsiveness reduces adolescents' susceptibility to peer influence mainly through an indirect effect by undermining their interdependent self-construal, fostering self-esteem and impairing self-monitoring. However, in collectivist cultures, responsive parenting reduces susceptibility primarily through a direct effect. These findings suggest a counterintuitive international marking strategy: in Western cultures such as in Canada or the United States, marketers should allocate larger budgets for interpersonal communications towards adolescents such as buzz marketing and opinion leaders. In Eastern cultures, it may be more profitable to target parents, who would in turn influence their adolescents. Furthermore, within each culture, parental responsiveness can be a meaningful segmentation variable to identify adolescents who are high or low in susceptibility to normative influence from peers (Yang and Laroche 2011). Ethnic marketers can use these insights in developing effective marketing strategies.

When the East meets the West: role of cultural adaption

Immigration to a new culture adds a new layer to the normal socialization process as it involves a cultural adaptation in aspects of social and psychological functioning (Taft 1986). The immigration case can be classified into one of the following situations: (1) the West meets the West (e.g., British migrating to the US), (2) the East meets the East (e.g. Philippines moving to Malaysia), (3) the West meets the East (e.g., Americans moving to Japan and living there) and (4) the East meets the West (e.g., the Chinese migrating to the US). Of these four conditions, this chapter mainly focuses on the forth category, 'the East meeting the West', as this is the major trend of the immigration in the world and is the focus of the literature when discussing about cultural adaptation.

According to Berry (1990), cultural adaptation is a special case of socialization that changes an immigrant's values, attitudes, abilities, motives, personal identity, ethnic identity and lifestyle preferences. A unique aspect of the socialization processes applicable for the immigrants under the 'the East meets the West' category is that migrants in such a situation may face somewhat contradictory socialization goals. For example, the socialization goal of the host (Western) country may require them to pursue individualism – a cultural orientation that promotes independence and an individual sense of being (e.g., Hofstede 1983). On the other hand, the socialization goals of their own country of origin can still be based on collectivistic cultural values and norms, whereby people are supposed to be interdependent, having strong and cohesive ties with in-group members (Kim, Yang and Lee 2009). While many have studied the acculturation processes and agents of cultural change in cultural encounters such as this (e.g., Peñaloza 1994), not many have investigated the role of contradictory socialization goals on socialization outcomes among migrant families facing the push and pull factors from original and host cultures.

Cultural adaptation and consumer socialization

To better understand how cultural adaptation affects socialization among immigrants, we need to first introduce two important concepts that capture the gist of cultural adaptation: acculturation and ethnic identification. While many conceptualizations exist, *acculturation* can be considered as the degree to which an immigrant learns the traits of the mainstream consumer culture, whereas *ethnic identification* refers to the extent to which one retains the cultural traits from the country of origin (Laroche *et al.* 2007). Through adaptation, coping and learning processes, some individuals are more acculturated than others, whereas others still keep a strong maintenance of original cultural traits.

There are two schools of thoughts regarding the relationship between acculturation and ethnic identification. One research camp holds the view that ethnic consumers who are highly acculturated behave similarly to the mainstream individualists. This view reflects the assimilation perspective of culture change (Laroche and Jamal, this volume), whereby the key assumption is the loss of cultural values associated with culture of origin. The view is supported by some research findings. For example, Tan and McCullough (1985) find that Chinese Americans high in acculturation are more similar to Anglo-Americans in terms of a high reliance on price and quality, whereas Chinese low in acculturation put more weight on image during their decision-making process. Highly acculturated Koreans, as compared with their less acculturated counterparts, are more likely to adopt American cultural styles in terms of observing friends' purchasing behaviour, taking peers' advice in selecting products and listening to advertising. Consistent results are also found based upon ethnic identification measure. For example, Deshpandé, Hoyer and Donthu (1986) report that significant differences exist in responses to ethnic advertising within the Hispanic subculture. Specifically, the preference for the ethnicity-congruency cues appears to be higher for respondents with stronger ethnic identity with their racial/ethnic group (Whittler 1989; Williams and Qualls 1989) than those with weak ethnic identity

The other research camp believes that acculturation and ethnic identification are not the bipolar ends of a single-continuum and, therefore, adopting cultural values of the host culture does not necessarily cause the loss of one's original ethnic identity (Lambert, Mermigis and Taylor 1986). To varying degrees, immigrants can incorporate two co-existing cultural self-identities (Ryder, Alden and Paulhus 2001). Along this bi-directional approach to cultural adaptation, Laroche et al. (2007) find that acculturation and ethnic identification are orthogonal and interact with each other to jointly affect children's purchase influence at home. Highly acculturated individuals with weaker ethnic identification tend to accept more individualistic values than those with stronger ethnic identification, whereas lowly acculturated individuals with stronger ethnic identification have more preference towards the collectivistic culture than those with weaker ethnic identification. Based on these findings, Laroche et al. suggest that advertisers, when targeting ethnic minority consumers, need to identify the primary target family member(s) based on the level of cultural adaptation the family has experienced. Advertisers of family products may be rewarded by launching advertisements whose messages are primarily targeted towards the parents for ethnic families who still largely identify with their traditional values. Messages reflecting traditional family values should be integrated into the promotion of products to enhance the market response. Advertisers may also use ethnic-congruent spokespeople in the advertisements, because high ethnic identifiers have been found to have more favourable responses to advertising that features ethnically similar actors or spokespeople (Whittler 1991; Torres and Briggs 2005), which in turn, elicits greater source honesty and attitudes towards the brand being advertised (Deshpandé and Stayman 1994; Toffoli and Laroche 2002).

Cultural adaptation and the effect of parental style on socialization

The socialization research has extensively used the authoritative-authoritarian-permissive-neglectful typology for examining the role of parental style in adolescents' adjustment with respect to a wide array of developmental factors. Many of the studies involving mainstream Western cultures find authoritative parenting to be the most effective style for a variety of socialization outcomes: pro-social development, psychological competence, school achievement and self-esteem. In contrast, authoritarian parental style has been associated with more negative outcomes: increased internalized distress, problem behaviour, drug use and poorer self-esteem (Lamborn *et al.* 1991). In consumer research, scholars (Carlson and Grossbart 1988; Rose 1999) have also associated parental styles with consumption-related socialization outcomes. They find that authoritative and permissive parents grant more consumption independence to their children and engage in higher levels of intergenerational communication about consumption than authoritarian parents. Focusing on children's use of influence strategies, Yang *et al.* (2014) find that children with neglectful parents tend to use more unilateral influence strategies than those with other parental strategies, including both stubborn persuasion and playing on emotions, whereas adolescents in authoritarian families use higher levels of both unilateral and bilateral strategies to get their way. This pattern exists in both Western societies and Eastern societies. In fact, a majority of studies involving diverse Western and non-Western cultures have shown support for the universal application of these parental styles (Chen 2000; Rohner 1986; Wu *et al.* 2002).

Although the parental style typology exists in both Western and Eastern cultures, two points are worthy of notification. First, the prevalent parental style differs in different cultures. Yang *et al.* (2014), for example, report that the most prominent parenting in Canada is authoritative parental style, followed by permissive parental style. By contrast, the most prevalent style in China is authoritarian, followed by authoritative parental style. Second, the effect of a specific parental style may be different in different cultures. Although authoritarianism is viewed as uniformly negative in the United States (Barber 1997), it is found to be more frequently used and more acceptable as a means of regulating children's behaviour in both China (Wu *et al.* 2002) and Japan (Rose 1999). For example, love withdrawal (e.g., threats of abandonment), shaming and guilt induction seem to be a prevalent part of Chinese children's socialization (Olsen *et al.* 2001). Not only do parents shame their children, but also primary schools use shaming (e.g., group ostracism or abandonment) as a principal moral training technique to correct children's misbehaviour (Fung 1999; Ho 1986).

An increasing number of researchers argue that the patterns found among White American families (e.g., link between authoritative parenting and positive outcomes, as well as between authoritarian parenting and negative outcomes) may not hold for ethnic minority groups (e.g., Asian Americans and African Americans) (Dornbusch *et al.* 1987). Sue and Abe (1995), for instance, find that although the majority of Chinese American parents tends to be authoritarian in parenting style, Chinese American children are likely to achieve higher test scores (e.g., SATs) and better school and college school grades. Similarly, focusing on the Chinese immigrant mothers living in the US, Wang and Phinney (1998) find that authoritarianism is positively associated with higher cognitive competence of pre-school children. Apparently, this explains why some researchers believe that the cultural traditions of the country of origin are so firmly entrenched among ethnic groups that their core cultural values do not change rapidly (Laroche *et al.* 2007). According to Ho, Peng and Lai (2001), the traditional values and ideologies, such as those concerning respect for authority figures and parents, continue to play a significant role in affecting socialization and child development among ethnic groups due to the enduring and resilient nature of the culture. For example, Wu (1996) shows that Chinese parents from Shanghai, Southern Taiwan, Bangkok, Singapore, Honolulu and Los Angeles share many basic traditional values, socialization goals and parenting practices, despite varying degrees of geographical and ideological differences. The recent debate on 'tiger mom' lends anecdotal evidence in this regard as well. However, as shown in the following, this view may be applicable for some ethnic groups, but not for others. Even in a particular ethnic minority group such as Chinese Americans, this view may only be applicable to high ethnic identifiers. Therefore, there is a need to exercise caution when generalizing findings from one cultural context to the other.

Potential issues and future research directions

Idiocentricity in the effect of parental style

Previous research involving effects of parental styles on socialization outcomes has mainly centred on the aggregated level of evidence while the idiocentricity of the immigrants is largely neglected. In an attempt to address this issue, Laroche *et al.* (2007) introduced the construct of 'generational dissonance' at the family, further segmenting the Chinese Canadian immigrants. Based on this measure, the Chinese Canadian families were classified into two categories: generationally dissonant families (i.e., dissimilar levels of acculturation between parents and children) and generationally consonant families (i.e., similar levels of acculturation between parents and children) (Portes and Rumbaut 1996). According to Laroche *et al.*, children in generationally consonant families had more influence over both frequently and infrequently purchased family product purchases than children in dissonant families. In addition, for members of consonant families, higher-acculturation and lower ethnic identification resulted in higher children's purchase influence on purchase decisions for all product categories. On the other hand, some of the findings for dissonant families were in the opposite direction. Specifically, acculturation affected children's influence negatively in dissonant families for both categories of the family products and infrequently purchased children products.

Future family research should consider idiocentricity in their studies. One way of doing so is to take both family-level and individual-level factors into consideration. By nature, families are multilevel entities where individuals (lower level units) are nested within families (higher level units). On the one hand, individuals are influenced by the families to which they belong. On the other hand, the properties of a family are in turn influenced by the individuals who make up that family. These kinds of interactions between the individuals and the families can be specified as a hierarchical system, in which individuals and families represent different hierarchical levels. This leads to research into the interplay between variables that describe the individuals and variables that describe the families. As shown in prior research (Laroche *et al.* 2007; Laroche, Yang, Kim and Chan 2006), including the family-level variables into the study opens a new avenue for research insights.

Another research avenue is to disentangle the differences among ethnic groups that share some common cultural values. Apparently similar looking cultures may not be the same. Let's use Hispanic Americans and Chinese Americans as an example. Similar to Chinese Americans, Hispanics are also under the category of collectivists (Hofstede 1983). However, readers should be cautious about the cultural difference between these two ethnic groups. For example, Koslow, Shamdasani and Touchstone (1994) find that among Hispanic consumers, there exists the effects of language-related inferiority complex (i.e., negative attitudes towards the advertisements when the ethnic language is exclusively used); nonetheless, prior research does not report similar effects among Chinese consumers. Such a cultural difference may cause the effects of parental style on consumer socialization to be dissimilar across these two groups.

Heterogeneity in responsiveness to parental influence among ethnic youth

The literature paints a mixed picture of the effect of parental style on children's behaviour. Some researchers argue that parenting strategies exert significant impact on children's behaviour after they become adults (Peters 1989; Shim 1996), while others suggest that parents have little influence on children's behaviour after they enter adolescence (McNeal 1991; Youniss and Smollar

1985; Yang, Schaninger and Laroche 2013). This chapter proposes that such mixed findings may be due to behavioural heterogeneity among children: different children may have different levels of sensitivity to parental influence. Parenting strategies may have positive, negative or null effects on children's behaviour, depending upon the characteristics of these children and, as such, may require marketers to use different strategies towards different types of families.

In the case of youth smoking, researchers show that intervention strategies that ignore this heterogeneity, ask the wrong questions, or those that take too harsh of an approach may actually exacerbate the maladaptive adolescent behaviour that they are designed to minimize (Berger and Rand 2008; Fitzsimons and Moore 2008; Yang and Netemeyer 2015). For example, delivering anti-smoking messages to the wrong audience may boost rather than curtail tobacco usage, which is termed as a 'boomerang effect' (Wakefield *et al.* 2006). To disentangle the behavioural heterogeneity among children's smoking, Yang and Netemeyer (2015) simultaneously examine the effects of parenting strategies on a child's: (1) probability to follow a specific trajectory for smoking growth; (2) growth pattern within a particular smoking trajectory; and (3) tobacco dependence at adulthood. Using nationally representative longitudinal data gathered over twelve years, they reveal five distinct smoking trajectories and demonstrate that parenting strategies have differential effects on these segments. Future researchers should examine how such heterogeneity is augmented or reduced by the process of cultural adaptation.

Future research may also want to examine the potential underlying mechanisms through which parental style affects socialization outcomes across different ethnic groups. Yang and Schaninger (2010) study the effects of a distal factor – parenting strategy – on child smoking development, after controlling for the effects of proximal factors. Findings suggest that parenting strategies have a direct impact only on the onset of smoking (smoking intercept), but not on smoking progression (smoking slope). However, after introducing the self-esteem trajectory as a mechanism, they find that parenting strategies affect child smoking progression indirectly – through child self-esteem trajectory factors. Similarly, from a developmental perspective, Yang and Laroche (2011) focus on how parental responsiveness affects adolescent susceptibility to normative influence both directly and indirectly through the key elements of adolescent self-concept (i.e., interdependent self-construal, self-esteem and self-monitoring). The findings suggest that, in individualist cultures such as Canada, responsiveness reduces susceptibility mainly through an indirect effect by undermining interdependent self-construal, fostering self-esteem and impairing self-monitoring. However, in collectivist cultures such as China, responsive parenting reduces susceptibility primarily through a direct effect (Yang and Laroche 2011). These findings indicate that one should use more interpersonal communications in individualist cultures than in collectivist ones; a suggestion that contradicts with conventional wisdom.

Moderating role of other socialization agents

Prior research has long considered parents, peers and mass media as the primary social influence sources for affecting the consumption-related behaviour among young consumers (Benezra 1995; Moschis 1987; Moschis and Churchill 1987; Shim 1996). More recently, the internet has become another important socialization agent, especially for university students. According to McKenna and Bargh (2000), the influence of the internet is so powerful that it even starts to erode the amount of human interactions among teenagers. In the context of ethnic marketing, a fruitful future research agenda could be to examine the extent to which parental styles moderate the effects of other socialization agents, such as mass media.

According to Peñaloza (1994), the media plays a significant role in socialization processes and acts as an important agent in the acculturation process. Extending previous research in this domain, this chapter argues to consider the role of parental style in enhancing media's impact on socialization outcomes. Consistent with this argument, research has shown that mass media health campaigns are most effective when utilized in conjunction with other sources of information (Wallack 1990). Family members have the ability to help young children understand what they see on television and in public, as well as understand what is true and what advertisers are trying to do in the commercials (Austin, Chen and Grube 2006). Furthermore, parental and family guidance can be a teaching aide in improving children's processing of information received via any media channel. As children further develop these skills, the pattern of influence becomes more effective and longer lasting (Austin, Chen and Grube 2006). When children and family experience messages via media channels together, there exists an opportunity to facilitate children's understanding and learning (Huston *et al.* 1992). However, further research is needed to investigate the interplay of new and old media, family roles, socializing goals, socialization agents and socializing outcomes among ethnic minority consumers.

Unique contribution of each dimension of parental style

A potential problem of the authoritative-authoritarian-permissive-neglectful typology is that multiple parenting behaviours co-exist within each style (Peterson and Hann 1999). This leads to the suggestion that more specific parenting behaviours, as opposed to broad all-inclusive parenting styles, can more accurately account for the relationship between parenting styles and socialization outcomes. In line with this reasoning, Darling and Steinberg (1993) propose that parenting styles should be disaggregated into their component parts to understand the processes through which styles influence child development. Parenting dimensions are relatively culture-free and therefore the examination of specific dimensions of parenting allows researchers to isolate relationships between specific parenting behaviours and socialization outcomes (Barber 1997; Peterson and Hann 1999), as well as to increase the explanatory power of socialization models among non-Western cultural groups (Steinberg *et al.* 1992).

In line with this reasoning, Yang and colleagues (Yang and Netemeyer 2015; Yang and Schaninger 2010; Yang, Schaninger and Laroche 2013) examine how three key parenting strategies – namely parental responsiveness, parental psychological control and parental monitoring (aka parental behavioural control) – affect children's smoking growth. Parental responsiveness refers to the extent to which parents show affective warmth, acceptance, involvement, nurturance and support. Parental *psychological control* reflects psychological manipulation aimed at obedience and conformity, accompanied by such specific parental behaviours as threats, physical discipline, withdrawal of love and guilt induction. Parental monitoring or behavioural control is the degree to which parents monitor, set and enforce limits on their child's activities and behaviours (Barber 1997). The general social orientation towards collectivism or individualism is reflected by the extent to which these parenting strategies are used. Relative to their Western counterparts, Chinese parents are less likely to use reasoning and induction in parenting (Chen 2000). They are more controlling and protective in child rearing (Kriger and Kroes 1972; Lin and Fu 1990; Kim, Yang and Lee 2009) and use more high-power strategies such as physical punishment and yelling in teaching adolescents (Kelley and Tseng 1992; Yang and Laroche 2011).

Using longitudinal panel data from parents and children aged ten through seventeen, Yang and Schaninger (2010) show that parental responsiveness decreases children's smoking development by enhancing the initial level and reducing the natural rate of deterioration in child self-esteem, while psychological control increases smoking development both directly, and indirectly, by reducing the initial level of child self-esteem. These findings support targeting parents as a complement to the present approach focusing on children/teens. Different from existing parent-oriented marketing practices, a new approach is suggested by this study – emphasizing the detrimental impact of psychological control in parent-targeted media and website campaigns, and targeting parents before their child reaches late grade school. By the time a child reaches late grade school, the damage to his/her self-esteem and parent–child relationships has been done and it may be too late to reverse, which is likely to lead to escalating smoking (Yang and Schaninger 2010). Parent-oriented programs should also be used in combination with effective segmentation strategies. These are hitherto unrecognized transformative implications for public policy and anti-smoking marketers.

Due to data constraint, Yang and Schaninger (2010) only examine the effect of parenting strategies on socialization outcome (smoking in this case) in the Western society. Future research can extend the model to the Eastern cultures to examine how culture plays an important role in enhancing or mitigating the effect of parenting styles. Also, cross-cultural research can examine such important variables as perceived attractiveness of smokers, perceived popularity of smokers and attitudes towards peers who quit smoking. Customized long-term longitudinal data sets can be developed in different cultures, measuring these and other variables that can reveal the process through which parenting strategies affect child smoking patterns in different countries and ethnic groups. Another research avenue is to examine how parenting strategies may moderate, or interact with child/adolescent-oriented marketing campaigns among ethnic youth. For example, children with particular parenting strategies in a specific ethnic group may be receptive to advert appeals that emphasize 'smoking is not cool', while others with different parenting strategies in another ethnic group may be receptive to advert themes emphasizing that quitting smoking shows 'you are independent' (Fitzsimons and Moore 2008).

Importance of collecting dyadic/triadic data

While some researchers (e.g., Minuchin 1985) warn about the potential biases in collecting parenting data from one parent, no empirical research has yet been conducted to examine the extent to which the results are distorted if such data are used. Acknowledging this potential problem, more recent research in consumer socialization (Kim, Yang and Lee 2009; Laroche et al. 2007; Yang and Schaninger 2010; Yang and Laroche 2011; Yang et al. 2014) use both parents' data and children's data. Gathering information from both parents and the child has at least the following three advantages over using only one informant from the family (most often the mother). First, collecting data from one single parent but interpreting the results at the parent level can be misleading. Yang (2008) gathers parenting information from three members in every family (i.e., father, mother, child) and compares the results of parenting measures derived from four resources: adolescents' reports of parenting, fathers' self-reported paternal parenting, mothers' self-reported maternal parenting and a combination of both parents' self-reported parenting. The results suggest that children's reports of parenting tend to have a greater predictive power than one single parent's self-reported parenting in studying the children's self-concept. Besides, it is the combination of both parents' parental behaviours, rather than any one of the parents alone, that has the strongest influence on children's self-concept.

Second, there are potential methodological concerns regarding using one single informant in a family. When using one parent, parents' self-reports may be subject to social desirability response biases by attempting to conceal certain behaviours that are socially sanctioned, such as harsh or punitive behaviours (Peterson and Hann 1999). However, using children as the single information of the family may result in distorted results caused by common method bias. As a result, it is unclear whether the stronger results observed from children's reports of parental behaviours on their self-reported self-concept are due to common method bias, or due to the fact that no matter what the actual parental behaviour was, the thing that mostly matters was how the child perceived the behaviour (Buri 1991).

Finally, not only do the multiple-informant family data reduce the common method bias in investigations of substantive relationships but also allow us to examine: (1) the differences in parental style between mothers and fathers, and (2) the differences between the parental styles more often practised with boys and those more often practised with girls (Yang *et al.* 2014). According to Meyers-Levy (1989), females are relationship/nurturing oriented, whereas males are agentic oriented. It seems natural to expect that fathers would be higher in controlling behaviours than mothers, and the reverse should be true for responsiveness. In addition, the collectivistic-oriented parents should be more controlling but less responsive than their individualistic-oriented counterparts, given the sex-role distinction is more pronounced in more traditional societies (Hofstede 1983). Furthermore, product type may set up boundary conditions for the effect of fathers' and mothers' influence on boys' versus girls' consumer socialization outcomes. Without the data from multiple informants in the family, these insights are not likely to be uncovered.

References

Aunola, K., Stattin, H. and Nurmi, J. E. (2000) 'Parenting styles and adolescents' achievement strategies'. *Journal of Adolescence*, 23: 205–22.

Austin, E. W., Chen, M. J. and Grube, J. W. (2006) 'How does alcohol advertising influence underage drinking? The role of desirability, identification and skepticism'. *Journal of Adolescent Health*, 38(4): 376–84.

Austin, M. J. and Reed, M. L. (1999) 'Targeting children online: Internet advertising ethics issues'. *Journal of Consumer Marketing*, 16(6): 590–602.

Barber, B. K. (1997) 'Introduction: Adolescent socialization in context – the role of connection, regulation, and autonomy in the family'. *Journal of Adolescent Research*, 12(1): 5–11.

Baumrind, D. (1968) 'Authoritarian vs. authoritative parental control'. *Adolescence*, 3(11): 255–72.

Baumrind, D. (1971) 'Current patterns of parental authority'. *Developmental Psychology Monograph*, 4 (1, Pt 2): 1–103.

Baumrind, D. (1978) 'Parental disciplinary patterns and societal competence in children'. *Youth and Society*, 9: 239–76.

Baumrind, D. (1991) 'The influence of parenting style on adolescent competence and substance use'. *Journal of Early Adolescence*, 11: 56–95.

Benezra, K. (1995) 'Don't mislabel gen X'. *Brandweek*, 36: 31–34.

Berger, J. and Rand, L. (2008) 'Shifting signals to help health: Using identity signaling to reduce risky health behaviors'. *Journal of Consumer Research*, 35: 509–18.

Berry, J. W. (1990) 'Psychology of acculturation: Understanding individuals moving between cultures'. In *Applied Cross-Cultural Psychology*, Volume 14. Cross-Cultural Research and Methodology Series, edited by R. W. Brislin. Newbury Park, CA: Sage Publications, pp. 232–53.

Buri, J. R. (1991) 'Parental authority questionnaire'. *Journal of Personality and Assessment*, 57: 110–19.

Carlson, L. and Grossbart, S. (1988) 'Parental style and consumer socialization of children'. *Journal of Consumer Research*, 15: 77–94.

Caruana, A. and Vassallo R. (2003) 'Children's perception of their influence over purchases: The role of parental communication patterns'. *Journal of Consumer Marketing*, 20(1): 55–66.

Chao, R. K. (1996) 'Chinese and European American mothers' beliefs about the role of parenting in children's school success'. *Journal of Cross-Cultural Psychology*, 27(4): 403–23.

Chao, R. K. and Sue, S. (1996) 'Chinese parental influence and their children's school success: A paradox in the literature on parenting styles'. In *Growing Up the Chinese Way*, edited by S. Lau. Hong Kong: The Chinese University Press, pp. 93–120.

Chen, X. (2000) 'Growing up in a collectivist culture: Socialization and socioemotional development in Chinese children'. In *International Perspectives on Human Development*, edited by A. L. Comunian and U. P. Gielen. Lengerich. Germany: Pabst Science Publishers, pp. 331–53.

Darling, N. and Steinberg, L. (1993) 'Parenting style as context: An integrative model'. *Psychological Bulletin*, 113(3): 487–96.

Deshpandé, R. and Stayman, D. M. (1994) 'A tale of two cities: Distinctiveness theory and advertising effectiveness'. *Journal of Marketing Research*, 31(1): 57–64.

Deshpandé, R., Hoyer, W. D. and Donthu, N. (1986) 'The intensity of ethnic affiliation: A study of the sociology of hispanic consumption'. *Journal of Consumer Research*, 13: 214–20.

Dornbusch, S. M., Ritter, P. L., Leiderman, P. H., Roberts, D. F. and Fraleigh, M. J. (1987) 'The relation of parenting style to adolescent school performance'. *Child Development*, 58: 1244–57.

Fitzsimons, G. J. and Moore, S. G. (2008) 'Should we ask our children about sex, drugs, and rock & roll? Potentially harmful effects of asking questions about risky behaviors'. *Journal of Consumer Psychology*, 18: 82–95.

Forehand, M. R. and Deshpandé, R. (2001) 'What we see makes us who we are: Priming ethnic self-awareness and advertising response'. *Journal of Marketing Research*, 38(3): 336–48.

Forehand, M. R., Deshpandé, R. and Reed, A. (2002) 'Identity salience and the influence of differential activation of the social self-schema on advertising response'. *Journal of Applied Psychology*, 87(6): 1086–99.

Fung, H. (1999) 'Becoming a moral child: The socialization of shame among young Chinese children'. *Ethos*, 27(2): 180–209.

Gao, G., Ting-Toomey, S. and Gudykunst, A. (1996) 'Chinese communication processes'. In *The Handbook of Chinese Psychology*, edited by M. H. Bond. Hong Kong: Oxford University Press, pp. 280–93.

Ho, D. Y. F. (1986) 'Chinese pattern of socialization: A critical review'. In *The Psychology of the Chinese people*, edited by M. H. Bond. New York, NY: Oxford University Press, pp. 1–37.

Ho, D. Y. F., Peng, S. Q. and Lai, A. C. (2001) 'Parenting in mainland China: Culture, ideology, and policy'. *International Society for the Study of Behavioral Development Newsletter*, 38: 7–9.

Hofstede, G. (1983) 'National cultures in four dimensions: A research-based theory of cultural differences among nations'. *International Studies of Management & Organization*, 13(1/2): 46–74.

Humes, K. R., Jones, N. A. and Ramirez, R. R. (2010) 'Overview of race and hispanic origin', *U.S. Census Bureau*. Available at http://www.census.gov/prod/cen2010/briefs/c2010br-02.pdf.

Huston, A., Donnerstein, E., Fairchild, H., Feshbach, N. D., Katz, P. A., Murray, J. P. Rubinstein, E., Wilcox, B. L. and Zuckerman D. (1992) *Big World, Small Screen: The Role of Television in American Society*. Lincoln, NE: University of Nebraska Press.

Kagitcibasi, C. (1996) 'Development in context'. In *Family and Human Development Across Cultures: A View from the Other Side*, edited by C. Kagitcibasi. Mahwah, NJ: Lawrence Erlbaum Associations, pp. 19–34.

Kelley, M. L. and Tseng, H. M. (1992) 'Cultural differences in child rearing: A comparison of immigrant Chinese and Caucasian American mothers'. *Journal of Cross-Cultural Psychology*, 23: 444–55.

Kim, C., Yang, Z. and Lee, H. (2009) 'Cultural differences in consumer socialization: A comparison of Chinese-Canadian and Caucasian-Canadian children'. *Journal of Business Research*, 62: 955–62.

Koslow, S., Shamdasani, P. N. and Touchstone, E. E. (1994) 'Exploring language effects in ethnic advertising: A sociolinguistic perspective'. *Journal of Consumer Research*, 20: 575–85.

Kriger, S. F. and Kroes, W. H. (1972) 'Child-rearing attitudes of Chinese, Jewish, and Protestant mothers'. *Journal of Social Psychology*, 86: 205–10.

Lambert, W. E., Mermigis, L. and Taylor, D. M. (1986) 'Greek Canadians' attitudes towards own group and other ethnic groups: A test of the multiculturalism hypothesis'. *Canadian Journal of Behavioral Science*, 18(1): 35–51.

Lamborn, S. D., Mounts, N. S., Steinberg L. and Dornbusch, S. M. (1991) 'Patterns of competence and adjustment among adolescents from authoritative, authoritarian, indulgent, and neglectful families'. *Child Development*, 62: 1049–65.

Laroche, M., Yang, Z., Kim, C. and Chan, C. (2006) 'A family level measure of acculturation for Chinese immigrants'. In *Marketing and Multicultural Diversity*, edited by C. P. Rao. Burlington, VT: Ashgate Publishing, pp. 154–66.

Laroche, M., Yang, Z., Kim, C. and Richard, M-O. (2007) 'How culture matters in children's purchase influence: A multi-level investigation'. *Journal of the Academy of Marketing Science*, 35(1): 113–26.

LeVine, R. A., Dixon, S., LeVine, S., Richman, A., Leiderman, P. H., Keefer, C. H., Braxelton, T. B. (1994) *Childcare and Culture: Lessons from Africa*. New York, NY: Cambridge University Press.

Lin, C. C. and Fu, V. R. (1990) 'A comparison of child-rearing practices among Chinese, immigrant Chinese, and Caucasian-American parents'. *Child Development*, 61: 429–528.

Maccoby, E. and Martin, J. (1983) 'Socialization in the context of the family: Parent–child interaction'. In *Handbook of Child Psychology (Socialization, Personality, and Social Development)*, Volume 4, edited by E. M. Hetherington. New York, NY: Wiley, pp. 1–101.

McKenna, K. Y. and Bargh, J. A. (2000) 'Plan 9 from cyberspace: The implications of the internet for personality and social psychology'. *Personality & Social Psychology Review*, 4(1): 57–75.

McNeal, J. U. (1991) *A Bibliography of Research and Writing on Marketing and Advertising to Children*. New York, NY: Lexington Books.

McNeal, R. B. (1999) 'Parental involvement as social capital: Differential effectiveness on science achievement, truancy and dropping out'. *Social Forces*, 78: 117–44.

Meyers-Levy J. (1989) 'Gender differences in information processing: A selectivity interpretation'. In *Cognitive and Affective Responses to Advertising*, edited by P. Cafferata and A. M. Tybout. Lexington, MA: Lexington Books, pp. 219–60.

Minuchin, P. (1985) 'Families and individual development: Provocations from the field of family therapy'. *Child Development*, 56: 289–302.

Moschis, G. P. (1987) *Consumer Socialization: A Life-Cycle Perspective*. Lexington, MA: Lexington Books.

Moschis, G. P. and Churchill Jr., G. A. (1978) 'Consumer socialization: A theoretical and empirical analysis'. *Journal of Marketing Research*, 15: 599–609.

Olsen, S. F., Yang, C., Hart, C. H., Robinson, C. C., Wu, P., Nelson, D. A., Nelson, L. J., Jin, S. and Wo, J. (2002) 'Maternal psychological control and preschool children's behavioral outcomes in China, Russia, and the United States'. In *Intrusive Parenting*, edited by B. K. Barber. Washington, DC: American Psychological Association, pp. 235–62.

Peñaloza, L. N. (1994) 'Atravesando fronteras/border crossing: A critical ethnographic exploration of the consumer acculturation of Mexican immigrants'. *Journal of Consumer Research*, 21(1): 32–54.

Peters, J. F. (1989) 'Youth clothes shopping behavior: An analysis by gender'. *Adolescence*, 24(95): 575–80.

Peterson, G. W. and Hann, D. (1999) 'Socializing parents and children in families'. In *Handbook of Marriage and the Family*, edited by S. Steinmetz, M. Sussman and G. W. Peterson. New York, NY: Plenum Press, pp. 327–70.

Portes, A. and Rumbaut, R. G. (1996) *Immigrant America: A Portrait*, Second edition. Berkeley, CA: University of California Press.

Rohner, R. P. (1986) *The Warmth Dimension: Foundation of Parental Acceptance-Rejection Theory*. Newbury Park, CA: Sage.

Rose, G. M. (1999) 'Consumer socialization, parental style, and development timetables in the United States and Japan'. *Journal of Marketing*, 63(3): 105–19.

Ryder, A. G., Alden, L. E. and Paulhus, D. L. (2001) 'Is acculturation uni-dimensional or bi-dimensional? A head-to-head comparison in the prediction of personality, self-identity, and adjustment'. *Journal of Personality and Social Psychology*, 79(1): 49–65.

Shim, S. (1996) 'Adolescent consumer decision-making styles: The consumer socialization perspective'. *Psychology and Marketing*, 13(6): 547–69.

Steinberg, L. (2001) 'We know some things: Parent–adolescent relationships in retrospect and prospect'. *Journal of Research on Adolescence*, 11(1): 1–19.

Steinberg, L., Lamborn, S. D., Darling, N., Mounts, N. S. and Dornbusch, S. M. (1994) 'Over-time changes in adjustment and competence among adolescents from authoritative, authoritarian, indulgent, and neglectful families'. *Child Development*, 65: 754–70.

Steinberg, L., Lamborn, S. D., Dornbusch, S. M. and Darling, N. (1992) 'Impact of parenting practices on adolescent achievement: Authoritative parenting, school involvement, and encouragement to succeed'. *Child Development*, 63: 1266–81.

Story, M. and French, S. (2004) 'Food advertising and marketing directed at children and adolescents in the US'. *International Journal of Behavioral Nutrition and Physical Activity*, 1: 17.

Sue, S. and Abe, J. (1995) 'Predictors of academic achievement among Asian American and white students'. In *The Asian American Educational Experience: A Source Book for Teachers and Students*, edited by D. T. Nakanishi and T. Y. Nishida. New York, NY: Routledge, pp. 303–21.

Taft, R. (1986) 'Methodological consideration in the study of immigrant adaptation in Australia'. *Australian Journal of Psychology*, 38: 339–46.

Tan, C. T. and McCullough, J. (1985) 'Relating ethnic attitudes and consumption values in an Asian context'. In *Advances in Consumer Research*, Volume 12, edited by M. B. Holbrook. Provo, UT: Association for Consumer Research, pp. 122–5.

Toffoli, R. and Laroche M. (2002) 'Cultural and language effects on Chinese bilinguals' and Canadians' responses to advertising'. *International Journal of Advertising*, 21(4): 505–24.

Torres, I. M. and Briggs E. (2005) 'Does Hispanic-targeted advertising work for services?' *Journal of Services Marketing*, 19: 150–6.

Triandis, H. C. (1995) *Individualism and Collectivism*. Boulder, CO: Westview Press.

United States Census Bureau (2012) 'The 2012 Statistical Abstract'. *U.S. Census Bureau*. Available at http://www.census. gov/compendia/statab/cats/population.html.

Wakefield, M., Terry-McElrath, Y., Emery, S., Saffer, H., Chaloupka, F. J., Szczypka, G., Flay, B., O'Malley, P. M. and Johnston L. D. (2006) 'Effect of televised, tobacco company–funded smoking prevention advertising on youth smoking-related beliefs, intentions, and behavior'. *American Journal of Public Health*, 96: 2154–60.

Wallack L. (1990) 'Two approaches to health promotion in the mass media'. *World Health Forum*, 11: 143–54.

Wang, C.-H. and Phinney, J. S. (1998) 'Differences in child rearing attitudes between immigrant Chinese Mothers and Anglo-American mothers'. *Early Development & Parenting*, 7(4): 181–9.

Ward, S. (1974) 'Consumer socialization'. *Journal of Consumer Research*, 1: 1–14.

Whittler, T. E. (1989) 'Viewers' processing of actors race and message claims in advertising stimuli'. *Psychology and Marketing*, 6: 287–309.

Whittler, T. E. (1991) 'The effects of actors' race in commercial advertising: Review and extension'. *Journal of Advertising*, 20(1): 54–60.

Williams, J. D. and Qualls, W. J. (1989) 'Middle class black consumers and intensity of ethnic identification'. *Psychology and Marketing*, 6(4): 263–86.

Wu, D. Y. H. (1996) 'Parental control: Psychocultural interpretations of Chinese patterns of socialization'. In *Growing Up the Chinese Way*, edited by S. Lau. Hong Kong: The Chinese University Press, pp. 1–28.

Wu, P., Robinson, C. C., Yang, C., Hart, C. H., Olsen, S. F., Porter, C. L., Jin, S., Wo, J. and Wu, X. (2002) 'Similarities and Differences in mothers' parenting of preschoolers in China and the United States'. *International Journal of Behavioral Development*, 26: 481–91.

Yang, Z. (2008) *The Parent-Self-Peer Model*. Saarbrücken, Germany: VDM Verlag Publishing Company.

Yang, Z. and Schaninger, C. M. (2010) 'The impact of parenting strategies on child smoking behavior: The role of child self-esteem trajectory'. *Journal of Public Policy & Marketing*, 29(2): 232–47.

Yang, Z. and Laroche, M. (2011) 'Parental responsiveness and adolescent susceptibility to peer influence: A cross-cultural investigation'. *Journal of Business Research*, 64: 979–87.

Yang, Z. and Schaninger, C. M. and Laroche, M. (2013) 'Demarketing teen tobacco and alcohol use: Negative peer influence and longitudinal roles of parenting and self-esteem'. *Journal of Business Research*, 66(4): 559–67.

Yang, Z., Kim, C., Laroche, M. and Lee, H. (2014) 'Parental style and consumer socialization among adolescents: A cross-national investigation'. *Journal of Business Research*, 67: 228–36.

Yang, Z. and Netemeyer, R. G. (2015) 'Differential effects of parenting strategies on child smoking trajectories: A longitudinal assessment over twelve years'. *Journal of Business Research*, 68(6): 1273–82.

Youniss, J. and Smollar, J. (1985) *Adolescent Relations with Mothers, Fathers, and Friends*. Chicago, IL: University of Chicago Press.

4

Ethnic minority consumers' responses to the web

Boris Bartikowski

Introduction

Ethnic minority consumers are growing in number in major economies around the world, along with their purchasing power. Moreover, ethnic minorities' increase in internet use rates outpaces that of majority consumers in developed countries (eMarketer 2013). Nielsen's (2012) 'State of the Hispanic Consumer' report shows that U.S. Hispanic broadband internet use at home grew 14 per cent within one year as compared to only 6 per cent in the general U.S. population. Many companies have recognized the increasing importance of the internet as a way to effectively reach the growing segments of ethnic minority consumers. For example, to target Turkish minorities in Germany, the German car producer Volkswagen launched the campaign 'Volkswagen speaks Turkish' ('Volkswagen Türkçe Konuşuyor') (Volkswagen 2011). On various occasions, the portal www.volkswagen.de offers consumers targeted information in Turkish, such as name and contact information of Turkish-German bilingual car sellers from all over Germany. Similarly, Kraft Canada launched Kraft Ka Khana (www.kraftcanada.com/kraftkakhana), a microsite that targets immigrants from South Asia. The website shows how easy it is to maintain ties with the home culture and traditional South Asian cooking, at the same time facilitating integration into Canadian life and society with products from Kraft. Although a wide array of theoretical and empirical investigations focuses on ethnic minority consumers in general (Grinstein and Nisan 2009; Jamal and Chapman 2000; Jamal, Peattie and Peattie 2012; Tsai 2011), surprisingly little research explores their behaviour on the internet (Becerra and Korgaonkar 2010).

Existing studies widely support that websites with a culturally congruent design generate positive outcomes such as favourable attitudes toward the website or enhanced intentions to purchase from the website (Baack and Singh 2007; Cyr 2008, Cyr and Trevor-Smith 2004; Lynch *et al.* 2001; Singh *et al.* 2006; Singh, Furrer and Ostinelli 2004). However, these studies resonate on country levels as cultural units – a view that is not without criticism, particularly with regards to targeting ethnic minorities. Indeed, many question the notion of cultural homogeneity within nations and hence call for conceptualizations that acknowledge cultural diversity and the existence of multicultural marketplaces (McSweeney 2009; Nakata 2009; Tung 2008; Witte 2012; Yaprak 2008). Although ethnic minority consumers can spread broadly through majority populations without forming unique bonds with their own culture, many associate strongly with their ethnic heritage and culture. In other words, ethnic minorities often retain ethnic cultural roots, but also reach for some degree of acculturation to their host culture (Mendoza 1989; Tsai *et al.* 2000). Hence, consumer segmentation and target marketing in terms of countries as homogeneous cultural units do not seem appropriate (Cleveland and Laroche 2007; Watson *et al.* 2002). Every country has its own unique mix of ethnic groups, suggesting a need for culturally specific approaches for effectively targeting ethnic minority consumers. Obviously, further academic research is needed in this area.

This chapter reviews and discusses literature related to how ethnic minority consumers behave on the web in an attempt to offer some guidance to ethnic marketing and to identify future research avenues. The remainder of the chapter is structured as follows: 'The digital divide' discusses literature relevant to the issue of the digital divide between mainstream and ethnic minority consumers; 'ethnic identity' reviews literature relevant to ethnic identity and the extent to which identity positions inform ethnic minority consumers' responses to online marketing communication; 'website cultural congruity and ethnic minorities' tackles issues of website cultural adaptation as a means to target ethnic minority consumers; finally, 'outlook and future research' describes further discussions and offers some propositions for future research.

The digital divide

Right from the beginning, the internet offered consumers significant digital opportunities in terms of job search, health information, education, entertainment, communication and product and price comparisons. However, not everyone had equal access to the internet, which created inequalities in the marketplace – or what is called the 'digital divide' (Fairlie 2004; Hoffman *et al.* 2001). The existing literature in this field focuses mostly on the situation in the United States and shows that ethnic minorities suffered the most from digital inequalities. For example, Morton *et al.* (2003) report that African Americans and Hispanics in the United States paid on average more for automobiles when they purchased offline, but they paid nearly the same price as non-Hispanic Whites when they bought online. Particularly in the earlier times of the internet, Hispanics, African Americans and Asian Americans in the United States were less likely to own computers and use the internet than the non-Hispanic White majority; they also often had had slower connections (Fairlie 2004; Hoffman *et al.* 2001). Such digital inequalities have important consequences for prosperity and economic development (Hsieh *et al.* 2008; Im and Chee 2008).

Studies also explored reasons for the digital divide and identified socio-economic and demographic factors as key differentiating influences. For example, Chinn and Fairlie's (2007) assessment of 161 countries shows that income differentials mainly explained the digital divide. Similarly, Porter and Donthu (2006) reveal that internet access barriers in the United States resonated mainly with lower income levels; they also show that race was one of the key factors that explained differences in consumer beliefs about the usefulness of the internet. Hoffman *et al.* (2001) found that gaps in internet access between ethnic minority and majority groups in the United States existed even after controlling for educational differences. Another study by Ono and Zavodny (2008), again conducted in the United States, suggests that a digital divide between ethnic minorities and majorities might be attributed to English language skills: ethnic minority consumers with a limited English proficiency used the internet significantly less often and less efficiently than those with more developed English language skills.

Recent studies also point to significant differences in how ethnic minority and majority consumers use interface devices and media. Although mainstream consumers in the United States use the internet more frequently at home, ethnic minority consumers are more likely to use mobile devices. In particular, in 2011, about 66 per cent of non-Hispanic Whites had broadband internet access at home compared to only about 50 per cent of African Americans or Hispanic Americans (Zickuhr and Smith 2012). However, during 2012, about 60 per cent of Hispanic households in the United States owned at least one internet-enabled cell phone compared to only 43 per cent of the general market (Nielsen 2013). Similarly, Lopez et al. (2013) report that in 2012 about 75 per cent of African Americans and Hispanics accessed the internet from mobile devices compared to only 60 per cent of the non-Hispanic White population. These studies also show that ethnic minority consumers used a much wider range of mobile applications (e.g. to access email, do social networking or listen to music) than majority consumers, and they were also more likely to use mobile devices for purchasing online (Nielsen 2012; Zickuhr and Smith 2012).

Significant differences among use patterns between ethnic minorities and mainstream consumers may also be related to structural or institutional factors that immigrants face within a specific host country. For example, minority consumers in Canada tend to fare either much better than the average Canadian in terms of education and earnings or much worse (Boudarbat and Lemieux 2010; Kaur 2011). Moreover, internet use within the ethnic minority groups could be a function of specific needs of minority groups. Ethnic minority consumers live and navigate in between multiple worlds and face the agents of acculturation aligned with original and new cultural environments (Jamal 2003a; 2003b). For example, Veenhof et al. (2008) showed that new immigrants in Canada use the internet significantly more for job searching and for making telephone calls than the Canadian mainstream population. This signifies that the internet is particularly useful for newcomers' transition into a new society, and at the same time enables them to keep bonds with family and friends in their home countries. Deeper understanding of factors that affect ethnic minority consumers' behaviour on the internet arguably requires insights into both collective- and individual-level phenomena, particularly in terms of acculturation processes.

Ethnic identity

Ethnic minority consumers' behaviour on the internet can be seen in relation to their ethnic identity (Appiah 2004; Deshpandé et al. 1986; Elias et al. 2011; Laroche et al. 1998). In this sense, ethnic minority consumers consume, not only for utilitarian reasons, but also to 'manifest their social identity, beliefs, and goals as minorities' (Grinstein and Nisan 2009, p. 105). The concept of ethnic identity emerged out of social identity theory (Tajfel and Turner 1986) and is defined as the 'self-constructed understanding of oneself in terms of one's ethnic group membership that changes in response to developmental and contextual factors' (Phinney 2005, p. 1987). Particularly, ethnic minority consumers may experience multiple ethnic identities that influence how they interact with others and how they consume (Jamal and Chapman 2000). Laroche et al. (2005) suggest that the impact of ethnic identity on consumer behaviour may be studied along two dimensions that consistently emerge in the literature: language use and ethnic attachment. Both dimensions have implications for how ethnic minority consumers respond to marketing communication on the internet, and they are discussed below.

Language use

Language plays an important role in the formation of cognitive processes and choice decisions (Craig and Douglas 2006; Schmitt and Zhang 1998; Sherry and Camargo 1987). Language is, according to Hofstede (2001, p. 21), 'the most clearly recognizable part of culture'.

Ethnic minority consumers differ with respect to their host-country language proficiency, suggesting that their website preferences may vary depending on the type of language used on a website. A study with a nationally representative sample of 1,220 Latino adults in the United States (Taylor *et al.* 2012) shows that immigrant Hispanics are least likely to be proficient in English; however, for the second and third generations, Spanish use falls as English use rises and English becomes the dominant language among the third generation. The study also shows that almost all third-generation Hispanics are either bilingual (29 per cent) or English dominant (69 per cent) – in other terms, only 2 per cent of third-generation Hispanics are primary Spanish speakers. Similarly, a research report by comScore consulting company (comScore 2010) shows that only 20 per cent to 30 per cent of Hispanics in the United States think they see 'not enough Hispanic advertising'. This suggests that language may not be a major factor that hinders successful online marketing to ethnic minority consumers. Accordingly, a study by La Ferle and Lee (2005) shows that English language media are generally effective for targeting African Americans and Hispanics in the United States. Similarly, based on data about U.S. Hispanics, Becerra and Korgaonkar (2010, p. 288) conclude that 'language used in web ads – English or Spanish – does not diminish their effectiveness on strong Hispanic identifiers'.

Luna and colleagues have extensively studied information processing of bilingual ethnic minorities. For example, Luna and Peracchio (2002) argue that second-language processing of marketing communication is more challenging and may, therefore, be less likely to be successful in persuading consumers than first- or native-language processing; however, this effect is contingent on consumers' processing motivation (need for cognition). Luna *et al.* (2003) show that both graphic congruity (the congruity between a website's graphics and its text) and cultural congruity (the congruity of the website's content and the visitor's culture) enhance the effect of second-language communication on persuasion. This again suggests that websites may not need to be translated to effectively reach bilingual ethnic minorities: graphic congruity may compensate effects of missing translations. Carroll and Luna's (2011) accessibility–fluency framework suggests that bilinguals' evaluations of marketing communication are contingent on interactions between what they speak as first and second languages and the content of advertising. Advertisements written in the language typically used in its content area (for example, 'job' is an English word typically used in the work content area) produce higher evaluations through processing fluency (the ease with which content can be decoded and processed).

One aspect that attracts particular research attention relates to mixed-language messages, such as, for example, a slogan that states 'Looking great doesn't have to cost a fortuna' (Luna and Peracchio 2005b, p. 43). According to the markedness model (Myers-Scotton 1998), language is associated with social meaning that people want to emphasize, for example, to express their social group membership. Mixed-language messages may generate greater contrast with the recipient's expectations and may therefore become more marked and more salient. Hence, mixed-language messages may be liked more for two reasons: they mark social group values and they are more salient. Similarly, communication accommodation theory (Giles *et al.* 1991) argues that adjusting speech, vocal patterns and gestures in communication signals to the recipients respect and awareness, which evokes positive responses. Accordingly, mixed-language messages may be preferred by ethnic minority consumers because such messages suggest that the sender has made an effort to appear as closer or as more similar to a well-respected ethnic target group.

Koslow *et al.* (1994) show that Spanish-language elements in advertising increase Hispanics' perceptions of the advertiser's sensitivity to the Hispanic culture, which leads to enhanced evaluations of the advertisement. Unexpectedly, the study shows that advertising exclusively in the Spanish language decreases affect toward the advertisement. Indeed, how mixed-language messages affect attitudes and behaviours may depend on the valence of the associations that people have with the target language or culture (Luna and Peracchio 2005a; 2005b). Native language use may activate an ethnic minority culture schema with positive as well as with negative associations (for example, stigmas associated with being Hispanic in the United States such as being lazy or belonging to a group with a lower socio-economic status). Luna and Peracchio (2005a) show that majority-language slogans that switch to the minority language are less persuasive than minority-language slogans that switch to the majority language; however, the effect is reversed when respondents have positive associations with the minority language.

Li and Kalyanaraman (2012) study a similar effect, namely, changes in attitudes that result from websites that display the editorial content in one language but show banner advertisements in another language. Their study involving Chinese minority consumers in the United States shows that websites and advertisements in English generally receive more attention and result in higher recall and purchase intentions than websites and advertisement in Chinese. It could be that a large number of Chinese consumers acculturate significantly to U.S. consumer culture, which results in their preferences for marketing messages in English language.

In summary, the preceding literature review suggests that ethnic minority consumers (mainly in the United States) can be targeted effectively with the use of (second-language) marketing communication in English. However, language preferences obviously vary with a number of factors such as language proficiency, type of information required, duration of stay in the host country or communication context, and should be taken into account. Further research is needed to compare and contrast those with low and high levels of individually felt acculturation and explore their preferences for language use in advertisements.

Ethnic attachment

Ethnic attachment, or the strength of felt identification to an ethnic group, is widely recognized as a key determinant of how consumers respond to marketing communications. Ethnic minority consumers with a strong and salient ethnic identity tend to be more sensitive to identity-relevant information (Appiah 2001; Deshpandé et al. 1986; Elias et al. 2011). This may be because such information activates social identity within a person's self-schema, particularly when the person strongly identifies with cultural identity (Forehand et al. 2002; Reed 2004). For example, Green (1999) shows that African American minorities in the United States who strongly identify with their ethnicity evaluate advertisements more positively when the advertisements feature people of their own ethnicity in positions of dominance; however, weak ethnic identifiers prefer advertisements that feature people from the majority population in positions of dominance.

On the internet, Appiah (2004) reports that African Americans in the United States with a strong ethnic identification spend more time on African American-targeted websites, and evaluate these websites more favourably than the ones targeting mainstream White consumers. Alternatively, African Americans with a weak ethnic identification show no such differences. Elias, Appiah and Gong (2011) find that African Americans in the United States display more favourable attitudes toward a website if the product presenter is African American instead of White and that this effect increases with the strength of the ethnic identity. Despite its undeniable importance, ethnic attachment alone may be insufficient to explain the effectiveness of ethnically targeted marketing communication on the internet. Other factors, such as language capabilities, host-country associations and the degree of host-culture acculturation, need to be considered as well.

Forehand and Deshpandé (2001) study effects of variability in the awareness or salience of ethnic identity. Consumers are likely to process more ethnically relevant information if they have a high degree of ethnic self-awareness, which is a 'temporary state during which a person is more sensitive to information related to his or her ethnicity' (Forehand and Deshpandé 2001, p. 336). Ethnic self-awareness may occur when people are prompted to categorize themselves along ethnic criteria. This process is oftentimes spontaneous or unconscious and can be aroused by individual variables, situational factors, or contextual primes (Forehand and Deshpandé 2001). Hence, culturally typical symbols, colours, visual images or other cultural markers displayed on a website may prime ethnic minority consumers' identities, make their identity more salient, and thereby increase website effectiveness.

Although ethnically targeted social media enable ethnic minorities to satisfy relational needs, such as creating and maintaining personal relationships, they also impel a sense of belonging to the ethnic group and may, therefore, be preferred over non-ethnically targeted social media sites. For example, migente.com is a website on which Latino people can meet; using the site may reinforce a sense of belonging to the Hispanic community and culture and thereby create 'stickiness' to the site. Similarly, Rovai and Gallien (2005) report that African American students who enrolled in an online class re-created a racial community that had a positive impact on their participation to the class.

Website cultural congruity and ethnic minorities

Ethnic minority consumers may respond favourably (in terms of positive attitudes toward the site or enhanced purchasing intentions) to websites that match with their cultural expectations, suggesting that targeting minorities on the internet requires different web content and design than what is used for the majority population (Grinstein and Nisan 2009; Mazaheri et al. 2011). Luna et al. (2002) argue that increased effectiveness from a website localization strategy is derived from the targeting possibilities by server tools that can identify the domain to which a visitor belongs: 'If the domain belongs, for example, to a Spanish internet service provider, marketers could serve certain culture-specific content that would not be available to visitors from a US domain' (p. 408). A website has high Website Cultural Congruity (WCC) when it communicates to consumers in their native language and when it displays graphical symbols, pictures or other markers that are typical for the target culture or otherwise suggests proximity to the target culture (Luna et al. 2002). The next sections discuss some theories that suggest overall positive effects of higher levels of WCC on consumers' attitudinal or behavioural responses to the web (such as greater liking of the site, greater trust, etc.). However, it should be mentioned that the suggested effects have not been tested explicitly in relation to ethnic minority consumers. Marketers should also be aware of potential undesirable non-target effects such as, for example, majority consumers' negative responses to brands that associate themselves to foreign cultures.

Flow experience

According to Luna et al. (2002), WCC is a content characteristic that influences the likelihood of users experiencing flow. Culturally congruent websites (as compared to incongruent ones) may be more familiar to visitors, thereby requiring them to use fewer resources for cognitive processing. This lower cognitive load may result in enhanced flow experiences. Flow is a state of focused attention and loss of self-consciousness in which the website user is completely engrossed in a browsing task (Csikszentmihalyi and LeFevre 1989). Hoffman and

Novak (1996) describe flow as an experience that is: (1) characterized by a seamless sequence of responses facilitated by interactivity, (2) intrinsically enjoyable, (3) accompanied by a loss of self-consciousness and (4) self-reinforcing. Flow creates stickiness to the site and encourages consumers to linger and revisit the site again in the future. Hence, when ethnic minority consumers surf a website that is culturally congruent with their ethnic culture, they may experience greater flow than majority consumers surfing the same website. However, when ethnic minority consumers surf a website that is culturally congruent to the host-country culture (hence incongruent to their ethnic culture), they may also experience some flow, perhaps as a consequence of habituation or acculturation to the host culture. Therefore, for websites that are culturally congruent to the host country, attitudes and preferences toward the site should be less distinctive between ethnic minority and majority consumers than for websites that are culturally incongruent to the host or the majority culture, but culturally congruent to the ethnic minority culture. Future research should explore this hypothesis while adjusting for potentially related predictors such as individually felt acculturation of ethnic minority consumers or their duration of stay in the host country.

Website usability and usefulness

Harris (2005) argues that search engines sometimes hinder ethnic minorities from using the web efficiently because they display information that may not be specifically relevant to them. Indeed, search engines commonly use geomarketing tools to determine the user's location and deliver region-specific content. Therefore, search queries can result in information or content suggestions that are more relevant to a local mainstream population but less relevant or less useful to ethnic minority consumers. As this example suggests, website usefulness and usability may be improved by ethnically tailored content. A study by Singh *et al.* (2006) involving majority consumers from three countries (Brazil, Germany and Taiwan) shows that these consumers perceive websites with a culturally congruent design as easier to use, more useful and efficient, and therefore they like them more. Similarly, for ethnic minorities, Detlefsen (2004), Lorence *et al.* (2006) and Miller *et al.* (2007) all show that African Americans in the United States, in comparison with White mainstream consumers, are less likely to use mainstream health information websites. According to Detlefsen (2004), this may be because of maladapted website content and design: health websites should address the specific needs of ethnic minority users and consider that on average they may have lower literacy rates than the mainstream population, less health literacy, as well as less computer experience. Digital divide research tackles such demographic influences extensively. Detlefsen also suggests that health information website content may be simplified, and therefore be more useful to ethnic minority consumers, when the site uses actual spoken language, such as 'sugar' instead of 'diabetes', 'pressure' for 'hypertension', or 'the blues' for 'depression'.

A relevant theoretical framework to explain usability aspects of culturally congruent websites is the Technology Acceptance Model (TAM) (Davis *et al.* 1989). TAM is one of the most influential models in information systems research and has been used frequently to study consumers' responses on the internet. It suggests that website acceptance results from two perceptual beliefs: perceived Ease Of Use (EOU) and Perceived Usefulness (PU). EOU is the degree to which a person believes that using a website is free of effort and PU is the belief that using a website increases task performance. These variables are interlinked: EOU affects PU, which in turn affects attitudes toward the website and ultimately use intentions. Singh *et al.* (2006, p. 94) suggest that researchers should draw on TAM 'to study the use and acceptance of portals and websites specifically targeted to ethnic minority consumers'.

Similarity attraction

Several studies (Appiah 2003; Baack and Singh 2007; Harris 2005; Marcus and Gould 2000) suggest that a greater match between a consumer's cultural identity with that of the website in terms of WCC accounts for positive effects of WCC on attitudes and behaviours. This resonates with the similarity effect (Byrne 1971), which states that people are attracted by people or objects that are similar to themselves. By contrast, objects or people that are perceived as dissimilar tend to be less liked. Similarity may be experienced in various ways, for example, in terms of similar personality traits, similar cultural values or similar attitudes.

Appiah (2003) reports that African Americans in the United States spend more time on, and recall more information from, ethnically targeted sites than on mainstream sites. Gevorgyan and Manucharova (2009) show that Chinese in the United States prefer websites that feature collectivistic values, whereas Americans favour websites that display individualistic values. Based on focus group interviews, Singh *et al.* (2008) offer extensive lists and examples of culturally specific themes and website design elements that are particularly relevant to U.S. Hispanics. For example, family themes (pictures of families, websites that are designed to be used by all family members) or important Hispanic role models ('triumphant Latinos') emerge as core themes from their focus group interviews. The authors recommend that marketers emphasize these themes when designing websites for targeting U.S. Hispanics in order to increase perceptions of cultural similarity and enhance website appreciation.

The similarity effect is known as a robust phenomenon in social psychology (Montoya and Horton 2004). It informs several theories that make similar predictions about how culturally congruent website design informs consumers' attitudes and website preferences. First, social categorization theory (Hogg and Abrams 1988) posits that people divide the world into 'us and them' categories. The in-group, which is the group that resembles oneself, tends to be preferred and the out-group is usually disliked (so-called in-group favouritism). For example, the theory predicts that when surfing a website with an Asian look and feel, consumers would make the same associations to the website as they make to Asian cultures in general. Hence, consumers may like a website more when it depicts cultural values of the culture to which they belong.

Second, balance theory (Heider 1958) posits that individuals strive for consistency or harmony. Accordingly, cognitive consistency (the urge to maintain one's values and beliefs over time) drives psychological balance. Balance may occur as a consequence of perceived similarity between the consumer and the website ('everything on the site is in the "right" order'). Hence, a culturally congruent design may evoke feelings of balance and harmony and may therefore be preferred over standardized or culturally incongruent ones.

Third, according to social comparison theory (Festinger 1954), people are driven by the need to hold 'correct' attitudes and beliefs. They may feel attracted by similar others because of social comparisons suggesting that agreement (similarity) satisfies this need. Therefore, culturally congruent websites may be seen as the confirmation of an internal self-evaluation in comparison with the website ('It is correct and good that I belong to this culture'), which ultimately results in liking culturally congruent websites.

Finally, the similarity effect may also be interpreted in terms of 'implied evaluation' (Aronson and Worchel 1966). Accordingly, when a person recognizes attitudinal similarity in another person, the similar person may be liked more because it is believed that the liking will be reciprocal (Layton and Insko 1974). Hence, a culturally congruent website may be liked more because viewers assume that they are part of the website's target and can therefore benefit from reciprocity ('The site will give me something positive back').

Although these theories generally support positive effects of higher levels of WCC, these relationships remain to be tested empirically for ethnic minority consumers.

Outlook and future research

Research into ethnic minority consumers' behaviour on the internet has broadly evolved in the following directions: studies that explore the extent of and reasons for the digital divide between ethnic minority and majority consumers, studies that investigate behaviour contingent on ethnic minorities' cultural identity and studies that investigate WCC as a driver of ethnic minority consumer behaviour. Despite the volume of research, research into ethnic minority consumers' behaviour on the internet is still in its infancy. The following discussion delineates some potentially fruitful areas for future investigations.

Given that most of the existing research on the digital divide has been conducted in the United States, there is an urgent need for more empirical insights involving ethnic minority consumers from other parts of the world. Insights from China would be particularly important because of the sheer size of the Chinese population. More than 40 per cent of the 1.3 billion people in China use the internet (Internetworldstats 2014) and almost half of them belong to ethnic minorities (China Statistical Yearbook 2012). Similarly, Europe, which is a mosaic of various cultures and ethnicities, remains widely under-researched in this regard. It would be interesting to see whether trends exemplified in the existing digital divide research (mainly from the United States) are the same as in other countries or regions of the world.

Recent statistics suggest that the emergence of smartphones makes it easier for ethnic minority consumers to access the internet, which arguably narrows the digital divide; at the same time, as mentioned previously, studies show that minorities use mobile devices more frequently than majority consumers (Nielsen 2013; Zickuhr and Smith 2012). These developments suggest a new form of digital divide in which minorities are no longer constrained by internet access problems but may be challenged by the device they use (Washington 2011). It is arguably more difficult to engage in thorough product or price comparisons or to follow an educational program on a smartphone than on a laptop or an office computer. Such differences between minorities and majorities may perpetuate segregation in the physical world, which future research should clarify. More research is also needed to reveal the consequences of the new digital divide in terms of price comparison activities or minority–majority differences in online product evaluation and choice processes.

Another important topic for future research is to clarify whether and when higher levels of WCC are needed to effectively target minority consumers. Existing studies suggest that effects of WCC may be contingent on the degree of ethnic identity, and that host-country language (mostly English in the United States) is in many instances an effective tool to target bilingual minorities. More insights are needed that guide practitioners' decisions on how to allocate resources toward standardized or culturally adapted website design in culturally diverse markets. Future studies may investigate the effectiveness of culturally congruent website design and language display depending on ethnic minority consumers' goals for using the internet. Such goals may be differentiated in terms of searching for information versus browsing for entertainment (Hoffman and Novak 1996; Schlosser 2003). Goal contingencies may also be researched along different product or service categories. For example, information related to ethnic and non-ethnic products may be processed differently and may therefore require different levels of WCC. In conjunction, future research may reveal the role of web translators on non-bilingual minority consumers' information processing and decision making. Studies may also consider minority consumers' degree of bilingualism (for example, measured by language tests such as the TOEFL), as well as their degree of bi-culturalism, which appears more realistic than categorizing minority and majority consumers into discrete bimodal categories (Luna *et al.* 2008). Research may also expand into multiculturalism and multi-lingualism. Indeed, many minorities live and work in multicultural environments in which they are confronted by more than one foreign language. For example, minority consumers in Canada deal in many instances with English and French, both of which may be second and third languages to them. How does ethnic minority consumers' multi-lingualism shape information processing of commercial information?

It would also be interesting to investigate further how the internet contributes to ethnic minority consumers' acculturation and socializing processes, particularly in relation to brands. Immigrants and ethnic minorities undergo processes of acculturation in which they add aspects of the host culture on to their traditional culture and potentially modify or even replace their existing value system (Hurh and Kim 1984; Teske and Nelson 1974). It has been shown that online social networks play an important role in the development of minorities' healthy sense of self-identity, which is necessary to adapt to a foreign environment (Byrne 2007). Studies also show that ethnic minorities use social media more frequently than majorities (Zickuhr and Smith 2012), that social media is increasingly important for brand building (Bernoff and Li 2008; Kaplan and Haenlein 2010), and that consumers embrace brand associations for improving their self-concept (Aaker 1997; Keller 1998). For example, Heehyoung *et al.* (2008) note that a brand achieves success when consumers express their personal characteristics through it as a result of online community membership. Drawing on this literature, researchers may interpret ethnic minorities' social media use in terms of a coping strategy that results from acculturative stress (Copeland and Hess 1995; Mena *et al.* 1987). Future studies may investigate if, and under which conditions, ethnic minority consumers may serve as brand ambassadors. With this in mind, studies may also answer questions about the role of social media for minority consumers' brand relationship building in relation to host- and home-country brands.

Another important, but under-researched area relates to the impact of religiosity on minority consumers' responses to the web. One of the rare articles in this field is by Zainul, Osman and Mazlan (2004), who offer a discussion on Muslims' e-commerce acceptance in regards to online payment systems. Because it is uncertain if credit card payments conform to the Islamic Shariah rulings, Muslims may prefer to use the 'Murabahah system', in which a buyer instructs an Islamic bank to make a purchase on one's behalf instead of directly using a credit card to make the payment (ibid.). Other faith groups may also have unique requirements potentially affecting the ways such groups engage with and use web-based marketing efforts. Future research should deepen this and other aspects related to religiosity and ethnic minorities' online behaviours.

Finally, marketing actions that target ethnic minorities can as well affect majority consumers with unwanted, potentially harmful, non-target market effects (Aaker *et al.* 2000; Antioco *et al.* 2012; Johnson and Grier 2011; Oakenfull *et al.* 2008). In many instances, marketers face the dilemma that culturally sensitive web content may be appreciated by members of one culture, but does not cause an effect on another culture – or can even offend another culture's value system. Cultural elements in advertising can also result in a lack of brand differentiation and dilute a brand's identity (Burgos 2008). An important question for marketers, therefore, is how they may use the internet to communicate with multiple cultures within the domestic market at the same time. Future research may adopt a processing fluency perspective (Carroll and Luna 2011; Fang *et al.* 2007; Janiszewski and Meyvis 2001) to investigate how cosmetic variations and repetitions of culturally laden web content and design interact with minority and minority consumers' preference formation on the internet.

References

Aaker, J. L. (1997) 'Dimensions of brand personality'. *Journal of Marketing Research*, 34(3): 347–56.

Aaker, J. L., Brumbaugh, A. M. and Grier, S. A. (2000) 'Non-target markets and viewer distinctiveness: The impact of target marketing on advertising'. *Journal of Consumer Psychology*, 9(3): 127–40.

Antioco, M., Vanhamme, J., Hardy, A. and Bernardin, L. (2012) 'On the importance of social integration for minority targeting effectiveness'. *International Journal of Research in Marketing*, 29(4): 380–89.

Appiah, O. (2001) 'Ethnic identification on adolescents' evaluations of advertisements'. *Journal of Advertising Research*, 41(5): 7–22.

Appiah, O. (2003) 'Americans online: Differences in surfing and evaluating race-targeted web site: By black and white users'. *Journal of Broadcasting & Electronic Media*, 47(4): 537–55.

Appiah, O. (2004) 'Effects of ethnic identification on web browsers' attitudes toward and navigational patterns on race-targeted sites'. *Communication Research*, 31(3): 312–37.

Aronson, E. and Worchel, P. (1966) 'Similarity versus liking as determinants of interpersonal attractiveness'. *Psychonomic Science*, 5(4): 157–58.

Baack, D. W. and Singh, N. (2007) 'Culture and web communications'. *Journal of Business Research*, 60(3): 181–88.

Becerra, E. P. and Korgaonkar, P. K. (2010) 'The influence of ethnic identification in digital advertising: How Hispanic Americans' respond to pop-up, e-mail, and banner advertising affect online purchase intentions'. *Journal of Advertising Research*, 50(3): 279–91.

Bernoff, J. and Li, C. (2008) 'Harnessing the power of the oh-so-social web'. *MIT Sloan Management Review*, 49(3): 36–42.

Boudarbat, B. and Lemieux, T. (2010) 'Why are the relative wages of immigrants declining? A distributional approach'. *Canadian Labour Market and Skills Researcher Network*. Available from: http://www.clsrn.econ. ubc.ca/workingpapers/CLSRN%20Working%20Paper%20no.%2065%20-%20Boudarbat%20and%20 Lemieux.pdf [accessed 18 March 2013].

Burgos, D. (2008) 'Use and abuse of cultural elements in multicultural advertising'. *Journal of Advertising Research*, 48(2): 177–8.

Byrne, D. E. (1971) *The Attraction Paradigm*. New York, NY: Academic Press.

Byrne, D. N. (2007) 'Public discourse, community concerns, and civic engagement: Exploring black social networking traditions on blackplanet'. *Journal of Computer Mediated Communication*, 13(1): 319–40.

Carroll, R. and Luna, D. (2011) 'The other meaning of processing fluency'. *Journal of Advertising*, 40(3): 73–84.

Chasin, J. (2010) 'A closer look at the US Hispanic online audience'. comScore. Available from: http:// www.comscore.com/Insights/Presentations-and-Whitepapers/2010/A-Closer-Look-at-the-US-Hispanic-Online-Audience [accessed 24 March 2013].

China Statistical Yearbook (2012) 'China Statistical Yearbook 2012'. *National Bureau of Statistics of China*. Available from: www.stats.gov.cn [accessed 18 March 2013].

Chinn, M. D. and Fairlie, R. W. (2007) 'The determinants of the global digital divide: A cross-country analysis of computer and internet penetration'. *Oxford Economic Papers*, 59(1): 16–44.

Cleveland, M. D. and Laroche, M. (2007) 'Acculturation to the global consumer culture: Scale development and research paradigm'. *Journal of Business Research*, 60(3): 249–59.

Copeland, E. P. and Hess, R. S. (1995) 'Differences in young adolescents' coping strategies based on gender and ethnicity'. *The Journal of Early Adolescence*, 15(2): 203–19.

Craig, C. S. and Douglas, S. P. (2006) 'Beyond national culture: Implications of cultural dynamics for consumer research'. *International Marketing Review*, 23(3): 322–42.

Csikszentmihalyi, M. and LeFevre, J. (1989) 'Optimal experience in work and leisure'. *Journal of Personality and Social Psychology*, 56(5): 815–22.

Cyr, D. (2008) 'Modelling website design across cultures: Relationships to trust, satisfaction and e-loyalty'. *Journal of Management Information Systems*, 24(4): 47–72.

Cyr, D. and Trevor-Smith, H. (2004) 'Localization of web design: An empirical comparison of German, Japanese, and United States web site characteristics'. *Journal of the American Society for Information Science & Technology*, 55(13): 1199–208.

Davis, F. D., Bagozzi, R. P. and Warshaw, P. R. (1989) 'User acceptance of computer technology: A comparison of two theoretical models'. *Management Science*, 35(8): 982–1003.

Deshpandé, R., Hoyer, W. D. and Donthu, N. (1986) 'The intensity of ethnic affiliation: A study of the sociology of hispanic consumption'. *Journal of Consumer Research*, 13: 214–20.

Detlefsen, E. G. (2004) 'Where am I to go? Use of the internet for consumer health information by two vulnerable communities'. *Library Trends*, 53(2): 283–300.

Elias, T., Appiah, O. and Gong, L. (2011) 'Effects of strength of ethnic identity and product presenter race on black consumer attitudes: A multiple-group model approach'. *Journal of Interactive Advertising*, 11(2): 13–29.

eMarketer (2013) *Among Hispanics, Who's Leading Digital Adoption Trends?* eMarketer. Available from: http://www.emarketer.com [accessed 25 March 2013].

Fairlie, R. W. (2004) 'Race and the digital divide'. *Contributions to Economic Analysis and Policy*, 3(1): 1–38.

Fang, X., Singh, S. and Ahluwalia, R. (2007) 'An examination of different explanations for the mere exposure effect'. *Journal of Consumer Research*, 34(1): 97–103.

Festinger, L. (1954) 'A theory of social comparison processes'. *Human Relations*, 7: 117–140.

Forehand, M. R. and Deshpandé, R. (2001) 'What we see makes us who we are: Priming ethnic self-awareness and advertising response'. *Journal of Marketing Research*, 38(3): 336–48.

Forehand, M. R., Deshpandé, R. and Reed, A. (2002) 'Identity salience and the influence of differential activation of the social self-schema on advertising response'. *Journal of Applied Psychology*, 87(6): 1086–99.

Gevorgyan, G. and Manucharova, N. (2009) 'Does culturally adapted online communication work? A study of American and Chinese internet users' attitudes and preferences toward culturally customized web design elements'. *Journal of Computer-Mediated Communication*, 14(2): 393–413.

Giles, H., Coupland, N. and Coupland, J. (1991) 'Accommodation theory: Communication, context, and consequence'. In *Contexts Of Accommodation: Developments in Applied Sociolinguistics*, edited by H. Giles, J. Coupland, and N. Coupland. Cambridge, MA: Cambridge University Press, pp. 1–68.

Green, C. L. (1999) 'Ethnic evaluations of advertising: Interaction effects of strength of ethnic identification, media placement, and degree of racial composition'. *Journal of Advertising*, 28(1): 49–64.

Grinstein, A. and Nisan, U. (2009) 'Demarketing, minorities, and national attachment'. *Journal of Marketing*, 73(2): 105–22.

Harris, K. L. (2005) *Searching For Blackness: The Effectiveness of Search Engines in Retrieving African American Websites*. Washington, DC: Howard University.

Heehyoung, J., Olfman, L., Islang, K., Joon, K. and Kyungtae, K. (2008) 'The influence of on-line brand community characteristics on community commitment and brand loyalty'. *International Journal of Electronic Commerce*, 12(3): 57–80.

Heider, F. (1958) *The Psychology of Interpersonal Relations*. New York, NY: Wiley.

Hoffman, D. L. and Novak, T. P. (1996) 'Marketing in hypermedia computer-mediated environments: Conceptual foundations'. *Journal of Marketing*, 60(3): 50–68.

Hoffman, D. L., Novak, T. P. and Schlosser, A. E. (2001) 'Evolution of the digital divide: How gaps in internet access may impact electronic commerce'. *Journal of Computer-Mediated Communication*, 5. doi: 10.1111/j.1083-6101.2000.tb00341.x

Hofstede, G. (2001) *Culture's Consequences: Comparing Values, Behaviors, Institutions, and Organization Across Nations*. Thousand Oaks, CA: Sage.

Hogg, M. A. and Abrams, D. (1988) *Social Identifications: A Social Psychology of Intergroup Relations and Group Processes*. London: Routledge.

Hsieh, J. J. P.-A., Rai, A. and Keil, M. (2008) 'Understanding digital inequality: Comparing continued use behavioral models of the socio-economically advantaged and disadvantaged', *MIS Quarterly*, 32(1): 97–126.

Hurh, W. M. and Kim, K. C. (1984) 'Adhesive sociocultural adaptation of korean immigrants in the US: An alternative strategy of minority adaptation'. *International Migration Review*, 18(2): 188–216.

Im, E.-O. and Chee, W. (2008) 'The use of internet cancer support groups by ethnic minorities'. *Journal of Transcultural Nursing*, 19(1): 74–82.

Internet World Stats (n.d.) 'Internet Users in Asia'. *Internet World Stats*. Avilable from: http://www.internet worldstats.com/stats3.htm [accessed 19 May 2013].

Jamal, A. (2003a) 'Marketing in a multicultural world: The interplay of marketing, ethnicity and consumption'. *European Journal of Marketing*, 37(11/12): 1599–620.

Jamal, A. (2003b) 'Retailing in a multicultural world: The interplay of retailing, ethnic identity and consumption'. *Journal of Retailing & Consumer Services*, 10(1): 1–11.

Jamal, A. and Chapman, M. (2000) 'Acculturation and inter-ethnic consumer perceptions: Can you feel what we feel?' *Journal of Marketing Management*, 16(4): 365–91.

Jamal, A., Peattie, S. and Peattie, K. (2012) 'Ethnic minority consumers' responses to sales promotions in the packaged food market'. *Journal of Retailing & Consumer Services*, 19(1): 98–108.

Janiszewski, C. and Meyvis, T. (2001) 'Effects of brand logo complexity, repetition, and spacing on processing fluency and judgment'. *Journal of Consumer Research*, 28(1): 18–32.

Johnson, G. D. and Grier, S. A. (2011) 'Targeting without alienating: Multicultural advertising and the subtleties of targeted advertising.' *International Journal of Advertising*, 30(2): 233–58.

Kaplan, A. M. and Haenlein, M. (2010) 'Users of the world, unite! The challenges and opportunities of social media'. *Business Horizons*, 53: 59–68.

Kaur, H. (2011) '*Income Gap Between Rich and Poor Immigrants: A Lesson for Canadians*, Canada Updates. Available from: www.canadaupdates.com [accessed 24 March 2013].

Keller, K. L. (1998) *Strategic Brand Management: Building, Measuring, and Managing Brand Equity*. Englewood Cliffs, NJ: Prentice-Hall.

Koslow, S., Shamdasani, P. N. and Touchstone, E. E. (1994) 'Exploring language effects in ethnic advertising: A sociolinguistic perspective'. *Journal of Consumer Research*, 20: 575–85.

La Ferle, C. and Lee, W.-N. (2005) 'Can English language media connect with ethnic audiences? Ethnic minorities' media use and representation perceptions'. *Journal of Advertising Research*, 45(1): 140–53.

Laroche, M., Kim, C. and Tomiuk, M. A. (1998) 'Italian ethnic identity and its relative impact on the consumption of convenience and traditional foods'. *Journal of Consumer Marketing*, 15(2): 125–51.

Laroche, M., Kim, C., Tomiuk, M. A. and Belisle, D. (2005) 'Similarities in Italian and Greek multidimensional ethnic identity: Some implications for food consumption'. *Canadian Journal of Administrative Sciences*, 21(4): 143–67.

Layton, B. D. and Insko, C. A. (1974) 'Anticipated interaction and the similarity-attraction effect'. *Sociometry*, 37(2): 149–62.

Li, C. and Kalyanaraman, S. (2012) 'What if web site editorial content and ads are in two different languages? A study of bilingual consumers' online information processing'. *Journal of Consumer Behaviour*, 11(3): 198–206.

Lopez, M. H., Gonzalez-Barrera, A. and Patten, E. (2013) 'Closing the digital divide: Latinos and technology adoption'. Pew Research Center. Available from: http://www.pewhispanic.org/2013/03/07/closing-the-digital-divide-latinos-and-technology-adoption/ [accessed 24 March 2013].

Lorence, D. P., Park, H. and Fox, S. (2006) 'Racial disparities in health information access: Resilience of the digital divide.' *Journal of Medical Systems*, 30(4): 241–49.

Luna, D. and Peracchio, L. A. (2002) '"Where there is a will . . .": Motivation as a moderator of language processing by bilingual consumers'. *Psychology & Marketing*, 19(7/8): 573–93.

Luna, D. and Peracchio, L. A. (2005a) 'Advertising to bilingual consumers: The impact of code-switching on persuasion'. *Journal of Consumer Research*, 31(4): 760–65.

Luna, D. and Peracchio, L. A. (2005b) 'Sociolingusitic effects on code-switched ads targeting bilingual consumers'. *Journal of Advertising*, 34(2): 43–56.

Luna, D., Peracchio, L. A. and de Juan, M. D. (2002) 'Cross-cultural and cognitive aspects of web site navigation'. *Journal of the Academy of Marketing Science*, 30(4): 397–410.

Luna, D., Peracchio, L. A. and de Juan, M. D. (2003) 'The impact of language and congruity on persuasion in multicultural e-marketing'. *Journal of Consumer Psychology*, 13(1/2): 41–50.

Luna, D., Ringberg, T. and Peracchio, L. A. (2008), 'One individual, two identities: Frame switching among biculturals'. *Journal of Consumer Research*, 35: 279–93.

Lynch, P. D., Kent, R. J. and Srinivasan, S. S. (2001) 'The global internet shopper: Evidence from shopping tasks in twelve countries'. *Journal of Advertising Research*, 41(3): 15–23.

Marcus, A. and Gould, E. W. (2000) 'Crosscurrents: Cultural dimensions and global web user-interface design'. *Interactions*, 7(4): 32–46.

Mazaheri, E., Richard, M.-O. and Laroche, M. (2011) 'Online consumer behavior: Comparing Canadian and Chinese website visitors'. *Journal of Business Research*, 64(9): 958–965.

McSweeney, B. (2009) 'Dynamic diversity: Variety and variation within countries'. *Organization Studies*, 30(9): 933–57.

Mena, F. J., Padilla, A. M. and Maldonado, M. (1987) 'Acculturative stress and specific coping strategies among immigrant and later generation college students'. *Hispanic Journal of Behavioral Sciences*, 9(2): 207–25.

Mendoza, R. H. (1989) 'An empirical scale to measure type and degree of acculturation in Mexican American adolescents and adults'. *Journal of Cross-Cultural Psychology*, 20(4): 372–85.

Miller, E., West, D. and Wasserman, M. (2007) 'Health information websites: Characteristics of US users by race and ethnicity'. *Journal of Telemedicine and Telecare*, 13(6): 298–302.

Montoya, R. M. and Horton, R. S. (2004) 'On the importance of cognitive evaluation as a determinant of interpersonal attraction'. *Journal of Personality and Social Psychology*, 86(5): 696–712.

Morton, F. S., Zettelmeyer, F. and Silva-Risso, J. (2003) 'Consumer information and discrimination: Does the internet affect the pricing of new cars to women and minorities?' *Quantitative Marketing and Economics*, 1(1): 65–92.

Myers-Scotton, C. (ed) (1998) 'A theoretical introduction to the markedness model'. In *Codes and Consequences: Choising Linguistic Varieties*. New York, NY: Oxford University Press, pp. 18–38.

Nakata, C. (2009) *Beyond Hofstede: Culture Frameworks for Global Marketing and Management*. Chicago, IL: Palgrave Macmillan.

Nielsen (2012) 'State of the Hispanic consumer: The Hispanic Market imperative'. Nielsen. Available from: http://www.nielsen.com/content/dam/corporate/us/en/reports-downloads/2012-Reports/State-of-the-Hispanic-Consumer.pdf [accessed 25 March 2013].

Nielsen (2013) 'The mobile consumer'. Nielsen. Available from: www.nielsen.com [accessed 25 March 2013].

Oakenfull, G. K., McCarthy, M. S. and Greenlee, T. B. (2008) 'Targeting a minority without alienating the majority: Advertising to gays and lesbians in mainstream media'. *Journal of Advertising Research*, 48(2): 191–98.

Ono, H. and Zavodny, M. (2008) 'Immigrants, English ability and the digital divide'. *Social Forces*, 86(4): 1455–79.

Phinney, J. S. (2005) 'Ethnic identity in late modern times: A response to Rattansi and Phoenix'. *Identity*, 5(2): 187–94.

Porter, C. E. and Donthu, N. (2006) 'Using the technology acceptance model to explain how attitudes determine internet usage: The role of perceived access barriers and demographics'. *Journal of Business Research*, 59(9): 999–1007.

Reed, A. I. (2004) 'Activating the self-importance of consumer selves: Exploring identity salience effects on judgments'. *Journal of Consumer Research*, 31: 286–95.

Rovai, A. P. and Gallien Jr, L. B. (2005) 'Blended learning and sense of community: A comparative analysis of African American and Caucasian online graduate students'. *The Journal of Negro Education*, 5(2): 53–62.

Schlosser, A. E. (2003) 'Experiencing products in the virtual world: The role of goal and imagery in influencing attitudes versus purchase intentions'. *Journal of Consumer Research*, 30(2): 184–98.

Schmitt, B. H. and Zhang, S. (1998) 'Language structure and categorization: A study of classifiers in consumer cognition, judgment, and choice'. *Journal of Consumer Research*, 25(2): 108–22.

Sherry, J. F. and Camargo, E. G. (1987) 'May your life be marvellous: English language labelling and the semiotics of Japanese promotion'. *Journal of Consumer Research*, 14(2): 174–88.

Singh, N., Furrer, O. and Ostinelli, M. (2004) 'To localize or to standardize on the web: Empirical evidence from Italy, India, Netherlands, Spain, and Switzerland'. *Multinational Business Review*, 12(1): 69–87.

Singh, N., Baack, D. W., Kundu, S. K. and Hurtado, C. (2008) 'US Hispanic consumer e-commerce preferences: Expectations and attitudes toward web content'. *Journal of Electronic Commerce Research*, 9(2): 162–75.

Singh, N., Fassott, G., Chao, M. C. H. and Hoffmann, J. A. (2006) 'Understanding international web site usage: A cross-national study of German, Brazilian, and Taiwanese online consumers'. *International Marketing Review*, 23(1): 83–97.

Tajfel, H. and Turner, J. (1986) 'The social identity theory of intergroup behavior'. In *Psychology of Intergroup Relations*, edited by S. Worchel and W. Austin. Chicago, IL: Nelson-Hall, pp. 7–24.

Taylor, P., Lopez, M. H., Martínez, J. H. and Velasco, G. (2012) 'When labels don't fit: Hispanics and their views of identity'. Pew Hispanic Center. Available at: http://www.pewhispanic.org/2012/04/04/when-labels-dont-fit-hispanics-and-their-views-of-identity/ [accessed 19 May 2013].

Teske, R. H. and Nelson, B. H. (1974) 'Acculturation and assimilation: A clarification'. *American Ethnologist*, 1(2): 351–67.

Tsai, W.-H. S (2011) 'How minority consumers use targeted advertising as pathways to self-empowerment'. *Journal of Advertising*, 40(3): 85–97.

Tsai, J. L., Ying, Y.-W. and Lee, P. A. (2000) 'The meaning of "Being Chinese" and "Being American" variation among Chinese American young adults'. *Journal of Cross-Cultural Psychology*, 31(3): 302–32.

Tung, R. L. (2008) 'The cross-cultural research imperative: The need to balance cross-national and intra-national diversity: commentary'. *Journal of International Business Studies*, 39(1): 41–6.

Veenhof, B., Wellman, B., Quell, C. and Hogan, B. (2008) 'How Canadians' use of the internet affects social life and civic participation?' *Statistics Canada*. Available from: http://www80.statcan.gc.ca/wes-esw/page1-eng.htm [accessed 18 March 2013].

Volkswagen (2011) 'Sustainability Report 2010'. Volkswagen. Available from: http://www.volkswagenag.com/content/vwcorp/info_center/en/themes/2011/03/Annual_Report_2010.html [accessed 30 December 2013].

Washington, J. (2011) 'New digital divide seen for minorities on internet'. *San Francisco Chronicle*. Available from: http://www.sfgate.com/business/article/New-digital-divide-seen-for-minorities-on-Internet-2459621.php [accessed 28 March 2013].

Watson, J., Lysonski, S., Gillan, T. and Raymore, L. (2002) 'Cultural values and important possessions: A cross-cultural analysis'. *Journal of Business Research*, 55(11): 923–31.

Witte, A. E. (2012) 'Making the case for a post-national cultural analysis of organizations'. *Journal of Management Inquiry*, 21(2): 141–59.

Yaprak, A. (2008) 'Culture study in international marketing: A critical review and suggestions for future research'. *International Marketing Review*, 25(2): 215–29.

Zainul, N., Osman, F. and Mazlan, S. H. (2004) 'E-commerce from an Islamic perspective'. *Electronic Commerce Research and Applications*, 3(3): 280–93.

Zickuhr, K. and Smith, A. (2012) 'Digital differences'. Pew Research Center. Available from: http://www.pewinternet.org/2012/04/13/digital-differences/ [accessed 18 March 2013].

Part III
Identity, space and ethnic entrepreneurship

5

Emplaced ethnicity

The role of space(s) in ethnic marketing

Luca M. Visconti

Emplacing ethnicity

In his article on the racialization of space and the spatialization of race, George Lipsitz (2007) captures the conceptual, experiential and economic porosity between space and ethnicity. As he writes (2007, p. 12):

> The lived experience of race has a spatial dimension, and the lived experience of space has a racial dimension. People of different races in the United States are relegated to different physical locations by housing and lending discrimination, by school district boundaries, by policing practices, by zoning regulations, and by the design of transit systems. The racial demography of the places where people live, work, play, shop, and travel exposes them to a socially shared system of exclusion and inclusion. Race serves as a key variable in determining who has the ability to own homes that appreciate in value and can be passed down to subsequent generations; in deciding which children have access to education by experienced and credentialed teachers in safe buildings with adequate equipment; and in shaping differential exposure to polluted air, water, food, and land.

Ethnicity and space are thus intertwined: space visualizes social representations of ethnicity (Lipsitz 1998; Peñaloza 2000; Peñaloza 2001; Visconti and de Cordova 2012); dwellers' ethnicities contribute to construct and modify the identity of the spaces in which they live, work, shop, consume and establish social and market interactions (Peñaloza and Gilly 1999; Üstüner and Holt 2007). In brief, construction of ethnicity entails at least three types of identities: (1) migrants'/ethnic minorities' identity (the term 'minority' here is used to signify 'disempowered ethnic groups'), (2) mainstream's (ethnic) identity, and (3) space identity, in which minorities' and mainstream's confrontation is emplaced. By space, I mean a large variety of spaces, ranging from the macro (e.g., nationscape, regionscape, cityscape; Paasi 2001) to the meso (e.g., marketplace, neighbourhood; Peñaloza 2004; Peñaloza 2007) to the micro level (e.g., servicescape, workplace, home; Jamal 2003; Üstüner and Thompson 2012; Veresiu *et al.* 2012; Visconti and de Cordova 2012; Visconti and Premazzi 2012). More importantly, in this chapter I classify space through its function in the construction of ethnicity and thus distinguish among physical, cultural, social, ideological, political and commercial space.

Discussion on emplaced ethnicity is overdue (Ping Hung Li and Figueiredo 2012). A recent special issue of *Landscape Journal* (2007) addresses the role of the built environment in the construction of race/ethnicity in the United States. The invited editor Dianne Harris (2007, p. 2) raises some thought-provoking questions:

> Why study race and space? What can the built environment tell us about the construction and maintenance of racial identities, or about the production of racism in the United States that we don't already know? . . . Can space really tell us anything new about this topic?

My answer is affirmative. I contend that by investigating the role of space in the construction of ethnicity, two main contributions unfold. First, such investigation advances current consumer and marketing literature on ethnicity – and its making, transformation or maintenance through market exchanges and consumption – as the following paragraph illustrates in further detail. Second, by addressing attention to space, we can better determine how 'minoritization', or the way certain ethnic groups are kept at the margins of society and the market, occurs. In doing so, forms of 'underground' – that is 'unspoken' – racism (Harris 2007) surface and can be more easily tackled.

The chapter comprises three main parts: first, I discuss different notions of space relevant to ethnicity and tie them together; second, from these notions of space, I draw implications for ethnic marketing strategy and practice; third, I question the commercial and social effects that space (im)permeability, or the extent to which different ethnic groups are equally entitled to use a given space, may determine.

Ethnicity and space(s)

Within ethnic marketing studies, ethnicity has been mostly addressed with reference to migration and ethnic minorities. Yet ethnicity does not concern just border-crossing people, nor does it exclude the mainstream (Lipsitz 1998; Peñaloza 2004; Peñaloza 2007). Thus, this chapter questions the role of space in the construction of ethnicity and ethnic identity for both migrant and non-migrant people as well as for ethnic minorities and the mainstream. In doing so, I rely on multidisciplinary contributions, in which research on consumer acculturation, cultural geography and urban studies are prominent.

With reference to the ethnic marketing literature, to date research on ethnicity has addressed the role of space either marginally or one-sidedly. Regany *et al.* (2012) comment on the marginality of space within consumer acculturation research. They contend that space has been mentioned in terms of, among others, 'boundary' (Oswald 1999; Peñaloza 1994), 'border' (Lindridge *et al.* 2004) and, more often, 'country of origin/destination' without being fully problematized. Featherstone *et al.* (2007, p. 383) also insist that research on ethnicity has repeatedly used 'spatial metaphors', which are elusive since they address space without really inspecting its mundane effects on 'everyday human experiences'.

When not treating it marginally, other ethnic marketing researchers have approached space in relation to ethnicity one-sidedly, by focusing on specific types of space. For example, Jamal (2003, p. 1) illustrates the role of the retailing-scape in the visualization of ethnic diversity and in promoting 'co-existence, tolerance and freedom of lifestyles among consumers of different ethnic backgrounds'. Peñaloza (2004; 2007) documents how the cityscape embeds consumption, labour and capital positions on which Latinos/as and the American mainstream build respective power positions. Similarly, Üstüner and Holt (2007) unveil how spatial segregation in a city leads to forms of dominated acculturation, and Üstüner and Thompson (2012) demonstrate the empowering role of a servicescape – namely, hair-saloons – in supporting the social promotion of underclass service workers in Turkey. Therefore, former contributions either treat space as a taken-for-granted concept or focus on circumscribed, specific spaces and their impact on ethnicity.

This chapter aims to (1) problematize space in ethnic marketing research and (2) provide a bigger picture, in which different types of space are included and tied together. Elaborating on Proshansky (1978, p. 150), Visconti and de Cordova (2012, p. 128) contend that any physical space is contextually a cultural, social, psychological, political and ideological space. Hereinafter and beyond any attempt of exhaustiveness, I discuss these key types of space and comment on their role in ethnic minorities' and mainstream's (market) confrontation around respective ethnic identities.

Physical and geopolitical space

Foundational to any discourse on space is physical space. Featherstone *et al.* (2007) suggest not conceptualizing physical space as a 'fixed container' but rather as a 'set of flows and networks' established across various physical spaces, which today may also be expanded to forms of 'cybermarket' (Venkatesh 1998). The authors examine physical space from a macro perspective and elaborate the notion of 'spatialities', defined as 'the diverse ongoing connections and networks that bind different parts of the world together and that are constituted through (and in fact constitute) particular sites and places' (pp. 383–4).

Despite Featherstone *et al.*'s (2007) invitation, political studies, geography and economic works on migration, and the majority of ethnic marketing studies have mostly interpreted physical space restrictively as a synonym of geopolitical space. There, physical space stands in lieu of the nation-state. Yet physical space is much more articulated. Scholars have proved that ethnic minorities and the mainstream use a large array of 'spatial scales' (Paasi 2001; Pierre 2000) to define the space they inhabit. Together with the national level, they use local, regional and supranational articulations of the physical space, which they intertwine so as to create more nuanced and richer ethnic identities. As Harris (2007, p. 2) observes, ethnic minorities and the mainstream interact within 'streets, freeways and the spaces they enclose, urban squares and antebellum public space, university campus landscapes, private estates, public parks, and housing developments'. Thus, a person's ethnic identity is at the same time an expression of the neighbourhood, the city, the region, the nation and the supranational level with which he or she identifies.

Last, sometimes the physical space is loaded with religious meanings, such as when religious groups choose real or metaphorical physical spaces as places to claim ethnic appurtance and mark identification (e.g., the Promised Land for Jews, the Vatican for Catholics, the Mecca for Muslims; Bowen 2004), beyond nationality and the spaces they currently inhabit. In paraphrasing Appadurai (1990), in these situations the physical space becomes a 'religious-scape'.

Cultural space

Physical space – either meant restrictively, as the nation, or more extensively, as suggested previously – always subtends a cultural space. By cultural space, I mean the complex of articulated meanings embedded in the physical space, which reflect the ways ethnic minorities and the mainstream think of personal and respective ethnic identity. I contend that the cultural space grants two substantive functions in relation to ethnicity: (1) it helps visualize how each ethnic group conceives of its ethnic identity and that of other ethnic groups and (2) it reflects power positions based on ethnic appurtance.

First, both anthropologists (e.g. Douglas and Isherwood 1979; McCracken 2005) and consumer researchers (e.g. Ahuvia 2005; Belk 1988; Belk 2013) have long documented how physical objects 'extend' the personal and the collective self. So does the physical space, to express either one's ethnicity or that of others. Typically, a person's home more fully reflects his or her ethnic identity. Research on Latinos (Peñaloza 1994) and Haitians (Oswald 1999) in the United States, Italians in Canada (Joy et al. 1995), South Asians in the United Kingdom (Lindridge et al. 2004), Greenlanders in Denmark (Askegaard et al. 2005) and Egyptians in Italy (Visconti 2008) has extensively documented how people adapt their dwellings to reflect their ethnic identity. Other times, the physical space mirrors the way a group sees another group's ethnic identity and thus incorporates stereotyping and prejudices about 'ethnic otherness' (what Oktem [2005] defines as an 'ethnocracy').

Commercial spaces may be the same, when others' ethnicity is staged to be 'sold' to both members and non-members of a given ethnic group (e.g., ethnic assortments in supermarkets, 'ethnic' restaurants and gift stores). Peñaloza and Gilly (1999) document how American shoppers adapt their stores to fit Mexican American ethnicity in cities or neighbourhoods densely populated by Latinos/as, Jamal (2003) highlights how the retailing-scape reflects the (presumed) market culture of multiple ethnic groups and Peñaloza (2000; 2001) illustrates how rodeo shows can stage the American West culture for both dwellers and tourists. The same happens with the cityscape more broadly. As Park and Burgess (1925/1984) contend, before being physical spaces cities are first and foremost spaces of mental imaginary. With reference to New York, Zukin (2010) unveils how flows of Black and White cultures in Harlem have left traces in the physical space, which make the city a multi-layered ethnic text to read. For more evidence on the ties between urban space and ethnicity, the anthology *Urban Culture*, edited by Chris Jenks (2004), proves insightful.

Second, the cultural dimension of the physical space also accounts for power positions different ethnic groups hold. The physical space then reveals and helps maintain ethnic inequalities and power imbalances. As Harris (2007, p. 3) states:

> For whom are most sites designed? Who is the presumed public that designers imagine? Where are designed landscapes situated and who has access to them? How are messages about access, belonging, and exclusion manifested in built form? How is the funding for public projects apportioned?

Similarly, other researchers have observed that, too often, the physical space inhabited complies with White privileges (Burton 2009; Lipsitz 1998). As Harris (2007, p. 4) remarks:

> White privilege literally hides in plain sight (invisible especially to those who enjoy the privileges), a situation that is exacerbated by the fact that landscapes are particularly well-suited to masking such constructions because they appear to be completely natural, God-given, and neutral.

Hise (2007) also demonstrates that the language urban planning adopts often reproduces situations of ethnic and social inequality and segregation. For example, he describes how embellished expressions, such as 'urban renewal', may actually dissimulate phenomena of marginalization and gentrification that often harm ethnic minorities. In conclusion, the cultural space directs attention to the use of the physical space to communicate ethnic groups' identity as well as to confirm or challenge established positions of ethnic privilege.

Social space

Physical space – in all its declinations (private, public and commercial) – provides ground for social encounters; it provides a social space. Notably, by temporarily or steadily sharing a physical space, different ethnic groups can engage in social interactions, compare respective ethnic identities and reinforce/modify ethnic stereotypes that others impose on them. Social interactions also help confront different 'spatial imaginaries' (Lipsitz 2007) – that is, different interpretations of the space these groups share in terms of how space can be appropriated, allocated and used. Therefore, social exchanges use physical space as a theatre in which to represent different ethnic identities as well as an object of dispute per se (i.e., who owns/can use this space). As Kostof (1992) notes, public space reflects purposes and ideas about the rituals and interactions it hosts.

When addressing the social space, two cautions are due. First, even when one ethnic group dominates the others, social exchanges remain bi-directional (Berry 1980; Padilla 1980). Thus, if ethnic minorities acculturate to the mainstream's cultural norms and social practices (Featherstone *et al.* 2007; Paasi 2001), the dominating ethnic group may also change through enduring interactions with the dominated ethnic groups. To date, ethnic marketing research has vastly accounted for ethnic minorities' (market) acculturation but has remained elusive on interethnic crossover effects (Grier *et al.* 2006), despite economic and cultural relevance of the phenomenon. Second, sometimes ethnic groups maintain relevant social exchanges with countries other than their country of residency. For example, Morosanu (2013) documents young Romanians' trying experiences in London due to stable socialization between their 'here' and 'there'. Research on 'transmigrants', or migrants steadily moving back and forth between their country of origin and destination (Üçok Hughes and Kjeldgaard 2006; Voigt-Graf 2004), and 'diasporic families' (Appadurai 1996) further illuminates the point. As a result, conceptualization of the social space must reflect the comprehensiveness of the relevant social exchanges in which different ethnic groups are engaged. This may transcend the boundaries of the nation in which these groups live.

With specific reference to migration in/outflows, both aspects/cautions can be visualized through the transformation of migrants' cities of origin and destination due to the maintenance of social relations with the hosting population as well as their community of origin. On the one hand, migrants transform the cities they inhabit (Zukin 2010) as they act as 'urban scale-makers' (Glick Schiller and Çaglar 2009, p. 177). On the other hand, they transform the cities they leave behind (Çaglar 2007). Depopulation and urban depletion go hand in hand with migrants' remittances, which sustain urban refurbishment and development (Üçok Hughes and Kjeldgaard 2006).

Ethnic marketing research shows that the social space may prove either beneficial to or detrimental for the construction of a sound, dynamic ethnic identity. On the positive side, the social space can reinforce ethnic identities (Peñaloza and Gilly 1999, p. 84), sustain ethnic groups' self-esteem and collective identity (Morosanu 2013), and increase opportunities to access the market (Visconti 2008). Prior research also documents the active processes of aesthetic adaptation that migrants/ethnic minorities frequently perform to beautify their neighbourhoods and reconnect with their homeland (Hadjiyanni 2009). Plastic manipulation of the residential space is a means to ritually appropriate the space (McCracken 1986). It is also a means to transmit culture down to the new generations (i.e. a form of 'performative memory'; Connerton 1989), a way to reproduce distinction (Bourdieu 1984) from other ethnic groups and a form of affiliation with one's ethnic community (Hadjiyanni 2009).

On the negative side, the social space may foster maintenance of ethnic stereotypes, over-emphasize the relevance of ethnic identity in people's lives and, ultimately, favour ethnic segregation. For example, in their critical enquiry on multiculturalism in major Canadian cities, Goonewardena and Kipfer (2005) explain that social exchanges in Canada can reproduce discourses on whiteness/non-whiteness. As they observe, the apparently innocent question 'Where are you from?' when meeting a foreigner underlies the persistence of ethno-racial interpretive schema used to locate the 'other', ethnically and socially. The space in which migrants inhabit also is typically the initial factor of environmental stress (Yan-chi Kwok and Ku 2008), since space design affects the mental, emotional and physical health among displaced people (Hadjiyanni 2009).

Ideological and political space

As noted, physical space conveys cultural interpretations of ethnicity and hosts social exchanges among different ethnic groups, which in turn construct ethnic identities as well as reflect power positions depending on ethnicity. The ideological dimension of space captures the transformative intentions that stand behind such meanings and social dynamics. As Sherry (1998, p. 6) writes, the physical space can include intentions, attitudes and purposes; thus, it has a normative content (Bowen 2004). When ideologies are used to derive implications for action (e.g., for behaviour, policy, marketing practice), the ideological space becomes a political space (Peñaloza 1995). Among others, sociologist Saskia Sassen (2006) identifies the role of global cities in improving migrants'/ethnic minorities' visibility and purposeful participation in social life. With reference to commerce, Maclaran and Brown (2005) comment on the Utopian marketplace and Kozinets (2002) provides evidence on emplaced ideologies of market resistance.

I contend that the physical space reflects ideologies of how different ethnic groups are entitled to be part of a nation, use the welfare system, contribute to the cultural life and access and play in the market. This can be true for ideologies that either empower or repress ethnic minorities. Taking an urban Marxist and antiracist feminist position, Goonewardena and Kipfer (2005, p. 671) also show that 'multiculturalism [is] an urban policy'. More often, physical space (re)produces ideologies of ethnic domination and/or segregation – that is, a whiteness discourse. I select here Oktem's (2005) study of Mardin, a multi-ethnic and multi-religious city located in southeast Turkey, to illustrate the point. The author performs a deep analysis of the ideological and political role of space and geography in the construction, hierarchical ordering and confrontation of ethnic groups. He comments on the use of the city in order to modify and negotiate power positions across different ethnic groups, and forges the notion of 'ethnocracy' as encapsulating the political and ideological tensions ethnicity fosters. According to him (2005, p. 243), ethnocracy appears any time ethnicity, instead of citizenship, 'determines the allocations of rights and privileges, despite several democratic features . . . A dominant "charter" ethnic group appropriates the state apparatus, determines most public policies, and segregates itself from other groups.'

Oktem (2005) describes how the political use of space (physical, cultural and social) in order to create an 'ethno-nation' – that is, a nation where one ethnic group rules over other ethnic minorities – is reflected into the social construction of 'ethno-classes' – that is, the establishment of social privileges, distinction (Bourdieu 1984) and separation due to ethnic difference. In doing so, he ties the political and the social spheres together and reveals the use of space as a means to upgrade/downgrade ethnically different groups beyond territorial citizenship, income and/or personal merits.

The strategic use of the physical space to emplace, communicate and reinvigorate ethnic ideologies is almost universal. First, this strategy characterizes several cities around the globe (Jenks 2004; Schein 2007). Second, both empowering and repressive ethnic ideologies tend to use space to accomplish their ideological aims. Third, all ethnic groups tend to use space to prevail over others. In the case of Mardin, Oktem (2005) unveils strategically similar but politically rival attempts that public administrations, private media and human rights organizations pursue in the reconfiguration of space and ethnicity in that city. Thus, the ideological use of space occurs regardless of geography, ideological purposes and ethnic appurtenance.

Implications for ethnic marketing: the commercial space

The former discussion on space(s) and ethnicity is not only conceptually engaging but also managerially relevant. It grounds implications about using space to improve companies' ethnic marketing competitiveness as well as ethnic groups' empowerment, self-esteem and self-efficacy. Indeed, consumers' ethnic identity stimulates a broad range of needs (utilitarian, emotional, ideological and symbolic) that commercial space design helps satisfy.

Table 5.1 summarizes ethnic marketing implications meant to be illustrative more than exhaustive. First, by critically considering the definition of physical space, marketing managers can improve the quality of their ethnic marketing decisions on an international scale. To date, international market segmentation predominantly relies on national/supranational criteria that

Table 5.1 Types of space and their implications for marketing

Types of space	Definition	Marketing implications
Physical and geopolitical space	The physical environment: – Macro level: nationscape, regionscape, cityscape – Meso level: marketplace, neighbourhood – Micro level: servicescape, workplace, home	For cross-cultural and international marketing decisions, remember that: – Notion of nation is dynamic – Notion of nation is constructed – Geopolitical spaces are interconnected – Physical spaces beyond the nation matter
Cultural space	The meanings embedded in the physical space, which visualize: – How ethnic groups conceive of their/others' ethnic identity – Power positions based on ethnic appurtenance	– Use of artifacts to visualize customers' ethnic identity – Check for how space design reflects ethnic stereotypes – Check for how space design supports ethnic folklore – Use of space design to control/empower ethnic groups
Social space	Social interactions allowed by shared space, which reflect: – Different ideas on the use of physical space – Social segregation and rivalry about space consumption	– Use of space design to cope with ethnic groups' entitlement on space use – Targeting decisions – Exploitation of consumption crossover
Ideological and political space	The transformative intentions that are pursued through space: – Space design – Space attribution – Space use	Attention for the implicit/explicit ideological intentions in marketing decisions such as: – Geomarketing decisions – Store layout decisions – Category management decisions

reflect a geopolitical acceptation of space. As the former discussion indicates, nation borders have become porous. The geopolitical spaces consumers use to define themselves can be interconnected and change at consumers' pace, regardless of geopolitical transformations (Featherstone *et al.* 2007). In addition, together with globalization, an increasing nostalgia for the local space (Emontspool and Kjeldgaard 2012) and the fragmentation of the global (Geertz 1983) have spread. As such, ethnic marketing decisions, including criteria to segment international markets, should reflect consumers' subjective interpretation of physical spaces that are deemed relevant to reflect their ethnic identity instead of using marketing managers' a priori geopolitical criteria (i.e., consumers' nationality/supranationality).

Second, when a company serves multi-ethnic markets, knowing that physical space is also a cultural space proves essential to take sound ethnic marketing decisions. In particular, this understanding should dictate how a company designs its commercial spaces (e.g. space for the service encounter, stores, experiential settings, corporate offices). Not only are commercial spaces places to exchange and shop, but they are also spaces in which established ideas of ethnic domination/subordination/empowerment can be conveyed through space design (Peñaloza and Gilly 1999; Visconti and Premazzi 2012). For example, Visconti and Üçok Hughes (2011) document banks (e.g. Banco de la Gente in the United States, Agenzia Tu in Italy, HSBC worldwide) that have used servicescape design to challenge shared ideas about migrants'/ethnic minorities' market irrelevance, dangerousness and subordination. Instead, their branches built environments that reflect positive images of migrants/ethnic minorities as diverse but integrated, successful and empowered citizens.

Third, space supports social exchanges (Tombs and McColl-Kennedy 2003), which may improve/diminish quality of interethnic confrontations and personal/collective ethnic self-esteem (Morosanu 2013). When targeting different ethnic groups, companies can decide either to serve their customers in separate spaces according to consumer ethnicity (e.g. 'ethnic stores' versus 'mainstream stores') or to welcome them within the same commercial space. In doing so, they can (de)emphasize ethnic difference and increase/limit ethnic segregation, respectively. They can also stimulate/limit social interactions across different ethnic groups within the commercial space. In addition, companies can decide the extent to which their personnel should mirror the ethnic diversity of their target markets.

Among other companies, IKEA has often employed a sales force as ethnically diverse as possible (Visconti 2007) to facilitate customers' identification and sentiment of inclusion during shopping. Social space also invites consideration of commercial opportunities stemming from consumption crossover (Grier *et al.* 2006), which to date have been scantly explored. Marketing managers usually follow common understanding that cultural adaptation occurs only on the side of ethnic minorities that get accustomed to the mainstream's market culture. Yet the mainstream also adapts to ethnic minorities' market cultures (e.g., 'ethnic' food, 'ethnic' design and 'ethnic' music) and modifies its consumption accordingly. Ethnic marketing managers able to escape such a biased, closed-minded interpretation of interethnic market acculturation will profit from consumption crossover opportunities.

Fourth, intentionally or subconsciously, commercial space can embed ideological discourses (Borghini *et al.* 2009; Maclaran and Brown 2005), including ethnic ideologies. Geomarketing decisions, about localization of a company's stores, respond to commercial as well as ideological criteria. Which types of customers does a company deem worthy? Ethnic minorities often live in separated city neighbourhoods, where high-quality commercial offerings may be scant. In the United States, 'food deserts' – areas in which the population has limited access to supermarkets or large grocery stores (Dutko *et al.* 2012) – arouse increasing preoccupation and often concern ethnic minorities. Category management decisions also reflect ideological motives. Think of supermarkets' organization of the 'ethnic' offering. Should 'ethnic' products be part of the respective product categories (e.g., pasta, sauces, drinks), or should they be included in a specific 'ethnic food' category (e.g., Mexican food assortment, Italian food)? The more a supermarket keeps ethnic minorities' 'typical' products separate from the main assortment, the more it helps 'folklorize' these groups by stressing their supposed diversity and market extraneousness.

In the following paragraphs, I contextualize ethnic marketing implications at two important levels: (1) the marketplace, in which economic exchanges occur within a space a plethora of economic agents has determined, and (2) the servicescape, in which consumers interact with the physical space a single company has designed.

The marketplace

Defining the marketplace is all but straightforward. This term may abstractedly stand as a synonym of the market or allude to the emplacement of the market and therefore refer to the physical space in which commercial exchanges occur. It can be a space for commerce but also a space for ideologies (Arnould and Thompson 2005, p. 871) and representations of the individual/collective self (Giesler 2008). It can be used as a metaphor for the Western capitalist market ideology or include any form of economic ideology (for non-Western market systems, see Part I in Peñaloza *et al.* 2011). Here, the marketplace indicates the physical space buyers, retailers and producers of different ethnicities, and across geographies, shared for their economic exchanges.

The marketplace serves a variety of purposes. First, it is a space for commerce. Migrants/ethnic minorities may act as shoppers as well as producers/retailers. When playing a consumer role, they navigate the marketplace looking for convenience, utility, entertainment, or involvement with products and brands, as any consumer does (Costa and Bamossy 1995). They also 'shop for identity' (Halter 2000) and try to improve their social and economic ethnic legitimation. Ethnic marketing research extensively illustrates the use of consumer goods in order to fulfil migrants'/ethnic minorities' identity projects, ranging from complete acculturation/assimilation to the local culture, to forms of rejection of the mainstream culture, to intermediate positions of cultural swapping (e.g. Askegaard *et al.* 2005; Oswald 1999; Visconti 2008). Thus, availability of ethnic products on the market fosters migrants'/ethnic minorities' economic legitimation – by being treated as an economically appealing segment (Visconti and Üçok Hughes 2011) – and attenuates their social invisibility (Jamal, 2003).

Second, when playing a producer/retailer role, migrants/ethnic minorities primarily look for business opportunities as any other entrepreneur. When native sellers do not serve the ethnic market, ethnic minorities may step in to offer products not available otherwise (Chaudhry and Crick 2005). This has been the case for halal or kosher butchery shops, internet and phone centres, ethnic grocery stores, ethnic media and more. In doing so, 'ethnic' companies/retailers act as 'cultural change agents' (Peñaloza and Gilly 1999, p. 101), which support ethnic minorities' market and social power, boost the local economy and even revitalize neglected areas of the cities they inhabit (Eroglu 2002).

The servicescape

If the marketplace notion is controversial, the definition of servicescape is relatively consensual and grounded on the foundational contribution of Canadian geographer Edward Relph (1976). Bitner (1992) is the first marketing scholar to define the servicescape as the built environment in which the service provision takes place. Her work directs attention to the 'language of the objects' (Bitner 1992, p. 62), which comprise: (1) ambient conditions, (2) spatial layout and (3) material artifacts. Taking an anthropological perspective, consumer researcher John Sherry (1998) expands the definition further by including: (4) the social interactions allowed by the space consumers and sellers share and (5) the emotional involvement (i.e. 'place attachment') that people can develop when spaces become special to them.

Notably, if all companies and consumers confront a similar marketplace, each company can design its own servicescape to develop relationships with specific consumers – including specific ethnic groups – and convey a distinctive ideology of what a servicescape is meant for. In doing so, the servicescape a company conceives can reflect, alter and even overturn ideologies and meanings the broader marketplace conveys. For example, by evoking a rural world, a historical heritage and an anticonsumerist ideology, Camper shoes stores create a disjuncture with the surrounding marketplace ideology (Dalli and Romani 2011). L'Occitane en Provence stores similarly cocoon shoppers within a commercial space that rejects the industrial society and reconnects with a lost (and hyper-real) preindustrial world (Visconti 2010). As Chin (1998, p. 612) observes:

> Shoppers are not anonymous, historyless individuals when they walk in the door, and stores are not monolithic spaces that affect all who enter in uniform and predictable ways. . . . In the confrontation between historically situated people and socially constructed spaces, people are repeatedly reconstructed as particular people in that place.

Ethnic marketing research has begun documenting the role of the servicescape in relation to ethnicity. In their ethnographic enquiry of the American Girl flagship store in Chicago, Borghini et al. (2009) discuss the company's choice of displaying historical doll models that comprise native 'American' women, which contests common understanding of American history as purely post-colonial. With reference to Turkish hair saloons, Üstüner and Thompson (2012) comment on hairdressers' progressive acquisition of cultural and aesthetic skills through ongoing interactions with customers from the upper classes. Thus, hair saloons facilitate realignment of social and ethnic disparities. Similarly, Veresiu and Giesler (2012, p. 126) report how Roma entrepreneurs in Toronto, Berlin and Pisa use the servicescape 'to leverage their ethnicity and expand their economic and social possibilities'. Visconti and de Cordova (2012) show how the design of health care servicescapes in Milan helps maintain situations of ethnic marginality, foster ethnic stereotyping or, conversely, stimulate migrants'/ethnic minorities' empowerment and self-esteem.

Each servicescape can thus work as a spatially situated 'factory of ethnicity'. Within a servicescape, different ethnic groups – in their multiple roles of producers, sellers and shoppers – can compare dominating meanings and ideologies about respective ethnic identities present in the general marketplace with the more specifically situated meanings and ideologies embedded in a given servicescape. Beginning in the eighties, Benetton stores and their multicultural ideology – recapped in the slogan 'United Colors of Benetton' – have served as spaces for commerce as well as spaces in which ethnic minorities could feel protected, recognized and empowered. Wal-Mart has invested massively to conquer the U.S. multi-ethnic market through, among others, in-store communication that reflects a multicultural credo. Starbucks has systematically designed its stores to reflect the local community in which each store is located.

Space (im)permeability

So far, I have identified four main types of space relevant to ethnic marketing. Then, by manipulating the physical, cultural, social and ideological aspects of commercial space, I have derived implications for ethnic marketing that deepen understanding of how commercial space design can affect the preferences and lives of a company's multi-ethnic customers. In this section, I examine the extent to which these spaces are appropriable by – and thus permeable to – different ethnic groups and comment on the effects of space impermeability. When targeting different ethnic groups, one of the key decisions marketing managers must consider is how much emphasis to put on the (presumed) ethnic diversity of their customers. This decision affects the rate of offer differentiation, the level of adaptation in communications directed to different ethnic markets and the extent to which a commercial space should include one or more ethnic groups. Thus, anticipating the positive/negative effects that may result from commercial space (im)permeability is essential to such ethnic marketing decisions.

I illustrate two forms of space impermeability: (1) space segregation and (2) lack of space accommodation. First, space segregation unfolds when given ethnic groups have limited access to a space. At an urban level, residential segregation implies the physical encapsulation of ethnic minorities within degraded neighbourhoods (for an updated overview, see Leal 2012). At a market level, the impermeability of a company's commercial space may result from: (1) the establishment of physical barriers (e.g., due to its positioning, bank Agenzia Tu in Italy is precluded to Italian customers); (2) the use of cultural and/or linguistic barriers that limit *de facto* the access to a commercial space for given ethnic groups (Visconti and de Cordova 2012); and (3) the creation of social and ideological barriers, when certain ethnic groups do not feel at ease or secured in a commercial space due to the store's brand ideology and/or the people shopping there (e.g., in 2013, Oprah Winfrey was denied the right to buy a luxury bag in a Swiss shop for the simple fact of being 'Black').

Second, an ethnic group can access a space but not be allowed to accommodate this space so as to express its ethnic identity. This is particularly true at an urban level, when ethnic minorities cannot adapt the inhabited space because of multiple factors 'including: spatiality, religious beliefs, regulations, income limitations, construction norms and availability of objects to purchase' (Hadjiyanni 2009, p. 541). By (not) providing desired goods necessary for homemaking, companies also affect the extent to which ethnic groups can accommodate space.

Effects of space impermeability can be both positive and negative. On the positive side, (commercial) spaces impermeable to other ethnic groups help preserve the historical and cultural heritage of the people entitled to those spaces (Oktem 2005). Notably, this can occur with both ethnic minorities and the mainstream, and even among ethnic minorities in countries characterized by high ethnic fragmentation (Noussia and Lyons 2009). For example, in a study on middle class Blacks in the United States, Lacy (2004) shows that many Black informants, living or working in White districts, preferred to maintain space segmentation in order to 'share in' (Belk 2010) their life with other middle class Blacks. Space impermeability can also foster commerce. Among others, the 'Chinatown' model represents one of the most recurrent and successful examples of space impermeability, from which Chinese entrepreneurs benefit through the preservation of ethnic homogeneity within their commercial space (Hatziprokopiou and Montagna 2012). On the negative side, (commercial) space impermeability boosts forms of 'privileged geography', 'environmental racism' (Lipsitz 2007) and 'White' domination (Lipsitz 1998) and thus puts at risk social mobility, intercultural exchanges and market citizenship.

To conclude, the profound cultural, religious, ideological, and political entailments of ethnicity – which space helps visualize and (de)emphasize – make ethnic marketing a particularly delicate field. As described, a differentiated marketing approach, which also implies granting secured and customized commercial spaces, can have positive returns for both consumers and the company (e.g., higher customization, market legitimation, maintenance of ethnic heritage) and negative effects (e.g., market ghettoization, over-'ethnicization').

To optimize marketing returns, a company should: (1) assess the extent to which a given ethnic group is willing to emphasize its diversity, (2) understand the extent to which the company's/brand's identity is consistent with the market endorsement of this ethnic group, (3) be aware that decisions about space design may reflect ideological and political meanings and (4) consider the indirect effect of this decision on other ethnic groups the company might be already targeting. A company should also consider forms of participatory space planning, thus involving its target customers in its decisions, as suggested by recent studies in urbanism (Yan-chi Kwok and Ku 2008), health management (Ozanne and Anderson 2010) and sociology (Lipsitz 2007). Only by attending to the role of commercial space can companies not only improve their competitiveness when targeting different ethnic groups but also limit the risk of using commercial space harmfully. As Harris (2007, p. 2) notes, 'The primary terms of racism – segregation, seclusion, marginalization, incarceration, hierarchy – are all spatial phenomena or have a spatial corollary'. Space is all but neutral when ethnicity is taken into consideration, within and beyond ethnic marketing decisions.

References

Ahuvia, A. C. (2005) 'Beyond the extended self: Loved objects and consumers' identity narratives'. *Journal of Consumer Research*, 32 (1): 171–34.

Appadurai, A. (1990) 'Disjuncture and difference in the global cultural economy'. In *Global Culture: Nationalism, Globalization and Modernity*, edited by M. Featherstone. London: Sage Publications, pp. 295–310.

Appadurai, A. (1996) *Modernity at Large: Cultural Dimensions of Globalization*. Minnesota, MN: University of Minnesota Press.

Arnould, E. J. and Thompson, C. J. (2005) 'Consumer Culture Theory (CCT): Twenty years of research'. *Journal of Consumer Research*, 31 (4): 868–82.

Askegaard, S., Arnould, E. J. and Kjeldgaard, D. (2005) 'Postassimilationist ethnic consumer research: Qualifications and extensions'. *Journal of Consumer Research*, 32: 160–70.

Belk, R. W. (1988) 'Possessions and the extended self'. *Journal of Consumer Research*, 15 (2): 139–68.

Belk, R. W. (2010) 'Sharing'. *Journal of Consumer Research*, 36 (February): 715–34.

Belk, R. W. (2013) 'Extended self in a digital world'. *Journal of Consumer Research*, 40 (October): 477–500.

Berry, W. J. (1980) 'Acculturation as varieties of adaptation'. In *Acculturation: Theory, Models and Some New Findings*, edited by A. M. Padilla. Boulder, CO: Westview Press, pp. 9–46.

Bitner, M. J. (1992) 'Servicescapes: The impact of physical surroundings'. *Journal of Marketing*, 56 (April): 57–71.

Borghini, S., Diamond, N., Kozinets, R. V., McGrath, M. A., Muñiz Jr., A. and Sherry Jr., J. F. (2009) 'Why are themed brand stores so powerful? Retail brand ideology at American girl place'. *Journal of Retailing*, 85 (3): 363–75.

Bourdieu, P. (1984) *Distinction: A Social Critique of the Judgment of Taste*. Cambridge, MA: Harvard University Press.

Bowen, J. R. (2004) 'Beyond migration: Islam as a transnational public space'. *Journal of Ethnic and Migration Studies*, 30 (5): 879–94.

Burton, D. (2009) 'Reading whiteness in consumer research'. *Consumption, Markets, & Culture*, 12 (2): 171–201.

Çaglar, A. (2007) 'Rescaling cities, cultural diversity and transnationalism: Migrants of Mardin and Essen'. *Ethnic and Racial Studies*, 30 (6): 1070–95.

Chaudhry, S. and Crick, D. (2005) 'An exploratory investigation into the entrepreneurial activities of Asian-owned franchises in the UK'. *Strategic Change*, 14 (6): 349–56.

Chin, E. (1998) 'Social inequality and the context of consumption: Local groceries and downtown stores'. In *Servicescapes: The Concept of Space in Contemporary Markets*, edited by J. F. Sherry Jr. Chicago, IL: NTC Business Books, pp. 591–617.

Connerton, P. (1989) *How Societies Remember*. New York, NY: Cambridge University Press.

Costa, J. A. and Bamossy, G. J. (eds) (1995) *Marketing in a Multicultural World: Ethnicity, Nationalism, and Cultural Identity*. Thousand Oaks, CA: Sage.

Dalli, D. and Romani, S. (2011) 'Mediterranean shoes conquer the world: Global branding from local resources – The camper case'. In *Marketing Management: A Cultural Perspective*, edited by L. Peñaloza, N. Toulouse and L. M. Visconti. London: Routledge, pp. 43–59.

Douglas, M. and Isherwood, B. (1978) *The World of Goods*. New York, NY: Basic Books.

Dutko, P., Ver Ploeg, M. and Farrigan, T. (2012) 'Characteristics and influential factors of food deserts'. *ERR-140, U.S. Department of Agriculture, Economic Research Service*. Available from: http://www.ers. usda.gov/publications/err-economic-research-report/err140.aspx (accessed on February 13, 2013).

Emontspool, J. and Kjeldgaard, D. (2012) 'Cultural reflexivity and the nostalgia for glocal consumer culture: Insights from a multicultural multiple migration context'. In *Research in Consumer Behavior*, Volume. 14, edited by R. W. Belk. Bingley, UK: Emerald, 213–32.

Eroglu, S. (2002) 'Impact of ethnic minority retailers on urban revitalization efforts: The buford corridor case'. *Journal of Shopping Center Research*, 9 (2): 53–75.

Featherstone, D., Phillips, R. and Waters, J. (2007) 'Introduction: Spatialities of transnational networks'. *Global Networks*, 7(4): 383–91.

Geertz, C. (1983) *Local Knowledge: Further Essays in Interpretive Anthropology*. New York, NY: Basic Books.

Giesler, M. (2008) 'Conflict and compromise: Drama in marketplace evolution'. *Journal of Consumer Research*, 34 (6): 739–53.

Glick Schiller, N. and Çaglar, A. (2009) 'Towards a comparative theory of locality in migration studies: Migrant incorporation and city scale'. *Journal of Ethnic and Migration Studies*, 35 (2): 177–202.

Goonewardena, K. and Kipfer, S. (2005) 'Spaces of difference: Reflections from Toronto on multiculturalism, bourgeois urbanism and the possibility of radical urban politics'. *International Journal of Urban and Regional Research*, 29 (3): 670–78.

Grier, S., Brumbaugh, A. M. and Thornton, C. (2006) 'Crossover dreams: Consumer responses to ethnic-oriented products'. *Journal of Marketing*, 70 (2): 35–51.

Hadjiyanni, T. (2009) 'Aesthetics in displacement: Hmong, Somali and Mexican home-making practices in Minnesota'. *International Journal of Consumer Studies*, 33: 541–49.

Halter, M. (2000) *Shopping for Identity: The Marketing of Ethnicity*. New York, NY: Shocken Books.

Harris, D. (2007) 'Race, space, and the destabilization of practice'. *Landscape Journal*, 26(1): 1–9.

Hatziprokopiou, P. and Montagna, N. (2012) 'Contested Chinatown: Chinese migrants, incorporation and the urban space in London and Milan'. *Ethnicities*, 12 (6): 706–29.

Hise, G. (2007) 'Identity and Social Distance in Los Angeles'. *Landscape Journal*, 26: 45–60.

Jamal, A. (2003b) 'Retailing in a multicultural world: The interplay of retailing, ethnic identity and consumption'. *Journal of Retailing & Consumer Services*, 10(1): 1–11.

Jenks, C. (2004) (ed) *Urban Culture: Critical Concepts in Literary and Cultural Studies*. London: Routledge.

Joy, A., Hui, M., Kim, C. and Laroche, M. (1995) 'The cultural past in the present: The meaning of home and objects in the homes of working-class Italian immigrants in Montreal'. In *Marketing in a Multicultural World: Ethnicity, Nationalism, and Cultural Identity*, edited by J. A. Costa and G. J. Bamossy. Thousand Oaks, CA: Sage, pp. 145–79.

Kostof, S. (1992) *The City Assembled: Elements of Urban Form Through History*. Boston, MA: Little Brown.

Kozinets, R. V. (2002) 'Can consumers escape the market? Emancipatory illuminations from Burning Man'. *Journal of Consumer Research*, 28 (1): 67–88.

Lacy, K. R. (2004) 'Black spaces, black places: Strategic assimilation and identity construction in middle-class suburbia'. *Ethnic and Racial Studies*, 27 (6): 908–30.

Leal, J. (2012) 'Residential segregation'. In *International Encyclopedia of Housing and Home*, edited by S. J. Smith. Cambridge, MA: Elsevier, pp. 94–9.

Lindridge, A. M., Hogg, M. K. and Shah, M. (2004) 'Imagined multiple worlds: How South Asian women in Britain use family and friends to navigate the "border crossings" between household and social contexts'. *Consumption, Markets & Culture*, 7 (3): 211–38.

Lipsitz, G. (1998) *The Possessive Investment in Whiteness: How White People Profit From Identity Politics*. Philadelphia, PA: Temple University Press.

Lipsitz, G. (2007) 'The racialization of space and the spatialization of race: Theorizing the hidden architecture of landscape'. *Landscape Journal*, 26: 10–23.

Maclaran, P. and Brown, S. (2005) 'The center cannot hold: Consuming the utopian marketplace'. *Journal of Consumer Research*, 32 (2): 311–23.

McCracken, G. (1986) 'Culture and consumption: A theoretical account of the structure and movement of cultural meaning of consumer goods'. *Journal of Consumer Research*, 13(June): 71–84.

McCracken, G. (2005) *Culture and Consumption 2: Markets, Meaning and Brand Management*. Bloomington, IN: Indiana University Press.

Morosanu, L. (2013) 'Between fragmented ties and "soul friendship": The cross-border social connections of young Romanians in London'. *Journal of Ethnic and Migration Studies*, 39 (3): 353–72.

Noussia, A. and Lyons, M. (2009) 'Inhabiting spaces of liminality: Migrants in Omonia, Athens'. *Journal of Ethnic and Migration Studies*, 35 (4): 601–24.

Oktem, K. (2005) 'Faces of the city: Poetic, mediagenic and traumatic images of a multi-cultural city in Southeast Turkey'. *Cities*, 22 (3): 241–53.

Oswald, L. R. (1999) 'Cultural swapping: Consumption and the ethnogenesis of middle-class Haitian immigrants'. *Journal of Consumer Research*, 25 (4): 303–18.

Ozanne, J. L. and Anderson, L. (2010) 'Community action research'. *Journal of Public Policy & Marketing*, 29 (1): 123–37.

Paasi, A. (2001) 'Europe as a social process and discourse: Considerations of place, boundaries and identity'. *European Urban and Regional Studies*, 8 (1): 7–28.

Padilla, A. M. (ed) (1980) *Acculturation: Theory, Models, and Some New Findings*. Boulder, CO: Westview Press.

Park, R. E. and Burgess, E. W. (1925/1984). *The City: Suggestions For Investigation of Human Behavior in the Urban Environment*. Chicago, IL: University of Chicago Press.

Peñaloza, L. N. (1994) 'Atravesando fronteras/border crossing: A critical ethnographic exploration of the consumer acculturation of Mexican immigrants'. *Journal of Consumer Research*, 21(1): 32–54.

Peñaloza, L. (1995) 'Immigrant consumers: Marketing and public policy considerations in the global economy'. *Journal of Public Policy & Marketing*, 14 (1): 83–94.

Peñaloza, L. (2000) 'The commodification of the American west: Marketers' production of cultural meanings at the trade show'. *Journal of Marketing*, 64 (4): 82–109.

Peñaloza, L. (2001) 'Consuming the West: Animating cultural meaning at a stock show and rodeo'. *Journal of Consumer Research*, 28 (December): 369–98.

Peñaloza, L. (2004) 'Multiculturalism in the new world order: Implications for the study of consumer behaviour'. In *Elusive Consumption: Tracking New Research Perspectives*, edited by K. Ekström and H. Brembeck. Oxford: Berg Publishers, pp. 87–109.

Peñaloza, L. (2007) 'Mainstreet U.S.A. revisited: Market targeting, politics, Latino/a consumer culture, and community'. *International Journal of Sociology and Social Policy*, 27 (5/6): 234–49.

Peñaloza, L. and Gilly, M. C. (1999) 'Marketer acculturation: The changer and the changed'. *Journal of Marketing*, 63: 84–104.

Peñaloza, L., Toulouse, N. and Visconti, L. M. (eds) (2011) *Marketing Management: A Cultural Perspective*. London: Routledge.

Pierre, J. (ed) (2000) *Debating Governance*. Oxford: Oxford University Press.

Ping Hung Li, E. and Figueiredo, B. (2012) 'Re-reading ethnicity in movement: When acculturation studies interrogate the space'. In *Advances in Consumer Research*, Volume 38, edited by D. W. Dahl, G. V. Johar and S. M. J. van Osselaer. Duluth, MN: Association for Consumer Research, pp. 67–71.

Proshansky, H. M. (1978) 'The city and self-identity'. *Environmental Behavior*, 10 (2): 147–69.

Regany, F., Visconti, L. M. and Fosse-Gomez M-H. (2012) 'A closer glance at the notion of boundaries in acculturation studies: Typologies, intergenerational divergences, and consumer agency'. In *Research in Consumer Behavior*, Volume 14, edited by R. Belk, S. Askegaard and L. Scott. Bingley, UK: Emerald, pp. 195–213.

Relph, E. (1976) *Place and Placelessness*. London: Pion Ltd.

Sassen, S. (2006) *Territory, Authority, Rights: From Medieval to Global Assemblages*. Princeton, NJ: Princeton University Press.

Schein, R. (ed) (2007) *Landscape and Race in the United States*. London: Routledge.

Sherry Jr., J. F. (1998) *Servicescapes: The Concept of Place in Contemporary Markets*. Chicago, IL: NTC Business Books.

Tombs, A. G. and McColl-Kennedy, J. R. (2003) 'The social-servicescape: A conceptual model'. *Marketing Theory*, 3 (4): 447–75.

Üçok Hughes M. and Kjeldgaard, D. (2006) 'Consumption in transnational social spaces: A study of Turkish transmigrants'. In *European Advances in Consumer Research*, Volume 7, edited by E. Karin and B. Helene. Duluth, MN: Association for Consumer Research, pp. 431–36.

Üstüner, T. and Holt, D. B. (2007) 'Dominated consumer acculturation: The social construction of poor migrant women's consumer identity projects in a Turkish squatter'. *Journal of Consumer Research*, 34 (1): 41–56.

Üstüner, H. and Thompson, C. J. (2012) 'How marketplace performances produce interdependent status games and contested forms of symbolic capital'. *Journal of Consumer Research*, 38 (5): 796–814.

Venkatesh, A. (1998) 'Cyberculture: Consumers and cybermarketscapes'. In *Servicescapes: The Concept of Space in Contemporary Markets*, edited by J. F. Sherry Jr. Chicago, IL: NTC Business Books, pp. 343–75.

Veresiu, E. and Giesler, M. (2012) 'Ethnic entrepreneurship: Creating an identity-enhancing assemblage of public and private servicescapes in the global city'. In *Advances in Consumer Research*, Volume 39, edited by R. Ahluwalia, T. L. Chartrand and R. K. Ratner. Duluth, MN: Association for Consumer Research, pp. 125–6.

Veresiu, E., Visconti, L. M. and Giesler, M. (2012) 'Servicescapes: Spaces of representation and dispute in ethnic consumer identity construction'. In *Advances in Consumer Research*, Volume 39, edited by R. Ahluwalia, T. L. Chartrand and R. K. Ratner. Duluth, MN: Association for Consumer Research, pp. 125–29.

Visconti, L. M. (2007) *Diversity Management e Lavoratori Migranti: Linee Guida per la Gestione del Caso Italia*. Milan: Egea, BEA.

Visconti, L. M. (2008) 'The social construction and play of ethnic minorities' identities: Antecedents and epiphany of cultural alternation'. In *Advances in Consumer Research*, Volume 35, edited by A. Y. Lee and D. Soman. Duluth, MN, Association for Consumer Research, pp. 31–5.

Visconti, L. M. (2010) 'Authentic brand narratives: Co-constructed Mediterraneaness for l'Occitane brand'. In *Research in Consumer Behavior*, Volume 12, edited by R. W. Belk. Bingley, UK: Emerald, pp. 231–60.

Visconti, L. M. and de Cordova, F. (2012) 'Culturally and linguistically appropriated servicescapes: The making of ethnicity in the context of healthcare services'. In *Advances in Consumer Research*, Volume 39, edited by R. Ahluwalia, T. L. Chartrand and R. K. Ratner. Duluth, MN: Association for Consumer Research, pp. 127–29.

Visconti, L. M. and Premazzi, K. (2012) 'Modern and ethnic retailing formats at *The Mirror*: Shoppers' domination, acculturation, distinction, and patronizing'. Paper presented at 19th International Conference on *Recent Advances in Retailing and Consumer Services Science*. Wien, July 2012.

Visconti, L. M. and Üçok Hughes, M. (2011) 'Segmentation and targeting revisited'. In *Marketing Management: A Cultural Perspective*, edited by L. Peñaloza, N. Toulouse and L. M. Visconti. London: Routledge, pp. 295–314.

Voigt-Graf, C. (2004) 'Towards a geography of transnational spaces: Indian transnational communities in Australia'. *Global Networks*, 4: 25–49.

Yan-chi Kwok, J. and Ku, H-B. (2008) 'Making habitable space together with female Chinese immigrants to Hong Kong: An interdisciplinary participatory action research project'. *Action Research*, 6 (3): 261–83.

Zukin, S. (2010) *The Naked City: The Death and Life of Authentic Urban Places*. New York, NY: Oxford University Press.

6

Ethnic marketing, ethnic entrepreneurship and social innovation

Abid Mehmood, Ahmad Jamal and Ven Sriram

Introduction

This chapter provides a novel perspective on ethnic marketing by looking at the specific case of social innovation as a marketing strategy employed by ethnic entrepreneurs. Ethnic marketing reflects the practice of marketing to one or more segments of consumers with a specific ethnicity. Such practices are often used by mainstream marketers interested in capitalizing on the opportunities arising out of a growing cultural diversity in the marketplace. In this context, Pires and Stanton (2005) emphasize the importance of understanding culturally specific needs and developing resonant ethnic marketing strategies. Ethnic minority entrepreneurs (henceforth, ethnic entrepreneurs) are best placed in serving the unique cultural needs of ethnic minority consumers given they share the same or similar cultural values, traditions and histories.

Steady rise in ethnic minority populations across the Western countries and subsequent growth in demand for ethnic products have provided significant entrepreneurial opportunities, as well as competitive advantage to those who know and share specific needs of ethnic minority cultures by moving into niche areas that require low economies of scale, have low or unstable market demand and are ignored by mainstream business enterprises (Jamal 2005; Morris and Schindehutte 2005). Networks of small ethnic enterprises act as distinct marketing systems within the national economies. Iyer and Shapiro (1999) and Jamal (2005) argue to consider the marketing strategies adopted by such enterprises as a benchmark against which to develop relevant ethnic marketing strategies. Others argue that ethnic minorities act not only as consumers but also as producers (e.g. Peñaloza and Gilly 1999) playing a significant role in the socio-economic development. Ethnic entrepreneurs take an active interest in identity-based relations acting as cultural intermediaries and facilitators of culture swapping (Oswald 1999) and 'frame switching' (Luna *et al.* 2008). They are hugely successful in developing and implementing innovative ethnic marketing strategies (Jamal 2003; 2005).

Despite this, the extant ethnic marketing literature largely ignores the creative and innovative practices (in particular those which are socially innovative in nature) adopted by ethnic entrepreneurs. This is surprising, given socially innovative initiatives potentially contribute not only to market co-creation of customer value but also help achieve wider social, economic and environmental sustainability of the markets (Peñaloza and Mish 2011). This chapter aims to fill this void in the literature by exploring some key social innovations especially through the norms, relationships and networks of trust and reciprocity adopted by ethnic entrepreneurs in their efforts to develop effective ethnic marketing strategies. In doing so, the chapter reviews literature relevant to ethnic entrepreneurship and highlights relevant issues for ethnic marketing. The aim is to further enrich theory development by advancing substantive understanding of intercultural market dynamics, knowledge generation and future research relevant to ethnic marketing. The main beneficiaries of this knowledge are likely to be the mainstream marketers interested in targeting ethnic minorities who can further enhance their understanding of the cultural mechanisms at play in developing socially innovative ethnic marketing programs.

The chapter also aims to contribute towards the extant entrepreneurship literature that tends to focus largely on discussing a) the impact of ethnic minority entrepreneurial actions on local economies and b) involvement of entrepreneurs within respective ethnic minority groups in a specific context or country. Examples include studying Brazilian and Hispanic entrepreneurs and their actions in the US (Siqueira 2007; Wang and Li 2007). The literature also places a considerable emphasis on the self-employment aspect of ethnic entrepreneurship as a survival strategy in the context of social and economic exclusion that ethnic minorities face in Western economies. However, the literature fails to take into account deliberative aspects of ethnic entrepreneurship and the extent to which highly motivated individuals and ethnic minority groups change and shape their careers and destinies by engaging in social innovation practices, and the impact their entrepreneurial actions have on local communities. The chapter aims to fill this gap in the literature by highlighting the ethnic marketing/ethnic entrepreneurship interface, and in particular the cultural networking and social innovation aspects of ethnic entrepreneurial marketing activities.

In the following sections, we first elaborate on the concept of ethnic entrepreneurship and its economic and social impacts in a multicultural marketplace. We then focus on discussing the role of social capital in building and bridging social and economic relations through ethnic entrepreneurship. Next, we argue for social innovation as a marketing mechanism for ethnic entrepreneurs. Finally, we examine the importance of ethnic entrepreneurship as an ethno-marketing strategy and its impact on social and economic development and prosperity.

Understanding ethnic entrepreneurs

One can develop a better understanding of ethnic entrepreneurs by looking at the notion of entrepreneurship, which can be defined in different ways and in different national social, cultural and economic contexts. The conventional approaches see an entrepreneur as a person who starts-up a small, successful business, but also as a risk taker who identifies opportunities and manages scarce capital and resources. For our purpose in this chapter, we adopt a more specific definition provided by Joseph Schumpeter (1934) who stresses the role of entrepreneurship in fostering innovation and change. His socio-economic views consider an entrepreneur as a creative innovator who can bring new ideas, approaches, objectives and procedures, or attempt a combination of all (Becker *et al.* 2011) especially for the purpose of market access and strategy-making.

Key defining features of ethnic entrepreneurs can also be better understood by looking into the ethnic entrepreneurship literature, which brings together two distant categories: a socio-cultural category such as ethnicity and a socio-economic category that reflects self-employment (Kloosterman 2010). Ethnicity and ethnic entrepreneurship thus are different but interlinked concepts. Ethnicity refers to a common identity that can be based on language, traditions, culture, heritage or norms (Tapsell and Woods 2008). Ethnic entrepreneurship brings together 'a set of connections and regular patterns of interaction among people sharing common national background or migration experiences' (Waldinger *et al.* 1990). It is not simply based on ethnic grouping, but refers to the levels of involvement of an entrepreneur in the community (Chaganti and Greene 2002).

A number of studies have looked at the patterns of relationships that lead to new marketing initiatives through a combination of various support mechanisms within specific communities of ethnic entrepreneurs. These particularly include, in the United States, Japanese Americans in California, Chinese Americans in New York, Cubans in Florida, Koreans in Atlanta and Pakistanis in Texas (Chaganti and Greene 2002). In Europe, there are examples of Turkish and Vietnamese entrepreneurs in Germany, Moroccans in Belgium, Algerians in France, Indonesians in Netherlands and generally South Asians in the UK. The processes of social and economic marginalization and exclusion also mean that ethnic enterprises tend to locate in the informal sector and specific areas (Samers 1998; Mingione 1999). Such initiatives can take advantage of the opportunity structures at the individual, community or institutional levels (Kloosterman 2010). Coming back to the statement by Chaganti and Greene (2002) on the importance of engagement in a community, it can be argued that this is the major distinguishing factor that sets ethnic entrepreneurship apart from other forms of entrepreneurial initiatives in terms of its innovative content and opportunity space for developing specific marketing strategies.

The literature has long recognized the 'push' and 'pull' motivations, sometimes character-ized as 'negative' and 'positive' motivations (Dawson and Henley 2012) that serve as an impetus for entrepreneurship. In the case of ethnic entrepreneurship, these factors are also important, although the specifics may be different in each case. For instance, while lack of employment opportunities or job dissatisfaction may 'pull' groups, language barriers or the non-acceptance of qualifications and credentials earned in another country are much more likely to be a factor that 'pushes' immigrants to become entrepreneurs. The Global Entrepreneurship Monitor (GEM) has a similar classification − 'necessity' entrepreneurs are those 'pushed' into self-employment as a result of limited available alternatives to earn an income whereas 'opportunity' entrepreneurs are 'pulled' into it by perceiving economic opportunity. Dawson and Henley (2012), however, caution that more clarity is needed in identifying these motives, whereas Williams and Williams (2014) argue for moving away from the necessity/opportunity dichotomy of entrepreneur-ial motivation since motivations change over time, frequently shifting between necessity and opportunity, and that the motivations are often a mixture of both compulsions. However, suc-cess or failure of ethno-marketing strategies may also depend on the extent ethnic entrepreneurs are pulled or pushed into the economic cycle.

Ethnic entrepreneurs contribute to society in many different ways, which can be broadly divided into economic and non-economic benefits. First, self-employment circumvents the bar-riers that exist in the form of fewer opportunities for employment, limited access to resources, insufficient knowledge of opportunities or discrimination from the employers. Second, there are opportunities for further job creation in the form of apprenticeships and employment from the self-employed ethnic entrepreneurs, sometimes leading to the emergence of local social networks and identification of new market potential. There tends to be a strong sense of social-capital-building for ethnic entrepreneurs through networks within their own ethnic communities and by bridging with their suppliers, customers and other networks associated with their businesses (Waldinger 1986; Deakins et al. 2007). Ethnic entrepreneurs also help fill the gaps left vacant by other entrepreneurs or businesses in specific sectors. In terms of non-economic benefits, the location of business helps shape a strong sense of citizenship and connection with the place, thus revitalizing and reviving local neighbourhoods and new marketing opportunities. There are also opportunities for more social and economic integration and cohesion within and among the communities in those neighbourhoods. This is particularly important in the wake of trans-national monopoly capitalism and the large business corporations that have restricted the role of entrepreneurship to the marginal sectors such as artisanal activities, craftsmanship, cottage industries and creative arts (Jenkins 2013).

Ethnic entrepreneurship and social capital

Social capital refers to such networks and norms of co-operation and reciprocity that offer opportunities for individual progress, ethnic entrepreneurship, civic engagement and economic advancement besides a number of personal and social benefits (Candland 2004). Pierre Bourdieu (1986) defines it as 'the aggregate of the actual or potential resources which are linked to possession of a durable network of more or less institutionalized relationships of mutual acquaintance and recognition – or in other words, to membership in a group'. Bourdieu designates social capital as benefits that can be obtained either from a sustainable and long-lasting network of relations or from belonging to a specific group. In this category, social capital brings its own exclusionary dynamics and hierarchical social relationships. Hence, ethnic entrepreneurs take advantage of the social capital when they have long standing relationships or strong internal contacts for marketing within the community.

On the other hand, James Coleman stresses that social capital does not belong to individual agents, but emerges from the network of relations between the actors. Accordingly 'persons' actions are shaped, redirected, constrained by the social context; norms, interpersonal trust, social networks, and social organization are important in the functioning not only of the society but also of the economy' (Coleman 1988, p. 96). Here, social capital is just one among the many resources available to an agent besides the human capital (own expertise), physical capital (tangible assets) and economic capital (investment and finance). Hence, ethnic entrepreneurs with good links in the community (based on trust, friendships and family ties) will have access to a specific form of social capital (and market) that may not be available to the others.

Robert Putnam defines social capital in terms of the 'features of social organization such as networks, norms, and social trust that facilitate coordination and co-operation for mutual benefit' (1995, p. 67). Personal trust, for Putnam, is transformed into social trust through the application of norms of reciprocity and networks of civic commitment. This provides a public and ethical face to ethnic entrepreneurship wherein community relations are bilateral and are based on real commitment of the entrepreneur towards the community and society. Ethnic marketing strategy in this instance would essentially build on mutual trust.

The literature also highlights the 'linking' role of social capital that refers to the 'norms of respect and networks of trusting relationships between people who are interacting across explicit, formal, or institutionalized power or authority gradients in society' (Szreter and Woolcock 2004). Examples may include vertical interaction relationship with the institutions and groups that are not on similar social, economic or power status. Based on these notions, the Organisation for Economic Co-operation and Development (OECD) defines social capital as comprising of 'networks together with shared norms, values and understandings that facilitate co-operation within or among groups' (OECD 2007, p. 103). These groups are defined by the UK's Office of National Statistics (ONS) as referring to: geographical groups (based on people living in a specific location), professional groups (based on occupations, or memberships of specific organizations), social groups (based on family, religious or ethnic ties) and virtual groups (linked through social media or special interests) (ONS 2013). The access to social capital can also determine the success or failure of ethnic marketing strategy, where personal relations that are based on ethnicity can provide more opportunities based on trust. Access to specific forms of social capital, therefore, helps ethnic entrepreneurs to become socially innovative. Subsequently, successful social innovations can contribute to social learning and help strengthen the stocks of social capital (Baker and Mehmood 2015). Peñaloza (2009), while making the case for the criticality of community development in social marketing, refers to the importance of social differences in terms of ethnicity, race, gender, religion and mobility in market development. This can help, she argues, to understand the role of cultural and social capital and social relations in specific consumer markets.

Entrepreneurship and innovation

The ethnic entrepreneurship literature has traditionally focused on the market-based economic aspects of self-employment through entrepreneurial activities (e.g., how the economic strategies of ethnic actors become more competitive to promote local economies by catering for co-ethnic groups, serving as middlemen entrepreneurs, or reaching out to the larger markets). However, an area that remains underexplored is the bottom-up initiatives for economic survival by accessing social capital for entrepreneurial activities (bonding and bridging social capital) and developing social relations and the possibility to engage with the society at large. This weakness can be mended by looking at the socially innovative character of an enterprise and the community (or market) it primarily serves. The social innovation lens here can help address the bipolar social/economic views of ethnic entrepreneurship and provide an integrated approach to the contributions of ethnic enterprises to the society and economy with more positive societal understandings and relations at different spatial scales (local, regional, national). Drawing on research from ethnic minority enterprises in Scotland, Deakins *et al.* (1997) argue that innovation plays a key role in the success and development of such enterprises and their marketing strategies. They further demonstrate that effective networks and personal contacts are a major source of bridging social capital in the peripheral markets. However, access to finance remains a crucial barrier to their effective marketization and diversification.

Social innovation and ethnic marketing

Social innovation can be generally defined as innovation in fulfilling social and economic needs that are beneficial to the communities (Phills *et al.* 2008; Murray *et al.* 2010). These innovations can be in the form of new ideas, products, services, management systems, marketing mechanisms or actions that are more effective than the conventional charitable, market-led or public policy approaches in meeting social and economic issues in a society (MacCallum *et al.* 2009). It therefore refers to the individual or collective entrepreneurial initiatives that have stood the test of time, space and geographical boundaries (Moulaert *et al.* 2013).

In market economy terms, social innovation can be seen as a set of social and economic practices embedded in the activities and institutions ranging from the everyday family and community life to the norms of production, consumption and social relations. These views require that the producers and consumers should not be looked at from pure economic rationale only. It demands taking into account the different kinds of social and economic capitals, relationships and practices from the micro to the macro level, thus providing a new vision to ethnic marketing. Such an approach can help ethnic marketers and entrepreneurs develop cultural relational capability (e.g. Ngugi *et al.* 2010), enabling them to cope with diverse cultural systems in the multicultural marketplace. The approach is also in line with the new service dominant logic in marketing (Vargo and Lusch 2004), which elaborates on how multiple actors co-create value together with emphasis on building relationships, sharing of knowledge resources and multiple interactions. As value can be created in different ways, ethnic marketers can build and operate alternative structures to provide goods and services addressing social and cultural needs and, hence, develop and maintain social harmony in situations where a lack of will by mainstream marketers prevent effectively addressing important social needs.

The focus on social marketing aspects of innovation can be traced to the emergence of Irish Loan Funds in the 1720s as socially innovative and independent microfinance institutions, complementing the banking system. Besides offering relatively higher loans at lower interest rates to the poor, their success is attributed to the use of social monitoring and peer pressure to ensure regular repayments and recovery at minimal costs in the wake of extreme social, economic, political and geographical conditions (Hollis and Sweetman 2001). The Funds proved a valuable measure during the Great Famine. Social innovation, therefore, emerged as a reformist ideology stemming from the theories of social, economic and political organization (Godin 2012). The approach re-emerged in the 1980s to describe 'practices that are more or less directly aimed at allowing an individual or a group of individuals to deal with a social need or a set of needs which could not be satisfied by other means' (Chambon *et al.* 1982, p. 8). More contemporary definition regards social innovation as 'a novel solution to a social problem that is more effective, efficient, sustainable, or just than existing solutions and for which the value created accrues primarily to society as a whole rather than private individuals'. (Phills *et al.* 2008, p. 36).

There are two conventional foci of social innovation in entrepreneurship literature and applications. The first focus is on the social nature of an enterprise, i.e. the firm as a point of interaction for social relations in a community. Here technological innovation goes hand in hand with the innovation in social relations. Technological innovations, such as new marketing strategies in this case, would remain ineffective if they do not take into account the social needs of the target customers. The second focus assumes the enterprise playing an active social role in a society. In ethnic marketing terms, the enterprise should establish its image as a socially responsible entity. Activities in this respect may range from corporate implementing social responsibility, to the promotion of social economy initiatives that are ecologically robust, socially sustainable and follow sustainable businesses models (Moulaert and Nussbaumer 2008).

These two foci are criticized by Moulaert (2009) as an attempt towards the commodification of social relations within and across the enterprises. Instead he suggests a model of social innovation that is practiced by social economy enterprises, i.e. to build bridges (bridging social capital) between the improvement in social relations and emancipation of collective action. He proposes three basic but interrelated tenets of social innovation for the benefit of communities: satisfaction of basic needs of the population, improvement in social relations among people and community empowerment. Empowerment in our case refers to how the needs of ethnic and minority communities are acknowledged and how migrant populations and ethnic groups can have equal opportunities to engage in the social and economic activities in a society (Moulaert *et al.* 2007). Not only does this provide an alternative in the cases where traditional market mechanisms of protectionism tend to fail, but also promotes the practices of social solidarity and reciprocity in a community (Moulaert and Nussbaumer 2005).

In a related domain, ethnic marketing can be seen as a vehicle of innovation through the role of social enterprise. From practitioners' perspective, any entrepreneurial initiative designed to help people, whether for- or non-profit, can be classified as a social enterprise. A more nuanced approach considers only those ventures that are socially innovative but have the vision for a transformational impact as social enterprises (Martin and Osberg 2007). Typically, these organizations have an 'enterprise' side and a 'mission' side where the former generates part or all of the revenues to fund the latter. In some cases, the enterprise is able to integrate the two. Nicholls (2006, p. 23) defines social entrepreneurship as 'innovation and effective activities that focus strategically on resolving social market failures and creating opportunities to add social value systematically by using a range of organizational formats to maximize social impact and bring about change'. In addition to creating economic value, social entrepreneurship focuses on creating social value although the innovative pursuit of social value can occur across different contexts, spaces and organization forms (Smith and Stevens 2010). However, our review of literature identifies little empirical research investigating the extent to which ethnic entrepreneurs engage in social entrepreneurial activities and the value of such activities for ethnic marketing. Despite many national governments promoting policies to support and increase the number of social enterprises, it remains a relatively excluded area for ethnic communities. From a study of third sector ethnic minority organizations in East London, Sepulveda *et al.* (2013) argue that there is very little policy support for ethnic entrepreneurs to establish and nourish social enterprises.

There are certain barriers to innovation that are typically faced by ethnic entrepreneurs in the marketing and promotion of their businesses. For smaller (or new) entrepreneurs these may include barriers to developing and establishing the enterprise, lack of sufficient information and training, problems with access to material goods, marketing to the larger consumer base and interpreting the legislative framework (Labie 2000). Based on a qualitative survey of new migrants in the UK, Jones *et al.* (2012) term such barriers as structural disadvantages. Ethnic entrepreneurs are particularly expected to suffer from these structural patterns of handicaps. It is here that social capital and network ties can be useful to such entrepreneurs both in navigating these barriers as well as providing a source of informal financing through embeddedness in ethnic and social groups.

There are some interesting cases of support mechanisms to counter such barriers. One of the pioneering research comes from Hillman (2009) who uses the examples of Turkish and Vietnamese migrants in Berlin to discuss how entrepreneurial initiatives for simple survival slowly achieve formal recognition in the society and become an integral part of the local economic revival. She illustrates the potential of social innovations – initiated in response to marginalization of ethnic entrepreneurs and unsatisfied needs of ethnic consumers – to achieve broader benefits and to help bring about progressive institutional change. Hillman criticizes the narrow interpretation of ethnic entrepreneurship in the literature as mere survival strategies from social and economic exclusion. She argues that ethnic entrepreneurs can become main agents in the processes of social innovation and contribute to the social economy. For example, ethnic communities as urban citizens can build close collaborations with advocacy groups to design inclusive local policies in accordance with the needs of such communities (Varsany 2006). Associated with the trend of ethnicization of cultural activities, Hillman (2009, pp. 159–60) refers to the rise of 'ethno-marketing' as a way to connect the ethnic entrepreneurs besides providing an advertising platform. One such example of success is the magazine *Ethnotrade* in Berlin (Germany). Since Autumn 2002, the magazine is published quarterly with a circulation of 20,000 copies of about fifty pages in each issue. The magazine forms part of a set of marketing strategies for ethnic entrepreneurs. It regularly organizes public fairs, annually awards the most successful entrepreneur of the year and considers the variety of ethno-cultures as stimulants for marketing strategies.

Ethnic entrepreneurs as ethno-marketers

Continuing with the approaches to ethnic entrepreneurship as a set of connections (Waldinger *et al.* 1990), social capital helps bond the ethnicity-based collaborative networks while bridging and extending the relations of respect and trust between individuals and networks outside the ethnic community. The socially innovative character of ethnic entrepreneurship provides ethnic entrepreneurs with alternative opportunities to promote their businesses and maintain their market shares. These alternative strategies may both emerge from informal networks as well as deliberative attitudes towards risk taking. These attitudes might also emanate from the specific cultural features of the respective ethnic and migrant groups in terms of dedication to hard work, strong sense of belonging to a community, solidarity relations, reciprocity and compliance with the social value systems (Masurel *et al.* 2004). It also helps with the opportunity space offered by the local environment in the local economy. This environment allows possibilities for absorption and economic mobility (Volery 2007).

These traits also potentially bring ethnic entrepreneurs in direct confrontation with large retailers. Although the scale economies of large retailers do not relate with the small niche entrepreneurs, the sense of mutual co-existence is often disrupted when larger stores start catering to the needs of geographic, cultural, ethnic and religious groupings in a city or neighbourhood. With wider infrastructure and price advantages, large stores tend to put the smaller ethnic retailers out of their comfort zones. This, however, is not always the case and there are examples of many ethnic enterprises that continue to innovate and survive in the difficult climates. They do so by means of innovative business practices (social innovations), strong community ties (social capital) and holding on to their market base.

Scholarly work exploring the marketing/entrepreneurship interface (Carson and Gilmore 2000) provides useful insights in highlighting the competency (using inherent and learned skills and knowledge in communicating to and with all parties in a timely manner), networking and innovation (in the whole spectrum of marketing) dimensions of ethnic entrepreneurial marketing. For example, Jamal (2005) explored the marketing strategies of ethnic entrepreneurs and found strong evidence in support of ethnic entrepreneurs engaging in social networking and innovation practices for satisfying personal, social and cultural needs of different stakeholders. At a social and cultural level, ethnic entrepreneurs take an active interest in identity-based relations in business and social life (Iyer and Shapiro 1999) and act as bi-cultural mediators facilitating the construction and maintenance of multiple identities in a multicultural marketplace (Jamal 2005).

Peñaloza and Gilly (1999) relate adaptability as a main characteristic of ethnic entrepreneurs. Their empirical model looks at the role of ethnic entrepreneurs as ethno-marketers through cultural mediation. The model uses patterns of consumption and ethnic cultural characteristics, and considers how these are transformed into the business, consumption and market patterns in the new place. Such interactions help create new cultural dynamics between the ethno-marketer and the local consumer. These new cultures can also contribute to market co-creation with new norms and practices, as well as contributing to social, economic and environmental sustainability of the markets (Peñaloza and Mish 2011). Ethnic entrepreneurs as ethno-marketers embedded in the communities, therefore, contribute to redefining the market logics by bringing new perspectives to the value systems, new market ethics, new relationships between marketers and consumers, reimagining the differences between local and international subcultures and spurring reflexivity for socio-cultural developments (Peñaloza and Venkatesh 2006).

There are also many empirical cases of how ethnic entrepreneurs embrace innovative strategies to transfer business cultures, marketing systems, management trends, shared values and adapt to their clientele in a global marketplace. From an empirical study of marketing strategies employed by family firms belonging to Chinese, Jewish, Korean and South Asian groups of entrepreneurs in the USA, Iyer and Shapiro (1999) argue that many of such small businesses have larger international social and economic impacts. These ethnic entrepreneurs are a key part of international supply chains besides creating market niches and transmitting business values. Often such firms become a major source of foreign direct investment.

An illustrative example is the role of ethnic entrepreneurship in the development of halal food supply chains across major cities in Europe, and particularly in the UK (Lever and Miele 2012). Studies document the perceived value and usefulness of halal labelling among the Muslim community (e.g. Jamal and Sharifuddin 2015). Islamic law specifies foods that are halal (lawful) or haram (unlawful). In particular Islam forbids consumption of pork and alcohol. The term halal, an all-encompassing concept with wide social and cultural connotations, encourages Muslims to use products that promote goodness and social welfare in all aspects of life (Alserhan 2010). Since the large scale migration of Muslim communities to Europe in the 1950s and 1960s, mainly from South Asia, Middle East and Africa, ethnic entrepreneurs have played a significant role in fulfilling an acute religious and cultural need that mainstream businesses were unable to fulfil. With the steady rise in the British Muslim population, demand for halal food and halal meat grew steadily not only for the in-home consumption but also for consumption at schools, hospitals, prisons, airlines, universities, work places, restaurants, takeaways and halal food supermarkets. An extensive network of ethnic enterprises now process and sell fresh halal meat across major cities in the UK, propelling some mainstream supermarkets to follow suit and sell packed halal meat in neighbourhoods with a substantial British Muslim population (Ahmed 2008). Ethnic entrepreneurs were also instrumental in developing halal certification bodies (e.g., Halal Food Authority, Halal Monitoring Committee, etc.) for monitoring, inspecting and certifying halal meat, and thus significantly adding value to overall shopping experiences of British Muslims. Similar examples can be traced in other product areas such as ethnic clothing, music, media and financial instruments where ethnic entrepreneurs serve important social, religious and cultural market related needs; areas largely ignored by other agencies, government and mainstream businesses.

Assessing the impacts

In order to continue to support social innovation and effective marketing strategy-making among ethnic entrepreneurs, it becomes important to understand whether these strategies and innovations, and the enterprises that deliver them, are successful and have a meaningful impact. While examples of successes abound, research needs to move from anecdotes to more robust and systematic assessments of impact and success. When measurement takes place, it is often the inputs and tasks completed that are measured – number of loans made, awards received, products distributed, etc – rather than output or specific changes such as increased social cohesion or increased well-being of target communities.

One potentially valuable approach to performance assessment is that outlined by London (2009). While originally developed to assess the impact of initiatives aimed for people at the Base of the Pyramid (BoP), the process can easily be adapted and expanded to marketing strategies and innovations that are targeted at other desirable social changes. For example, Mersha *et al.* (2014) apply a modified BoP Impact Assessment process to evaluate the activities of three social enterprises in Africa. London (2009) argues that his framework is a forward-looking tool rather than one based on justifying past results, and looks at both the positive and negative impacts, just as any social innovation should. Impact is determined based on:

- 'Who' is being affected? Three potential beneficiaries are identified – sellers, customers and the community in which the enterprise or innovation operates.
- 'How' are they affected? London suggests that the one impact could be economic – access to borrowing, increased or reduced debt, income, prices, etc. Another potential impact could be on capabilities such as skills, education, increased self-esteem and well-being of the

community. Finally, social inclusion, new partnerships and networks within the community and enhanced social status could be relationship impacts. There is of course the possibility that some of these impacts may be negative – greater gender and social equality could cause tensions and disrupt traditions in some communities, resulting in social exclusion.

Once the full gamut of the social innovation effects are understood, London recommends that each effect be evaluated on two dimensions: the anticipated magnitude of the effect and the likelihood of it occurring. Clearly, high-magnitude and high-likelihood outcomes are most important in assessing the impacts of ethnic enterprise or their ethno-marketing innovation and the low-magnitude, low-likelihood ones merit the least attention.

Conclusion

From the discussion above, it can be argued that ethnic entrepreneurs are unique in the sense that they are able to identify the gaps in the market and are in a position to fill those gaps through socially innovative actions and strategies. They are proactive risk takers, aware of the potential competition in the market. They are resilient, although there can be a steep learning curve with high chances of failure, but as social innovators they have the ability to adapt their strategies with new business approaches, environments, demands, and the shifts in consumer base.

This chapter has attempted to explore key academic literature and empirical examples in social innovations especially through the norms, relationships and networks of trust and reciprocity by ethnic entrepreneurs in developing and implementing ethno-marketing strategies. These entrepreneurs increasingly face competition with large retailers over the niche market segments, often through cultural mediation market co-creation and building new relationships with customers through community engagement and sustainable market ethics.

While social innovations can arise from many places and organizations, including social, ethnic and community entrepreneurships, the focus here has been on how ethnic entrepreneurs can leverage their social capital and embeddedness in social networks to create innovative and sustainable solutions that produce value for the local communities as well as for society as a whole. Whereas the anecdotal evidence for the existence of these innovations is strong, we have also proposed a more systematic process for assessing the impact of these innovations and the enterprises that often drive them. By these means, ethnic marketers can also embrace socially innovative strategies to co-produce and transmit business cultures, marketing systems, management practices and shared values, and even broaden their prospects to a global marketplace.

References

Ahmed, A. (2008) 'Marketing of halal meat in the United Kingdom: Supermarkets versus local shops'. *British Food Journal*, 110: 655–70.

Alserhan, B. A. (2010) 'Islamic branding: A conceptualization of related terms'. *British Journal of Management*, 18: 34–49.

Baker, S. and Mehmood, A. (2015) 'Social innovation and the governance of sustainable places'. *Local Environment: The International Journal of Justice and Sustainability*, 20(3): 321–34.

Becker, M., Knudsen, T. and Swedberg, R. (eds) (2011) *The Entrepreneur: Classic Texts by Joseph A. Schumpeter*. Palo Alto, CA: Stanford University Press.

Bourdieu, P. (1986) 'The forms of capital'. In *Handbook of Theory and Research for the Sociology of Education*, edited by J. Richardson. New York, NY: Greenwood, pp. 241–58.

Carson, D. and Gilmore, A. (2000) 'Marketing at the interface: Not "what" but "how"'. *Journal of Marketing Theory and Practice*, 8(2): 1–8.

Candland, C. (2004) 'Social capital'. In *The Oxford Companion to Politics of the World*, Second edition, edited by J. Krieger. Oxford: Oxford University Press. Available at: http://www.oxfordreference.com/view/10.1093/acref/9780195117394.001.0001/acref-9780195117394-e-0695 [accessed 4 November 2014].

Chaganti, R. and Greene, P. G. (2002) 'Who are ethnic entrepreneurs? A study of entrepreneurs' ethnic involvement and business characteristics'. *Journal of Small Business Management*, 40(2): 126–43.

Chambon, J. L., David, A. and Devevey, J. M. (1982) *Les Innovations Sociales*. Paris: Presses Universitaires de France.

Coleman, J. S. (1988) 'Social capital in the creation of human capital'. *American Journal of Sociology*, 94: S95–S120.

Dawson, C. and Henley, A. (2012) '"Push" versus "Pull" entrepreneurship: An ambiguous distinction?' *International Journal of Entrepreneurial Behaviour & Research*, 18(6): 697–719.

Deakins, D., Ishaq, M., Smallbone, D., Whittam, G. and Wyper, J. (2007) 'Ethnic minority businesses in Scotland and the role of social capital'. *International Small Businesses Journal*, 25(3): 307–26.

Deakins, D., Majmudar, M. and Paddison, A. (1997) 'Developing success strategies for ethnic minorities in business: Evidence from Scotland'. *Journal of Ethnic and Migration Studies*, 23(3): 325–42.

Godin, B. (2012) 'Social innovation: Utopias of innovation from *c*.1830 to the present', *Working Paper 52, Project on the Intellectual History of Innovation*. Quebec: INRS.

Hollis, A. and Sweetman, J. (2001) 'The life-cycle of a microfinance institution: The Irish loan funds'. *Journal of Economic Behavior & Organization*, 46(3): 291–311.

Hillman, F. (2009) 'How socially innovative is migrant entrepreneurship? A case study of Berlin'. In *Social Innovation and Territorial Development*, edited by D. MacCallum, F. Moulaert, J. Hillier and S. Vicari-Haddock. Aldershot: Ashgate, pp. 101–14.

Iyer, G. R. and Shapiro, J. M. (1999) 'Ethnic entrepreneurial and marketing systems: Implications for the global economy'. *Journal of International Marketing*, 7(4): 83–110.

Jamal, A. (2003) 'Marketing in a multicultural world: The interplay of marketing, ethnicity and consumption'. *European Journal of Marketing*, 37(11/12): 1599–620.

Jamal, A. (2005) 'Playing to win: An explorative study of marketing strategies of small ethnic retail entrepreneurs in the UK'. *Journal of Retailing and Consumer Services*, 12: 1–13.

Jamal, A. and Sharifuddin, J. (2014) 'Perceived value and usefulness of halal labelling: Role of religion and culture'. *Journal of Business Research*, 68(5): 933–41.

Jenkins, R. (2013) *Transnational Corporations and Uneven Development: The Internationalization of Capital and the Third World*. London: Routledge.

Jones, T., Ram, M., Edwards, P., Kiselinchev, A. and Muchenje, L. (2012) 'New migrant enterprise: Novelty or historical continuity?' *Urban Studies*, 49(14): 3159–76.

Kloosterman, R. (2010) 'Matching opportunities with resources: A framework for analysing (migrant) entrepreneurship from a mixed embeddedness perspective'. *Entrepreneurship and Regional Development*, 22(1): 25–45.

Labie, M. (2000) *La Microfinance en Questions: Limites et Choix Organisationnels*. Brussels: Luc Pire.

Lever, J. and Miele, M. (2012) 'The growth of halal meat markets in Europe: An exploration of the supply side theory of religion'. *Journal of Rural Studies*, 28: 528–37.

London, T. (2009) 'Making better investments at the base of the pyramid'. *Harvard Business Review*, (May): 106–13.

Luna D., Ringberg, T. and Peracchio, L. A. (2008) 'One individual, two identities: Frame switching among biculturals'. *Journal of Consumer Research*, 35: 279–285.

MacCallum, D., Moulaert, F., Hillier, J. and Vicari-Haddock, S. (eds) (2009) *Social Innovation and Territorial Development*. Aldershot: Ashgate.

Martin, R. L. and Osberg, S. (2007) 'Social entrepreneurship: The case for definition'. *Stanford Social Innovation Review*, 5(2): 29–39.

Masurel, E., Nijkamp, P. and Vindigni, G. (2004) 'Breeding places for ethnic entrepreneurs: A comparative marketing approach'. *Entrepreneurship & Regional Development*, 16: 77–86.

Mersha, T., Sriram, V. and Elliott, R. (2014) 'Africa's third sector: Assessing the impact of Africa's social enterprises'. In *Routledge Companion to Business in Africa*, edited by S. Nwankwo and K. Ibeh. Oxford: Routledge, pp. 102–16.

Mingione, E. (1999) 'Introduction: Immigrants and the informal economy in european cities'. *International Journal of Urban and Regional Research*, 23(2): 209–11.

Morris, M. and Schindehutte, M. (2005) 'Entrepreneurial values and the ethnic enterprise: An examination of six subcultures'. *Journal of Small Business Management*, 43(4): 453–479.

Moulaert, F. (2009) 'Social innovation: Institutionally embedded, territorially (re)produced'. In *Social Innovation and Territorial Development*, edited by D. MacCallum, F. Moulaert, J. Hillier and S. Vicari-Haddock. Aldershot: Ashgate, pp. 11–24.

Moulaert, F., MacCallum, D., Mehmood, A. and Hamdouch, A. (eds) (2013) *The Handbook of Social Innovation: Collective Action, Social Learning and Transdisciplinary Research*. Cheltenham: Edward Elgar.

Moulaert, F., Martinelli, F., González, S. and Swyngedouw, E. (2007) 'Introduction: Social innovation and governance in European cities: Urban development between path dependency and radical innovation'. *European Urban and Regional Studies* 14(3): 195–209.

Moulaert, F. and Nussbaumer, J. (2005) 'Defining the social economy and its governance at the neighbourhood level: A methodological reflection'. *Urban Studies*, 42(11): 2071–88.

Moulaert, F. and Nussbaumer, J. (2008) *La Logique Spatiale du Développement Territorial*. Sainte-Foye: Presses Universitaires du Québec.

Murray, R., Caulier-Grice, J. and Mulgan, G. (2010) *The Open Book of Social Innovation*. London: NESTA and The Young Foundation.

Ngugi, I. K., Johnsen, R. E. and Erdelyi P. (2010) 'Relational capabilities for value co-creation and innovation in SMEs'. *Journal of Small Business and Enterprise Development*, 17(2): 260–78.

Nicholls, A. (2006) *Social Entrepreneurship: New Models of Sustainable Social Change*. Oxford: Oxford University Press.

OECD (2007) 'OECD Insights: Human capital'. OECD. Available at: http://www.oecd.org/insights/37966934.pdf [accessed 19 May 2013].

ONS (2013) 'The Social Capital Project'. Office of National Statistics. Available at: http://www.ons.gov.uk/ons/guide-method/user-guidance/social-capital-guide/the-social-capital-project/guide-to-social-capital.html [accessed 4 November 2014].

Oswald, L. R. (1999) 'Cultural swapping: Consumption and the Ethnogenesis of middle-class Haitian immigrants'. *Journal of Consumer Research*, 25(4): 303–18.

Peñaloza, L. (2009) 'And the beat goes on! Critical marketing for community development'. *Journal of Marketing Management*, 25(7/8): 855–59.

Peñaloza, L. and Gilly, M. C. (1999) 'Marketer acculturation: The changer and the changed'. *Journal of Marketing*, 63: 84–104.

Peñaloza, L. and Mish, J. (2011) 'The nature and processes of market co-creation in triple bottom line firms: Leveraging insights from consumer culture theory and service dominant logic'. *Marketing Theory*, 11(1): 9–34.

Peñaloza, L. and Venkatesh, A. (2006) 'Further evolving the new dominant logic of marketing: From services to the social construction of markets'. *Marketing Theory*, 6(3): 299–316.

Phills, J. A., Deiglmeier, K. and Miller, D. T. (2008) 'Rediscovering social innovation'. *Stanford Social Innovation Review*, 6(4): 34–43.

Pires, G. and Stanton, J. (2005) *Ethnic Marketing, Accepting the Challenge of Cultural Diversity*. London: Thomson Learning.

Putnam, R. D. (1995) 'Bowling alone: America's declining social capital'. *Journal of Democracy*, 6: 65–78.

Samers, M. (1998) 'Immigration, "ethnic minorities", and "social exclusion" in the European Union: A critical perspective'. *Geoforum* 29(2): 123–44.

Schumpeter, J. A. (1934) *The Theory of Economic Development*. London: Oxford University Press.

Sepulveda, L., Syrett, S. and Calvo, S. (2013) 'Social enterprise and ethnic minorities: Exploring the consequences of the evolving British policy agenda'. *Environment and Planning C: Government and Policy*, 31(4): 633–48.

Siqueira, A. C. O. (2007) 'Entrepreneurship and ethnicity: The role of human capital and family social capital'. *Journal of Developmental Entrepreneurship*, 12(1): 31–46.

Smith, B. R. and Stevens, C. E. (2010) 'Different types of social entrepreneurship: The role of geography and embeddedness on the measurement and scaling of social value'. *Entrepreneurship & Regional Development*, 22(6): 575–98.

Szreter, S. and Woolcock, M. (2004) 'Health by association? Social capital, social theory, and the political economy of public health'. *International Journal of Epidemiology*, 33(4): 650–67.

Tapsell, P. and Woods, C. (2008) 'A spiral of innovation framework for social entrepreneurship: Social innovation at the generational divide in an indigenous context'. *Emergence: Complexity & Organization*, 10(3): 25–34.

Vargo, S. L. and Lusch, R. F. (2004) 'Evolving to a new dominant logic for marketing'. *Journal of Marketing*, 68(1): 1–17.

Varsany, M. (2006) 'Interrogating "urban citizenship" vis-á-vis undocumented migration', *Citizenship Studies*, 10(2): 229–49.

Volery, T. (2007) 'Ethnic entrepreneurship: A theoretical framework'. In *Handbook of Research on Ethnic Minority Entrepreneurship: A Co-evolutionary View on Resource Management*, edited by L. P. Dana. Cheltenham: Edward Elgar, pp. 30–41.

Waldinger, R. D. (1986) *Through the Eye of the Needle: Immigrants and Enterprise in New York's Garment Trades*. New York, NY: New York University Press.

Waldinger, R., Aldrich, H. and Ward, R. H. (1990) *Ethnic Entrepreneurs, Immigrant Business in Industrial Societies*. London: Sage Publications.

Wang, Q. and Li, W. (2007) 'Entrepreneurship, ethnicity and local contexts: Hispanic entrepreneurs in three US southern metropolitan areas'. *GeoJournal* 68(2–3): 167–82.

Williams, N. and Williams, C. C. (2014) 'Beyond necessity versus opportunity entrepreneurship: Some lessons from English deprived urban neighbourhoods'. *International Entrepreneurship and Management Journal*, 10(1): 23–40.

7

The landscape of ethnic marketing in the UK

*Sanya Ojo, Sonny Nwankwo
and Ayantunji Gbadamosi*

Introduction

Unabating mobility of populations across national frontiers has become as much a hot and challenging issue globally as it is to Britain. Peculiarly to Britain, its adventurous history, especially in Africa and Asia, positioned the country as a magnate for people from the erstwhile colonies. The consequence is that Britain is discernibly multi-ethnic and multicultural, demographically. Coupled with the shifting contours of colour, the concept of creed, ethnicity and culture is the heterogeneity of the market system, evoked and orchestrated through marketing aphorisms. Exacerbated by the growing population of immigrants from far-flung territories, the resulting ethnoscapes requires that marketing must keep track of the behavioural signals and attitudinal attributes overtly or covertly emitted by these groups. Therefore, attention is now, more than ever, focused on ethnic marketing and the imperatives of developing successful marketing strategies to serve the needs of ethnically diverse markets. In this regard, ethnic marketing is gaining space in contemporary marketing literature as marketers struggle to cope with the increasing diversity of markets. However, as both conceptual and empirical boundaries are pressed, the inadequacies of conventional marketing paradigms are constantly exposed.

The need to focus on this aspect of marketing lies in the fact that many modern social institutions are characterized by plurality of contrasting and sometimes contradictory interests. Consumers are not all the same and cannot be expected to share a common value system. Ethnic marketing thus offers a conceptual platform within which to re-examine the strategies for coping with the heterogeneity of the modern marketing system. After all, marketing is partially a social activity and must accordingly acknowledge the inherent diversity of cultures and value systems. This chapter highlights those critical issues that account for the shifting landscape of ethnic marketing in Britain. The aim is to draw attention to the dynamically evolving marketing system and thus illuminate how such an understanding can be of value as the marketing implications of a diverse society are manifesting themselves.

Gaps in ethnic marketing research

From the 1990s, there appeared to be a welcome flourishing of research in ethnic marketing in the UK (e.g. Watson 1992; Dwek 1997; Nwankwo and Lindridge 1998; Burton 2000; Altinay 2010;

Jamal *et al.* 2012; Gbadamosi 2012). Paradoxically, the subject does not seem to generate much attention in the mainstream research in the UK. A constellation of factors may explain this: for example, (a) lack of a critical mass of researchers working in the topic area, (b) thematic research is slow in catching up with practice (the classic theory–practice gap) and/or (c) something to do with the position well-articulated over twenty years ago (and still relevant) by Brownlie, Saren, Whittington and Wensley (1994, p. 8), although in a different context but quoted liberally:

- Marketing academics are so busy running around engaging in empirical work with the aim of getting us closer to the apparent needs of the managerial community, that the theoretical soil from which many new ideas spring is in danger of losing fertility.
- The soils is being very thinly spread over a wide-range of applications without much appreciation of the limitation of marketing ideas and tools in contexts for which they were not originally conceived.
- Mainstream marketing journals reinforce a set of norms among the marketing academy, which is in danger of driving out the qualities of openness, tolerance and critique that, in turn, facilitate innovation and new ways of thinking.

Essentially, the marketing study of 'marginal populations' in the UK has not received as wide attention as the case with the US. Ironically, while ethnic composition of the British population attracts vibrant interests in social and political policy discourses (oftentimes in the guise of 'immigrant overflow'); the business case is seemingly drowned in the cacophony of contestations even among the major political parties. Equally, concerns have trailed theoretical and discursive aspects of ethnic marketing development (Nwankwo 1996). Arguably, this resonates with the argument that marketing concepts are encumbered, among other things, with ethnocentric biases (Fırat and Dholakia 1989). In particular, partly because marketing, as conventionally espoused, is tinted and framed by Western hues, some of the practices within ethnic enclaves are quickly falling off the radar of 'conventional researchers'. The consequence is that situated practices in marginal populations and non-Western accounts are neutralized (Nwankwo 2004). What we then see happening, as Fullerton (1988) remarked with regard to developments in marketing history, is that the study of ethnic marketing in Britain in non-ethnic terms is leading to the application (more appropriately, imposition) of constructs and ideas without regard to the need to study the phenomenon on the basis of its own distinctiveness.

Nevertheless, for the community of scholars who read marketing as discursive practice rather than as 'hard' objective science, the subject is seen to be snugly tied to the goals and practices of specific social agents and embedded in socio-economic relations within a given cultural context. This means that, as a social construct, marketing custom is bound to have profound implications on marketing praxis as well as its societal transformative potentials. Thus, making a case for re-evaluating ethnic marketing research in the UK is tantamount to advocating reflexivity and contextual relevance in how we seek to understand the dynamics of marketing within diverse populations. There is probably nothing new in staking out this position except that, sometimes, marketing scholars need to remind themselves of the entreatment by Berlin (1991, p. 15) that 'any study of society shows that every solution creates a new situation which breeds its own new needs and problems'. It is doubtful that marketing can be studied in a meaningful way without deep contextualization, linking with the paradigms in which practices are situated.

Problematizing ethnic markets

Generally, the ever-increasing growth in the population of ethnic minorities' in Europe/ Western societies leads to continuous rise in ethnic products and markets over the years. But it is not so much the population that is critical in terms of marketing but the market spread. It is clear, using the UK's experience, that there are now pockets of ethnic consumer markets that may be different or similar to the mainstream market. From this perspective, it will be interesting to analyze the level of differences and interfaces between ethnic and mainstream markets. Also, interest in ethnic marketing in the UK assumes greater relevance given the context of Patterson's (1969) contrasting trajectories which suggests that the British Asians are destined for a 'Jewish future' in business and the professions, while the African Caribbean groups are set for an 'Irish' future through the organized working class. Suffice it to say that the African Caribbean groups' entrepreneurial venturing is on the rise and visible in many leading edge sectors (Smith 2006). They are also visible in innovative market sectors of the economy (e.g., printing and nursery businesses) previously unpenetrated by ethnic entrepreneurs. Invariably, situated practices in terms of which markets are emerging and which groups are dominant in what market are areas of immense value to ethnic marketing research.

Furthermore, within the context of the globalization effects on contemporary patterns, ethnic marketing and enterprising could be useful tools to understand issues of ethnicity and diversity in developed societies. In order to achieve this, there is a need for more intracultural research. This is because a more integrative research in relation to ethnic integration/diversity studies will aid the understanding of the dynamism of ethnic marketing. In essence, the discernment of the issues of ethnic assimilation and the culture which shapes it are crucial to marketing/entrepreneurial success in a multicultural society like the UK.

Conceptual boundaries

The conceptual boundary of the study is set to examine how the changing nature of the British society in the context of evolving global pattern of social relations exemplified in Appadurai's (1998) imagination of global cultural flows (i.e., ethnoscapes, mediascapes, technoscapes, financescapes, ideoscapes), ethnicity and identity might be exploited in marketing theory and practice. Appadurai's '-scapes' signpost fluidity and variability as they are in constant change. The flexibility of ethnoscapes is evidenced in cross-border migration of people; technoscapes promotes new types of cultural interactions and exchanges through the power of technology; financescapes change is effected as capital moves around in the global economy. Expansion and transformations of the media from different places account for mediascapes change, and ideoscapes change is fostered when ideas are exchanged and spread. The five factors thus form an aggregate mode that constantly define and redefine the dynamic global cultural and structural patterns and it is appealing to know how all of that coalesced into creating newer markets.

In addition, the exploration will obviously link back to the concepts of ethnic hegemony, entrepreneurial capital, acculturation, bi-culturalism and so on. British ethnic entrepreneurs are used as exemplar, and the diffusion of their entrepreneurship defines the contextual limit. However, the point has to be made of the volatility of situating ethnic marketing within the margin of 'ethnic minorities', given the evolving notion of 'superdiversity' (Vertovec 2007). Superdiversity underscores a type of complex and dynamic interplay of variables among a growing number of new, small and dispersed multiple-origin, transnationally connected, socio-economically segregated and legally stratified immigrants who have arrived over the last decade in Britain (Vertovec 2007). Even so, it is safe to assume that the term 'ethnic minority' could be a productive operational phrase on the basis that it is how reality is formed institutionally.

Consequently, a number of questions consequently arise. These include: how is ethnic marketing in Britain constructed in pedagogical terms? Does the populist ontology marginalize questions relating to the interaction between marketing and society (using ethnic minority

99

settings as a standpoint)? To what extent does the massed body of knowledge on general marketing help to inform, influence and inspire critical reflections? What are the implications in pressing the boundaries of ethnic marketing thought (promoting epistemological reflexivity and theoretical/methodological pluralism)? How do we plug the 'contextual relevance' issues (e.g. effect of environmental factors) that are well established in the literature given that contexts can and do affect the study and practice of marketing? Essentially, we will be exploring what may be unique about ethnic marketing in the UK and the implications for future research. Broadly, the chapter is arranged into six sections including: contextual re-articulation; the dialectics of ethnic marketing; issues in ethnic marketing; ethnic entrepreneurship congregation; synthesis and discussion; and conclusions.

Contextual re-articulation

Britain, likewise many major European nations such as France, Germany, Sweden and the Netherlands, have tried to integrate immigrants into their societies and managed ethno-cultural plurality using a variety of social and economic approaches. The dominant notion was that encouraging immigrants (mainly ethnic minority groups) into business would afford a veritable platform to achieve their integration into host countries, at least, economically. As a result, nurturing ethnic-owned businesses became a flagship policy of Her Majesty's governments especially during the past decade.

All the same, the relationship between economic activities and social behaviour is not new and has been highlighted in several studies such as those by Karl Marx (e.g. Marx 1964) on the effect of economic activities on the social and cultural system of a society. Nonetheless, the multiplication of research into ethnic assimilation, business development and marketing behaviours in Western industrialized economies appears to assume a sort of convergence. Points of convergence manifest in the integration of migrants and the management of ethno-cultural plurality in the host society through a variety of social and economic approaches.

The most common social frameworks are the pluralist and the assimilation options. Each consists of different possible group interactions and pathways along which group relations might develop. Pluralism indicates groups remain separate and preserve their individual socio-cultural identities over time, whereas assimilation refers to groups coming to share a common culture and the differences between them decreasing. Nevertheless, both concepts have been discredited in some parts of Western Europe. For instance, the failure of the assimilation approach in France has been acknowledged (Silverman 2007); while in Britain and Germany multiculturalism is deemed unsuccessful (Connolly 2010; Lerman 2010).

Research drift

Trajectories of ethnic business development and marketing ethos have been severally focused in research (e.g. Nwankwo *et al.* 1998; Jamal 2005). Some of the works have sought to unravel the variety of motivating factors, growth of key sectors, development and sustenance of ethnic-based networks and cultural capital, and how these are, in turn, harnessed for marketing purposes. Sectoral studies include Kalra's (2000) study conducted on Pakistanis' taxi drivers and takeaways; Bhachu's (2004) description of Indians' women fashion designers and entrepreneurs networks of supply; Madichie's (2007) examination of Nigerians' restaurant sector; and Bagwell's (2008) analysis of Vietnamese nail business.

However, studies on ethnic participation in markets that are not ethno-culturally specific, such as the property market, pharmaceuticals, hotels, information technology (IT) and media remain largely invisible. This is mainly due to the fact that ethnic entrepreneurship studies are by and large mostly embedded and mired in ethnic orientation and sensitivity, that is, particularly focused on ethnic products/services. Nevertheless, research attention is increasingly directed to emerging sectors such as: Ram and Carter's (2003) research on Asian ethnic accountants' that looks at the acceleration of Asians into professional pursuits and Smallbone *et al.*'s (2005) analysis of ethnic entrepreneurs in creative industries and so on. What is apparent is that ethnic markets are now in the ascendancy and controlling some sectors of the economy. It is then the case that ethnic markets generate challenging niches of investigation in many interdisciplinary contexts.

Ethnic market trends

While felt ethnicity remains a solid marketing base in the UK (Jamal *et al.* 2012), the ground is somewhat malleable and shifting in time and space. This, in part, reflects a sort of generalized appreciation of the diffusion of ethnic marketing into the mainstream along the dimensions of integration and multicultural conceptualization. The expectation in assimilation theory is that ethnic marketing would propel ethnic businesses to metamorphose into mainstream enterprise undertakings over a period of time.

In contemporary Britain, the attraction towards ethnic products and markets in recent years has gradually become significant to the extent that ethnic entrepreneurs and entrepreneurship have diffused into the mainstream marketplace. For example, ethnic food is now a growing market in the UK, with estimated sales of US$2.6 billion (approximately £1.75 billion) and accounts for more than half of the market share in Europe (Datamonitor 2005). Recent data on the overall ethnic foods market recorded a 24 per cent increase in sales value between 2007 and 2011, showing a growth rate of a solid 6.6 per cent in 2011 compared with 0.2 per cent of the overall economy (Mintel 2012). Basically, the ethnic market has transformed to a large part of the local economy with broader coverage of urban demands, particularly in big cities. For instance, 7 per cent of the total small and medium enterprises (SMEs) in the UK are minority ethnic group controlled (BMG Research 2013).

More and more ethnic businesses are branching out to and benefiting from visible success and fast growth in fields hitherto uncharted such as private health care, training and self-employed professional lines like accountancy (Ram and Carter 2003). Furthermore, several new energetic ethnic entrepreneurs are engaging in cutting edge of new economy like software manufacturers, IT and business consultants (Castells 2000). Much as the ethnic market/economy is vibrant and on the upward trajectory, it is nevertheless becoming difficult to delineate markets along the ethnic/non-ethnic divide in a number of sectors such as transport, property investments, forecourt/garages, IT and so on.

As a consequence, the influence of ethnic businesses pervades all spheres of British society, including cultural and the food industries. Such businesses are said to be contributing an estimated £20 billion to the UK economy yearly, even when discounting the large corporations such as Tata and Mittal (Nottingham Post 2011). Aside from adding to Britain's cosmopolitan endowment, these groups are shaping its contemporary multicultural pretences while at the same time contributing to its innovativeness and connectedness with the rest of the world.

Research protocol

Marketing has been studied from a variety of perspectives, including industries, companies, communities and clans or at analytical levels such as ideas, concepts, theories or schools of thought (e.g. Golder 2000; Shaw and Jones 2005). Therefore, using an ethnic prism in knowledge production and dissemination enjoys support in the literature. Migration to the UK has become more diffused in recent years as more people are now migrating from other European Union countries as well as from far-flung corners of the world. But this chapter focuses on ethnic groups other than those from the EU/Western world. This is because the issues of ethnicity, identity and acculturation are arguably not as complex for migrating groups from the non-EU/Western world as compared to other groups that have a very different cultural profile (Burton 2000). Within this context is the analysis of the ways in which ethnic market changes and transforms over time. Invariably, what might be perceived and measured as changes in market structure could instead be the dynamics of ethnic cultural adaption or/and mainstream cultural change over time.

Essentially, in order to satisfy the aims of drawing attention to new realities nurtured in a multicultural society such as Britain (in terms of a new ethnic marketing and theoretical imagination) some thematically relevant sectoral studies are appraised. The intention is guided by the logic of 'exploration and classification of some phenomena where accurate information is lacking' (Forcese and Richer 1973, p. 79). Towards this end, three industries (professional services, food and media) in which ethnic groups actively participate are chosen as illustrative templates of the diffusion of general ethnic entrepreneurship in the UK. These templates are presented in the form of sectoral studies assembled from multiple data sources. The professional services and media sectors are selected because they represent a new frontier of ethnic minorities' active participation in supposedly mainstream markets.

On the other hand, the food/catering sector, dominated by ethnic operators, presents a good platform to study the extent of marketing-reach of ethnic businesses. This is relevant because Britain, unlike other European countries, has no strong culinary traditions of its own and seems to have acquired a huge appetite for foreign food (Benedictus 2005). Basically, data are extracted from a variety of sources, including secondary material such as official statistical data, previous reports and sector-specific data gathered from trade sources.

However, as a caveat, this study's protocol is not informed by an 'ethno-divisional' perspective, which has a tendency to differentiate between ethnic minority groups' sectoral/entrepreneurial affinity and business practices. Rather, recent studies (e.g. Basu 2010) have attached greater explanatory weight to the context in which ethnic minority businesses achieve breakthrough into the mainstream's more promising markets. Hence, instead of attempting a static assessment of the experiences of different ethnic groups, this study presents holistic analysis of ethnic minority businesses' diffusion into the mainstream. It is concerned with understanding something of shifting opportunity structure in relation to ethnic minority groups' participation and expansion into the larger and lucrative mainstream base.

The dialectics of ethnic marketing

There are tensions and contestations surrounding the subject of ethnic marketing, and it is imperative to examine some of them for better understanding of issues under discussion. Few of these are analyzed, as below.

The ambivalence of the term 'ethnic minority'

Ethnic marketing could be complicated by the extent of ethnic groups' embeddedness and their cultural assimilation within the mainstream. For instance, some sections, such as new immigrants, may concentrate in enclaves and prefer to stick with their 'home' culture rather than that of the 'host'. Others, such as second or third generation, may be bi-cultural and be more geographically dispersed. This can be problematic in deciphering 'what is' and 'what is not' ethnic marketing. In that sense, there is need to question the stability of the phrase 'ethnic minority': Is there anything like 'ethnic minority' now? As a constructed social reality, ethnicity is considered to be a fluid concept under constant change and reinterpretation whose significance might be influenced by the external environment (Habermas 1994). The vagueness underlining the concept is aptly summed up by Weber (1978, p. 389): 'The whole conception of ethnic groups is so complex and so vague that it might be good to abandon it altogether'.

However, this is not a problem. For analytical purposes, one can still argue that it is relevant to talk of ethnicity and ethnic minorities. This is because ethnicity, just as class or gender, seems to be a central category that shapes people's opportunities in the society. It is the case that in many instances the 'ethnic minority' status often refers to belonging to a category of disadvantage in contemporary Western multi-ethnic societies. From this perspective, it could still be relevant to refer to ethnicity or its perception in the discourse of the 'ethnic minority' as a dividing line between people and a mechanism of social stratification and inequality of opportunities. Even if ethnicity itself is a contested terminology full of intellectual tension because of the fluidity in its usage, it has the potential to have implications for every aspect of marketing theory and practice, for instance, ethnic and tribal loyalties always exist to complicate and compromise (Burton 2000).

Ethnic marketing as an oxymoron

The study of ethnicity in consumption is a recent trend (Ogden *et al.* 2004), but the concept itself remains a subject of shifting interpretations (Brown and Langer 2010). For instance, its derivative, 'ethnic minority' as a concept is de rigueur. In its usage, the concept lumps all non-mainstream groups together, thus suggesting a commonality. But, in the day-to-day usage, the term tends to overstate the significance of similarities while simultaneously understating the differences in ethnic identity of groups. Essentially, ethnicity cannot be reductively defined although it can be phenomenologically described – that is, its conditions can be specified and characterized. Against this background, the ontological boundaries of ethnic marketing are hugely difficult to delineate, especially in the face of the fluidity in migration and integration patterns of the global epoch.

The increase in the amount of temporary, repeated and circulatory migration is reflected in the emergence of transnationalism and transnational communities as new modes of migrant belonging. This trend is highlighted in Castells' (1996, p. 407) depiction of a change in the spatial configuration of the world from 'a space of places' to a 'space of flows'. Basically, transnational communities are groups whose identity is not primarily based on attachment to an exclusive domain. Invariably, migrants' assimilation has been weakened by the proliferation of transnational activities and cross-border flows that stem from globalization such that the frequent and multi-directional flows of people, ideas and cultural symbols are blurring the boundaries between different categories of ethnic groups. Thus, the transformation of material and cultural practices stemming from migration and community formation is directing new forms of mobility and incorporation, especially the advent of transnational communities, multiple identities and multi-layered citizenship (Castles 2002).

Integration and market exchanges

Against the background of Enoch Powell's 'river of blood' diatribe (Graham 2014) and Lord Tebbit's infamous 'cricket test' (Carvel 2004), the issue of ethnic integration in the UK has always been topical. For instance, various opinions still mirror Trevor Phillips' argument that Britain is 'sleepwalking into segregation' (Casciani 2005) and many studies (e.g. Cantle 2008) have demonstrated that ethnic groups in the UK live parallel lives. Invariably, the analysis of market exchanges within the contexts of multiculturalism, acculturation and integration concepts directs attention to the fluidity of the exchange process between the microculture and the dominant culture.

In other words, investigating the ambivalence inherent in contemporary society, exhibited in the tension between convergence and divergence patterns, could help in unpacking the dynamics of ethnic marketing in the UK. For example, aside from the ability to resolve how consumption or market-mediated exchanges unfold, one would be able to unpick whether ethnic market is diffusing into the mainstream, growing in parallel or both. All the same, thriving ethnic markets exist that provide sources of economic independence for many entrepreneurs in contemporary multicultural Britain. It is then the case that individuals' beliefs about the constructs (multiculturalism, assimilation, integration and acculturation) define their state of orientation toward ethnic marketing either as consumers or producers.

This is an important starting point for ethnic marketers and researchers because it will help them in assessing individuals' decision domain and strategic orientation. Furthermore, from a managerial perspective, many mainstream marketers are discovering that exploiting opportunities in ethnic markets could lead to greater success. From that it can be seen that marketers must have an understanding of how minority cultures impact product-specific consumptions by consumers in order to be more effective in reaching their target markets.

Issues in ethnic marketing

Relevant to this paper's discussions are a number of issues and concepts such as ethnic economy (breakout, ethnic identity and business positioning) and entrepreneurial capital. Focusing on them is germane and will enable a deeper perspective on the topic of ethnic marketing.

Ethnic economy

Ethnic economy has been variously defined. Some of the definitions emphasize ethnic-level entrepreneurship (Portes and Bach 1985), composition of co-employers and employees (Bonacich and Modell 1980), importance of ethnic employees' concentration in certain industries (Zhou and Logan 1989), and ethnic enclave (Sanders and Nee 1987). Nevertheless, shared ethnicity is the common thread weaving all these standpoints together (Light *et al.* 1993), such as the predominance of Chinese in the catering sector, or Pakistani in mini-cabbing or Indians cornershops.

However, a useful perspective is offered by Jiobu (1988, p. 353). It introduces the concept of 'ethnic hegemony' referring to 'the situation in which an ethnic group achieves economic control over an important economic arena that interfaces with the majority'. An example abounds in the medical profession as exemplified in the mass recruitment of foreign medical workers into the NHS (Oakeshott 2013). Five provisions underlined ethnic hegemony, these are: an internal labour market, middleman minority activity, ethnic economic control, ethnic saturation and an interface between minority output and majority customers.

In middlemen minority activity, ethnic entrepreneurs assume intermediate positions operating as agents linking ethnic products to consumers and also linking ethnic employers with co-ethnic employees (Bonacich 1973). The Asian grocery businesses in the UK are typical middlemen minority. They interphase between different ethnic groups by marketing their (e.g., White mainstream and Black groups) products. Ethnic economic control alludes to the minority group's assumption of entrepreneurial and managerial roles. Ethnic saturation depicts group members' propensity to concentrate as labour in particular activities (Model 1992). Ethnic concentration is also construed in enclave economy (e.g. Southall, Brixton and Peckham in London). This refers to a large number of co-ethnic businesses in a single economic networked cluster producing particular goods, along with the connected ethnic firms supplying and servicing the cluster. Basu and Werbner (2009) assert that the triadic relationship engendering an ethnic enclave economy is person/good/networked space, and that ethnic enclave economies may be localized or dispersed in different places. Thus, ethnic enclave may involve several different ethnic groups located differentially in the supply line. It is typified by aggressive competition, and underscored by circles of credit and trust.

Deriving from ethnic enclave is the notion of ethnic niche signifying a protected market space that can only be supplied by members of a particular cultural community (Ward 1987). The protected market space alludes to ethnic monopoly of supplies of ethnic particular cultural products such as hair and body care products or preferences for distinct ethnic foods, for instance Chinese cuisine. Ethnic niches are however constrained by the size of the minorities served, as this is very small compared with the overall mainstream market, even with increase in the population of some minorities. Besides, many ethnic minorities are not as rich as others, judging by their unemployment and economic activity rates; this also limits the value of a protected market.

Conversely, and central to the notion of customer-centric marketing, ethnic niches could often compensate for lack of volume/scale by exclusivity and margin. Essentially, researchers have variously suggested that breaking out into serving mainstream markets is the key to expansion and prosperity (Ram and Hillin 1994). However, this process is contingent on the regulatory framework, which can exert considerable pressure on its direction, shape and form. For instance, McEvoy and Hafeez (2009) argue that changes in the UK's regulatory structure often tend to tilt in support of large companies to the detriment of ethnic businesses. A good example is the legislation on Sunday opening hours, which favours large firms (e.g., Tesco and ASDA) against independent small cornershops, thus expanding the competitive intensity of the sector (Friends of the Earth 2005).

Breakout, ethnic identity and business positioning

Despite the overwhelming support for ethnic entrepreneurship breakout concept, a strand of opinion in the literature argues the importance of limiting ethnic business operations within ethnic enclave/economy. This perspective is anchored on the unique opportunities and resources available for ethnic businesses only within the ethnic community social networks and capital, which are based on mutual trust and solidarity deriving from a common ethnic origin (Basu and Werbner 2009). In essence, the authors contend that breaking out of ethnic enclave may be unnecessary for entrepreneurial success. Thus, the point is made that ethnic enclaves can provide viable market segments; meaning, long segmentation strategy, targeting and positioning are strategically driven. For example, Curry Mile in Wilmslow Road in Manchester's Rusholme or Brick Lane in London's Tower Hamlet as a hub for Bangladeshi cuisines.

Moreover, the imperative of expansion (breakout) of ethnic enterprises into the mainstream markets is undermined by difficulties. For instance, problems of ethnic businesses 'breakout' could reflect problems of market acceptance deriving from the cultural specificity of the product/service being offered (Smallbone et al. 2005). Research on ethnic migrants' identity and culture often emphasises the notion that migrants awkwardly negotiate between two cultures. This concept has its origin in the bounded perception of cultures as constituting distinct entities, plainly detached from one another. Ethnic migrants are then assumed to suffer incongruity between their culture and that of the host society (Pécoud 2002). However, the idea of cosmopolitanism speaks to the ability of ethnic entrepreneurs to adopt identities that enable cultural competencies (Vertovec and Rogers 1998) in juggling ethnic identity and business positioning in a socio-economic context characterized by prejudice and economic difficulties.

From a marketing standpoint, ethnic entrepreneurs take advantage of their ethnic solidarity and network to acquire resources and at the same time, through cosmopolitan competencies, position their businesses outside the confines of their ethnic community in order to get in contact and deal with non-ethnic customers. This necessitates knowing these customers' tastes and being able to meet their expectations. Nevertheless, there is a difference between breaking out of local ethnic customer markets, as advocated in the principle of 'breakout' concept, and breaking out of local ethnic factor markets and co-ethnic networks (Basu 2010). An ethnic business may diffuse outside its co-ethnic and local customers' base while remaining attached to its ethnic root through reliance on co-ethnic labour, co-ethnic sources of capital and co-ethnic suppliers. Ethnic entrepreneurs have the tendency of relying on co-ethnic labour, which could also impede growth when more skilled employees are needed to serve market demands (Drori and Lerner 2002).

Ethnic entrepreneurial capital

According to Firkin (2003, p. 65) the 'concept of entrepreneurial capital is based on the total capital that an individual possesses' and the value placed on this fused form of capital. The notion of entrepreneurial capital then suggests that entrepreneurship is engendered through accessibility to financial and non-financial resources. Other non-financial capitals identified by scholars (e.g., Davidsson and Honig 2003; Firkin 2003; Cope *et al.* 2007) include: physical, organizational, technological, human, cultural and social capital of business owners and their firms. Invariably, in competitive marketplace such capitals are employed. Consequently, it is recognized that the assortment and amount of capital available and controlled by entrepreneurs could considerably affect their business experiences and performance (Davidsson and Honig 2003; Firkin 2003).

Bourdieu's (1977) viewpoint on structuralism contributed to the understanding of the relationship between business ownership and entrepreneurial capital. He contends that social phenomena develop from the complex interchange between human interactions and objective and subjective structures. The former comprises resources and capitals such as economic, social, cultural and symbolic, while the latter is created by the subliminal categorizations that individuals use as symbolic prototypes for engaging in and interpreting practical activities. In the emerging social structure, the individual positions are determined by the quantity and types of capital controlled by them, and also by the value assigned to such capital by others. It then follows that the different forms and quantity of capital owned by entrepreneurs may have different values attached to them, possibly resulting in owners possessing similar levels of capital but having different values placed on their entrepreneurial capital. Ultimately these differing values will impact upon their entrepreneurial experiences, possibly producing better opportunities for those entrepreneurs in control of a mix of capitals that is more highly valued (Bourdieu 1977).

However, capitals are deemed convertible; that is, 'each form of capital can be converted from and into other forms of capital' (Firkin 2003, p. 5). The notion of convertibility of capitals and the overlap between them suggests that individuals may possess various forms of capital and it may be difficult to isolate and separate them. But eventually, each form of non-financial capital converts to economic capital, especially the convertibility of social capital into symbolic capital (Bourdieu 1986). For brevity, two apropos capitals, symbolic and cultural capitals are discussed below.

Symbolic capital

Symbolic capital is a form of non-financial resource of the entrepreneurial capital base. Bourdieu (1993, p. 37) describes the concept of symbolic capital as 'being known and recognised and is more or less synonymous with: standing, good name, honour, fame, prestige and reputation'. These are cumulatively regarded as the actor's 'credit of renown' (Bourdieu 1990, p. 120). The credit of renown can be symbolic power through authority, prestige and reputation that opens up new markets (Gergs 2003). Examples can be found in the restaurant sector where the Asians' curry and stir-fries dominate UK's cuisine preferences.

Thus, symbolic capital is defined through its function of mediating power through prestige, and can consist of economic, social or cultural capital. A few studies have indicated some connection between symbolic capital and entrepreneurship; for instance de Clercq and Voronov (2009, p. 400) use the paradox of 'fit in' and 'stand out' to explicate how cultural and symbolic capital influences the ability to gain legitimacy for entrepreneurs; the ability to fit in depending on cultural capital and the ability to stand out on symbolic capital. On their part, Fuller and Tian (2006) investigate the connections between social capital and symbolic capital and responsible entrepreneurship.

Cultural capital

Bourdieu and Passeron's (1979, p. 14) conceptualization of cultural capital contends that apart from economic factors, innate 'cultural habits and dispositions' are essentially important to success. They maintain that culture shares many of economic capital properties and, in particular, cultural habits and dispositions consist of a resource capable of producing profits and potential source of monopoly by individuals and groups. In addition, given the right situation, cultural habits/dispositions can be diffused from one generation to the next (Lareau and Weininger 2003).

Essentially, the concept suggests a familiarity with the dominant culture in a society and exists in three forms: in the embodied state (in the form of long-lasting dispositions of the mind and body), in the objectified state (in the form of cultural artifacts, e.g., food, clothes and music) and in the institutionalized state (a form of objectification that is a criteria for cultural evaluation) (Bourdieu 1986). Rettab (2001) extends and describes the concept as cultural attitudes that act to enrich entrepreneurial competence within a group. Further declaring that these attitudes consist of personal desire for economic independence (a major determinant of migration) and this strengthens the chances of business creation. For instance, the gap between ethnic entrepreneurs and financial institutions could be rooted in the cultural background and group characteristics of immigrants, as well as their attitudes, resulting in both the rejection of outside control over their businesses and the desire to be self-directing and be self-employed (Rettab 2001). Cultural capital is then perceived to have the possibility of being utilized in an entrepreneurial sense to provide goods and services in specific ways and forms that are desired and valued by groups.

Ethnic entrepreneurship congregation

Several ethnic entrepreneurs are to be found in all sectors of the British economy, and a number of them robustly partaking in a variety of businesses serving non-ethnic markets, including gas stations for vehicles, travel/news agencies and retail opticians/pharmacists. Nevertheless, certain ethnic entrepreneurship's sectional congregations are evidenced, for example, Indians and Pakistanis are heavily involved in retailing, especially convenience grocery stores, confectionery, tobacco and newsagents.

The South Asian groups are known to dominate this sector: an area where their assiduousness has been duly noted (Jones *et al.* 1994). The Chinese and Bangladeshis are more renowned in the restaurant trade (Barrett *et al.* 2003). In this sector, ethnic restaurants enjoy a monopoly as they are supposed to be authentic purveyors of ethnic cuisine (although same could not be said of some Italian cuisine, e.g. pizza). This cements their remarkable strong position to manipulate the tastes of their customers, while simultaneously accommodating the cuisine itself to those tastes (Jamal 1996). Pakistanis are strongly represented in transport, with taxi driving as the predominant activity (Cabinet Office 2002). Bangladeshis and Blacks (African Caribbean) are equally prominent in this sector, as taxi business seems a popular example of ethnic minorities' entry to mainstream markets (Bank of England 1999).

Key sectors

Following the trend in ethnic enterprising and marketing, three sectors, media, professional services and catering/food, are clear exemplars of the changing nature of ethnic markets in the UK. Also, the emerging trend towards transnational marketing and cross-border market platforms are particularly interesting because these unfurling developments reveal how ethnic minority marketers are navigating multiple market spaces, sometimes connecting their countries of origin with the UK market space.

The media sector

It is the case that ethnic groups maintain interest in their country of origin, even after years of their settlement in the UK through ethnic media sources and choices (Husband *et al.* 2000). Ethnic media are often deemed to be vital for minorities' empowerment and for nourishing cultural particularity, though it has been claimed that they challenge the domination of mainstream culture (Riggins 1992; Husband 1994). For example, large scale events/festivals attracting tens of thousands among ethnic communities (e.g., Notting Hill Carnival, Diwali, Chinese New Year Festivals, etc.) offer special media appeal for both ethnic and mainstream business communities in the UK. Essentially, the imagination and the mediation of self-representation increasingly take place in media cultures; hence, the media progressively shape identity and diasporic consciousness developments (Jordanova 2001).

Consequently, the popularity of ethnic media in the UK is growing and fragmenting into different segments, for instance, in the last ten years, there have been over fifty Asian broadcasters in the UK at any one time and there are now ten Afro-Caribbean TV channels available to view (de Napoli 2013). New technologies have a direct impact on the expansion and output; the digital switchover that has led to increase in the number of ethnic TV channels is a case in point. There exist some ethnic media with substantial audiences rivalling those of the mainstream (ibid.); popular ones include Zee TV, Choice FM, Sunrise Radio, Spectrum Radio, The Voice and Eastern Eye among others. Relatedly, the popularity of cinema is rising particularly among Asians and Africans. For example, Nollywood (Nigerian film industry) now trails Bollywood as the world's second-largest producer of movies (Chakrabortty *et al.* 2012). Accordingly, cinema and commercial activities surrounding it (e.g., production, marketing, sales and promotion), not only provide investment opportunities for ethnic entrepreneurs but also offer avenues for cross-cultural interaction with the mainstream.

However, the point has to be made that the fragmentation of the media markets due to multiculturalism colliding with technological advancement puts ethnic minorities, more than ever before, in the driver's seat. Also, the ubiquity of satellite television and the internet allows diasporas to maintain contact, thus possibly dampening the pace of acculturation from (reduced) exposure to mainstream from (mainstream) media sources.

Professional services

Ethnic self-employment activities are recorded in particular industries or sectors and mostly in non-culturally specific markets that are often spatially dispersed. Instances of these abound in many professionals sectors such as law, accountancy, general medical practice and those in the leisure, cultural and media industries (Barclays Bank 2006). As illustration, the latest figures from the General Medical Council (GMC) list of registered medical practitioners' shows that 48.1 per cent are from the ethnic minority groups (GMC 2013). Expectedly, generational change is contributing to the emergence of these new areas of ethnic entrepreneurship (Modood *et al.* 1995), especially in business and professional services, hospitality and entertainment and creative industries.

Although some of these sectors attract heavy funding, the intergenerational resource accumulation over time (Janjuha-Jivraj 2005) helps to prop up ethnic ventures in such cases. This generous financial investment is frequently supplied by the business parents of the owner (Ram *et al.* 2003). Invariably, developing and growing sectors of the economy, such as telecoms, software, media, IT or mobile phone technologies, are witnessing increased participation of ethnic entrepreneurs (Deakins and Freel 2003). Probably reflecting the level of acculturation or assimilation of the younger generations in the mainstream, these sectors appear to be popular among second and third generations of immigrants. Their potential (sectors) to bridge ethnic boundaries (i.e. their cross-cultural appeal) could account for ethnic entrepreneurs' growing engagement with them.

Catering/food sector

There is an exceptional growth of ethnic food manufacturing firms in the UK, supplying both ethnic and non-ethnic markets. This market is particularly unique, as it produces the 'entrepreneurial movement' that facilitates a cultural revolution in British eating habits (Basu and Werbner 2009, p. 60). This 'entrepreneurial movement' describes the claim that 'innovations have been the product of an entrepreneurial movement whose members were individually unknown' (Light and Rosenstein 1995, p. 4). The term was coined in reference to the rapid rise in new food consumption habits facilitated by the growth of the fast food industry in the twentieth century. Ethnic restaurants have become ubiquitous in many cities in the UK pandering to the tastes of all and sundry.

The stranglehold of ethnic food on the palate of the British populace is such that its status as 'exotic' became 'common' some time ago. Many Britons are now consuming more Chinese, Thai, Indian, West Indian and Japanese cuisines and buying more foreign garnishes and seasonings to replicate these cuisines at home (Chakrabortty *et al.* 2012). The dominance of Chinese stir-fry and chicken tikka masala as British national dishes in polls over the years (Hills 2012) could be presumed to be testimony to ethnic control of this sector. Essentially, the strong demand in the UK's ethnic food is such that six in ten adults enjoy eating foreign food and 44 per cent of users are continually looking for new and interesting ethnic foods (Mintel 2012). Most popular ethnic foods are flourishing because of their successful adjustment to British taste.

For instance, many Asian cuisines have notably modified the range of foods offered and advanced the alteration of British tastes; for example, curry is now regarded as almost as British as roast beef (Fishlock 1994). This creativity in tweaking ethnic products to accommodate the sensitivity of the mainstream has profound implication for ethnic marketing and business breakout.

Cross-border market platforms

Transnational activities of ethnic entrepreneurs are growing and facilitated by increasing volume of ethnic social networks located outside the boundaries of the host country (Henry *et al.* 2002). These cross-border marketing/business relations by ethnic minorities looking to their countries of origin for new economic opportunities or extend UK-based businesses are currently in vogue (Ojo 2012). Transnational activities, aside from providing the means for ethnic entrepreneurs to adjust and integrate into the host country (Min 2005), also enable them to exploit different markets rather than limiting their businesses to the co-ethnic market (Menzies *et al.* 2007).

By operating both physically and virtually, transnational entrepreneurs participate concurrently in two or more socially embedded environments (Ojo 2012). This enables them to sustain crucial global relations that augment their ability to creatively and economically exploit their resource base. Scholars (e.g. Yeung 2002) have attached the increasing impact of transnational entrepreneurship to the changing nature of international migration and diasporas, and to the intricate nature of international business activities. Essentially, transnational entrepreneurs' efforts to convert, innovate and transform structures simultaneously functioning in two or more distinctive cultural contexts embody entrepreneurial engagements that take advantage of an emergent globalized and interconnected world (Drori *et al.* 2009).

However, this dimension of breaking through into larger markets need not necessarily follow the route of breaking out of ethnic customer markets (Ram and Jones 1998). Ethnic entrepreneurs could spread out to co-ethnic customers in diverse locations. As a result, the notion of market 'break through' contends that ethnic entrepreneurs can supply larger, national or international markets immediately after business start-up and do not necessarily have to 'break out' into mainstream markets at a later period.

Synthesis and discussion

Whereas in the past, ethnic businesses often target ethnic customers, employing ethnic labour and were situated in ethnic enclaves, nowadays many now sell their products and services to all ethnic groups while employing non-ethnic labour and operate anywhere in society. Then again, many enterprises in some sectors (e.g. retail) still cater largely to ethnic customers, especially in cultural items and artifacts that appeal to ethnic desire. Other industrial sectors, such as manufacturing, creative, telecoms and professional services mainly have customers that belong to the majority population. These sectors are now witnessing increasing number of ethnic entrepreneurs, so much so that they now appear to be dominating a few of them; for example, the catering/food (Hills 2012) and taxi service sectors (Bank of England 1999) in the UK. It is then the case that ethnic hegemonized economic arena has been established in particular spheres of the British economy. In these hegemonized arenas ethnic entrepreneurs are in control since the mainstream customers must now deal with them as discrimination is largely absent.

To what can we attribute this trend to? It appears the disadvantage theory argument that ethnic minorities are driven to entrepreneurship because of their marginal social position is unable to offer credible explanation to the observed diffusion of ethnic products and markets into the mainstream. It seems the case that the trigger for new firms' start-ups is as a result of a deliberate and intentional act or a result of rational decision-making. Starting a business has moved beyond the inability to adapt to a social system and occupation of marginal social position by ethnic minorities. Furthermore, current technological developments in internet telecommunication and wireless connectivity are facilitating the expansion of ethnic entrepreneurs businesses to a much larger customer base across several countries, while operating at comparatively low cost. This trend justifies Ram and Jones' (2008) submission that ethnic entrepreneurs need to advance into sectors (e.g., high order retailing, manufacturing and producer services) that extend beyond local ranges to further afield spanning regional, national and even international orbits. The authors regarded this as the ultimate breakout market; entirely mainstream custom neither constrained by locality nor ethnic relationship.

Other cogent factors are identified as steering the breakout process. One of these is the entrepreneurial activities of the second and third generations that are driving the pace of entry into the mainstream markets in many emergent sectors such as information technology, professional services, mobile phone and so forth (Deakins and Freel 2003). One can also infer that expansion into mainstream markets is also strengthened by the increasing economic power of emerging countries such as China and India whose huge investments in the UK are bolstering ethnic entrepreneurship (Nottingham Post 2011) in many sectors. Of note is the observation that only six out of the twenty football clubs in the English Premiership League (2013–2014 season) are wholly owned by the natives, others are fully/part owned by rich individuals among the ethnic minority groups. Lastly, it seems that growing maturity in erstwhile focused sectors is beginning to inspire entrepreneurial diversity (Barclays Bank 2005). This could signify the increasing fluidity in the nature and character of ethnicity and ethnic market in Britain.

Then again, breaking out is not necessarily the panacea to success, since ethnic businesses still have to negotiate survival in the market place like any other SME. Essentially, it is the case that many ethnic businesses (and non-ethnic ventures, admittedly) in the supposedly mainstream sectors (e.g., clothing manufacture and restaurant catering) are frantically struggling for survival (Ram and Jones 2008). The implication seems to be that though market breakout is perhaps a necessity, it is definitely not enough reason for ethnic enterprises to expand and thrive. Other resources are essential, least of which is access to adequate funding (ibid.).

Suffice it to reiterate the difficulties in accessing mainstream finance and effective business support initiatives for certain ethnic groups. Different ethnic groups have different experience in those regards with African Caribbean businesses in particular encountering bigger difficulties than others (ibid.). It is the case that the process of breakout is laboured, with several promising markets proving, in the event, to be damagingly competitive. Also, in general, it must be conceded that too much of ethnic marketing/enterprising is still trapped in declining or otherwise unattractive sectors of the economy where strenuous hard work is required to survive (ibid.).

The opportunities that come in the form of transnational entrepreneurship by ethnic entrepreneurs could be ascribed to a number of trajectories. These include the notion of competitiveness, environmental munificence or nostalgic investment/attraction for country of residence. Thus, by becoming transnational entrepreneurs, ethnic entrepreneurs acquire quite different entrepreneurial roles than other entrepreneurs who are not engaged in cross-border business ventures. By navigating transnational dimension, ethnic entrepreneurs negotiate two diverse environments to create value. This enables them to develop different strategies to circumvent some of the barriers they may encounter in host countries.

In reflection, there is awareness of policy and research related issues, especially as the study exposes the conceptual inadequacy in the current knowledge base of ethnic marketing/ entrepreneurship in the UK. The constant and dynamic changes to which ethnic businesses are subjected have had major impact on their ability to grow and sustain themselves. Hence, there is a need for ethnic marketing/entrepreneurship theories to appreciate the changing dynamics of their fields and challenge existing stereotypes. It is the case that research and policy frameworks are lagging behind the profound ethnic market and entrepreneurial diversification and associated socio-economic integration patterns; but remaining rooted within erstwhile perceptions of ethnic market/entrepreneurship expressed largely in terms of contentious multiculturalism framework.

Conclusions

The chapter presented a conceptual discussion on the issue of ethnic marketing in a multicultural society, in which new realities are evoked as erstwhile ethnic boundaries are becoming blurred. Fundamentally, what is commonly tagged 'ethnic market' is mutating to mainstream market to reflect the phenomenon of globalization in its cultural sense. In essence ethnicity is safely expressed through the successes of ethnic market/entrepreneurship and, by being expressed, it is reinforced. The reinforcement of ethnicity could then account for the vagaries of multiculturalism in societies such as the UK. Although ethnicity can achieve vital functions in the start-up of ethnic ventures, it also tends to become an encumbrance on successful enterprises. Contemporarily, ethnic-transcending business organizations are emerging, but they oscillate between functions; that is, as conveyors of custom on the one hand and heralds of integration on the other. Thus, studying the social consequences of participating in ethnic economy will further clarify and extends the understanding of the role of ethnic economy in the assimilation process.

Invariably, in a research exercise of this nature, some limitations are unavoidable. A major weakness is identified in the study's exclusive attention on ethnic markets and enterprises of migrants from (or background from) the so-called developing/emerging economies. Ethnic minorities' markets and enterprises from Europe (e.g., Poland, Bulgaria) or Americas (e.g., Brazil, Argentina) are excluded. Particularly, analysis of enterprises by new arrivals from 'high-income' countries (e.g., Australia, France, Germany, Japan or USA) could extend our understanding of the characteristics of diversity in the UK's ethnic groups' markets. Sepulveda et al. (2011) assert that their ('high-income' groups) entrepreneurship not only add different important elements in the diversification of entrepreneurial activity in the UK, but also exhibit further differences in terms of types of sector of operation, migratory status and the trajectories of their development.

Some implications become apparent from this study; one, the facade of ethnic market/entrepreneurship study in the developed world is changing and the term 'ethnic entrepreneurs' may be becoming extinct. The distinction between mainstream and ethnic markets/entrepreneurs is becoming blurred, just as it is increasingly difficult to draw neat boundaries within ethnic groups. Second, the fluidity surrounding contemporary global epoch is such that the shape and form of entrepreneurship and entrepreneurial phenomena remain indeterminate and speculative. This creates problems and prospects; emerging vistas and 'newer challenges' apposite for engaging researchers' attention for the foreseeable future. In other words, areas for further research exist in the necessity for marketers to rethink strategies that take cognizance of the volatility in the ethnoscape of contemporary Britain, and in the need for the academia to react to the same. It behoves researchers to arrange a sort of ontological denaturalization, through offering alternative representations of marketing and effectively unpacking the cultural syncretism and hegemonic power of contemporary mainstream discourse.

References

Altinay, L. (2010) 'Marketing orientation of small ethnic minority-owned hospitality firms'. *International Journal of Hospitality Management*, 20: 140–56.

Appadurai, A. (1996) *Modernity at Large: Cultural Dimensions of Globalization*. Minnesota, MN: University of Minnesota Press.

Bagwell, S. (2008) 'Transnational family networks and ethnic minority business development: The case of Vietnamese nail-shops in the UK'. *International Journal of Entrepreneurial Behaviour & Research*, 14(6): 377–94.

Bank of England (1999) *The Financing of Ethnic Minority Firms in the United Kingdom: A Special Report*. London: Bank of England.

Barclays Bank (2005) *Black and Minority Ethnic Business Owners: A Market Research Perspective*. London: Barclays Bank.

Barclays Bank (2006) *Asian Entrepreneurs in the UK*. London: Barclays Bank.

Barrett, G., Jones, T. and McEvoy, D. (2003) 'United Kingdom: Severely constrained entrepreneurialism'. In *Immigrant Entrepreneurs: Venturing Abroad in the Age of Globalization*, edited by R. Kloosterman and J. Rath. Oxford: Berg, pp. 101–22.

Basu, A. (2010) 'From "break out" to "breakthrough": Successful market strategies of immigrant entrepreneurs in the UK'. *International Journal of Entrepreneurship*, 14: 59–81.

Basu, D. and Werbner, P. (2009) 'Who wants to be a millionaire? Gendered entrepreneurship and British South Asian women in the culture industries'. *Revue Europeenne des Migrations Internationales*, 25(3): 53–77.

Berlin, I. (1991), *The Crooked Timber of Humanity: Chapters in the History of Ideas*. Waukegan: Fontana Press.

Benedictus, L. (2005) 'Every race, colour, nation and religion on Earth.' *The Guardian*. Available at: http://www.theguardian.com/uk/2005/jan/21/britishidentity1.

Bhachu, P. (2004) *Dangerous Designs: Asian Women Fashion the Diaspora Economies*. London: Routledge.

BMG Research, (2013) *2012 Small Business Survey: Employers Report*. London: Department for Business, Innovation and Skills.

Bonacich, E. (1973) 'A Theory of Middleman Minorities'. *American Sociological Review*, 37: 547–59.

Bonacich, E. and Modell, J. (1980) *The Economic Basis of Ethnic Solidarity*. Berkeley, CA: University of California Press.

Bourdieu, P. (1977) *Outline of a Theory of Practice*. Cambridge, UK: Cambridge University Press.

Bourdieu, P. (1986) 'The forms of capital'. In *Handbook of Theory and Research for the Sociology of Education*, edited by J. Richardson. New York, NY: Greenwood, pp. 241–58.

Bourdieu, P. (1990) *The Logic of Practice*. Cambridge, MA: Polity Press.

Bourdieu, P. (1993) *Social Sense*. Frankfurt: Suhrkamp.

Bourdieu, P. and Passeron, J. C. (1979) *The Inheritors: French Students and their Relations to Culture*. Chicago, IL: University of Chicago Press.

Brown, G. K. and Langer, A. (2010) 'Conceptualizing and measuring ethnicity'. *Oxford Development Studies*, 38(4): 411–36.

Brownlie, D., Saren, M., Whittington, R. and Wensley, R. (1994) 'The new marketing myopia: Critical perspectives on theory and research in marketing – Introduction'. *European Journal of Marketing*, 28(3): 6–12.

Burton, D. (2000) 'Ethnicity, identity and marketing: A critical review'. *Journal of Marketing Management*, 16: 853–77.

Cabinet Office (2002) 'Ethnic minorities in the labour force'. Interim Analytical Report, Performance and Innovation Unit. London: The Stationery Office.

Cantle, T. (2008) *Community Cohesion: A New Framework for Race & Diversity*. London: Palgrave Macmillan.

Carvel, J. (2004) 'Tebbit's cricket loyalty test hit for six'. *The Guardian*. Available at: http://www.theguardian.com/uk/2004/jan/08/britishidentity.race.

Casciani, D. (2005) 'Analysis: Segregated Britain?'. *BBC News*. Available at: http://news.bbc.co.uk/1/hi/uk/4270010.stm.

Castles, S. (2002) 'Migration and community formation under conditions of globalization'. *International Migration Review*, 36(4): 1143–68.

Castells, M. (1996) *The Rise of The Network Society*. Oxford: Blackwell Publishers.

Castells, M. (2000) *End of Millennium*. Oxford: Blackwell.

Chakrabortty, A., Sims, J. M. and Shabi, S. (2012) *2012 Multicultural Britain*. London: IPA.

Connolly, K. (2010) 'Angela Merkel declares death of German multiculturalism'. *The Guardian*. 18 October 2010, p. 16.

Cope, J., Jack, S. and Rose, M. B. (2007) 'Social capital and entrepreneurship: An introduction'. *International Small Business Journal*, 25(3): 213–19.

Datamonitor (2005) *Insights into Tomorrow's Ethnic Food and Drinks Consumers*. Available at: http://www. datamonitor.com/.

Davidsson, P. and Honig, B. (2003) 'The role of social and human capital among nascent entrepreneurs'. *Journal of Business Venturing*, 18: 301–31.

de Clercq, D. and Voronov, M. (2009) 'The role of cultural and symbolic capital in entrepreneurs' ability to meet expectations about conformity and innovation'. *Journal of Small Business Management*, 47(3): 398–420.

de Napoli, J. (2013) 'Ignored: The 14% of consumers big firms do not target'. *The Guardian*. Available at: http://www.theguardian.com/media-network/media-network-blog/2013/jan/16/british-advertisers-ignore-ethnic-minorities.

Deakins, D. and Freel, M. (2003) *Entrepreneurship and Small Firms*, Third edition. London: McGraw-Hill.

Drori, I. and M. Lerner (2002) 'The dynamics of limited breaking out: The case of the Arab manufacturing businesses in Israel'. *Entrepreneurship and Regional Development*, 14: 135–54.

Drori, I., Honig, B. and Wright, M. (2009) 'Transnational entrepreneurship: An emergent field of study'. *Entrepreneurship Theory and Practice*, 33(5): 1001–22.

Dwek, R. (1997) 'Losing the Race'. *Marketing Business*, March: 10–15.

Firat, A. and Dholakia, N. (1989) 'Rewriting marketing history: Why?' *Proceedings of the 4th Conference on Historical Research in Marketing and Marketing Thought*. April 29–May 1, pp. 107–19.

Firkin, P. (2003) 'Entrepreneurial capital'. In *Entrepreneurship: New Perspectives in a Global Age*, edited by A. de Bruin and A. Dupuis. Aldershot: Ashgate: 57–75.

Fishlock, T. (1994) 'Hot Spots'. *The Telegraph Magazine*, 23 July.

Forcese, D. and Richer, S. (1973) *Social Research Methods*. Englewood Cliffs, NJ: Prentice-Hall.

Friends of the Earth (2005) 'Briefing: Good neighbours? Community impacts of supermarkets'. *Friends of the Earth*. Available at: http://www.foe.co.uk/sites/default/files/downloads/good_neighbours_community.pdf.

Fuller, T. and Tian, Y. (2006) 'Social and symbolic capital and responsible entrepreneurship: An empirical investigation of SME narratives'. *Journal of Business Ethics*, 67(3): 287–304.

Fullerton, R. (1988) 'Modern Western marketing as a historical phenomenon: Theory and application'. In *Historical Perspectives in Marketing*, edited by T. Nevett and R. Fullerton. Lexington, MA: Lexington Books, pp. 71–89.

Gbadamosi, A. (2012) 'Acculturation: An exploratory study of clothing consumption among Black African women in London (UK)'. *Journal of Fashion Marketing and Management*, 16(1): 5–20.

Gergs, H. J. (2003) 'Economic, social, and symbolic capital'. *International Studies of Management and Organisation*, 33(2): 22–48.

GMC, (2013) 'List of registered medical practitioners' Statistics'. *General Medical Council*. Available at: http://www.gmc-uk.org/doctors/register/search_stats.asp.

Golder, Peter N. (2000) 'Historical method in marketing research with new evidence on long-term market share stability'. *Journal of Marketing Research*, 37: 156–72.

Graham, G. (2014) 'Nigel Farage: "The basic principle" of enoch powell's river of blood speech is right'. *The Telegraph*. Available at: http://www.telegraph.co.uk/news/uknews/immigration/10552055/Nigel-Farage-the-basic-principle-of-Enoch-Powells-River-of-Blood-speech-is-right.html.

Habermas, J. (1994) 'Struggles for recognition in the democratic constitutional state'. In *Multiculturalism*, edited by A. Gutman. Princeton, NJ: Princeton University Press.

Henry, N., McEwan, C. and Pollard, J. (2002) 'Globalisation from below: Birmingham – Post-colonial workshop of the world?' *Area*, 34: 117–27.

Hills, S. (2012) 'Vindawho? Chicken tikka masala knocked off top spot by chinese stir-fry as Britain's favourite dish'. *The Daily Mail*. Available at: http://www.dailymail.co.uk/news/article-2089796/Britains-favourite-dish-Chicken-tikka-masala-knocked-spot-Chinese-stir-fry.htm.

Husband, C. (1994) *A Richer Vision: The Development of Ethnic Minority Media in Western Democracies*. Paris: UNESCO.

Husband, C., Beattie, L. and Markelin, L. (2000), 'The key role of minority ethnic media in multiethnic societies: Case study, UK'. *Research Paper for the International Media Working Group Against Racism and Xenophobia (IMRAX)* and The International Federation of Journalists (IFJ).

Jamal, A. (1996) 'Acculturation: The symbolism of ethnic eating among contemporary British consumers'. *British Food Journal*, 98(10): 14–28.

Jamal, A. (2005) 'Playing to win: An explorative study of marketing strategies of small ethnic retail entrepreneurs in the UK'. *Journal of Retailing and Consumer Services*, 12: 1–13.

Jamal, A., Peattie, S. and Peattie, K. (2012) 'Ethnic minority consumers' responses to sales promotions in packaged food market'. *Journal of Retailing and Consumer Services*, 19: 98–106.

Janjuha-Jivraj, S. (2005) *Succession in Asian Family Firms*. Basingstoke: Palgrave.

Jiobu, R. M. (1988) 'Ethnic hegemony and the Japanese of California'. *American Sociological Review*, 53: 353–67.

Jones, T., McEvoy, D. and Barrett, G. (1994) 'Labour intensive practices in the ethnic minority firm'. In *Employment, the Small Firm and the Labour Market*, edited by J. Atkinson and D. Storey. London: Routledge, pp. 172–205.

Jordanova, D. (2001) 'Diasporas-in-the-making: Global cinematic representations of new migrations'. Presentation at BFI Conference: Global Village or Global Image? July 2001.

Kalra, V. S. (2000) *From Textile Mills to Taxi Ranks: Experiences of Migration, Labour and Social Change*. Aldershot: Ashgate.

Lareau, A. and Weininger, E. B. (2003) 'Cultural capital in educational research: A critical assessment'. *Theory and Society*, 32: 567–606.

Lerman, A. (2010) 'In Defence of Multiculturalism'. *The Guardian*. Available at: http://www.guardian.co.uk/commentisfree/2010/mar/22/multiculturalism-blame-culture-segregation.

Light, I. and Rosenstein, C. (1995) *Race, Ethnicity and Entrepreneurship in Urban America*. New York, NY: Aldene de Gruyter.

Light, I., Sabagh, G., Bozorgmehr, M. and Der-Martirsian, C. (1993) 'Internal ethnicity in the ethnic economy'. *Ethnic and Racial Studies* 16(4): 581–97.

Madichie, N. (2007) 'Nigerian restaurants in London: Bridging the experiential perception/expectation gap'. *International Journal of Business and Globalisation*, 1(2): 258–71.

Marx, K. (1964) *Selected Writings in Sociology and Social Philosophy*. London: McGraw-Hill.

McEvoy, D. and Hafeez, K. (2009) 'Ethnic minority entrepreneurship in Britain'. *Management & Marketing*, 4(1): 55–64.

Menzies, T. V., Filion, L. J., Brenner, G. A. and Elgie, S. (2007) 'Measuring ethnic community involvement: Development and initial testing of an index.' *Journal of Small Business Management*, 45(2): 267–82.

Min, P. G. (2005). *Asian Americans: Contemporary Trends and Issues*. Thousand Oaks, CA: Sage Publications.

Mintel (2012) *Ethnic Food UK 2012 Report*. London: Mintel Group.

Model, S. (1992) 'The ethnic economy: Cubans and Chinese reconsidered'. *The Sociological Quarterly*, 33(1): 63–82.

Modood, T., Virdee, S. and Metcalf, H. (1995) *Asian Self-Employment in Britain: The Interaction of Culture and Economics*. London: Policy Studies Institute.

Nottingham Post (2011) 'Ethnic minorities make significant contribution to local and national economy'. *Nottingham Post*. Available at: http://www.nottinghampost.com/Ethnic-minorities-make-signifiant-contribution/story-13713696-detail/story.html.

Nwankwo, S. (1996) 'Marketing in diversity: Ethnography of two cultures'. In *Proceeding of the Multicultural Marketing Conference*, edited by P. Choudhury. Switzerland: Springer International Publishing, pp. 359–64.

Nwankwo, S. (2004) 'Apocalypse in marketing practice: Uncovering socio-cultural embeddedness of market orientation African economies'. *International Journal of Applied Marketing*, 3(1): 58–77.

Nwankwo, S., Aiyeku, J. and Ogbuehi, A. (1998) 'The marketing challenge of multiculturalism: An exploratory study'. *Journal of International Marketing and Exporting*, 3(1): 47–61.

Nwankwo, S. and Lindridge, A. (1998) 'Marketing to ethnic minorities in Britain'. *Journal of Marketing Practice: Applied Marketing Science*, 4(7): 200–16.

Oakeshott, I. (2013) '4,000 foreign staff join NHS in the last year'. *The Daily Mail*. Available at: http://www.dailymail.co.uk/health/article-299257/4-000-foreign-staff-join-NHS-year.html#ixzz2dp7H0S5k.

Ogden, D. T., Ogden, J. R. and Schau, H. J. (2004) 'Exploring the impact of culture and acculturation on consumer purchases decisions: Toward a microcultural perspective'. *Academy of Marketing Science Review*, 8(3): 1–22.

Ojo, S. (2012) 'Ethnic enclaves to diaspora entrepreneurs: A critical appraisal of black British Africans' transnational entrepreneurship in London'. *Journal of African Business*, 13(2): 145–156.

Patterson, S. (1969) *Immigration and Race Relations in Britain*. London: Oxford University Press.

Pécoud, A. (2002) '"*Weltoffenheit Schafft Jobs*": Turkish entrepreneurship and multiculturalism in Berlin'. *International Journal of Urban and Regional Research*, 26(3): 494–507.

Portes, A. and Bach, R. L. (1985) *Latin Journey*. Berkeley, CA: University of California Press.

Ram, M. and Carter, S. (2003) 'Paving professional futures: Ethnic minority accountants in the United Kingdom'. *International Small Business Journal*, 21(1): 55–71.

Ram, M. and Hillin, G. (1994) 'Achieving "break-out": Developing mainstream ethnic minority business'. *Small Business Enterprise and Development*, 1: 15–21.

Ram, M. and Jones, T. (1998) *Ethnic Minorities in Business*, Small Business Research Trust Report. Milton Keynes: Open University Business School.

Ram, M., Smallbone, D., Deakins, D. and Jones, T. (2003) 'Banking on "break-out": finance and the development of ethnic minority businesses'. *Journal of Ethnic and Migration Studies*, 29(4): 663–81.

Rettab, B. (2001) 'The emergence of ethnic entrepreneurship: A conceptual framework'. *EIM/Business & Policy Research*. Netherlands: Zoetermeer.

Riggins, S. H. (1992) *Ethnic Minority Media: An International Perspective*. London: Sage.

Sanders, J. M. and Nee, V. (1987) 'Limits of ethnic solidarity in the enclave economy'. *American Sociological Review*, 52: 745–67.

Sepulveda, L., Syrett, S. and Lyon, F. (2011) 'Population superdiversity and new migrant enterprise: The case of London'. *Entrepreneurship & Regional Development*, 23(7–8): 469–97.

Shaw, E. H. and Jones, D. G. B. (2005) 'A history of schools of marketing thought'. *Marketing Theory*, 5(3): 239–81.

Silverman, M. (2007) 'The French Republic unveiled'. *Ethnic and Racial Studies*, 30(4): 628–42.

Smallbone, D., Bertotti, M., & Ekanem, I. (2005) 'Diversification in ethnic minority business: The case of Asians in London's creative industries'. *Journal of Small Business and Enterprise Development*, 12(1): 41–56.

Smith, L. (2006) 'Black entrepreneurs break through the red line'. *The Guardian*. Available at: http://www.theguardian.com/money/2006/may/15/discriminationatwork.discrimination.

Vertovec, S. (2007) 'Super-diversity and its implications'. *Ethnic and Racial Studies*, 29(6): 1024–54.

Vertovec, S. and Rogers, A. (1998) 'Introduction.' In *Muslim European Youth: Reproducing Ethnicity, Religion, Culture*, edited by S. Vertovec and A. Rogers. Aldershot: Ashgate, pp. 1–24.

Ward, R. (1987) 'Ethnic enterprises in Britain and Europe'. In *Entrepreneurship in Europe*, edited by R. Coffee, and R. Scase. London: Croom Helm, pp. 83–104.

Watson, M. (1992) 'Researching minority'. *Journal of the Market Research Society*, 3(4): 337–44.

Weber, M. (1978) *Economy and Society*. Berkeley, CA: University of California Press.

Yeung, H. (2002) 'Entrepreneurship in international business: An institutional perspective'. *Asia Pacific Journal of Management*, 19(1): 29–61.

Zhou, M. and Logan, J. R. (1989) 'Returns on human capital in ethnic enclaves'. *American Sociological Review*, 54: 809–20.

8

An ethnoconsumerist approach to Hispanic small business' adoption of internet technology

Cecilia Ruvalcaba and Alladi Venkatesh

Introduction

Small businesses need simple solutions that are timely and efficient. As new technologies come into play, small businesses find new market opportunities and challenges. Apart from cost and resource considerations involved in Information Technology (IT) related operations, small businesses lack qualified IT staff and the resources to train employees on new technologies. In this digital age, these issues become critical especially because of the resulting digital divide, the gap between those with access to information, the 'haves', and those without access, the 'have-nots', that leaves certain segments (e.g., small businesses, minorities, low-income consumers) out of current trends (Companie 2001; Peterson and Dibrell 2002; U.S. Congress 2012). Studies suggest the gap among ethnic minorities is larger than that for the dominant culture (Hoffman *et al.* 1997; Zickuhr and Smith 2012). Thus it is important to understand not only small business adoption of such technologies, but the adoption and use of such technologies by minority-owned small businesses. This is indeed the focus of this chapter.

Hispanic-owned small businesses are a significant contributor to the U.S. economy and to the overall Hispanic community by increasing access to capital (Light and Gold 2000). According to the Small Business Administration, Hispanic small businesses earn nearly $300 billion in annual revenue by approximately two million businesses (U.S. Bureau of the Census 2012). The number of Hispanic small businesses is expected to increase 60 per cent to 4 million, and generate a combined $550 billion in revenue by 2014. In response to these impressive statistics, it is important for researchers to study how emerging trends in IT impact these businesses (Middleton and Byus 2011).

The purpose of this study is to investigate internet and e-commerce related business opportunities and challenges facing an ethnic business community – Hispanic-owned small businesses located in the South Western region of the United States, specifically in Southern California. We look to understand what technological tools are used, how these tools are integrated into their business operations and what barriers to adoption are faced. In understanding how technology is used by Hispanic small businesses, we look to identify the challenges in adoption and thus provided policy implications and recommendations for marketing, or, more specifically, ethnic marketing. The research questions we look to address are: (1) What are the current practices and needs of Hispanic small business regarding internet-based operations, specifically as they relate to business development and transactions, customer contacts, online

117

communications, scheduling, calendaring and event planning?; (2) What gaps exist among Hispanic small businesses and how can these gaps be addressed?; (3) What are the cultural issues that arise in Hispanic small businesses adoption of information technology? and (4) What are the policy implications and recommendations?

We use an ethnoconsumerism (Venkatesh 1995; Meamber and Venkatesh 2000) and ethno-marketing perspective (Korzenny and Korzenny 2005; Morse 2009) to address these research questions. Our study is based on empirical work conducted in Southern California from 2009 to 2010. We chose this region based on several factors: high proportion of Hispanic population and Hispanic small businesses, digitally disadvantaged nature of the business community and the expected growth of the population and issues concerning access to technology and resources. The remainder of this chapter will proceed as follows. First we provide a review of our theoretical framework. Then we describe the process of our current study and present our findings. Lastly we provide implications and recommendations for future research.

Ethnoconsumerism, ethnic marketing and Hispanic small businesses

Ethnoconsumerism and ethnic marketing

There has been much discussion on how to study markets as culturally constituted economic entities (Elyachar 2005; Burton 2009). Venkatesh (1995), and later elaborated by Meamber and Venkatesh (2000), proposed ethnoconsumerism as a theoretical and methodological approach to the study of market and consumption culture. The focus of this methodology is to gain an understanding of the subject's point of view while at the same time identifying the contextual/environmental factors contributing to their position, what is described as the field view and the text view respectively. Adding an ethno-marketing perspective to the ethnoconsumerism approach permits us to study (business) culture, not merely as providing the context for the study of market/consumption practices but to study market behaviours as culturally constituted (Korzenny and Korzenny 2005). Being members of a shared cultural group structures inter-actions in the market (Barth 1998). Understanding how these structures govern marketplace activities will allow us to construct marketing activities to fit within these inherent conceptions. In this context we also refer to Peñaloza's (1994) study on the Mexican immigrant population in the US, which examines acculturation issues in reference to the dominant culture. Using Southern California as the site for her study, Peñaloza analyzes how culture constitutes the Mexican immigrant's market behaviours as they adjust to their new environment. For the purposes of this study, the ethnoconsumerism approach is easily adaptable to a business setting as the foundation of the methodology is not context-specific.

In discussing cultural issues relating to ethnic marketing and consumption, we are faced with a variety of concepts and terminology such as 'cross-cultural marketing', 'comparative studies' and 'cultural analysis'. These are related but do not have the same meaning (Burton 2009). What is common to all these approaches is that the focus is on 'culture' or an ethnic segment and can include marketplace or consumption practices, customs, value systems, social arrangements, communities and institutional histories, meaning systems and ethnic configurations associated with any population or cultural group under study. Ethnicity is a complex construct which can include any number of identifiers. What originated as a term to define individuals who were not part of the dominant majority (Nash 1989) is now used to describe a group which identifies as having a shared set of social and cultural identifiers (Zmud and Arce 1992). The growth of ethnic market segments require ethnicity no longer be treated as a variable to be checked-off in a box. It is a complex aggregation of factors that are unique to each individual market segment and can be both homogeneous and heterogeneous (Deshpandé *et al.* 1986). Therefore ethnicity is dynamic and influenced by both the internal individual and its external environment (Stayman and Deshpandé 1989).

Focusing on an ethnicity as a vital influence on individuals actions is not new (Hirschman 1981; Stayman and Deshpandé 1989; Holland and Gentry 1999) though most of these studies focus on the consumer. Studies on marketing to these ethnic markets have looked at issues such as the differences within and among ethnic markets (Hirschman 1981; Deshpandé *et al.* 1986), consumers reaction to targeted marketing using ethnic cues (Deshpandé and Stayman 1994; Holland and Gentry 1999), assimilation of the ethnic consumer in comparison with the dominant market (Wallendorf and Reilly 1983), and acculturation of the marketer to the ethnic market (Peñaloza and Gilly 1999). This study looks to add another perspective by focusing on small businesses – more specifically, Hispanic small businesses – using the foundations of the ethnoconsumerist framework to identify ethnic marketing implications. Doing so will help us gain a cultural understanding of ethnic small business owners adoption of IT into their business practices.

Hispanic small businesses – some trends and cultural issues

Hispanic small businesses in the US can be contextualized in terms of their ethnic identities, acculturation and business practices (Lofstrom 2009). Due to their growing size and significant contribution to the U.S. economy, this is a growing sector that requires attention. Although there are some resources for Hispanic small businesses, options for this market are currently very limited, but are growing. There are a number of websites (www.sba.gov; www.nfib.com) designed to serve this community and provide advice on how to startup, manage and grow one's business. These include discussions on the different types of technology out there, but there is very little mention on how to actually use this technology. What is found on all of these websites is how to utilize one's network to make a successful business, a theme that seems to echo throughout the community. The lack of available resources is consistent with Light and Gold's (2000) discussion of the differences among varying amounts of success by ethnic entrepreneurs. Access to financial, human, social and cultural capital is a product of class and ethnic resources. Ethnic economies lacking such capital, such as the Hispanic market, will struggle to survive.

Training programs and tutorials are rather scarce and there seems to be a definite need for such series to educate business owners. However, the small number of such programs may be due to the fact that there is very little research on Hispanic small businesses and their needs, technology or otherwise. We know that ethnicity influences consumption decisions (Stayman and Deshpandé 1989; Hirschman 1981) and research has shown that the Hispanic culture differs from non-Hispanics in the US (Valencia 1989). For example, although there is growth in consumption of technologies such as cell phones by Hispanics in the US (Nielsen 2012), internet usage still lags compared to non-Hispanics and the differences are even greater once country of birth and education are considered (Pew Hispanic Center 2009). When it comes to business transactions, Hispanics are more likely to do business with someone who was referred to them through a social connection (Hofstede *et al.* 2010). Lastly, it is estimated that the majority of the Hispanic market speaks Spanish at home; therefore language is also an important variable when dealing with the Hispanic consumer (Pew Hispanic Center 2009). Though these studies give us an overall look at the make up of the Hispanic market, it is important to gain deeper insight into how consumption decisions are impacted by cultural variables such as language and community. The research outlined in this chapter tries to fulfill this gap.

Methodology

For the purposes of our study, twenty Hispanic-owned small businesses in Southern California were selected from a larger list provided to us by the Hispanic Chamber of Commerce of Orange County. These businesses were selected based on consultations with the Hispanic Chamber of Commerce and on the type of business in an effort to acquire an adequate representation of the larger community of small businesses. We conducted site visits and in-depth interviews of the businesses on a one-to-one basis. Interviews lasted approximately ninety minutes and took place at either the interviewee's place of business or a local coffee shop. All interviews were tape recorded, transcribed and analyzed using the qualitative data analysis software NVIVO.

Interview questions

Interview questions revolved around technology use, as that was the main area of focus, but along with the IT questions we included questions regarding issues of technology use and adoption by this specific ethnic community (Appendix 8.1). In probing these questions further we are able to get at certain cultural intricacies that would have not appeared had this been done in a survey format. The ethnoconsumerism approach encourages the researcher to investigate at the micro level in order to gain an intracultural understanding while also paying mind to the meso-level factors to gain a cross-cultural understanding and ideally be able to gain a macro-level view through a combination of field and textual understanding. In this case, the micro-level questions focused specifically on the participant's technology use while the meso-level questions looked to understand the cultural influences of use by the Hispanic community.

Participants

A wide of range of businesses were interviewed from a mortgage company serving the Spanish-speaking California residents to a DJ/entertainment service company (see Figure 8.1). The average business had ten employees and had been in business for seven years. Of the participants interviewed, 75 per cent of them were male and the rest female. Nearly all of our interviewees (93 per cent) were owners/presidents/CEOs. They had an average of six computers and two laptops, with a median of one computer and one laptop. One-third of the companies conducted business predominantly in Spanish.

Findings

User typologies

Previous work on technology adoption and use allows us to define such use along a continuum from limited to intense users of technology (Shih and Venkatesh 2004). Similarly, we use the Use-Diffusion framework to define the categories of IT users from our sample.

Intense users

Intense users of technology were those that are ahead of the technology curve. These businesses were early adopters of technology and use it effectively to enhance their business. Only three of our participants were in this category. These businesses had integrated the use of technology into their daily operations – so much so that their business would not be able to run without the

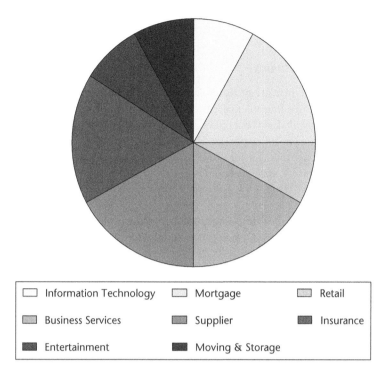

Figure 8.1   Types of businesses

use of computers or the internet. The majority of their business operations and communications with business partners and customers were done through the internet.

Specialized users

We identified six of our participants as specialized users of technology. These businesses used computer and internet technology to assist their daily operations but these technologies were not fully integrated into the business. Use of these technologies was reserved for specific activities such as managing their web presence and use of email. Most of their business operations and communications were done either in person or through printed communication.

Limited users

The majority of our informants were behind the curve of technology use. Computer and internet use was limited to checking email and, on occasion, doing research on their industry. Though some did have a website, basic users relied solely on personal, face-to-face communication.

Use of technology

The participants discussed three main uses of technology and the internet in their business: to enhance their business processes, to market their business online and to stay connected with their customers. Though the level integration of technology into these processes varied among the different groups, their goal was the same. They each look to find a way to enhance their business processes with minimal cost.

Supporting business operations

The participants discussed their use of technology to support business operations. Uses ranged from simple tasks, such as sending an email, to more complex tasks, such as bookkeeping. As an intense user of technology, Rafael Garcia (pseudonym) runs the majority of his business through his computer. As a company that provides Hispanic businesses with technical assistance and guidance for growth, it is critical for him to be at the cutting edge of technology. Vital to his business operations are the use of a variety of tools that assist with file sharing, instant messaging, video conferencing, online training, bookkeeping and contact management. Specialized users will also use their computers for complex tasks, but on a less regular basis. On the other hand, light users use their computers for simple tasks and personal use. Their business use is limited to email and one or two other use(s), such as conducting research.

Marketing activities online

Use of technology for marketing purposes was also a prevalent theme from interviewees. The extent of a web presence and use of analytical tools varied considerably depending on level of technology use. Intense users of technology participated in online advertising in addition to having a web presence through a company website. These users had sophisticated websites that offered a variety of services and made use of web analytics. In contrast, specialized users did have a web presence, but did not utilize analytic tools to measure the effectiveness of their website traffic. As a marketing consultant, Fernando Lopez (pseudonym) uses the internet to promote his services through the use of a website and blog. He had never heard the term 'web analytics', but he does some basic analytics to get an idea of who subscribes to his email list. Fernando is not aware how many subscribers are on his list are actually Hispanic, but he can sometimes tell from their email address. Any data mining he does stay in his head and he does not have a system of how to better target his market segment. Specialized users do not participate in or fully understand the concept of web advertisements or how to incorporate this marketing tool into their traditional marketing mix. As for limited users, some may have a website but do not measure its effectiveness. They generally prefer to do business in person, thus minimizing the centrality of a web presence to the success of the business.

Communicating with customers

The majority of computer uses discussed by informants were directed at methods of communicating with customers. Whether through teleconferencing or simply by email, individuals stressed the importance of staying connected with their customers. Businesses that were ahead of the curve had a wider variety of methods they used to communicate with customers. Those who integrated technology with their business, such as Rafael, had moved to mostly paperless communication processes. With business partners spread all over the country (one is even located in Mexico), Rafael relied heavily on internet-based networking. His company has a Virtual Private Network (utilizing FTP) for sharing files, and has championed innovative communications such as free-web conferencing. Although he used these technologies heavily in order to communicate with his business partners, Mr. Garcia relied primarily on phone and email communications to reach his clients. Similarly, Fernando Lopez also relied heavily on email communication to reach his customers. As a specialized user of technology, Fernando still relied heavily on paper, although he had adopted some paperless processes. His primary method of communication with customers was through an email service, which allows him to send out weekly email blasts to a subscriber list of 6000+. He did not use the more sophisticated methods of communication, such as Rafael Garcia, but expressed a desire to integrate more technologically advanced methods of communication. Limited users such as Maria Rocha (pseudonym), an insurance salesperson, did use email but mostly to communicate with family and friends and not for business.

Barriers to use

Throughout the interviews, we noted that although some of these businesses had the technological resources available to them, they were not adopting them into their business processes. In probing further, we found several issues hindering technology and internet usage that kept coming up in almost all interviews. The main issues were: staying connected with the community, the power of word-of-mouth, the trust in IT mediums and the risk of implementing IT systems. These issues were discussed by all the interviewees, but the level of problem varied between the different levels of technology adoption and use.

Staying connected with the community

The most prominent issue was maintaining a social connection with their customers. Personal interaction in community-based cultures, such as the Hispanic culture, are a priority (Peterson and Dibrell 2002). As Hispanic small businesses whose client base is Hispanic, personal interaction is critical to their business. Many of the interview participants favoured face-to-face networking and connecting to people in the real world versus the virtual world. Limited users of technology really stressed the importance of meeting people face-to-face, shaking hands and exchanging business cards. These participants valued real-world connections and did not think that the virtual world could offer the same benefits. Individuals such as Maria considered face-to-face interaction to be more powerful than other sources of communication. Generally, participants who fell into this category believed in the power of attending networking events and contacting people by phone using a rolodex and business cards as their 'database'.

Language was also a challenge in connecting with customers. Rafael's company targets Hispanic business owners and business is predominantly conducted in Spanish. The company utilized some software and internet resources in Spanish, such as Wikipedia en Español. Internet communications are woven into the fabric of his company's operations, but there is limited Spanish content on their website, which limits their online operations. Language is not a barrier for his business, but the technology often is. For this reason the company's internet site, which only contains content in English, was not effective. Maria also conducted the majority of business in Spanish (she estimated about 90 per cent). Although one of her associates did not speak Spanish at all, Maria did not think this was a problem since she was usually around to translate for her associate.

Access to technology is also a major issue for maintaining social connections. Many of the companies mentioned that their clients do not own computers. Thus companies risk limiting their access to customers by only using internet-based communication mediums. Fernando Lopez connects and stays connected with clients through his email system, website and blog. Therefore, his access to customers outside of a computer medium was limited. He knew that his target market was people who will not necessarily go to his website so he attends a lot of networking events himself. When discussing the technology she used in her business, Maria Rocha shared that her customers (and Hispanics in Orange County in general) were not as tech savvy as the rest of the population. For this reason, she felt that businesses like hers that serve mostly Hispanic customers had to use minimal technology to avoid confusing or frustrating customers unnecessarily.

The power of word-of-mouth

Getting word-of-mouth recommendations from trusted friends and networking contacts was another issue expressed by interview participants as being very important. Hispanics tend to consult with other individuals before making important purchases (Korzenny and Korzenny 2005). Personal recommendations are valued higher than expert knowledge. Many of the interview participants felt a strong sense of community both in a cultural and territorial sense. Most of the time, they would buy or implement new technologies based on a recommendation from a friend or family member. A few of them had someone working in the office who was the 'go-to' person when it came to recommending a technology or internet-based product. Thus using technology they trusted was very important.

Trust in IT mediums

Trust is a major issue for Hispanic small businesses. Understanding where individuals get their information from is important. Hispanics rely highly on both English and Spanish media as sources of information (Pew Research Hispanic Center 2008). Thus issues of online security are difficult to resolve when the news media fuels uncertainties by reporting online security issues such as identity theft, fraud and online scams.

Online security was a common concern expressed by nearly all interview participants. This concern was consistent across all categories of participants. However, participants in the intense and specialized user categories were more inclined to continue using internet resources such as online banking and online shopping, despite their concerns. The limited users identified online security concerns as a motivating factor in why they did not partake in internet banking and/or shopping. Most of the participants who expressed online security as a major concern had learned about online security issues through media related sources (e.g., television news or newspaper stories).

Having the resources to combat online security concerns made a difference in technological adoption. For example, having an in-house IT expert greatly reduced the insecurity of using technology. Experience with the technology also played a role in trust in the technology. Rafael kept two different contact databases because the online contacts management system accidentally crashed. Some of our informants also adopted alternatives methods to combat IT insecurities. Due to concerns over identity theft, another informant does not do any online banking but will purchase items online only through a pre-paid credit card.

It is interesting to point out that 67 per cent of participants did use online banking and 76 per cent of participants had at some point bought something online. However, online security concerns are probably not specific to Hispanic-owned small businesses but a general concern of everyone because of the recent outbreak of identity theft reported in the media.

Risk of implementing IT

Lastly, along the same lines as trust is individuals' adversity to risk. According to Hofstede *et al.* (2010), Hispanic cultures tend to be more collectivist cultures and rank higher on uncertainty avoidance scale. They represent a collective culture of low risk taking. All informants discussed issues of weighing out the cost over the benefits of investing in technology. Without a recommendation from a trusted source, or personal expertise, the businesses find it difficult to justify the investment. This is not surprising since most small businesses are more cost sensitive than bigger corporations. Yet, intense users saw more value to implementing new technology versus those who fell into the specialized and limited technology use categories. Fernando Lopez discussed how he looked for free ways to implement technology and felt reluctant incorporating anything that cost money. Interestingly enough, Fernando started a weekly email blast service on a computer donated by a friend, a dial-up connection and Yahoo! Mail. When we interviewed him, Fernando had recently upgraded to using an online email blast software program for approximately $35/month. Yet, many of the interview participants carefully analyzed the benefit of implementing new technologies versus the cost involved.

Another issue contributing to their risk adversity is the lack of technological knowledge. As a software engineer, Rafael was an early adopter of technology for his business, although he admitted he was not an expert. He noted that both partners and clients needed training in order to use their online tools. Fernando also discussed his lack of technological knowledge as hindering his eagerness to adopt more technological tools. He said that he would like to learn how to streamline videos and use web analytics to better target his market segment.

Our informants understood that the adoption of technology was a benefit to their company, but the investment needed to implement these technologies successfully was hindering their progress. These companies must not only make the monetary investment but take the time to educate themselves, their partners and their customers. Many of these technologies also require a reciprocal investment by their customer base, which is a large risk for small companies not wanting to alienate their customers.

Future strategies

Using an ethnoconsumerist view, we were able to not only capture the use of technology in Hispanic small businesses, but also gain an understanding of their primary barriers to use. In understanding these barriers and their origins, we can better address how to help Hispanic small businesses navigate them by adapting business practices to the specific environment in order to meet their needs (Deshpandé and Webster 1989).

Extrapolating from the results of the study, Hispanic small business owners are prepared to adopt new technologies, but they are concerned about staying connected with their customers, obtaining information from trusted sources, trusting the technology and minimizing their risk for implementing such technology. However, all Hispanic small businesses are not equally prepared. Our interviews indicated that only the organizations classified as 'intense' users of technology have the ability to fix and update IT internally. This is because this group of organizations tend to have a trusted in-house IT expert to adopt new technology and the resources to provide support for this technology as their requirements necessitate. Apart from those who are ahead of the curve, others fear that the time, learning and financial costs to adopt and maintain new technology will be overwhelming. In addition, many business owners fear that additional technology will cause their customers to be confused, thus alienating them. The challenge is to introduce new technologies and modes of communication to the 'specialized' group and, the further challenge, the 'limited' users, who are behind the technology curve.

Overall, businesses look to find ways to decrease costs and increase value for themselves and their customers. Based on our findings, we generated future strategies regarding how Hispanic small businesses could be supported to improve technologically and participate in a more fully fledged e-commerce type environment without alienating their customers.

Demonstrate the relevance of technology to their company

Adoption of technology can help small businesses run their operations more efficiently and enhance communication with customers. A common remark from our interviewees was that they knew that technology was an important and useful tool in increasing a business's chance for success. However, they did not know how (or believe) technology could be applied in their industry, or in their business in particular. As a result, it is important to tailor the value proposition of technology products so that is resonates with Hispanic small businesses (Soto 2006). There is an opportunity here for the IT industry to demonstrate the relevance of technology specific to their company and show how it can be used in a way that is personally meaningful to Hispanic small business owners.

The most personal way of doing this would be to offer on-site consultations at business sites for the business owner. By sending IT specialists directly to business sites, the business owner will learn how technology can be implemented in the environment in which it will be used. In addition, owners can be provided with suggestions on how their business can be improved with specific software and tools with the option to purchase.

Free trials of the recommended technology may further convince the owner of the technology's value. Such trials could introduce technology to the audience and demonstrate the need for use in their businesses. They should be marketed to business owners as a necessary tool to become their own IT expert and increase their business's potential for success. These benefits should be emphasized in great detail before discussing the associated price. If the perceived benefits of such an offering were truly internalized as a necessity, the value is thereby increased and the associated costs may be seen as a one-time small price to pay to enhance one's business.

Conducting personalized visits to demonstrate how technology can be customized to their businesses will help reduce the feelings of risk to implementing. Product trials can also help further reduce this risk by showing how actual implementation of technology can enhance their business. Lastly, explaining how it can be used to enhance communication with their customers will help minimize the uncertainty of adoption due to perceived alienation of their customers.

Provide the tools to use the technology

One of the major concerns of Hispanic business owners are the many perceived costs associated with implementing technology, in particular the cost to learn to use the product and train employees. Research on formal and informal business incubators stress the importance of such structures in providing services that assist entrepreneurs. These structures are even more essential for advancing minority enterprises by providing access to a variety of services including education and technical consulting (Greene and Butler 2004; Greenhalgh and Lowry 2011). Therefore, agencies like the Hispanic Chamber of Commerce or SBA (Small Business Administration) can be instrumental in providing a way to ease this burden for small businesses. One way of accomplishing this could be to offer no-cost or low-cost training sessions as part of the purchase of products. Getting a cluster of educational institutions involved to provide such classes would be a less expensive way of making these classes available.

As on-site training can be an expensive way of personalizing the technology, industry-specific training sessions at a central site may be more feasible. Most of the Hispanic small businesses we encountered were, in one way or another, in the services industry. Training sessions on what technology is the most useful to bolster customer relationship management in retail or summits on how to use software to automate insurance forms would definitely increase the relevance factor and demonstrate how technology directly applies to their specific industry.

Because many of the Hispanic small business we encountered that were not categorized as 'intense users' did not have their own IT expert, they were hesitant to step into the unknown world of technology. However, if they had someone they could rely on when they encountered difficulties, they may be more willing to take risks. Therefore, we recommend that IT companies provide a Spanish-speaking local representative that business owners can contact when they encounter IT problems. This representative could serve as the IT expert and service a cluster of businesses within an area in the language they prefer. Adopting new technology can be a daunting task, especially for those with much ground to make up in order to get up-to-date; but, with someone to rely on to walk them through the process or manage crises, the experience can be a much less stressful one.

Another opportunity for technology companies is to take advantage of building alliances with other companies such as, for example, HP's (Hewlett Packard) initiative on their Centro Empresarial Hispano de HP (HP Hispanic Business Center) training series. This could be a valuable relationship in which other companies like Microsoft can leverage a program that has already been established. Since HP is already providing tutorials on how to use Microsoft products to enhance business processes, a relationship may ensure that the right products are being marketed and the right message is being communicated.

Training sessions offered with the purchase of products not only increases the value of the products that consumers are purchasing, but also equips purchasers with the knowledge they will need to effectively use the products in which they have invested. Having a 'go-to' person when an in-house IT expert is not available is necessary to continue use and implementation of products. Therefore making this available to small businesses is necessary to reduce the perceived risk of implementation and also help build trust in using the technology.

Utilize the community

There was a great deal of ambivalence among Hispanic small business owners toward technology. To combat this, technology companies must position their products as useful and trusted tools to enhance businesses within this population. Accomplishing this is not just an issue of marketing, major IT companies must make use of the most important entities to Hispanic business owners – the community.

Community influencers, such as Hispanic community leaders and non-profit organizations, are central to effectively marketing to this Hispanic community (Tovar 2005). Most of the Hispanic small businesses we contacted for interviews were assisted by the Hispanic Chamber of Commerce in various day-to-day and planning activities. Consequently, collaborating with the Hispanic Chamber of Commerce of Orange County to bring technology and its education to this population is heavily recommended to establish trust within the community.

Secondary research has indicated there are not many major corporations that sponsor Hispanic entrepreneur events or have a presence on Hispanic resource websites. Such a presence would communicate awareness and support for the business community and its efforts. Often, companies that do reach out to the Hispanic community do so ineffectively because they provide a mere extension of a current effort instead of tailoring programs to reach this market (ibid.). Therefore, reaching out to the Hispanic market would require a focused effort. Sponsoring existing community programs such as Casa Cyber Technology to provide software and training at incubator sites may be the avenue to explore such support programs without going at it alone.

Another way of taking advantage of the benefits of the close-knit Hispanic business community is through the recruitment of other business owners to share their business success stories from using IT products. Such business owners should be trusted members of the community who are at least moderate technology users. Their success stories may inspire others that they, too, have the ability to increase the visibility, impact and efficiency of their business, and this also allows IT companies to get their message across while being delivered by a trusted source within the community.

It is necessary to value the importance of personal relationships to the Hispanic community. Since word-of-mouth recommendations are more favourable than company or industry recommendations, connecting with the community is crucial in order to build trust for a product or company. Doing so will lead to positive evaluations of the company and thus increase word-of-mouth recommendations.

Entry into the world of social media

A prevalent statement among interviewees was that, although websites and other technologies may be useful in obtaining new business, they could never take the place of word-of-mouth referrals and old fashioned networking. In many cases, technology was not even considered as a tool to network or generate buzz, and this mentality must be addressed. With the rapid growth of social media, there are many opportunities and challenges for small businesses to utilize their potential. To quote Michaelian (2013):

> It's no secret that new and social media are important marketing tactics for small businesses in 2013. While new media encompasses video, podcasting, blogging and mobile media, social media is about the conversations that occur in comments and updates on these platforms and others like Twitter, Facebook, Google+ and LinkedIn. Businesses that want to stay relevant and be seen as leaders in their industries in 2013 must have an active presence in the majority of these platforms, etc.

The IT industry must highlight the importance of websites and other marketing tools (e.g. blogs) to increase visibility, generate 'buzz' and referrals, and increase their network. According to Michaelian, participating in social media can help a business connect with customers through a myriad of sophisticated platforms. Many of these applications now have capabilities for more localized target marketing, allowing the business to target individuals within walking distance and offer them a discount. By understanding who the key influencers are among their customers and targeting them specifically, businesses can utilize these individuals to connect to the larger customer base (Kutchera 2011). Social media also helps businesses create a personality for their company and generate buzz through blogs and real-time postings of pictures, comments and feedback. Lastly, social media allows businesses to connect with other businesses and create a virtual network for customers to engage.

Furthermore, the IT industry can emphasize the enhanced impact of traditional word-of-mouth coupled with web presence to improve and grow their business. Though nothing may be able to completely replace in-person networking, the combination of several media to market their products or services allows them to cast a much larger net and, therefore, capture a greater quantity of potential customers.

No matter what approach or combination of approaches IT companies use to introduce technology to Hispanic small businesses in Orange County, they must utilize the most valuable element – the community. The community and the social networking that goes on within the community, we believe, are a key factor. Among the number of challenges that Hispanic small businesses face and the plethora of reasons why they fear technology, there are many opportunities for improvement and change.

The study is an attempt to understand the adoption and use of technology by Hispanic small businesses. Based on our sample of twenty small businesses located in Southern California, our study identified three segments of technology use: intense, specialized and limited. Although not an exhaustive study, our aim was to identify important issues and questions for further investigation.

While this work helped shed some light on IT adoption by Hispanic small businesses, there are limitations to our study. Although our informants varied in the type of small business, they are not representative of all Hispanic small businesses. These businesses are all members of the Orange County Hispanic Chamber of Commerce and, although they have a large membership base, the number of small businesses in Orange County that are not members is larger. Thus we cannot say that our study reflects all Hispanic small businesses in Southern California and much less those across the United States.

Second, technology is constantly changing. Therefore from the time our data was collected there have been new innovations to the use of technology in small businesses. More specifically, the rise of social media as a marketing tool has grown significantly in the past year. Media that were popular initially have now been rendered obsolete, and newer technologies have made it easier to connect with the customer base. Thus many questions remain about the evolution of social media use in Hispanic small businesses.

Further research that investigates the integration of social media in Hispanic small businesses is needed. It is likely that our initial study was not able to capture this phenomenon to the extent it is at present day. Thus a more in-depth examination is necessary to understand not only the adoption of social media, but also the types and to what extent businesses are able to connect with their customer base. Along the same line, future research can look at the customers' receptivity to interacting with these businesses thorough the varied media. There is something to be said about the growth of social media adoption by Hispanics in general and the implications of this on their interaction with businesses. Perhaps what was once perceived as an initial barrier to adoption of IT by Hispanic small businesses is now a pathway to an evolved customer base.

References

Barth, F. (1998) *Ethnic Groups and Boundaries*. Long Grove, IL: Waveland Press, Inc.

Burton, D. (2009) *Cross-Cultural Marketing: Theory, Practice and Relevance*. New York, NY: Routledge.

Companie, B. M. (2001) *The Digital Divide: Facing a Crisis or Creating a Myth?* Cambridge, MA: MIT Press.

Deshpandé, R., Hoyer, W. D. and Donthu, N. (1986) 'The intensity of ethnic affiliation: A study of the sociology of hispanic consumption'. *Journal of Consumer Research*, 13: 214–20.

Deshpandé, R. and Stayman, D. M. (1994) 'A tale of two cities: Distinctiveness theory and advertising effectiveness'. *Journal of Marketing Research*, 31(1): 57–64.

Deshpandé, R. and Webster Jr., F. E. (1989) 'Organizational culture and marketing: Defining the research agenda'. *Journal of Marketing*, 53: 3–15.

Elyachar, J. (2005). *Markets of Dispossession: NGOs, Economic Development, and the State in Cairo (Politics, History, and Culture)*. Durham, NC: Duke University Press.

Greene, P. G. and Butler, J. S. (2004) 'The minority community as a natural business incubator'. In *Immigrant and Minority Entrepreneurship*, edited by J. S. Butler and G. Kozmetsky. Westport, CT: Praeger Publishers.

Greenhalgh, L. and Lowry, J. (2011). *Minority Business Success*. Stanford, CA: Stanford University Press.

Hirschman, E. C. (1981) 'American Jewish ethnicity: Its relationship to some selected aspects of consumer behavior'. *The Journal of Marketing*, 45(3): 102–10.

Hoffman, D. L., Novak, T. P. and Venkatesh, A. (1997) 'Diversity on the internet: The relationship of race to access and usage'. In *Investing in Diversity: Advancing Opportunities for Minorities and the Media*, edited by A. K. Garmer. Maryland: The Aspen Institute.

Hofstede, G., Hofstede G. J. and Minkov M. (2010). *Cultures and Organizations: Software of the Mind*. New York, NY: McGraw-Hill.

Holland, J. and Gentry, J. W. (1999) 'Ethnic consumer reaction to targeted marketing: A theory of inter-cultural accommodation'. *Journal of Advertising*, 28(1): 65–77.

Korzenny, F. and Korzenny, B. A. (2005) *Hispanic Marketing: A Cultural Perspective*. Burlington, MA: Elsevier.

Kutchera, J. (2011) *Latino Link: Building Brands Online With Hispanic Communities and Content*. Ithaca, NY: Paramount Market Publishing, Inc.

Light, I. and Gold, S. (2000) *Ethnic Economies*. San Diego, CA: Academic Press.

Lofstrom, M. (2009) 'Latina entrepreneurship'. *Small Business Economies*, 33(May): 427–39.

Meamber, L. and Venkatesh, A. (2000) 'Ethno-consumerist methodology for cultural and cross-cultural consumer research'. In *Interpretive Consumer Research*, edited by S. C. Beckmann and R. H. Elliott. Denmark: Copenhagen Business School Press.

Michaelian, B. (17 January 2013) 'New and social media trends for small business in 2013'. *Huffington Post*. Available from: http://www.huffingtonpost.com/britt-michaelian/social-media-small-business_b_2491821.html [accessed 30 March 2013].

Middleton K. L. and Byus, K. (2011) 'Information and communications technology adoption and use in small and medium businesses: The influence of Hispanic ethnicity'. *Management Research Review*, 34(1): 98–110.

Morse, D. R. (2009) *Multicultural Intelligence*. Ithaca, NY: Paramount Market Publishing, Inc.

Nash, M. (1989) *The Cauldron of Ethnicity in the Modern World*. Chicago, IL: The University of Chicago Press.

Nielsen (2012) 'State of the Hispanic consumer: The Hispanic Market imperative'. Nielsen. Available from: http://www.nielsen.com/content/dam/corporate/us/en/reports-downloads/2012-Reports/State-of-the-Hispanic-Consumer.pdf [accessed 25 March 2013].

Peñaloza, L. N. (1994) 'Atravesando fronteras/border crossing: A critical ethnographic exploration of the consumer acculturation of Mexican immigrants'. *Journal of Consumer Research*, 21(1): 32–54.

Peñaloza, L. and Gilly, M. C. (1999) 'Marketer acculturation: The changer and the changed'. *Journal of Marketing*, 63: 84–104.

Peterson, R. M. and C. Dibrell (2002) 'Consumers and technology in small businesses: Are we creating relationships or distance?' *Academy of Entrepreneurship Journal*, 8(1): 31–45.

Pew Hispanic Center (13 August 2008) 'Hispanics and health care in the United States'. Pew Research Center. Available from: http://www.pewhispanic.org/2008/08/13/iv-sources-of-information-on-health-and-health-care/ [accessed 13 November 2013].

Pew Hispanic Center (22 December 2009) 'Latinos Online, 2006–2008, Narrowing the Gap'. Pew Research Center. Available from: http://www.pewhispanic.org/2009/12/22/latinos-online-2006-2008-narrowing-the-gap/ [accessed 30 March 2013].

Shih, C. F. and Venkatesh, A. (2004) 'Beyond adoption: Development and application of a use-diffusion model'. *Journal of Marketing*, 68(1): 59–72.

Soto, T. J. (2006) *Marketing to Hispanics*. Chicago, IL: Kaplan Publishing.

Stayman, D. M. and Deshpandé, R. (1989) 'Situational Ethnicity and Consumer Behavior'. *Journal of Consumer Research*, 16(3): 361–71.

Tovar, D. O. (2005) 'Hispanic public relations and its emergence as an industry'. In *Hispanic Marketing & Public Relations*, edited by E. del Valle. Boca Raton, FL: Poyeen Publishing.

U.S. Bureau of the Census (21 September 2010) 'Census bureau reports Hispanic-owned businesses increase at more than double the national rate'. U.S. Bureau of the Census. Available from: http://www.census.gov/newsroom/releases/archives/business_ownership/cb10-145.html [accessed 30 March 2013].

U.S. Congress (2012). *Digital Divide: Expanding Broadband Access to Small Businesses*. Washington, DC: U.S. Government Printing Office.

Valencia, H. (1989) 'Hispanic values and subcultural research'. *Journal of the Academy of Marketing Science*, 17(1): 23–8.

Venkatesh, A. (1995) 'Ethno-consumerism: A new paradigm to study cultural and cross-cultural consumer behavior'. In *Marketing in a Multicultural World*, edited by J. A. Costa and G. J. Bamossy. Thousand Oaks, CA: Sage Publications, pp. 26–67.

Wallendorf, M. and Reilly M. (1983) 'Ethnic migration, assimilation, and consumption'. *Journal of Consumer Research,* 10(December): 292–302.

Zickuhr, K. and Smith, A. (13 April 2012). 'Digital Differences'. *Pew Internet & American Life Project*. Available from: http://pewinternet.org/Reports/2012/Digital-differences.aspx.

Zmud, J. and Arce, C. (1992) 'The ethnicity and consumption relationship'. *Advances in Consumer Research*, 19(1): 443–50.

Appendix 8.1: interview protocol

- What are the current and emerging trends of online communications in your business?
- What are the practices and needs pertaining to your business regarding online communications, scheduling, calendaring, event planning and contact management?
- What are the online networking tools that you are using?
- What are the new technology trends that you might be aware of?
- How do you become educated or acquire skills and knowledge in internet skills and online communication?
- What are your practices and needs of small businesses regarding online communications, scheduling, calendaring and event planning?
- What are your social and professional networking patterns? What online tools do you use?
- What is the interrelationship between professional and personal online communication? Where and how do they overlap for you?
- How are new technologies (including mobile) appropriated and adapted by you as a socio-cultural group?
- Online and offline communications habits and practices: email, messenger, intranet blogging/ wiki (blogging as communication tool), scheduling/calendaring, organizing events, phone use, postal mail, address books/contacts (contact management).
- Internet use (including mobile internet use).
- Internet services (training, setting up own website and email) and online infrastructural needs.
- Mobile technology use.
- Technology adoption and consumption.
- Special technology needs (Spanish-language services and software).
- Email and internet safety, protection and privacy.

Part IV

Globalization, religion and materialism

9

Rethinking religion and ethnicity at the nexus of globalization and consumer culture

Elif Izberk-Bilgin

Introduction

Religion and ethnicity are two critical topics shaping the agendas of world leaders, public policy makers and academics. Increasing ethnic and religious diversity brought about by transnational migration poses many challenges to most nation states. For example, the US alone has taken in 22 million immigrants since the 1980s (Rytina 2009), not only pressing policy makers to urgently address issues such as housing, employment and education for the newcomers, but also rendering timid encounters with the 'ethnic/religious-other' unavoidable in everyday life. More importantly, religiously and ethnically charged activism appear to be a leading source of conflict throughout the world; the recent street riots in the French banlieues and the ongoing Arab–Jew, Hindu–Muslim conflicts are only a few examples of such social conflict.

Religion and ethnicity are also intriguing topics from a scholarly view. First of all, both concepts are prominent markers of identity; our religious and ethnic background shapes our attitudes, values and lifestyles, while also informing our political views and consumption choices. Second, religion and ethnicity are complexly intertwined in the way they influence our everyday practices and social relations. Religious practices play a fundamental role in constructing a distinct ethnic identity and forming social alliances (e.g., Jews, Amish, Mormons), while ethnicity is manifested in great variations in religious practices (e.g., Muslim Shias and Sunnis). Despite the close association between the two topics, religion and ethnicity have been largely studied separately in social sciences. Perhaps due to this silo effect, modernist scholars declared the demise of religion and ethnicity decades ago (Berger 1967; Park 1950).

Yet, in a rapidly globalizing world, religion and ethnicity have become more relevant than ever. For example, the need for ethnic and religious anchors grows with increased border cross-ings as more migrants grapple with the anxieties related to the diaspora experience. Moreover, as the global popularity of the 'om' amulets and the 'ethno/gypsy-bohemian' look suggest, religious and ethnic identifiers have also become important tools for the non-religious and non-immigrant consumers who want to pursue an authentic identity in an increasingly sterile consumer culture. As marketers readily accommodate the demand for authenticity, ethnicity and religion become a choice that is exercised through consumption; one that can be worn like a garment and swapped as needed (Bouchet 1995; Oswald 1999). Lastly, religious and ethnic discourses have become effective ideological tools to negate the discontent with poverty and asymmetrical economic growth brought about by globalization (Bandarage 2004). In short, globalization has created tremendous social, cultural and economic change that directly influences the role of religion and ethnicity in the contemporary era. As such, we need to reconsider our existing assumptions on these topics, with particular emphasis on how religion and ethnicity interact in complex ways to materialize in everyday life through consumption.

With this goal in mind, this chapter explores several questions at the intersection of religion, ethnicity, market, culture and politics. Drawing from the theory of prominent globalization scholar, Sassen, the following pages examine how the transnational mobility of people and capital has been informing the way religion and ethnicity interact in myriad ways within contemporary society to offer implications for the study of religion and ethnicity in consumer research. The remainder of this chapter is organized in four sections. The first section reviews the existing literature on religion and ethnicity in marketing. While this review provides a representative portrayal of extant literature, it is not exhaustive of the entire body of knowledge on these concepts in marketing. The second section briefly discusses the shortcomings of the past studies and offers an alternative theoretical lens, through which consumer researchers may study the role of religion and ethnicity in everyday life. The third section offers research implications with respect to the intriguing relationships among the rise of ethno-religious ideologies, consumer activism, the emergence of faith-based markets and the spread of capitalist ideals to the developing world. The last section offers some concluding thoughts.

Religion and ethnicity in marketing literature

Early examinations of religion in marketing focused on examining the relationship between religious affiliation and aspects of consumer behaviour such as price sensitivity and perceived risk (Delener 1990; Delener 1994; Delener and Schiffman 1988; Hirschman 1981; Hirschman 1982; Hirschman 1983), retail store evaluative criteria (McDaniel and Burnett 1990), shopping behaviour (Bailey and Sood 1993; Essoo and Dibb 2004; Sood and Nasu 1995) and lifestyle measures (Wilkes *et al.* 1986). Religiosity has also been studied in the contexts of materialism (Burrough and Rindfleisch 2002; Cleveland and Chang 2009; La Barbera and Gürhan 1997), ethical decision making (Swimberghe *et al.* 2011), as well as brand loyalty (Rindfleisch *et al.* 2005; Rindfleisch *et al.* 2010) and brand reliance (Shachar *et al.* 2011). Collectively, these quantitative studies found a significant effect of religious orientation and strength of religious affiliation on several aspects of consumer behaviour, confirming that examining religiosity is integral to marketing practice and theory.

Interpretive scholars, on the other hand, have explored how consumption can facilitate transcendent experiences. Belk *et al.*'s (1989) seminal work, which offers a comprehensive analysis of the processes through which the ordinary can be deemed sacred, has suggested that mundane objects like brands can become vehicles of transcendent experience. Building on this, a series of studies have demonstrated how iconic and lifestyle brands such as Harley Davidson, Apple, Jeep and Saab have become a sacred totem in the eyes of loyal consumers (Belk and Tumbat 2005; Kozinets 2001; Muniz and Schau 2005; Schouten and McAlexander 1995). Another group of consumer studies have examined the implications of 'secularization of religion'. As Belk *et al.* (1989) note, examples of secularization include the discontinuance of Latin in Catholic mass, decline in religious traditions such as prayer at meal and bed time, and the increasing use of TV and radio for communication of religious messages. More current examples include the growing emphasis on entertainment in religious service, particularly in mega churches (Robertson 2002) and the emergence of 'pick-and-mix' religion (Hamilton 2000) or new age spirituality. In consumer research, the commercialization, cross-cultural adoption and changing consumer interpretations of religious holy days (e.g., Ramadan, Christmas and Passover) are examined in various studies (Belk 1987; Belk 2001; Belk 2013; Deshen 1997; Hirschman and LaBarbera 1989; Hirschman *et al.* 2011; Kimura and Belk 2005; Sandıkçı and Ömeraki 2007; Touzani and Hirschman 2008; Touzani *et al.* 2009; Sherry and McGrath 1989). Aside from religious celebrations, increasing secularization of the sacred can also be noted in the fashionable meanings consumers and marketers assign to religious symbols such as the Islamic veil and the Catholic rosary (Rinallo *et al.* 2012; Sandıkçı and Ger 2010).

A close reading of the marketing literature on religion shows that religion and modernity (and by implication consumption) have been treated as two opposing forces. This might be attributed to the influence of secularization theory (Berger 1967; Weber 1922/1978), which argued that modernization, with its emphasis on science and rationality, will bring about the demise of religion. The reflections of this theoretical perspective, which poses modernity as a rival to religion can be observed in the two main themes that emerged in consumer research: the secularization of the sacred and the sacralization of the profane. Consumer researchers have, on the one hand, demonstrated how modern ideas infiltrate the realm of the sacred, for example, in the increasing commercialization and secularization of religious traditions (Belk 1987; Belk 2001; Kimura and Belk 2005) and, on the other, have offered examples of how religious discourses and the human need for the sacred permeate the modern life (Izberk-Bilgin 2012a; Muniz and Schau 2005). Yet, a more comprehensive understanding of the complex ways in which religion operates in contemporary consumer culture, which is significantly shaped by globalization, requires us to move beyond the modernity–religion duality and the theoretical limitations it poses.

Modernization has also influenced the theoretical foundations of ethnicity research. Early ethnicity research and migration studies, particularly those of Park (1950) and Warner and Srole (1945) are guided by the assumption that modernization, more specifically urbanization, democracy and increasing equality among different social groups, would eventually erode ethnic identity markers and social conflicts, yielding to cultural assimilation to the dominant culture. These studies had a lasting effect on the early development of the consumer acculturation research in marketing. Building on the assumptions of assimilation theories, as Luedicke (2011) notes, early consumer acculturation research has been preoccupied with measuring the level of immigrant consumers' assimilation to a new cultural context. The second wave of acculturation studies notably depart from previous literature by demonstrating that immigration does not necessarily lead to assimilation (Peñaloza 1994); migrants draw from home, host and Global Consumer Cultures (GCC) as they negotiate a migrant identity (Askegaard *et al.* 2005); these identities are not fixed, but rather migrants can wear their ethnicity as a garment and can swap it as needed, moving between different identity positions (Oswald 1999); and lastly, that the process of constructing an ethnic identity is not always voluntary and, in the absence of sufficient social and economic capital, migrants cannot realize the social mobility they desire (Üstüner and Holt 2007).

While these later works were groundbreaking and stood apart from the first wave of consumer acculturation studies in terms of their phenomenological scope and methodology, they were still deeply influenced by modernist thinking and thus suffer from what Glick Schiller, Çaglar and Guldbrandsen (2006, p. 613) call 'methodological nationalism'. Wimmer and Glick Schiller (2002) argue that the nation-state building processes of the eighteenth century and the subsequent immigration and integration policies developed at the time have fundamentally influenced the academic discourse on immigration such that we have come to believe that 'nation state' is the only natural social and political organization. As such, Glick Schiller *et al.* (2006, p. 613) critically observe that: 'Through an extension of the logic of methodological nationalism, migrants were, by definition, culturally and socially different because they originated in other national territories; natives, by this same logic, became a homogeneous whole'. This confining analytical lens is reflected in many disciplines, including the consumer acculturation research in marketing, most notably in the form of dualistic home–host country notation. To move beyond this duality, Glick Schiller *et al.* (2006) recommend focusing on the processes of building and maintaining social networks and the social fields created by these networks, instead of ethnic identity or culture, which are bound to entail reductionist and dualistic perspectives. The authors argue that studying social networks and related social fields opens up possibilities to realize how these networks might transcend local/national and ethnic boundaries and thus, better account for how globalization – through new technologies, media and institutions – inform the immigrant experience. Economic, political, religious and class interests – be it at the local or global level – can cut across ethnic, racial and national ties to mobilize individuals around shared goals. Dávila (2012) shows, for example, how Hispanic advertisers in the US assembled Cuban, Mexican, Puerto Rican, Caribbean and Central American identities under the Hispanic pan-ethnic identity to convince corporate clients that Latinos make a substantive consumer group. Likewise, regardless of ethnic-racial differences and religious inclinations, increasing numbers of African Americans and Latinos are associating with the Evangelical church in pursuit of social mobility (Dias 2013). These examples remind us to leave behind our modernist conceptualization of ethnicity as confined to a particular locality and consider its dynamic nature as constructed through social interactions and global movements.

Moving beyond existing debates

The above literature review shows that marketing discipline has gained considerable theoretical ground over the years in the study of religion and ethnicity. Yet, the review also suggests that these two very important topics, which play a foundational role in consumer identity formation, have been studied separately to a great extent. Further, investigations of both religion and ethnicity have been marked by a modernist perspective; consumer research on religion is confined to accounts of sacralization of the secular or the secularization of the sacred, while modernist and nationalist thinking prevalent in ethnicity research has produced methodological and conceptual confines that overlook how ethnic identities, communities and social fields are formed transnationally through consumption. Developing a more comprehensive and dynamic understanding of religion and ethnicity in relation to consumption in today's world requires us to move beyond these theoretical and methodological limitations. Rather than focusing on modernity and its dualisms, investigating how globalization facilitates the complex ways in which religion and ethnicity interact and operate in everyday life might allow us to advance the state of research on these topics.

The economic, social, cultural and political implications of globalization have been extensively addressed usually in the form of a debate on cultural homogenization versus cultural pluralism, hypercapitalism, polycentrism and hybrid identities (Bauman 1998; Klein 2000; Korten 2001; Ritzer 2003; Scholte 2005; Sklair 2001; Oncu and Wayland 1997). Within this wide literature, Sassen's works (1988; 1991; 1998) are noteworthy for thoroughly analyzing the interrelations among globalization, transnational mobility of people and internationalization of production and deregulation of capital flows. In *The Mobility of Labor and Capital* (1988) and *The Global City* (1991), Sassen argues that developed countries' shift from manufacturing to service economies has led to the emergence of, on the one hand, global cities – new centres of economic power like New York, London and Tokyo with a rising professional class – and, on the other hand, export-processing zones with an increasing demand for low-skill, low-wage workers. Facilitating this economic restructuring has been the financial deregulation and transnational expansion of capital; the global expansion of multinational firms and growing foreign direct investment in commercial agriculture left many rural dwellers unemployed and induced massive waves of transnational migration.

Sassen's thesis of transnational mobility of people and capital offers an interesting organizational framework to explore how globalization facilitates the multitude of ways in which religion and ethnicity work within contemporary consumer culture. More specifically, looking through this theoretical lens allows us to investigate how different parties in a market system (e.g., consumers, religious institutions, cultural interpreters and governments) are forming new interpretations of religious teachings and creating new religious practices to cope with the socio-economic transformations brought about by transnational flows of people and capital. The increasing border crossings of migrant workers, tourists, expatriates, refugees and students have profound implications on marketplace expressions of religious and ethnic identity. For example, the formation of diasporic communities in Europe and North America has significantly shaped the political, cultural and economic landscapes in these countries as exemplified in the proliferation of Muslim-friendly products in Europe (Pink 2009) and in the increasing numbers of Hispanic Americans shifting from Catholicism to Protestantism (Dias 2013). Such developments propelled by globalization have not been sufficiently explored in consumer research literature; yet they pose critical implications on our existing theories of identity, authenticity, community, ritualistic consumption and market formation. Utilizing Sassen's analytical framework of globalization, the rest of this chapter explores the interrelations between religion, ethnicity, markets, culture and politics in the context of transnational mobility of people and capital to offer some potentially interesting research implications for advancing the study of religion and ethnicity in consumer culture.

Research implications

Consumer activism and ethno-religious ideologies

Following the post-colonial era, particularly during the reconstruction period after the Second World War, many Western European countries and the US have witnessed an influx of migrants (Sassen 1988). In addition to its economic and political implications, migration has significantly stimulated discussion on the role of religion in everyday life from the public display of conspicuous religious symbols, as observed in the French law on secularity and the Swiss ban on the building of minarets, to the use of free speech, as in the case of the Danish cartoon crisis, and the attack at the *Charlie Hebdo* headquarters in France in 2015. As a result, some secular-minded locals have started to re-examine their assumptions about the relevance of religious teachings in modern life, while others have embraced their Christianity as a counter-identity, mostly in response to cultural confrontation with Muslim, Hindu and Jewish immigrants. In this tense environment, the migrants have also faced complex questions related to their religious identity and have been forced to examine what it means to belong to a minority faith. Removed from their social networks and home cultures, the migrants have encountered many cultural tensions leading to heightened consciousness of their religious 'otherness'. This increased awareness reflexively lends itself to the use of religious symbols and discourses as an important marker of identity, which, in turn, has important ramifications in the marketplace.

One example is the rise of ethno-religious discourses of activism such as Hindu nationalism, Gitano (Spanish gypsy) Evangelism, African American Islamism, Latino Pentecostalism and Sunni Wahhabism in Europe and Americas (Spohn 2003). In particular, the case of Islamic consumer activism offers a telling illustration of how consumption mediates the formation of the transnational networks and social fields that Glick Schiller *et al.* (2006) discuss. Muslims have long quietly refrained from buying Western brands, mostly owing to religious and moral qualms such as concerns about the halal compliance of a Big Mac or the perceived indecency of Barbie. However, the recent cultural denigration of Islam through the Danish cartoons and the movie *Innocence of Muslims* has stirred up long-held ideological and historical tensions emanating from a history of colonialism and Western involvement in Middle East, which fuelled a wave of consumer activism targeting a wide range of global brands (Izberk-Bilgin 2012a; Sandıkçı and Ekici 2009). Diaspora Muslims have played a critical role in organizing and sustaining these boycotts owing to their growing size and spending power as well as to their effective utilization of new media to bring visibility to Muslim causes in the marketplace. By using web-based technologies, Islamic activists have turned local conflicts into transnational issues and, more importantly, have fostered transnational links among dispersed Muslim communities. Activist Muslims in Europe and United States can now connect virtually with like-minded Muslims in Indonesia, Saudi Arabia, Egypt and elsewhere to vocalize their concerns on new platforms, using new tools. As noted in Izberk-Bilgin (2012b), diaspora-based Islamic websites, forums, blogs and Facebook pages have been instrumental in mobilizing a transnational boycott by disseminating certain fundamentalist scholars' *fatwas* (religious rulings), which declare multinational brands *haram*, developing a peculiar religious rhetoric that constructs the consumption of global brands as sinful. Likewise, Lindekilde (2010) shows that in the aftermath of the cartoon crisis Danish Muslims used email campaigns, chain text messaging and transnational media such as al-Jazeera to mobilize a multinational, pan-ethnic response that resulted in a boycott of Danish products throughout the Muslim world. As both studies suggest – in addition to activist consumers – religious scholars, governments, NGOs, media organizations and marketers are transnationally connected around shared ideological interests that cut across class, national and ethnic alliances.

While the case of Islamic consumer activism is informative in revealing interesting interactions at the nexus of migration, ethnicity, religion, markets and politics, it seems that increased academic and public interest in Islam following the tragic events of September 11 has drawn attention away from other forms of ethno-religious activism. For example, what are the implications of Hindu nationalism, Latino Pentecostalism and Jewish activism for marketers and consumers? Given how deeply the last of these is embedded in the marketplace, as exemplified in the 'Buy Israel Goods' campaign and its ties to prominent organizations like the American-Israel Chamber of Commerce, it is surprising that researchers have not sufficiently explored the marketing ramifications of this form of activism. Other interesting research questions include how the diaspora experience, in light of the global socio-political and economic context, shapes migrant consumers' interpretation of religious teachings as well as the way they perform religion. Or what are the different roles that consumers, marketers, governments, NGOs, religious scholars and other cultural intermediaries play in the way religious narratives are constructed, manipulated and disseminated? How do web-based technologies like Facebook, Twitter and blogs facilitate the way religious and ethnic identity is expressed and performed through consumption? These and many other interesting questions represent largely uncharted territory in consumer research, and thus, offer new possibilities for advancing the research on religion and ethnicity in marketing.

Emergence of faith-based markets and marketing

Transnational flows of people and capital have also significantly stimulated the emergence of faith-based markets and faith-based marketing. Two socio-cultural phenomena are driving these trends. First, the influx of migrants has been steadily diversifying the 'homogeneous' nature of national cultures, leading to increased fragmentation in consumer tastes and lifestyles. Second, there has been a surge of interest in religion, partly due to migration and flows of ideas, as evinced in the rise of Pentecostalism in Africa and Latin America, Christianity in China and Islam in Europe and Asia, while new age spirituality attracts followers throughout the world (Spohn 2003). Marketplace examples of this religious renaissance can be found in the popularity of offerings such as Kabbalah bracelets, Dolce & Gabbana rosaries, Christian rock, Buddha amulets and faith-based diet books. It is in this particular context of growing diversity of consumer tastes, the proliferation of media and the rise of interest in authentic consumption goods that faith-based markets are blooming. Astute marketing practitioners are finding that not only appealing to faith-based consumer segments is a profitable endeavor with over 2.1 billion Christians, 1.6 billion Muslims, 1 billion Hindus and 14 million Jews in the marketplace, but also that marketing activities carried out through religious networks (e.g., priests, bible study groups, religious websites and broadcasting channels) lends firms more credibility and affords them a more easily reached (as congregations routinely meet) and, presumably, more loyal audience.

One prominent example of a faith-based market is the halal industry. Halal refers to what is permissible under Islamic law, and the demand for halal products has paralleled the growth of the Muslim population worldwide (1.6 billion), particularly in diasporic lands where, unlike in many Muslim-majority countries, halal manufacturing and slaughtering standards are not mandatory. The global halal market is estimated to be worth 2.1 trillion dollars (ogilvynoor. com) and offers a wide range of products from Shariah-compliant credit cards to halal whiskey. The surge of interest in halal can be attributed to the growing spending power and increasing aptness of Muslims in engaging with GCC. Young, tech-savvy and globally travelled Muslims, while often conservative in values, are quite similar to their Western counterparts in constructing consumption-mediated identities. Particularly for middle and upper-middle class Muslims, the most convenient and prominent way of enacting their identity position is through the consumption of halal and other Muslim-friendly products (Izberk-Bilgin 2013; Pink 2009). The marketplace has been quick to accommodate this demand, as multinationals such as Nestlé, Unilever, Wal-Mart, McDonald's, KFC, Novartis, Whole Foods and HSBC have begun offering halal versions of everyday consumer goods such as toothpaste, cosmetics, over-the-counter drugs and interest-free bank accounts.

Examples of faith-based marketing are not confined to the case of halal and products manufactured according to religious standards. Advertising through faith-based networks and sponsoring religious events help ordinary businesses to access ethnic communities that are hard to reach due to cultural and communication barriers. One particular case of interest is the Latino population in the US. Despite their substantial buying power, many Latino immigrants lack access to mainstream financial services such as business loans, credit cards and mortgages, as they do not always have the necessary documents to open bank accounts. Further, unbanked Latinos have no choice but to stash savings at home and use informal channels to send remittances to their home countries, which translates into lost service opportunities for financial institutions (Bair 2003). Banks in particular are keen on establishing long-term relationships with the Latino community and are turning to partnerships with faith-based organizations and their communication initiatives to overcome the lack of trust that some Latino immigrants harbor about financial institutions. For example, Bair (2003) notes that some banks operate part-time teller windows in churches, while Kelderhouse (2002) reports that several banks have been partnering with a local church in a historic Latino neighbourhood in Chicago to offer financial literacy education, free tax preparation and help in opening new bank accounts.

While our knowledge of faith-based marketing is growing with bourgeoning academic research (e.g. recent research on Islamic finance and marketing) and a few practitioner resources in this area, consumer researchers have yet to explore faith-based markets in a systematic way.

For example, how are faith-based markets formed, and what are the role of consumers and various institutions (e.g., producers, advertising agencies, governments, market research firms, religious organizations) in the formation of faith-based markets? A quick glance at the halal industry, for example, reveals the vested interests of multiple actors, from halal certifiers to national governments (Izberk-Bilgin 2013). How do these interests inform consumer demand for halal? Likewise, we might ask what kinds of cultural meanings consumers assign to faith-based products like Dolce & Gabbana rosaries (Rinallo *et al.* 2012). Consumer researchers can also make significant contributions to public policy formation by studying exemplary cases of faith-based marketing. Following in the footsteps of Peñaloza and Barnhardt (2011), researchers might investigate the consequences of financial literacy and consumer debt among the immigrant communities and the poor, as well as exploring how effective the partnerships between marketers and faith-based organizations are in providing infrastructure and support to overcome such societal problems.

Globalization, religion and capitalism

Economic globalization, as summarized in Sassen's 'transnational mobility of capital' argument, is characterized by increasing decentralization of production, surging foreign direct investment by multinational corporations and international subcontracting by industrialized nations. However, the deregulation of financial transactions and internationalization of corporations' operations represent more than global economic restructuring. The mobility of capital also indicates the spread of market ideals (e.g., capitalism, economic liberalization and privatization) to developing countries like China, Kenya and Ghana. At the same time, the strengthening of these ideals in developed countries leads to 'hypercapitalism', transforming many aspects of everyday life into 'paid-for experiences' according to Rifkin (2000). Yet little is known about how the ideological consequences of these capital flows impact the relations between the minorities and the 'locals' or about the role of religion in mediating that relationship. Research indicates that religious teachings may be used either to numb or to exacerbate ethnic and racial tensions, to mobilize social change, or to champion economic agendas (Harris 1994; Wald 1987). Given that, a series of interesting questions can be explored at the nexus of globalization, capitalism, religion and ethnicity: How do consumerist aspirations in developing countries fuel religious-ethnic tensions, particularly in locales where socio-economic status largely depends on ethnicity? Relatedly, how do consumers from different social strata make use of religious teachings and various forms of spiritualities as they cope with the economic, social and cultural transition imposed by globalization? Do they interpret religious texts literally, or form new interpretations to negotiate their lifestyles with capitalist ideals? And how do these various takes on religion play out in the marketplace? How do priests, imams, rabbis or Buddhist clergy respond to the logic of the market societies; do they appropriate religious teachings to make them suitable to the existential realities of the context? And if so, how are markets and market relationships contextualized within these appropriated accounts?

Such questions remain largely unanswered in consumer research. Studies on the rise of Pentecostalism in Ghana and Kenya by Bonsu and Belk (2010) and Dolan (2012) represent notable exceptions. Bonsu and Belk (2010) show how Pentecostalist clergy and their prosperity gospel are not only changing Ghanaian religious practice and norms, but also contributing to the economic impoverishment of the poor. Also vividly demonstrated in the authors' account is how such imported religious ideals are restructured to accommodate conditions of poverty, as in the example of religious discourse and popular songs that advocate prostitution over thievery, legitimizing prostitution as a way of utilizing God's gift to women. Dolan (2012) offers an equally interesting account of how Pentecostalism blurs the boundaries among religion, market and the domestic sphere in Kenya by popularizing the idea that God bestows single women with marriage proposals from wealthy men in return for their generous tithes (obligatory donations), thus rendering marriage a site for spiritual and financial transformation. In short, both studies show how Pentecostalism, a peculiarly capitalist interpretation of God, can be restructured to suit various local contexts and capitalist aspirations. Building on these studies, consumer researchers might also investigate how the close encounters between different religious ideologies and ethnic groups (e.g., in the case of Ghana, Islamic influence in the north among the Sunni and Ahmadi Muslims and Pentecostalism among the Asante in the southern part of the country) inform consumer identity work and are thereby reflected in consumption choices.

While African Pentecostalism offers a nice illustration of the spread of capitalist ideologies through Christian discourses, Haenni's (2005) Market Islam argues that the lure of the prosperity gospel is not limited to Pentecostals and that young and upwardly mobile Muslims with neoliberalist ideals are forging an Islamic version of the 'earthly wealth' discourse. Indeed, the consumption patterns of the rising Islamic bourgeoisie class in Turkey and in Asia (Ergu 2009; O'Neill 2010) are revealing of how religious rhetoric is used to advance personal salvation. Advocating the idea that prosperity indicates divine ordination, based on selective readings of the Qur'an and the Prophet Muhammad's life, wealthy Turkish Islamists are splurging on plasma screens that project 24/7 live views from Mecca, gold-plated faucets adorned with Swarovski crystals, and bathroom tissues imprinted with designer logos (Ergu 2009). Additional reflections of this prosperity gospel can be found in the rhetoric developed by business associations, publications and broadcasting channels owned by the Islamist bourgeoisie (Buğra 1998). Needless to say, this interesting intermingling of capitalism, consumer culture and Islam provides fertile ground for a morality contest between Yuppie Muslims and their poorer brethren. Indeed, the earthly wealth rhetoric of the well-to-do Turkish Islamists has effectively created its own counter-culture: anti-capitalist Muslims, a group of pious activists, who recently received public attention when they collaborated with pro-secularists in the Taksim square protests against the increasingly authoritarian pro-Islamist AKP government in Turkey. As the Turkish case shows, the fragmentations within a religious movement (e.g., Islamic bourgeoisie, anti-capitalist Muslims, environmental Muslims) reflect competing interpretations of capitalism, morality, religion, consumer culture and ethnicity (e.g. Sunni-Shiite), offering consumer researchers ample opportunities for empirical investigation of the complex theoretical relationships among markets, religion, ethnicity and politics.

Conclusion

Ethnicity and religion are two topics of critical importance to marketing scholars. Yet, to a great extent, these topics have been examined separately and through modernist lenses. Until recently, this modernist view prevalent in social sciences, where key theories of ethnicity and religion originate, claimed the demise of the role of ethnicity and religion in modern life. However, such a modernist view disregards the fundamental human need for spirituality and ethnic allegiances, particularly under trying socio-economic and cultural conditions brought about by the processes of globalization. As such, past studies are not in a position to address neither how complexly intertwined ethnic and religious issues are in contemporary societies nor how globalization facilitates the way religion and ethnicity manifest in everyday life. This chapter suggests that consumer researchers can develop a more comprehensive understanding of how religion and ethnicity inform consumer identity work in contemporary society by focusing on the way globalization, through its cultural, social and economic implications, facilitates consumers' pursuit of spirituality, appropriation of religious discourses for national, ethnic and class-based interests, as well as formation of new markets.

References

Askegaard, S., Arnould, E. J. and Kjeldgaard, D. (2005) 'Postassimilationist ethnic consumer research: Qualifications and extensions'. *Journal of Consumer Research*, 32: 160–70.

Bailey, J. M. and Sood, J. (1993) 'The effects of religious affiliation on consumer behavior: A preliminary investigation'. *Journal of Managerial Issues*, 5: 328–52.

Bair, S. C. (2003) 'Improving access to the U.S. banking system among recent Latin American immigrants.' *Consumer Bankers Association*. Available from: http://idbdocs.iadb.org/wsdocs/get document.aspx?docnum=547516 [accessed March 20 2015].

Bair, S. C. (2005) 'Improving the Access of Recent Latin American Migrants to the US Banking System'. In *Beyond Small Change: Making Migrant Remittances Count*, edited by D. F. Terry and S. R. Wilson. IDB, pp. 95–132.

Bandarage, A. (2004) 'Beyond globalization and ethno-religious fundamentalism'. *Development*, 47: 35–41.

Bauman, Z. (1998) *Globalization: The Human Consequences*. New York, NY: Columbia University Press.

Belk, R. W. (1987) 'A child's Christmas in America: Santa Claus as deity, consumption as religion'. *Journal of American Culture*, 10: 87–100.

Belk, R. W. (2001) 'Materialism and the making of the modern American Christmas'. In *Consumption: Critical Concepts in the Social Sciences*, edited by D. Miller. New York, NY: Routledge, p. 319.

Belk, R. W. (2013) 'The sacred in consumer culture'. In *Consumption and Spirituality*, edited by D. Rinallo, L. Scott, and P. Maclaran. New York, NY: Routledge, pp. 69–81.

Belk, R. W., Wallendorf, M. and Sherry Jr, J. F. (1989) 'The sacred and the profane in consumer behavior: Theodicy on the odyssey'. *Journal of Consumer Research*, 16: 1–38.

Belk, R. W. and Tumbat, G. (2005) 'The cult of Macintosh'. *Consumption, Markets & Culture*, 8: 205–17.

Berger, P. L. (1967) *The Sacred Canopy: Elements of a Sociological Theory of Religion*. New York, NY: Doubleday.

Bonsu, S. K. and Belk, R. W. (2010) 'Marketing a new African god: Pentecostalism and material salvation in Ghana'. *International Journal of Nonprofit and Voluntary Sector Marketing*, 15: 305–23.

Bouchet, D. (1995) 'Marketing and the redefinition of ethnicity'. In *Marketing in a Multicultural World*, edited by J. A. Costa and G. J. Bamossy. London: Sage Publications: pp. 68–104.

Buğra, A. (1998) 'Class, culture, and state: An analysis of interest representation by two Turkish business associations'. *International Journal of Middle East Studies*, 30: 521–39.

Burroughs, J. E. and Rindfleisch, A. (2002) 'Materialism and well-being: A conflicting values perspective'. *Journal of Consumer Research*, 29: 348–70.

Cleveland, M. and Chang, W. (2009) 'Migration and materialism: The roles of ethnic identity, religiosity, and generation'. *Journal of Business Research*, 62(10): 963–71.

Dávila, A. (2012) *Latinos, Inc. The Marketing and Making of a People*, Second edition. Berkeley, CA: University of California Press.

Deshen, S. (1997) 'The Passover celebrations of secular Israelis'. *Megamot*, 38: 528–47.

Delener, N. and Schiffman, L. G. (1988) 'Family decision making: The impact of religious factors'. *AMA Educators' Proceedings*, pp. 80–3.

Delener, N. (1990) 'The effects of religious factors on perceived risk in durable goods purchase decisions'. *Journal of Consumer Marketing*, 7: 27–38.

Delener, N. (1994) 'Religious contrasts in consumer decision behaviour patterns: Their dimensions and marketing implications'. *European Journal of Marketing*, 28: 36–53.

Días, E. (2013) 'Evangélicos!' in *Time*, April 15.

Dolan, C. (2013) 'Economies of expectation: Men, marriage, and miracles in Kenya's religious market-place'. In *Consumption and Spirituality*, edited by D. Rinallo, L. Scott and P. Maclaran. New York, NY: Routledge, pp.144–65.

Ergu, E. (2009) 'İslami Burjuvanın Şatafatlı Ev Hayatı', (The Pompous Domestic Life of Islamic Bourgeoisie) in *Tempo*, April 12.

Essoo, N. and Dibb, S. (2004) 'Religious influences on shopping behaviour: An exploratory study'. *Journal of Marketing Management*, 20: 683–712.

Glick Schiller, N., Çaglar, A. and Guldbrandsen, T. C. (2006) 'Beyond the ethnic lens: Locality, globality, and born-again incorporation'. *American Ethnologist*, 33(4): 612–33.

Haenni, P. (2005) *Islam De Marché: Láutre Révolution Conservatrice*. Seuil.

Hamilton, M. (2000) 'An analysis of the festival for mind-body-spirit, London'. In *Beyond New Age: Exploring Alternative Spirituality*, edited by S. Sutcliffe and M. Bowman. Edinburgh: Edinburgh University Press, p. 188.

Harris, F. C. (1994) 'Something within: Religion as a mobilizer of African American political activism'. *The Journal of Politics*, 56: 42–68.

Hirschman, E. C. (1981) 'American Jewish ethnicity: Its relationship to some selected aspects of consumer behavior'. *The Journal of Marketing*, 45(3): 102–10.

Hirschman, E. C. (1982) 'Ethnic variation in hedonic consumption'. *The Journal of Social Psychology*, 118: 225–34.

Hirschman, E. C (1983). 'Cognitive structure across consumer ethnic subcultures: A comparative analysis'. *Advances in Consumer Research*, 10: 97–102.

Hirschman, E. C. and la Barbera, P. A. (1989) 'The meaning of Christmas'. In *Interpretive Consumer Research*, edited by E. Hirschman. Provo, UT: Association for Consumer Research, pp. 136–47.

Hirschman, E. C., Ruvio, A. A. and Touzani, M. (2011) 'Breaking bread with Abraham's children: Christians, Jews and Muslims' holiday consumption in dominant, minority and diasporic communities'. *Journal of the Academy of Marketing Science*, 39: 429–48.

Izberk-Bilgin, E. (2012a) 'Infidel brands: Unveiling alternative meanings of global brands at the nexus of globalization, consumer culture, and Islamism'. *Journal of Consumer Research*, 39: 663–87.

Izberk-Bilgin, E. (2012b) 'Cyber-Jihad: Islamic consumer activism on the web'. *Advances in Consumer Research*, 40: 532–9.

Izberk-Bilgin, E. (2013) 'Theology meets the marketplace'. *Consumption and Spirituality*, edited by D. Rinallo, L. M. Scott and P. Maclaren. London: Routledge, pp. 16–41.

Kelderhouse, E. R. and Region, K. C. (2002) 'Banking Latino immigrants: A lucrative new market for progressive financial institutions'. *Federal Reserve Bank of St Louis*. Available from: https://www.stlouisfed.org/publications/bridges/fall-2002/banking-latino-immigrants-a-lucrative-new-market-for-progressive-financial-institutions.

Kimura, J. and Belk, R. W. (2005) 'Christmas in Japan: Globalization versus localization'. *Consumption Markets & Culture*, 8: 325–38.

Klein, N. (2000) *No Logo: Taking Aim at the Brand Bullies*. New York, NY: Picador.

Korten, D. C. (2001) *When Corporations Rule The World*. San Francisco: Berrett-Koehler Publications.

Kozinets, R. V. (2001) 'Utopian enterprise: Articulating the meanings of star trek's culture of consumption'. *Journal of Consumer Research*, 28: 67–88.

la Barbera, P. A. and Gürhan, Z. (1997) 'The role of materialism, religiosity, and demographics in subjective well-being'. *Psychology & Marketing*, 14: 71–97.

Lindekilde, L. (2010) 'Soft repression and mobilization: The case of transnational activism of danish muslims during the cartoons controversy'. *International Journal of Middle East Studies*, 42(03): 451–69.

Luedicke, M. (2011) 'Consumer acculturation theory: (Crossing) conceptual boundaries'. *Consumption Markets & Culture*, 14(3): 223–44.

McDaniel, S. W. and Burnett, J. J. (1990) 'Consumer religiosity and retail store evaluative criteria'. *Journal of the Academy of Marketing Science*, 18: 101–12.

Muniz Jr, A. M. and Schau, H. J. (2005) 'Religiosity in the abandoned Apple Newton brand community'. *Journal of Consumer Research*, 31: 737–47.

Ogilvynoor.com (n.d.) 'Why Islamic branding?' Ogilvynoor. Available from: http://www.ogilvynoor.com/index.php/why-islamic-branding/.

O'Neill, M. 'Meet the New Muslim consumer'. October 2010, www.campaignasia.com [accessed 28 May 2015].

Oncu, A. and Wayland, P. (1997) *Space, Culture, and Power: New Identities in Globalizing Cities*. London: Zed Books.

Oswald, R. L. (1999) 'Culture swapping: Consumption and the ethnogenesis of middle-class Haitian immigrants'. *Journal of Consumer Research*, 25: 303–18.

Park, R. E. (1950). *Race and Culture*. New York, NY: Free Press.

Peñaloza, L. N. (1994) 'Atravesando fronteras/border crossing: A critical ethnographic exploration of the consumer acculturation of Mexican immigrants'. *Journal of Consumer Research*, 21(1): 32–54.

Peñaloza, L. and Barnhart, M. (2011) 'Living US capitalism: The normalization of credit/debt'. *Journal of Consumer Research*, 38(4): 743–762.

Pink, J. (ed) (2009) *Muslim Societies in the Age of Mass Consumption*. Newcastle upon Tyne: Cambridge Scholars.

Rifkin, J. (2000) *The Age of Access: The New Culture of Hypercapitalism Where All of Life is a Paid-For Experience*. New York, NY: Penguin Putnam.

Rinallo, D., Borghini, S., Bamossy, G. and Kozinets, R. V. (2012) 'When sacred objects go B® a (n) d'. In *Consumption and Spirituality*, edited by D. Rinallo, L. Scott, and P. Maclaran. New York, NY: Routledge, pp. 29–41.

Rindfleisch, A. Burroughs, J. E. and Wong, N. (2005) 'Religiosity and brand commitment: A multicultural perspective'. In *Asia Pacific Advances in Consumer Research*, edited by Y. Ha and Y. Yi. Duluth, MN: Association for Consumer Research, p. 153.

Rindfleisch, A., Wong, N. and Burroughs, J. E. (2010) 'God & Mammon: The influence of religiosity on brand connections'. In *The Connected Customer: The Changing Nature of Consumer and Business Markets*, edited by S. Wuyts, M. G. Dekimpe, E. Gijsbrechts, and R. Pieters. New York, NY: Routledge, p. 163.

Ritzer, G. (2003) *The Globalization of Nothing*. Thousand Oaks, CA: Sage.

Robertson, C. K. (ed) (2002) *Religion as Entertainment*. New York, NY: Peter Lang Publishing.

Rytina, N. 2009. 'Estimates of the legal permanent resident population in 2008', Office of Immigration Statistics.

Sandıkcı, Ö. and Ekici, A. (2009) 'Politically motivated brand rejection'. *Journal of Business Research*, 62(2): 208–17.

Sandıkcı, Ö. and Ger, G. (2010) 'Veiling in style: How does a stigmatized practice become fashionable?' *Journal of Consumer Research*, 37: 15–36.

Sandıkcı, Ö. and Ömeraki, S. (2007) 'Islam in the marketplace: Does Ramadan turn into Christmas?' In *Advances in Consumer Research*, edited by G. Fitzsimons and V. Morwitz. Duluth, MN: Association for Consumer Research, pp. 610–15.

Sassen, S. (1988) *The Mobility of Labor and Capital: A Study in International Investment and Labor Flow*. Cambridge, MA: Cambridge University Press.

Sassen, S. (1991) *The Global City: New York, London, Tokyo*. Woodstock: Princeton University Press.

Sassen, S. (1998) *Globalization and Its Discontents: Essays on the New Mobility of People and Money*. New York, NY: The New Press.

Shachar, R., Erdem, T., Cutright, K. M. and Fitzsimons, G. J. (2011) 'Brands: The opiate of the nonreligious masses?' *Marketing Science*, 30: 92–110.

Scholte, J. A. (2005) *Globalization: A Critical Introduction*. New York, NY: Palgrave Macmillan.

Schouten, J. W. and McAlexander, J. H. (1995) 'Subcultures of consumption: An ethnography of the new bikers'. *Journal of Consumer Research*, 22: 43–61.

Sherry Jr., J. F. and McGrath, M. A. (1989) 'Unpacking the holiday presence: A comparative ethnography of two gift stores'. In *Interpretive Consumer Research*, edited by E. C. Hirschman. Provo, UT: Association for Consumer Research, pp. 148–67.

Sklair, L. (2001) *Transnational Capitalist Class*. Malden, MA: Blackwell Publishing Ltd.

Sood, J. and Nasu, Y. (1995) 'Religiosity and nationality: An exploratory study of their effect on consumer behavior in Japan and the United States'. *Journal of Business Research*, 34: 1–9.

Spohn, W. (2003) 'Multiple modernity, nationalism and religion: A global perspective'. *Current Sociology*, 51(34): 265–86.

Swimberghe, K., Flurry, L. A. and Parker, J. M. (2011) 'Consumer religiosity: Consequences for consumer activism in the United States'. *Journal of Business Ethics*, 103: 453–67.

Touzani, M. and Hirschman, E. C. (2008) 'Cultural syncretism and Ramadan observance: Consumer research visits Islam'. In *Advances in Consumer Research*, edited by A. Y. Lee and D. Soman. Duluth, MN: Association for Consumer Research, pp. 374–80.

Touzani, M., Hirschman, E. C. and Ruvio, A. (2009) 'Looking for Christmas in a Muslim country'. In *Advances in Consumer Research*, edited by A. McGill and S. Shavitt. Duluth, MN: Association for Consumer Research, pp. 210–13.

Üstüner, T. and Holt, D. B. (2007) 'Dominated consumer acculturation: The social construction of poor migrant women's consumer identity projects in a Turkish squatter'. *Journal of Consumer Research*, 34(1): 41–56.

Wald, K. D. (1987) *Religion and Politics in the United States*. New York, NY: St. Martin's Press.

Warner, W. L. and Srole, L. (1945). *The Social Systems of American Ethnic Groups*. New Haven, CT: Yale University Press.

Weber, M. (1922/1978) *Economy and Society: An Outline of Interpretive Sociology*. Berkeley, CA: University of California Press.

Wilkes, R. E., Burnett, J. J. and Howell, R. D. (1986) 'On the meaning and measurement of religiosity in consumer research'. *Journal of the Academy of Marketing Science*, 14: 47–56.

Wimmer, A. and Glick Schiller, N. (2002) 'Methodological nationalism and beyond: Nation–state building, migration and the social sciences'. *Global Networks*, 2(4): 301–34.

10

Wanting things and needing affiliation

Ethnic consumers and materialism

Mark Cleveland

Introduction

> He who dies with the most toys wins.
>
> *—Popular American bumper sticker*

Ethnicity and culture affect perceptions and priorities, and consequently, consumers' attitudes and behaviours. Cultural theorists envisage consumption as 'an inherently communicative act, a form of symbolic behaviour that creates and expresses meaning' (Wilk 1998, p. 320). Consumer goods are needed for 'making visible and stable the categories of culture' (Douglas and Isherwood 1979, p. 59). Measured against purely ideological or behavioural aspects, tangible cultural features disseminate far more readily to other cultures. Consumption-related values are pertinent for understanding the formation and expression of ethnic identities. Globalization, particularly the internationalization of markets and media, potentially heralds the loosening of cultural bonds. A contrarian perspective maintains that present circumstances not only motivate, but facilitate, the preservation of cultural differences. Whichever holds true, the ways consumers identify themselves is clearly an important managerial issue (Bouchet 1995).

Corporations are intensifying their efforts to develop and extend international brands. Advertisers employ numerous themes connected with materialism: achievement and success, abundance and wealth, gratification and happiness, glamour and exclusivity; which operate to reinforce status, social class and the desirability of upward social mobility. Researchers have long noted the association between brands and social status. In emerging economies, possessing Western brands often enhances the owner's social standing and can buttress their self-perceptions of sophistication and cosmopolitanism (Ger and Belk 1996a; Ger and Belk 1996b; Wong and Ahuvia 1998). The enormous potential afforded by economic prosperity in the developing world (and among ethnic minorities within developed nations) drives promotional efforts targeting consumers living in these countries. Rising discretionary income and the pervasiveness of media promoting hedonism and status ostensibly motivate people to seek recognition by conspicuously displaying consumption symbols (Dubois and Duquesne 1993; Sharma 2011). A visit to Nanjing Road (Shanghai), Causeway Bay (Hong Kong), the Ginza (Tokyo), the Dubai Mall (the world's largest) or for that matter, l'avenue des Champs-Élyssés (Paris, where the upscale shops of Cartier, etc. are thronged with East-Asian and Middle-Eastern shoppers) will persuade any sceptic that materialistic passion has been enthusiastically embraced by collectivist peoples. Indeed, *BCG* predicts that China will soon become the world's largest luxury market, overtaking the United States.[1] Following decades of material deprivation under Maoism, the Chinese 'are now hungry for material possessions, making up for lost time' (Yang and Stening 2011, p. 449).

The uncertainties that accompany rapid social change encourage materialism (Ger and Belk 1996b; Cleveland and Chang 2009). Hirschman (1992) opined that materialistic tendencies (e.g., conspicuous or compulsive consumption) represent attempts to restore a sense of self-concept when undergoing major life transitions or during moments of personal crisis. Belk *et al.* (2003) wrote that '[s]ocial control of consumer desire, either in the form of external control or self-control, is thought to decline in a consumer society . . . [this] desire is no longer a sin or vice but an attractive and sought after state of being' (p. 331). The *Cultural imperialism hypothesis* (Tomlinson 1991) – also denoted as *Coca-Colanization* (Hannerz 1992) and *McWorld* (Barber 1996) – evokes an assimilationist standpoint, assuming that because individuals are easily indoctrinated by the seductive powers of marketing, the natural desire of humans to seek material enrichment coupled with the global penetration of Western media or styled on Western ideals propels consumers to emulate the materialistic lifestyle of their counterparts living in Western nations. An opposing argument claims that some individuals recoil from globalization, retreating to their established values and ways of life, partly through fear of inundation by a homogenizing culture of consumption. Other consumer trajectories have been proposed, ensuing from the permutation of indigenous values with global cultural forces. With the globalization of markets and the multiculturalism of societies, international and domestic marketing managers are challenged to detect consumer segments with similar dispositions, preferences and behavioural responses; and to incorporate this understanding when constructing marketing strategies.

It is curious, against this background, that quantitative research examining ethnicity and materialism is meager, and cross-cultural studies are rarer still (Douglas and Craig 2010; Sharma 2011; Cleveland *et al.* 2009a; Shrum *et al.* 2012). The limited findings are confounded by different conceptualizations of materialism. Most literature positions materialism as an individual-level construct, although it is arguably as much the product of social forces. It is certainly true that 'important possessions reflect personal values and the inner self', yet these private meanings 'are shaped by and reflect one's culture' (Watson *et al.* 2002, p. 925). Embodying socio-cultural symbols, products and brands signal identity as well as indicating cultural complexity and change, particularly for consumers buffeted by several cultural spheres. The homogenous communities and ethnic identities of earlier ages are giving way to pluralistic societies and, for some individuals, polysemous identities. Consumers may oscillate between these identities, be they local, ethnic, religious or transnational. At other times, these entwined identities are inseparable; converging or conflicting depending on the context. Collectively, these issues inhibit generalizing materialism theories to international and intranational contexts.

Is the nature of materialism uniform across ethnic groups? How do materialistic tendencies amend over consumer lifecycle stages and changes in economic and social circumstances; how consistent are these patterns across ethnic conditions? Does globalization inexorably disseminate materialistic values? Are some ethnic traditions revitalizing in the face of globalization and if so, which ones and under which consumption contexts? Is there evidence that insular consumers have immunity to materialistic passion? How does ethnic affiliation and acculturation combine to advance materialism and could these relationships vary across cultures and situations? This chapter conceives materialism as an individual-level disposition that is regulated by the cultural values and behavioural norms operational in a particular social situation. Figure 10.1 summarizes the concepts considered. Reviewing the literatures on materialism, ethnicity and culture change, the focus is on elucidating the multifarious interrelationships of these constructs. I clarify how materialism is a product of enculturation and culture change. I explain how materialism differentially manifests at the intersection of social norms and the consumption situation, and offer reasons why these vary across ethnic groups. The chapter concludes with a discussion of the challenges facing cross-cultural inquiries on materialism, the implications for marketers and topics requiring research.

Materialism

The philosopher Sartre (1943) conjectured that the entire corpus of human conduct is reducible into three interrelated cardinal categories: 'being', 'doing', and 'having'. The terms 'consumer' and 'consuming' have progressively become the foundation for describing the human experience (Firat 1995), and for better or for worse, a person's sense of self or identity is interlaced with their material possessions (Domzal and Kernan 1993). It is therefore not surprising that in the past four decades, hundreds of papers have been published on materialism (Yang and Stening 2011; Cleveland and Chang 2009). Belying this intense activity, very little work has examined the innateness of materialism. Researching twins, Giddens et al. (2009) found an independent relationship with genetics. They concluded that individual differences in materialism must therefore stem principally from environmental causes.

Whereas some researchers conceive materialism as a personality trait (e.g. Belk 1985) or representing an attitude constellation (e.g. Kilbourne et al. 2005), others envisage it as a personal

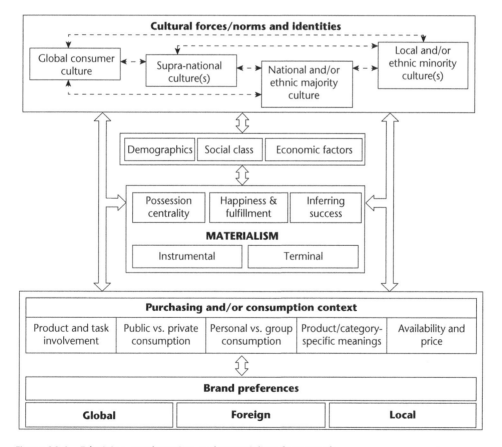

Figure 10.1 Ethnicity, acculturation and materialism framework

value (e.g., Richins and Dawson 1992; Kasser 2002; Burroughs and Rindfleisch 2002) or as a cultural characteristic (e.g. Inglehart 1990). Some envision materialism as relatively stable (Belk 1985), other authors contend that it is manifested situationally (Wallendorf and Arnould 1988; Hirschman 1992; Cleveland *et al.* 2009a). Uncertainty exists as to whether materialism is antecedent or consequent to consumption. Most papers depict materialism as ultimately negative for consumer well-being, yet a few persuasively claim that material pursuits potentially yield positive outcomes (Hudders and Pandelaere 2011; Karabati and Cemalcilar 2010; Richins and Rudmin 1994). The multiplicity of theories, conceptualizations and operationalizations (Shrum *et al.* 2012) has frustrated efforts to coherently link materialism to culture and ethnicity – concepts that themselves are fraught with ambiguity. The nature of materialism across cultures and how social forces affect materialism across ethnicities remains indefinite. Social groups may readily embrace or resist the consumption-based orientation characterizing Global Consumer Culture (GCC). The same consumer may be variably prone to materialistic tendencies, as per the social setting enveloping the consumption situation.

Materialism is 'the importance ascribed to the ownership and acquisition of material goods in achieving major life goals or desired states' (Richins 2004, p. 210). The most widely adopted characterizations are those advanced by Belk (1985), Csikszentmihalyi and Rochberg-Halton (1981) and Richins and Dawson (1992). Belk (1985) conceives materialism as a personality trait, consisting of three facets. *Possessiveness* refers to the 'inclination and tendency to retain control or ownership of one's possessions' (Ger and Belk 1990, p. 186). The other two dimensions entail negative connotations towards others. Whereas *envy* embodies the 'displeasure and ill will at the superiority of [another person] in happiness, success, reputation or the possession of anything desirable', *non-generosity* represents 'an unwillingness to give possessions to or share possessions with others' (p. 186). Envy is distinguishable from jealousy as the former relates to others' possessions (wanting something of another) and the latter, on personal possessions (not wanting to share your own possessions; Belk 1985).

From a motivational perspective, Csikszentmihalyi and Rochberg-Halton (1981) distinguish instrumental and terminal materialism. The latter describes consumption as an end, and stereotypically reflects how materialism negatively associates with consumer well-being. Achieving happiness through possessions is unattainable because this form of materialism is habit-forming and thus insatiable. Whereas a moderate level of envy is potentially beneficial for motivational purposes, at the extreme envy is a destructive trait, connected to several psychological disorders and anti-social behaviours (Burroughs amd Rindfleisch 2002). Non-generosity has also been empirically associated with unhappiness (Belk 1984). *Terminal materialism* intimates valuing stuff more than people (Ger and Belk 1996b), and for some, possessions substitute for deficient interpersonal relations (Rindfleisch *et al.* 1997). Achievement that is principally socially oriented implies that the pursuit of material goods stems from a deep-seated motivation to fulfill the expectations of relevant others, e.g., family (Markus and Kitayama 1991). *Instrumental materialism* is thus more a consequence of socialization relative to terminal materialism, which is perhaps primarily idiosyncratic. With instrumental materialism, objects are valued because they operate to achieve other objectives: a gift serves to strengthen a relationship; a creative or sacred object provides an aesthetic experience or enables fulfilment of a cultural ritual, and so forth (Zinkhan 1994). In this way, materialism needn't negatively impact subjective well-being. It is interesting to note that the opposite state of materialism – *asceticism* – has also been linked to mental disorders and maladaptive behaviours, which might ensue from self-denial of materialistic satisfaction (Belk 1985).

While some researchers cling to the trait perspective, the majority depict materialism as a value (Yang and Stening 2011). As defined by Rokeach (1973), values are 'enduring beliefs that a specific mode of conduct or end-state of existence is personally or socially preferable to an opposite or converse mode of conduct or end-state of existence' (p. 5). Value systems exist at the psychological and sociological levels (Schwartz 1999). Values underpin a large part of human cognition. Values are less circumstantial than attitudes, transcending particular objects. Like most values and norms, materialistic values are believed to be instilled in children by parents and other socialization agents, for example, in terms of giving/receiving gifts for birthdays and cultural occasions, as well as rewarding/withholding material items (e.g. toys) as a response to (or to encourage) appropriate conduct and to punish (discourage) inappropriate behaviours (Belk 1985). Consistent with the socialization argument, Rindfleisch et al. (1997) linked materialism in young adults to their experiences growing up under various forms of family structure. Richins and Dawson (1992) conceptualize materialism as an enduring personal value, inculcated by various socialization agents. Analogous to Belk's (1985) tripartite conceptualization, this value spans three domains: (1) the centrality of possessions in a person's life, (2) the belief that acquiring possessions yields happiness and fulfillment and (3) the use of belongings to infer the success of oneself and others.

Long ago, Veblen (1899) and Weber (1904–05[1947]) reasoned that *conspicuous consumption* (and its doppelganger, conspicuous waste)[2] was a tactic employed by individuals as a way to signal their identity and place within the social network. Baudrillard (1968) was among the first to explicitly expound the social meanings within consumer objects. These items are used by materialists to communicate information about themselves to other people, e.g., for signaling social status, adherence to group norms and indicating identity (Hudders and Pandelaere 2011). According to the *theory of planned behavior* (Ajzen 1985) the fulfillment of any behaviour is determined by behavioural intention and perceived behavioural control. The former stems from attitudes, subjective norms and the motivation to comply with these norms; whereas the latter concerns perceptions of ability to behave in a certain way (i.e. volition). Individual consumption behaviours, therefore, are shaped by and exert influence upon, the opinions and consumption activities of other members in the social network. Despite this reality, 'consumption's role in larger collectives, such as social networks and communities that operate within and across identity categories, is comparatively under-researched' (Crockett et al. 2011, p. 47).

Shrum et al. (2012) recently advocated a functional perspective on materialism, which they defined as 'the extent to which individuals attempt to engage in the construction and maintenance of the self through the acquisition and use of products, services, experiences, or relationships that are perceived to provide desirable symbolic value' (p. 2). They identified six motives that can be satisfied by material means: self-esteem, efficacy, meaning, continuity, distinctiveness and belonging. The latter three strongly connect with social membership. *Continuity* refers to identity-maintenance efforts over time and situations (e.g. purchasing 'home-country' products, keeping objects as nostalgic markers). *Distinctiveness* entails consumption rituals that signal differentiation; e.g. when immigrants wear traditional apparel. *Belonging* is motivated by the need for affiliation and acceptance, and for immigrants this could also enact towards the mainstream society (e.g. embracing a local sports team). All three represent 'identity construction motives fulfilled through *other signaling*' (Shrum et al. 2012, p. 4), for social comparison purposes or to obtain social approval.

Consumption embodies symbolism, revealing the formation or conservation of selfhood and affiliation, as well as denoting social and occupational status. Several authors have hinted that materialism is aggravated by worries of social condemnation and negative evaluations by others (Karabati and Cemalcilar 2010; He et al. 2012). Social behaviours are principally determined by norms guiding appropriate conduct (including the consequences of performing or not conforming) in a given situation (Triandis 1994).

Culture and ethnic identity

Attitudes, values and behaviours are a coproduction of idiosyncratic ingredients (personality traits, experiences) and shared cultural factors (Schwartz 1999). Since culture is so 'entwined with all facets of human existence . . . it is often difficult to determine how and in what ways its impact is manifested' (Craig and Douglas 2006, p. 322). Culture is antecedent to human thought and behaviour (Berry 1997; Triandis 1994). Due to its inherent complexity and intangibility, culture cannot be measured *per se*; one can only measure proxy signifiers. These typically consist of the degree to which value and belief systems and associated behavioural trappings are maintained, promoted and move across social boundaries.

Identity 'is the idea one has about oneself, one's characteristic properties, one's own body, and the values one considers to be important' (de Mooij 2004, p. 109). Ethnic and other forms of social identity incorporate culture into a person's self-concept, fundamentally permeating the feelings and actions of cultural members (Markus and Kitayama 1991). The inculcation of Ethnic Identity (EID) occurs throughout childhood, rooted in the contrasts children make between their own group and other groups, and reinforced by the socializing efforts of parents to infuse in their child a feeling of group membership (Rosenthal and Cichello 1986). This belongingness is indispensable to the development of the child's self-definition, which in turn eases the acquisition of cultural values and behaviours. With changes in social expectations, physical development and effects on self-esteem, identity assumes greater significance during adolescence (Erikson 1959). Studying EID requires examining how group members themselves understand and interpret their own ethnicity (Phinney 1990). EID must therefore be conceptualized as a psychological variable consisting of individuals' perceptions of social belongingness, as opposed to an objective descriptor of precise meaning, e.g., race, nationality, religious or language group (Venkatesh 1995). Eriksen (1993) reasons that ethnicity is a relational construct, best examined from the standpoint of group formation, maintenance and interaction with other groups. Consequently, members' sense of self-identification is 'mediated by the perceptions of others' (Venkatesh 1995, p. 33). As per Oswald (1999, p. 312), 'language, customs, representations of the past, religious beliefs, a sense of common origin, rules of comportment, behaviours that contrast with those of outsiders – all symbolize boundaries of inclusion and exclusion between social groups, levels and modes of belonging, leadership modalities and social identity'.

Due to mixed ethnicities and exposure to external cultures individuals can identify with multiple groups, and variably acquire, adhere or reject few, some, or many aspects from each group (Phinney 1990). Over successive generations, central and invisible facets (i.e. values) tend to be preserved by immigrants and their progeny, with erosion more likely along peripheral and visible facets such as language and media usage (Rosenthal and Feldman 1992). Moreover, people can switch back and forth between loci of identity (Stayman and Deshpandé 1989; Askegaard *et al.* 2005). Role theory (Wilson and Bozinoff 1980) posits that individuals are composed of multiple selves (ideal vs. actual, independent vs. interdependent, etc.), and different roles activate various identities. Analogous to a play, the same person can act quite differently (following a particular script) and use different props and costumes (products), depending on the situational requirements. The more salient a given identity, the more the individual will partake in identity-related activities. The stronger the level of socio-cultural identification, the greater is the dedication to group values/norms and hence, the group's sway on the person's attitudes/behaviours (Phinney 1990; Jamal 2003). Frideres and Goldenberg (1982) observed that EID was most prominent during religious/secular holidays, when travelling and when spending time with family. According to Oswald (1999, p. 303), 'consumers routinely "culture swap" – they borrow or buy the cultural trappings of other groups . . . since goods take on different meanings as consumers move between one identity and another'. Here, EID is a voluntary choice; negating the customary belief that consumers are merely culture bearers by recognizing that they are also culture producers (Arnould and Thompson 2005).

Ethnic identity thus embodies a higher-order, subjective construct, reflecting the idea that a person's identity builds around numerous aspects, which are inadequately summarized by uni-dimensional, objective criteria. Focusing on the relationships to materialism, the ensuing paragraphs discuss key ethnicity aspects.

The notion that consumption is contingent on ethnicity and culture change is well established. Influencing perceptions, configuring priorities and translating consumer needs into wants, culture also reinforces behavioural expectations via social norms. Certain norms are formal and explicit (e.g., laws, club regulations); most are implicit and informal, with such knowledge (including possible rewards/sanctions for conformity/deviance) acquired gradually through group engagements. These norms affect behavioural intentions, ultimately shaping behaviour. Thus within a given context, whether materialism is perceived as a moral indiscretion by the relevant in-group combined with the individual's degree of adherence to group values/norms – including appropriateness of autonomous opinions – determines whether materialism will be enacted.

Social psychologists describe the need to belong as a deep-seated, pervasive human motivation and the foundation for comprehending interpersonal behaviour. Two requirements are implicated to satisfy this drive: '[f]irst, there is a need for frequent, affectively pleasant interactions with a few other people, and, second, these interactions must take place in the context of a temporally stable and enduring framework of affective concern for each other's welfare' (Baumeister and Leary 1995, p. 497). For immigrants and ethnic minorities, *social networks* are indispensable for ethnic maintenance/expression and for consumer acculturation (Peñaloza 1989; Peñaloza 1994). Ethnic associations, neighbourhoods and other networks established by minorities also enable members to live somewhat isolated from mainstream society. The importance of maintaining *interpersonal relationships* with in-group members may elevate materialism. Possessions 'are a convenient means of storing the memories and feelings that attach to our sense of past' (Belk 1988, p. 148). Nostalgia is connected to many consumption experiences (Holbrook 1993). Associated products, particularly when consumed with kin and kind, help the consumer relive cherished moments. Assimilating the symbolic meaning inherent to valued possessions, these objects form part of the extended self (Belk 1988), enhancing self-concept and constructing identity (Hudders and Pandelaere 2011).

It is not only the owner that defines materialistic goods, but also the owner's impression of how s/he thinks others will evaluate the goods. Researching advertising memory in social contexts, Puntoni and Tavassoli (2007) found that the presence of others activated impression management concerns. *Evaluation-apprehension theory* (Baumeister and Leary 1995) and *social capital theory* (Bourdieu 1984) imply that the perceptions of relevant others mediates individual materialism levels. Materialistic consumers 'are concerned about displaying their status and possessions in their relevant social groups' (Sharma 2011, p. 289). Command over economic resources supports and is reinforced by social capital. Immigrant and ethnic minority consumers might cultivate a *conspicuous consumption* lifestyle, to gauge and convey their own success (Cleveland and Chang 2009). Alternatively, an inconspicuous consumption strategy could emphasize adherence to cultural norms emphasizing austerity, or reduce the risk of being categorized into the wrong ethnic group (Shrum et al. 2012). In public, individuals generally abstain from expressing opinions or engaging in behaviours that could convey a negative impression or invite disapproval from others. Studies show that felt emotions (e.g., conceit, humiliation) are felt more acutely when in the presence of others (He *et al.* 2012). Lastly, from a *social exchange theory* perspective, the exchange of material goods might substitute for direct interactions with another/others, or an attempt to compensate for perceived inadequacies thereof (Wilk 1998; Rindfleisch *et al.* 1997).

Indispensable for communication, language comprises a channel for conveying the intangible components of culture – activities and histories, as well as their interpretations – across place and time (Craig and Douglas 2006). Individuals modify their verbal expressions to conform to social expectations and to coordinate in-group activities. This interactivity distinguishes from the passive, uni-directional flow characterizing most media (Cleveland *et al.* 2015). *Media consumption* is another prominent ethnicity dimension, particularly since it is somewhat volitional (Lee and Tse 1994). Satellite television and the internet enable individuals to select from a set of alternatives. Reference group exposure depends in part on media choices, which is both a cause and effect of the individual's worldview. Holt (1998) distinguishes the media habits of high and low *cultural capital* consumers. The former, with their cosmopolitan disposition, consume international media and gain exposure to foreign reference groups; enabling adoption of products/styles from elsewhere. This group sets or modifies the standards (the subjective, elaborated codes) dictating suitable patterns of consumption, including those regulating status and hedonic goods, which then trickle down to lower social strata. Low cultural-capital consumers tend to confine their media and reference groups to local or ethnic sources. Subsequently, the parochial group relies heavily on objective forms of meaning inherent to consumption (i.e. restricted codes). Thus, the dual role played by cultural capital, in terms of establishing and assigning significance to status goods, ensures that the objects and connotations employed as markers will normally vary across social classes and potentially, cultural groups.

Other ethnic aspects commonly invoked include *ethnic customs, aesthetics and rituals* (Phinney 1990). The multiplicity and variability of customs makes it impractical to postulate specific relationships; some activities may encourage materialistic tendencies, whereas others might inhibit the same. *Family structure* and adherence to traditional *gender roles* have both served as ethnicity indicators. These resemble several cultural values discussed later.

Most studies report negative links between materialism and happiness (Millar and Thomas 2009). The unquenchable nature of terminal materialism is clearly detrimental; however, a positive relationship could exist. Some motives driving instrumental materialism (economic security, affiliation, self-improvement, upward mobility, etc.) associate positively with social well-being (Karabati and Cemalcilar 2010; Richins and Rudmin 1994). The valence 'may depend on what other values one holds central, particularly if these other values are antithetical to a materialistic lifestyle' (Burroughs and Rindfleisch 2002, p. 349), for example, religious ideals.

The self-promotion, consumption-based orientation embodied by materialism is regarded as an aspect of economic affluence, secularism and Western post-industrial life (Ger and Belk 1990). Most religions are diametrically opposed to materialistic desires, and religious values hold more sway in traditional societies (Watson *et al.* 2002; Burroughs and Rindfleisch 2002). Nearly all consumers worldwide identify with a particular religious creed, yet few studies examine how religion guides consumer behaviour. World religions share an emphasis on subordinating personal objectives to focus on the betterment of others, and demoting the significance of material belongings in favour of embracing spiritual aspirations. Catholic teachings, for example, are irreconcilable with the self-centredness of materialism; a point repeatedly preached by Pope John Paul II (Tobacyk *et al.* 2011). Conversely, contemporary North American culture – preponderantly individualist and Christian – has been linked to the anthropocentric concept that humans possess dominion over the Earth, as stated in the Bible (Genesis I). Most Americans affiliate with Protestantism, of which the tenets find some compatibility with materialism. As per the *Protestant work ethic* (Weber 1947), 'personal financial success is a divine blessing' (Tobacyk *et al.* 2011, p. 946). Describing the 'prosperity gospel' preached by several evangelical denominations, Stillman *et al.* (2012) wrote that 'religious and spiritual pursuits are not inimical to spending and wealth, but are explicitly linked to financial and materialistic rewards' (p. 6). This contrasts against the notions of harmony and submission espoused by Islam (Sarigöllü 2009). The doctrines of numerous faiths incorporate fatalistic perspectives. Expressions equivalent to 'God Willing' are found in Latin (*Deus Vult*) in reference to Catholicism and in Arabic (Inšā' Allāh) regarding Islam (Bloom and Blair 2002). Buddhism distinguishes fate from karma. The former denotes the inevitability of a chain of events (according to the master plan of a Supreme Being), whereas karma springs from intention (Chapple 1986). Unlike fate, karma is volitional; a consequence of the motives (good or bad) behind an action. Good deeds sow positive rewards whereas bad conduct reaps negative outcomes. Venkatesh (1995) contends that in Indian culture, spiritualism is not incompatible with materialism, 'instead they belong to the same realm of experience' (Gupta 2011, p. 253).

Frequently spanning ethnic groups, different faiths are often practised by members of the same ethnic group. Individuals vary in the intensity to which they internalize and practise religious-relevant aspects, depending on the motives underlying religious fulfillment. For instance, immigrants will often join congregations soon after their arrival for spiritual comfort, but also to obtain support for the difficult transition and to make in-group connections. Stillman *et al.* (2012) distinguish between intrinsically religious people (for whom faith is a fundamental part of their self-concept) and those practicing religion for external reasons (e.g. for social benefits). This explains equivocal findings on the relationship between religiosity and materialism. Burroughs and Rindfleisch (2002) and Stillman *et al.* (2012) reported reduced materialism among those with higher levels of spirituality. Cleveland and Chang (2009) reported an inverse (non-significant) relationship among first- (second-) generation Koreans, whereas Cleveland, Laroche and Hallab (2012b) documented positive relationships for both Muslim and Christian Lebanese. Contrary to their predictions, Tobacyk *et al.* (2011) reported similar materialism – for both success/centrality and happiness sub-dimensions – among Catholic Poles and chiefly Protestant Americans. These latter findings support the idea that materialism advances in places facing rapid social change, despite conflicting traditional values.

Ethnically salient consumers should presumably be more traditional and consequently, have greater immunity to external influences transmitting materialism. Then again, traditional societies tend to be collectivistic and this may foster materialism when the self-promotion component is understood to include in-group members in terms of achieving status and acquiring possessions for kith and kin. Ger and Belk (1990; Ger and Belk 1996b) believe that the Protestant work ethic is now stronger in certain developing nations and weaker in the post-industrial West. Ger and Belk (1996b) speculated that evolving social conditions enhances materialism. Cleveland and Chang (2009) found that materialism was higher among first-generation immigrants from a collectivist country (Korea) vs. their second-generation (Canadian-born) counterparts, even though the earlier generation predictably expressed higher Korean EID. They concluded that this was due to acculturative stress and anxiety of separation from their native land. As immigrants move away from their home country, a greater burden is laid upon material possessions to anchor EID and to fashion a new identity, 'especially when the move is voluntary and reflects upward social mobility' (Mehta and Belk 1991, p. 400). Crises of identity from acculturation pressures, and the relative anonymity of modern society, precipitate identity-seeking behaviours, whereby possessions compensate for an insecure identity or low self-esteem (Kasser 2002).

To recap, materialism is not necessarily incompatible with traditional identity. Indeed, some authors maintain that materialism embodies a latent, universal human desire for material and status enrichment (Belk *et al*. 2003), although genetic research (Giddens *et al*. 2009) fails to support this explanation. As evidenced by the equivocal results, exactly how ethnicity and culture intertwine with materialism is still not well understood. This ambiguity arises from two inter-related issues: differences in the values underlying culture and EID, and differences ensuing from contact with external cultures.

Ethnic values and materialism

Cross-national investigations ordinarily omit scales for cultural phenomena. True cross-cultural studies integrate such measures, normally operationalized along dimensions denoting the guiding principles/standards and associated life goals (Rokeach 1973; Triandis 1994). These values underpin social arrangements and practices, and thus consumption-related attitudes and activities. Indeed, the bumper-sticker slogan opening this chapter is laden with value elements, commencing with 'He' (masculinity and individualism due to singular tense), 'the most' (dominance, epitomizing hierarchy) and concluding with 'wins' (mastery). The discussion centres on the connections of materialism to the typologies proposed by Hofstede (1991), Schwartz (1999) and Hall (1976).

The most fundamental distinction between societies concerns the respective roles of the individual vs. the group. Under *individualism*, people are supposed to take care of themselves and of their immediate family only. Persons adhering to this independent self-construal are 'individualist, egocentric, separate, autonomous, idiocentric, and self-contained' (Markus and Kitayama 1991, p. 226). Individualists' behaviours arise from cost/benefit calculations (Triandis *et al*. 1993). Consequently, they are susceptible to the rewards ensuing from personal effort and less disposed towards rewards reflecting the group. Individualists, according to Furnham (1984) should be more materialistic than collectivists, since becoming rich and obtaining material goods are desirable end-states for those questing for economic independence. Within individualistic societies, marketing caters to consumers' wishes for personal gratification, selection and novelty (Nakata and Sivakumar 2001). Roth (1995) confirmed that individualists have a proclivity for variety-seeking and hedonistic experiences. Moreover, asserting autonomy encourages individualists to desire materialistic objects that are consistent with the goal of self-differentiation (Watson *et al*. 2002).

Cultures high in *collectivism* emphasize group harmony, social order, loyalty and reputation (Hofstede 1991). In-groups and out-groups are more stable and concrete for collectivists. If individualists are stereotypically more materialistic then ethnic consumers with an interdependent self-construal should be less so, given their propensity to subordinate personal desires – especially when in conflict with the group – and presumably, their better capability to resist the materialistic appeals associated with the individualist West. Yet, as noted earlier, collectivists could be more materialistic when what is valued is the admiration and status accruing to kin and kind from possession ownership (Ger and Belk 1990). Collectivists' higher levels of generosity and willingness to share may encourage materialistic passion (Cleveland and Chang 2009). Employing Belk's (1985) materialism scale, Turan (2007, c.f. Karabati and Cemalcilar 2010) reported a positive link between collectivism and acquisition-centrality, and an inverse relationship between individualism and the success facet, though individualists did score higher on the happiness subscale.

Kagitcibasi (1997) contends that instead of representing fixed states or polar opposites, individualism-collectivism (I-C) simultaneously exist within the same person, with one or the other subject to context factors. Triandis and Gelfand (1998) alternatively proposed vertical and horizontal I-C components. Under vertical individualism (e.g., American society), an acute sense of competition with others underscores the motivation to distinguish oneself and acquire status. Under horizontal individualism (e.g., Swedish society), self-reliance and uniqueness are valued, although these are not necessarily obtainable through competition but rather through self-transcendence (Karabati and Cemalcilar 2010). Whereas personal goals are subordinated for both horizontal and vertical forms of collectivism (e.g., Israeli *kibbutz* and Korean society, respectively), people within the latter form are predisposed to 'support competitions of their in-groups with out-groups', and – unlike horizontal collectivists – they will yield to authorities if this is deemed necessary to achieve superiority over competing groups, even when the methods are seen extremely objectionable by in-group members (Triandis and Gelfand 1998, p. 119).

I-C resembles Schwartz's (1999) continuum of autonomy vs. conservativism. *Intellectual autonomy* portrays the appropriateness of personal freedom vs. embeddedness within the collectivity, in terms of the engagement of intellectual pursuits and the fostering ideas. *Affective autonomy* denotes the independent quest for pleasure and other emotionally positive experiences, presumably whetting material desire. With *conservativism*, individual needs are fulfilled by partaking in a shared way of life and striving towards communal aspirations, rather than pursuing personal outcomes that might conflict with the traditional order. Product choices, including luxuries, status markers and gifts, should closely reflect social norms; whereas idiosyncratic attitudes and tastes are liable to steer selection in less conservative circles (Wong and Ahuvia 1998).

Materialism's relationship to intellectual autonomy and conservativism is ambivalent. Conservativism can imply valuing material goods due to their historical significance (e.g., heirlooms, nostalgia) and their ability to render concrete intangible cultural values. Several of the sub-values associated with conservativism are clearly inconsistent with materialism (self-discipline, obedience, moderateness and devoutness), yet others are conducive (preservation of public image, reciprocation of favours and honouring parents/elders). Belk (1985) noted that traits associated with conservativism (e.g., Protestant work ethic) link to an aversion towards charitable acts, consistent with his non-generosity subscale. Connected to intellectual autonomy, people accrue status by exhibiting cultural capital (Bourdieu 1984), e.g., displaying comparatively rare customs. The value of aesthetic possessions partly stems from their capacity for social differentiation (Wallendorf and Arnould 1988). These private meanings could encourage materialism through the acquisition of products necessary to exhibit and perform cultural knowledge and rituals. As Belk (2000, p. 137) declares, the 'rise of global consumption ideals potentially makes the elite among Third World consumers into cosmopolitans who are more concerned with how they compare to the world's most privileged consumers than they are to compare themselves locally'. For impression management purposes, materialists may amass and display discretionary experiences similar to how they would exhibit possessions (Millar and Thomas 2009). Yet, versus their counterparts that have endured pecuniary scarcity, consumers who have consistently experienced affluence ought to have broader horizons. In line with Inglehart's (1990) *post-materialism theory* and consistent with striving for intellectual autonomy, they are motivated by abstract concerns (e.g., environmentalism, self-actualization) and less fixated on materialistic matters.

The context continuum advanced by the anthropologist Hall (1976) closely parallels the I-C divide. The explicit exchange of information is the chief purpose fulfilled by communication within *low-context* societies. Communication is principally for constructing and preserving in-group relationships within *high-context* cultures: 'most of the information is either in the physical context or internalized in the person, while very little is in the coded, explicit, transmitted part of the message' (Hall 1976, p. 79). Individualistic societies typically speak low-context Germanic languages (e.g., English). High-context languages (e.g., Chinese, Arabic, Spanish) prevail within collectivistic societies. This has many marketing implications, especially regarding information search and advertising appeals. Germans prefer (low-context) detailed product-attribute facts when acquiring information in conjunction with an automobile purchase whereas their Italian counterparts favour (high-context) imagery and subjective allusions to car-usage situations (de Mooij 2004). High-context collectivists place greater reliance on word-of-mouth, interpersonal sources, whereas individualists favour explicit media information (Laroche *et al.* 2005). Cleveland *et al.* (2015) recently reported higher materialism among consumers living in high-context societies. This, the authors speculated, was partly due to global media exposure (promoting secular consumption values), which was also higher for respondents from high-context countries. Interestingly, these respondents outscored their low-context counterparts on the importance of preserving their EID.

To summarize, the individualist is predisposed towards materialism when consumption activities are connected to accomplishment/status for the self, whereas the collectivist is prone to materialism when conspicuous consumption achieves status for the (extended) family and other in-groups, provided that this orientation is not irreconcilable with in-group behavioural expectations and finds congruency with other core societal values. Whereas individualists crave material items consistent with the objective of standing apart from the crowd, the collectivist desires materialist objects enabling compliance with social expectations and favourable comparisons with others occupying similar status. The horizontal individualism of German society explains why Germans 'do not see material possessions as a distinguishing factor in social institutions of society' as much as their vertical-individualist American counterparts (Kilbourne *et al.* 2005, p. 638). Consistent with evaluation-apprehension theory, sensitivity to norms elevates materialism among collectivists if fellow members also embrace the same, especially within public settings.

Power distance (PD) associates with traditional notions of dominance, stratification and rigidity. Within high PD societies, superiors exhibit authoritarian tendencies and subordinates are expected to be passively obedient. Attempts to thwart the social order, dividing the 'haves' from the 'have-nots', are regarded harshly. These aspects impede susceptibility to outside cultural influences; however, they advance materialism by encouraging the display of goods to designate social stratification (Hofstede 1991; Roth 1995). Low PD cultures value fairness, equal opportunity and merit through ability, as well as initiative over birthright, nepotism and class (Nakata and Sivakumar 2001). Here, Roth (1995) argues that advertising appeals centred on social roles and ethic affiliation should be deemphasized.

Schwartz's second continuum is analogous to PD. *Hierarchy* emphasizes the pecking order and uneven distribution of resources; accepted as legitimate by societal members. The sub-values of social power, influence, wealth and authority are prominent within hierarchical societies, as are the virtues of humility and accepting one's place. *Egalitarianism* implies recognizing other societal members as moral equals and a concern for their prosperity and welfare. Conspicuous consumption is an obvious tactic to indicate one's relative standing within relatively misanthropic, hierarchical societies. Consumers pursuing status through consumption should be more sensitive to group opinions and apt to conform to in-group norms (Goldsmith and Clark 2012). Symbolic goods indicate the person's echelon within the social strata, relative to more egalitarian environments where such goods aid in expressing the person's unique, internal self (Wong and Ahuvia 1998).

Somewhat similar to hierarchy, traditional sex roles and male dominance are pronounced in *masculine* (MAS) societies; and mannish values/aims are stressed, e.g., boldness, achievement, as well as acquiring status, money and possessions (Nakata and Sivakumar 2001). Within such cultures (e.g., Japan), 'people consume for show' (de Mooij 2004, p. 35), whereas within *feminine* societies such as Denmark, consumption modesty is encouraged, and there is more of an emphasis on helping others, improving the quality of life and shunning self-recognition. At the national level, MAS and PD are strongly correlated (Hofstede 1991). Anchored by mastery and harmony, Schwartz's third continuum is conceptually similar. *Mastery* implies advancement through self-assertion and dominating the world; and, consistent with materialism, 'gaining control of objects and making them possessions is a key way of accomplishing this' (Belk 1985, p. 268). Self-direction, social recognition and accomplishment are embraced by societies emphasizing mastery. Products denoting social status are readily justifiable within cultures stressing ambition, achievement and audaciousness (Gutterman 2009). From an immigration standpoint, mastery implies successful integration with mainstream society, in terms of 'becoming adept at both its elements and relational rules' (Peñaloza 1994, p. 42). Societies positioned towards the opposite pole, *harmony*, espouse an ecumenical perspective towards the natural and social worlds. These ideals are not necessarily incompatible with individual autonomy; however self-enhancement objectives should not entail exploitation. Harmony can manifest for objects that 'allow aesthetic and physical awareness of the environment' (Watson *et al.* 2002, p. 925).

Cultures with high *Uncertainty Avoidance* (UA) (e.g., Greece) are aversive to new ideas, products, technologies and practices (Hofstede 1991), and place greater weight on word-of-mouth communications as a means of reducing risk (Nakata and Sivakumar 2001). To minimize ambiguity, UA societies adhere to strictly defined laws and measures. Globalization is fraught with uncertainty, in terms of breaking down barriers and reorganizing societies. Tensions arising from the intersection of different customs and modes of expression are acutely experienced by members of UA societies; leading to disorientation, apprehension about the future and perhaps xenophobia (Mau *et al.* 2008). According to Hofstede (1991), '[t]he more anxious cultures tend to be the most expressive cultures' (p. 115). He goes on to say that money (and what it buys) conveys extrinsic meaning. Empirical findings uphold the positive materialism–UA link (Cleveland 2007). Then again, because low UA societies have fewer formal rules, people are more tolerant of behaviours and ideals that differ from their own (Hofstede 1991), which could include materialism.

Confucian-dynamism (Hofstede 1991) is more commonly labelled *long-* versus *short-term orientation* (LTO vs. STO). STO societies attach importance to obligations and reciprocity, concern for face, etc. *Hyperbolic discounting theory* (Thaler 1981) refers to the general tendency of human beings to prefer rewards sooner rather than later, hence discounting the worth of the later reward. Materialistic gratification may be preferred within STO societies, even to the detriment of long-term goals (Hudders and Pandelaere 2011). Discounting should be moderate in LTO cultures. LTO societal members value thrift and perseverance, live within their means and save 'for a rainy day'. The pressure to keep up appearances is more pronounced among their STO counterparts; they may even overspend to maintain their social image (Cleveland 2007).

Beyond temporality, Yau (1988) delineated Chinese values stemming from Confucianism: spirituality (personal dignity ensuing from spiritual supremacy), face-saving (respectability and/or deference obtained from others, though one's position in the social network and by exhibiting behaviour befitting one's station), group orientation and power distance. Yang and Stening (2011) empirically examined materialism's association with these facets and Maoism (a political ideology epitomizing selflessness, extreme egalitarianism and complete renunciation of capitalistic society), conjecturing diminished materialism among Chinese valuing spirituality, group orientation and Maoism. Materialism, they argued, should be higher for those concerned with maintaining face and social status and, particularly, for those embracing post-Maoism ideology (espoused by Deng Xiaoping who famously said: 'To be rich is glorious', and 'It doesn't matter if a cat is black or white, so long as it catches mice' cited in Yang & Stening 2011, p. 443). As expected, materialism positively linked to power distance and post-Maoism, and negatively with subjective well-being. Contrary to hypotheses, face associated negatively with materialism. As China is drawn into the global capitalist system, 'the rhetoric of wealth as achievement . . . [supplants] the Confucian language of humility' (Wong and Ahuvia 1998, p. 428).

Researching twelve countries, Ger and Belk (1996b) resolved that materialism is neither exclusively Western, nor directly related to affluence, but is coupled with unsettled social conditions. A subsequent study reinforced these conclusions (Belk *et al.* 2003). Burroughs and Rindfleisch (2002) assert that materialism levels have plateaued within advanced (primarily individualistic) economies, whereas materialistic desires are escalating among emerging-market consumers (Sharma 2011). Consumers in advanced economies may be moving towards abstract post-material aspirations (Inglehart 1990); however, recent findings provide only equivocal support for this conjecture (Cleveland *et al.* 2009a).

Ethnic change and materialism

Identity positions are fluid and in motion: a product of reconciling the various acculturation factors facing individuals under different contexts (Askegaard *et al.* 2005). The nature and extent of culture change depends on situational factors encouraging or inhibiting socialization, including length of time in the host country, employment, residence (ethnic vs. mixed neighbourhood), marital status and lifecycle stage, etc. Furthermore, explicit and/or implicit institutional policies regarding immigration and ethnic minorities abet or hinder the expression of diversity. Because minority groups face the prospect of cultural assimilation, members are motivated to maintain solidarity with and patriotism towards the group(s) with which they identify most strongly, so that they and future generations can maintain their distinctive values and traditions (Cleveland and Chang 2009). Acquiring new traits does not mean inexorable desertion of ethnic traits. EID 'may be retained or even strengthened despite acculturation' (Cleveland *et al.* 2009b, p. 208). Contemporary theorists envisage multiple and more complex culture-change outcomes. The most prominent framework, promulgated by Berry (1997), describes four patterns from the permutation of two issues: (1) maintenance of original cultural identity/traits and (2) contact with, and participation in, the host culture.

Assimilation is when host traits steadily replace those of the original entity. Overshooting describes cases when the adopted behaviour extends beyond the host society (Stayman and Deshpandé 1989), transpiring when the immigrant craves mainstream acceptance and willingly disassociates from their original culture (Triandis 1994). At the other extreme lies *separation* (or segregation), when the individual actively refrains from participating in or adopting from the host – or is otherwise unable to engage with the alternate culture due to discrimination, prejudice or lingering animosity – in favour of ethnic affirmation. This can produce hyper-identification: zealous adherence to the values and behavioural norms of the original group exceeding levels found in the home country (Mehta and Belk 1991; Askegaard *et al.* 2005).

Marginalization implies disengagement from original and alternative cultural identities (e.g. counter-cultures). Ethnic attachment hinges partially on the perceived responses of mainstream members. Researching marginalized rural-to-urban migrants, Üstüner and Holt (2007) determined that those living in the deprived neighbourhoods experienced social stigmatism, which diminished ethnic identity and dignity. From a consumer behaviour standpoint, this pattern may reflect the lifestyles of ascetic individuals who eschew consumption except that required for survival. At the societal level, marginalization finds resonance with the past and current political ideologies of China (Maoism) and North Korea (Juche), respectively.

Integration describes blending without loss of distinction. Jamal (2003) explains how non-ethnic ties facilitate immigrants' exposure to unfamiliar products, which are adopted, then modified to suit their tastes. This applies to mainstream cultures when they are permeated by outside influences, e.g., as a consequence of globalization (Cleveland *et al.* 2011c; Gillespie *et al.* 2010). For example, affluent, young urban Chinese consumers 'are shifting from collective values to greater individualism, and have aspirations of modernizing, but on their own terms' (Douglas and Craig 2010, p. 446). Mendoza and Martinez's (1981) framework differentiates between incorporation and transmutation (or creolization). The latter depicts hybridized social entities (and related artifacts and behaviours, e.g., hip-hop music, *Ganguro* subculture) forged over an indeterminate period of time from the amalgamation of cultural elements.

Consumer acculturation 'primarily focuses on cultural adaptation as manifest in the marketplace' (Peñaloza 1989, p. 111). Direct agents comprise family, peers and other reference groups; indirect agents include media, marketing and retail businesses (Lee and Tse 1994).[3] Peñaloza and Gilly (1999, p. 101) aver that marketers have their own culture, 'with values including initiative, consummating exchanges, competing, [and] making money'. Consumer culture amplifies the importance accorded to individual pursuits/desires and the escalation of consumer expectations (Ger and Belk 1996a), potentially to the detriment of ethnic and religious values. Emerging-market consumers are discounting utilitarian needs in favour of satisfying hedonic ideals and consigning priority to status symbols (Sharma 2011). Douglas and Isherwood (1979) proposed the envy theory of needs, essentially stating that *we want what others have*. This spreading ideology of desire is said to have its origins in modern American culture (Hirschman 1988; Belk *et al.* 2003), whereby the latter was shaped by a relative absence of a rigid class strata and a moderation of religious opposition towards conspicuous consumption (Wilk 1998).

Intercultural contact and cultural artifacts help to confirm identity. With a significance extending well beyond 'their utilitarian character and commercial value' (McCracken 1986, p. 71), consumer goods are cherished because of their implicit semiotic qualities that express social standing (Bourdieu 1984) and inclusion or exclusion with social groupings (Oswald 1999; Shrum *et al.* 2012). These objects substantiate otherwise intangible cultural meaning.

As migrants, immigrants are predisposed to be adaptive, and this presumably carries over to product adoption. Whether relocation is motivated by lifestyle, or for economic or socio-political reasons, it will impact the acculturation style as well as the absorption of materialistic values, ultimately having an effect on social well-being. The stress of adapting a new cultural environment may precipitate low self-esteem and insecurity. These psychological states have been associated with a materialistic orientation, insofar that possessing goods is envisaged as a means to achieving happiness (Hudders and Pandelaere 2011). Peñaloza (1989) proposed that 'uncertainty due to the effects of multiple role demands of multiple reference cultures may result in the accelerated adoption and conspicuous consumption of products associated with the new culture' (p. 112).

Most people hitherto lived their lives in accordance with parochial values and behavioural expectations. The perspective of culture change as a dichotomous process involving home/host cultural elements neglects to consider how contemporary global forces impel social transformation (Cleveland and Laroche 2007; Askegaard *et al.* 2005). Cultural intermingling now encompasses whole regions whereas previously it applied only to an echelon of global metropolises. Consumer acculturation theory needs revision to elucidate the 'contestations of cultural presence and meanings in an increasingly global arena' (Peñaloza 1994, p. 51).

Global consumer culture and materialism

Representing the implicit flattening of the planet into a single consciousness, globalization describes an uncoordinated process of accelerating and cumulative interactions of markets, companies and, increasingly, cultures and individuals (Robertson 1992). Globalization is championed as mechanism for pecuniary advancement, as Firat (1995, p. 110) describes:

> the most important thing in modernity was to expand the pie . . . so that all subjects could get a larger piece of the pie and thus take greater control over their material conditions and improve their lives. [. . .] In this society, the most important determinant, the all-important provider of the promised 'better life', was material wealth and accumulation.

Superseding nation-states, marketing, technology and globalization are coming together to level the economic playing field. The penetration of social spheres is equally noteworthy. Cultural adjustments arising from globalization are everywhere but incomplete, occurring at different speeds and magnitudes. Consumers living in emerging economies have felt these effects most intensely (Gupta 2011). The social-anthropological critique of globalization proceeds from *world-system theory* (Wallerstein 1989). This perspective portrays the asymmetry existing among social blocs: 'key conceptual pairs have been center (or core) and periphery, metropolis and satellite' (Hannerz 1992, p. 219). The core describes the leading cities of economically dominant countries while the periphery depicts the poorer regions and hinterlands. The power disparity favouring Western countries – above all, the United States – means that they disproportionately direct global cultural flows (Venkatesh 1995; Ger and Belk 1996a).

Globalization casts doubt on individuals' sense of self, identities and cultural belongingness (Arnett 2002). Four decades ago Bell insisted that ethnicity 'is best understood not as a primordial phenomenon in which deeply held identities have to reemerge, but as a strategic choice by individuals who, in other circumstances, would choose other group memberships as a mean of gaining some power and prestige' (1975, p. 171). Economic interests may supersede ethnicity observance unless the latter advances the former. Identity positions are dynamic, as the individual strives to reconcile the multiplicity of societal influences manifesting differentially across contexts (Askegaard *et al.* 2005). Individuals could adopt a hybridized identity or uphold independent identities; switching as suitable to the situation (Oswald 1999). EID and acculturation are seen here as malleable or mutable rather than fixed. Arnett (2002) contends that a growing number of people worldwide are to some extent bi-cultural, with one identity part derived from the local cultural narrative and the other extracted from global culture. Minorities may acculturate to the global consumer culture (GCC) to circumvent acculturation vis-à-vis the mainstream society, or draw upon their GCC knowledge to help them figure out the host culture (Cappellini and Yen 2012).

Presupposing that GCC is more materialistic (vis-à-vis territorially derived cultures), when and how does this orientation diffuse into mainstream and minority populations? Assuming GCC elevates individual aspirations, does this erode adherence to traditional, communal and religious values and in what ways across ethnic groups? Bouchet (1995, p. 93) explains that the cultural tensions experienced by minorities will increasingly play out among mainstream groups:

> What is happening in the subcultures of descendants of immigrants might well be harbingering the situation of many people on this planet who, confronted with the postmodern sources of identity making such as international marketing and satellite television and with the difficulties of political expression on a world market dominated by transnational companies, will have to define new ways of being persons and groups.

According to Firat, the result 'is a globalization of fragmentation in all respects. Poverty is everywhere, wealth and riches everywhere – America is in every country and every country in America' (1995, p. 116). Lévi-Strauss (1978) proposed that to the human mind, meaning ensues from the tensions of seemingly contradictory positions. His concept of binary *oppositions* is relevant to the internal conflicts underlying consumer desire in terms of the struggles between: secularism and faith, materialism and asceticism, and traditional affiliation and GCC. Numerous GCC conceptualizations are relevant to grasping the dissemination of materialism. The first stems from the proliferation of transnational corporations marketing consumer commodities (Levitt 1983). The second originates from the interdependencies among countries and the spread of global capitalism (Appadurai 1990). Global consumerism, the third angle, depicts the 'widespread and unquenchable desire for material possessions' (Ger and Belk 1996a, p. 275). The final viewpoint characterizes GCC as the homogenization of consumption patterns. GCC is 'a transnational set of cultural ideas and practices . . . inspired notably by U.S. consumer culture' (Askegaard *et al.* 2005, pp. 165–66). Studying Greenlandic immigrants living in Denmark, the authors invoke world-system theory to describe GCC radiating from the American centre to the Danish periphery. Respondents expressed overlapping social identities: traditional Greenlandic, mainstream Danish and GCC sources, which were variably resurrected or assumed subject to the consumption context. Cleveland and Laroche's (2007b) acculturation to GCC (AGCC) scale incorporates seven facets reflecting the drivers of GCC. The ensuing paragraphs describe each from the perspective of materialism.

Global mass media is predictably paramount as the chief agent diffusing GCC and materialism. The boundaries imposed by national frontiers are wearing down due to the pervasiveness of global media and programming (Hannerz 1992); principally from satellite television and the film industry, and joined nowadays by a virtual explosion in the number of internet-ready devices. The imagery broadcast facilitates the construction and sharing of GCC symbols (e.g., brands, lifestyles) and associated consumption-laden values (Alden *et al.* 1999; Ger and Belk 1996a; Walker 1996). Promoting self-indulgence and immediate gratification, media abet consumer desire for luxuries and other objects; valued more for their symbolic benefits than for their hedonic qualities. Researching the semiotic properties conveyed by media, Hirschman (1988) has this to say regarding the antagonist of Dallas, the hugely popular, syndicated 1980s American television show: 'J. R. Ewing not only acts, he consumes, and what he consumes tells us as much about him and about what he symbolizes as his actions do' (p. 346).

Theories regarding the role of media split into two perspectives. The *Frankfurt School* holds that consumers passively absorb media. Consumers attempt to emulate the individuals depicted and strive to satisfy the drives primed by the advertising appeals. Media with a worldwide presence are disproportionately Western, although Asian-based sources are growing swiftly. The excessive hedonism and preoccupation with social status characterizing programming depicts an exaggerated image of Western society (Ger and Belk 1996b). Emulation based on these stereotypes advances desire for luxury goods, possibly to the detriment of basic physiological safety and social needs (Ger and Belk 1996b; Burroughs and Rindfleisch 2002). Levitt's (1983) extreme stance avers that *exposure to the marketing activities of multinationals* will ultimately amalgamate everyone into a uniform GCC in which consumers purchase, use and value the same repertoire of products, permitting marketing strategies to be further standardized worldwide. As expressed by Steingard and Fitzgibbons (1995, p. 34):

> The values of Globalization, transmitted through satellite television and the distribution of worldwide publications, permeate everyone's life. Global marketing, international stock markets, and the availability of nomadic world-wide venture capital complete the scene for the rise of a global market value system. No culture is protected by topography, tradition or just plain disinterest – essentially nobody is out of reach of the extended arm of Globalization.

The second viewpoint contends that consumers are active manipulators, selectively filtering programming and engaging in counter-argumentation. This perspective refutes convergence; rather, ethnic values and other distinctions are reasserted in response to globalization (de Mooij 2004). As Huntington (1993, p. 40–1) declared: 'Western efforts to propagate such ideas produce instead a reaction against "human rights imperialism" and a reaffirmation of indigenous values, as can be seen in the support for religious fundamentalism by the younger generation in non-Western cultures'. Ger (1999, p. 65) avows that 'consumers are returning to their roots, reconfiguring global goods and their meanings to better fit local culture and, especially, mixing the old and the new from disparate sources'. Waters (1995, p. 130) similarly claims that the social changes are likely more nuanced than Western cultural hegemony or utter rejection thereof, with tensions arising from the concurrence of cultural forces:

> the uneasy balance between the persistence of unique local cultural identities and the reshaping of such uniqueness by totalizing transnational cultural influences ranging from Coca-Colarization to the universalisation of western ideological and political concepts.

The debate continues as to whether advertising is the cause of materialism or merely intensifies it (Belk 1985). Marketing channels convey meaning transfer: overtly and clandestinely disseminating cultural signs, values and behavioural norms (McCracken 1986; Peñaloza and Gilly 1999). Materialism can be primed by advertising, and triggered by cues embedded in the purchasing, consumption and social environments. Adverts persuade us that 'we will be happier, that our lives will become somehow more satisfying – if we accumulate more and more things' (Swinyard, Kau and Phua 2001, p. 27). Don Draper, the fictional protagonist of the Sterling-Cooper Advertising Agency explains:

> Advertising is based on one thing: happiness. And do you know what happiness is? Happiness is the smell of a new car. It's freedom from fear. It's a billboard on the side of a road that screams with reassurance that whatever you're doing is OK.
>
> [Advertising] creates an itch. You simply put your product in there as a kind of . . . calamine lotion.[4]

Changing consumption values mirror shifting advertising appeals, and the most striking changes have occurred within emerging markets. The prominence of utilitarian appeals (i.e. satisfying basic physiological and safety needs) has given way to emphasizing the social and hedonic consumption values fulfilled by products (Tse *et al.* 1989). These latter ideals are characteristic of GCC (Alden *et al.* 1999).

Tourism lists among the world's largest industries; directly or indirectly employing 10 per cent of the world's labour force (Graddol 2000). Relaxing barriers, cost reductions and increasing pecuniary resources encourage mobility; escalating the incidence of intercultural contacts, the transmission of GCC and, its lingua franca, English. While satisfying hedonistic motives, tourists normally confine their experiences to aesthetically pleasing situations, which may warp their perceptions of material abundance (similar to drawing lifestyle impressions TV programming), whetting consumer desire. Belk (1985) found that people scoring highly on the possessiveness dimension of materialism tended to be avid travellers. He surmised that travelling episodes represented accumulating experiences, which is analogous to acquiring possessions. Displaying material goods acquired from abroad is a strategy used by migrants to accentuate social status.

Language is a framework for organizing social activities and interpretations (Hall 1976). In 1780 the world contained fewer than 13 million English speakers (Belich 2009); today a third of the planet speaks or is learning English (Graddol 2000).[5] English is the lingua franca of international business and institutions, sciences, media and thus, GCC (Huntington 1996). Even in places where few speak the language, English appears in advertisements, symbolically denoting modernism, sophistication and upward mobility (Alden *et al.* 1999).

Cleveland and Laroche (2012) conceive *cosmopolitanism* as a learnable disposition:

> reflecting a specific set of values, opinions, and competencies held by certain individuals; specifically a genuine, humanitarian appreciation for, desire to learn from, and ability to engage with, peoples of different cultures; in short, an affinity for cultural diversity and the proclivity to master it.
>
> *(p. 55)*

Tourists are simply cultural spectators, whereas cosmopolitans actively interface with discrete social entities and serve as conduits for conveying external values. Global media fosters this disposition, discounting the need for foreign travelling (Hannerz 1992). Cosmopolitanism has been described as a secular force and as a taste orientation. Cosmopolites demonstrate luxurious cultural capital (Ong 2009) by virtue of their skill at decoding foreign symbols. Displaying the accoutrements and rituals of foreign cultures enhances social standing (Thompson and Tambyah 1999).

A dissenting view considers cosmopolitanism a post-materialism value. Cosmopolites accord higher priority to achieving intellectual autonomy associated with self-transcendence (vs. self-enhancement), which is antithetical to materialism (Cleveland *et al.* 2011a). Cosmopolitanism correlates with education, which also fosters post-materialistic values (Cleveland and Laroche 2012a). The less tangible, experiential consumption cherished by cosmopolitans may supplant or – consistent with the hedonism typifying affective autonomy – reinforce materialistic predilections.

Cleveland and Laroche's (2007b) sixth dimension was labelled *openness to GCC*. Globalization disseminates themes, ideologies and aspirations, which are selectively adopted by individuals worldwide (Robertson 1992). Individuals are seduced by experiences and marketplace objects (e.g., the iPhone) serving as points of common reference to the consumer culture conveyed by global media (Appadurai 1990; Alden *et al.* 1999; Walker 1996). Luxury brands 'like Vuitton purses fulfill the need to conform . . . teenage girls want Vuitton because "everyone has it"' (de Mooij 2004, p. 163). Materialism is instrumental for building and strengthening relationships among initiates and members of consumer tribes (Schouten and McAlexander 1995). As Oswald (1999, p. 310) states, 'consumers cruise the malls to go "lifestyle shopping" . . . to acquire the outward signs of culture for a lack of a more permanent identity'. Wee (1999) reported that young Asian consumers eagerly embrace a lifestyle reflecting such Western ideals as individualism, competition, self-indulgence and cynicism. Other research identifies global segments regarding advertising appeals, fashion and lifestyle traits (Cleveland *et al.* 2011c; Alden *et al.* 2006; Zhou and Belk 2004; Belk *et al.* 2003).

Globalization amplifies the role played by the marketing system in shaping consumer identity (Bouchet 1995). Following *social identity theory* (Tajfel and Turner 1986), *self-identification with GCC* extends beyond experimentation with the symbols of global culture. As with EID, a strong global identity affects members' thoughts, values and behaviours. Global consumers act out their lives according to the belief structures intrinsic to GCC, drawing products from the global bazaar to fashion and express this self-affirmation, and to distinguish themselves from the local masses. This phenomenon is more likely among younger consumers (due to incomplete identities or generation gap perceptions) and among sub-groups experiencing a sense of exclusion from (or conversely, feeling superiority towards) mainstream society, due to their occupation, class/caste, or race/ethnicity/religion. Xenocentrism – the perception that one's local/ethnic culture is inferior to the culture of the out-group (e.g., global culture) – is thought to be more prevalent among citizens of developing countries (Ger and Belk 1996a; Ger and Belk 1990; Batra *et al.* 2000).

Empirical findings

Concerning materialism's association with EID and AGCC, Cleveland *et al.* (2013) surveyed consumers living in the Americas, Europe and Asia. Robust support emerged for the proposition that AGCC drives materialistic values. The positive correlation obtained for the overall sample on the composite AGCC construct replicated across all eight country sub-samples. Most constituent AGCC dimensions linked positively with materialism; although merely speaking more English did not, which was positively associated only among French-speaking Canadians. Consistent patterns emerged for global mass media and self-identification with GCC: these constructs' relationships to materialism were strongly positive for all countries. Likewise, the link between materialism and exposure to multinational marketing was significantly positive overall, and for seven countries. These results testify to the power of media and marketing to transmit materialistic values, especially regarding the ubiquity of American media conveying GCC values and promoting identification with GCC. With positive links uncovered for five countries, materialism was reinforced via first-hand intercultural encounters (travelling abroad); and, for a subset of samples, through openness to GCC (four countries) and exposure to European global media (also four countries).

Mixed results emerged for the relationship of materialism to ethnic identity. The linkage was non-significant overall (aggregate data), yet was positively significant in four countries. In no case did materialism negatively link to the composite EID factor. Across the countries, almost all the significant links uncovered for the sub-facets of EID to materialism were positive. This clearly demonstrates that cultural traditions are compatible with materialism, and debunks the notion that GCC is solely responsible for the spread of acquisitive tendencies. This was particularly true for interpersonal relationships with fellow ethnic members, whereby positive associations with materialism emerged in four countries. Identification with/desire to maintain local culture positively associated with materialism in three countries (and negatively in only one country). For two cases local language use positively associated with materialism; only for French-speaking Canadians was the relationship negative. Local media usage positively related to materialism in two countries. Studying Korean Canadians, Cleveland and Chang (2009) reported a strong positive relationship between materialism and ethnic media exposure for first-generation (Korean-born) immigrants, but this finding was not sustained for their second-generation (Canadian-born) counterparts. The authors' finding of a positive relationship between materialism and overall (Korean) EID was replicated in a study of ethnic Lebanese living in Lebanon, but only for the Christian sub-sample, whereas for Muslims the link was insignificant (Cleveland *et al.* 2012). Research on Japanese consumers – a collectivistic society – found a positive link between EID and materialism (Cleveland *et al.* 2009c), which was considerably stronger in magnitude than the relationship between AGCC and materialism. Another study revealed a positive link between materialism and Iranian EID; here, the magnitude was slightly lower than that observed between materialism and AGCC (Cleveland *et al.* 2011b).

Individual differences

The nature of materialism and ethnicity is also informed by demographic variables, including: length of residency, generation, education, income, social class, occupation and gender. Income is confounded by social class, wealth, age, education, family size and purchasing power. Within Western countries, individuals typically achieve their peak earnings during their fifth decade; however, older (vs. younger) individuals tend to be relatively less materialistic (Keillor, d'Amico and Horton 2001). This explains the lack a significant relationship between materialism and income reported in numerous studies (Cleveland *et al.* 2009a; Richins and Dawson 1992; Belk 1985; Ger and Belk 1996b). Regarding gender, males are said to employ conspicuous consumption to signal success, with the goal of attracting females (Stillman *et al.* 2012). Gender differences in materialism are documented (Gupta 2011; Cleveland *et al.* 2009a), yet these findings are equivocal across ethnic groups. Parental guidance and family structure affects the socialization of children, and elevated materialism evidences among children of divorced parents (Rindfleisch *et al.* 1997).

Individual-level values and other idiosyncratic differences also combine with social factors to foster materialism. Personality traits associated with conformity that encourage materialism include: susceptibility to interpersonal influence, need for uniqueness, opinion-seeking and self-monitoring.[6] Schwartz's (1992; 1999) value inventory contains ten motivationally distinct and universal values applicable at the individual level, and studies have linked some of these values to materialism (Burroughs and Rindfleisch 2002; Karabati and Cemalcilar 2010; Kilbourne *et al.* 2005). Cleveland *et al.* (2012b) reported numerous differences between Muslim and Christian Lebanese on the relationship of materialism to these values. Whereas *power* (*benevolence*) was strongly positively (negatively) associated for both groups, *hedonism* was positively linked only for Christians. *Tradition* (*universalism* and *self-direction*) was (were) inversely associated to materialism only for Christians (Muslims).

Studying Turks, Karabati and Cemalcilar (2010) reported positive relationships of *power*, *achievement* and *hedonism* to materialism; although the strength of these linkages varied across the subscales (happiness, success and centrality: Richins and Dawson 1992). Contrary to expectations, they documented a positive effect of tradition on the success facet; which the authors suggest, points towards a less austere, more status-driven form of conservativism. Elaborating the complexity of these individual-social interactions and materialistic outcomes is delegated to future authors.

Consumption contexts and culture

Schwartz (1992) holds that although values steer consumption behaviour, these should not be context-specific. However, the earlier review of ethnicity and acculturation implies that the prominence and behavioural outcomes of materialism are dependent on the situation, rather than absolute. Products operate as dramaturgical props that define and display the consumer's self-image, and the particular social role that is operational (Oswald 1999; Bouchet 1995), which brings into play different reference groups. Ethnic awareness and the salience of other groups can be inconstant, activated in part by verbal/visual cues (e.g., propinquity of other culturally similar/dissimilar individuals, ethnic holidays and religious events, and cultural signals present within advertising), coinciding with purchasing and consumption settings (Forehand and Deshpandé 2001). Moreover, private and public self-concepts co-exist and the researcher must reflect on which aspect(s) of the self will dominate in different social circumstances (Triandis 1994; Wong and Ahuvia 1998).

Peñaloza's (1994) research on Mexican American immigrant acculturation found that readily adopted products were low in cost but high in visibility. Traditional consumption behaviours revealed when celebrating ethnic heritage and familial ties, whereas consumer acculturation readily occurred with culturally inert activities. Askegaard *et al.* (2005) described how marketplace offerings enabled Greenlandic-Danish immigrants to resurrect ethnic traditions. This supports Firat's (1995) argument that the persistence of cultural forms is contingent upon rendering traditions into consumable forms, and Bouchet's (1995) assertion that ethnicity in the contemporary period is primarily about responding to social change, whereas beforehand it was a mechanism for avoiding it.

The meanings incorporated into material goods can also be dynamic (McCracken 1986). Certain objects assume static meanings, e.g., heirlooms symbolize continuity, religious artifacts denote spirituality. Others, including branded products, assume different meanings to both the same and different people, across time and place (Kleine and Baker 2004). Evoking cultural values, Watson *et al.* (2002) give the example of how conservativism and mastery engender equivalent importance to an antique Hamilton pocket watch for different, often private, meanings. Regarding the former, the watch is valued for symbolizing family ties and heritage; whereas for the latter, the significance derives from the object's prestige and capacity to enhance self-concept. Likewise, whereas someone might value a bicycle for enhancing athletic prowess (an expression of mastery), another person might value the object for providing the sensory pleasures associated with experiencing, via leisurely bikerides, the natural environment (thus, harmony; Watson *et al.* 2002). Because cultural values affect self-image – which is partly the product of how others see the individual as well as the person's perceptions of themself – these values have some bearing on the individual's selection and definition of their most important belongings (Markus and Kitayama 1991). To the bearer, consumer goods infuse with symbolic properties incorporating social (and economic) risk. Reference group influence is not equally powerful for all types of information, products and consumption contexts. Also, the role(s) of different social power bases (referent, legitimate, expert, etc.) vary according to the situation.

Materialism is also triggered by retailing cues. Copious inventories, numerous brand choices, category assortments and the full shopping carts of other customers signal material abundance and convey impressions regarding the social acceptability of consumer desire. People weave in and out of a materialistic orientation and therefore, materialism influences certain behaviours but not others. Where a relationship exists, it is usually, but not always, positively valenced.

Karabati and Cemalcilar (2010) speculate that high materialists engage in consumption that publically signals status, whereas low materialists are apt 'to value private meanings of possessions . . . [such as] books, memorabilia, and other possessions displayed privately rather than in public' (p. 631). Luxuries are the category of products most obviously associated with materialism. In addition to satisfying hedonic needs, luxuries are purchased for symbolic reasons, to promote idiosyncratic expression and invidious distinction, to convey personal success and status and so forth. Several authors have cogitated about cultural differences concerning the motives underlying luxury consumption. Wong and Ahuvia (1998) proposed that individualist Western consumers accord importance to achieving hedonic experiences, whereas collectivist Asians – with their enhanced concern for 'face' – stress publically visible possessions. Clothing, jewellery and other wearables signify personality, ethnic affiliation, occupation and social status; possibly communicating intentions regarding a particular situation.

In their eight-country study, Cleveland *et al.* (2009a) reported that for the aggregated dataset, materialism was a significant predictor for most of the forty-eight consumption behaviours considered, and the relationship was positive in all but two cases (Appendix 10.1). Materialism's role was pronounced for the consumption of luxury goods, apparel, consumer electronics and applicances. Materialism also linked positively with media and communication behaviours. Yet, the magnitude (and sometimes, direction) of these relationships varied considerably across nations. The most consistent findings ensued for hedonistic, socially visible and status-enhancing consumer objects: luxuries, media devices, durables and appliances. In all but one country, automobile ownership was a positive function of materialism. On the other hand, purchasing athletic shoes positively linked with materialism in some countries, but the relationship was negative one country (Korea). These and other inconsistent findings are probably due to cultural differences in product meaning as well as the norms guiding the satiation of materialism.

The results demonstrate that cultural homogenization is not the inevitable outcome of marketplace globalization. When consumer goods are introduced, the recipient society modifies the meaning of these objects in ways that can enhance or compliment rather than diminish existing cultural identity (Akaka and Alden 2010; Miller 1996; Hannerz 1992). Increasingly, consumers in affluent societies are curious about foreign cultures, cuisines and products; whereas some studies point to a revival of localism in the consumption habits of those living in less prosperous environs (Ger 1999). Describing the evolution of habits in Romania following the overthrow of Ceauşescu, Belk (1996) stated that despite the influx of Western brands, media and other influences, 'significant differences in foods, clothing, religion, vehicles, and celebrations act as ethnic markers that are used by the Romanian majority and the Hungarian and Gypsy minorities to proclaim their ethnic identities and thereby resist assimilation to each other, much less to global culture' (p. 26).

Levitt (1983) foretold inexorable cultural convergence and synchronization of attitudinal/behavioural outcomes. Certain segments (e.g., global teens) may embrace a lifestyle congruent with GCC while spurning local norms (Alden *et al.* 1999). De Mooij (2004) counters that unique cultural affiliations and predilections are not waning: 'the spread of global symbols . . . does not necessarily include homogeneity of people's habits or values' (p. 4). Juxtaposing with affirmation to traditional identities, globalization produces marketplace tensions; e.g., deliberating between local/foreign product alternatives. Ethnic members strive to maintain identity and pride towards their ethnic heritage. This entails adhering to cultural customs/values and enculturating these aspects into their offspring (Mehta and Belk 1991).

The allure of *neoethnicism* partly stems from its reductivism (Miyoshi 1993), and assumes greater salience in the current, perplexingly intricate phase of globalization. Social identity theory posits that when individuals encounter complex social environments, they will search out and identify with the group that they feel most at ease (Tajfel and Turner 1986). Supposed cultural encroachment or economic vulnerability motivates compels certain individuals to 'promote a resurgence of, and renewed commitment to, indigenous cultures' (Huntington 1996, p. 37); and perhaps eschew global influences and associated media/marketing, and abstention of foreign products. Modernization and economic expansion is not interchangeable with cultural Westernization. Foreign products, ideas and even values are indigenized. Researching consumer acculturation in Belize, Wilk (1995) found that the adoption of foreign behaviours was highly selective, and in certain instances, consumers reacted strongly against Western standards. Partaking in rituals and consuming symbolic products help establish group solidarity. One corollary is that minorities may develop exaggerated perceptions of the importance/quality of brands emanating from their original country, as they strive to affirm their traditional identity (Guzmán and Paswan 2009).

How do consumers reconcile manifold value systems, particularly if one ethos is conducive to materialism while the other is hostile? One way that these ambivalent feelings are revealed is through *consumer ethnocentrism* (CET).

> [Ethnocentrism] represents the universal proclivity for people to view their own group as the center of the universe, to interpret other social units from the perspective of their own group, and to reject persons who are culturally dissimilar while blindly accepting those who are culturally like themselves.
>
> *(Shimp and Sharma 1987, p. 280)*

169

CET specifically refers to individuals' penchant towards local products, and aversion to foreign alternatives, which are seen as perilous to the in-group economy and culture. Ethnocentric consumers will even forfeit the higher quality or lower prices offered by foreign goods so as to 'enjoy the psychological benefit of avoiding contact with the out-group' (Steenkamp *et al.* 2003, pp. 56–7). CET alternatively denotes compliance to injunctive norms. A person might stifle their private preference towards a foreign product in light of perceived reference group pressure to select the domestic/ethnic alternative (Rawwas *et al.* 1996).

Norms critically impact behaviour, but prognosticating the nature of influence requires specifying the type(s) apt to be operational in a given context. Descriptive norms denote typical behaviours (what is *usually* done), whereas injunctive norms signify morally appropriate behaviours (what *ought* to be done) as defined by society (Cialdini *et al.* 1990). It is also helpful to distinguish between prescriptive norms (dictating what people *should* do) and proscriptive norms (decreeing what people *should not do*; Argyle *et al.* 1985). The extent to which a societal member is motivated to conform to social expectations (gaining approval by imitating others or affirming norms) and to avoid disapproval from the group – risking sanctions for violating values and deviating from accepted norms – independently or jointly affect the degree that materialistic temptations are embraced or suppressed.

Because many ethnocentric consumers, especially those acquiescing to in-group norms, still desire materialistic objects, local/ethnic options will be sought to fulfill acquisitive needs, assuming that conspicuous consumption does not openly violate cultural sensibilities. Support for this contention emerged in Cleveland *et al.*'s (2009a) study, which revealed an independent link between CET and materialism in most countries examined. CET positively predicted numerous consumer behaviours prototypically thought of as satisfying hedonic and status needs, including several luxuries, consumer electronics, appliances and durables. Relevant for product positioning, a four-fold classification was suggested based on the combined influence of materialism and CET (Table 10.1). Still, ethnocentrism does not always drive preferences for local/ethnic brands over foreign/host alternatives. Consumers may perceive local brands as more responsive to their unique in-group needs. Traditional ethnic consumers may also spurn brand options that explicitly emphasize status or hedonism in their promotional appeals (Cleveland and Laroche 2012a).

Table 10.2 summarizes the principal linkages of materialism to ethnic identity, cultural values and acculturation.

Implications and conclusions

Researching materialism

Despite the abundant materialism literature, few studies focus on the consistency and drivers across countries/cultures. This is a glaring oversight, given the pervasiveness of materialistic-laden

Table 10.1 Materialism, consumer ethnocentrism, and consumer behavior

		Materialism	
		Negative*	Positive
Consumer ethnocentrism	Negative*	Necessity consumption	Hedonistic-global consumption
	Positive	Traditional consumption	Hedonistic-local consumption

Source: Adapted from Cleveland *et al.* (2009a).

Note
*or not significant.

Table 10.2 Summarizing ethnicity and materialism relationships

Antecedent variable/construct		Relationship to materialism
Ethnic identity (EID)	▲▼	Depends on whether materialism is acceptable to fellow ethnic group members, within a given situation. Perceptions differ across ethnicities due to cultural traditions, interacting with religion and attitudes towards upward mobility, majority vs. minority ethnicity status, demographics, consumption situational effects (e.g., public vs. private consumption), etc.
Religiosity	▼	An orientation towards consumption fundamentally conflicts with most forms of religious fulfillment.
High (vs. low) context	▲▼	Low-context communication may explicitly reference materialistic values, although symbolism present in high-context communication may covertly convey materialistic appeals (e.g., status-marking objects).
Hofstede's dimensions		
• Individualism	▲▼	Acquiring goods is consistent with individual pursuits; collectivists can be materialistic when benefits of status/possessions accrue to family/group.
• Power distance	▲	Status goods reinforce power/wealth differences.
• Uncertainty avoidance	▲	Consumer goods help to anchor identity under ambiguous situations and social upheaval.
• Masculinity	▲	Agentic needs, e.g., material enrichment, are emphasized in masculine societies; feminine cultures are comparatively communally oriented.
• Long-term orientation	▼	Time horizon affects consumption priorities, i.e., delaying gratification vs. satisfying immediate, hedonic needs.
Schwartz's cultural values		
• Harmony	▼	Symbiotic societies less likely engage in exploitive consumption as well as restrain consumer envy and the display of status markers.
• Egalitarianism	▼	The importance of status markers should be muted in relatively classless societies.
• Intellectual autonomy	▲▼	Advanced as a post-materialistic value, self-actualization is also consistent with the enhancement of cultural capital, which encourages materialism via flaunting social sophistication.
• Affective autonomy	▲	The pursuit of hedonistic experiences is coherent with the belief that material goods are instrumental to achieving happiness and fulfillment.
• Mastery	▲	Similar to achieving control over the environment, mastery implies command over (conspicuous evidence of) resources.
• Hierarchy	▲	As with power distance, conspicuous consumption expresses one's place in the social hierarchy.
• Conservativism	▲▼	Conforming to ethnic traditions could suppress or encourage materialistic tendencies depending on social norms and consumption context.

(continued)

Table 10.2 (continued)

Antecedent variable/construct	Relationship to materialism
Acculturation	
• Host society	▲▼ Depends in part on whether expressions of materialism are embraced or frowned upon by mainstream/host cultural entity in a given consumption situation, and host society attitudes towards the acculturating group.
• Global consumer culture (AGCC)	▲ This ideology of consumption aggressively promotes consumer desire. Globalization and culture change links with rising materialism.
Consumer ethnocentrism	▲▼ Ethnocentric consumers shun outside cultural influences; however, they still place value on material enrichment for conveying social status.

Note
▲ = increasing/positive, ▼ = reducing/negative.

product appeals, and the awareness that cultural forces fundamentally shape consumer behaviour. As nations converge along socio-economic indicators, cultural variables take on greater significance for explaining consumer variability (de Mooij 2004). There is a dearth of research on societies characterized as culturally distant from the West: Africa, much of Asia, Latin America, etc. These neglected regions represent almost 90 per cent of the world's populace and most of its future economic growth. Conducting research into these regions 'requires both understanding and sensitivity to differences in the marketing environment as well as an ability to deal with the lack of a well-developed market research infrastructure' (Craig and Douglas 2001, p. 84); and requires the employment of instruments that are 'readily understood and unambiguously interpreted, and, as far as possible, devoid of cultural bias' (p. 85).

Many studies suffer because the treatment of culture is exploratory, lacking a priori specification of the influence it will take. Innovative uses of and novel meanings for products/brands strengthens the need for emic (anthropological) research approaches. Acculturation processes are difficult to describe with quantitative methodologies. Longitudinal and qualitative designs enable documentation of the dynamic evolution of identity, culture change and materialism (Askegaard *et al.* 2005). The *Diderot effect* (McCracken 1988) implies that it is necessary to research consumption constellations: the meaning ensuing from the interaction of complimentary consumer possessions. Consumer values and lifestyles are revealed when objects are assessed in concert. The beneficial insights offered by such approaches must be balanced against the inability to generalize. The nature of identity varies across ethnic groups, further complicating etic cross-cultural comparisons of materialism. Most consumer research employs the individual as the unit of analysis; however many decisions are made at the household level. This requires insights into decision-making and gender roles within families, which also vary across ethnic groups.

Hofstede's data – drawn from *IBM* employees – dates from the 1960s onwards. Scores may have shifted, especially within societies experiencing economic change or sustaining high immigration. Cultural indices are limited by their aggregation. Within-country variation is often as great as between-country differences. Most marketing research positioned as cross-cultural is essentially cross-national. Ethnicity and nationality are not interchangeable concepts. Many nation-states are multi-ethnic: aggregated country-sample data obscures individual-level discrepancies as well as regional and subcultural differences. The ecological fallacy (Robinson 1950) occurs when inferences are made about the nature of individuals based upon aggregate-level data findings. This error is the bane of deductive quantitative research, whereas inductive, qualitative methodologies risk the exception fallacy (Damer 2012), whereby group conclusions are confounded because they are based on exceptional/anecdotal cases. These issues inform as to the brevity (Cleveland *et al.* 2011c) of ethnicity-based segmentation relative to more objective demographic and/or country-level approaches, despite ample theoretical justification and practical significance for utilizing ethnicity to craft marketing strategy.

The literature upholds the superior psychometric properties of Richins' (2004) material values scale vs. Belk's (1985) trait-based scale. Studies employing either scale report deviations from the posited tripartite structure, and several report issues regarding the interpretation of negatively valenced statements, especially when translated (Cleveland and Chang 2009; Wong *et al.* 2003; Tobacyk *et al.* 2011; Karabati and Cemalcilar 2010). Cross-cultural validation requires assessing equivalence in the meaning and structure of construct measures (i.e. measurement invariance; Steenkamp and Baumgartner 1998). Researchers must also be on guard for elements or manifestations of materialism unique to a particular culture, and avoid pseudo-etic operationalizations whereby measures developed in one cultural context are applied with only minimal adaptation (i.e., translation) to others without due consideration of social and behavioural context-effects (Triandis 1994). To clarify materialism's effects on personal and social well-being, it would be advantageous to develop a materialism scale conceptualized from a motivational perspective; one that distinguishes between instrumental and terminal functions, and that is reliable/valid across ethnic groups, social contexts and consumption circumstances.

Practical implications

As economies become affluent, advertising appeals shift from primarily utilitarian themes towards emphasizing hedonistic values (Tse *et al.* 1989). Rising materialism augers well for globally branded luxuries seen as universal symbols of social status. For most other products, product attributes and appeals require modification to fit into existing consumer values. Global advertising 'can only be effective if there are global consumers with universal values' (de Mooij 2004, p. 16). Demirbag *et al.*'s (2010) findings indicated that materialism moderated the relationship between country image and preferences for local vs. foreign products; however this relationship varied across product categories. Increasing discretionary income enables greater freedom of expression; nevertheless, articulations of social identity and manifestations of materialism are shaped principally by or in reaction to value systems. Jamal (2003) described the crucial role played by ethnic marketers in terms of providing the 'emotional glue' that binds members to their original culture, in contrast to mainstream marketers' activities that encourage integration into the consumer culture.

The challenge facing managers of global status brands is to sustain consumer desire. Sony and Cadillac once had the brand insistence levels currently enjoyed by Apple and BMW. The majority of status brands are unlikely to achieve such universal appeal as social markers, even ephemerally. Because consumption unfolds within socio-cultural circumstances, the connotation of materialism will often be dissimilar across cultures (Venkatesh 1995; Cleveland *et al.* 2009a). Certain products/brands may be deemed materialistic/hedonistic in one culture, but not in another. What one group deems as impeccable taste may be gaudy or ostentatious for another. *Symbolic self-completion theory* (Wicklund and Gollwitzer 1982) avers that goods allow for substantiating or innovating identity, through selective use and experimentation with existing cultural meanings (e.g., the juxtaposition of clothing materials in unconventional ways). Episodes of meaning re-contextualization emerge as ethnic members' negotiate between traditional and host cultural spheres (Oswald 1999).

Existing international market segmentation information tends to be organized from the nation-state perspective. This is poorly diagnostic for uncovering transnational or intranational segments, which – as is the case with domestic environments – are likely to be specific to particular product categories (Cleveland *et al.* 2011c; Jamal 2003). The ethnic fragmentation occurring at the societal level is paralleled by identity fragmentation occurring at the individual consumer level. Analogous to the tossed-salad metaphor, and drawing from Bouchet's (1995) concept of *bricolage*, each individual is a mosaic: a blend of various cultural pieces that can be ill-fitting due to incompatibility amid the constituent values, competing ethnic norms and marketing messages prescribing acceptable behaviour. Research is necessary to illuminate how, where, when and for whom this amalgam of identities fuses over time, leading to creolization, and to identify factors encouraging oscillation between identities. Ethnicity is 'not just who one is but how one feels in and about a particular situation' (Dion *et al.* 2011, p. 311). Managers seeking to exploit materialistic desire must recognize the circumstances favouring the dominance of ethnic/national vs. other/global identities and vice-versa, and to tailor brand strategies to suit the values/dispositions operating under these contexts. When taken together, the possible outcomes of materialistic goal pursuits are legion across times, places and individuals, depending on a complex interchange of cultural norms, socialization forces and marketing intermediaries, further interacting with personality, other individual differences and aspirations.

Social implications and conclusions

Members of mainstream Western (vs. emerging-market) societies are likely socialized earlier in life to consumerism. Consequently, they may be somewhat inoculated to overt materialistic appeals, or possess an enhanced capacity to restrain materialistic urges. Negative affect (anxiety, unhappiness, depression, etc.), compulsive buying and a host of other risky behaviours have been positively linked with materialistic dispositions, whereas several intrinsic pursuits seen as beneficial to subjective well-being – such as social participation and self-actualization – have been inversely associated with materialism.[7] Conversely, Hudders and Pandelaere (2011) surmise that consuming luxuries leads to happiness when individuals believe that conspicuous consumption 'provides them with a higher status, not only within their own reference groups but also within their aspirational groups' (p. 416). Regardless, the direction of causality remains ambiguous: 'it is also possible that those who have for various reasons experienced dissatisfaction in life turn to materialism in their effort to find happiness' (Belk 1985, p. 274). Despondency may result from the trials and prejudice facing ethnic minorities. Immigrants employed in jobs for which they lack intrinsic motivation (insufficiently engaging tasks, etc.) could have a greater susceptibility towards extrinsic, materialistic-laden rewards.

Drawing from the concepts discussed herein, there is a plethora of issues warranting enquiry. Regarding immigration and ethnic minority groups, what situations (e.g., migration motives, ethnic stigmatization) exacerbate or alleviate instrumental and terminal forms of materialism? How do cultural values work in concert to affect materialism, and how does materialism manifest when different ethos intersect, under varying social situations and consumption contexts? What forms of materialism drive or are reinforced by the multifarious gift-giving behaviours across ethnic groups and cultural norms (reciprocity, etc.) for different occasions? Does materialism occur when social needs are reasonably satiated, or develop as a substitute for interpersonal relationships? What acculturative stressors lead to ethnic ambivalence and identity confusion (as well as coping mechanisms), when the relentlessly secular materialistic character of GCC collides with inviolable cultural traditions, including religious mores? Researching how individuals cope with cultural fracture, and consistent with social capital theory, Davies and Fitchett (2010) conclude that people 'who live in consumer cultures and have therefore developed abilities to read, encode, and interpret consumption symbolism are likely also to be better able to cope with the transnational movement' (p. 1016).

What materialistic subcultures – deriving from shared allegiance to a particular constellation of brands and display of associated rituals (Schouten and McAlexander 1995) – are emerging and transcending boundaries hitherto imposed by ethnicity and nationality? What factors encourage anti-materialistic sentiments to arise at the vortex of cultural ideologies? Counter-culture movements, ironically, are often subsumed by GCC in due course (e.g., hip-hop), and when they are not, the frenzied antagonism to consumerism demonstrated by these groups hastens their marginalization. The impact of another six billion people consuming at levels enjoyed by the one billion of the West would clearly be ecologically catastrophic. It is imperative to identify techniques that effectively dampen ecologically harmful manifestations of consumer desire. Lastly, in terms of measuring materialism, existing scales need refinement to ensure reliability and construct validity across cultures, languages and consumption contexts.

With globalization, cultural homogeneity is waning within many nation-states. Technology and tolerance of multiculturalism emboldens ethnic groups to express their distinctiveness. Birds of a feather still flock together, but now roost in a greater number and variety of trees. This chapter argues that the spread of global consumption symbols does not inevitably insinuate homogeneity of consumers' values and habits. Whereas the need to belong *is innate* to human kind (Baumeister and Leary 1995), the accumulating evidence suggests that materialism by and large *is not* (Cleveland *et al.* 2013; Giddens *et al.* 2009). Researchers have only scratched the surface of the connection between materialism and ethnicity, in this period of pervasive marketplace globalization.

Notes

1 BGC perspectives. "Luxe redux: Raising the bar for the selling of luxuries" https://www.bcg perspectives.com/content/articles/consumer_products_automotive_luxe_redux/ (accessed 2 January 2013).
2 E.g., Potlatch ceremony of native tribes living along the Pacific north-western coast of North America.
3 See Peñaloza (1994) for a review.
4 AMC's Mad Men TV show. http://www.imdb.com/character/ch0031457/quotes (accessed 12 February 2013).
5 Mandarin and Spanish have greater and similar numbers of native-speakers, yet the dispersion of English is unparalleled.
6 See Kleine and Baker (2004) for a review.
7 See Hudders and Pandalaere (2011) for a review.

References

Ajzen, I. (1985) 'From intentions to actions: A theory of planned behavior'. In *Action Control: From Cognition to Behavior*, edited by J. Kuhl and J. Beckmann. Heidelberg, Germany: Springer-Verlag, pp. 11–39.

Akaka, M. A. and Alden, D. L. (2010) 'Global brand positioning and perceptions'. *International Journal of Advertising*, 29(1): 37–56.

Alden, D. L., Steenkamp, J.-B. and Batra, R. (1999) 'Brand positioning through advertising in Asia, North America, and Europe: The role of global consumer culture'. *Journal of Marketing*, 63(1): 75–87.

Alden, D. L., Steenkamp, J.-B. E. M. and Batra, R. (2006) 'Consumer attitudes toward marketplace globalization: Structure, antecedents and consequences'. *International Journal of Research in Marketing*, 23(3): 227–39.

Appadurai, A. (1990) 'Disjuncture and difference in the global economy'. *Theory Culture & Society*, 7(2/3): 295–310.

Argyle, M., Henderson, M. and Furnham, A. (1985) 'The rules of social relationships'. *British Journal of Social Psychology*, 24: 125–39.

Arnett, J. J. (2002) 'The psychology of globalization'. *American Psychologist*, 57(10): 774–83.

Arnould, E. J. and Thompson, C. J. (2005) 'Consumer Culture Theory (CCT): Twenty years of research'. *Journal of Consumer Research*, 31(4): 868–82.

Askegaard, S., Arnould, E. J. and Kjeldgaard, D. (2005) 'Postassimilationist ethnic consumer research: Qualifications and extensions'. *Journal of Consumer Research*, 32: 160–70.

Barber B. R. (1996) *Jihad Versus McWorld: How Globalism and Tribalism are Reshaping the World*. New York, NY: Ballentine Books.

Batra, R., Ramaswamy, V., Alden, D. L., Steenkamp, J. B. E. M. and Ramachander, S. (2000) 'Effects of brand local/non-local origin on consumer attitudes'. *Journal of Consumer Psychology*, 9(2): 83–95.

Baudrillard, J. (1968) *The Consumer Society: Myths and Structures*. Newbury Park, CA: Sage.

Baumeister, R. F. and Leary, M. R. (1995) 'The need to belong: Desire for interpersonal attachments as a fundamental human motivation'. *Psychological Bulletin*, 117(3): 497–529.

Belich J. (2009) *Replenishing the Earth: The Settler Revolution and the Rise of the Angloworld*. Oxford, UK: Oxford University Press.

Belk, R. W. (1984) 'Three scales measure constructs related to materialism: Reliability, validity, and relationships to measures of happiness'. In *Advances in Consumer Research*, Volume 11, edited by T. Kinnear. Provo, UT: Association for Consumer Research, pp. 291–97.

Belk, R. W. (1985) 'Materialism: Trait aspects of living in the material world'. *Journal of Consumer Research*, 12 (December): 265–80.

Belk, R. W. (1988) 'Possessions and the extended self'. *Journal of Consumer Research*, 15(2): 139–68.

Belk, R. W. (1996) 'Hyperreality and globalization: Culture in the age of Ronald McDonald'. *Journal of International Consumer Marketing*, 8(3–4): 23–37.

Belk, R. W. (2000) 'Consumption patterns of the new elite in Zimbabwe'. In *Marketing Contributions to Democratization and Socioeconomic Development, Proceedings of the 25th Macromarketing Conference*, C. L. Shultz and B. Grbac. Lovran, Croatia, pp. 120–37.

Belk, R. W., Ger, G. and Askegaard, S. (2003) 'The fire of desire: A multisited inquiry into consumer passion'. *Journal of Consumer Research*, 30(3): 326–51.

Bell, D. (1975) 'Ethnicity and social change'. In *Ethnicity: Theory and Experience*, edited by N. Glazer and D. P. Moynihan. Cambridge, MA: Harvard University Press, pp. 141–34.

Berry, J. W. (1997) 'Immigration, acculturation, and adaptation'. *Applied Psychology: An International Review*, 46(1): 5–68.

Bloom, J. M. and Blair, S. S. (2002) *Islam: A Thousand Years of Faith and Power*. New Haven, CT: Yale University Press.

Bouchet, D. (1995) 'Marketing and the redefinition of ethnicity'. In *Marketing in a Multicultural World*, edited by J. A. Costa and G. J. Bamossy. London: Sage Publications, pp. 68–104.

Bourdieu, P. (1984) *Distinction: A Social Critique of the Judgment of Taste*. Cambridge, MA: Harvard University Press.

Burroughs, J. E. and Rindfleisch, A. (2002) 'Materialism and well-being: A conflicting values perspective'. *Journal of Consumer Research*, 29(December): 348–70.

Cappellini, B. and Yen, D. A. (2012) 'Little emperors in the UK: Acculturation and food over time'. *Journal of Business Research*, 66(8): 968–74.

Cialdini, R. B., Reno, R. R. and Kallgren, C. A. (1990) 'A focus theory of normative conduct: Recycling the concept of norms to reduce littering in public places'. *Journal of Personality and Social Psychology*, 58(6): 1015–26.

Chapple, C. (1986) *Karma and Creativity*. New York, NY: Suny Press.

Cleveland, M. (2007) *Globals, Locals, and Creoles: Acculturation to Global Consumer Culture, Ethnic Identity, and Consumptionscapes*. Saarbrücken, Germany: VDM Publishing House.

Cleveland, M. and Chang, W. (2009) 'Migration and materialism: The roles of ethnic identity, religiosity, and generation'. *Journal of Business Research*, 62(10): 963–71.

Cleveland, M., Laroche, M. (2007) 'Acculturation to the global consumer culture: Scale development and research paradigm'. *Journal of Business Research*, 60(3): 249–59.

Cleveland, M. and Laroche, M. and Papadopoulos, N. (2009a) 'Cosmopolitanism, consumer ethnocentrism, and materialism: An eight-country study of antecedents and outcomes'. *Journal of International Marketing*, 17(1): 116–46.

Cleveland, M., Laroche, M., Pons, F. and Kastoun, R. (2009b) 'Acculturation and consumption: Textures of cultural adaptation'. *International Journal of Intercultural Relations*, 33(3): 196–212.

Cleveland, M., Laroche, M. and Takahashi, I. (2009c) 'The interplay of local and global cultural influences on Japanese consumer behavior'. In *Proceedings of the 2009 Academy of Marketing Science World Marketing Congress*, edited by C. L. Campbell. Oslo, Norway.

Cleveland, M., Erdoğan, S., Arıkan and Poyraz, T. (2011a) 'Cosmopolitanism, individual-level values and cultural-level values: A cross-cultural study'. *Journal of Business Research*, 64(9): 934–43.

Cleveland, M., Laroche, M., Naghavi, P. and Shafia, M. A. (2011b) 'Globalization, culture, consumer dispositions, and consumption: The case of Iran'. In *Proceedings of the 2011 Academy of Marketing Science World Marketing Congress*, edited by C. L. Campbell. Reims, France.

Cleveland, M., Papadopoulos, N. and Laroche, M. (2011c) 'Identity, demographics, and consumer behaviors: International market segmentation across product categories'. *International Marketing Review*, 28(3): 244–66.

Cleveland, M. and Laroche, M. (2012a) 'Becoming and being a cosmopolitan consumer'. In *Consumer Cosmopolitanism in the Age of Globalization*, edited by M. Prince. New York, NY: Business Expert Press, pp. 51–100.

Cleveland, M., Laroche, M. and Hallab, R. (2013) 'Globalization, culture, religion and values: Comparing consumption patterns of Lebanese Muslims and Christians'. *Journal of Business Research*, 62: 958–67.

Cleveland, M., Laroche, M. and Papadopoulos, N. (2013) 'Cross-cultural examination of the psychographic drivers of materialism'. In *Proceedings of the 2013 Academy of Marketing Science World Marketing Congress*, edited by C. Campbell, and J. Ma. Melbourne, Australia.

Cleveland, M., Laroche, M. and Papadopoulos, N. (2015) 'You are what you speak? Globalization, multilingualism, consumer dispositions, and consumption'. *Journal of Business Research*, 68(3): 542–52.

Craig, C. S. and Douglas, S. P. (2001) 'Conducting international marketing research in the twenty-first century'. *International Marketing Review*, 18(1): 80–90.

Craig, C. S. and Douglas, S. P. (2006) 'Beyond national culture: Implications of cultural dynamics for consumer research'. *International Marketing Review*, 23(3): 322–42.

Crockett, D. Anderson, L., Bone, S. A., Roy, A., Wang, J. J. and Coble, G. (2011) 'Immigration, culture, and ethnicity in transformative consumer research'. *Journal of Public Policy and Marketing*, 30(1): 47–54.

Csikszentmihalyi, M. and Rochberg-Halton, E. (1981) *The Meaning of Things: Domestic Symbols and the Self*. New York, NY: Cambridge University Press.

Damer, T. E. (2012) *Attacking Faulty Reasoning*, seventh edition. Boston, MA: Wadsworth, Cengage Learning.

Davies, A. and Fitchett, J. A. (2010) 'Material man is not an island: Coping with cultural fracture'. *Journal of Marketing Management*, 26(11–12): 1005–20.

Demirbag, M., Sahadev, S. and Mellahi, K. (2010) 'Country image and consumer preference for emerging economy products: The moderating role of consumer materialism'. *International Marketing Review*, 27(2): 141–63.

de Mooij, M. (2004) *Consumer Behavior and Culture: Consequences for Global Marketing and Advertising*. Thousand Oaks, CA: Sage.

Dion, D., Sitz, L. and Rémy, E. (2011) 'Embodied ethnicity: The ethnic affiliation grounded in the body'. *Consumption Markets & Culture*, 14(3): 311–31.

Domzal, T. J. and Kernan, J. B. (1993) 'Mirror, mirror: Some postmodern reflections on global advertising'. *Journal of Advertising*, 22(4): 1–20.

Dubois, B. and Duquesne, P. (1993) 'The market for luxury goods: Income versus culture'. *European Journal of Marketing*, 27(1): 35–44.

Douglas, S. P. and Craig, C. S. (2010) 'Global marketing strategy: Past, present, and future'. In *The Past, Present, and Future of International Business & Management*, Volume 23, edited by T. Devinney, T. Pedersen and L. Tihanyi. Bingley, UK: Emerald Group Publishing, pp. 431–57.

Douglas, M. and Isherwood B. (1979) *The World of Goods: Towards an Anthropology of Consumption*. London: Allen Lane.

Erikson, E. H. (1959) 'Identity and the life cycle'. *Psychological Issues Monograph*, 1(1): 1–171.

Eriksen, T. H. (1993) *Ethnicity and Nationalism*. London: Pluto.

Firat, A. F. (1995) 'Consumer culture, or culture consumed?' In *Marketing in a Multicultural World*, edited by J. A. Costa, and G. J. Bamossy. Thousand Oaks, CA: Sage Publications, pp. 105–23.

Forehand, M. R. and Deshpandé, R. (2001) 'What we see makes us who we are: Priming ethnic self-awareness and advertising response'. *Journal of Marketing Research*, 38(3): 336–48.

Frideres, J. and Goldenberg, S. (1982) 'Ethnic identity: Myth and reality in Western Canada'. *International Journal of Intercultural Relations*, 6(2): 137–151.

Furnham, A. (1984) 'The Protestant ethic: A review of the psychological literature'. *European Journal of Social Psychology*, 14(1): 27–33.

Ger, G. (1999) 'Localizing in the global village: Local firms competing in global markets'. *California Management Review*, 41(4): 64–83.

Ger, G. and Belk, R. W. (1990) 'Measuring and comparing materialism cross-culturally'. In *Advances in Consumer Research*, Volume 17, edited by G. Gorn and R. Polly. Provo, UT: Association for Consumer Research, pp. 186–92.

Ger, G. and Belk, R. W. (1996a) 'I'd like to buy the world a Coke: Consumptionscapes of the "less affluent world"'. *Journal of Consumer Policy*, 19(3): 271–304.

Ger, G. and Belk, R. W. (1996b) 'Cross-cultural differences in materialism'. *Journal of Economic Psychology*, 17(1): 55–77.

Giddens J. L., Schermer, J. A. and Vernon, P. A. (2009) 'Material values are largely in the family: A twin study of genetic and environmental contributions to materialism'. *Personality and Individual Differences*, 46(4): 428–31.

Gillespie, K., McBride, J. B. and Riddle, L. (2010) 'Globalization, biculturalism and cosmopolitanism: The acculturation status of Mexicans in upper management'. *International Journal of Cross Cultural Management*, 10(1): 37–53.

Goldsmith, R. E. and Clark, R. A. (2012) 'Materialism, status consumption, and consumer independence'. *Journal of Social Psychology*, 152(1): 43–60.

Graddol, D. (2000) *The Future of English*. London: The British Council.

Gupta, N. (2011) 'Globalization does lead to a change in consumer behavior: An empirical evidence of impact of globalization on changing materialistic values in indian consumers and its aftereffects'. *Asia Pacific Journal of Marketing and Logistics*, 23(30): 251–69.

Gutterman, A. S. (2009) *Organizational Management and Administration: A Guide for Managers and Professionals*. New York, NY: Thomson Reuters/West.

Guzmán, F. and Paswan, A. K. (2009) 'Cultural brands from emerging markets: Brand image across host and home countries'. *Journal of International Marketing*, 17(3): 71–86.

Hall, E. T. (1976) *Beyond Culture*. New York, NY: Anchor Press/Doubleday.

Hannerz, U. (1992) *Cultural Complexity: Studies in the Social Organization of Meaning*. New York, NY: Columbia University Press.

He, Y., Chen, Q. and Alden, D. L. (2012) 'Social presence and service satisfaction: The moderating role of cultural value-orientation'. *Journal of Consumer Behavior*, 11(2): 170–76.

Hirschman, E. C. (1988) 'The ideology of consumption: A syntactical analysis of "Dallas" and "Dynasty"'. *Journal of Consumer Research*, 15(3): 344–59.

Hirschman, E. C. (1992) 'The consciousness of addiction: Towards a general theory of compulsive consumption'. *Journal of Consumer Research*, 19(2): 155–79.

Hofstede, G., Hofstede, G. J. and Minkov, M. (2010) *Cultures and Organizations: Software of the Mind*. New York, NY: McGraw-Hill.

Holbrook, M. B. (1993) 'Nostalgia and consumption preferences: Some emerging patterns of consumer tastes'. *Journal of Consumer Research*, 20(2): 245–56.

Holt, D. B. (1998) 'Does cultural capital structure American consumption?' *Journal of Consumer Research*, 25(1): 1–25.

Hudders, L. and Pandelaere, M. (2011) 'The silver lining of materialism: The impact of luxury consumption on subjective well-being'. *Journal of Happiness Studies*, 13(3): 411–37.

Huntington, S. P. (1993) 'The clash of civilizations?' *Foreign Affairs*, 72(3): 22–49.

Huntington, S. P. (1996) 'The West: Unique, not universal'. *Foreign Affairs*, 75(6): 28–46.

Inglehart, R. (1990) *Culture Shift in Advanced Industrial Society*. Princeton, NJ: Princeton University Press.

Jamal, A. (2003) 'Marketing in a multicultural world: The interplay of marketing, ethnicity and consumption'. *European Journal of Marketing*, 37(11/12): 1599–620.

Kagitcibasi, C. (1997) 'Individualism and collectivism'. In *Handbook of Cross-Cultural Psychology*, Volume 3, edited by J. W. Berry, M. H. Segall and C. Kagitcibasi. Boston, MA: Allyn & Bacon, pp. 1–50.

Karabati, S. and Cemalcilar, Z. (2010) 'Values, materialism, and well-being: A study with Turkish university students'. *Journal of Economic Psychology*, 31(4): 624–33.

Kasser, T. (2002) *The High Price of Materialism*. Cambridge, MA: MIT Press.

Keillor, B. D., d'Amico, M. and Horton, V. (2001) 'Global consumer tendencies'. *Psychology & Marketing*, 18(1): 1–19.

Kilbourne, W., Grünhagen, M. and Foley, J. (2005) 'A cross-cultural examination of the relationship between materialism and individual values'. *Journal of Economic Psychology*, 26(5): 624–41.

Kleine, S. S. and Baker, S. M. (2004) 'An integrative review of material possession attachment'. *Academy of Marketing Science Review*, (1). Available at http://www.amsreview.org/articles/kleine01-2004.pdf.

Laroche, M., Kalamas, M. and Cleveland, M. (2005) '"I" versus "we": How individualists and collectivists use information sources to formulate their service expectations'. *International Marketing Review*, 22(3): 279–308.

Lee, W.-N. and Tse, D. K. (1994) 'Changing media consumption in a new home: Acculturation patterns among Hong Kong immigrants to Canada'. *Journal of Advertising*, 23(1): 57–68.

Lévi-Strauss, C. (1978) *Myth and Meaning*. London: Routledge and Kegan Paul.

Levitt, T. (1983) 'The globalization of markets'. *Harvard Business Review*, 61(3): 92–102.

Markus, H. R. and Kitayama, S. (1991) 'Culture and the self: Implications for cognition, emotion, and motivation'. *Psychological Review*, 98(6): 224–53.

Mau, S., Mewes, J. and Zimmermann, A. (2008) 'Cosmopolitan attitudes through transnational social practices?' *Global Networks*, 8(1): 1–24.

McCracken, G. (1986) 'Culture and consumption: A theoretical account of the structure and movement of cultural meaning of consumer goods'. *Journal of Consumer Research*, 13(June): 71–84.

McCracken, G. (1988) *Culture and Consumption: New Approaches to the Symbolic Character of Consumer Goods and Activities*. Bloomington, IN: Indiana University Press.

Mehta, R. and Belk, R. W. (1991) 'Artifacts, identity, and transition: Favorite possessions of Indians and Indian immigrants to the United States'. *Journal of Consumer Research*, 17(4): 398–411.

Mendoza, R. H. and Martinez Jr., J. L. (1981) 'The measurement of acculturation'. In *Explorations in Chicano Psychology*, edited by A. Baron Jr. New York, NY: Praeger, pp. 71–82.

Millar, M. and Thomas, R. (2009) 'Discretionary activity and happiness: The role of materialism'. *Journal of Research in Personality*, 43(4): 699–702.

Miller, D. (1996) 'The myth of cultural erosion'. In *Consumption and Macromarketing*, edited by R. W. Belk, N. Dholakia and A. Venkatesh. Cincinnati, OH: Southwestern, pp. 153–65.

Miyoshi, M. (1993) 'A borderless world? From colonialism to transnationalism and the decline of the nation-state'. *Critical Inquiry*, 19(4): 726–51.

Nakata, C. and Sivakumar, K. (2001) 'Instituting the marketing concept in a multinational setting: The role of national culture'. *Journal of the Academy of Marketing Science*, 29(3): 255–75.

Ong, J. C. (2009) 'The cosmopolitan continuum: Locating cosmopolitan in media and cultural studies'. *Media, Culture & Society*, 31(3): 449–66.

Oswald, R. L. (1999) 'Culture swapping: Consumption and the ethnogenesis of middle-class Haitian immigrants'. *Journal of Consumer Research*, 25: 303–18.

Peñaloza, L. N. (1989) 'Immigrant consumer acculturation'. In *Advances in Consumer Research*, Volume 16, edited by T. K. Srull. Provo, UT: Association for Consumer Research, pp. 110–18.

Peñaloza, L. N. (1994) 'Atravesando fronteras/border crossing: A critical ethnographic exploration of the consumer acculturation of Mexican immigrants'. *Journal of Consumer Research*, 21(1): 32–54.

Peñaloza, L. and Gilly, M. C. (1999) 'Marketer acculturation: The changer and the changed'. *Journal of Marketing*, 63: 84–104.

Phinney, J. S. (1990) 'Ethnic identity in adolescents and adults: Review of research'. *Psychological Bulletin*, 108(3): 499–514.

Puntoni, S. and Tavassoli, N. T. (2007) 'Social context and advertising memory'. *Journal of Marketing Research*, 44(2): 284–96.

Rawwas, M. Y. A., Rajendran, K. N. and Wuehrer, G. A. (1996) 'The influence of worldmindedness and nationalism on consumer evaluation of domestic and foreign products'. *International Marketing Review*, 13(2): 20–38.

Richins, M. L. (2004) 'The material values scale: Measurement properties and development of a short form'. *Journal of Consumer Research*, 31(1): 209–19.

Richins, M. L. and Dawson, S. (1992) 'A consumer values orientation for materialism and its measurement: Scale development and validation'. *Journal of Consumer Research*, 19(3): 303–16.

Richins, M. L. and Rudmin, F. W. (1994) 'Materialism and economic psychology'. *Journal of Economic Psychology*, 15(2): 217–231.

Rindfleisch, A., Burroughs, J. E. and Denton, F. (1997) 'Family structure, materialism, and compulsive consumption'. *Journal of Consumer Research*, 23(4): 312–25.

Robertson, R. (1992) *Globalization: Social Theory and Global Culture*. London: Sage.

Robinson, W. S. (1950) 'Ecological correlations and the behavior of individuals'. *American Sociological Review*, 15: 351–57.

Rokeach, M. J. (1973) *The Nature of Human Values*. New York, NY: The Free Press.

Rosenthal, D. A. and Cichello, A. M. (1986) 'The meeting of two cultures: Ethnic identity and psychosocial adjustment of Italian-Australian adolescents'. *International Journal of Psychology*, 21(1–4): 487–501.

Rosenthal, D. A. and Feldman, S. S. (1992) 'The nature and stability of ethnic identity in Chinese youth: Effects of length of residence in two cultural contexts'. *Journal of Cross-Cultural Psychology*, 23(2): 214–27.

Roth, M. S. (1995) 'The effects of culture and socioeconomics on the performance of global brand image strategies'. *Journal of Marketing Research*, 32(2): 163–75.

Sarigöllü, E. (2009) 'A cross-country exploration of environmental attitudes'. *Environment and Behavior*, 41(3): 365–86.

Sartre, J.-P. (1943) *Being and Nothingness: A Phenomenological Essay on Ontology*. New York, NY: Philosophical Library.

Schouten, J. W. and McAlexander, J. H. (1995) 'Subcultures of consumption: An ethnography of the new bikers'. *Journal of Consumer Research*, 22(1): 43–61.

Schwartz, S. H. (1992) 'Universals in the content and structure of values: Theoretical advances and empirical tests in 20 countries'. In *Advances in Experimental Social Psychology*, Volume 25, edited by M. P. Zanna. San Diego: Academic Press, pp. 1–65.

Schwartz, S. H. (1999) 'A theory of cultural values and some implications for work'. *Applied Psychological International Review*, 48(1): 23–47.

Sharma, P. (2011) 'Country of origin effects in developed and emerging markets: Exploring the contrasting roles of materialism and value consciousness'. *Journal of International Business Studies*, 42(2): 285–306.

Shimp, T. A. and Sharma, S. (1987) 'Consumer ethnocentrism: Construction and validation of the CETSCALE'. *Journal of Marketing Research*, 24(3): 280–89.

Shrum, L. J., Wong, N., Arif, F., Chugani, S. K., Gunz, A., Lowrey, T. M., Nairn, A., Pandeleaere, M., Ross, S. M., Ruvio, A., Scott, K. and Sundie, J. (2012) 'Reconceptualizing materialism as identity goal pursuits: Functions, processes, and consequences'. *Journal of Business Research*, 66(8): 1179–85.

Stayman, D. M. and Deshpandé, R. (1989) 'Situational ethnicity and consumer behavior'. *Journal of Consumer Research*, 16(3): 361–71.

Steenkamp, J.-B. E. M. and Baumgartner, H. (1998) 'Assessing measurement invariance in cross-national consumer research'. *Journal of Consumer Research*, 25(1): 78–107.

Steenkamp, J.-B. E. M., Batra, R. and Alden, D. L. (2003) 'How perceived globalness creates brand value'. *Journal of International Business Studies*, 34(1): 53–65.

Steingard, D. S. and Fitzgibbons, D. E. (1995) 'Challenging the juggernaut of globalization: A manifesto for academic praxis'. *Journal of Organizational Change Management*, 8(4): 441–46.

Stillman, T. F., Fincham, F. D., Vohs, K. D.; Lambert, N. and Phillips, C. A. (2012) 'The material and immaterial in conflict: Spirituality reduces conspicuous consumption'. *Journal of Economic Psychology*, 33(1): 1–7.

Swinyard, W. R., Kau, A. K. and Phua, H. Y. (2001) 'Happiness, materialism, and religious experience in the U.S. and Singapore'. *Journal of Happiness Studies*, 2(1): 13–32.

Tajfel, H. and Turner, J. C. (1986) 'The social identity of inter-group behavior'. In *Psychology of Intergroup Relations*, edited by S. Worchel and W. Austin. Chicago, IL: Nelson-Hall, pp. 7–24.

Thaler, R. (1981) 'Some empirical evidence on dynamic inconsistency'. *Economic Letters*, 8(3): 201–7.

Tobacyk, J. J, Babin, B. J., Attaway, J. S., Socha, S., Shows, D. and James, K. (2011) 'Materialism through the eyes of Polish and American Consumers'. *Journal of Business Research*, 64(9): 944–50.

Tomlinson, J. (1991) *Cultural Imperialism: A Critical Introduction*. Baltimore, MA: Johns Hopkins University Press.

Thompson, C. J. and Tambyah, S. K. (1999) 'Trying to be cosmopolitan'. *Journal of Consumer Research*, 26(3): 214–41.

Triandis, H. C. (1994) *Culture and Social Behavior*. New York, NY: McGraw-Hill.

Triandis, H. C. and Gelfand, M. J. (1998) 'Converging measurement of horizontal and vertical individualism and collectivism'. *Journal of Personality and Social Psychology*, 74(1): 118–28.

Triandis, H. C., McCusker, C., Betancourt, H., Iwao, S., Leung, K., Salazar, J. M., Setiadi, B., Sinha, B., Touzard, H. and Zaleski, Z. (1993) 'An etic-emic analysis of individualism and collectivism'. *Journal of Cross-Cultural Psychology*, 24(3): 366–83.

Tse, D. K., Belk, R. W. and Zhou, N. (1989) 'Becoming a consumer society: A longitudinal and cross-cultural content analysis of print ads from Hong Kong, the people's republic of China, and Taiwan'. *Journal of Consumer Research*, 15(4): 457–72.

Üstüner, T. and Holt, D. B. (2007) 'Dominated consumer acculturation: The social construction of poor migrant women's consumer identity projects in a Turkish squatter'. *Journal of Consumer Research*, 34(1): 41–56.

Veblen, T. (1899). *The Theory of the Leisure Class*. New York, NY: Penguin.

Venkatesh, A. (1995) 'Ethnocentrism: A new paradigm to study cultural and cross-cultural consumer behavior'. In *Marketing in a Multicultural World*, edited by J. A. Costa and G. J. Bamossy. Thousand Oaks, CA: Sage, pp. 27–63.

Walker, C. (1996) 'Can TV save the planet?' *American Demographics*, 18(5): 42–9.

Wallendorf, M. and Arnould, E. J. (1988) '"My favorite things": A cross-cultural inquiry into object attachment, possessiveness, and social linkage'. *Journal of Consumer Research*, 14(4): 531–47.

Wallerstein, I. (1989) *The Modern World-System III: The Second Era of Great Expansion of the Capitalist World-Economy, 1730-1840s*. New York, NY: Cambridge.

Waters, M. (1995) *Globalization*. London: Routledge.

Watson, J., Lysonski, S., Gillan, T. and Raymore, L. (2002) 'Cultural values and important possessions: A cross-cultural analysis'. *Journal of Business Research*, 55(11): 923–31.

Weber, M. (1947) *The Theory of Social and Economic Organization*. Translated by Parsons, T. (1904–1905), reprint. New York, NY: Charles Scribner's Sons.

Wee, T. T. T. (1999) 'An exploration of a global teenage lifestyle in Asian societies'. *Journal of Consumer Marketing*, 16(4): 365–71.

Wicklund, R. A. and Gollwizter, P. M. (1982) *Symbolic Self-Completion*. Hillsdale, NJ: Erlbaum.

Wilk, R. (1995) 'Learning to be local in belize: Global systems of common difference'. In *Worlds Apart: Modernity Through the Prism of the Local*, edited by D. Miller. London: Routledge, pp. 110–31.

Wilk, R. (1998) 'Emulation, imitation, and global consumerism'. *Organization & Environment*, 11(3): 314–33.

Wilson, D. T. and Bozinoff, L. (1980) 'Role theory and buying–selling negotiations: A critical overview'. In *Marketing in the 80's*, edited by R. Bagozzi. Chicago, IL: American Marketing, pp. 118–21.

Wong, N. Y. and Ahuvia, A. C. (1998) 'Personal taste and family face: Luxury consumption in Confucian and Western societies'. *Psychology & Marketing*, 15(5): 423–41.

Wong, N. Y., Rindfleisch, A. and Burroughs, J. (2003) 'Do reverse-worded items confound measures in cross-cultural consumer research? The case of the material values scale'. *Journal of Consumer Research*, 30(1): 72–91.

Yang, S. and Stening, B. W. (2011) 'Cultural and ideological roots of materialism in China'. *Social Indicators Research*, 108(3): 441–52.

Yau, O. H. M. (1988) 'The Chinese cultural values: Its dimensions and marketing implications'. *European Journal of Marketing*, 22(5): 44–57.

Zhou, N. and Belk, R. W. (2004) 'Chinese consumer readings of global and local advertising appeals'. *Journal of Advertising*, 33(3): 63–77.

Zinkhan, G. M. (1994) 'From the editor: Advertising, materialism, and quality of life'. *Journal of Advertising*, 23(2): 1–4.

Appendix 10.1: materialism and consumer behaviour consistency across countries

	Canada	Mexico	Greece	Korea	Hungary	India	Chile	Sweden	Overall
Traditional meals									
Traditional beverages			−c	+c	+b				
Traditional food items									
Traditional snack items				+c	+a		+b	+a	+a
Traditional restaurants	+a			+c					+a
Tea		−a						−a	−a
Coffee					+c	−c			
Soft drinks		+a	+b		+a		+b	+a	+a

(continued)

(continued)

	Canada	Mexico	Greece	Korea	Hungary	India	Chile	Sweden	Overall
Beer	+c	+a				+c			
Wine (table)									
Champagne/expensive wine	+a				+a	+a		+c	+a
Pizza	+b	+c		-c	+b	+a	+a	+a	+a
Hamburgers	+b	+c	+a		+a	+a	+a	+a	+a
Boxed chocolates			+a	+a		+a	+b		+a
Personal portable stereo	+a	+b	+a		+a	+a		+a	+a
VCR	+a		+a		+a				+a
Washing machine						+a			
Clothes dryer			+a	+a	+a	+a		+a	+a
Dishwasher			+a		+b	+a			+a
Hairdryer		+c	+b	+a	+b	+b	+a		+a
Vacuum						+b	+c		
CD player	+a	+a	+a		+a	+a		+c	+a
Bicycle	-b		-b						_a
Videogame console	+a	+a	+b		+a	+b	+b	+a	+a
DVD player	+a	+c	+a	+b	+a			+a	+a
Refrigerator									
Microwave oven	+a		+a	+b	+a		+a	+a	+a
TV set	+a	+a	+a		+a	+c	+a	+a	+a
Digital camera	+a		+a	+a	+a	+b	+b	+a	+a
PC/laptop computer	+a		+c		+a	+a			+a
Food processor	+a		+a	+a	+a	+a	+a		+a
Automobile	+b	+b	+a	+b	+a	+a	+b		+a
Blue jeans	+a				+c	+b	+a	+a	+a
Athletic shoes				_c	+c		+a	+a	+a
Business attire			+a					+b	+a
Traditional fashion		+b	+a					+c	+b
Fur/leather coats	+a		+a	+a	+a	+a	+a		+a
Fragrances	+a		+a	+a	+a	+a	+a	+a	+a
Cosmetics	+a		+a +c		+a	+a	+a	+a	+a
Jewelry	+a		+a	+a	+a	+c	+a		+a
Antique furniture			+b	+a		+a	+c		+a
Purchase DVD's	+c		+b	+b	+b	+a		+c	+a
Watch television	+a		+b	+b	+a		+b	+a	+a
Use mobile phone	+a		+a				+b	+a	+a
Use PC/laptop	+b		+b			+b			+a
Surf internet	+a						+a	+a	+a
Send email	+a							+b	+b
Use ATM	+a	+a			+a	+b		+a	+a

Source: Using data derived from Cleveland et al. (2009a).

Note

+/–: Sign direction for significant standardized path coefficients, AMOS multi-group SEM (baseline model for overall; for country-sample results: structural models with measurement-weights constrained, see Cleveland et al., 2009a). a means p<.01, b means p<.05, c means p<.10 (N=2015).

Part V
Market segmentation and targeting

11

Demographics and ethnic minority lifestyles

Miguel A. Zúñiga and Ivonne M. Torres

Introduction

Ethnic minority consumers (e.g., Hispanics, African Americans and Asian Americans) are defined as consumers that share an ethnicity distinct to the mainstream population (Pires and Stanton 2002). In the United States (US), Hispanics, African Americans and Asian Americans are the main ethnic minority consumer groups with the largest economic impact and highest population growth. The marketing literature has studied these ethnic minority groups due to their positive impact on the economy and businesses (ibid.). Culture and ethnicity are factors that influence consumer behaviour and seller–buyer behaviour (Hui *et al.* 1992; Zúñiga and Torres 2015c). As a result each ethnic group's consumer behaviour might be unique due to cultural differences. In this context, many called for ethnic marketing taking into account the cultural differences of ethnic groups for developing successful targeted marketing programs (e.g., Nwankwo *et al.* 1998).

Ethnic marketing is 'to treat ethnic consumers as distinctive markets separate from the macro market and to reach them using differentiated marketing mix strategies' (Cui 1998, p. 87) or 'differentiated marketing towards an ethnic group' (p. 88).

With the growing diversity of the U.S. population, ethnic marketing has become an increasingly crucial component of marketing strategy (Pires *et al.* 2003; Demangeot *et al.* 2013). Targeting consumers on the basis of ethnicity is essential as latest demographic trends suggest that the population of ethnic minority consumers is increasing in numbers. For example, an estimated 53 million Hispanics currently live in the US, totaling 17% of the U.S. population (Taylor *et al.* 2012a). It is estimated that by 2050, Hispanics will total 29% of the U.S. population (Passel and Cohn 2008). As of 2005, Whites totalled 67% of the U.S. population and will only make up 47% in 2050. In 2050, African Americans will make up the same proportion of 13% as they did in 2005, while Asian Americans will see their proportion increase to 9% from 5% in 2005 (ibid.). In light of these trends, it is important to examine both the demographics and lifestyles of ethnic minorities and their implications for ethnic minority consumer behaviour. The chapter aims to provide a comprehensive overview of such trends providing useful insights for ethnic marketing development and implementation. The chapter first considers the impact of ethnicity and acculturation on ethnic minority consumer behaviour.

Targeting ethnic minority consumers

Role of ethnicity and ethnic identification

Marketers have used ethnicity in advertising as a tool to appeal to consumers who self-identify with a specific ethnicity (Hirschman 1981; Broderick *et al.* 2011b). Deshpandé and Stayman (1994) tested the distinctiveness theory developed by McGuire (1984) to study its application to advertising. Distinctiveness theory is defined as the process in which ethnically targeted stimuli becomes more effective when the proportion of consumers from a specific ethnic group is lower in the overall population (Deshpandé and Stayman 1994). For instance, using a Hispanic ethnic spokesperson in an advert becomes more effective in creating positive attitudes toward the advert among Hispanics if the Hispanics are small in comparison to the overall population. Additionally, distinctiveness theory has found that consumers feel more different when the consumers' ethnic group is a minority leading to a strong identification with their ethnic group. McGuire (1984) found that consumers' distinctive traits related to the overall population were more relevant and important to the consumers than the more common traits. Therefore, advertising with Hispanic cues may be more effective when targeted toward a Hispanic ethnic group.

Ethnic self-awareness is also an important factor which influences consumers' perceptions and responses to adverts. In this context, the concept of ethnocentrism has been employed in understanding the behaviours of minorities. Ethnocentrism refers to a tendency to believe that one's own ethnic group is superior to all other ethnic groups (Guo and Schwing 2009) or to judge other cultures or ethnic groups using your own cultural values and standards. Such tendencies are expected to impact advert attitudes, product attitudes, retail attitudes and purchase intentions. In a multicultural context, some ethnocentric consumers may develop less favourable attitudes toward retailers and products that employ bilingual advertising or signage that does not relate to their ethnicity (ibid.). Moreover, including product or retailer associations of another ethnic group may also diminish the appeal, perception of validity, quality and preference for those products or retailers. In the case of Hispanic minorities, for example, advertisers may create more effective adverts by using code-switching, Hispanic models, Hispanic cues, and other cultural relevant cues such as family, social and business settings and relationships. This phenomenon is a result of Hispanic consumers relating to the cultural cues found in the advert (Zúñiga and Torres 2015a; 2015b; 2015c).

Whittler (1989) suggests that ethnic minority consumers respond positively when ethnicity is used in advertising. As a result of the U.S. market being more diverse, marketers have responded by representing various multicultural groups and using ethnic cues (e.g., ethnic actors (Zúñiga 2015; Zúñiga and Torres 2015b)). Forehand and Deshpandé (2001) argued that the more often ethnicity is used in adverts, the more consumers will become conditioned to the use of ethnicity and the less sensitive they will be toward this tactic. Therefore, the use of ethnicity in adverts is not always the most appropriate strategy (ibid.). This conditioning effect may be mitigated when consumers relate the ethnic cues in adverts to their self-identity (ibid.). In other words, consumers are more susceptible to adverts with ethnic cues if they possess high levels of ethnic self-awareness.

Forehand and Deshpandé (2001) found that ethnic self-awareness occurs when consumers are more sensitive to information that relates to their specific ethnicity. The related process in which consumers self-identify with a specific ethnicity is known as self-categorization. Self-categorization is the unconscious process of consumers comparing the similarities and dissimilarities between their ethnic group and others. Ethnic identification, which is shaped from consumers' past social and cultural experiences, is a factor that affects ethnic self-awareness (ibid.). Strength of ethnic identification is defined as the extent to which a member of an ethnic group identifies with their ethnic group (Deshpandé and Stayman 1994). Moreover, the higher the level of ethnic identification a consumer holds the more sensitive the consumer is to products and adverts with ethnic cues. The social situation or environment also affects the strength of ethnic identification (Stayman and Deshpandé 1989). It is important to understand that the measurement of ethnicity is more accurate if ethnicity and strength of ethnic identification is studied in combination with the environmental or situational ethnicity.

Ethnic minority groups are more likely to identify with their ethnicity if they are surrounded by a majority of consumers belonging to another ethnicity. Consumers living in such situations are characterized as having a strong ethnic self-awareness and in being more sensitive to ethnic cues in adverts. For example, if the social environment has a majority of Hispanics, Hispanic consumers tend to consume more products that relate to their Hispanic ethnicity compared to situations where their social environment is composed of diverse ethnic groups and Hispanic consumers don't represent the majority. Consumers with strong ethnic group identification don't not always possess a strong ethnic self-awareness (Forehand and Deshpandé 2001). Forehand and Deshpandé argue that advertisers often assume that consumers with a strong ethnic group identification always possess a strong ethnic self-awareness and this is not the case. Advertisers need to be cautious and not assume such relationships, and instead research their target audience carefully in order to determine small details (e.g., the relationship between ethnic group identification and self-awareness) that are essential for the effectiveness of their adverts (Zúñiga 2015). Besides factors related to the consumer or social environment, contextual or stimulus primes are also known to influence ethnic self-awareness (Zúñiga and Torres 2015b). For instance, cues in an advertising context such as code-switched words and ethnic images directed toward Asian Americans might affect the levels of consumer self-awareness.

The use of specific ethnic group members as spokespeople for advertising is a factor that impacts the effectiveness of adverts (Whittler 1989). More specifically, viewers of adverts prefer those that use spokespeople from their own ethnic group. Furthermore, viewers can be differentiated by the level of strength of identification with their ethnic group. For instance, viewers prefer a spokesperson belonging to their own ethnic group when they identify more strongly with that group. The relationship between distinctiveness theory and the influence of ethnicity on advertising effectiveness is vital for developing effective marketing messages. A model was developed by Deshpandé and Stayman (1994) that states an ethnic situation affects ethnic salience, which moderates the influence of the spokesperson's ethnicity on the spokesperson's trustworthiness – ultimately influencing brand attitude.

In essence, marketers may be more successful by tailoring their marketing messages to each distinct ethnic group. Accommodation theory indicates that ethnic minority consumers are more likely to consider someone they perceive as similar as more attractive and influential (Koslow *et al.* 1994).

Role of acculturation

Acculturation is a process that influences the effectiveness of targeted messages toward ethnic minority groups. The process of acculturation is the cultural change that occurs when consumers with diverse cultural backgrounds interact (Gibson 2001). Consumers form their identities via diverse acculturation modes, meaning that the acculturation process is an ongoing process and not a homogenous one (ibid.).

Berry (1997; 2003) and Berry *et al.* (1986) depict one of the most popular models of acculturation. Such models in particular highlight the resulting acculturation categories from the interactions of ethnic groups of consumers. Acculturation results in either positive or negative attitudes toward 'ancestral' and 'host' cultures (Poulis *et al.* 2013). Those consumers that strive for cultural maintenance typically are those that consider their cultural identity important enough to maintain. On the other hand, those consumers that do not strive for cultural main-tenance typically make an effort to be involved with the majority culture. Four modes of acculturation exist: integration, assimilation, separation and marginalism. The fours modes of acculturation result because differences in consumers' attitudes toward their ancestral culture and host culture. There are some consumers that strive to maintain their ancestral cultural back-ground, some that strive to be involved with the host culture, some hold positive attitudes, and some hold negative attitudes toward the acculturation process.

Integration results when consumers maintain their ancestral culture and also become involved in the host culture (Kipnis *et al.*; Broderick *et al.* 2011a). On the other hand, *assimilation* results when consumers reject their ancestral culture and become involved in the host culture (ibid.). *Separation* is the process that occurs when consumers make efforts to maintain their ancestral cultural identity and do not engage with the host culture (ibid.). *Marginalism* occurs when con-sumers reject both their own cultural identity and the host culture as well. The different modes of acculturation have implications on firms' marketing strategy. Additionally, Ownbey and Horridge (1997) found that acculturation modes have a stronger effect on consumer behaviour than ethnicity. Therefore, marketers have to consider the acculturation mode besides ethnicity to effectively target ethnic groups.

This chapter reviews the three major minority groups (i.e., Hispanics, African Americans and Asian Americans) because they represent the largest groups and economically most impact-ful. The chapter then reviews changing trends in demographics and ethnic minority lifestyles in the areas of education, poverty, economics, health, politics, immigration, ethnic media, homeownership, technology and religion that may be used by marketers to develop more effective messages targeted at each distinct ethnic group.

Hispanics

Important issues

Categorization of the U.S. Hispanic population with roots to Spanish-speaking countries has typically involved the use of the terms Hispanic or Latino. In order to clarify this further, Taylor *et al.* (2012b) held a telephone-based national bilingual survey of a nationally representative sample of 1,220 Latinos 18 years and older. Of the 1,220 total respondents 436 were born in the US (this excludes Puerto Rico) and 784 were born outside the US including Puerto Rico. The margin of error is 3.6% for this study. The authors found that 51% (vs 24% of Hispanics who prefer a pan-ethnic label) of Hispanics identify by their family's country of origin using terms such as Mexican or Venezuelan, not fully agreeing with the pan-ethnic labels Hispanic and Latino (Taylor *et al.* 2012b). Additionally, 36% identify their race as White and 3% as African American (ibid.). Those that use the term American to describe their identity totaled 21%. When choosing between the terms Hispanic or Latino, 51% of Hispanics indicated they have no preference while those that did have a preference were divided, 33% preferred Hispanic and 14% preferred Latino (ibid.).

Taylor *et al.* also found that 69% of Hispanics believe that U.S. Hispanics have different cultures compared to 29% who believe that one culture is shared among the ethnic group. All respondents did however agree that they shared a strong relationship with the Spanish lan-guage. A total of 82% of Hispanic adults studied speak Spanish and 95% said it is important for Hispanics to continue speaking Spanish in the future (ibid.).

In comparison to those who identified as a typical American, 47% of Hispanics believe that they are very different from a typical American (ibid.). Only 21% indicated that they use the term American to describe their identity. Currently 48% of Hispanics are U.S. born; these U.S. born Hispanics tend to have a stronger American identity than those Hispanics that immigrated to the US (ibid.). A total of 66% U.S. born Hispanics identify as a typical American compared to only 34% of those Hispanics born outside the US (ibid.).

Use of the Spanish or English language varies among Hispanics. Taylor *et al.* found that 38% of Hispanics are Spanish dominant, 38% are bilingual and 24% are English dominant. The majority of those born in the US (51%) are English dominant. Overall, Hispanics have positive perceptions of the US and 87% of Hispanics believe that Hispanic immigrants should learn English in order to be successful (ibid.). A total of 55% believe it is very important that future generations learn to speak Spanish if they want to be successful and 20% believe it is somewhat important (ibid.).

Economic power

Though companies' dollars allocated to Hispanics remain small as a percent of total general domestic advertising spending, more than 78% of blue chip companies have recognized the potential of the Hispanic market in the US (Torres 2007). The Hispanic consumers' annual purchasing power totals $1 trillion and is the fastest growing demographic in the US (Fahmy 2010). Their purchasing power is expected to increase to $1.5 trillion by the year 2017, becoming the world's nineth largest economy (ibid.). Hispanics are characterized as one of the most brand loyal segments of the U.S. general population, making it an even more valuable market for advertisers (Zúñiga and Torres 2015c). These attributes of Hispanics are vital for economic growth and business success. As a result, advertisers have viewed the Hispanic segment as an attractive and high potential market segment to target.

When Hispanics compare their minority group to other minorities, 55% say their group is as successful as other ethnic minority groups. Only 22% indicate that they believe the Hispanic group is less successful, and 17% believe the Hispanic group has been more successful than other minority groups (Taylor *et al.* 2012b). The perception of the US, compared to their country of origin, differs among Hispanics. Hispanics perceive life in the US to be of higher quality than in their family's country of origin, regardless if they are U.S. born or have immigrated to the US. A majority 87% of Hispanics believe that the US offers more opportunities for progress in life than their country of origin (ibid.). Additionally, 72% of Hispanics view the US as a better country for raising children compared to their country of origin and 69% believe that the US treats the poor better (ibid.). When looking at moral values, 44% of Hispanics believe that they are higher in the US, but 39% believe that the strength of family ties is higher in their country of origin (ibid.). Hispanics' perceptions of the US being an overall positive country to live in were also analyzed. For example, 79% of Hispanic immigrants would immigrate again despite the reasons for immigration. Of these, 55% immigrated for economic reasons and 24% for family reasons (ibid.).

African Americans

Important issues

A content analysis by Bailey (2006) found that African Americans have more commonly appeared in advertising, and their presence has become more significant in recent years. Research regarding African Americans in advertising over the years (Taylor and Lee 1995; Cox 1970; Bush *et al.* 1980; Green 1999; Lee *et al.* 2002; Martin *et al.* 2004) has found that their presence in advertising has increased consistently. Many of these studies have looked at the frequency in which African Americans appear in advertising (Bush *et al.* 1980; Licata and Biswas 1993; Stevenson 2002; Bailey 2006) and they all agree that African Americans have become more prominent in both TV and print advertising.

Appiah (2001) examined whether the strength of ethnic identification influenced adolescents' responses to adverts, and found that subjects with strong ethnic identities identified more strongly with and responded more favourably towards adverts with characters matching their own ethnicity. The relevance of this finding becomes clearer when advertisers consider evidence that ethnic identification is high among minority group members in the US (Deshpandé *et al.* 1986).

The role of a model's race has been well researched and its role as a peripheral cue has previously been established (Whittler and Spira 2002). The study by Whittler and Spira (2002) explored the role of ethnicity in an advertising context based on the Elaboration Likelihood Model (ELM) and Social Categorization Theory. Their study examined minority viewers' evaluations of products and adverts containing ethnic cues. Specifically, African American adults rated an advert that featured either a White or an African American model. Consistent with distinctiveness and ethnic identification theory, product and advert evaluations were more favourable when an African American model was present compared to when a White model was, but only for African American participants who identified strongly with their culture. African Americans who identified weakly with their culture evaluated the product and advert similarly for both situations in which either a White or African American model were present. The results also showed that the African American model's ethnicity motivated African Americans, especially those with strong racial attitudes, to process the message in a biased manner. In particular, the African American (versus White) model's ethnicity positively influenced the African American participants' thoughts about the product, which in turn yielded more favourable product evaluations.

Whittler and Spira (2002) explored how the model's ethnicity, consistent with the ELM's contention, may play different roles (i.e. as a peripheral cue, to increase the level of elaboration or as an argument). By collecting thought listing data and measuring both valence of thoughts and elaboration, they found that a model's ethnicity may influence persuasion in more than one way. Their research suggests that a model's ethnicity can play two roles. In one role, the model's ethnicity may operate as a peripheral cue. With respect to model ethnicity, its role as a peripheral cue has been established in several past studies (e.g., Whittler 1989; Whittler and DiMeo 1991). Their study supports a second but limited role for model ethnicity. In this second role, a model's ethnicity may affect the direction of argument elaboration by producing a positive or negative motivational bias to related thoughts. This role is limited because it only emerged with racially sensitive viewers.

Economic power

As marketers begin planning their future campaigns and strategic approach, the list of the most desirable consumer targets is not necessarily a copy of years past. With a significant spending power, the African American segment is one of the most lucrative, interesting and complex targets for national and local advertisers. Reaching the African American consumer can help marketers expand their consumer base, increase revenue and build brand awareness. African Americans comprise more than 13% of the U.S. population today (i.e. totaling 39.2 million) and are expected to spend more than $1 trillion in 2013 alone from approximately $318 billion in 1990, according to the U.S. Census Bureau and the Selig Center for Economic Growth at the University of Georgia's Terry College of Business (Humphreys 2007). The estimated spending power of $1 trillion in 2013 is expected to result from an increase of 41% from 2007, the largest increase among other ethnic groups (ibid.). By July 2050, census estimates indicate 61.4 million African Americans will live in the US. The population growth in this segment gives marketers reason enough to market to African Americans and create inventive ways of reaching out to them.

As this consumer segment continues to grow in importance, marketers need to focus on determining what types of products could benefit from African American-targeted advertising. Major corporations have certainly taken notice. Marketing giants such as Coca-Cola, Ford and L'Oreal have instituted special divisions within their marketing departments to develop targeted strategies for communicating to African Americans through traditional advertising media and other diverse channels. Marketers are definitely paying attention. These days whenever we watch TV or look through a magazine African Americans appear in more adverts than ever before. African Americans have become more and more prominent in advertising in recent years (Torres 2007). In the 2012 Super Bowl alone Coca-Cola paid close to $4 million each for three commercials celebrating African American History Month. Advertising in ethnic media increased in the last decade at a pace dramatically beyond increases in advertising as a whole. Price (2005) reported that in 2004, marketers spent about $1.8 billion in advertising to communicate specifically with African American consumers. African American media receives the largest share of ethnic media spending.

Armed with the U.S. Census data that indicates the large and increasing purchasing power and population size of the African American market, more corporations – including Pepsi, GM and Johnson & Johnson – are investing more marketing dollars into the African American market than ever before (TNS Media Intelligence 2005). Also, corporations who have targeted these buyers for some time have increased their investment. Examples include Procter & Gamble, Wal-Mart and Dell (TNS Media Intelligence 2005). In 2007 L'Oreal USA Beauty Company teamed up with Essence magazine as a way to target African American women (Nagel 2007).

Asian Americans

Important Issues

As indicated by the U.S. Census Bureau, the term Asian refers to a person having an origin in Southeast Asia, Far East or the Indian sub-continent (Humes *et al.* 2011). Some countries in this geographic location include China, India, Pakistan, Cambodia, Japan, Korea, Malaysia, Philippine Islands, Vietnam and Thailand. Chinese, Asian Indian, Japanese, Vietnamese or Other Asian are the terms used by Asian Americans to indicate their race.

The 2010 Census estimated there were 17.3 million U.S. residents of Asian descent (Pew Research Social & Demographic Trends 2013). This number is 5.6% of the U.S. population. The Asian population is expected to increase to 33.4 million by 2050 (Zhang 2010). A total 14.7 million indicated they were Asian alone and the other 2.6 million indicated they were a combination of Asian with one or more race (Humes *et al.* 2011). California has the largest Asian population, totaling 5.6 million; New York the second largest with 1.6 million; and the highest proportion exists in Hawaii making up 57% of the population (U.S. Census Bureau 2010). The U.S. Asian population can be divided into different sub-groups in the following fashion: Chinese Americans (4.0 million) are the largest group, followed by Filipinos (3.4 million), Asian Indians (3.2 million), Vietnamese (1.7 million), Koreans (1.7 million) and Japanese (1.3 million) (Pew Research Social & Demographic Trends 2013). According to the U.S.

Census Bureau (2010), the Asian American population is expected to increase from 10.7 million in 2000 to 40.6 million in 2050, a 279% increase. Additionally, the Asian American population is expected to increase 162% from 2008 to 2050 compared to a 44% increase of the total U.S. population (ibid.).

Country of origin, immigration rates and local availability of native-language media are factors that affect the choice of whether Asian Americans view media in English or their native language. For instance, Japanese Americans have lower rates of immigration, and most families tend to have established themselves in the US several generations ago compared to other Asian American sub-groups (Nielsen 2012). As a result, they are more likely to consume English language media and tend to speak English at higher rates than other Asian American sub-groups. However, while Japanese families established themselves in the US several generations ago, Chinese, Vietnamese and Korean current immigration rates are higher than those of the Japanese (Nielsen 2012). As a result, Chinese, Vietnamese and Koreans prefer to speak in their native language rather than English. According to Nielsen (2012), a total 61% of all Asian Americans indicate they speak English very well compared to 50% of those who are foreign born. Additionally, a total of 77% of all Asian Americans speak another language besides English at home (ibid.).

More specifically, in 2008 there were 2.5 million people aged 5 or older who spoke Chinese in their home (U.S. Census Bureau 2010). In the US, this ranks the Chinese language second only behind Spanish as the most widely spoken language besides English (ibid.).

Younger Asian Americans are more likely to use English as their primary language compared to the older generations, who are more likely to stick to their native tongue (Kaufman-Scarborough 2000). Additionally, many Asian Americans use their native tongue in normal situations such as reading, entertainment and product evaluations. Specifically, about 24% primarily use their native language and more than half of Asian Americans feel comfortable speaking their native language (ibid.).

In terms of brand attitudes, both brand loyalty and price sensitivity are high among Asian Americans (Cohen 1992). When making buying decisions, Asian American consumers do not buy the lowest priced item but instead search for the best item for the lowest price (Kaufman-Scarborough 2000). Additionally, Berkowitz (1994) found that Asian Americans are high in brand loyalty. A survey of 1,600 Asian Americans showed that 72% reported brand names influencing their purchase decisions. Premium products are high on the list of items to buy among Asian American consumers – one example being automobiles, as they represent status to a great extent.

In mainstream media, Asian Americans are under-represented compared to other ethnic groups, but when they do appear in media they are more commonly in stereotypical roles (Zhang 2010). Asian women, for example, are depicted in a variety of stereotypes including silent, humble, obedient, exotic or hyper-sexualized dolls, or the total opposite, being evil, deceitful, seductive or ruthless dragon ladies (Park *et al.* 2006). Men are portrayed as asexual, culturally ignorant, effeminate, hardworking, intelligent, thrifty, technologically savvy and as the model minority (Yuen *et al.* 2005; Paek and Shah 2003). It is important to note that these stereotypes affect the acculturation of Asian Americans. Therefore, in understanding the stereotypes, as well as their current lifestyles, marketers can more effectively target Asian Americans. For instance, Paek and Shah (2003) indicate that marketers are more than ever targeting Asian Americans with stereotypes, such at the model minority stereotypes, in order to increase advert effectiveness. Language use, price sensitivity, brand loyalty and status are other factors that influence Asian Americans' lifestyles, and that should be considered to effectively develop persuasive adverts.

Economic power

Buying power for Asian Americans in 2012 was $718.4 billion, a dramatic increase of 523% between 1990 and 2012 (Nielsen 2012). At this rate, the buying power is expected to reach $1 trillion in 2017 (ibid.). This buying power can be compared to individual countries and would make it the world's eighteenth economy in buying power (ibid.). Asian Americans are considered to be one of the fastest growing, most educated and affluent ethnic group. The 2008 median household income for Asian Americans was $70,069 for those that identify as single race (U.S. Census Bureau 2010). The median household income for the sub-groups differed. For instance, Asian Indians had a median household income of $90,528 and Vietnamese-Americans had a median household income of $55,667 (ibid.). In comparison to the 2012 U.S. median household income, Asian American median household income was 28% higher (ibid.). According to Nielsen, a total of 28% of all Asian American households had incomes greater than $100,000 compared to only 18% of U.S. households. As far as education is concerned, a total of 50% of Asian Americans aged twenty-five years or older have a Bachelor's degree compared to 28% of the U.S. population (ibid.). Nielsen also reported that within the working Asian American population, 50% hold professional or managerial roles compared to 40% of the U.S. population. In 2007, the author reports that Asian American owned businesses generated revenues of more than $506 billion, which is more than any other ethnic group in the US. There were over 1.6 million Asian American owned businesses in 2007, a 41% increase from 2002 compared to the 18% increase for the general U.S. growth (ibid.).

Education

Enrollment rate

U.S. college enrollment of 18 to 24 year old students recently hit a record of 12.2 million in October 2010 (Fry 2011). In 2010, 1.8 million (15%) of students enrolled in either two or four year colleges were Hispanic making this a record as well (ibid.). In one year, from 2009 to 2010, the number of Hispanic students enrolled in college increased by 349,000 compared to an increase of 88,000 African American students, 43,000 Asian American students, and a decrease of 320,000 White students. For Whites, the 320,000 students decline is the largest percentage decline since 1993 when the historical comparison study began (ibid.).

Another record for the year 2010 is that for the first time Hispanic students outnumbered African American students enrolled in college, despite the increase in enrollment for African American students. For instance, in 2010 among 18 to 24 year old African American students a total of 38% were enrolled in college compared to 32% in 2008 and 13% in 1967 (ibid.). Hispanic students' enrollment rate has been growing faster than for African Americans because of higher birth rates and higher levels of immigration. Based on U.S. Census data, Fry found that in 2010, 19% of 18 to 24 year olds were Hispanic compared to 5% in 1972. Even though Hispanic enrollment rate has grown rapidly to 32%, a record for Hispanics, it is still lower than other ethnic groups such as 38% for African Americans, 62% for Asian Americans and 43% for Whites (ibid.).

The share of Hispanics who have completed high school has improved for the 18 and 24 year old Hispanic demographic; the rate increased to 73% in 2010 from 70% a year earlier in 2009 (Fry 2011). Of those Hispanic high school graduates, the share who attended college increased from 39% in 2009 to 44% in 2010 (ibid.). The growth of Hispanic students attending college was focused on two year colleges. In 2010, 46% of Hispanic 18 to 24 year olds attending college were enrolled at two year colleges and 54% attended a four year college. This can be compared to the 18 to 24 year old cohorts from other ethnic groups that attended four year colleges, which included 73% Whites, 78% Asian Americans and 63% of African Americans (ibid.).

The economic recession that started in 2007 impacted 18 to 24 year olds with high unemployment levels. As a result, this recession helped with increased college enrollment of young adults of all three major minority groups due to high unemployment rates (Fry 2009).

Completion rate

Enrollment rates have been increasing for ethnic minority young adults but the question now is whether that translates to increased completion rates. Fry (2011) used data from the National Center for Education Statistics to compare the completion rate of the various ethnic groups in 2010. The findings showed that 25 to 29 year old Hispanic students who completed at least a Bachelor's degree consisted of only 13% compared to 53% of Asian Americans, 39% of Whites and 19% of African Americans (ibid.). This lower completion rate of Hispanics was attributed to Hispanic immigrants and the challenges they encounter learning a new language. A total 20% of those U.S. born 25 to 29 year old Hispanics completed at least a Bachelor's degree (ibid.).

Economics

Kochhar *et al.* (2011a) used data from the Pew Research Center's Social and Demographic Trends and found that household wealth for Hispanics suffered the largest decrease of 66% among all ethnic groups from $18,359 in 2005 to $6,325 in 2009. African Americans suffered a household wealth decrease of 53% and Whites 16% (ibid.). The main factor that impacted the household wealth of Hispanics was the drop in household values. Interestingly, Hispanic's net worth was heavily focused on home equity – about 66% of their net worth (ibid.). Additionally, a majority of Hispanics live in states that were hit the hardest by the housing market crash.

Based on research conducted using data from the Survey of Income and Program Participation (SIPP), the median wealth of Whites is 18 times greater than that of Hispanics and twenty times greater than that of African Americans (Kochhar *et al.* 2011b). These discrepancies are the largest in twenty-five years since the U.S. government started publishing such data and studies (ibid.). Additionally, in 2009, a total of 31% of Hispanic households and 35% of African American households had either a zero or negative net worth compared to only 15% of White households (ibid.). In 2005 prior to the recession of 2007, those percentages were 23% for Hispanic households, 29% for African Americans compared to only 11% of Whites (ibid.). In 2009, a total of 24% of Hispanics and 24% of African Americans had no assets besides a vehicle compared to 6% Whites (ibid.). From 2005 to 2009, the wealth disparity among Hispanics increased as well. For instance, in 2005 the top 10% Hispanic households accounted for 56% of all Hispanic household wealth compared to 72% in 2009 (ibid.).

Poverty

The World Bank defines poverty as deprivation in well-being and involves several dimensions (Poverty 2014). For example, it involves low incomes and the inability to access basic goods and services to survive with dignity (ibid.). Additionally, poverty involves the inability to access health and education, clean water and sanitation, physical security, voice and the inability to have the capacity and opportunity to improve one's well-being (ibid.). In the US, poverty levels of families are determined by family size and income (DeNavas-Walt *et al.* 2011). The U.S. Census Bureau specifically determines poverty levels based on family composition and the Consumer Price Index. The official poverty line for a family of four was $22,113 in 2010 (ibid.).

In 2010, the U.S. Census Bureau released the results of a study that analyzed the poverty status of U.S. ethnic groups using the Supplemental Poverty Measure (SPM). This measure was developed by the U.S. Census Bureau so that factors such as medical expenses, tax credits, non-cash government benefits (e.g., food stamps, housing subsidies, school lunch programs) and cost-of-living adjustments are considered when determining poverty status (Lopez and Cohn 2011a). The poverty status results showed that the national poverty rate for 2010 was 16% or 49.1 million people. Currently Hispanics have the highest rate of people living in poverty. The poverty rate in 2010 for Hispanics was 28.2%, 11.1% for Whites, 16.7% for Asian Americans, and 25.4% for African Americans (ibid.).

Childhood poverty

Hispanic children have been the most affected by the increasing poverty levels in the U.S. Hispanic children are the largest group in poverty compared to children in other ethnic groups, amounting to 6.1 million in 2010 (Lopez and Velasco 2011b). In percentage terms, 37.3% of children in poverty were Hispanic, 30.5% were White, and 26.6% were African American during the year 2010 (ibid.). This is the first time in history that the largest proportion of poor children was not White. This result is attributed to the growing Hispanic population, high birth rates and increasing economic problems in the Hispanic community.

Hispanic children aged 17 years and younger total 23.1% of the nation's children (Passel *et al.* 2011a). Of other groups, White children total 53.5% of the U.S. children and African Americans only 14.6% (Lopez and Velasco 2011b). An estimated 6.1 million Hispanic children live in poverty and 4.1 million of those born in the US have immigrant parents (ibid.).

The economic downturn that was experienced in 2007 greatly impacted the Hispanic community's unemployment rates, mostly among Hispanic immigrants (Kochhar 2008). In 2011, the Hispanic unemployment rate was 11.0%, which was higher than the 8.5% national unemployment rate (Taylor *et al.* 2012c). During the period 2005–9, household wealth decreased the most among Hispanic consumers compared to the household wealth among Whites and African Americans (Taylor *et al.* 2011). In 2008, a study by the U.S. Department of Agriculture found that food insecurity among Hispanics increased drastically during the recession that was experienced in 2007. For instance, in 2008, 32.1% of Hispanic households with children were affected compared to 23.8% of similar households in 2007 (Nord *et al.* 2009). Moreover, before the recession more White children lived in poverty, but after the recession Hispanic children in poverty outnumbered White children. From 2007 (when the recession started) to 2010, there was an increase of 1.6 million (36.3%) Hispanic children living in poverty. In the same period, the increase for White children was 17.6%, and 11.7% for African American children (Lopez and Velasco 2011b).

By 2010, 35% of Hispanic children, 39.1% of African American children and 12.4% of White children were living in poverty (ibid.). The poverty rate changes that resulted from the 2007 recession affected Hispanic children the most. For instance poverty rates increased by 9.7% for those children with parents with a high school diploma or less and only 0.6 percentage points for those that had parents with a college degree. Additionally, Hispanic children with single mothers had a poverty rate of 57.3%. Hispanic children with one parent unemployed had a poverty rate of 43.5% in 2010, whereas children with one parent that had at least a college degree had a poverty rate of 8.7% (ibid.).

Health

In order to further understand health care access of ethnic minorities, the Pew Research Hispanic Center held a nationwide survey in 2007. A high proportion of Hispanics, similar to other minority groups, lack health insurance. According to Livingston (2009), an estimated 60% of non-U.S. citizens or legal permanent residents lacked health insurance in 2007. In comparison, 28% of Hispanics that are legal permanent residents or citizens and 17% of the adult U.S. population lack health insurance (ibid.). In general, Hispanic adults who are non-U.S. citizens or legal permanent residents tend to be younger and healthier when compared to the adult U.S. population. These Hispanic adults are also less likely (57%) than U.S. citizens or legal permanent residents (76%) and the adult U.S. population (83%) to have a regular health care provider (ibid.).

Community health centres that are funded by federal and state governments as well as private donations have been very helpful to vulnerable populations such as Hispanics. A total of 41% of Hispanics who are non-U.S. citizens or non-legal permanent residents attended such community health centres for health care (ibid.). Of those adult Hispanics that are U.S. citizens or legal permanent residents, 15% attended private health centres or hospital outpatient facilities for health care (ibid.). These facilities require the patients to pay by either insurance or out of pocket means.

Emergency rooms, in general, are required by law to accept and provide health services to most patients. Most of the time, patients are responsible for payment of the services, but on occasion, the Federal government reimburses the hospitals' part of the expenses for some patients who do not have the financial means to make the payment. Only 6% of Hispanic adults who are non-U.S. citizens or legal residents attended emergency rooms for health care services (ibid.). It is also estimated that a total of 37% of Hispanics who are non-U.S. citizens or legal permanent residents have no health care provider. Out of that 37%, about 28% of the group state that financial problems are the reason for having no health care provider, another 17% indicate the reason is the lack of health insurance and a futher 12% state that the high medical costs are the reason (ibid.). Additionally, 56% of Hispanics with no health care provider state that they do not need one, so therefore do not have one. Not understanding the U.S. health care system was a reason provided by 5% of the group for not having a health care provider (ibid.). In the US, there are about 46 million Americans who lack health insurance, out of which, 17% are unauthorized immigrants and their children (Passel and Cohn 2009).

Health status

In general, the Hispanic U.S. population is considered to be young compared to other ethnic groups. Livingston (2009) found that 43% of Hispanics that are non-U.S. citizens or legal permanent residents are younger than 30 compared to 27% of those Hispanics who are U.S. citizens or legal permanent residents and 22% of other U.S. adults. Their young age is a factor in the healthiness of Hispanics in the US. Only 34% of Hispanics that are non-U.S. citizens or legal permanent residents missed work or spent at least half a day in bed due to illness or injury within the past year (ibid.). The rate increases for those Hispanics that are U.S. citizens or legal permanent residents to 42% and even further to 52% for the remainder of the U.S. adult population (ibid.).

Health care system experiences

Livingston (2009) also found that the majority of Hispanics (76%) who are non-U.S. citizens or non-legal permanent residents experienced an excellent or good medical care experience within the past year. About 78% of Hispanics that are U.S. citizens or legal permanent residents were satisfied with their medical care that they had within the last year. In a related survey, Hispanics were asked whether they had experienced any poor medical treatment in the past five years. Results show that Hispanics who are non-U.S. citizens or non-legal permanent residents were less likely to report any bad experiences (16%) compared to those U.S. citizens or legal permanent residents (24%; ibid.). Out of the 16% of Hispanics that are non-U.S. citizens or non-legal permanent residents and expressed a poor medical care experience, 46% stated they believed that their English proficiency was a reason for the poor medical care experience (ibid.). Another 43% believed that their financial limitations to pay for the medical care was a reason, 37% attributed their poor medical care to their race or ethnicity and 25% attributed their poor experience to their medical history (ibid.).

Out of the Hispanic non-U.S. citizens or non-legal permanent residents, 76% felt comforted by their medical care visit, 69% felt reassured, 31% felt frustrated, and 27% felt confused (ibid.).

Political attitudes

2012 Election and the impact of the Hispanic electorate

Taylor *et al.* (2012a) relied on data from the Pew Research Hispanic Center, U.S. Census Bureau data, Election Day exit polls and nationwide surveys of Hispanics to develop an understanding of the Hispanic electorate in 2012. The Hispanic electorate is estimated to double by the year 2030 (ibid.). In the 2012 election, Hispanics only comprised 10% of the total U.S. voters. This electorate share is expected to increase rapidly due to several reasons. One main reason is the current Hispanic median age of 27 years and 18 years for those who are native born, making them the youngest ethnic group (ibid.). In comparison, Whites have a median age of 42 years. As more Hispanics reach voting age their electorate is expected to increase rapidly.

Hispanics are projected to account for 40% of the growth that is expected in the U.S. electorate up until the year 2030. In the year 2030, the current 23.7 million Hispanics that are eligible to vote is expected to reach 40 million (ibid.). During the 2012 election, voter participation rates and naturalization rates of Hispanics were low compared to other ethnic groups. The Hispanic electorate could potentially double in twenty years if those voter participation and naturalization rates of Hispanics increase to equivalent levels to those of other ethnic groups (ibid.).

According to the national exit polls of the 2012 election, an estimated 10%, or 12.5 million, of all voters were Hispanic (ibid.). This indicates that more than 40 million Hispanics did not vote or were not eligible to vote. The significance of this to the future of the Hispanic electorate can be described by understanding the characteristics of the more than 40 million Hispanics that did not cast any ballots. There were 11.2 million eligible adult voters who did not vote (44% to 53% turnout rate is below the turnout rate of Whites and African Americans), 5.4 million were adult legal permanent residents that were not eligible to vote because they were not naturalized U.S. citizens (naturalization rate of 49% is below the rate for other ethnicities, which is 72%), 7.1 million were adult unauthorized immigrants (if Congress passes a law that allows citizenship they will become eligible voters) and 17.6 million were under the age of 18 (93% of youths are U.S. born and will be eligible to vote once they turn 18; ibid.). Currently 800,000 Hispanics turn 18 each year and by 2030 this could be more than 1 million per year (by the year 2030 new Hispanic voters of this type could total 16 million; ibid.). This demonstrates reasons why the Hispanic electorate has a great potential to increase dramatically.

2012 Election Hispanic voters

In the 2012 election, 71% of Hispanics voted for Democrat Barack Obama compared to 27% for Republican Mitt Romney (Lopez and Taylor 2012). In comparison to all other presidential elections, the largest share of Hispanic votes (71%) was the highest percentage since the 72% of Hispanics who voted in the 1996 elections for President Bill Clinton (ibid.). The electorate in the 2012 election consisted of 10% Hispanics compared to 9% in 2008 and 8% in 2004 (ibid.). Non-White voters also increased from 26% in 2008 to 28% in 2012 (ibid.).

In key battleground states, the majority of Hispanic voters voted for President Barack Obama. In Florida, 60% of eligible Hispanic voters voted for President Barack Obama compared to 39% for Mitt Romney. Similarly, the majority of eligible Hispanics (75%) voted for President Barack Obama in Colorado and 23% for Mitt Romney, in Nevada 70% for President Barack Obama and 25% for Mitt Romney and 68% in North Carolina, 65% in Wisconsin, 64% in Virginia and 53% in Ohio for Barack Obama (ibid.).

According to Lopez and Taylor, national exit polls using CNN's 2012 data showed that 60% of Hispanics considered the economy to be the most important issue facing the US compared to the 59% of the general U.S. electorate. Healthcare followed with 18% of Hispanics, the federal budget deficit then followed with 11% and 6% for foreign policy. A total of 77% (vs 65% of general U.S. electorate) of Hispanic voters preferred that unauthorized immigrants currently working in the US should be offered an opportunity for legal status and only 18% (vs 28% of general U.S. electorate) thought that the unauthorized immigrants should be deported (ibid.).

Demographics and political views

As general politics go, 30% (vs 21% of the general U.S. public) of Hispanics identify their political views as 'liberal' or 'very liberal' (Taylor *et al.* 2012b). Lopez and Taylor (2012a) studied the 2012 national exit polls and found 76% of Hispanic women voted for President Barack Obama compared to 65% of Hispanic males. A total of 74% Hispanic youth voted for President Barack Obama compared to 23% who voted for Mitt Romney (ibid.). When considering all the U.S. youth, 60% voted for President Barack Obama and 37% for Mitt Romney. When talking about Hispanic college graduates, 62% voted for President Barack Obama and 35% for Mitt Romney. Those Hispanics without a college degree, 75% voted for President Barack Obama and 24% for Mitt Romney (ibid.). Income was also a factor of division. A total of 82% (vs 17% for Romney) of Hispanic voters with family income below $50,000 voted for President Barack Obama (ibid.). In comparison, 59% (vs 39% for Mitt Romney) of Hispanic households with family incomes of more than $50,000 voted for President Barack Obama (ibid.).

Immigration

According to the Pew Research Hispanic Center (2013a), a study using U.S. Census Bureau data found there were 40.4 million immigrants in 2011. Overall, immigration rates have seen a steady increase in the past decade. For instance, there was an increase of 2.4 million immigrants from 2007 to 2011 (ibid.).

Unauthorized immigration rates also experienced a steady increase in the past decade. For instance, in 2000 there were 8.4 million immigrants, but by 2011 that number had increased to 11.1 million (ibid.). Since 2000, the peak of unauthorized immigrants reached 12 million in 2007 but saw a decrease in 2009 to 11.1 million (Passel and Cohn 2012). More immigrants reach the US than any other country in the world. Russia has the second most immigrants, totaling 12.3 million per year (Pew Research Hispanic Center 2013a). The 40.4 million authorized and unauthorized immigrants in the US totalled 13% of the U.S. population in 2011. This percentage is just slightly smaller than the 15% of immigrants that made up the U.S. population after the large immigration of Europeans from 1890 to 1920 (ibid.). The majority of immigrants are a result of the 1965 legislation that facilitated border crossing; most are from Latin America (50%) followed by Asia (27%) (ibid.).

In order to better understand the characteristics of foreign-born immigrants, the Pew Research Hispanic Center performed a study using data from the 2011 American Community Survey held by the U.S. Census Bureau. This survey includes details about characteristics such as citizenship, nativity, age, origin, language proficiency, living arrangements, marital status, fertility, schooling, health insurance coverage, earnings, poverty and employment.

An estimated 11.1 million unauthorized immigrants resided in the US by 2011 according to the Pew Research Hispanic Center and reached a peak of 12 million in 2007. The decrease that was seen after 2007 was attributed to the decreased immigration of unauthorized immigrants from Mexico (Passel and Cohn 2012). In 2010, Mexican unauthorized immigrants totalled 58% of all the U.S. unauthorized immigrants (Passel and Cohn 2011a). There were a total of 1 million unauthorized immigrants that were under 18 years old and 4.5 million U.S.-born children whose parents were unauthorized immigrants (Passel and Cohn 2011a). It was also estimated in 2010, that about 66% of unauthorized immigrants had been living in the US for at least a decade and 46% of those immigrants had young children (Taylor *et al.* 2011). According to the Pew Research Hispanic Center (2013a), about 25% of unauthorized immigrants end up working as farm workers (Passel and Cohn, 2009).

In comparison to Hispanic population growth, Asian American population growth is attributed to immigration. In 2012, 74% of Asian American adults were foreign born (Brown 2014). A total 61% of the change in the Asian American population from 2012 to 2013 was attributed to international migration (Brown 2014). The factor of immigration responsible for the Asian American population change has also affected the age of this population. For example, the median age for Asian Americans is 36.3 compared to 28.1 of Hispanics (Brown 2014).

Immigration attitudes

U.S. adults surveyed by the Pew Research Hispanic Center (2013b) found that 39% believed that illegal immigration should be a priority for the President and Congress. Based on this study, illegal immigration ranked seventeenth on the list of priorities for U.S. adults (ibid.). On the other hand, 33% of Hispanics believed that immigration should be a priority but ranked the economy, jobs, education and health care higher (Lopez and Gonzalez-Barrera 2012b).

Perceptions as to strategies to deal with unauthorized immigration vary among U.S. adults. For instance, 28% of adults believe that tighter restrictions should be implemented, while another 27% believe that the opportunity for citizenship should be given (Pew Research Center for the People & the Press 2012). The majority (42%) agree that both strategies should be priorities. The strategy of giving unauthorized immigrants the opportunity for citizenship is more popular among Hispanics (42%) compared to the general U.S. population (27%; Pew Research Hispanic Center 2013a). Only 10% of Hispanics believe that tighter restrictions, such as border security and enforcement, should be a priority to deal with unauthorized immigration. When comparing Hispanics and the general U.S. population, 46% of Hispanics believe that both enforcement and legalization should be priorities compared to 42% of the general U.S. population (Lopez *et al.* 2011c).

A majority of Hispanics disapproved of Obama's deportation policy (59%) compared to 25% who approved (Lopez *et al.* 2011c). Under the Obama Administration, since 2009, there have been 400,000 unauthorized immigrants deported a year. These deportations affected many U.S. Hispanics: 26% of Hispanic U.S. citizens, 32% of Hispanics non-U.S. citizens or legal residents, and 22% of Hispanics who are registered voters indicated that they personally know someone who has been deported or detained in the past 12 months (ibid.).

Ethnic media

Media selection

Hispanics are known to navigate from English to Spanish media to access news stories. For instance, about 50% of those foreign-born Hispanics access some of their news in English, and even English-fluent Hispanics access some news related to Latin America and U.S. Latin communities in Spanish (Suro 2004). Suro found that those Hispanics who are likely U.S. voters prefer English media, with 53% accessing their news via English media, 40% from media in both languages and only 6% accessing their news from Spanish-only media (ibid.)

Hispanics indicate that news media influences society in various ways. The majority of Hispanics believe that Spanish-language media is very important for the economic and political development of U.S. Hispanics. Many Hispanics also believe that English language media portrays Hispanics in ways that influence the negative image that English-speaking Americans have of Hispanics (ibid.).

News

A media content analysis study of more than 34,000 news stories by the Pew Research Hispanic Center (2009) found that event-driven news stories is the main way that the U.S. public learns about Hispanics and not through focused coverage of Hispanics. During the period of February 9 to August 9, 2009, only 57 stories out of 34,452 analyzed focused directly on the lives of Hispanics and only 645 contained measurable references to Hispanics (ibid.). During the 2009 period studied, the main story or 39% of the news stories and 33% of news coverage that related to Hispanics was regarding the nomination of Supreme Court Justice Sonia Sotomayor as the first Hispanic. In comparison, immigration was the subject in 8% of the news stories during the same period, reflecting the priority of this subject to the Obama Administration. The Mexican Drug War was the subject in 15% of the news stories and the H1N1 outbreak represented 13% of the news stories (ibid.).

Homeownership

An analysis of housing, economic and demographic data in 2009 by Kochhar, Gonzalez-Barrera and Dockterman (2009) found that the U.S. housing market over the past fifteen years has resulted in larger gains and losses for minority groups compared to Whites. At the onset of the housing market crash in 2005, homeownership rates for African Americans and U.S.-born Hispanics decreased the greatest compared to that for the U.S. population in general. In 2008, 48.9% of Hispanics owned homes compared to 59.1% of Asian Americans, 47.5% of African Americans and 74.9% of Whites (ibid.).

Hispanics and African Americans also have higher rates of borrowing in the subprime market. A total of 27.6% of the mortgages to Hispanics and 33.5% to African Americans were considered subprime mortgages compared to 10.5% to Whites in 2007 (ibid.). These are considered higher priced loans. Specifically, Hispanic homeowners had mortgages with an annual percentage rate (APR) of 2.5 percentage points higher than a 30-year, fixed-rate conventional mortgage while African American homeowners' APR was three percentage points higher (ibid.).

Kochhar and colleagues also indicated that U.S. homeownership experienced an increase from 1994 to 2004, but has declined since 2004. In 2004, it was estimated that 69% of all U.S. households owned a home compared to 64% earlier in 1994 (ibid.). The homeownership rate (measure of the percent of householders living in owner-occupied homes) decreased after 2004 and reached 67.8% in 2008 (ibid.).

The authors found that Hispanic homeownership increased at a higher rate and for a longer period than the overall U.S. homeownership rate with U.S.-born Hispanics tending to have higher homeownership rates. Homeownership rates among this group increased from 47.2% in 1995 to 56.2% in 2005 and remained the same rate in 2008. Foreign-born Hispanics increased their homeownership rates from 47.2% in 1995 to 56.2% in 2005 and they experienced a decrease in 2008 to 53.6% (ibid.).

In comparison, African American homeownership rates increased from 41.9% in 1995 to 49.4% in 2004. Similar to Hispanics, in 2008 the African American homeownership rate decreased to 47.5% (ibid.).

In general, U.S. born citizens have a higher likelihood to be homeowners than foreign-born immigrants. For instance, immigrant homeownership experienced an increase from 46.5% in 1995 to 53.3% in 2006, while in 2008 there was a decrease to 52.9%. In comparison, home-ownership rates of U.S.-born citizens increased from 66.1% in 1995 to 71.5% in 2004 and in 2008 the rate decreased to 70.0% (ibid.).

Home purchase loans

Loan applications among the various ethnic groups also varied. Loan applications by Hispanics decreased 38.2% from 2006 to 2007 compared to African Americans who saw a 34.4% decrease and Whites only experienced an 18.9% decrease (Kochhar *et al.* 2009). Within the Hispanic group, those with highest incomes experienced a greater decrease of 41.0% compared to those with lowest income of 23.8% from 2006–7 (ibid.). In 2007, the median home purchase loan by Hispanics was $197,000 compared to $168,000 for African Americans and $180,000 for Whites. As a result, the loan-to-income ratios are higher within the Hispanic and African American groups compared to Whites. Between 2006 and 2008, the national foreclosures tripled from 0.6% to 1.8% (ibid.).

Technology

Internet

A majority (95%) of Hispanic families with annual incomes of $50,000 or more and 93% of those with annual incomes between $30,000 and $50,000 indicated they occasionally use the internet (Lopez, Gonzalez-Barrera, and Patten 2013). An estimated 93% of Hispanics between the ages of 18 and 29 also occasionally use the internet. Only 33% of Hispanics aged 65 and older use the internet at least occasionally. A total of 50% of Hispanics that use the internet are U.S. born and 50% are foreign born (Lopez *et al.* 2013). Of those Hispanics that do not use the internet, 21% are U.S. born and 79% are foreign born. Considering the Hispanic population of internet users, a total of 31% are English dominant, 41% are bilingual and 28% are Spanish dominant. Compared to Hispanics that are not internet users, 13% are English dominant, 29% are bilingual, and 58% are Spanish dominant (ibid.).

When it comes to African Americans, 80% are internet users compared to 87% of Whites (Smith 2014). About 62% of African Americans have some form of broadband connection at home compared to 74% of Whites (ibid.). Asian Americans, on the other hand, have higher rates of technology use. For example, 87% of Asian Americans use the internet and 80% have broadband at home (Rainie 2011).

Accessing internet using mobile devices

According to Lopez *et al.* (2013), an estimated 76% of Hispanic internet users access the internet via a mobile device compared to 60% of White internet users and 73% of African Americans. A total of 87% of Hispanic internet users from families with annual incomes of $50,000 or more as well as Hispanics ages 18 to 29 get access to the internet via a mobile device at least occasionally (ibid.). Only 29% of Hispanic internet users of ages 65 and older indicated that they accessed the internet via a mobile device. On the other hand, about 90% of Asian Americans access the internet via a mobile device and 77% connect to the internet wirelessly (Rainie 2011).

Cell phone ownership

A total 86% of U.S. Hispanics indicated they owned a cell phone compared to 84% of Whites and 90% of African Americans (ibid.). Hispanic families with annual incomes above $50,000 had the highest cell phone ownership rate of 97%. Families with annual incomes between $30,000 and $50,000 had a cell phone ownership rate of 95% and 96% of Hispanics ages 18 to 29 owned a cell phone (ibid.). Spanish-dominant Hispanics have a lower cell phone ownership rate of 78%, Hispanics with less than a high school diploma have a 77% cell phone ownership and those Hispanics ages 65 and older have a cell phone ownership of 56% (ibid.). Out of those Hispanics that do not own cell phones, a total of 76% are foreign born and 24% are U.S. born. Additionally, only 13% are English dominant, 30% are bilinguals, and 57% are Spanish dominant (ibid.).

Smartphone ownership

Smartphone ownership among Hispanic adults is 49%, among Whites it is 46% and among African American it is 50% (ibid.). Hispanic families with annual incomes of $50,000 or more have the highest smartphone ownership of 76% (ibid.). In comparison, Hispanics ages 65 or older have the lowest smartphone ownership rate of 14%. A total of 54% of Hispanic smartphone users are U.S. born and 58% of those that do not own a smartphone are foreign born (ibid.).

Computer ownership

When it comes to computer ownership, 95% of those Hispanic families with incomes of $50,000 or more own either a desktop or laptop computer (ibid.). Only 35% of Hispanics ages of 65 or older own either a desktop or laptop computer. Half of Hispanic computer owners are foreign born and 73% of those that do not own a computer are foreign born (ibid.).

Social networking

A total 68% of Hispanic internet users use Facebook, Twitter and other social networking sites at least occasionally compared to 66% of Whites and 69% of African Americans (ibid.).

A large proportion or 84% of Hispanic internet users 18 to 29 years of age indicated that they use Facebook, Twitter and other social networking sites (ibid.). Only 27% of Hispanic internet users 65 years and older indicated they use a social networking site. A total of 54% of Hispanics that use social media are born in the US and 57% of those that do not use social media are foreign born (ibid.). In regards to those Hispanics that use social networking sites, 29% do so mostly or only in Spanish, 60% do so mostly or only in English and 11% do so in both English and Spanish (ibid.). Out of those U.S.-born Hispanics that use social networking sites, a majority (86%) do so mostly or only in English. In comparison, the majority of immigrant Hispanics (55%) who use social networking sites do so mostly or only in Spanish (ibid.). When it comes to Asian Americans, 20% of internet users used Twitter, 65% used social networking sites, 44% used social networking yesterday, 78% of Asian Americans online are women and 57% are men, 73% are under age 40 and 43% are older than 40 (Rainie 2011).

Religion

Results from the Pew Research Hispanic Center (2007) showed 68% of Hispanics in the US identified as being Roman Catholic. Another 15% identify as evangelical Protestants and 8% do not identify with any religion (Pew Research Hispanic Center 2007). There was a relationship between religious identification and demographic characteristics. For instance, the U.S. Catholic group had a higher percentage of immigrants than the evangelical Protestants.

As it relates to the general U.S. Hispanic population of all religious affiliations, the majority regard God as an influence in life's daily activities. Additionally, most Hispanic households are devoted to praying on a daily basis, hold religious objects and attend religious service at least once a month (Pew Research Hispanic Center 2007). Hispanics that identify with a religion also are more likely to believe that miracles in current times are the same as in the past. According to the Pew Research Hispanic Center, 18% of all U.S. Hispanics indicated that they have converted to another religion or simply dropped their religion. Religious conversion rates are high among Hispanics. Among those Hispanics that identified as evangelicals, a total of 51% had converted from another religion and 43% previously identified as Catholics (ibid.). Out of all the Hispanics who converted, 82% indicated they converted because they sought a more direct and more personal experience with God. When analyzing the population of Hispanics who became evangelicals, a total of 90% indicated that the reason they did so was a spiritual search. Most of this same population of evangelical converts (61%) state that Catholic mass can be unexciting and not lively but only 36% indicate that they converted because of this reason (ibid.). Religion is perceived differently among U.S.-born Hispanics compared to those born outside the U.S. For instance, 69% of immigrant Hispanics perceive religion as very important in life while only 49% of U.S.-born Hispanics perceive religion as important, this compared to the 58% of the U.S. general population (Taylor *et al.* 2012b).

In the US, the increased growth rate of the Hispanic population has been attributed to the increase of Hispanic-oriented churches of all religious denominations. Those churches who are most frequented by Hispanics also consist of congregations with the majority of clergy being Hispanic (ibid.). A total of 77% of foreign-born Hispanics attend churches with Hispanic majority congregations compared to only 48% of U.S.-born Hispanics (ibid.).

Religion was found to impact political views of Hispanics; a total of 66% of U.S. Hispanics indicated so. More than 50% say that churches should incorporate social and political questions in their services (ibid.). Two-thirds of Hispanics strongly believe that political leaders don't express religious faith enough. Based on a study by the Pew Research Hispanic Center, religious affiliation impacts political beliefs. Results showed that Hispanic Catholics tend to be less conservative than Hispanic evangelicals on social issues, foreign policy and the poor (ibid.). Hispanic Catholics are also less likely to be Republicans than Hispanic evangelicals. The majority of the Hispanic electorate is Catholic (63%) and the strength of this segment is even more important when we consider that 70% of all Hispanics eligible to vote are Catholic (ibid.).

African Americans tend to be more religious in the following measures compared to the U.S. population as a whole: level of affiliation with a religion, attendance at religious services and frequency of prayer and religion's importance in life (Sahgal and Smith 2009). Additionally, African Americans compared to other racial and ethnic groups have the highest rates of religious affiliation, 87% reported they belonged to a religious affiliation compared to 85% of Hispanics and 83% for the overall population (ibid.).

Religion in general plays a very important role in the lives of African Americans. Sahgal and Smith (2009) found that 79% of African Americans compared to 56% of the overall population regard religion as playing an important role in their lives. Additionally, a total 72% of African Americans who do not affiliate with a specific religion regard religion as somewhat important in their lives, 45% of this population regard religion as very important in their lives compared to 16% of the overall population (ibid.). A majority, 78%, of African Americans are Protestant compared to 53% of Whites, 27% of Asian Americans, 23% of Hispanics and 51% of the overall population (ibid.).

The largest religious group among the Asian American community are Christians (42%; Funk 2012). An estimated 26% of Asian Americans are unaffiliated with a religion, 14% affiliate with Buddhism, 10% affiliate with Hinduism, 4% are Muslim, 1% are Sikhs and about 2% are followers of other religions.

Asian Americans who do not affiliate with a religion have lower levels of religious commitment compared to the overall U.S. population who do not affiliate with any religion (ibid.). For example, 76% of these Asian Americans indicate that religion is not too important or not at all important in their lives compared to 58% of the overall U.S. population who do not affiliate with a religion (ibid.).

Conclusion

Consumer diversity in the US has created a substantial challenge for advertisers. As a result of the increased diversity of consumers in the US, managerial and social implications need to be examined by advertisers when pursuing their advertising strategies (Torres 2007). This examination is important as each consumer market segment differs in culture, language usage, values, ideologies, preferences, customs, historical perspectives and consumption behaviour (Zúñiga and Torres 2015a). According to Torres it is vital to consider the differences in the diverse consumer markets that compose the US. Trends in health, politics, immigration and media choices among minority segments are especially important in recent years given the enactment of the Affordable Care Act, the size of the minority electorate (which has been very important in the most recent elections), the increasingly polarizing immigration debate and the broad spectrum of media choices available on everything from TV to the internet. In light of recent events, it is important to examine both the demographics and lifestyles of ethnic minorities and the strategies marketers are using to target the Hispanic, African American and Asian American segments.

With the growing diversity of the U.S. population, ethnic target marketing has become an increasingly crucial component of marketing strategy (Pires *et al.* 2003). Such targeting responds not only to current diversity, but also to census estimates that by 2050 the Hispanic, African American and Asian American segments of the U.S. population will collectively exceed 50%, compared to less than 30% in 2003 (Passel and Cohn 2008). Our chapter tries to describe these trends to give both academics and practitioners a better picture of how these three ethnic minority segments are changing in the different areas. For instance, in the area of education there seems to be a trend of increased enrollment for 18 to 24 year olds. Despite this trend, Whites and Asian Americans still have higher rates of enrollment at four year colleges compared to Hispanics and African Americans (Fry 2011). The economic recession that started in 2007 impacted 18 to 24 year olds with high unemployment levels. As a result, this recession helped with increased college enrollment of young adults of all three major minority groups due to high unemployment rates (Fry 2009). Additionally, Whites and Asian Americans have higher rates of Bachelor's degree completion than Hispanics and African Americans. This lower completion rate of Hispanics was attributed to immigrant Hispanics and the challenges they face learning a new language.

Purchasing power is a factor that is considered by marketers when targeting potential consumers. A study by the Survey of Income and Program Participation found that the median wealth of Whites is 18 times greater than that of Hispanics and 20 times greater than that of African Americans (Kochhar et al. 2011b). These discrepancies are changing (i.e. the gap is closing) and should be factored in when determining the most valuable consumers.

Related to the economic power of consumers is the rate of homeownership. In 2008, Asian Americans had higher rates of homeownership, followed by Hispanics and African Americans, respectively. As the homeownership rates increase among minorities, the demand for homeownership services and products increase. Both academics and practitioners should consider investigating how this trend affects minority consumers' responses to targeted marketing messages.

Considering the Hispanic population of internet users, the highest rate of users is among those that are bilingual followed by those that are English dominant and Spanish dominant, respectively (Lopez et al. 2013). When it comes to African Americans, a similar percentage of African Americans to Whites are internet users (Smith 2014). Asian Americans on the other hand have higher rates of internet use compared to Whites (Rainie 2011). An important trend related to technology is smartphone ownership. Smartphone ownership among Hispanics, Whites and African Americans is very similar (Lopez et al. 2013). Hispanic families with annual incomes of $50,000 or more have the highest smartphone ownership of 76% (ibid.). Again the families with higher incomes typically have a higher demand for technology and specifically smartphone services and products. Minority groups have an increased rate of smartphone ownership and internet use. These technology trends among ethnic minority groups might assist marketers with their segmenting and targeting efforts.

Religious affiliations and practices might also be used to target minority groups effectively. For example, religion was found to impact political views of Hispanics; a total 66% of U.S. Hispanics indicated so. African Americans tend to be more religious in the following measures compared to the U.S. population as a whole: level of affiliation with a religion, attendance at religious services, frequency of prayer and religion's importance in life (Sahgal and Smith 2009). The largest religious group among the Asian community is Christians, followed by those that are unaffiliated, 42% and 26% respectively (Funk 2012). Knowing the religious affiliations of these three major minority groups provides valuable segmentation information that could be useful in the political marketing area since religion was found to impact political views.

We believe the trends in this chapter are likely to provide useful guidance to marketers as they increase their efforts to selectively target ethnically defined segments in an increasingly diverse population. This chapter is an initial step in developing a better understanding of ethnic demographic trends. The ethnic marketing literature will benefit from future research that takes into account these demographic trends. Future research should look at the effects of ethnic identification on every major minority audience (i.e., Hispanics, African Americans and Asian Americans) examining several product and service categories (Zúñiga and Torres 2015b; 2015c).

The strength of ethnic identification construct can be useful in several ethnic marketing contexts (e.g. Zúñiga et al. 2015). Future research should look at the effects of ethnic identification using several ethnic cues (e.g., ethnic actors, language, symbols, etc.) as this may provide a stronger argument for the use of ethnic identification as a segmentation tool (Zúñiga and Torres 2015b). Future research should also look at what factors may heighten minorities' ethnic identification. Feelings of being ethnic fluctuate, as evidenced by studies that show ethnic respondents who report feeling varying degrees of ethnicity depending on the situation they encounter and the people with whom they interact (Deshpandé and Stayman 1994). Market researchers and practitioners should consider the implications that situational or context factors can have in the ethnic marketing area (Zúñiga 2015).

Future research might explore other viewer/advertising matches like gender, age, lifestyle, etc., and combine those with ethnicity to see how the combination of these factors influence consumer responses to ethnic marketing (Zúñiga 2015b). Researchers should also explore the effects of brand prestige, brand meaning, language used, media placement and other product characteristics that could further support the value of measuring the impact of ethnic identification (Zúñiga 2015). The effects of brand meaning should be specifically addressed since different brands mean different things to different segments. Some brands are so laden with meaning that they can have an overpowering effect on ethnic identification and acculturation. Researchers should be careful to not only take into account but also measure the effects that brand meanings can have.

Finally, research might be profitably directed to explore whether and when saturation/diminishing marginal returns might affect the responses to ethnic marketing. These are all issues in what is likely to be not only a rich area for research, but also one with significant practical implications as ethnic minorities continue to increase their share of the total U.S. population.

References

Appiah, O. (2001) 'Ethnic identification on adolescents' evaluations of advertisements'. *Journal of Advertising Research*, 41(5): 7–22.

Bailey, A. A. (2006) 'A year in the life of the African American male in advertising'. *Journal of Advertising*, 35(Spring): 83–104.

Berkowitz, H (1994) 'Cornering a market'. *Newsday*, 5(December), p. 4.

Berry, J. W. (1997) 'Immigration, acculturation and adaptation'. *Applied Psychology: An International Review*, 46(1): 5–34.

Berry, J. W. (2003) 'Conceptual approaches to acculturation'. In *Acculturation: Advances in Theory, Measurement, and Applied Research*, edited by K. Chung, P. Balls-Organista, G Marin. Washington, DC: American Psychological Association Press, pp.17–37.

Berry, J. W., Trimble, J. E. and Olmedo, E. L. (1986) 'Assessment of acculturation'. In *Field Methods in Cross-Cultural Research*, edited by W. J. Lonner and J. W. Berry. Beverly Hills, CA: Sage, pp. 291–324.

Broderick, A. J., Demangeot, C., Adkins, N. R., Ferguson, N. S., Henderson, G. R., Johnson, G., Kipnis, E., Mandiberg, J. M., Mueller, R. D., Pullig, C., Roy, A. and Zúñiga, M. A. (2011a) 'Consumer empowerment in multicultural marketplaces: Navigating multicultural identities to reduce consumer vulnerability'. *Journal of Research for Consumers*, 19: 1–13.

Broderick, A. J., Demangeot, C., Kipnis, E., Zúñiga, M. A., Roy, A., Pullig, C., Mueller, R. D., Mandiberg, J. M., Johnson, G., Henderson, G. R., Ferguson, N. S. and Adkins, N. R. (2011b) 'No harm done? Culture-based branding and its impact on consumer vulnerability: A research agenda'. *Social Business*, 1(3): 263–80.

Brown, A. (26 June 2014) 'U.S. Hispanic and Asian populations growing, but for different reasons'. Pew Research Center. Available from: http://www.pewresearch.org/fact-tank/2014/06/26/u-s-hispanic-and-asian-populations-growing-but-for-different-reasons/ [accessed 20 July 2014].

Bush, R. F., Resnick, A. J. and Stern, B. L. (1980) 'A content analysis of the portrayal of black models in magazine advertising in marketing in the '80s: Changes and challenges'. *AMA Educators' Conference Proceedings*, edited by R. P. Bagozzi *et al.* Chicago, IL: American Marketing Association, pp. 484–87.

Cohen, J. (1992) 'White consumer response to asian models in advertising'. *Journal of Consumer Marketing*, 9: 17–27.

Cox, K. (1970) 'Changes in stereotyping of negroes and whites in magazine advertisements'. *Public Opinion Quarterly*, 33(Winter): 603–6.

Cui, G. (1998) 'Ethical issues in ethnic segmentation and target marketing'. In *Proceedings, 1998 Multicultural Marketing Conference* (Academy of Marketing Science, Montreal), edited by J.-C. Chebat and A. B. Oumlil, pp. 87–91.

Demangeot, C., Adkins, N. R., Mueller, R. D., Henderson, G. R., Ferguson, N. S., Mandiberg, J. M., Roy, A., Johnson, G. D., Kipnis, E., Pullig, C., Broderick, A. J. and Zúñiga, M. A. (2013) 'Toward intercultural competency in multicultural marketplaces'. *Journal of Public Policy & Marketing*, 32(special issue): 156–64.

deNavas-Walt, P. and Smith (2011) 'Income, poverty, and health insurance coverage in the United States: 2010. Current population reports'. *U.S. Census Bureau*. Available from: from http://www.census.gov/prod/2011pubs/p60-239.pdf [accessed 15 June 2014].

Deshpandé, R., Hoyer, W. D. and Donthu, N. (1986) 'The intensity of ethnic affiliation: A study of the sociology of hispanic consumption'. *Journal of Consumer Research*, 13: 214–20.

Deshpandé, R. and Stayman, D. M. (1994) 'A tale of two cities: Distinctiveness theory and advertising effectiveness'. *Journal of Marketing Research*, 31(1): 57–64.

Fahmy, S. (2010) *Despite Recession, Hispanic and Asian Buying Power Expected to Surge in U.S.* Georgia: University of Georgia, Terry College of Business: Selig Center.

Forehand, M. R. and Deshpandé, R. (2001) 'What we see makes us who we are: Priming ethnic self-awareness and advertising response'. *Journal of Marketing Research*, 38(3): 336–48.

Fry, R. (29 October 2009) 'College enrollment hits all-time high, fueled by community college surge'. Pew Research Social and Demographic Trends. Available from: http://www.pewsocialtrends.org/2009/10/29/college-enrollment-hits-all-time-high-fueled-by-community-college-surge/ [accessed 29 March 2013].

Fry, R. (25 August 2011). 'Hispanic college enrollment spikes, narrowing gaps with other groups'. Pew Research Hispanic Center. Available from: http://www.pewhispanic.org/2011/08/25/hispanic-college-enrollment-spikes-narrowing-gaps-with-other-groups/ [accessed 30 March 2013].

Funk, C. (19 July 2012) 'Asian Americans: A mosaic of faiths'. Pew Research Center. The Pew Forum on Religion and Public Life. Available from: http://www.pewforum.org/2012/07/19/asian-americans-a-mosaic-of-faiths-overview/ [accessed 24 June 2014].

Gibson, M. A. (2001) 'Immigrant adaptation and patterns of acculturation'. *Human Development*, 44(1): 19–23.

Green, C. L. (1999) 'Ethnic evaluations of advertising: Interaction effects of strength of ethnic identification, media placement, and degree of racial composition'. *Journal of Advertising*, 28(1): 49–64.

Guo, C. and Schwing Jr., L. C. (2009) 'Cultural ethnocentrism and its effect on shopping tendency with bilingual signage: An empirical investigation'. In *American Marketing Association Summer Educators' Conference*, edited by M. Kamins and I. M. Martin. Chicago, IL: American Marketing Association, p. 190.

Hirschman, E. C. (1981) 'American Jewish ethnicity: Its relationship to some selected aspects of consumer behavior'. *The Journal of Marketing*, 45(3): 102–10.

Hui, M. K., Joy, A., Kim, C. and Laroche, M. (1992) 'Acculturation as a determinant of consumer behavior: Conceptual and methodological issues'. In *AMA Winter Educators' Conference Proceedings*, Volume 3, edited by C. T. Allen and T. J. Madden. Chicago, IL: American Marketing Association, pp. 466–73.

Humes, K. R., Jones, N. A. and Ramirez, R. R. (March 2011) 'Overview of race and Hispanic Origin: 2010'. *US Census Bureau*. Available from: http://www.census.gov/prod/cen2010/briefs/c2010br-02.pdf [accessed 18 April 2013].

Humphreys, J. M. (31 July 2007) 'Minority groups' share of $10 trillion U.S. consumer market is growing steadily, according to annual buying power study from Terry College's Selig Center for Economic Growth'. Terry College Selig Center for Economic Growth. Available from: http://www.terry.uga.edu/news/releases/minority-groups-share-of-10-trillion-u.s.-consumer-market-is-growing-steadi [accessed 29 March 2013].

Kaufman-Scarborough, C. (2000) 'Asian-American consumers as a unique market segment: Fact or fallacy?' *Journal of Consumer Marketing*, 17(3): 249–62.

Kipnis, E., Broderick, A. J., Demangeot, C., Adkins, N. R., Ferguson, N. S., Henderson, G. R., Johnson, G., Mandiberg, J. M., Mueller, R. D., Pullig, C., Roy, A. and Zúñiga, M. A. (2013) 'Branding beyond prejudice: Navigating multicultural marketplaces for consumer well-being'. *Journal of Business Research*, 66(8): 1186–94.

Kochhar, R. (4 June 2008) 'Latino Labor report, 2008: Construction reverses job growth for Latinos'. Pew Research Hispanic Center. Available from: from http://www.pewhispanic.org/2008/06/04/latino-labor-report-2008-construction-reverses-job-growth-for-latinos/ [accessed 1 April 2013].

Kochhar, R., Fry, R. and Taylor, P. (26 July 2011a) 'Hispanic household wealth fell by 66% from 2005 to 2009'. Pew Research Hispanic Center. Available from: from http://www.pewhispanic.org/2011/07/26/the-toll-of-the-great-recession/ [accessed 29 March 2013].

Kochhar, R., Gonzalez-Barrera, A. and Dockterman, D. (12 May 2009) 'Minorities, immigrants and homeownership'. Pew Research Hispanic Center. Available from: http://www.pewhispanic.org/2009/05/12/through-boom-and-bust/ [accessed 29 March 2013].

Kochhar, R., Fry, R. and Taylor, P. (26 July 2011b) 'Wealth gaps rise to record highs between whites, African Americans, Hispanics'. Pew Research Hispanic Center. Available from: http://www.pewsocialtrends.org/2011/07/26/wealth-gaps-rise-to-record-highs-between-whites-Africanamericans-hispanics/ [accessed 31 March 2013].

Koslow, S., Shamdasani, P. N. and Touchstone, E. E. (1994) 'Exploring language effects in ethnic advertising: A sociolinguistic perspective'. *Journal of Consumer Research*, 20: 575–85.

Lee, C. K-C., Fernandez, N. and Martin, B. A. S. (2002) 'Using self-referencing to explain the effectiveness of ethnic minority models in advertising'. *International Journal of Advertising*, 21: 367–79.

Licata, J. W. and Biswas, A. (1993) 'Representation, roles, and occupational status of black models in television advertisements'. *Journalism Quarterly*, 70(December): 868–92.

Livingston, G. (25 September 2009) 'Hispanics, health insurance and health care access'. Pew Research Hispanic Center. Available from: http://www.pewhispanic.org/2009/09/25/hispanics-health-insurance-and-health-care-access/ [accessed 2 April 2013].

Lopez, H. M. and Cohn, D. (8 November 2011a) 'Hispanic poverty rate highest in new supplemental census measure'. Pew Research Hispanic Center. [online] Available from: http://www.pewhispanic.org/2011/11/08/hispanic-poverty-rate-highest-in-new-supplemental-census-measure/ [accessed 31 March 2013].

Lopez, H. M. and Velasco, G. (28 September 2011b) 'Childhood poverty among Hispanics sets record, leads nation'. Pew Research Hispanic Center. Available from: http://www.pewhispanic.org/2011/09/28/childhood-poverty-among-hispanics-sets-record-leads-nation/ [accessed 31 March 2013].

Lopez, H. M., Gonzalez-Barrera, A. and Motel, S. (28 December 2011c) 'As deportation rise to record levels, most Latinos oppose Obama's policy'. Pew Research Hispanic Center. Available from: http://www.pewhispanic.org/2011/12/28/as-deportations-rise-to-record-levels-most-latinos-oppose-obamas-policy/ [accessed 28 March 2013].

Lopez, H. M. and Taylor P. (7 November 2012a) 'Latino voters in the 2010 election'. Pew Research Hispanic Center. Available from: http://www.pewhispanic.org/2012/11/07/latino-voters-in-the-2012-election/ [accessed 27 March 2013].

Lopez, H. M. and Gonzalez-Barrera, A. (11 October 2012b) 'Latino voters support Obama by 3-1 ratio, but are less certain than others about voting'. Pew Research Hispanic Center. Available from: http://www.pewhispanic.org/2012/10/11/latino-voters-support-obama-by-3-1-ratio-but-are-less-certain-than-others-about-voting/ [accessed 26 March 2013].

Lopez, H. M., Gonzalez-Barrera, A. and Patten, E. (7 March 2013) 'Closing the digital divide: Latinos and technology adoption'. Pew Research Hispanic Center. Available from: http://www.pewhispanic.org/2013/03/07/closing-the-digital-divide-latinos-and-technology-adoption/ [accessed 1 April 2013].

Martin, B. A. S., Lee, C. K.-C. and Yang, F. (2004) 'The influence of ad model ethnicity and self-referencing on attitudes'. *Journal of Advertising*, 33(4): 27–37.

McGuire, W. J. (1984) 'Search for the self: Going beyond self-esteem and the reactive self'. In *Personality and the Prediction of Behavior* edited by, R. A. Zucker, J. Aronoff and A. I. Rabin. New York, NY: Academic Press, pp. 73–120.

Nagel, A. (2007) 'SoftSheen takes consumers to heart'. *WWD: Women's Wear Daily*, 193(122), p. 18.

Nielsen (2012). 'State of the Asian-American consumer'. Nielsen. Available from: http://www.nielsen.com/us/en/reports/2012.html?sortbyScore=true&tag=Category%3AConsumer [accessed 18 April 2013].

Nord, M., Andrews, M. and Carlson, S. (November 2009) 'Household food security in the United States, 2008'. Economic Research Service, United States Department of Agriculture. Available from: http://www.ers.usda.gov/publications/err-economic-research-report/err83.aspx [accessed 31 March 2013].

Nwankwo, S., Aiyeku, J. and Ogbuehi, A. (1998) 'The marketing challenge of multiculturalism: An exploratory study'. *Journal of International Marketing and Exporting*, 3(1): 47–61.

Ownbey, S. F. and Horridge, P. E. (1997) 'Acculturation levels and shopping orientations of Asian-American consumers'. *Psychology and Marketing*, 14: 1–18.

Paek, H. J. and Shah, H. (2003) 'Racial ideology, model minorities, and the "not-so-silent partner": Stereotyping of Asian Americans in U.S. magazine advertising'. *The Howard Journal of Communication*, 14: 225–43.

Park, J. H., Gabbadon, N. G. and Chernin, A. R. (2006) 'Naturalizing racial differences through comedy: Asian, black, and white views on racial stereotypes in rush hour 2'. *Journal of Communication*, 56: 157–77.

Passel, J. and Cohn, D. (2008) 'US population projections: 2005–2050'. Pew Research Hispanic Center. Available from: http://www.pewhispanic.org/2008/02/11/us-population-projections-2005-2050/ [accessed 27 March 2013].

Passel, J. and Cohn, D. (2009) 'A portrait of unauthorized immigrants in the United States'. Pew Research Center. Available from: http://www.pewhispanic.org/2009/04/14/a-portrait-of-unauthorized-immigrants-in-the-united-states/ [accessed 2 April 2013].

Passel, J. and Cohn, D. (2011a) 'Unauthorized immigrant population: National and state trends, 2010'. Pew Research Center. Available from: http://www.pewhispanic.org/2011/02/01/unauthorized-immigrant-population-brnational-and-state-trends-2010/ [accessed 30 March 2013].

Passel, J., Cohn D. and Lopez, M. (2011b) 'Hispanics account for more than half of nation's growth in past decade'. Pew Research Center. Available from: http://www.pewhispanic.org/2011/03/24/hispanics-account-for-more-than-half-of-nations-growth-in-past-decade/ [accessed 31 March 2013].

Passel, J. and Cohn, D. (2012) 'Unauthorized immigrants: 11.1 million in 2011'. Pew Research Center. Available from: http://www.pewhispanic.org/2012/12/06/unauthorized-immigrants-11-1-million-in-2011/ [accessed 3 April 2013].

Pew Research Center for the People and the Press (2012) 'Any court health care decision unlikely to please'. Pew Research Center for the People and the Press. Available from: http://www.people-press.org/2012/06/18/any-court-health-care-decision-unlikely-to-please/ [accessed 27 March 2013].

Pew Research Hispanic Center (2007) 'Changing faiths: Latinos and the transformation of American religion'. Pew Research Center. Available from: http://www.pewhispanic.org/2007/04/25/changing-faiths-latinos-and-the-transformation-of-american-religion/ [accessed 1 April 2013].

Pew Research Hispanic Center (2009) 'Hispanics in the news: An event-driven narrative'. Pew Research Hispanic Center. Available from: http://www.pewhispanic.org/2009/12/07/hispanics-in-the-news-an-event-driven-narrative/ [accessed 29 March 2013].

Pew Research Hispanic Center (2013a) 'A nation of immigrants'. Pew Research Hispanic Center. Available from: http://www.pewhispanic.org/2013/01/29/a-nation-of-immigrants/ [accessed 4 April 2013].

Pew Research Hispanic Center (2013b) 'Immigration rises on Washington's agenda, not the public's'. Pew Research Hispanic Center. Available from: http://www.pewresearch.org/2013/01/28/immigration-rises-on-washingtons-agenda-not-the-publics/ [accessed 23 March 2013].

Pew Research Social & Demographic Trends (2013) 'Demographics of Asian Americans'. Pew Research Social & Demographic Trends. Available from: from http://www.pewsocialtrends.org/2013/04/04/asian-groups-in-the-u-s/ [accessed 18 April 2013].

Pires, G. D. and Stanton, J. (2002) 'Ethnic marketing ethics'. *Journal of Business Ethics*, 36: 111–18.

Pires, G., Stanton, J. and Cheek, B. (2003) 'Identifying and reaching an ethnic market: Methodological issues'. *Qualitative Market Research: An International Journal*, 6(4): 224–35.

Poulis, K., Poulis, E. and Yamın, M. (2013) 'Multicultural markets and acculturation: Implications for service firms'. *Journal of Services Marketing*, 27(7): 515–25.

Poverty (2014) 'The work bank, working for a world free of poverty'. The World Bank. Available from: http://www.worldbank.org/en/topic/poverty/overview#1 [accessed 8 July 2014].

Price, M. (2005) 'Some analysts expect surge in corporate spending on African American-targeted advertising. Daily News'. *High Beam Research*. Available from: http://www.highbeam.com/doc/1G1-127172358.html [accessed 3 August 2014].

Rainie, L. (2011) 'Asian-Americans and technology'. Pew Research Internet Project. Available from: http://www.pewinternet.org/2011/01/06/asian-americans-and-technology/ [accessed 22 January 2014].

Sahgal, N. and Smith, G. (2009) 'A religious portrait of African Americans'. Pew Research Religion and Public Life Project. Available from: http://www.pewforum.org/2009/01/30/a-religious-portrait-of-African Americans/ [accessed 24 June 2014].

Smith, A. (2014) 'African Americans and technology use'. Pew Research Internet Project. Available from: http://www.pewinternet.org/2014/01/06/African Americans-and-technology-use/ [accessed 24 June 2014].

Stayman, D. M. and Deshpandé, R. (1989) 'Situational ethnicity and consumer behavior'. *Journal of Consumer Research*, 16(3): 361–71.

Stevenson, T. H. (2002) 'The portrayal of African Americans in business-to-business catalog advertising'. *Journal of Current Issues and Research in Advertising*, 24: 41–9.

Suro, R. (2004) 'Changing channels and crisscrossing cultures'. Pew Research Hispanic Center. Available from: http://www.pewhispanic.org/2004/04/19/changing-channels-and-crisscrossing-cultures/ [accessed 30 March 2013].

Taylor, C. R. and Lee, J. U. (1995) 'Portrayals of African, Hispanic, and Asian Americans in magazine advertising'. *American Behavioral Scientist*, 38(April): 608–21.

Taylor, P., Lopez, M., Passel, J. and Motel, S. (2011) 'Unauthorized immigrants: Length of residency, patterns of parenthood'. Pew Research Hispanic Center. Available at: http://www.pewhispanic.org/2011/12/01/unauthorized-immigrants-length-of-residency-patterns-of-parenthood/ [accessed 5 April 2013].

Taylor, P., Gonzalez-Barrera, A., Passel, J., & Lopez, M. (2012a) 'An awakened giant: The Hispanic electorate is likely to double by 2030'. Pew Research Hispanic Center. Available from: http://www.pewhispanic.org/2012/11/14/an-awakened-giant-the-hispanic-electorate-is-likelyto-double-by-2030/ [accessed 27 March 2013].

Taylor, P., Lopez, M. H., Martínez, J. H. and Velasco, G. (2012b) 'When labels don't fit: Hispanics and their views of identity'. Pew Hispanic Center. Available from: http://www.pewhispanic.org/2012/04/04/when-labels-dont-fit-hispanics-and-their-views-of-identity/ [accessed 18 March 2013].

Taylor, P., Lopez, M., Velasco, G. and Motel, S. (2012c) 'Hispanics say they have the worst of a bad economy'. Pew Research Hispanic Center. Available from: http://www.pewhispanic.org/2012/01/26/hispanics-say-they-have-the-worst-of-a-bad-economy/ [accessed 2 April 2013].

TNS Media Intelligence (2005) *Ethnic Marketing News*, 39(12), p. 23.

Torres, I. M. (2007) 'A tale of two theories: Sympathy or competition'. *Journal of Business Research*, 60: 197–205.

U.S. Census Bureau. (2 March 2010) 'Asian/Pacific Asian heritage month: May 2010'. U.S. Department of Commerce, U.S. Census Bureau. Available from: http://www.census.gov/newsroom/releases/archives/facts_for_features_special_editions/cb10-ff07.html [accessed 1 April 2013].

Whittler, T. E. (1989) 'Viewer's processing of source and message cues in advertising stimuli'. *Psychology & Marketing*, 6: 287–309.

Whittler, T. E. and diMeo J. (1991) 'Viewers reactions to racial cues in advertising stimuli'. *Journal of Advertising Research*, 31: 37–46.

Whittler, T. E. and Spira, J. (2002) 'Model's race: A peripheral cue in advertising messages?'. *Journal of Consumer Psychology*, 12: 291–301.

Yuen, N. W., Chin, C., Deo, M., Lee, J. and Milman, N. (2005) *Asian Pacific Americans in Prime Time: Lights, Camera, and Little Action*. Washington, DC: The National Asian Pacific American Legal Consortium.

Zhang, Q. (2010) 'Asian Americans beyond the model minority stereotype: The nerdy and the left out'. *Journal of International and Intercultural Communication*, 3(1): 20–37.

Zúñiga, M. A. (2015) 'African-American consumers' evaluations of ethnically primed advertisements'. Working Paper, Earl G. Graves School of Business and Management, Department of Business Administration, Morgan State University, Baltimore, MD.

Zúñiga, M. A. and Torres, I. M. (2015a) 'Cultural cues in Hispanic-targeted magazines: A content analysis from 1998 to 2013'. Working Paper, Earl G. Graves School of Business and Management, Department of Business Administration, Morgan State University, Baltimore, MD.

Zúñiga, M. A. and Torres, I. M. (2015b) 'Generation Y college aged Hispanic and white cohorts' ethical ideology effects on alcohol advertising appraisals: The role of strength of ethnic identification and ethical appraisal'. Working Paper, Earl G. Graves School of Business and Management, Department of Business Administration, Morgan State University, Baltimore, MD.

Zúñiga, M. A. and Torres, I. M. (2015c) 'Influence of collectivist and individualist cultural orientation and regulatory construal fit on brand attitudes'. Working Paper, Earl G. Graves School of Business and Management, Department of Business Administration, Morgan State University, Baltimore, MD.

Zúñiga, M. Z., Torres, I. M. and Niculescu, M. (2015) 'Boundary conditions to the effect of fluency and comprehension on AAD when targeting hispanics vs whites with single meaning vs polysemous slogans'. *Journal of Consumer Marketing*, 32(3).

12

Ethnic consumer decision making

Yasmin K. Sekhon

Introduction

This chapter aims to explore the influences and main characteristics of ethnic consumer decision making and what factors, whether directly or indirectly, influence the decisions made. Globally, we have witnessed a rapidly expanding multicultural landscape. With the growth in Hispanic, African American, Asian American, Black and ethnic minorities (BME), understanding ethnic decision making is vital for many. The rise in migrant numbers over the years is considerable, as is the change in the type of migration – from flows of people in particular eras to 'more people are now moving from more places, through more places, to more places' (Vertovec 2010, p. 86). The migration scene has changed with larger groups migrating in the mid-1950s to late-1970s from countries such as India, Pakistan and Africa to more recently smaller groups moving from one country to another. Understanding ethnic consumption and decision making is more challenging. The traditional distinct attributes of ethnic groups have become blurred; in addition, transnationalism blurs the boundaries further. Also Venkatesh draws attention to the role of ethnicity: 'Ethnicity becomes a cultural condition with profound consequences to the nature of consumption experiences among different people' (1995, p. 36).

The changing face of consumption and the challenges facing the consumption process have been discussed by many:

> Consumption is evoked as a meta-concept, used to explain the most disparate phenomena. At once part of debate on industrial and commercial restructuring, over the language and meaning of contemporary politics and about the reordering of identity, space and place, consumption is glossed as a composite and synthetic term.
>
> *(Mort 1996, p. 7)*

This evokes the depth and complexity of the concept of consumption and how it can affect different aspects of a person and the environment.

Central to consumption theory is motivation. Motivation is regarded as a basic concept in 'human behaviour and also in consumer behaviour' (Evans *et al.* 2009, p. 4). There are many different motivations that drive the consumer to buy. Belk and Xin (2003) argue that 'want' is the basic motivator in contemporary consumption. Others have argued that ultimately consumption is used as a means of fulfilling one's satisfaction, as Marx (1867/1967) wrote, 'A commodity is, in the first place, an object outside us, a thing that by its properties satisfies human wants of some sort or another. The nature of such wants, whether for instance they spring from the stomach or from fancy, makes no difference' (p. 33).

This chapter focuses on ethnic consumer decision making; and in doing so, culture, identity, ethnicity, influence of reference groups, considering transnationalism and superdiversity.

Ethnicity and ethnic identity

'Ethnicity is a dynamic concept related to changing social relations. Today, ethnicity is not so much the expression of existing roots but the provocative avowal and claim of a disturbed identity' (Bouchet 1995, p. 97). In addition, ethnicity is similarly described as 'pertaining to a social group within a cultural and social system that claims or is accorded special status on the basis of complex, often variable traits, including religion linguistics, ancestral or physical characteristics' (Engel et al. 1991).

Weber's (1961) work focused on ethnicity and ethnic identity. Ethnicity was regarded as a construct that included a sense of common custom, language, religion, values, morality and etiquette. Horowitz (1985, p. 41) regarded ethnicity as a concept of individual and group identity that 'embraces differences identified by colour, language, religion, or some other attribute of common origin'. Ethnicity is complex in nature; Webster (1994, p. 321) states that the term 'ethnicity has implied several dimensions, including a sense of common customs, language, religion, values, morality and etiquette and has subsequently been measured in a myriad of ways'. Horowitz's work (1985, p. 53) on the concept of ethnicity has referred to 'tribes', 'races', 'nationalities', and 'castes'. Parsons (1975, p. 53) related nationalism to group and ethnic identity, in which there is 'a coincidence of . . . common culture and territory of residence'. The many aspects of ethnicity accentuate its complexity. Notably when discussing ethnicity, the author refers to one's ethnicity as well as one's ethnic identity.

Research shows that 'ethnicity' and 'ethnic identity' are often used interchangeably. Venkatesh (1995) also argued that identity is influenced by self-identification and belonging. He presented ethnicity as self-identification influenced by others, which raises the difficult area of identity also being impacted by how others see us. Identification is both an individual response and one affected by the groups we relate to. This notion is an important issue to consider. Rossiter and Chan (1998) support Venkatesh, defining ethnicity as a means of self-identification by individuals categorizing themselves and others into groups using ethnic labels.

The discussion of ethnicity also leads to work on multiculturalism. Historically, heterogeneous groups from different cultural and religious backgrounds with linguistic differences have been the focus of multicultural studies. The discourse on multiculturalism has meant that there are a number of different labels of multiculturalism: from difference multiculturalism (Turner 1993) and public space multiculturalism (Vertovec 1996) to Delanty (2003) detailing nine kinds of multiculturalism. However, it has been argued that the term 'multiculturalism' is outdated (Vertovec 2010), and with the need to consider 'superdiversity', which questions the neat categorization of ethnic groups based on ethnicity, marketers now need to consider the diversity of migrants as well as the delineation of migrant groups.

Consumption: identity and ethnicity

A number of consumption studies focusing on one's ethnicity have been undertaken, including Hirschman's (1981) analysis of Jewish consumption patterns, Stayman and Deshpandé (1989), Zmud and Arce (1992), as well as Peñaloza's (1994) research on Hispanics and Venkatesh (1996).

These studies have all considered ethnicity and its role in the consumption process. Consumption is regarded as a personal and social process helping to express feelings of belonging and identity in private and public (Douglas and Isherwood 1979; Belk 1988; Lunt and Livingstone 1992).

Tomlinson (1991) linked identity to marketing, suggesting that marketing has a role in creating identity. Zmud and Arce (1992) make a direct link between identity and consumption, suggesting that 'social and cultural identity are affected by the social surroundings and the type of product being purchased' (cited in Burton 2000, p. 859).

The interplay between consumption and identity was also discussed by Askegaard and Arnould's (1999, p. 335) study of consumer acculturation of Greenlandic people living in Denmark. Consumption was regarded as a 'domain through which immigrants seek to hold on to certain patterns of culture and identity perceived to link them to their culture of origin'. Askegaard and Arnould's research is in fact highlighting the dual identity held by ethnic groups. Through acculturation and the transition from one culture to another, consumption patterns help form and shape this identity and so play a fundamental role in the socialization process. The research found that 'border crossings produce persistent identity constructions that may nonetheless alternate in Danish and Greenlandic social contexts' (1999, p. 335).

Ger and Ostegaard's (1998) study also links consumption with acculturation and identity. Arguably, different forms of cultural transition impact ethnic consumption. The findings suggest that consumption helps to negotiate the cultural differences and becomes the basis of constructing a new and more modern identity. Identity for ethnic audiences is constantly evolving, developing and changing over time. Ger and Ostegaard (1998, p. 48) studied Turko-Danish students and found that their participants were 'negotiating their identity in their consumption of clothes, with cultural and sub-cultural forces being felt and reflected in their dress'. Findings from this study implied that global consumption patterns were influencing identity formation among immigrants on a day-to-day basis. Here, clothing served 'the construction and expression of identity for the second-generation Turkish immigrants in Denmark' (Ger and Ostegaard 1998, p. 45). Hence, consumers were seeking and developing their identity through consumption (Friedman 1994).

Appostolova-Blossom (1999, p. 333) found that particular forms of consumption allowed the groups to hold on to country-of-origin culture or to further assimilate with the new culture. Ethnic groups, whether recent or more established, hold dual and fluid identities. These identities were also discussed by Lindridge et al. (2004) in their study of South Asian women living in Britain, highlighting how consumption is used 'to negotiate different cultural settings in postmodern ethnic families and households' (2004, p. 212). However, Lindridge and colleagues argue that consumption is only one part of identity formation and that acculturation levels, with the influence of family/households and generations, are also important in the process. In addition Lindridge and Dhillon (2005) argue that while previous studies show immigrants using consumption to create 'multiple identities', certain groups 'actively disengaged from any consumption they felt had cultural association with British White society or their own communities' (p. 413). Consumption is a part of one's identity; the complexity of influences ranges from community, family and a desire to belong and be accepted.

Another aspect of consumption is discussed by Joy and Dholakia (1991). In their study of home and possessions of Indian professionals in Canada, they found that a more individualistic ethic is being adopted by ethnic groups as they acculturate to the host country.

> Acculturation, it is argued, has ushered in a reconsideration of identity based on the supremacy and the sovereignty of the individual over community, such a concept allows for the recognition of the individualistic ethic within which property and possessions have begun to dominate.
> *(Joy and Dholakia 1991, p. 385)*

However, as Berry (1980) and Wallendorf and Reilly (1983) have argued, such individualism does not necessarily result in cultural loss and displacement, but rather is a process of growth in the new country. The study by Joy and Dholakia indicates that the second generation's identity and values are learned more from their Canadian peers and so are eroding their Indian identity. 'The second generation are in part tempered by the demands made by the milieu in which they live – Canada, they learn to value individual material gains over community with greater ease than their parents' (1991, p. 397). The study reveals that identity formation is therefore closely linked to consumption, and consumption is being influenced by acculturation and the desire to assimilate with the host country to help create belonging. This desire to conform appears to be without pressure. There is arguably a need to possess a hybrid style of culture and values that take into account the host country with a strong country-of-origin foundation. Home- and host-country integration and consideration of values is also discussed later in the chapter.

Understanding identity through consumption is problematic and challenging, as it is an ever-changing and developing phenomenon. As Gould's (1994, p. 306) work on Asian post-modern consumer culture shows, the 'consumer in post-modern culture is engulfed in a tidal wave of disorienting dilemmas which challenge his/her identity'. Firat (1995, p. 116) has attempted to explain this idea of post-modern consumer culture by classifying identity and ethnicity as a commodity. 'In post-modern consumer culture, ethnicity has been commodified, alienated from history, reified, and reduced to a set of symbols circulating on the global market and available to everyone'. This so-called 'fragmentation of the self' theoretically allows the possibility of building and ordering one's identity through the market (Firat 1995, p. 115).

This idea of building one's own identity piece by piece was also put forward by Bouchet (1995, p. 84), arguing that consumers' ethnicity in 'post-modern Europe is more bricolage than ever. It is not the continuation or the importation of an already existing cultural system, but rather the creation of a lifestyle. Ethnicity in today's Europe is, like religiosity, à la carte'. He argues that consumption is being used to form and express identities. However, these identities are more than just the home and host country's influences but are rather the 'building of a new and often individual identities on the basis of elements from a diversity of cultural representations and practices' (Bouchet 1995, p. 84).

Oswald (1999) develops the subtlety of ethnic identity formation by stating that 'immigrants negotiate differences between home and here by choosing when and where to wear their ethnicity' (p. 315). Oswald provides empirical evidence to support the co-existence of consumers' mixed emotions arguing that 'in consumer culture, ethnicity can be bought, sold, and worn like a loose garment' (p. 304).

Ethnicity and identity have been discussed here in the context of consumption. Consumption, it is argued, helps to construct one's ethnicity and identity. In essence it is not only ethnicity influencing consumption, but consumption impacting one's affiliation and ethnic identity. Consumption decisions may be made to express one's loyalty to the home country or to demonstrate one's assimilation; however, this may be a moveable and changing process. The meaning of consumption in identity terms is multi-faceted. It includes the need to possess certain goods as well as symbolize one's cultural affiliation in different contexts. Moreover, it is the formation of a hybrid identity that takes into account one's personal, public and cultural needs, and so as Oswald (1999) states, we are in fact 'theorizing about the movement of ethnic identity between several worlds at once' (p. 303). We see how ethnic consumer decision making is influenced by one's acculturation, identity and feelings of ethnicity. In addition the transnational consumer (discussed later in the chapter) needs to be considered, the influences are varied and diverse and so challenge traditional consumption thinking.

Bi-cultural self and culture

The study undertaken by Sekhon and Szmigin (2005; 2009) found their participants – second-generation Asian-Indian Punjabis—when making consumption decisions did not require subordination of their own needs to those of the group as traditional collectivistic theory has indicated (Hofstede 1984; Triandis 1989; Triandis et al. 1988); however, the findings did demonstrate how their 'bicultural self' has to take into account the Punjabi culture in their decision making. They use the term the '"bicultural self' to refer to a mixture of home- and host-country influences along with the integration of individualistic and collectivistic thinking. These factors, they found, impacted the intensity of the acculturation of this ethnic group, which oscillates between strong and weak depending on the ongoing cultural context – whether it be more Western or more Eastern. Additionally, Brewer and Chen (2007) explore the cultural discourse of individualism and collectivism, calling for a need to further investigate these distinctions as well as understand the relational networks that exist in different cultures.

Bhatia's (2002) work discussed the complex nature of identity, labelling it 'hyphenated' identity. In particular, he suggests that 'immigrant parents and their native-born children are constantly negotiating their multiple, and often conflicting, dialogical voices, histories and I positions' (2002, p. 57), once again supporting the ever-evolving and changing notion of identity. In a bi-cultural world, ethnic consumer decision making is influenced by a number of factors that are embedded into an individual's being, both at a personal and at a social level.

Consequently, consumption, culture and identity are interrelated. Consumption is shaped by culture, which then influences one's identity and levels of ethnicity. This, however, varies in both the private and the public context. Joy and Dholakia's (1991) work examined the close relationship between culture and consumption and how it then influences identity formation, particularly among the second generation, succinctly highlighting the ever-changing and developing nature of identity across generations. Similarly, Jamal and Chapman (2000, p. 377) identify consumption as indicative of the 'multiple identities held within and across groups'. Zmud and Arce (1992), in researching the relationship between ethnicity and consumption, argued that social and cultural identity is affected by the 'social surroundings and the type of product being purchased' (cited in Burton 2000, p. 859). This view has been supported by Lindridge et al. (2004), whose research indicates that culture is part of and influenced by ethnicity, identity and consumption. Bhatia (2002) argues that those living as a part of two cultures are constantly negotiating their cultural identities, defying categorization such that the individual may experience multiple identities at any one time.

A more recent study by Sekhon and Szmigin (2011) found that ethnic consumer decision making, particularly those from the first- and second-generation Indian Punjabi background, was influenced by a number of factors. Indeed, these were well managed; the influence of two cultures, *izatt* (family honour), parents, family, community, friends and peers was accepted in a consumption context but was found to be more challenging in developing one's identity. The participants are explicit in stating that Punjabi cultural norms and expectations influence their decision making, which stems from their collectivistic thinking of the role of *izatt* in their lives. The participants deal with the pressures of both cultures with greater ease in the context of consumption than they do in the context of defining their own identity. In addition, consumer decision making is also inextricably linked to the need to gain approval from others. Sekhon (2007) in her work looking into the consumption patterns of first- and second-generation Asian Indian Punjabis found that the identity for these participants was to seek belonging. Being accepted, one's image in the public and private domain, is linked to history (parents' migration), to the present (feelings of belonging with different groups) and the future (one's level of achievement and success and affiliation in a bi-cultural context).

As the previous sections have highlighted, consumer acculturation is also a fundamental part of identity and consumption. Acculturation can impact ethnic groups as they grapple with two distinct cultures, both home and host. Acculturation is strongly linked to consumption. There has been significant consumer acculturation research, including Deshpandé et al. (1986); Venkatesh (1994); Peñaloza (1989; 1994); Askegaard et al. (2005); and Luedicke (2011). The cultural interactions influence ethnic consumer decision making. The 'cultural viewpoint', the mix of cultures impact consumption; as Sekhon and Szmigin stated, ethnic groups are influenced by a number of factors, 'the between two cultures generation' who do not just juggle situations between East and West (home and host country) but rather juggle life continuously, sometimes integrating and acculturating and other times deliberately alienating and identifying with one's ethnicity for a sense of belonging and identity (2005, p. 13).

Historically Peñaloza (1989) also discusses consumer acculturation, describing it as a 'two-level phenomenon' (1989, p. 114), a phenomenon that can occur at an individual and group level, and at a psychological and social-psychological level. At a psychological level, cognitive development theory is used to explain age and generational differences in immigrant consumer acculturation. For example, the first-generation immigrant typically demonstrates lower levels of cultural assimilation than proceeding generations (Padilla 1980). Social-psychological theories place emphasis on the importance of 'interpersonal relationships and exchanges of information which then affect individual consumer theory' (Peñaloza 1989, p. 117). Peñaloza (1989) suggests that consumer acculturation may also result in accelerated adoption and display behaviours related to conspicuous consumption because of products associated with the new culture. Hence, ethnic groups, whether recent settlers or more established communities, are influenced by different levels of acculturation and assimilation. This in turn impacts their decision making, in terms of who and what influences their choices. In addition, Berry discusses acculturation strategies (1980), consisting of two components, attitudes and behaviours; however, the author states that often individuals do not always have complete freedom because of dominant cultural constraints – for example, language and other structural factors, that is attitudes of dominant culture members, all of which influence consumption patterns and behaviour.

Gronhaug et al. (1993) report that 'through observation, imitation and interactions with socialising agents, individuals learn the culture brought up in and they become socialised as consumers' (1993, p. 279). Consumers are socialized and their resultant consumption patterns are directly linked to this socialization process, such that 'consumer acculturation refers to the subset of acculturation related to consumption activities' (1993, p. 280).

Sandıkçı and Ger (2002) suggest, because of culture, the creation of a hybrid post-modern tone to consumption. On the one hand, this hybridity is regarded as a result of globalization, but on the other, it is regarded as a state that is a result of forced acculturation or forced adoption of behavioural patterns due to structural mandates and conditions. Jun et al. (1993) also argued that individuals might choose a particular brand simply because of its availability over another; however, this does not necessarily imply acculturation assimilation of the host country, but rather consumption based on the choices available to the individuals. This is similar to other previous studies, for example Wallendorf and Reilly's (1983) work on assimilation, suggesting that an individual may be forced to participate with the host country's culture because of 'structural constraints that force compliance' (p. 293). These studies distinguish between consumption choices that are made freely with no restriction and those that are forced, arguing that those based on structural constraints do not accurately measure acculturation in a consumption context. The neat categorization of ethnic groups as either integrated or marginalised as proposed by the dominant Berry model (Berry 1997) is questioned. If we are to question the neat categorization of ethnic groups, it would be timely to consider transnationalism, 'the cross-border and homeland links maintained by migrants' (Vertovec 2010, p. 89).

Traditionally, acculturation theory has suggested that ethnic groups acculturate with the host country, adapting to new traditions' values and experiences, or decide, due to a number of circumstances, to remain closely associated to their home country with little integration with the host country. This has made marketing to these groups very distinct because of a number of factors, from the more obvious language differences, clothing for some groups, health and beauty (because of skin and hair differences) and even the consumption of public services, especially in relation to health, fitness and well-being. However, in more recent arrivals, smaller groups are consumers of multiple retailers, from both their host and their home country. Decision making is not so neatly categorized and there is a clear blurring of boundaries.

Additionally, transnational practices of these groups encourage increased mobilization, whether it be for personal, business or professional services. Locality is not necessarily the anchor or the key factor that influences decision making. Community is not just those in their locale, but through the development of technology and communication they remain rather connected and integrated to their homeland. Furthermore, in-groups, as well as social networks, may vary (Brewer and Chen 2007). Transnationalism does not necessarily alienate individuals or discourage them to integrate; rather, there is a greater level of multiple identity formation. As Vertovec (2010, p. 93) neatly summarized, 'While migrants continue to feel powerfully bound to homelands and communities elsewhere, they are now more able to maintain and enhance these feeling, while at the same time being quite capable of developing a new life, livelihood and social ties'. Vertovec (2010) labelled this as 'superdiversity', a more sophisticated and a less demarcated way of thinking, moving beyond multiculturalism; in essence, regarding ethnic decision making as a complex, diverse and nonlinear process. The social capital of individuals and ethnic groups is enlarged, and so decision making is more complex than ever before (Jones et al. 2010). There is thus a need to consider both traditional cultural studies along with the findings of transnationalism and 'superdiversity' if we are to better comprehend ethnic consumption at the present and in the future.

Cultural consumption

Luna and Gupta (2001) proposed an individual's behaviour as directly linked to their cultural value system. These value systems develop over time through the socialization process. The individual's cultural value system is formed of societal culture, regional subculture and family values. This cultural value system then influences an individual's consumer behaviour. Luna and Gupta also suggest that an individual's consumption patterns may influence their cultural value system. They further suggest that an individual's consumption behaviour may be 'viewed and imitated or rejected by others. It can then become the group's norm of behaviour and be identified as part of the culture of a given population' (Luna and Gupta 2001, p. 46).

Ethnic groups are thus influenced by norms and values that are not only accepted but also respected by their peers and reference groups. A strong reference group for ethnic groups is family; a number of studies have investigated Hispanic consumers being influenced by family and peers (Hoyer and Deshpandé 1982; O'Guinn and Meyer 1983; Deshpandé et al. 1986). Others have also looked at Indian family influences (Lindridge et al. 2004; Sekhon and Szmigin 2005; 2011). These studies demonstrate how a mixture of ethnic identity and social belonging as well as peer and reference group influence impacts ethnic consumer decision making. Culture-specific consumption behaviour has also been observed in a number of product categories, from food to clothing to entertainment.

This cultural significance of consumer goods was also discussed by Pyssler (1992), focusing on the study of the Indian two-wheeler (scooter). This study revealed how the same physical object can materially take on a very different cultural meaning, 'operating within different political economic structures, seen by different people, at different times, from differing perspectives, the scooter has generated diverse meanings, pleasures, and identities' (1992, p. 440). Pyssler, although in agreement with McCracken's (1986) statement that 'consumer goods have a significance that goes beyond their utilitarian value' (p. 71), also states that it is not only culture that differentiates a product and its meaning but also the country's infrastructure, availability of resources, and labour. Consumption and culture are thus interlinked.

Summary and conclusion

Ethnic identity construction is impacted by the individual's social environment. This context consists of one's social and personal world. One's identity is formed both at an individual and wider social level; it has a number of influences from family, community, peer groups, mass media and the extended family, all of whom influence the forging of a new identity (Oswald 1999, p. 314). In particular, for many ethnic groups, identity is 'bicultural' in nature; additionally, acculturation in its many forms impacts consumer decision making as well as the significance of possessions to individuals as well as their communities.

Consumer acculturation studies highlight the various ways in which migrant identity is constructed as well as the interactions with cultures impacting consumer decision making. Social experiences together with these interactions influence identity construction. Peñaloza (1994) and Berry (1980; 1989; 2001) as well as Luedicke (2011) continue to dominate acculturation discussions.

In summary, consumption decisions are closely linked to and an expression of one's identity. Individuals wish to consume products that enhance their image and help to facilitate belonging within both one's ethnic group and the wider population. The chapter outlines how consumption, identity and acculturation are interrelated, impacting ethnic consumer decision making. The complexities of acculturation demonstrate how consumption helps to facilitate belonging and affiliation with other members. Consumption from an ethnic perspective is ever evolving as an individual's identity develops over time and with different interactions. Socialization theory and levels of ethnic affiliation as well as the influence of transnationalism and 'superdiversity' impact consumption decisions of ethnic groups. It is clear that these factors impact culture-specific consumption and, in understanding the interplay of all these factors, we can better appreciate ethnic consumption.

These discussions also highlight practical implications for marketing to ethnic groups. Marketers need to consider 'superdiversity' and ensure that they too question the neat categorization of ethnic groups, considering the diversity of ethnic groups (both smaller and larger groups). Targeting to these groups requires an in-depth understanding of the relationship networks that exist in these communities and the influence of these relationships as well as individual's transnational identities.

The constant negotiation of oneself is also a fundamental consideration for marketers; identity is negotiated in different contexts and situations. Decision making for different product categories may vary considerably and cannot be assumed to be consistent across all industries, products and categories. The negotiation of one's identity is ever present but differs across sectors.

Future research directions

As we question and continually develop the different aspects of consumption, identity and culture, it would be appropriate to examine further these concepts across different generations. Consideration needs to be given to the constant negotiation experienced by different generations as consumption patterns vary considerably, from the first generation to subsequent generations influenced by a mix of cultural values. A greater level of understanding is required of the network of relationships that exist within these groups: questioning where the strength of ties lie and how these ties impact opinion leaders, as well as developing a meaningful understanding of and identifying in-group influences, will help to understand the complexities of ethnic consumer decision making.

References

Appostolova-Blossom, E. (1999) 'Identity and modern consumption: Special edition summary'. *European Advances in Consumer Research,* 4: 332–35.

Askegaard, S. and Arnould, E. (1999) 'Consumer acculturation of Greenlandic people in Denmark'. *European Advances in Consumer Research*, (IV). Provo, UT: Association for Consumer Research, pp. 332-35.

Askegaard, S., Arnould, E. J. and Kjeldgaard, D. (2005) 'Postassimilationist ethnic consumer research: Qualifications and extensions'. *Journal of Consumer Research*, 32: 160–70.

Belk, R. W. (1988) 'Possessions and the extended self'. *Journal of Consumer Research*, 15(2): 139–68.

Belk, R. W. and Zhao, X. (2003) 'China's first global advertising encounter: Pre-Communist Shanghai'. In *The Romance of Marketing History*, edited by E. H. Shaw. Boca Raton, FL: Association for Historical Research in Marketing, pp. 220–28.

Berry, W. J. (1980) 'Acculturation as varieties of adaptation'. In *Acculturation: Theory, Models and Some New Findings*, edited by A. M. Padilla. Boulder, CO: Westview Press, pp. 9–25.

Berry, J. W. (1990) 'Psychology of acculturation'. In *Cross-Cultural Perspectives. Proceedings of the Nebraska symposium on motivation*, edited by J. J. Berman. Lincoln, NE: University of Nebraska Press, pp. 201–34.

Berry, J. W. (1997) 'Immigration, acculturation and adaptation'. *Applied Psychology*, 46: 5–68.

Berry, J. W. (2001) 'A psychology of immigration'. *Journal of Social Issues*, 57: 611–27.

Bhatia, S. (2002) 'Acculturation dialogical voices and the construction of the diasporic self'. *Theory and Psychology*, 12(1): 55–77.

Bouchet, D. (1995) 'Marketing and the redefinition of ethnicity'. In *Marketing in a Multicultural World*, edited by J. A. Costa and G. J. Bamossy. London: Sage Publications, pp. 68–105.

Brewer, M. B. and Chen, Y. R. (2007) 'Where (who) are collectives in collectivism? Toward conceptual clarification of individualism and collectivism'. *Psychological Review*, 114: 133–51.

Burton, D. (2000) 'Ethnicity, identity and marketing: A critical review'. *Journal of Marketing Management*, 16: 853–77.

Delanty, G. (2003) *Community*. London: Routledge.

Deshpandé, R., Hoyer, W. D. and Donthu, N. (1986) 'The intensity of ethnic affiliation: A study of the sociology of hispanic consumption'. *Journal of Consumer Research*, 13: 214–20.

Douglas, M. and Isherwood B. (1979) *The World of Goods: Towards an Anthropology of Consumption*. London: Allen Lane.

Engel, J. F., Warshaw M. R. and Kinneart. C. (1991) *Promotional Strategy: Managing the Marketing Communications Process*. Homewood, IL: Irwin Professional Publishing.

Evans, M., Jamal A. and Foxall G. (2009) *Consumer Behaviour*. Hoboken, NJ: Wiley & Sons.

Firat, A. F. (1995) 'Consumer culture or culture consumed'. In *Marketing in a Multicultural World*, edited by J. Costa and G. Bamossy. Thousand Oaks, CA: Sage, pp. 106–25.

Ger, G. and Ostergaard, P. (1998) 'Constructing immigrant identities in consumption: Appearance among the Turko-Danes'. In *Advances in Consumer Research*, edited by J. W. Alba, and J. W. Hutchinson. Provo, UT: Association for Consumer Research, pp. 48–52.

Gould, S. J. (1994) 'An Asian-based perspective on postmodern consumer culture and consciousness: The nature of mind'. *Asia Pacific Advances in Consumer Research*, 1: 306–10.

Gronhaug, K. Gilly M. L. and Peñazola L. (1993) 'Barriers and incentives in consumer acculturation'. *European Advances in Consumer Research*, 1: 278–86.

Hirschman, E. C. (1981) 'American Jewish ethnicity: Its relationship to some selected aspects of consumer behavior'. *The Journal of Marketing*, 45(3): 102–10.

Hofstede, G. R. (1984) *Culture's Consequences: International Differences in Work Related Values*. Beverly Hills, CA: Sage.

Horowitz, D. (1985) *Ethnic Groups in Conflict*. Berkeley, CA: University of California Press.

Hoyer, W. D. and Deshpandé, R. (1982) 'Cross-cultural influences on buyer behavior: The impact of Hispanic ethnicity'. In *An Assessment of Marketing Thought and Practice*, edited by B. J. Walker, W. O. Bearden, P. E. Murphy, J. R. Nevin, J. C. Olson and B. D. Weitz. Chicago, IL: American Marketing Association, pp. 89–92.

Jamal, A. and Chapman, M. (2000) 'Acculturation and inter-ethnic consumer perceptions: Can you feel what we feel?' *Journal of Marketing Management*, 16(4): 365–91.

Jones, T., Ram, M. and Theodorakopoulos, N. (2010) 'Transnationalism as a force for ethnic minority enterprise: The case of Somalis in Leicester'. *International Journal of Urban and Regional Research*, 24(3): 565–85.

Joy, A. and Dholakia, R. R. (1991) 'Remembrances of things past: The meaning of home and possessions of Indian professionals in Canada'. In *To Have Possessions: A Handbook on Ownership and Property*, edited by F. W. Rudmin. Corte Madeira, CA: Select Press, pp. 385–402.

Jun, S. A., Ball, D. and Gentry, J. W. (1993) 'Modes of consumer acculturation'. *Advances in Consumer Research*, 20: 76–82.

Lindridge, A. M. and Dhillon K. (2005) 'Cultural role confusion and memories of a lost identity: How non-consumption perpetuates marginalisation'. *Advances in Consumer Research*, Volume 32, edited by G. Menon and A. R. Rao. Duluth, MN: Association Consumer Research, pp. 408–14.

Lindridge, A. M., Hogg, M. K. and Shah, M. (2004) 'Imagined multiple worlds: How South Asian women in Britain use family and friends to navigate the "border crossings" between household and social contexts'. *Consumption, Markets & Culture*, 7(3): 211–38.

Luedicke, M. (2011) 'Consumer acculturation theory: (Crossing) conceptual boundaries'. *Consumption Markets & Culture*, 14(3): 223–44.

Luna, D. and Gupta, S. F. (2001) 'An integrative framework for cross-cultural consumer behaviour'. *International Marketing Review*, 18(1): 45–69.

Lunt, P. K. and Livingstone, S. M. (1992) *Mass Consumption and Personal Identity*. Buckingham: Open University Press.

Marx, K. (1867/1967) *Capital: A Critique of Political Economy*, Volume 1. New York, NY: International Publishers.

McCracken, G. (1986) 'Culture and consumption: A theoretical account of the structure and movement of cultural meaning of consumer goods'. *Journal of Consumer Research*, 13(June): 71–84.

Mort, F. (1996) *Cultures of Consumption: Masculinities and Social Space in Late Twentieth-Century Britain London*. New York, NY: Routledge.

O'Guinn, T. C. and Meyer, T. P. (1983) 'Segmenting the Hispanic market: The use of Spanish-language radio'. *Journal of Advertising Research*, 23(6).

Oswald, R. L. (1999) 'Culture swapping: Consumption and the ethnogenesis of middle-class Haitian immigrants'. *Journal of Consumer Research*, 25: 303–18.

Padilla, M. A. (ed) (1980) *Acculturation: Theory, Models and Some New Findings*. Boulder, CO: Westview Press.

Parsons, T. (1975) 'Some theoretical considerations on the nature and trends of change of ethnicity'. In *Ethnicity: Theory and Experience*, edited by N. Glazer, and D. P. Moynihan. Cambridge, MA: Harvard University Press, pp. 53–83.

Peñaloza, L. N. (1989) 'Immigrant consumer acculturation'. In *Advances in Consumer Research*, Volume 16, edited by T. K. Srull. Provo, UT: Association for Consumer Research, pp. 110–18.

Peñaloza, L. N. (1994) 'Atravesando fronteras/border crossing: A critical ethnographic exploration of the consumer acculturation of Mexican immigrants'. *Journal of Consumer Research*, 21(1): 32–54.

Pyssler, B. D. (1992) 'The cultural and political economy of the Indian two-wheeler'. *Advances in Consumer Research*, Volume 19, edited by J. F. Sherry Jr. and B. Sternthal. Provo, UT: Association for Consumer Research, pp. 437–42.

Rossiter, J. R. and Chan, A. M. (1998) 'Ethnicity in business and consumer behaviour'. *Journal of Business Research*, 42: 127–34.

Sandıkçı, Ö. and Ger, G. (2002) 'Interrogating non-Western consumer cultures: Are we really talking about postmodern plurality, multiple modernities or pre-modern transformations?' *Special Session Summary: Advances in Consumer Research*, Volume 29: 463–64.

Sekhon, Y. K. (2007) '"From saris to sarongs" Ethnicity and intergenerational influences on consumption among Asian Indians in the UK'. *International Journal of Consumer Studies*, 31: 60–167.

Sekhon, Y. and Szmigin, I. (2005) 'Conceptualising ethnicity and acculturation of second generation Asian Indians in Britain'. *Academy of Marketing Science Review* (US), 3: 1–18

Sekhon, Y. K. and Szmigin, I. (2009) 'The bicultural value system'. *International Journal of Market Research*, 51: 751–71.

Sekhon, Y. K. and Szmigin, I. (2011) 'Acculturation and identity: Insights from second-generation Indian Punjabis'. *Consumption, Markets, and Culture*, 14: 79–98.

Stayman, D. M. and Deshpandé, R. (1989) 'Situational ethnicity and consumer behaviour'. *Journal of Consumer Research*, 16(3): 361–71.

Tomlinson, J. (1991) *Cultural Imperialism*. Baltimore, MA: Johns Hopkins University Press.

Triandis, H. C (1989) 'The self and social behavior in differing cultural contexts'. *Psychological Review*, 96: 506–20.

Triandis, H. C., Bontempo, R. Villareal, M. J., Asai M. and Lucca, N. (1988) 'Individualism and collectivism: Cross-cultural perspectives on self-in group relationships'. *Journal of Personality and Social Psychology*, 54(February): 323–38.

Turner, T. (1993) 'Anthropology and multiculturalism: What is anthropology that mulitculturalists should be mindful of it?' *Cultural Anthropology*, 8: 411–29.

Venkatesh, A. (1994) 'India's changing consumer economy: A cultural perspective'. *Advances in Consumer Research*, 21: 323–28.

Venkatesh, A. (1995) 'Ethno-consumerism: A new paradigm to study cultural and cross-cultural consumer behavior'. In *Marketing in a Multicultural World*, edited by J. A. Costa and G. J. Bamossy. Thousand Oaks, CA: Sage Publications, pp. 26–67.

Vertovec. S. (2010) *Towards Post-Multiculturalism? Changing Communities, Conditions and Contexts of Diversity*. UNESCO: Blackwell Publishing Ltd.

Wallendorf, M. and Reilly M. (1983) 'Ethnic migration, assimilation, and consumption'. *Journal of Consumer Research*, 10(December): 292–302.

Weber, M. (1961) *General Economic History*. Glencoe IL: Free Press.

Webster, C. (1994) 'Effects of Hispanic ethnic identification on marital roles in the purchase decision process'. *Journal of Consumer Research*, 21: 319–31.

Zmud, J. and Arce, C. (1992) 'The ethnicity and consumption relationship'. *Advances in Consumer Research*, 19(1): 443–50.

13

Marketing financial services to the ethnic minority customers

Intekhab (Ian) Alam

Introduction

Many markets in both developed and developing countries are culturally diverse, containing sizable populations of a variety of ethnic minority groups. High levels of immigration in different parts of the world are partly responsible for this cultural diversity that has resulted in intermingling of values, interests and consumption patterns of consumers from diverse backgrounds (Grier and Deshpandé 2001; Ouellet 2007; Peñaloza and Gilly 1999). The improvements of technology, such as the growth of satellite communications and the internet, have also contributed to greater interchanges and linkages among various minority groups. This has indeed led to blurring of the social boundaries of culture (Craig and Douglas 2006). However, despite this cultural intermingling, ethnic minority groups have been found to maintain their own unique consumption patterns due to the intangible elements of societal values and beliefs as shown in the extant literature (e.g. Jamal *et al.* 2012; Goldman and Hino 2005; Jamal 2003; Burton 2000; Ackerman and Tellis 2001). These rather unique and conflicting views on the cultural shifts make the issue of marketing to ethnic minorities an important area of enquiry (Emslie *et al.* 2007; Jamal and Shukor 2014; Pires *et al.* 2011).

Consumption of services or service-based products is largely based on cultural and ethnic orientation of the customers (Pires and Stanton 2000; Rossiter and Chan 1998). Therefore, to ensure success in introducing new services, ethnic and cultural issues must be incorporated while developing new services (Jaw *et al.* 2010). Additionally, of all the service sectors, financial services have been the focus of intense scrutiny and research in the extant literature because of the high level of innovation in the industry resulting from deregulation and technological advancements (Alam 2013; Lyons *et al.* 2007). Over the past few years, a considerable amount of research has focused on new service development (NSD) (see reviews by Johne and Storey 1998; de Jong and Vermeulen 2003). Most studies in this area discuss the structured process of NSD and suggest that a firm must use such a process model for developing successful new services (for example, Alam and Perry 2002; Scheuing and Johnson 1989). Yet, relatively little effort has been expended on studying how the financial service organizations develop new services to address the needs of ethnic minority customers in different parts of the world (Chaudhry and Crick 2004). This gap in the literature and growing needs of ethnic minority customers make service innovation, specifically for ethnic customers, a key issue for financial service firms. In a related domain, a stream of research highlights the important role played by ethnic minority enterprises in serving the unique needs of ethnic minority consumers (e.g. Jamal 2005). Others point to product development issues in specific sectors like Islamic banking (e.g. Ahmed 2011). However, very little research investigates the NSD process as used and applied by those who are interested in targeting ethnic minority consumers. The current chapter is an attempt to identify the significance of NSD process in ethnic marketing and consider future research avenues.

The Shariah-compliant financial service that adheres to the tenets of Islamic law is a growing niche within the financial service sector of countries having a sizeable Muslim population (Ford 2012; Long 2013). Therefore, the use and application of a structured NSD process for developing new financial services, such as mortgages, business loans and share investments for a growing number of ethnic Muslim customers in different parts of the world, is an important issue facing many financial institutions. Currently, the issue of Shariah-compliant banking is attracting more attention in the big emerging market and Muslim minority country, India (Ahmed 2013; Hammond 2012). This is because India's central bank, known as the Reserve Bank of India (RBI), has agreed to allow the commercial banks to explore the possibility of offering new interest-free banking services to its ethnic minority customers (Bose and Yedukumar 2013). With the enormous Muslim population and the significant requirement of the capital in the country, there is a scope for massive growth in Islamic banking in India. As a result, there is a scurry among many financial services firms, both from India and abroad, to develop new services to address the need of Muslim customers and cash in on the increasing openness of the Indian capital market (Hammond 2012). Yet, to the best of our knowledge, no study has explored the process of developing new services for the minority customers in India as well as other parts of the world.

Against this backdrop, the objective of this chapter is to provide a review of the literature with a view to develop an understanding of the process of developing new financial services for the minority customers and offer practical guidelines to service managers. The rest of the chapter is organized as follows. We first analyze the strength of Muslim customers and discuss the need for new financial services for them, especially in a country in which they are in minority. Subsequently, we review the extant literature related to global service innovation and customer interaction. We conclude the chapter with a discussion of implications for the service managers and policy makers.

Marginalization of the Muslim minority

India is a country of multi-religious, multi-lingual and multi-ethnic people. Because of the large variety of the ethnic origins of her people, the country is often called an ethnic museum (Fazlie 1995). Muslims are the second-largest religious group after the majority Hindu community and thus the largest minority in India. There are over 160 million Muslims in India, which constitutes about 13.4% of the total population according to the 2011 census. In essence, India has the largest concentration of the Muslims outside the member countries of the Organization of the Islamic Conference (OIC) and the second-largest (after Indonesia) in the world. However, despite their population and a strong political clout, the socio-economic condition of this ethnic minority is somewhat pitiable (Bagsiraj 2003). An extensive study of the economic, social and educational conditions of the Muslim ethnic minority in India by the high-level prime ministerial committee headed by Justice Rajinder Sachar reported an extremely low level of penetration of banking and financial services among this largest minority group (Sachar Committee Report 2006). The RBI's efforts to extend banking and credit facilities under the Prime Minister's 15-point program of 1983 has mainly benefited other minorities, while completely marginalizing a large section of the Muslim population (ibid.). According to a recent RBI report, the public sector banks in fact are failing to cater to the need of the Muslim minority community, partly because the bank employees are not sensitized to address the exclusive needs of the minority community. This case of banking discrimination is consistent with the issues in developed countries, including the USA, where minority customers face tougher standards in borrowing and lending due to biases and prejudices (e.g. Black et al. 2003; Horne 1997; Munnell et al. 1996). In a broader sense, the issue of marginalization of ethnic minorities has been a pressing problem worldwide, and India is no exception. There seems to be abundant literature demonstrating the marginalization of ethnic customers in marketing practices. The literature suggests that the Muslim minority in particular is marginalized due to general prejudice and a lack of assimilation efforts initiated by the Muslims themselves in many Western countries (El-Bassiouny 2014; Knight et al. 2009; Lee et al. 2011). The reflection of this marginalization of a minority in India is exemplified, for example, by the unavailability of interest-free banking services for its 160 million Muslim customers.

In summary, the flow of bank credit to the Muslim community is inadequate, and this exclusion of Muslims has far-reaching implications for their socio-economic advancement and the country as a whole. Realizing the negative consequences of the marginalization of the ethnic minority customers as documented in the literature (e.g. Lee et al. 2011; Russell and Russell 2010) the RBI has started to take some measures to remove the barriers in credit flow to the Muslim minority (Hammond 2012). Two key barriers for the low penetration of banking services among the minority customers are the lack of education among the minority community and the failure of both public and private sector banks to offer the products that suit their needs (Sachar Committee Report 2006). Many have argued that the existing minority financial institutions have been a failure and, therefore, it is desirable to create separate financial institutions for Muslim entrepreneurs offering Shariah-compliant services.

Islamic financial service sector of India

Currently the largest markets for Islamic banking products are Indonesia and Malaysia, yet several secular and industrialized countries such as Singapore, Hong Kong, France and the UK have already accommodated Islamic finance and banking along with other conventional banking practices (Chin et al. 2008; Ihsanoglu 2011; Long 2013; Mcaughtry 2013). Service firms in these countries are responding to the needs of ethnic customers because they are looking for growth outside the North America and European Union (Chittenden 2010; Colvin 2009; El-Bassiouny 2014; Ferguson 2011). Although the population of Muslims in the UK is only three million, London has become a hub for Islamic finance (Volk and Pudelko 2010; Bershidsky 2013).

The number of Muslims in India is about 160 million, accounting for about 10% of the world's total Muslim population, which provides a larger platform for the use of Shariah-compliant services than any other countries in the world. In addition, India is a big emerging market, having a GDP growth rate of almost 9% that, in turn, leads to the need of large capital requirement. Given the growth rate in the financial service sector, India has the great potential to become the largest market for Islamic finance worldwide. Although Islamic finance has been around in the Indian sub-continent for many years (see for example Khan [2004] and Siddiqui [2006] for India; Khan and Bhatti [2008] for Pakistan and Sarker [1999] for Bangladesh), it has not thrived in an unregulated environment, specifically in developing countries such as India. With this in phenomenon in mind, recently a panel of economists recommended the introduction of interest-free banking in India, and the RBI on principle gave approval for developing new financial products based on the principles of Shariah. The Raghuram Rajan Committee, appointed by the RBI, also recommended Islamic finance and banking for the Muslim minority customers in India. This development has led to flurry of activities in the Indian financial service sector, as is evident from the formation of National Minorities Development Finance Corporation (NMDFC), Islamic Finance Organization (IFO) and introduction of Shariah-compliant mutual and venture capital fund products by organizations such as Taqwaa Advisory and Shariah Investment Solutions (TASIS). These developments point towards the systematic approach the Indian policy makers have adopted in allowing the banks to offer financial products specifically for the minority customers to further boost India's financial service sector.

However, a pertinent question to ask is: why should global banks enter into the Islamic banking market in a Muslim minority country? The answer to this question can be gleaned from the fact that finding growth and prosperity is a pressing issue in virtually all financial institutions worldwide. If the global financial institutions are searching for new ways to grow, reaching the ethnic minority customers should be a priority for them (Emslie et al. 2007). They should assess the appeal of the Indian financial service sector and investigate the possibility of developing new financial services for the Muslim minority customer, because this very large customer segment has been neglected for far too long. In the next section, we review the process of developing new services that can be applied for developing Shariah-compliant new services for the Muslim minority customers.

New service development process

Use of a systematic process for developing new financial services is considered as a key success factor (e.g. Cooper and Edgett 1996; Edgett 1994; Storey and Easingwood 1993). Therefore, several studies have proposed formal development models for developing new services. One development model described eight stages in developing new products in the financial and health services industries (Bowers 1987; 1989). This model for services is similar to Booz et al.'s (1982) model of tangible product development, although the service characteristics of intangibility, heterogeneity, perishability and inseparability set services apart from tangible goods (Shostack 1977). Therefore, recognizing these unique characteristics of services, Scheuing and Johnson (1989) proposed several new stages for service development and expanded the model to fifteen stages. Later, Alam and Perry (2002) proposed a more simplified and improved model for financial services containing ten development stages, which seem to capture the intricacies of NSD very well. The ten stages in this model are: strategic planning, idea generation, idea screening, business analysis, formation of cross functional team, product design and process/system design, personnel training, product testing and pilot run, test marketing and commercialization. This model also suggests that customers' input into the new services should be obtained throughout the development process. Hence, the literature of customer interaction is reviewed next.

Customer interaction in new service development

Over the last few decades, there has been a growing recognition among scholars and managers that customer interaction during new product or service development represents a source of competitive advantage. Therefore, several empirical studies have investigated the benefits of customer interaction in both new product and service development and report that customer input may lead to high-quality innovations (e.g. Alam 2002; 2006; Gruner and Homburg 2000).

As buyers of current and future new services, the customers may contribute to all the stages of NSD, from idea generation to commercialization. For instance, Gruner and Homburg (2000) studied customer interaction in tangible product development and reported that customer interaction during the early stages of a development process significantly influenced the performance of new products. Therefore, they argued for intense interaction between customers and product developers during the innovation process. Likewise in the case of NSD, Alam (2002) suggested that the intensity of service producer-customer interactions during the idea generation stage should be higher than all other stages. He also suggested that customer interaction results in important benefits such as reduced cycle time, superior services and customer education. In addition, Alam (2006) reports that customer interaction during the fuzzy front end (i.e. the first three stages of idea generation, idea screening and concept development) are more important than other later stages. Most firms have many different types of customers each with a unique set of characteristics and needs. Thus a key question arises: what types of customers should be selected for interaction? A firm may obtain input from the customers with whom they have a close relationship because confidentiality can be a major issue. A service manager can trust close customers to keep sensitive information confidential. Close customers may also display their commitment in conducting NSD activities efficiently. In summary, formal NSD process and customer interaction are two important strategic choices in any NSD decision strategy. These two key issues are applied in the case studies reported in this chapter.

How to develop new services for the minority customers?

This chapter is based on several case studies of NSD and customer interaction employed by multinational financial institutions providing Shariah-compliant and other diverse ranges of financial services to the minority Muslim customers in India. These financial institutions wanted to tap into a neglected market segment of the Muslim minority customers by developing new services. The managers of these banks, using the recent changes in the RBI's ruling on Shariah-compliant products as an opportunity, decided to increase their customer base by offering new Shariah-compliant services. However, to be successful, managers recognized that they would need to adopt a new and unique approach to service innovation. For example, they realized the need to obtain inputs from Muslim customers for the new services because of the unique needs of this minority group. In all the cases, the research team applied the ten-step comprehensive NSD process of Alam and Perry (2002) to develop new Shariah-compliant services. The companies participating in the case studies also interacted with the minority Muslim customers to obtain their input for the new services. During the case studies we followed several actual NSD projects in real time and interviewed the managers and customers and analyzed several documents and archival records. Based on the cases studied, we have identified several key issues related to NSD and customer interaction that a service firm must consider while developing new financial services for the minority customers in India and other parts of the world.

Which stages of new service development are important?

Service managers are required to develop new services that meet the growing needs of the ethnic Muslim customers in India. To achieve this objective, they need to follow a structured NSD process model as reported in the literature; particularly the one containing ten NSD stages proposed by Alam and Perry (2002). Service managers may conduct all the above ten stages of the NSD model, although they should put more emphasis on the idea generation, idea screening, service design and process system design, service testing and commercialization stages. Overall the management attention seems to be most critical for idea generation than any other stages of the development process. One reason is that the managers must gain an in-depth understanding of the needs of the minority customers that are vastly different from the other mainstream majority customers. Next, the test marketing is another important stage because banks needed to obtain key information about the new services potential, viability and other marketing information prior to its final launch. During the case studies, several bank managers reported that a large number of their Muslim customers routinely (a) do not invest in mutual funds with a debt component, (b) donate the interest earned on their salary savings accounts to the charity and (c) use zero interest current accounts instead of high yielding and interest bearing savings account. These phenomena buttress the argument that many Muslim customers are in fact creating their own methods to develop Shariah-compliant financial services. Thus, customer interaction during NSD becomes a key strategic choice for many service firms, as discussed next.

Process of customer interaction

Overall, customers can be involved in most of the ten stages of NSD reported previously in this chapter. However, the three initial NSD stages, including idea generation, service and system design, and service testing/pilot run, are more important than other stages for the purpose of customer interaction. In particular, the customer input into the stage of idea generation is more important and complex than in other later stages. Therefore, service managers should interact with the minority customers more intensely in the earlier stages of the NSD process. Additionally, the interaction with customers is also more intense during the last three stages of service design, test marketing and commercialization of the development process. Thus, the beginning and end of a NSD process are considered to be crucial. In contrast, the intensity of interaction is very low at the business analysis and strategic planning stages of the development process. In summary, the service managers need to be more proactive in collaborating with the Muslim customers from idea generation to the launch of their new services.

Muslim customers can perform a number of activities and provide valuable inputs into all the stages of NSD process as shown in the table below. A detailed analysis of Table 13.1 shows that the customers can contribute to most of the stages of NSD process. However, the number of activities is the highest in the initial two stages of idea generation and idea screening. This is followed by service design, service testing, test marketing and commercialization stages. Service managers can use this detail of customer activities as a checklist of the customer interaction activities for their NSD projects.

Modes of customer interaction

A service firm can solicit input from ethnic customers through several interaction modes as reported in the literature (e.g. Alam 2002): observations, management retreat, focus group, brainstorming, in-depth interviews and team meetings. Essentially, there are six customer interaction tactics that are particularly critical to developing an effective interaction strategy: (1) conducting several initial face-to-face interviews and team meetings for idea generation and screening, (2) conducting innovation retreats, summits and mini conferences for new service concept development that may uncover customers' latent or unspoken needs, (3) increasing the amount of communication and informal interactions among the front-line employees/bank officers and Muslim customers. This also underscores the need for managers to foster a culture of idea hunting among front-line employees of their respective firms, (4) developing a

Table 13.1 Activities performed by the customers at various stages of the NSD process

NSD stages	Activities performed by the minority customers
1. Strategic planning	Limited feedback on proposed plan for new service development.
2. Idea generation	Describe needs, problems and possible solutions; suggest desired features, benefits and preference in a new service via brainstorming or focus group sessions; identify financial problems not solved by the existing services; evaluate existing services by suggesting likes and dislikes; identify gaps in the market; provide a new service wish list.
3. Idea screening	Suggest rough sales guide and market size of various new service ideas; rate the liking, preference and purchase intents of all the new service concepts; critically react to the concepts by analysing how they would meet customers' needs; compare the concepts with competitor's offerings; examine the overall saleability of a new service.
4. Business analysis	Limited feedback on financial data, including profitability of the concepts, competitors' data.
5. Formation of cross functional team	Join top management in selecting team members.
6. Service design and process/system design	Jointly develop initial service blueprints; review and evaluate the initial service blueprints to crystallize the concepts; suggest improvements by identifying fail points in service delivery; observe a mock service delivery process by the key contact employees; participate in a simulated service delivery process as a customer; compare their wish list with the proposed initial service blueprints.
7. Personnel training	Observe and participate in mock service delivery process; suggest improvements.
8. Service testing and pilot run	Participate in a simulated service delivery processes; suggest final improvements and design change.
9. Test marketing	Comments and feedback on various aspects of the marketing plan; detailed comments about their satisfaction with marketing mixes; suggest desired improvements.
10. Commercialization	Adopt the service as a trial; feedback about overall performance of the service along with desired improvements, if any; word of mouth communications to other potential users.

close relationship with customers who are experts and innovative, (5) holding periodic progress update meetings to remain up-to-date on new developments and emerging needs. While the initial meeting sets the stage in building trust and establishing a close relationship, continual efforts to increase communications serve to reinforce and expand these behaviours that are so crucial to effective NSD and (6) using customer interaction strategy to educate customers about the new services or to develop a long-term relationship.

Criteria for customer selection

When selecting the customer for the purpose of interaction, existing relationships with the customers and their expertise and knowledge are the key selection criteria because the customers are required to act as development partners and co-developers of new services. Therefore, we recommend that the managers target customers with strong ties for the purpose of interaction because commitment and trust are very important considerations in any customer interaction strategy. Customers with strong ties are also highly motivated to provide input and ideas for NSD. Furthermore, expert and knowledgeable customers already exist among Muslim minority groups and only need to be identified (instead of being 'grown' from the innovative effort itself). These customers will willingly provide their input if they feel part of a team and believe that they are influencing a firm's innovation process. Because they stand to benefit from the new services, the ethnic customers are willing to participate actively in the NSD process, bringing in required resources, expertise and information.

Cultural challenges in developing new services for the minority customers

Service managers should be cognizant of several cultural factors that may impact the customer interaction process in a NSD project. The way of thinking among Muslim customers is analytical rather than holistic in nature. There is a general tendency among the customers to strive to solve problems through the use of logic rather than relying on finding a common middle ground. A related implication is that this style of thinking promotes never-ending debate and argumentation. They find it all too easy to discover flaws in other customers' arguments. Thus there is a need for a strong team leader who will step in to resolve any unending debates and move forward with the common tasks of developing new services. Customers may be very agreeable on some occasions and make concerted efforts to find common ground, while on other occasions they may be singularly focused on attaining their own goals. In this situation, service managers are advised to take a firm stand on the need to focus on common goal, which is obtaining input from the customers to generate new service ideas and ultimately converting those ideas into new services.

Hall and Hall (1990) identify three dimensions of culture: high/low context, high/low space and monochronic/polychronic use of time. They argue that in high space culture such as the United States, people that are engaged in conversation will assume a wider social distance. But in low space culture such as Asia the expected social distance is much narrower. Similarly, low-context cultures communicate in direct, explicit and informative ways. In contrast, in high context cultures, messages include other communicative cues such as body language, nonverbal communications and the use of silence. The concept of monochronic and polychronic time is used to describe two contrasting ways of handling time in different cultures. Typically, monochronic time people do one thing at a time. Polychronic time people, on the other hand, like to be involved in many things at once and are committed to socializing and personal relationships.

Applying one of these dimensions of cultural values to India and its minority customers, it becomes apparent that India is a polychronic country and because of the polychronic use of time by the Muslim customers, service managers may face meeting scheduling problems. It is common among the Indian customers to either cancel the interviews at the last minute or come rather late to the team meetings. Because of these scheduling issues, NSD projects may be delayed. Second, in contrary to the general belief about the polychronic nature of the Indians customers, the Muslim customers may provide detailed and explicit information about new services which can be very helpful in generating innovative service ideas. Third, as with most high-context cultures, the relationships may play a key role in customer selection and the overall success of customer interaction strategy. Therefore, the service firms might consider investing time and resources in developing a close relationship with their customers. It will assist in selecting the right customers and gaining their co-operation for NSD projects.

Problems in customer interaction and new service development process

The service managers can however be cognizant of various problems and risks associated with developing new Shariah-compliant services with customer interaction. For instance, we provide a caution to service developers that listening to customers too closely may create a risk of over-customization of new services. To avoid this risk, the emerging trends in the marketplace as a whole need to be weighed against individual customer suggestions. Thus, the new service concepts must be tested with the larger group of customers that are representative of the ethnic population.

Locating appropriate minority customers for interaction is another major problem because an intimate knowledge of the market and customer contacts is necessary. Additionally, customers may be disinclined to co-operate because of the conflicting objectives and intents of managers versus customers. Managers typically have the objective of developing a service that would yield maximum profit, whereas customers have the objective of developing a service that would serve his/her needs. Some Muslim customers may need extra motivation for their co-operation. Both monetary and non-monetary incentives can be useful to get full customer co-operation. Managers can also solve the above problems by selecting the customers with whom their firm has a close relationship. These problems may also be solved by entrusting the task of customer selection to the product champions in the firm because product champions are often well connected to the industry and may have forged relationships with customers already. By virtue of their position and connections in the industry, product champions may be able to more easily identify key customers and get appropriate assistance from them.

Implications for managers

Global financial service firms can achieve growth and prosperity by integrating ethnic minority customers into their NSD programs. Marginalization of ethnic customers and recent initiatives by the Indian government to solve the marginalization and exclusion problems offer opportunities for many service firms. In addition, slowed population growth of the majority group coupled with the population increase of the minority group means it is time to target this growing niche more aggressively. Financial service firms that can successfully develop new services for the Muslim minority market will create a win-win situation for their business and for their customers. Our findings have implications for other parts of the world with sizable Muslim population as well, because the growth in Islamic banking and the neglect of minority customers are global phenomena (Bershidsky 2013; El-Bassiouny 2014).

The ten-step NSD model is a good starting point for idea generation and introduction of the new financial services for minority customers. Despite the use of NSD model, there may be uncertainty on the ultimate shape and make of the new services. Some of these uncertainties can be alleviated by involving the minority customers in the NSD process. The managers need to interact extensively with their customers to obtain key input and information as detailed in this chapter. The customers can help crystallize service concepts and critically evaluate the overall service delivery blueprints and final offerings that are relevant to their needs.

Interaction with minority customers also offers two additional advantages: (1) customer interaction is a way of developing a relationship with the customers because minority customers respond more favourably to products and services targeted exclusively at them (Grier and Deshpandé 2001) and (2) customer interaction may also dispel the perception of exclusion and marginalization of the minority customers, a problem experienced by the Muslims and other ethnic minorities in many parts of the world (Knight et al. 2009; Wilson and Liu 2011).

Therefore, we have proposed a systematic process to search and involve minority customers in NSD. The task of interaction can be assigned to the product champions belonging to the minority community because of their contact and knowledge of the market. Managers may take note of this process and apply it to their NSD programs.

Implications for policy makers

India is ripe for the formal introduction and massive penetration of financial services among the growing ethnic Muslim minority population. This process will contribute to greater financial stabilization and open the door for better inclusion of the economically weak and downtrodden minority community. In particular, Indian policy makers will be interested to increase the flow of finance to the Muslim community for several reasons. First, it will reduce the economic disparities between the Muslim minority and other religious and ethnic groups leading to the reduction of poverty in the country, which has been the slogan of the Indian government for many years. Second, Islamic finance will further boost the Indian economy because it will result in the free flow of finance to the millions of new and emerging customers. Third, it will introduce a new mode of banking in India, making the Indian financial market more robust, competitive and mature. Finally, it will offer diplomatic advantages in dealing with the Muslim-dominant and rich nations in the Middle East, especially to attract more lucrative foreign direct investment in the country. For example, due to the several geopolitical reasons, many investors from the Middle East are now reluctant to invest in institutions based in Europe and North America. India can easily offer a viable alternative to those investors, once it opens the door for Shariah-compliant services and establishes itself as a regional hub of Islamic banking and finance.

Future research agenda

Although the introduction of new Shariah-compliant services poses political, regulatory and administrative constraints to many service firms worldwide, developing new services for ethnic customers is a worthwhile venture and needs to be investigated further. Indeed, there is a dearth of infrastructure and technical knowhow for managing Shariah-compliant banking worldwide. This chapter is an initial attempt to forge better understanding of the process of developing new services for the ethnic minority customers. There is a need to replicate this study in other countries and in the context of other ethnic minority groups to further contribute to the literature of both NSD and ethnic marketing. Identifying within-country differences in the NSD process that might be due to ethnic and cultural factors is another research issue that deserves more attention. In this chapter we have focused only on one type of service, the financial services, so therefore further studies of NSD across different service categories and tangible products is another avenue of further research.

In summary, many firms are discovering that previously ignored ethnic customers are growing in power because of the rapid increase of minority population in various parts of the world (Geng and Choudhury 2002). Yet ethnic marketing as an area remains largely in need of empirical research. Particularly, there is much work yet to be done in the area of NSD for the ethnic customers because, as the ethnic groups grow in size and purchasing power, they will demand that the firms be responsive to their needs for financial and other types of services. We believe that this chapter is only a catalyst for future research in a field growing in theoretical and practical importance. It is hoped that the themes that emerged from this chapter will help lay the foundation upon which later analysis and research of this topic can be built.

References

Ackerman, D. and Tellis, G. (2001) 'Can culture affect prices? A cross-cultural study of shopping and retail prices'. *Journal of Retailing*, 77(1): 57–82.

Ahmed, H. (2011) *Product Development in Islamic Banks*. Edinburgh: Edinburgh University Press.

Ahmed, S. S. (2013, October) 'Asia focus: Sun rises in the east'. *Islamic Finance News Asia*, 7–8.

Alam, I. (2002) 'An exploratory investigation of user involvement in new service development'. *Journal of the Academy of Marketing Science*, 30(3): 250–61.

Alam, I. (2006) 'Removing the fuzziness from the fuzzy front-end of service innovations through customer interactions'. *Industrial Marketing Management*, 35(4): 468–80.

Alam, I (2013) 'Customer interaction in service innovation: Evidence from India'. *International Journal of Emerging Markets*, 8(1): 41–64.

Alam, I. and Perry C. (2002) 'A customer-oriented new service development process'. *Journal of Service Marketing*, (16)6: 515–34.

Bagsiraj, M. G. I (2003) *Islamic Financial Institutions of India: Progress, Problems and Prospects*. Jeddah, Saudi Arabia: Scientific Publishing Centre.

Bershidsky, L (2013) 'Islamic finance can save the world'. *Bloomberg News*, October 29.

Black, H., Robinson, B. L, Schlottmann, A. M, Schweitzer, R. L, (2003) 'Is race an important factor in bank-customer preferences? The case of mortgage lending'. *Journal of Real Estate Finance & Economics*, 26(1): 5–26.

Booz, E., Allen, J. and Hamilton, C. (1982) *New Product Management for the 1980s*. New York, NY: Booz Allen Hamilton Inc.

Bose, S. and Yedukumar, P. (2013) 'Finally waking up to Islamic finance opportunities'. *Islamic Finance Asia*, February 15.

Bowers, M. R. (1987) 'Developing new services for hospitals: A suggested model'. *Journal of Health Care Marketing*, 7(2): 35–44.

Bowers, M. R. (1989) 'Developing new services: Improving the process makes it better'. *Journal of Services Marketing*, 3(1): 15–20.

Burton, D. (2000) 'Ethnicity, identity and marketing: A critical review'. *Journal of Marketing Management*, 16: 853–77.

Chaudhry, S and Crick, D (2004) 'Attempts to more effectively target ethnic minority customers: The case of HSBC and its South Asian business unit in the UK'. *Strategic Change*, 13(1): 37–49.

Chin, V., Storholm K., Vathje, S. Razali, N. H and Badi, M. (2008) *Islamic Banking, Can you Afford to Ignore It?* Boston, MA: The Boston Consulting Group Inc.

Chittenden, O. (2010) *The Future of Money*. London: Virgin Books.

Colvin, G. (2009) *The Upside of the Downturn: Ten management strategies to prevail in the recession and thrive in the aftermath*. New York, NY: Portfolio.

Cooper, R. G. and Edgett, S. J. (1996) 'Critical success factors for new financial services'. *Marketing Management*, 5(3): 26–37.

Craig, C. S. and Douglas, S. P. (2006) 'Beyond national culture: Implications of cultural dynamics for consumer research'. *International Marketing Review*, 23(3): 322–42.

de Jong, J. P. J and Vermeulen, P. A. M (2003) 'Organizing successful New Service Development: A literature review'. *Management Decision*, 41(9): 844–58.

Edgett, S. J. (1994) 'The traits of successful new service development'. *Journal of Services Marketing*, (8)3: 40–9.

El-Bassiouny, N. (2014) 'The one-billion-plus marginalization: Toward a scholarly understanding of Islamic consumers'. *Journal of Business Research*, 67(2): 42–9.

Emslie, L., Bent, R. and Seaman, C. (2007) 'Missed opportunities? Reaching the ethnic consumer market'. *International Journal of Consumer Studies*, 3(2): 168–173.

Fazlie, M. B. J (1995) *Muslims in India: Past and Present*. Jeddah, Saudi Arabia: Abul Qasim Publishing House.

Ferguson, N. (2011) *Civilization: The West and the Rest*. London: Allen Lane.

Ford, N. (2012) 'The rise and rise of Islamic finance'. *African Banker*, September, 24.

Geng, C and Choudhury P. (2002) 'Marketplace diversity and cost-effective marketing strategies'. *The Journal of Consumer Marketing* 19(1): 54–73.

Goldman, A. and Hino, H. (2005) 'Supermarkets vs. traditional retail stores: Diagnosing the barriers to supermarkets' market share growth in an ethnic minority community'. *Journal of Retailing and Consumer Services*, 12: 273–284.

Grier, S. and Deshpandé, R. (2001) 'Social dimensions of consumer distinctiveness: The influence of social status on group identify and advertising persuasion'. *Journal of Marketing Research*, 38(2): 216–224.

Gruner K. E and Homburg C. (2000) 'Does customer interaction enhance new product success?'. *Journal of Business Research*, 49(1): 1–14.

Hall, E. T. and Hall, R. M. (1990) *Understanding Cultural Differences: Germans, French and Americans.* Yarmouth, ME: Intercultural Press.

Hammond, C (2012) 'Could India allow offshore Islamic bonds?' *Asia Money*, November.

Horne, D. K (1997) 'Mortgage lending, race and model specification'. *Journal of Financial Services Research*, 11: 43–68.

Ihsanoglu, E. (2011) *The Islamic World in the New Century: The Organization of the Islamic Conference, 1969–2009.* London: Hurst & Company.

Jamal, A. (2003) 'Marketing in a multicultural world: The interplay of marketing, ethnicity and consumption'. *European Journal of Marketing*, 37(11/12): 1599–620.

Jamal, A. (2005) 'Playing to win: An explorative study of marketing strategies of small ethnic retail entrepreneurs in the UK'. *Journal of Retailing and Consumer Services*, 12: 1–13.

Jamal, A., Peattie, S. and Peattie, K. (2012) 'Ethnic minority consumers' responses to sales promotions in the packaged food market'. *Journal of Retailing & Consumer Services*, 19(1): 98–108.

Jamal, A. and Shukor, S. (2014) 'Antecedents and outcomes of interpersonal influences and the role of acculturation: The case of young British-Muslims'. *Journal of Business Research*, 67: 237–45.

Jaw, C., Lo, J., and Lin, H. (2010) 'The determinants of new service development: Service characteristics, market orientation, and actualizing innovation effort'. *Technovation*, 30(4): 265–77.

Johne, A. and Storey, C. (1998) 'New Service Development: A review of the literature and annotated bibliography'. *European Journal of Marketing*, 32(3/4): 184–251.

Khan, M. M. and Bhatti, M. I. (2008) *Development in Islamic Banking.* Hampshire, UK: Palgrave MacMillan.

Khan, O (2004) 'A proposed introduction of Islamic banking in India'. *International Journal of Islamic Financial Services*, 5(4): 1–10.

Knight, J., Mitchell, B. and Gao, H. (2009) 'Riding out the Muhammad cartoons crisis: Contrasting strategies and outcomes'. *Long Range Planning*, 42(1): 6–22.

Lee, K., Kim, H. and Vohs, K. (2011) 'Stereotype threat in the marketplace: Consumer anxiety and purchase intentions'. *Journal of Consumer Research*, 38(2): 343–357.

Long, K. (2013) 'The global growth of Islamic finance'. *Trade Finance*, October.

Lyons, R. K, Chatman, J. A. and Joyce, C. K. (2007) 'Innovation in services: Corporate culture and investment banking'. *California Management Review*, 50(1): 174–191.

Mcaughtry, L. (2013) 'Late to the table: Which Asian nations are going hungry at the feast?' *Islamic Finance Asia*, October 7.

Munnell, A. H., Browne, L. E, McEnearny, J. and Tootel, G. M. B (1996) 'Mortgage lending in Boston: Interpreting HMDA data'. *American Economic Review*, 86: 25–53.

Ouellet, J. (2007) 'Consumer racism and its effects on domestic cross-ethnic product purchase: An empirical test in the United States, Canada, and France'. *Journal of Marketing*, 71(1): 113–128.

Peñaloza, L. and Gilly, M. C. (1999) 'Marketer acculturation: The changer and the changed'. *Journal of Marketing*, 63: 84–104.

Pires, G. and Stanton, J. (2000) 'Marketing services to ethnic consumers in culturally diverse markets: Issues and implications'. *Journal of Services Marketing*, 14(7): 607–18.

Pires, G., Stanton, J., and Stanton, P. (2011) 'Revisiting the substantiality criterion: From ethnic marketing to market segmentation'. *Journal of Business Research*, 64(9): 988–996.

Rossiter J. R. and Chan A. M. (1998) 'Ethnicity in business and consumer behavior'. *Journal of Business Research*, 42(2): 127–34.

Russell, C. and Russell, D. (2010) 'Guilty by stereotypic association: Country animosity and brand prejudice and discrimination'. *Marketing Letters*, 21(4): 413–25.

Sachar Committee Report (2006) *Social, Economic and Educational Status of the Muslim of India.* Prime Minister's High Level Committee, Cabinet Secretariat, Government of India.

Sarker, M. A. A. (1999) 'Islamic banking in Bangladesh: Performance, problems and prospects'. *International Journal of Islamic Financial Services*, 1(3): 1–21.

Scheuing, E. E. and Johnson, E. M. (1989) 'A proposed model for New Service Development'. *Journal of Services Marketing*, 3(2): 25–35.

Shostack, G. L. (1977) 'Breaking free from product marketing'. *Journal of Marketing*, 41(2): 73–80.

Siddiqui, N. (2006) 'Islamic banking and finance in theory and practice: A survey of the arts'. *Islamic Economics Studies*. Jeddah, Saudi Arabia: King Abdul Aziz University.

Storey, C. and Easingwood, C. J. (1993) 'The impact of the New Product Development project on the success of financial services'. *Service Industries Journal*, 13(3): 40–54.

Volk, S., Pudelko M. (2010) 'Challenges and opportunities for Islamic retail banking in the European context: Lessons to be learnt from a British–German comparison'. *Journal of Financial Services Marketing*, 15: 191–02.

Wilson, J. and Liu, J. (2011) 'The challenges of Islamic branding: Navigating emotions and Halal'. *Journal of Islamic Marketing*, 2(1): 28–42.

14

Market segmentation by ethnicity

Is it really feasible?

Andrew Lindridge

Introduction

Cultural, historical and social differences and similarities between and within ethnic groups present both an opportunity and difficulty for marketers. In this chapter we relate the topic of ethnicity to the marketing strategy of segmentation. This approach views the market as consisting of heterogeneous groups that can be identified and separated into homogeneous segments by their different needs and benefits sought. By identifying these differing segments, organizations can decide whether or not to target their resources at these segments in similar or different ways to achieve their marketing objectives.

Applying market segmentation to ethnic groups is not a recent marketing initiative. Indeed, by the early 1900s North American marketers were readily developing market segments based around ethnic differences aimed at encouraging assimilation into American society. For example, Halter (2000) notes how Jewish migrants to America were encouraged to cook and consume pastry-orientated foods symbolic of American culture. However, as these recipes often included the prohibited use of pork fat, the brand Crisco responded by launching a product that offered assimilating Jews a kosher vegetable-derived fat substitute.

Where initial market segmentation offerings encouraged ethnic group assimilation, by the 1970s a combination of commercial pressures and environmental changes led to the market encouraging ethnic group differences. The origins of this change partially lied in the demise of the mass market and consumers seeking different products required new, alternative, markets to sustain mass production and deliver profitability. Ethnicity and its related differences offered such a market, resulting in organizations using market segmentation to reach differing ethnic groups. Complimenting this market change were various socio-political changes. First, the introduction of legislation by various countries supported and encouraged ethnic equality. For example, the Ethnic Heritage Act (1974) in the USA supported funding initiatives that encouraged ethnic group distinctiveness through protecting their cultures and histories. Second, the 1960s and 70s witnessed an increased politicization of ethnic groups. As Halter (2000) notes, the late 1960s in America witnessed a political outburst of oppressed ethnic groups starting with the Black Nationalism, followed by the American Indian movement and Chicano militancy; movements that demanded recognition and self-determination within a White dominated society.

By the twenty-first century, the allure of market segmentation by ethnicity had become a mainstream part of marketing education, practice and research. Yet this allure is was not without its critics. Fennell *et al.* (1992), in a scathing review entitled 'Do Hispanics Constitute a Market Segment?', argued that many market segmentation variables applied to the Latino market, such as brand loyalty, were not valid. Instead what marketers were effectively undertaking was product differentiation. Product differentiation relies upon increasing product attractiveness for the target audience by adding value to the consumer experience and/or distinguishing the product from its competitors. The relationship between product differentiation and market segmentation is problematic owing to their inherent similarities (Dickson and Ginter 1997).

We can understand these similarities through the 2012 announcement by Proctor and Gamble that its 'Gain' washing detergent brand had become its twenty-third brand to generate annual sales revenue of US$1 billion. While this was a remarkable achievement in its own right, the fact that the brand is solely sold in North America made this result even more outstanding. Originally introduced in 1969 as an enzyme-driven stain removing detergent, its increasing sales success ensured it became America's second best-selling detergent. As Kevin Burke, P&G Laundry Marketing Director (PR Newswire 2012) noted:

> Gain consumers demonstrate an extraordinary passion for the brand. We work hard to understand our Gain consumers and work even harder to deliver the amazing scent experience they find in Gain. That's the secret to Gain's remarkable growth.

While there may be many reasons for Gain's success, perhaps the biggest reason can be attributed to Gain deliberately targeting African American and Latino market segments through targeted promotions. However, the use of English and Spanish narratives on the packaging also suggests that Gain is using an undifferentiated approach to ethnic differences within the market by ignoring ethnic differences between English and Spanish speakers. To what extent then is Gain's increasing popularity attributable to market segmenting ethnicity or simply undertaking effective product differentiation?

The answer to this question lies within market segmentation principals and their applicability to ethnic groups and forms the remainder of this chapter. In reviewing the feasibility of market segmenting ethnic groups we take a traditional, managerial perspective. (For those wanting an alternative perspective to ethnic market segmentation, such as using cultural frames, Visconti and Hughes [2011] offer a satisfying read). We begin by reviewing the market segmentation criteria, discussing the appropriateness of various market segmentation variables. This is followed by a discussion on the need to consider acculturation in ethnic groups' market segmentation. We then conclude with the key steps marketing managers should follow for successful ethnic market segmentation.

The market segment process

Dickson and Ginter (1987), in a seminal paper on market segmentation, lamented the continued inability of marketing academics and practitioners to specifically define with clarity what market segmentation is. Taking a historical perspective, they argued that market segmentation is identifiable with differing consumer groups having differing needs and levels of demand. These segments are characterized as having minimal within-group differences, in contrast to other segments. As each segment has differing needs and demand levels, organizations can allocate their marketing resources more effectively. By segmenting the market, organizations are able to satisfy segment needs by becoming more market orientated (Albert 2003; Freytag and Clarke 2001) and competitive (Wong and Saunders 1993).

To undertake market segmentation a number of criteria need to be satisfied. These and other relevant issues regarding ethnicity and market segmentation are summarized in Table 14.1 (Dibb *et al.* 2006; Lancaster and Massingham 2001; Kotler and Armstrong 2008).

If an organization is satisfied that an ethnic group can be segmented using the previous criteria, it must then decide how to proceed. There are four groups of variables that an organization can use to segment ethnic groups: demographic, geographic, psychographic and behaviouristic. Each of these market segmentation variables, as we shall see, offer opportunities and limitations to segmenting ethnic groups.

Demographic variables

Demographic variables represent the most obvious approach to market segmenting ethnic groups. Indeed, Dibb *et al.*'s (2006) classification of ethnicity and race, within this category, reflects a widely held perspective of their relevance to market segmentation (for example: Donthu and Cherian 1994; Cui 1997; Jamal 2003). Yet using ethnicity and race as marketing segmentation variables is problematic.

The term 'race' is widely used, and sometimes inconsistently, to categorize geographically separate populations (such as 'Africans'), a cultural group (such as 'Hindus') and nationality (such as 'German') (Singh 1997). Scientific advances in DNA analysis (for example, Hirschman and Panther-Yates 2008) have discredited the concept of race, with studies indicating greater racial differences within supposed racial groups (such as African) than between differing racial groups (Zuckerman 1990). Indeed the use of the term 'race' within cultural dialogues is politically problematic in Western societies (Molnar 1992) largely because racial categorizations are often determined by an external source (Betancourt and Lopez 1993). One external source would be an organization determining market segments based upon racial characteristics, which may be prone to accusations of racism (Wilk 2006). For example, racially categorizing all Far East Asians as a market segment of 'rice eaters' based upon higher rice consumption ignores important cultural differences. Furthermore, when we consider the earlier market segmentation criteria, measurability becomes an issue owing to its reliance on grouping individuals with differing needs into homogenous groups. For example, it is highly unlikely that all Far East Asians, as a racial group, share the same needs for a product, let alone the same religion or national identity. Instead, ethnicity as a market segmentation variable may be more appropriate.

The emergence of ethnicity arose from the belief that differences in humans should not be ascribed to racial categories, but instead ethnic categories (Huxley *et al.* 1935). The term ethnicity is derived from the Greek words 'ethnos' referring to a nation or a tribe, and 'ethnikos', referring to a national (Betancourt and Lopez 1993). These two words form the basis of typical definitions of ethnicity as a nation or a group who share one or all of the following shared variables: culture, nationality, language, religion or common descent. Alternative definitions of ethnicity locate the individual from a minority perspective and status. Researchers such as Weber (1968) and Venkatesh (1995) note that ethnicity is an ideologically fashioned term describing a group that is culturally or physically outside the dominant group.

Yet applying ethnicity to categorize and segment a market is problematic owing to such categorizations being imprecise and arbitrary 'social constructions rather than natural entities that are simply "out there" in the real world' (Waters and Eschbach 1995, p. 421). The need to categorize ethnic minorities by natural entities recognizes changes that may reflect wider societal changes,

Table 14.1 Market segmentation criteria and applicability to ethnic minority markets

Segmentation criteria	Relevance	Suitability of criteria for ethnic minorities
Measurability	Can the market segment be measured in terms of size, profitability, purchasing power and needs?	Applying measurability to ethnic groups is problematic owing to a lack of appropriate demographic information. For example, whilst Britain and the United States measure ethnicity, France does not. Information regarding purchasing power is often unavailable, resulting in speculation.
Differentiability	Market segment requires group homogeneity and notable differences when compared to other groups.	At simplistic level differences between various ethnic groups ensures differentiability. So, a British-born Indian would be expected to classify with this ethnic group and not with a British-White ethnic group. Differentiability, however, is problematic because it assumes that ethnic groups, such as British-born Indians, are similar. As we will explore later in this chapter, this is not necessarily true.
Accessibility	A market segment must be easily accessible allowing for cost-efficient distribution of the organization's product.	Ethnic groups, to varying extents, live in concentrated urban areas. This geographical concentration may ensure accessibility.
Exhaustiveness	Each customer can only be attributed to one market segment only.	The extent that an individual can be attributed solely to a segment based upon their ethnicity is problematic. Acculturation, as we discuss later in this chapter, in particular suggests that exhaustiveness may not be possible.
Stability	Organizations seek market segments that will not radically change or break up into smaller, less profitable segments.	Stability is problematic for market segmenting ethnic groups. If an ethnic minority market segment is determined by physical characteristics, such as skin colour, then these characteristics are unlikely to change for a millennium, ensuring market segment stability. However, when non-physical characteristics are considered, such as behaviour change arising from acculturation, then changes may result in ethnic market segments becoming unstable.
Profitability	A key marketing objective is maximizing an organization's profitability. Ethnic groups' market segment will only be relevant if it results in an appropriate return on investment on the resources invested in that market segment.	Whether an ethnic group's market segment is profitable is highly subjective. What is sufficiently profitable for one organization may not be for another. In some instances, ethnic groups may have a higher socio-economic status than others, but have a smaller population. Whether this group offers more profitability, as a market segment, than a poorer but larger ethnic group will be for individual organization's to decide.
Competition	Fewer competitors in a segment suggest a higher level of attractiveness for the organization. However, does fewer competitors indicate that the segment has not been previously identified, or because that segment offers little profitability?	What constitutes competition within an ethnic market segment may differ from other segments. For instance, a competitor in an ethnic market segment may be a local organization who understands the needs of that ethnic community. As we shall discuss later, in a study amongst Chinese Americans and White Americans, the former were more likely to shop at their local Chinese supermarket within their community than at a national supermarket chain.
Organizational capabilities	Does the organization have the capability and resources to satisfy the needs of the segment? If not then the organization should target other, more attractive, segments.	Targeting an ethnic group's market segment requires more than an organization's financial and human resources. The organization needs to ask itself whether it is open to understanding cultural and ethnic differences in a sensitive and empowering way. If it is incapable then the organization should perhaps look for alternative segments that match its capabilities.

such as differing education levels, geographical regions, generation of migration, and the size and composition of the ethnic community (Harrison *et al.* 1990). This argument then prohibits the use of ethnicity as a market segmentation variable using the stability criteria.

While organizations ideally should not use race and ethnicity as a segmentation variable it may still be relevant for some products. Products associated with religious beliefs or cultural festivals may still find some value in demographic segmentation. Foods specifically produced for religious festivals like Eid, or cultural ones such as Thanksgiving, may discover that consumer shared needs and values take precedence over ethnic differences.

Geographic variables

Differing geographic regions may result in differing needs and benefits sought from a product. At its most simplistic level, geographic regions are segmented according to population needs, such as India consuming skin lightening creams and European countries consuming sun tan lotion. Alternatively, differing ethnic groups' concentration in geographic regions, such as inner-cities, may offer small scale market segmentation opportunities. For instance, research indicates that many ethnic groups in the UK tend to experience lower levels of income, higher levels of unemployment and live in areas of higher socio-economic deprivation in inner-city areas (Clark and Drinkwater 2007; Modood *et al.* 1997). While poverty and its concentration in geographic areas may not initially appear to be an attractive market segmentation variable, it may offer some organizations a marketing opportunity.

Alternatively, countries and governments may actively create geographic areas that lend themselves to market segmentation of ethnic groups. For example, London's China Town based around Gerald Street arose partially from Chinese businesses locating there and local government's desire to develop a commercial and tourist attraction. Geographic concentration offers then opportunities for market segmentation measurability with segments potentially being of a substantial size, accessible because of their concentration and relatively stable (as ethnic minorities may choose to remain in a similar area), satisfying the earlier segmentation criteria.

Psychographic variables

Psychographic variables segment the market based upon differences regarding consumer lifestyles and/or ethnocentrism.

Consumer lifestyle refers to the activities, attitudes, opinions and values that an individual or a group identify with and is typically measured using the Activities, Interests, Opinions (AIO) Scale (Wells and Tigert 1977). An ethnic group that has differing AIO's will consume products for differing reasons, therefore constituting a separate market segment and warranting the attention of marketers. For example, African Americans are disproportionately more likely to suffer from smoking-related diseases than White Americans, even though they smoke less (HHS 1998). A difference attributed to African Americans differing AIO's leading to a higher tendency to smoke menthol cigarettes; a combination of tobacco mixed with mint oil (i.e. menthol), which anesthetizes the throat from the burning effect of inhalation. The reasons for these lifestyle differences and why they represent a psychographic segment lies in a combination of historical/cultural factors and savvy marketing by tobacco organizations.

The cultural/historical associations with menthol cigarettes and African Americans lies in the latter's history of poverty and their inability to purchase medicines. Menthol cigarettes were deliberately misclassified by the tobacco industry not as a tobacco-based product but instead, owing to its anesthetic and cooling properties, as a cough suppressant (MentholKillsYou 2014). Poverty stricken African Americans in the 1920s unable to purchase expensive medicines were encouraged through marketing to positively view menthol cigarettes as a cheaper medicinal substitute. Smoking then served a medicinal need. Complimenting this deliberate misclassification of menthol cigarettes was the tobacco industry's classification of African Americans as a market segment. Cigarette brands such as B&W and Kool produced advertisements targeting African Americans located in poor socio-economic environments. For example, a study into Californian neighbourhoods with secondary schools found that as the proportion of African American secondary school students increased, this was accompanied by an increase in menthol cigarette advertising (Henriksen *et al.* 2011). In particular the Newport menthol cigarette brand was most likely to undertake promotional activities, including a lower selling price for a packet of cigarettes in these areas (Henriksen *et al.*). The effectiveness of using African Americans differing AIO's towards menthol cigarettes and tobacco organizations marketing activities is evident in Dauphinee *et al.*'s (2013) study revealing that African American youth are three times more likely to recognize the Newport menthol cigarette brand than youths from other ethnic groups.

Ethnic groups' relationship with food represents another important lifestyle difference to White society. For example, Delva, Johnston and O'Malley (2007), in a study among American youths, noted how non-White ethnic groups had a greater propensity for obesity. This lifestyle difference may be attributable to cultural differences, where higher body weight is not only associated with wealth but also femininity and sexual attractiveness (Ghannam 1997; Tovée *et al.* 2006). Consequently, Black ethnic groups drawn from Africa and the Caribbean tend to have more favourable attitudes towards body fat than their White counterparts (Furnham and Baguma 1994). While obesity may represent negative market segment variables for some ethnic groups, research also indicates some positive lifestyle variables. For instance, research has indicated that ethnic minorities tend to have healthier eating patterns compared to the White majority (Gibbens and Julian 2006; Sharma and Cruickshank 2001). A lifestyle difference that may be reflected in religious differences, such as Hindu religious doctrine discouraging meat consumption in favour of vegetarianism, among South Asians.

In contrast, ethnocentrism, which is associated with lifestyles, assesses the extent that an individual or their group judges, through comparing and contrasting, another culture or ethnic group. This judgment allows a group to define their own unique cultural identity (Andersen and Taylor 2006). From a marketing perspective, consumer ethnocentrism represents an individual and their group's attitudes and behaviours towards purchasing domestic versus foreign products (Shimp and Sharma 1987). Ethnocentrism, as a market segmentation tool, can be either encouraged directly by organizations or through socio-economic and cultural factors affecting consumers. An example of the former would be nationalistic marketing campaigns with products featuring labels stating 'Proudly made in America.'

Previous studies reflecting consumers' socio-economic and cultural factors support the use of lifestyle and ethnocentrism to segment a market, with two studies from Turkey illustrating their relevance. Researching the Turkish food market, Kavak and Gumuslouglu (2007) identified numerous ethnocentric market segments regarding food consumption. For example, when income was considered, the people in the segment with a higher income were more likely to be pro-Western (lifestyle) and less ethnocentric in their food consumption choices. In a similar study, Kucukemiroglu (1999) also identified differing market segments based upon lifestyle, with consumers belonging to the 'Liberals/trend setters' having lower ethnocentric tendencies, resulting in purchasing behaviours that were similar to consumers in Western societies.

In a rare study on ethnocentrism within a contrasting ethnic group, Goldberg (2012) studied the role of ethnocentrism among middle class Blacks living in South Africa – hence forth called 'Black Diamonds', a term used to describe South Africa's fast-growing, affluent Black middle class consumer segment (Ndanga *et al.* 2010). This choice of population is interesting because Black Diamonds represent a small, but important, growing segment in a society where wealth is still predominately held by White South Africans. Unlike Kavak and Gumuslouglu (2007) and Kucukemiroglu's (1999) studies in Turkey where higher levels of wealth equated to more Western centric behaviours, Goldberg's results differ markedly. Instead, Goldberg argues that moderately high levels of ethnocentric behaviour are evident with a consumption preference for South African products over imports. Although Goldberg (2012) provides no explanation for the reasons for this, one possibility may lie in feelings of Black Nationalism arising from South Africa's historical context of apartheid, with Black Diamonds asserting their new found socio-economic status, as a minority group, through identification with a Black South African identity.

The use of psychographic variables to market segment ethnic groups presents the recurring problem of within-group heterogeneity. Quite simply, individuals within an ethnic group will have differing AIO's that will affect their consumer behaviour. Consequently, the marketer is once again faced with the problem of identifying sufficient similarities within an ethnic group to ensure the market segment meets the earlier stated criteria. Consequently, psychographic variables infer a high level of heterogeneity within and between ethnic groups that fail to address the earlier market segmentation criteria.

Behaviouristic variables

Behaviouristic variables segment the market by assessing levels of price sensitivity, brand loyalty, benefits sought and how the product is used.

Using price sensitivity to market segment an ethnic group is supported by research. In a study from the U.S., Latinos were found to be more sensitive to price increases in cigarettes than Whites were, suggesting that the higher the price the less likely they were to smoke (Myers *et al.* 2012), while a lower price for internet providers is likely to encourage greater uptake from ethnic minorities (Joshi *et al.* 2012). Ackerman and Tellis (2001), in their study on the relationship between ethnicity, culture and price sensitivity among American Chinese and Whites, found that American Chinese cultural needs to handle food prior to purchase created an affiliation not only with the need to shop in Chinese-owned stores, but also encouraged lower price offerings. The authors attribute this price difference to cultural differences with Chinese shoppers who, regardless of their affluence, are more willing to spend time undertaking searches for the lowest prices.

In a similar vein, brand loyalty may also offer a valuable means of market segmenting ethnic groups. For example, in 2006 the American research firm 'Yankelovich' declared that:

> The ability to reach African Americans and Hispanic consumers in a way that truly strikes a chord and connects with their deep-seated cultural values and beliefs is critical . . . brands must show that they understand the ethnic consumer by crafting culturally appropriate and targeted messaging that speaks directly to them.
>
> *(c.f. from Reyes 2006)*

Part of this understanding lies in the need for brands to reflect differing ethnic groups needs and identities. Indeed Yankelovich claim that 58 per cent of Latinos and 55 per cent of African

Americans were brand loyal and were less inclined to purchase private label brands. Using brand loyalty as a market segmentation variable is also supported by Rickard (1994), who noted that American Latinos and Asians were not only brand loyal but tended to purchase higher-priced brands than their White counterparts.

The extent that ethnic groups are brand loyal may depend on how strongly they identify with their own culture. In two similar studies – Donthu and Cherian (1994) researched Latino brand loyalty, while Podoshen (2006) investigated American Jewish brand loyalty towards automobiles – both researchers identified strength of ethnic affiliation to be important. For instance, Donthu and Cherian noted how Latinos who strongly identified with Latino culture would seek out Latino retailers, while remaining loyal to brands that their family and friends used. Similarly, Podoshen noted how American Jews who strongly identified with their Jewish culture tended to be more brand loyal than their counterparts who had a weaker Jewish identification. These findings suggest that brand loyalty among ethnic minorities should not be assumed, but instead considered as a sub-segment within the respective ethnic group's segment.

Benefits sought from consuming a product may also represent a means of segmenting ethnic groups. Health provides a good example, with many ethnic groups experiencing lactose intolerance (the natural occurring sugar found in milk and related products that cannot always be digested easily) (National Dairy Council 2011). Market offerings such as lactose-free diary milk or non-dairy alternatives, such as soya or almond milk, effectively segment ethnic groups through health benefits.

A wider review of the literature on ethnic minorities and benefits sought returns to the issue of brands, ethnic identification and acculturation (discussed later). In two related studies, Wallendorf and Reilly (1983; 1984) undertook an analysis of Latino garbage (rubbish) to identify products purchases, noting how Latinos extensively consumed products identifiable with White American consumers. A consumer behaviour, they concluded, arose from the Latino sample identifying with, and attempting to acculturate into, American White culture. However, it should also be considered whether these participants were also expressing their own sense of modernism and/or social mobility embodied in American society and reflected in the consumption of particular brands.

Another benefit sought, and one that presents an attractive segmentation variable for prestige brands, is the concept of the collective self. The collective self can be defined as the 'need to gain a favourable evaluation from a reference group by fulfilling one's role in a reference group and achieving group goals' (Yamaguchi et al. 1995, p. 659). Inherently identifiable with collectivist cultures, such as those found in India, individuals within these cultural systems tend to have a stronger affiliation with a group to derive their sense of identity from (Wong and Ahuvia 1995), such as the family (Kitayama et al. 1997). Indeed, ethnic minority studies on Indian immigrants to Canada by Joy and Dholakia (1991) and Indians living in Britain by Lindridge and colleagues (Lindridge et al. 2004; Lindridge et al. 2005; Lindridge and Hogg 2006), noted how the Indian diaspora actively purchased brands that enhanced their collective self. However, these studies did not particularly look at acculturation's influence on these behaviours, and the extent this variable affected their sense of collective self remains unclear. However, the role of the collective self does offer an attractive means of market segmentation for prestigious brands that are dependent on exclusivity and wider public recognition as a means to increase their market share.

The final behaviouristic segmentation variable refers to how a product's consumption may represent a more global perspective, but also be reinterpreted and consumed by local communities to suit their specific needs (Ger, Kravets and Sandıkçı2011). While research has tended not to investigate this area, sufficient anecdotal information is available to illustrate this variable.

For instance in the 1980s, Smith and Nephew, the then owners of the skin cream brand Nivea, noted as part of their regular monthly sales analysis disproportionate sales of Nivea hand cream in specific British cities. When this consumption pattern was repeated on a monthly basis, Smith and Nephew undertook market research to understand further these localized sales increases. The results indicated that the sales were attributable to African Caribbean's purchasing Nivea hand cream to use as an all-over body skin cream. Apparently Nivea hand cream was thicker and more suitable for African Caribbean skin than the standard Nivea or other competitors body cream products, which targeted a predominately White audience.

In a different but related example, the launch of Cola Turka in Turkey was attributable to opposition to Americanization of cultures and a need to develop a cola drink that represented and benefited Turkish society (ibid.). After initial commercial success, sales began to fall in response to the brand's Islamic associations, ensuring that loyal drinkers identified with both the brands Turkish and Islamic associations. Both examples, of how product usage can offer a means to market segment ethnic groups through behaviour variables satisfies the earlier segmentation criteria of being substantial and accessible.

Market segmentation and the need to consider acculturation

The approaches to market segmenting ethnic groups discussed so far have relied upon a fundamental assumption – that the ethnic group being discussed represents a homogenous group who demonstrate similar behaviours. An assumption supported by the three segmentation criteria presented at the beginning of this chapter:

Differentiability a segment requires group homogeneity.

Stability the population forming the segment does not radically change over time.

Exhaustiveness a population can only be ascribed to one segment only.

Yet this assumption, along with these segmentation criteria, is unrealistic when we consider acculturation as a variable (Palumbo and Teich 2004). One of the oldest and still most relevant definitions of acculturation was given by the Social Science Research Council (1954, p. 974), who defined acculturation as:

> Culture change that is initiated by the conjunction of two or more autonomous cultural systems. Acculturative change may be the consequence of direct cultural transmission; it may be derived from non-cultural causes, such as ecological or demographic modification induced by an impinging culture; it may be delayed, as with internal adjustments following upon the acceptance of alien traits or patterns; or it may be a reactive adaption of traditional modes of life. Its dynamics can be seen as the selective adaptation of values systems, the process of integration and differentiation, the generation of developmental sequences, and the operation of role determinants and personality factors.

Acculturation then generates changes among ethnic groups in three different ways:

Behavioural the types of clothes and foods bought and consumed, along with what cultural festivals are celebrated, for example, will begin to differ between and within ethnic groups and wider society.

Affective   how emotions are demonstrated and experienced towards other people, communities and products will change. Ethnoconsumerism, as discussed earlier, may produce varying levels of emotional attachment towards products and brands from the ethnic minority's country of origin in contrast to their new society.

Cognitive   language choice, between their ancestral and societal choices, has been shown to affect ethnic groups' beliefs and values in how they perceive a situation (Farb 1975).

We can illustrate these themes and the importance of acculturation to ethnic groups' market segmentation through a number of studies undertaken among the Latino market in the United States. O'Guinn and Faber (1986) noted how less acculturated Latinos, compared to those who were highly acculturated, were more brand loyal and price conscious. In a similar study IRI (2012) found that less acculturated Latinos, when compared to their highly acculturated counterparts, were less influenced by promotional sales (8 per cent compared to 52 per cent), demonstrated higher levels of ethnoconsumerism (27 per cent compared to 6 per cent) and were more likely to seek out bilingual signage on packaging (22 per cent compared to 6 per cent). The latter finding is supported by the Cheskin Research (cited from Malaghan 2003), which found that among 6,000 Latinos, 76 per cent favoured communicating in Spanish.

If varying levels of acculturation effect ethnic groups' consumer behaviours then instead of perceiving them as a homogenous market segment, we should perhaps view them as a collection of sub-segments. For example, Cheskin Research analyzed the 2002 Hispanic Opinion Tracker Study to segment the American Latino market by acculturation level identifying three segments: Latino Dominant (56 per cent), Bi-cultural (20 per cent) and English Dominant (23 per cent). In another report, using similar categories, Lokpez (2010) identified that Latinos, and, we argue, ethnic groups per se, can be segmented into three categories on the basis of how their acculturation affects their consumption:

Unacculturated Latinos

- Are Spanish-dominant (language)
- Have recently arrived in the United States
- Reside in neighbourhoods with a high density of Hispanics
- Conduct business in Spanish
- Rely on Spanish media
- Purchase products that are familiar – i.e. available in their homeland
- Practise Hispanic traditions

Bi-cultural Latinos

- Are bilingual
- Are born in the United States or have been in the country for several years
- Live in metropolitan areas
- Use English as their primary language for business
- Are comfortable with Spanish and English media
- Purchase products that are not exclusive or distinctive to Hispanic consumers
- Remain loyal to Hispanic traditions and customs

Acculturated Latinos

- Are English-dominant
- Are born in the United States or have been here for ten or more years
- Live in suburban areas
- Conduct business in English
- Prefer English media
- Have similar purchase behaviour as the general market
- Observe few or no Hispanic traditions

Classifying an ethnic minority group as 'unacculturated, bicultural or acculturated', while offering some value to the marketer, also makes a number of fundamental assumptions. First, Lokpez's (2010) segment criteria fails to consider socio-economic and demographic criteria. For example, under the 'acculturated' segment the only demographic criterion given is propensity to speak English. To understand the relationship between these variables and the importance of acculturation to segmentation we need to return to the academic literature. Second, and most importantly, is the assumption that an individual's ethnic identity and their acculturation are static.

Using Lokpez's segment categorizations, an acculturated Latino would be expected to identify with the dominant American culture, effectively ignoring their Latino identity and associated behaviours; this is an acculturation proposition that is widely disputed within academic literature. For instance, Szapocznik *et al.*'s (1980) bi-directional acculturation model identifies an ethnic minority individual's behaviours and identity with both their own ethnic and the dominant culture. Ethnic minority and dominant cultural behaviours and identities are not apparent on either side of a bi-directional scale, but instead represent dimensions that are interdependent and orthogonal of each other (Zak 1973; 1976). An individual can then identify with their ethnic culture or dominant culture, and demonstrate (or otherwise) behaviours reflective of their identity. In other words, an individual may identify themselves as a Latino but demonstrate behaviours indicative of American White society.

Developing Szapocznik *et al.*'s model further, Berry (1990; 1992; 1997) proposed a 2 x 2 matrix that categorized individuals into four distinct categories based upon the retention of their cultural identity and their behaviours relative to the dominant society. This comparison then produced four acculturation outcomes: (1) *integration*: the individual is equally interested in engaging with both their ethnic and dominant cultures, (2) *separation*: the individual rejects the dominant culture and accepts the ethnic culture, (3) *assimilation*: in contrast to the previous point, the individual rejects their ethnic culture in favour of the dominant culture and (4) *marginalization*: where both cultures are rejected.

Berry's acculturation model offers an attractive proposition for market segmenting ethnic groups, recognizing that ethnic identity may not necessarily reflect acculturation related behaviours. Rudmin (2003) argued that those ethnic groups from a culture similar to the dominant culture were more likely to be reflected in Berry's integrated categories, compared to those who are from less similar cultures. Indeed, in a study into Latino acculturation, Maldonado and Tansuhaj (2002) using Berry's acculturation categories assessed their relevance in determining brand loyalty towards brands indicative of Latino and American culture. Indeed, they concluded that Berry's acculturation categories did explain variances within Latinos brand loyalty. In particular, the individuals within the 'assimilation' category (identity and behaviour reflecting American society) demonstrated low ethnoconsumerist traits, with 73 per cent choosing U.S.

brands. In comparison, those individuals who demonstrated 'separation' were more ethnocentric, with only thirty-two per cent choosing American brands instead of a Latino brand. Of interest is the 'integration' category, where identities and behaviours were reflective of both their Latino and their American cultures, reflected in 48 per cent choosing U.S. and 52 per cent choosing Latino brands.

It should be noted that Maldonado and Tansuhaj make no mention of 'marginalization' as a category in their research (nor offer any explanation as to why). Indeed, the limited research into marginalized ethnic minorities does suggest the appropriateness of this category as an ethnic minority sub-segment. In a study undertaken by Lindridge, Dhillon and Shah (2005) among second-generation Punjabi Sikh alcoholics living in Britain, their findings noted how participants' rejection of both their Sikh and British cultures was compensated through constructing an identity around alcoholism. Linked to this, and not mentioned in the paper, was how the local alcohol shops had effectively recognized this group as a sub-segment, among the wider Sikh community, offering these participants exclusive price discounts for larger quantities of alcohol purchases.

Maldonado and Tansuhaj further expand and contradict Lokpez's (2010) acculturation categories by introducing generational differences into segment categorizations. While it may be assumed that being born in a country is more likely to result in ethnic groups becoming more 'assimilated' than say 'separated', this was not borne out by Maldonado and Tansuhaj. Once again applying Berry's (1990; 1992; 1997) acculturation categories, they found that 34 per cent of individuals belonging to the 'integrated' and 'separation' categories were born in the United States. A finding that suggests that generational level should not be used as a segmentation measure, while supporting the use of Berry's acculturation categories as a tool to market segment ethnic groups.

Berry's acculturation model has been criticized by Turner, Oakes, Haslam and McGarty (1994) for assuming that acculturation categories represent static, fixed states. Instead they argue that ethnic groups and their members exist in a constant state of flux, often alternating in their positions regarding their cultural identity and related behaviours. Indeed, such behaviour is identifiable with Stayman and Deshpandé's (1989) situational ethnicity, where the environmental context experienced by an individual with a different ethnicity to the majority adapts their consumer behaviour to conform. Developing this perspective further, Bhatia (2002) proposed the Dialogical Model of Acculturation, arguing that individuals from minority ethnic groups move continuously between opposing cultural values, while holding simultaneously positions of assimilation, marginalization and separation. Consequently the ethnic minority individual creates multiple identities depending on the situation and other individuals encountered (Phinney 1996). From a consumption perspective, Lindridge, Hogg and Shah (2004) noted how second-generation Indians living in Britain selectively used culturally value-laden consumption to assist them in constructing appropriate acculturated identities for the differing contexts encountered. Consequently, the Dialogical Model of Acculturation raises issues surrounding the segmentation criteria of 'stability'. After all, if the ethnic group being segmented continuously shifts in how it perceives its own identity and behaviour, reflected in what they consume, then segmentation will have to be undertaken on a product by product basis.

The introduction of acculturation into our discussion on the feasibility of market segmentation among ethnic groups presents a challenge. By recognizing that acculturation ensures ethnic groups are not homogenous, we must recognize the need for sub-market segments. While Maldonado and Tansuhaj (2002) offer us a way forward, their reliance on Berry's acculturation categories also assumes a level of in-group homogeneity, that situational ethnicity, encapsulated within the Dialogical Model of Acculturation, claims does not exist. How then should marketers market segment ethnic groups? We posit that the approach to undertake should accept the need for sub-segments primarily based around acculturation. Acculturation variables such as language and media usage offer a means to initially categorize an ethnic group by their behaviours, with further investigation required to assess an individual's sense of ethnic identity. From here, organizations could then assess the extent and reasons why situational ethnicity may affect product consumption. Finally, once these acculturation categories have been determined, they could be applied to more traditional market segmentation approaches. For example, an ethnic minority sub-segment identifiable with Berry's 'separated' acculturation category may live in certain geographical areas, lending themselves to geographic segmentation.

Resolving the market segmentation of ethnic groups

How, if at all, can ethnic groups be market segmented? Throughout this chapter various researchers have questioned fundamental assumptions about ethnic groups and their related consumption (for example, Furnham and Baguma 1994; Lindridge *et al.* 2004; 2005; 2006; Podoshen 2006). These assumptions have been based around ethnic groups representing a homogenous group, with cultural differences only being evident when compared to others. Yet as we have noted, acculturation recognizes cultural differences exist within ethnic groups. Considering this potential lack of group homogeneity among ethnic groups then acculturation may offer an appropriate approach to market segmentation.

Acculturation was identified as the interaction between two cultures, with ethnic minority individuals differing in their identification with their native and dominant culture. This identification may be relatively fixed (as suggested by Berry) or more fluid depending upon the context the individual encounters (as suggested by Bhatia). Yet these differences, as noted earlier, may be problematic for market segmentation. The question then arises 'How then can this dilemma be resolved?'

In resolving this dilemma it is important to recognize that some ethnic groups are not a homogenous group ensuring their market segmentation remains a challenge. While Maldonado and Tansuhaj (2002) offer us a way forward, their reliance on Berry's (1990; 1992; 1997) acculturation categories also assumes a level of in-group homogeneity that situational ethnicity, encapsulated within the Dialogical Model of Acculturation, claims does not exist. How then should marketers market segment ethnic groups? We posit that the approach to undertake should accept the need for sub-segments primarily based around acculturation. Acculturation variables (that space does not permit to discuss here) such as language and media usage, offer a means to initially categorize an ethnic minority group based upon their behaviour, with further investigation required to assess an individual's sense of ethnic identity. From here organizations could then assess the extent and reasons why situational ethnicity may affect how their product is consumed. Finally once these acculturation categories have been determined, these could be applied to more traditional market segmentation approaches. For example, an ethnic group's sub-segment that was identified under Berry's acculturation category as 'separated' may live in certain geographical areas, lending themselves to geographic segmentation.

At this point we can return to our earlier example of Gain washing powder – an example of effective market segmentation or product differentiation? The answer lies in the various targeted ethnic groups acculturation. For those consumers who can be identified as assimilated (whose identity and behaviours are similar to the dominant culture) we can identify Gain's use of Spanish on its packaging as an example of 'segment-based product differentiation' (Dickson and Ginter 1987). However, for those ethnic minorities who would be identified as 'integrated' or 'separated' or who need to demonstrate their ethnicity (within situational ethnicity, such as other ethnic minorities visiting the consumer's house) Gain is demonstrating a market segmentation strategy. Perhaps most importantly is that Gain's ability to target Latinos and African Americans has delivered strong financial results.

Separating ethnic minorities into sub-segments, mediated through demographic, geographic, psychographic and behaviour variables, however, raises feasibility problems. For most countries, differing ethnic group populations tend to be small and geographically diverse. For an organization to segment an already small heterogeneous population into smaller sub-segments may render those market segments unviable.

Having identified a possible resolution on how to market segment differing ethnic groups, future research would be well advised to explore further the relationship between acculturation and consumer behaviour within, as well as between, different ethnic groups, particularly to what extent market segmentation is viable for these groups or whether organizations are likely to leave them as a diverse, heterogeneous group who, while different, do not represent a financially viable segment.

In conclusion: the key steps marketing managers can undertake in ethnic market segmentation

This chapter concludes by discussing how marketing practioners can undertake effective market segmentation through a seven step process.

Step one: why do you want to market segment an ethnic group?

Market segmenting an ethnic group has been shown to be a difficult undertaking therefore an organization should ask 'What do we wish to achieve from segmenting this ethnic group?' The reasons may vary but could include:

- Increasing the organization's competitiveness
- Identifying new marketing opportunities
- Defending market share
- Encouraging customer brand loyalty
- Attracting new customers

Step two: take some time to understand your own customers

An organization's existing customer base is likely to include a range of different ethnicities. Using available information organizations should undertake an in-depth analysis to identify which ethnic groups are purchasing your products, how often, where from and in what quantities. If you have access to Mosaic you may wish to apply this marketing research tool to further elaborate upon your customers.

By identifying which ethnic groups are purchasing your products and their characteristics the organization will potentially be able to develop this information into profitable market segments.

Step three: now focus on the value of these ethnic groups to your organization

Having recognized the reasons for undertaking marketing segmentation of ethnic minorities and identified which ethnic groups are already purchasing your product, we now need to calculate their value to the organization. After all, regardless of which ethnic groups purchase your products, if they do not represent a current or future profit source or positively contribute towards the organization's marketing objectives then the organization should not consider developing them into a market segment.

In assessing the value of an ethnic group to an organization, three variables should be considered:

Financial value   what is the financial value offered by each individual ethnic customer? This should be considered on a monthly and annual basis. In particular, profit and sale levels need to be considered here.

Customer potential   to what extent is the individual ethnic customer susceptible to purchasing different organizational products? The greater their propensity to purchase related products, the higher their financial value to the organization.

Customer loyalty   what is the customer loyalty for this ethnic group? The greater the loyalty the more profit and value they offer the organization increasing their commercial attractiveness.

Step four: now undertake some marketing research

While step two involved collecting secondary data to identify potential market segments, this step now requires the organization to undertake some primary research. Step three should have identified which potential ethnic market segments offer the organization opportunities for increased profit and achieving marketing objectives. In this step, the organization now needs to understand what the needs, wants and benefits are that are sought from the potential ethnic market segments.

Step five: recognize which segmentation approaches will work

In this step, the organization reviews the marketing research data gathered previously and identifies whether demographic, geographic, psychographic and behaviouristic variables will be effective in targeting ethnic market segments. In some instances, more than one variable may be applicable. For example, where an ethnic group lives in a country (demographic) but is dispersed into specific geographical areas (geographic) with differing lifestyles (psychographic). In these instances the organization needs to evaluate which segmentation variable is most likely to achieve the profit and marketing objective outcomes sought.

We should also consider at this step whether acculturation needs to be considered and what the implications of this would be.

Step six: implement marketing activities that will appeal to your ethnic market segments

This step involves developing a marketing strategy and tactics that address the ethnic market segment needs. For example, if the segment is less acculturated then it would be expected to be more ethnocentric. Consequently the marketing strategy would need to draw upon symbolisms indicative of that group's cultural values to ensure the strategy's success.

Step 7: evaluate

The final stage involves evaluating the effectiveness of the ethnic market segments to the original aims agreed upon in step one. In this step the organization should decide what changes need to be made to the ethnic market segments to improve their effectiveness.

Summary

This chapter reviewed the feasibility of market segmenting ethnic minorities. Market segmentation relies upon the premise that a heterogamous group can be separated into separate homogenous sub-groups. An approach that lends itself to ethnic minorities who as a group either self-identify or have an ethnic identity imposed upon them by wider society. Yet market segmentation variables when applied to ethnic minorities have been criticized for effectively undertaking product differentiation. To resolve this criticism careful consideration must be undertaken to ensure that different behaviours required to justify market segmentation are evident.

Effective market segmentation of ethnic minorities requires two themes to be considered. First is whether the ethnic minority group's behaviour truly is different from the dominant ethnic group. Second, if the ethnic minority's behaviour is different, then acculturation needs to be considered, in particular, how the ethnic minority group's acculturation affects their behaviour and related consumption. Only if acculturation results in different behaviour should market segmentation be undertaken.

References

Ackerman, D. and Tellis, G. (2001) 'Can culture affect prices? A cross-cultural study of shopping and retail prices'. *Journal of Retailing*, 77: 57–82

Albert, T. C. (2003) 'Need based segmentation and customised communication strategy in a complex industry: A supply chain study'. *Industrial Marketing Management*, 32(4): 281–90.

Andersen, M. L. and Taylor, H. F. (2006) *Sociology: Understanding a Diverse Society*. London: Wadsworth.

Berry, J. W. (1990) 'Psychology of acculturation'. In *Cross-Cultural Perspectives. Proceedings of the Nebraska symposium on motivation*, edited by J. J. Berman. Lincoln, NE: University of Nebraska Press, 201–34.

Berry, J. W. (1992) 'Acculturation and adaption in a new society'. *International Migration*, 30: 69–85.

Berry, J. W. (1997) 'Immigration, acculturation and adaptation'. *Applied Psychology: An International Review*, 46(1): 5–34.

Betancourt, H. and Lopez, S. R. (1993) 'The study of culture, ethnicity, and race in American psychology'. *American Psychologist*, 48: 629–37.

Bhatia, S. (2002) 'Acculturation, dialogical voices and the construction of the diasporic self'. *Theory and Psychology*, 12(1): 55–77.

Clark, K. and Drinkwater, S. (2007) *Ethnic Minorities in The Labour Market: Dynamics and Diversity*. London: Joseph Rowntree Foundation.

Cui, G. (1997) 'Marketing strategies in a multi-ethnic environment'. *Journal of Marketing Theory and Practice*, 5(1): 122–34.

Dauphinee, A., Doxey, J. R., Schleicher, N. C., Fortmann, S. P. and Henriksen, L. (2013) 'Racial differences in cigarette brand recognition and impact on youth smoking'. *BMC Public Health*, 13: 170.

Delva J., Johnston, L. D, O'Malley, P. M. (2007) 'The epidemiology of overweight and related lifestyle behaviors: Racial/ethnic and socioeconomic status differences among American youth'. *American Journal of Preventative Medicine*, 33(4 special supplement): 178–86.

Dibb, S., Simkin, L, Pride, W. M. and Ferrell, O. C. (2006) *Marketing Concepts and Strategies*, 5th Edn. Abingdon, UK: Houghton Mifflin.

Dickson, P. R. and Ginter, J. L. (1987) 'Market segmentation, product differentiation and marketing strategy'. *Journal of Marketing,* 51(April): 1–10.

Donthu, N. and Cherian, J. (1994) 'Impact of strength of ethnic identification on Hispanic shopping behaviour'. *Journal of Retailing*, 70(4): 383–93.

Farb, P. (1975) *Word Play: What Happens When People Talk*. New York, NY: Knopf.

Fennell, G., Piron, F, Saegert, J. and Jimenez, R. (1992) 'Do Hispanics constitute a market segment?' *Advances in Consumer Research*, 19: 28–33.

Freytag, P. V. and Clarke, A. H. (2001) 'Business to business market segmentation'. *Industrial Marketing Management*, 30(6): 473–86.

Furnham, A. and Baguma, P. (1994) 'Cross-cultural differences in the evaluation of male and female body-shapes'. *International Journal of Eating Disorders*, 15: 81–9.

Ger, G, Kravets, O and Sandıkçı, Ö. (2011) 'International marketing at the interface of the alluring global and the comforting level'. In *Marketing Management: A Cultural Perspective,* edited by L. Peñaloza, N. Toulose and l. M. Visconti. London: Routledge.

Ghannam, F. (1997) 'Fertile, plump and strong: The social construction of female body in low income Cairo'. *Monographs in Reproductive Health Number 3*. Cairo: Population Council Regional Office for West Asia and North Africa.

Gibbens, C. and Julian, G. (2006) *Family Spending: A Report on the 2004–05 Expenditure and Food Survey*. London: The Stationary Office.

Goldberg, R. H. (2012) 'Determining consumer ethnocentrism and lifestyle among Black Diamonds in Sandton', *Thesis (M. Com – Marketing Management)*, North-Western University. Available from: http://dspace.nwu.ac.za/handle/10394/7003?show=full [accessed 19.02.2014].

Halter, M. (2000) *Shopping for Identity: The Marketing of Ethnicity*. New York, NY: Shocken Books.

Harrison, A. O., Wilson, M. N., Pine, C. J., Chan, S. Q. and Buriel, R. (1990) 'Family ecologies of ethnic minority children'. *Child Development,* 61: 347–62.

Henriksen, L., Schleicher, N. C., Dauphinee, A. L. and Fortmann, S. P. (2012) 'Targeted advertising, promotion, and price for menthol cigarettes in California high school neighborhoods'. *Nicotine & Tobacco Research*, 14(1): 116–21.

Hirschman E. C. and Panther-Yates, D. (2008) 'Peering inward for ethnic identity: Consumer interpretation of DNA test results'. *Identity: An International Journal of Theory and Research*, 8(1): 47–66.

HHS (1998) 'Tobacco use among US racial/ethnic minority groups – African Americans, American Indians and Alaskan Natives, Asian Americans and Pacific Islanders, and Hispanics: A report of the Surgeon General'. *U.S. Department of Health and Human Services*. Available from: http://www.cdc.gov/tobacco/data_statistics/sgr/1998/complete_report/pdfs/complete_report.pdf [accessed 27.07.2014].

Huxley, J. S., Haddon, A. C. and Carr-Saunders, A. M. (1935) 'We Europeans'. *The New Republic*, 86 (March 11).

Jamal, A. (2003) 'Marketing in a multi-cultural world'. *European Journal of Marketing*, 37(11/12): 1599–620.

Joshi, D., McGovern, R., Noriega, E., Riesser, H. S. and Walker, J. (2012) 'Let's make a deal: Price sensitivity and optical subsidies among broadband non-adapters'. Available from: https://prodnet.www.neca.org/publicationsdocs/wwpdf/113012bbpaper.pdf [accessed 23.03.2013].

Joy, A. and Dholakia, R. R. (1991) 'Remembrances of things past: The meaning of home and possessions of Indian professionals in Canada'. In *To Have Possessions: A Handbook on Ownership and Property*, edited by F. W. Rudmin. Corte Madera, CA: Select Press, 385–402.

IRI (2012) 'IRI Finds Expanding Hispanic Market Presents Exceptional Opportunity'. *IRI*. Available from: http://www.iriworldwide.com/NewsEvents/PressReleases/tabid/97/ItemID/1496/View/Details/Default.aspx [accessed 20.02.2014].

Kavak, B. and Gumuslouglu, L. (2007) 'Segmenting food markets: The role of ethnocentrism and lifestyle in understanding purchasing intentions'. *International Journal of Market Research*, 49(1): 71–94.

Kitayama, S., Markus, H. R., Matsumoto, H. and Norasakkunkit, V. (1997) 'Individual and collective processes in the construction of the self: Self-enhancement in the United States and self-criticism in Japan'. *Journal of Personality and Social Psychology,* 72: 1245–67.

Kotler, P. and Armstrong, G. (2008) *Principles of Marketing*, 12th Edn. Upper Saddle River, NJ: Prentice-Hall.

Kucukemiroglu O. (1999) 'Market segmentation by using consumer lifestyle dimensions and ethnocentrism'. *European Journal of Marketing*, 3(55): 470–87.

Lancaster, G. and Massingham, L. (2001) *Marketing Management,* 3rd Edn. Berkshire, UK: McGraw-Hill Inc.

Lindridge, A. M., Dhillon, K. and Shah, M. (2005) 'Cultural role confusion and memories of a lost identity: How non-consumption perpetuates marginalisation'. *Advances in Consumer Research*, 32(1): 408–14.

Lindridge, A. M. and Hogg, M. K. (2006) 'Parental gatekeeping in diasporic Indian families: Examining the intersection of culture, gender and consumption'. *Journal of Marketing Management*, 22(9–10): 979–1009.

Lindridge, A. M., Hogg, M. K. and Shah, M. (2004) 'Imagined multiple worlds: How South Asian women in Britain use family and friends to navigate the "border crossings" between household and social contexts'. *Consumption, Markets & Culture*, 7(3): 211–38.

Lokpez, E. (2010) 'Reaching Hispanics: First segment by acculturation, then speak their language'. *MarketingProfs*. Available from: http://www.marketingprofs.com/authors/955/ederick-lokpez [accessed 20.02.2014].

McCracken, G. (1986) 'Culture and consumption: A theoretical account of the structure and movement of cultural meaning of consumer goods'. *Journal of Consumer Research*, 13(June): 71–84.

Malaghan, T. (2003) 'Keys to segmenting the U.S. Hispanic market', *DirectMarketing IQ*. Available from: http://www.directmarketingiq.com/article/keys-segmenting-us-hispanic-market-630/2 [accessed 20.02.2014].

Maldonado, R. and Tansuhaj, P. (2002) 'Segmenting a local Latino market using Berry's acculturation taxonomy'. *Advances in Consumer Research*, 29: 414–20.

MentholKillsYou (2014) Available from: https://twitter.com/mentholkillsyou [accessed 12.05.2014].

Modood, T., Berthoud, R. and Lakey, J. (1997) *Ethnic Minorities: Diversity and Disadvantage*. London: PSI.

Molnar, S. (1992) *Human Variation: Races, Types and Ethnic Groups*, 3rd Edn, New Jersey, NJ: Prentice Hall.

Myers, M. M., Edland, S. D., Hofstetter, C. R. and Delaimy, A. L. (2012) 'Perceived price sensitivity by ethnicity and smoking frequency among California Hispanic and Non-Hispanic white smokers'. *Nicotine & Tobacco Research*. Available from: http://ntr.oxfordjournals.org/content/early/2012/11/03/ntr.nts240.abstract [accessed 23.03.2013].

National Dairy Council (2011) 'Lactose intolerance among different ethnic groups'. *National Dairy Council*. Available from: http://www.nationaldairycouncil.org/SiteCollectionDocuments/LI%20and%20Minorites_FINALIZED.pdf [accessed 13.03.2013].

Ndanga, L. Z. B., Louw, A. and van Rooyen, J. (2010) 'Increasing domestic consumption of South African wines: Exploring the market potential of the "black diamonds"'. *Agrekon*, 49(3): 293–315.

O'Guinn, T. C. and Faber, R. J. (1986) 'Advertising and sub-culture: The role of ethnicity and acculturation in market segmentation'. *Current Issues in Research and Advertising*, 9(1): 149–68.

Palumbo, F. A. and Teich, I. (2004) 'Market segmentation based on level of acculturation'. *Marketing Intelligence and Planning*, 22(4): 472–84.

Phinney, J. S. (1996) 'When we talk about American ethnic groups, What do we mean?' *American Psychologist*, 51(9): 918–27.

Podoshen, J. S. (2006) 'Word of mouth, brand loyalty, acculturation and the American Jewish community'. *Journal of Consumer Marketing*, 23(5): 266–82.

PR Newswire (2012) 'Procter & Gamble Announces Gain(R) As Its 23rd Billion Dollar Brand'. *PR Newswire*. Available from: http://www.prnewswire.com/news-releases/procter—gamble-announces-gainr-as-its-23rd-billion-dollar-brand-57811677.html [accessed 27.07.2014].

Reyes, S. (2006) 'Brand loyalty strong among minorities'. *Adweek*, August 16. Available from: http://www.adweek.com/news/advertising/brand-loyalty-strong-among-minorities-86092 [accessed 24.03.2013].

Rickard, L. (1994) 'Study: Minorities show brand loyalty, spend more on food'. *Advertising Age*. Available from: http://adage.com/article/news/study-minorities-show-brand-loyalty-spend-food/87228/ [accessed 13.04.2013].

Rudmin, F. W. (2003) 'Another mystery in our history: Who was Sarah Emma Simmons?'. *Cross-Cultural Psychology Bulletin*, 37(4): S26.

Sharma, S. and Cruickshank, J. K. (2001) 'Cultural differences in assessing dietary intake and providing relevant dietary information to British African-Caribbean populations'. *Journal of Human Nutrition Dietetics*, 14: 449–56.

Shimp, T. A. and Sharma, S. (1987) 'Consumer ethnocentrism: Construction and validation of the CETSCALE'. *Journal of Marketing Research*, 24(August): 280–9.

Singh, S. P. (1997) 'Ethnicity in psychiatric epidemiology: Need for precision'. *Journal of Psychiatry*, 171: 305–8.

Social Science Research Council (1954) 'Acculturation: An exploratory formulation'. *American Anthropologist*, 56(6): 973–1002.

Stayman, D. M. and Deshpandé, R. (1989) 'Situational ethnicity and consumer behavior'. *Journal of Consumer Research*, 16(3): 361–71.

Szapocznik, J., Kurtines, W. and Fernandez, T. (1980) 'Biculturalism and adjustment among Hispanic youths'. *Journal of Psychiatry*, 164: 474–80.

Tovée, M. J., Swami, V., Furnham, A. and Mangalparsad, R. (2006) 'Changing perceptions of attractiveness as observers are exposed to a different culture'. *Evolution and Human Behaviour*, 27: 443–56.

Turner, J., Oakes, P., Haslam, S. A. and McGarty, C. (1994) 'Self and collective: Cognition and social context'. *Personality and Social Psychology Bulletin,* 20: 454–63.

Venkatesh, A. (1995) 'Ethno-consumerism: A new paradigm to study cultural and cross-cultural consumer behavior'. In *Marketing in a Multicultural World,* edited by J. A. Costa and G. J. Bamossy. Thousand Oaks, CA: Sage Publications: 26–67.

Visconti, L. M. and Üçok Hughes, M. (2011) 'Segmentation and targeting revisited'. In *Marketing Management: A Cultural Perspective,* edited by L. Peñaloza, N. Toulouse and L. M. Visconti. London: Routledge: 295–314.

Wallendorf, M. and Reilly M. D. (1983) 'Ethnic migration, assimilation, and consumption'. *Journal of Consumer Research,* 10(December): 292–302.

Wallendorf, M. and Reilly, M. D. (1984) 'A longitudinal study of Mexican-American assimilation'. *Advances in Consumer Research,* 11: 735–40.

Waters, M. and Eschbach, K. (1995) 'Immigration and ethnic and racial inequality in the United States'. *Annual Review of Sociology,* 21: 419–46.

Weber, M. (1978) *Economy and Society: An Outline of Interpretive Sociology.* Berkeley, CA: University of California Press.

Wells, W. D. and Tigert, D. J. (1977) 'Activities, interests and opinions'. *Journal of Advertising Research,* 11(4): 27–34.

Wilk, R. (2006) *Home Cooking in the Global Village: Caribbean Food from Buccaneers to Ecotourists.* New York, NY: Berg Publishers.

Wong, N. and Ahuvia, A. (1995) 'Self-concepts and materialism: A cross cultural approach'. *Winter Educators' Conference,* American Marketing Association: 112–19.

Wong, V. and Saunders, N. (1993) 'Business orientation and corporate success'. *Journal of Strategic Marketing,* 1(1): 20–40.

Yamaguchi, S., Kuhlman, D. M. and Sugimori, S. (1995) 'Personality correlates of allocentric tendencies in individualist and collectivist cultures'. *Journal of Cross-Cultural Psychology,* 26: 658–72.

Zak, I. (1973) 'Dimensions of Jewish-American identity'. *Psychological Reports,* 33: 2891–900.

Zak, I. (1976) 'Structure of ethnic identity of Arab-Israeli students'. *Psychological Reports,* 38: 239–46.

Zuckerman, J. (1990) 'Some dubious premises in research and theory on racial differences'. *American Psychologist,* 45(December): 1297–303.

Ethnicity marketed to and consumed by the transcultural consumer

*Esi Abbam Elliot, Joseph Cherian
and Hernan Casakin*

Introduction

> . . . *As we begin to love people in another culture, we can begin to identify with them and see the truth they understand. As we make their truth our own, we become new people, formed by the synthesis of two cultures.*
>
> Adeney 1995: 165

Rampant globalization and immigration has created transcultural consumers who seek to consume ethnicity; the cosmopolitan consumers move beyond the confines of their cultures, embracing the global, the local, and their intersections (Epstein 2009). Such situations allow transcultural consumers to expand their repertoires by perceiving differences not as disconcerting, but as opportunities to adapt their old selves. The consumers, who participate in an ethnic festival that celebrates an important occasion with spicy food and after the experience look at spicy food differently, have become transformed in a small cultural way. This transcultural thinking embraces diversity and brings the possibility of transformation from the affordances of diverse ethnic attitudes and behaviours (Ghisi 2010).

Transcultural consumers wander through an ethnicity cafeteria with an eagerness to sample and partake at will. They cobble together an identity by taking the best selves offered across the transcultural spectrum they encounter; their exposure to multiple cultures enables them to (re) work their multiple, nested or elective identities. For example, a traveller from a 'masculine' culture (in the Hofstede sense) who visits a 'feminine' culture and therefore modifies their mental model of work relationships has essentially transformed their work-related elective identity. Generally speaking, ethnicity is how 'we' think the world does work and should work and our related behaviours; identity is how 'I' think I actually work and should work within this ethnic context; and here the 'we' and 'I' refer to a construal of the group one belongs to and of the self. Despite such observable phenomena, there has been limited research on consumption of ethnicity in and through the transcultural arena. Therefore, this chapter investigates the marketing and consumption of ethnicity in the context of transcultural consumption.

We propose an approach to marketing ethnicity that considers its consumption as integral to the construction of a transcultural identity. Our work differs from previous research on ethnic consumption in at least two ways. First, where existing studies on ethnic marketing focus mostly on marketing to marginalized or niche groups (Peñaloza and Venkatesh 2006), we suggest a transcultural perspective that is inclusive of all cultures. Second, where prior studies have been inspired by observation of ethnic practices (e.g. Askegaard *et al.* 2005), our ideas are grounded in two streams of research: the theories of transculture and consumption of ethnicity. Given the limited attempts by existing research in addressing transcultural aspects of ethnic consumption, it seems useful to evaluate ethnic consumption through the eyes of consumers as they absorb elements of ethnicity provided by artists who are considered in this study as producers and marketers of ethnicity.

Our investigation was carried out in the Pilsen community in Chicago, a Mexican enclave with a rich cultural heritage. The sample included a group of American tourists (i.e. transcultural consumers) and a group of Mexican cultural workers – artisans who produce artistic cultural products for sale and also offer cultural services (i.e. culture producers and marketers). To investigate such phenomenon a qualitative approach is most suitable, and therefore our methods included phenomenological interviews, field observations and photography.

Theoretical foundations

In this section we present key studies on transcultural perspectives, consumer mental models, visual cultural metaphors and destination image. The relation between transcultural perspectives and ethnic consumption is discussed, and current theoretical gaps in literature are further delineated.

Ethnic consumption and transcultural perspectives

Consumer ethnicity is made manifest through customary behaviours, values, patterns of thinking and communication (Levy 1981). Marketers socially validate ethnic groups by targeting them as market niches or segments and by exchanging relevant artifacts and sentiments (Peñaloza and Gilly 1999; Peñaloza 1994). Naturally, marketers tend to focus on those artifacts and behaviours that are more marketable. This predilection towards marketability can create distortions when people consuming a certain culture are not a member of the ethnic group (Peñaloza and Venkatesh 2006).

The production and consumption of ethnicity by individuals from different cultures creates 'agency' and 'subjectivity' as a prelude to transcultural experiences. Agency refers to the way individuals in one ethnic group act with those of another group, and how they shape their actions to sustain their culture and develop their communities (Peñaloza and Venkatesh 2006); in essence, they are the 'selling' agents of their culture. Subjectivity, on the other hand, refers to the individual's position with respect to the larger group, the way the individual feels about the ethnic group and the position of the ethnic group in relation to other groups (Venkatesh 1995); in essence, it is the sense of how it feels to an individual to belong to an ethnicity. Because cultures are not mutually exclusive (Yeo 1996), consumers belong simultaneously to multiple cultures influencing their preferences and behaviour. The interaction between consumers from different cultures can lead to the emergence of transcultural perspectives, which may have an effect in the materialization of new concepts and visions. According to Voss (2003), transcultural perspectives are ideal for the creation of a space where the interrelation between consumers is enhanced and a transcultural identity can emerge.

Such transcultural experiences can lead to the formation of an identity where one is no longer bounded by a single relatively closed culture but can be part of other cultures as well (Appadurai 1996). An example is the common saying that 'everyone is Irish on St. Patrick's Day'. Bianchini (2004) also argues that transcultural perspectives endow consumers with a capacity for self-transcendence, i.e. to be open to the world, to transcend cultural differences, to fit themselves in another's position and to embrace new meanings. Such transcendence is reflected in 'the capacity of individuals to stand outside of their immediate sense of time and place to view life from a larger, more objective perspective' (Piedmont 1999, p. 988).

Epstein (2009) notes that being transcultural enables consumers to share common elements that make it possible to establish cosmopolitan relationships. In this regard, the chapter presents and discusses transcultural perspectives identified by studying consumers in the process of consuming ethnicity. The study provides insights to the understanding of ethnic consumption in a transcultural context and to the development of relevant marketing strategies.

(Visual) cultural metaphors in ethnic markets

Metaphors are essential building blocks of cognition that enable individuals to creatively comprehend an ever-changing world (Lakoff and Johnson 1980). Metaphorical reasoning embraces tacit knowledge (Zaltman and Coulter 1995), which has deep implications for unconscious thinking and emotions (Zaltman 1997). Metaphor fleshes out our understanding (Nonaka and Takeuchi 1995) and has the power to assist in reflection by providing representative insights (Lakoff 1987). This mechanism assists in analyzing information (Zaltman 1997) and in the depiction of emotions and thoughts (Elliot, Elaydi and Cherian 2014).

Metaphors have their roots in culture (Morris and Waldman 2011). Gannon *et al.* (2005) define cultural metaphors as 'an institution, phenomenon, or activity with which most citizens in each national culture identify cognitively or emotionally, and through which it is possible to describe the culture and its frame of reference in depth'. Cultural metaphors entail words, visual patterns, shapes and colours. Denny and Sunderland (2005) suggest that cultural metaphors have the potential to unveil relevant categories of meaning among consumers.

Studies on metaphors that derive from symbolic anthropology focus on cultural images and visual metaphors (e.g. Hirschman 2007). Visual metaphors are often seen in visual media; for example, flags metaphorically evoke the ideals of a nation through symbolic colours and/or elements (Elliot, Cherian and Casakin 2013). The prevalence of national flags at cultural destinations is a strong visual reminder of national ideals. Hirschman (2007) indicates that metaphors are cultural and symbolic ways of structuring reality in the marketplace. These devices enable one to gain new and deeper insights into cultural aspects of another nation or ethnic group (Gannon 2002). An advantage of cultural metaphors is that they allow transcultural consumers become familiar with a foreign culture in a quick and friendly way.

At many neighbourhood ethnic festivals it is possible to see a cornucopia of nostalgic items and themes visually presented. Flags and foods, signs and symbols – all cultural metaphors – cram into the space of a few days the transcultural experience of visiting a country. For the span of these days, a hard-core native coming home for a visit would revel in the all-consuming experience. An expatriate coming home for a visit could become more fervently ethnic, at least during the visit. The transcultural tourists encounter a wide-spectrum of ethnic behaviours all available for consumption – looking at how 'they' greet each other, how 'they' relate to food, how 'they' express ethnic pride, etc. and they might wonder how those behaviours could be adapted to their home contexts. Each of these (can) have a metaphoric content: greeting each other with a kiss and a hug signifies the closeness of members, a metaphor for solidarity; the predominance of a food-type, say meat, a metaphoric stand-in for strength and valor in some ethnicities; the overt expression of ethnic pride through tattoos visually expresses an allegiance to ideals or group identity and endorses the idea that the visual representation of solidarity is desirable, perhaps even expected.

Visual cultural metaphors thus affect the quality of a transcultural experience. According to Zaltman and Coulter (1995), specific metaphors are filled with symbols and imagery that bring relevant reasoning processes and mental models to life. Through imagery, metaphors provide a vivid and, therefore, memorable emotion-arousing representations of the ethnic experience. Despite its prevalence, the influence of visual cultural metaphors on ethnic markets has not yet been fully investigated. This study investigates the effect of these cultural metaphors on ethnic production and consumption.

Metaphors and mental models

While a metaphor is, in essence, seeing one thing as another (Lakoff and Turner 1989), a mental model can be thought of as a coherent linkage of many metaphors (Hill and Levenhagen 1995). For example, seeing one country's citizenry as being consumers and another's as being producers is a simple metaphor that equates a citizenry to one or the other function; seeing a nation as being a 'kingdom of consumers' combines, coherently, two metaphors: citizen is consumer and consumer is king.

Teichert *et al.* (2006) propose three roles of metaphors in affecting mental models: (1) mental model communication, which occurs by enabling a metaphoric transfer from previously unassociated knowledge domains to create new meanings; (2) mental model matching, which takes place when metaphors are used as a shaping device to overcome deeply ingrained viewpoints that seek to influence mental models of consumers; and (3) mental model creation, that occurs when metaphors are used as cognitive frameworks to imbue meaning. Accordingly, visual cultural metaphors have the potential to influence consumer mental models and, in consequence, to affect the destination image. The role of mental models, closely informed by how visual cultural metaphors impact destination image and transcultural consumers, has yet to be deeply investigated.

Destination image

The destination image is a consumer's mental representation of knowledge and beliefs, of feelings and of the overall perception of a particular destination (Fakeye and Crompton 1991). A destination, which can vary in scale, can be a building, a city, a region, etc. Image formation is based on the information, images and experience that a consumer has about the destination (Gartner 1993; 1989). Indeed, the image can even be formed more by imagination than by information from the real world. The destination image formed by a transcultural consumer will then affect the subjective perception, behaviour and destination choice of the consumer (Han 2005).

A number of studies have examined how cultural tourism impacts the destination image for the consumer. This included investigations of iconic structures and mega-events (e.g. Richards and Wilson, 2004), thematization (e.g., Arnould and Price 1993; Joy and Sherry 2003) and heritage mining (e.g. Russo 2002). Destination images in consumer minds can develop to the extent that little of the local or original culture remains (Richards and Wilson, 2004). Such a loss of authenticity leads the purist cultural consumer to seek out archaic communities that are imagined to be culturally unadulterated (Berger 1996). Other studies showed that consumers are weary of finding the serial reproduction of their home cultures in different destinations all over the world and as a consequence they direct their efforts to find destinations alternative to their native and conventional ones (Richards and Wilson 2004); in other words, a destination may be valued to the extent that it does not have familiar fast food outlets. Seeing familiar signage from domestic fast food chains at a destination could entangle the destination image with the origination image. This entanglement is not necessarily bad as it could have the dual effect of helping create a sense of familiarity ('they like fries too') and a sense of difference ('they like their fries spicier'). To what extent then do universal symbols and metaphors, like global brands, institutions, personalities and such render the unfamiliar familiar?

Despite the relevance of this topic, few investigations have looked at transcultural consumption as a mechanism for enhancing destination image. If there are consistent mechanisms of improving destination images via reproducible aspects of transcultural consumption, then it is likely that global consumers and marketers can benefit from this; for example, can destination images of a popular movie star from home assuage natural tensions transcultural consumers no longer feel at home. In order to deal with the above issue, the present study explores transcultural consumption as a non-conventional way of leveraging culture to enhance the destination image.

Methodology

Research context

The setting of the Pilsen Mexican community was selected for our exploration due to its past role as a port of entry for many immigrant ethic groups. The Pilsen community, previously inhabited by Jewish, Italian, Polish, Greek, Czechs and Poles, has now become a major centre of the Latino population, primarily Mexican Americans. In this community, cultural workers play an inspiring role of using murals, museums, galleries and other forms of material culture to communicate transcultural values and to enhance destination images. Hence, many members of this ethnic community have taken on the profession of cultural workers to portray the rich culture, history and values of their ethnic community *to visitors*.

Research method

The main goal of this study was to investigate the production and consumption of ethnicity through transcultural consumption and to look at the specific mechanisms of destination image enhancement, visual cultural metaphors and consumer mental models. A phenomenological qualitative methodology and interpretive approach were considered suitable to deal with the research questions. These approaches combine aesthetics, ethics and epistemologies, and at the same time exhibit representational adequacy that is free from race, class or gender, and represent many voices (Christians 2000).

A qualitative approach based on phenomenological interviews, observations and photographs was used to collect the research data. Insights gleaned from the phenomenological interviews allowed the identification of not only cognitive themes, but also of emotions, attitudes, goals, values and sensory aspects of the assessed phenomenon (Christensen and Olson 2002). Given that cultural metaphors are characterized by numerous visual elements, photography was a particularly important complementary research technique.

Interviews carried out with twelve participants lasted from forty-five minutes to one hour. Due to the qualitative nature of the interviews, there was no canonical sample size required. Therefore, the interviews were considered complete when no novel information could be obtained and a saturation point was reached. Table 15.1 provides personal information for the participants. Five of the participants were Latino cultural workers and seven others were American tourists.

Table 15.1 Personal information for the participants

Name	Age	Gender	Education	Status
Gabriel Villa	53	Male	High School	Muralist/teacher
Hector Duarte	62	Male	Undergraduate	Artist
Jose Guerrero	65	Male	High School	Muralist/tour guide
Rolando	47	Male	High School	Artist/performer
Alejandro	36	Male	Ninth grade	Artist/photographer
Alison	30	Female	Graduate	American tourist
Monique	25	Female	Undergraduate	American tourist
Freddie	32	Male	Undergraduate	American tourist
Sarah	33	Female	Graduate	American tourist
John	37	Male	Graduate	American tourist
Tom	32	Male	Undergraduate	American tourist
Linda	41	Female	Undergraduate	American tourist

Note
Original names used in the table of participant information are those of Gabriel Villa, Hector Duarte and Jose Guerrero. All other names are pseudonyms.

Three different strategies were used for conducting the interviews. First, we interviewed three artists exhibiting their work at the National Museum of Mexican Art. Second, we approached two artists in their art galleries and interviewed them about their artwork. Third, we joined a guided tour looking at the murals of Pilsen streets, where we interviewed seven American tourists about their experiences. The tourists were recruited through snowball sampling from introductions made by one of the participating cultural workers, who was a tour guide. Based on research directions by Thompson *et al.* (1989), each interview was recorded, transcribed, analyzed and interpreted to identify emergent themes. A list of the sample questions asked during the interviews are attached in Appendix 15.1.

Findings and analysis

Our approach to the data is grounded in procedures for rigorous interpretive analysis, including individual analysis, iterations and part-to-whole comparisons (Thompson *et al.* 1989). We analyzed data, including both text and images, and discussed emerging interpretations. Findings were coded and classified into main themes using an interpretative phenomenological analysis approach. Coding was performed based on meaningful key words, phrases or sentences that generated themes related to the research objectives. The resulting interpretation was evaluated and modified as a function of supportive data, as well as by triangulation between the researchers. Transcripts of in-depth interviews and field notes provide the basis for the iterative analysis. This included tacking between the data and the literature (Glaser and Strauss 1967) to develop further an explanation of ethnic consumption in the transcultural context. Themes relating to production and consumption of ethnicity interplaying with transcultural perspectives emerged from the data. The initial codes concerned with ethnic consumption included worldview, cultural identity and cultural aesthetics, as well as those relating to transculture included humanity, idealism and interrelatedness. These emergent categories are used to organize and group codes into meaningful clusters (Patton 2002). Our findings are presented through the themes emerging from the codes.

In our presentation of findings, we build up three thematic dimensions that allow us to explain how transcultural perspectives impact and transform the consumer. These include:

(1) use of cultural metaphors; (2) mental model transcendence and (3) enhancement of the destination image. The identified themes, which are detailed below, showed that artists and workers use cultural metaphors to create a transcultural space that generates an awareness of the consumers' self and leads to a mental model transcendence.

Cultural metaphors and symbolic consumption

The consumption of cultural metaphors is an integral aspect of the consumption of ethnicity. The cultural metaphors are displayed through the Latino artworks. As explained before, cultural metaphors are associations that convey shared beliefs and understandings of a particular group or society. According to Morgan (1987), metaphors can serve to narrate an event, describe a scene, illustrate a concept, effect an emotive persuasion or present a logical argument. In our study, the artworks were used as visual images to convey metaphors. Langer (1980) describes art as the practice of creating observable symbolic forms representing the human feeling in a way that cannot be expressed using verbal language. The use of metaphors in art leads to a view of these tools as containers of cultural ideals.

Cultural metaphors capture essential characteristics of ethnicities (Gannon 2002) and connect consumers with the experiences and feelings of the ethnic communities. Features such as social sustainability, globalized culture, world peace, poverty elimination and environmental sustainability are characteristics of the Latino cultural metaphors. The construction of cultural metaphors is a process where meanings from different cultural domains are connected to each other to create, or recreate transcultural understanding. The consumption of cultural metaphors has the following components: a) *altruistic*: messages are conveyed to help the consumer; b) *agnostic*: cultural workers derive a positive emotional pleasure from sharing messages; c) *instrumental*: cultural workers want the consumers to share their interpretations; d) *obligatory*: cultural workers feel the situation demands it; e) *relationship mending*: messages are used to alleviate hard feelings; and f) *antagonistic*: used to disturb the consumer. In this process the consumer can be transformed by the transcultural perspective. An example of this is illustrated below.

The Latino culture uses the beating heart in many metaphors; for example, the eaten heart is used to signify a faithless wife, a shrinking heart to indicate a feeling of fear or pity. The use of heart of gold or big heart is more universal and may not be particular to any one ethnic group. Hector Duarte (age 62, male artist) expresses his feelings and wishes by means of cultural metaphors of a pumping heart in order to inspire ideals, and create a transcultural way of thinking. He says:

> I like to create optical illusions in my artwork. This [work] represents the idea of a closure of spaces between cultures. This mural creates an optical illusion of a pumping heart wrapped in chains. [But there are glimmers] of hope . . . on each side of the heart, where [there can be seen] metal hands holding broken chains . . . I would like tourists to admire the love for nature and life in my culture, and a love for people so they can be treated with respect and dignity.

The connection between the production and consumption of ethnicity and transcultural communications can be perceived by the use of cultural metaphors. Hector Duarte uses optical illusions to communicate his ideals as transcultural, which creates a platform for the production and consumption of ethnicity (see Figure 15.1). Ethnicity shapes and is shaped by the artworks through which Hector Duarte, like other Latino artisans, expresses his views and ideals, and establishes social interactions with consumers of culture. Hector Duarte uses several

Figure 15.1 Mural of a heart breaking chains
Note
Artwork by Hector Duarte. Image used with permission from Mr. Duarte.

cultural metaphors to communicate universal ideals such as love for life and people, courage, social conscience and liberation. In the Latino culture, a heart represents love and warmth. Metaphorically speaking, the heart signifies connections with people, while the chains depict the opposite. Thus, the breaking of chains can be seen to convey a transcultural message of hope, love, respect and dignity. Such ideals, represented through a set of principles and values, are interpreted as personal goals strongly connected to ethical issues.

American tourists perceive the artwork exhibited by Hector Duarte as a multiplicity of transcultural issues – including cultural, social, psychological, political and ideological ones. For example, Freddie (age 32, male American tourist) refers to how the cultural metaphors inspire universal ideals as he consumes the Latino ethnicity:

> I appreciate these older murals for their beauty and detail, and that they show a historic spectrum of mural creation in this neighbourhood. Some of the older, fading murals are more symbolic and depict signs and forms from ancient Aztec culture. When I look at the murals and artwork I distinctly see in them a desire to communicate certain ideals . . . These murals are a big part of what makes Pilsen so special, so unique and so desirable.

Freddie notices the desire to communicate ideals as he consumes artworks from the 'ancient Aztec culture'. This is transcendental for him as a tourist in the sense that his interpretation is about a (universal) cultural drive to communicate while he imagines the lives of Latino immigrants in between multiple worlds. Freddie also shows an understanding of the evolution of the culture by referring to the 'historic spectrum' of the murals in this neighbourhood.

Sarah (age 33, a female American tourist) provides further insights into how cultural metaphors inspire universal ideals. This involves issues relating to humanity, which encourages the compatible co-existence and integration of culturally diverse groups:

> . . . the aesthetics are very colourful . . . things they make their art out of is very fascinating. They pay a lot of attention to nature and also to religion, and I find their religious depictions like these paintings and other pieces of art really cool – and it makes me wish America could go back to what it was . . . the colours are fascinating. We can identify with the culture, and I am just blown away with all this faith and culture. I have read about it, but never experienced it, and that is why this is all awesome for me. I really feel emotional when I see this and hearing the descriptions of the artists, you really seem to get an idea of what this is all about – humanity and in a way it is very touching. It means to me that different cultures perceive things differently. I think that it is good to realize that things are different, to be aware of what other cultures are like and to understand them.

Consumers of culture like Sarah are inspired by cultural metaphors representing ideals that celebrate different cultures. Transcultural aspects transport consumers beyond cultural differences, to focus on issues that unify humanity (Epstein 2009). In order to provide further insights into how cultural metaphors serve as symbolic consumption through the inspiration of universal ideals, Morgan's (1987) exposition on the properties of metaphors are considered. According to Morgan, metaphors invite the generation of a 'constructive falsehood' that inspires a conversation outside the constraints of normal discourse. When consumers perceive artworks, their sensory, emotional and cognitive systems are immediately engaged and experiential information is transferred in rich and vivid detail. The richness of ethnic consumption is therefore underlined by the cultural metaphors.

Mental model transcendence

The findings presented in this section indicate how the consumption of ethnic artworks as cultural metaphors creates mental model transcendence for the consumer. The consumption of ethnicity exposes the ways of being and knowing of marginal groups, the relations between social groups, and how members of other groups treat a marginalized group and its members, both informally in personal interactions and in formal settings (Peñaloza and Venkatesh 2006). The findings depict that the awareness of social issues made possible by the cultural metaphors leads to a mental model transcendence that allow to see such social issues in a new light. Schon (1979), who investigated the 'generative' role of metaphors, promoted the view that by constructing a new way of looking at 'problems' it is possible to reconcile conflicting situations. This process that takes place by finding new metaphorical ways of understanding transcultural situations, which can be characterized as a blending of cultural frames that causes consumers to break free from their previous conceptions.

The existing differences between artworks from the Latino and American cultures create a distance from the so-called 'conventional' understanding. The intentional vagueness of the Latino images offers new and unorthodox points of view to understand reality, and this leads consumers to introspection. That novel way of perceiving the world has the potential to evoke a richer set of associations in the memory and the self of the consumer. Self-awareness is a phenomenon that can cause a revolution in the consumer's thinking. It can open up new horizons when the consumer is able to identify his or her 'self' as the 'other' – a person from a different culture. Consequently, interpretation is an important component of the consumption of ethnicity that is crucial to the consumer's mental model transcendence.

Insights from two informants – Gabriel Villa (age 49, male artist) and Linda (age 41, female tourist) – illustrate how the metaphorical images are used to create a self-awareness that changed their prior mental models. Gabriel Villa's desire to instill a social conscience leads him to use cultural metaphors in his paintings to help encourage a change or an update of mental models, which in turn helps to transcendence:

> I am very concerned about disparities in social contemporary life and vices in society that lead to a deterioration in human life. I have learned to play with new concepts relating to my culture and add new dimension to my work that stimulate social conscience. An example is my painting showing the different human heads under the cactus plants . . . If people come to the gallery and they don't know about the issue, then I want them to walk away a little more knowledgeable . . . It's about values . . .

Gabriel Villa uses human heads under a cactus plant to represent a transcultural identity that embraces all humanity (see Figure 15.2). He suggests that the human heads forming a circle under the cactus show human condition of interaction. The self-confessed intention of the artist is to

Figure 15.2 Cactus and heads

Note
Artwork by Gabriel Villa. Image used with permission from Gabriel Villa.

make the consumer feel a sense of responsibility for the creation of a better world. Through his art-work, Gabriel Villa embodies ethnicity connecting physical, cultural and social spaces. The cultural objectification of the artworks is presented as a form of social confrontation. In this way, this cul-tural worker opens up a discourse of ethnic domination/subordination/empowerment and creates a framework for the production and consumption of social exchanges (Peñaloza and Gilly 1999).

The process of consuming and producing ethnicity causes the consumer to 'live in the blend' and establishes an interaction with the unpleasant visceral connotations of social injustice. Linda explains her impressions of Gabriel Villa's paintings thus:

> I perceive these images as crucial tools for storytelling and for exposing both the struggles and beauty of the Mexican culture. As a non-Mexican, I can appreciate the experience of coming upon these murals, being curious about their meaning, and wanting to learn more . . . So you become more personally engaged, and this provokes me to become more interested in this issue.

Linda's words show that the murals emotionally touch her and that, by being curious about their meanings, her self-awareness is raised. Although the mural is one of a confrontation, in its consumption Linda transcends the ethnic segregation and stereotyping. Despite there being no long-term engagement or shared experience between Linda and the cultural workers, her curiosity is aroused. This creates a platform for changing her mindset about Latino ethnicities.

Creative work by Hector Duarte also provides further support for explaining how transcul-tural perspectives create self-awareness, leading to mental model transcendence (see Figure 15.3). This is illustrated in the following quote:

> Images associated with my concept of transformation are a whirlpool, the breaking of a barbed wire, and butterflies . . . Paintings such as *Awakening of the Americas* have images that represent our roots as well as new horizons. I like to [dismantle] the psychological fron-tiers of the mind . . . This picture shows a man with a DNA fingerprint where his face is supposed to be. The DNA represents the exterior identity of mankind while on the other hand, the fingerprint represents the interior identity.

Figure 15.3   Barbed wire and butterflies
Note
Artwork by Hector Duarte. Image used with permission from Mr. Duarte.

Butterflies and whirlpools in Mexican culture are associated with a mystical transformation of one form of life into another. In his approach, Hector Duarte represents the DNA as
a human identity (Figure 15.4), which triggers an awakening to a new sense of self. With the
consumption of ethnicity through these ideologically loaded paintings, cognitive processes and
communication structures of the consumer change to embrace a transcultural perspective.

Similarly, Jose Guerrero (age 65, male artist/tour guide) speaks about his mural painting
depicting a skeleton tangled in barbed wire. Jose indicates that this painting represents Gulliver
who travelled around the world with no borders and as a result he was maltreated. Making reference to a barbed wire that leads to death, a death of conscience, Jose suggests that the human
species needs to be liberated from prejudice. This artist adorns the alleyways and garage doors in
Pilsen with his painting of Mexican history, which he shares with people from all races in order
to provide a transcultural perspective.

Peñaloza (2007) considers the subjectivity and agency of 'whiteness' as a mental model that
creates discrimination against ethnic minorities and cripples knowledge of ethnicity and consumption. Artwork such as that of Hector Duarte and Jose Guerrero prompts White American
consumers to look beyond this subjectivity, question White values of individual autonomy,
achievement and meritocracy, and contrast them with transcultural perspectives. In this way,
mental model transcendence can be achieved.

Tom (age 32, male tourist) illustrates the transformation that he experienced after being
exposed to the barbed wire and butterfly image (see Figure 15.3):

> I have been inspired and would like to acquire this ability to take care of one's community
> while appreciating and understanding the diversity and differences of others in the world:
> local action and global consciousness. I realize that one should appreciate all the world has
> to offer but try not to change others to your ways.

Figure 15.4 DNA fingerprint
Note
Artwork by Hector Duarte. Image used with permission from Mr. Duarte.

Similarly, the immediate effect for Tom after consuming the ethnicity in this artwork was an awareness of the self that led him to a mental model transcendence. The new perception Tom has is different from the nostalgic and romantic characterizations of the ethnic cultures. His inspiration takes him to reflections of issues such as ethnic community welfare.

In order to explain mental model transcendence caused by ethnic consumption, we consider Fauconnier and Turner's (2002) blending theory. This theory is concerned with the concept of stimulated elaboration, which refers to the imaginative processes based on novel conceptualizations for learning, understanding and other creative sense-making activities. We relate the narratives of the cultural workers about the production of ethnicity to three different stages that take place in the process of stimulated elaboration. The first stage deals with the use of metaphorical images to stimulate thinking. Metaphorical images help people look at themselves and those involved (Morgan 1997). Stimulated elaboration evokes a rich set of associations in memory, which leads to a greater persuasion and a higher agreement with the message that metaphors convey.

The second stage is concerned with the creation of distance from conventional understandings of the cultural metaphor by means of an intentional vagueness that raises open issues and unanswered questions. The third stage is the ownership of insights, which in turn lead to a sense of self-awareness. At this stage, an opportunity is offered to attempt to deal with the unknown, and in so doing to internalize unfamiliar knowledge and new meanings. Rather than being distant and abstract, the emergent meaning is considered to be immediate and personal, and thus allows the creation of a sense of self-awareness. Consequently, the sense of self-awareness that involves cognition (revelation, knowledge) and emotions is able to evoke a mental model transcendence. Teichert *et al.'s* (2006) concept of mental model matching helps to understand how mental model transcendence is achieved. In their role in mental model matching, metaphors act as a trigger to break up entrenched mental models that are no longer in line with changing mental representations. The narratives of cultural workers show how cultural metaphors are used to create new collectively shared mental models focusing on universal ideals. Once the connection to an ideal reality is made, mental paradigms are changed in such a way that they lead to mental model transcendence into a transcultural space. In this study, we aimed at extending Teichert *et al.'s* (2006) model to include metaphors as major triggers of consumers' mental model transcendence.

Enhancement of destination image

Interviews with three informants illustrate how the consumption of ethnicity through cultural metaphors creates awareness of transcultural identity. This in turn results in a mental model transcendence that enhances the destination image. According to the informants, the importance of awareness of transcultural identity is to make consumers transcend the traditional concept of culture, characterized by social homogeneity, and intercultural divisions. The aim of, awareness is therefore an attempt to encourage a respect for, and enjoyment of, diversity. This appreciation of, diversity was identified as a major factor enhancing the destination image. Jose Guerrero vividly illustrates how the cultural metaphors represented in the public murals are used to signal a deeper level of thinking that moves beyond cultural and gender boundaries. He notes:

> You can see symbols in these murals, which are meant to encourage [the youth] to understand history and utilize it for a better life in harmony with other cultures. *Choc mol* is a metaphor for knowledge and belief. The crack running down from top to bottom has the symbolic importance of separating belief from knowledge.

From Jose Guerrero's words, it can be understood that the use of cultural metaphors depicting belief and wisdom creates an awareness of a transcultural identity for the youth that contributes to enhance the destination image. The opportunity to obtain transformative learning enhances the destination image for consumers. Transformative learning does not simply add to the reservoir of knowledge, but changes the consumer fundamentally. As stated by Clark (1993), 'transformative learning shapes people: they are different afterward, in ways both they and others can recognize. The process can be gradual or sudden' (p. 47).

Rolando (age 47, male artist) describes the way he uses cultural metaphors in his artwork in order to evoke something 'magical' that makes tourists more aware of who they are. He says:

> People are absorbed in the textures and sizes of my pieces. A lot of my images go back to the magic of the Mexican theatre and also scenic designs. My work [operates between] figuration and abstraction, leaving more questions unanswered than answered. I leave my audience with direction to think about a specific idea or situation and try to evoke a response that would come from them . . .

Rolando's allusion refers to a magic that is partially staged, but closely based on reality. He shows the way that the Mexican culture considers people to feel affection for nature. This is perceived as a call to awake to a sense of self characterized by elements of love inviting to a transcendence experience.

Alison (age 30, female tourist) who admires Victor's works comments:

> The bright, bold colours and the range of faces and stories [are] absolutely beautiful. I value that there is some history here that you normally don't see in other parts of Chicago. You definitely have some homely, warm feelings when you experience the culture . . . there's the murals, gardens, the style of the building, the way people paint their homes, the potted humble plants upfront. Or like the Virgins of Guadalupe . . . What other neighbourhood has that in Chicago?

In her words, both the physical and symbolic features of the paintings provide a transcultural perspective that contributes to enhance the destination image of the neighbourhood far away than its physical borders. Transcultural consumers such as Alison, most of who have achieved the American dream of owning a beautiful house with aesthetic gardens, are fascinated by the effect/impact of this imagery in their consumption of ethnicity. The aesthetics of ethnic communities often represent 'the better life', one that closely resembles the American dream. Such perceptions grant social legitimacy to ethnic groups in targeting them as market niches (Peñaloza 1994).

John (age 37, male tourist) shares similar sentiments:

> I would say that my emotions range with the different murals – some of which are very serious, quite literal . . . I often feel curious as I feel that these images are communicating deeply powerful stories about the Mexican immigrant experience, both in Mexico and here in the U.S. Some of them portray a sense of strength and courage stemming from community and faith . . . These stories touch me deeply, and draws me to this community . . .

John makes an interpretation of the stories reflected in the different murals of the neighbourhood, indicating that his destination image is enhanced. The metaphorical images of the Pilsen community play a major role in evoking feelings and emotions that contribute to his transcultural experience. The richness of the ethnic themes captured in the historical images of the murals shows John that the 'other' also lived the heroic lives they aspired to. As a result John is emotionally moved and his destination image is favourably affected.

Fauconnier's (1997) work concerned with the uncovering of the conceptual blend is fundamental for the interpretation of consumption of ethnicity that leads to transcultural awareness and the enhancement of the destination image. According to this researcher, the basic principles of conceptual blending can be described as operating in two input mental spaces that yield to a third space: the blend. Mental spaces are conceived as being cognitively processed and constructed in the memory of the consumers as they think, talk and act in different settings. Mental spaces draw partly on background knowledge acquired through past events and are stored in the form of image schemas that endow meaning to the consumer experience (Johnson and Lehman 1997). Furthermore, the conceptual blend helps analyze how consumption of ethnicity through cultural metaphors plays a role in shaping the transcultural experience. Most cultures have some dominant metaphors about life and how it is to be lived; some may see life as a game, some as a journey and so on. Seeing how others view life through a metaphorical lens brings one's own guiding metaphors into question.

In the concept of Fauconnier and Turner's (2002) conceptual blending, the metaphorical space is the transcultural exposure and the source domain is the cultural artworks. Then the blend can be understood as the resultant transcultural space, with altered image schemas. The transcultural artist (Rolando) specifically tries to 'evoke a response that would come from them (the transcultural tourist)', which leads to 'homely, warm feelings when you experience this culture' (Alison) and that 'touch me deeply, and draws me to this community' (John). Clearly then, Rolando's attempt to evoke a response created felicitous reactions in terms of destination image in Alison and in John, who are left with altered image schemas with respect to the cultural destination they had visited.

Discussion and conclusions

In this chapter, we investigated the production and consumption of ethnicity in a transcultural context from three different angles. First, we explored how cultural metaphors represent the consumption of ethnicity. Second, we found how the consumption of cultural metaphors can be an important medium for enhancing understanding of ethnic cultures, and hence resulted in mental model transcendence. We showed how cultural workers managed to make use of powerful means to communicate thought-provoking messages dealing with open and unresolved issues. In their attempt to understand the conflicts and contradictions represented in the artworks, consumers were able to gain self-awareness as transcultural beings, and this led to mental model transcendence. Third, the findings depicted how the transcultural perspective from the metaphorical images and the mental model transcendence enhances the destination image. Such enhancement of the destination image is an integral part of the process, by which ethnicity is consumed. Consumers found the messages retrieved from the metaphorical sources as inspirational and stimulating as they evoked novel ideas that were radically different from those of their cultural milieu. The messages transmitted by these works of art embraced the co-existence of the local and the global, the modern and the traditional, as well as the historical and aesthetic at the same time. All these generated positive perceptions and favourable evaluations of the destination image by positively and emotionally moving the consumer.

Implication for theory

The themes that arose in this investigation have important implications for research and practice. In terms of research, the notions of cultural metaphors, mental models and destination image are central to the understanding of the consumption of ethnicity. The first finding of this study – consuming ethnicity – shows how this leads to motivations and ideals that transcend cultures and groups to endow transcultural meaning to consumers, and enriches their lives. Personal meanings and understandings may be essentially metaphorical, cobbled together from a palette of more universal metaphors; the most likely ones used are the ones selected through acculturation. This suggests that one can consume a new ethnicity via the predominant metaphors that these ethnicities use (as suggested by Zaltman [2003] in *How Consumers Think*). Thus, new ethnicities can be better introduced in a wide array of forms and places if the reigning metaphors are explicated.

The mechanism suggested above provides an avenue for the exploration of how cultural metaphors can be used to consume salient issues relating to ethnicity and even to marginalized consumers. For example, does the consumer need to be accosted by an 'other', one that uses a starkly different metaphoric view of the world, to realize that everyone is guided by their own metaphors? How different does the 'other' need to be to provoke a possibility of rapprochement? How important is the degree of difference in this process? What processes can attune a consumer to an awareness of the other and, therefore, of oneself?

The second finding – transcending culture – suggests the same pattern as the first finding of consuming ethnicity. To an extent, consumption of ethnicity can be considered a larger version of the project of creating the self – that there are guiding metaphors for ethnic cultures like there are for selves; that cultures have cosmologies of metaphors that are sanctioned ways for its members to construe the world. Then, it could be asked what ethnic cultures are more likely to generate cosmopolitan consumers, those more willing to accept a transcendent encounter? What makes some ethnic cultures more likely than others to accept that which is different? Are (some) ethnic and cultural dimensions more related to acceptance of other cultures than others (e.g. are masculine cultures more resistant to the 'other' than feminine cultures?) Are some ethnic metaphors more acceptable to others for absorption? And what aspects of metaphors are these based on?

The final finding – transcending the local – was driven by the notion that seeing the 'other' as being the same as oneself would lead to favourable evaluations while consuming ethnicity. Whereas this was one of the outcomes of this study, there are several conditions under which seeing the 'other' as same as 'us' could lead to a dislike; this is especially true when the 'other' is a romanticized ideal – this happens when such transcultural consumers are chasing 'differentness', not seeking a 'sameness'. Transcultural consumers who loathe their own ethnicity and seek escape in some destination perceived as exotic are primed to see differences, and will likely balk at anything that has actual or perceived familiarity with their own culture. This raises questions such as: 'Are consumers of some ethnicities more likely to appreciate the essential sameness of different cultures while consuming ethnicity?' and 'What makes the social reality constructed by cultural metaphors constraining enough to preclude seeing the oneness?' Within the context of our study, one could ask whether the reactions of Latino tourists visiting an American village would lead to the same kinds of transformations that the American tourists had when visiting a Latino enclave, based on the guiding metaphors within the source and destination cultures.

Implications for practice

Our findings can have important implications for marketers. The first one is the opportunity to leverage the intersections of marketing and ethnicity, such as in the context of tourism. Transcultural consumption, e.g. through tourism, is pervasive and therefore is becoming one of the largest industries. Mainstream and minority ethnic subcultures are likely to benefit from contact and cross-fertilization with each other through such marketing initiatives.

Additionally, the consumption of ethnicity can be modified so that the consumers' ways of relating to the world are packaged and sold, much in the same way that other products are consumed. Similarly, configuring opportunities for transcendence will make other cultures and ethnicities more likeable, i.e. improvement of destination images; this can also help to properly calibrate, and rehabilitate, the country-of-origin or country-of-destination effects. Images of the 'other' are not fixed but (trans)mutable. Thus, rich and complex transcultural resources can be used as transformational tools for influencing the mental models of consumers.

Second, transcultural marketers can profit from applying the findings of this study to create a distinctive destination image and gain a favourable differentiation from competitors. A transcultural perspective with an emphasis on diversity makes possible the recognition of cultural universals, those that link consumers to common values and ideals. This phenomenon is in line with Benjamin et al.'s (2006) concept of culturally adaptive communities, in reference to those cultural groups that, after identifying what makes them unique, develop distinctiveness from others. Awareness on this issue can be beneficial for ethnic marketers, who can enhance the destination image influenced by diverse cultures. Transcultural strategies could be encouraged by placing consumption of ethnicity and transcultural perspectives as important priorities of policy-making. Such an approach may have an important impact on marketing, not only in the field of tourism but also in other areas relating to multicultural activities such as consumer entertainment, i.e. development of multicultural theatre, dance, literature and the crafts. Cultural metaphors can also play a key role to create mental model transcendence, enhance destination images and inspire universal ideals that unite ethnic and transcultural markets. These transcultural values could be embodied in other public displays, such as the symbols located in central areas of the city, flagship buildings, public art and information services.

Finally, this study has implications for the segmentation, targeting and positioning of ethnic markets. Marketers must understand what the critical cultural metaphors are and the mental models of their target segments. Different cultures, or ethnic groups, will have different metaphors undergirding the consumer experiences, and this will require the marketer to engage in sense-making any product that goes between cultures in terms of the guiding metaphors of each culture.

In a culture where a breakfast is an occasion for the family to gather (metaphorically, gathering the tribe before going off to combat), the multinational company cannot simply barge in and offer breakfast cereals in a variety of local flavours; the meaning of the meal is not in the flavours but in the gathering, and to make it about flavours is to misconstrue it at its metaphoric core.

References

Adeney, B. T. (1995) *Strange Virtues: Ethics in a Multicultural World*. Downers Grove, IL: Inter-Varsity Press.

Appadurai, A. (1996) *Modernity at Large: Cultural Dimensions of Globalization*, (Vol. 1). Minnesota, MN: University of Minnesota Press.

Arnould E. J. and Price, L. L. (1993) 'River magic: Extraordinary experience and the extended service encounter'. *Journal of Consumer Research*, 20(June): 24–45.

Askegaard, S., Arnould, E. J. and Kjeldgaard, D. (2005) 'Postassimilationist ethnic consumer research: Qualifications and extensions'. *Journal of Consumer Research*, 32: 160–70.

Benjamin, S., Cerere, J., Granier, M. and Tang, L. (2006) *New Fundamentals in Local Economic Development Planning: Culturally Adaptive Communities*. Atlanta, GA: Georgia Institute of Technology, City and Regional Planning Program.

Berger, A. A. (1996). *Narratives in Popular Culture, Media and Everyday Life*. Thousand Oaks, CA Sage Publications.

Bianchini F. (2004) 'The cultural impacts of globalization and the future of urban cultural policies'. In *New Horizons in British Urban Policy: Perspectives on New Labour's Urban Renaissance*, edited by C. Johnstone, M. Whitehead: 215–28.

Christensen, G. L. and Olson, J. C. (2002) 'Mapping consumers' mental models with ZMET'. *Psychology & Marketing*, 19(6): 477–501.

Christians, C. G. (2000) 'Ethics and politics in qualitative research'. *Handbook of Qualitative Research*, 2: 133–155.

Clark, M. (1993) 'Transformational learning'. *New Directions For Adult and Continuing Education*, No. 57, edited by R. Brockett and S. Merriam. Californian, CA: Jossey-Bass: 47–56.

Denny, R. and Sunderland, P. L. (2005) 'Researching cultural metaphors in action: Metaphors of computing technology in contemporary U.S. life'. *Journal of Business Research*, 58(10): 1456–63.

Elliot, A. E., Cherian, J. and Casakin, H. (2013) 'Cultural metaphors: Enhancing consumer pleasure in ethnic servicescapes'. *Journal of Business Research*, 66(8): 1004–12.

Elliot, E. A., Cherian, J. and Elaydi, R. (2014) 'Microcredit and metaphors in subsistence markets'. *Journal of Macromarketing*, 34(2): 133–4.

Epstein M. (2009) 'Transculture: A broad way between globalism and multiculturalism'. *American Journal of Economics and Sociology*, 68(January): 327–51.

Fauconnier, G. (1997). *Mappings in Thought and Language*. Cambridge, UK: Cambridge University Press.

Fauconnier, G. and Turner, M. (2002) *The Way We Think*, New York, NY: Basic.

Fakeye, P. C. and Crompton, J. L. (1991) 'Image differences between prospective first-time, and repeat visitors to the Lower Rio Grande Valley'. *Journal of Travel Research*, 30(2): 10–16.

Gannon, M. J. (2002) 'Cultural Metaphors: Their use in management practice and as a method for understanding cultures'. In *Online Readings in Psychology and Culture*, edited by W. J. Lonner and D. N. Sattler. Washington, WA: Western Washington University.

Gannon, M. J., Locke, E. A., Gupta, A., Audia, P. and Kristof-Brown, A. L. (2005) 'Cultural metaphors as frames of reference for nations: A six-country study'. *International Studies of Management and Organization*, 35(4): 37–47.

Gartner, W. C. (1989) 'Tourism image: Attribute measurement of state tourism products using multidimensional scaling techniques'. *Journal of Travel Research*, 28(2): 16–20.

Gartner, W. C. (1993) 'Image formation process'. *Journal of Travel and Tourism Marketing*, 2(2/3): 191–215.

Ghisi, M. L. (2010). 'Towards a transmodern transformation of our global society: European challenges and opportunities'. *Journal of Future Studies* 15(1): 39–48.

Glaser, B. and Strauss, A. (1967). *The Discovery of Grounded Theory*. London: Weidenfeld & Nicolson.

Han, J. Y. (2005) 'The relationships of perceived risk to personal factors, knowledge of destination, and travel purchase decisions in international leisure travel'. *Doctoral Dissertation*. Virginia Polytechnic Institute and State University.

Hill, R. C. and Levenhagen, M. (1995) 'Metaphors and mental models: Sensemaking and sensegiving in innovative and entrepreneurial activities'. *Journal of Management*, 21(6): 1057–1074.

Hirschman, E. (2007) 'Metaphor in the marketplace'. *Marketing theory*, 7(3): 227–48.

Johnson, M. D. and Lehmann, D. R. (1997) 'Consumer experience and consideration sets for brands and product categories'. *Advances in Consumer Research*, 24: 295–300.

Joy, A. and Sherry Jr., J. F. (2003) 'Speaking of art as embodied imagination: A multisensory approach to understanding aesthetic experience'. *Journal of Consumer Research*, 30(Sept): 259–82.

Lakoff, G. (1987) *Women, Fire and Dangerous Things: What Categories Reveal about the Mind?* Chicago, IL/London: University of Chicago Press.

Lakoff, G. and Johnson, M. (1980) *Metaphors We Live By*, Chicago, IL: Chicago University Press.

Lakoff, G. and Turner, M. (1989) *More Than Cool Reason: A Field Guide to Poetic Metaphor*. Chicago, IL: University of Chicago Press.

Langer, S. (1980) *Philosophy in a New Key: A Study in the Symbolism of Reason, Rite, and Art*. Cambridge, MA: Harvard University Press.

Levy, S. J. (1981). 'Intepreting consumer mythology: A structural approach to consumer behavior'. *The Journal of Marketing*, 45(Summer): 49–61.

Morgan, G. (1997) *Images of Organization*. Beverly Hills, CA: Sage Publications.

Morris, P. K. and Waldman, J. A. (2011) 'Culture and metaphors in advertisements: France, Germany, Italy, the Netherlands, and the United States'. *International Journal of Communication*, 5: 27.

Nonaka, I. and Takeuchi, H. (1995) *The Knowledge-Creating Company: How Japanese Companies Create the Dynamics of Innovation*. Oxford, UK: Oxford University Press.

Patton, M. Q. (2002) *Qualitative Research and Evaluation Methods*. Thousand Oaks, CA: Sage.

Peñaloza, L. N. (1994) 'Atravesando fronteras/border crossing: A critical ethnographic exploration of the consumer acculturation of Mexican immigrants'. *Journal of Consumer Research*, 21(1): 32–54.

Peñaloza, L. N. (2007) 'Researching ethnicity and consumption'. In *Handbook of Qualitative Research Methods in Marketing*, edited by R. W. Belk. North Hampton, MA: Edward Elgar Publishing.

Peñaloza, L. N. and Gilly, M. (1999) 'Marketers' acculturation: The changer and the changed'. *Journal of Marketing*, 63(3): 84–104.

Peñaloza, L. N. and Venkatesh, A. (2006) 'Further evolving the new dominant logic of marketing: From services to the social construction of markets.' *Marketing Theory*, 6(3): 299–316.

Piedmont, R. L. (1999) 'Does spirituality represent the sixth factor of personality? Spiritual transcendence and the five-factor model'. *Journal of Personality*, 67: 985–1013.

Richards, G. and Wilson, J. (2004) 'The impact of cultural events on city image: Rotterdam, cultural capital of Europe 2001'. *Urban Studies*, 41(10): 1931–51.

Russo, A. P. (2002) 'The "vicious circle" of tourism development in heritage cities'. *Annals of Tourism Research*, 29(1): 165–82.

Schon, Donald A. (1979) 'Generative metaphor: A perspective on problem-setting in social policy'. In *Metaphor and Thought*, edited by A. Ortony. Cambridge, UK, Cambridge University Press, 254–83.

Teichert, T., Wartburg, I. V. and Braterman, R. (2006) 'Tacit meaning in disguise: Hidden metaphors in new product development and market making'. *Business Horizons*, 49: 451–61.

Thompson, C., Locander, W. B. and Pollio, H. R. (1989) 'Putting consumer experience back into consumer research: The philosophy and method of existential-phenomenology'. *Journal of Consumer Research*, 16(September): 133–46.

Venkatesh, A. (1995) 'Ethno-consumerism: A new paradigm to study cultural and cross-cultural consumer behavior'. In *Marketing in the Multicultural World*, edited by J. A. Costa and G. Bamossy. Thousand Oaks, CA: Sage Publications.

Voss, K.-C. (2003) 'Transculture: The emergent property of intercultural encounters'. *Paper Presented At the Research Institute for Austrian and International Literature and Cultural Sciences Conference*, November: 7–9.

Yeo, A. (1996). 'Cultural user interfaces: A silver lining in cultural diversity'. *ACM SIGCHI Bulletin* 28(3): 4–7.

Zaltman, G. and Coulter, R. H. (1995) 'Seeing the voice of the customer: Metaphor-based advertising research'. *Journal of Advertising Research*, 35: 35–51.

Zaltman, G. (1997) 'Rethinking market research: Putting people back in'. *Journal of Marketing Research*, 34(November): 424–37.

Zaltman, G. (2003) *How Customers Think: Essential Insights into the Mind of the Market*. Cambridge, MA: Harvard Business School Press.

Appendix 15.1: interview questions: Latino and American participants

Interview questions: Latino cultural workers

Description of creative expression

1. How would you describe your artwork?
2. Why did you choose to design and make these?

Description of value created with artwork (cultural and symbolic value):

1. What are the thoughts and feelings behind the design of this mural?
2. What would you like the tourists to admire about your work?
3. Can you relate your artistic movement to the enhancement of Pilsen as a touristic destination?
4. How is your culture reflected in the form and function of your art work?
5. What is the symbolism of these designs?

Interview questions: American tourists

1. What are your thoughts and feelings when you look at these murals? What do you admire most about these works?
2. How do these artworks influence your perception of the community?
3. How do these artworks influence your perception of the world?

Part VI
Advertising

16

Multicultural advertising and ethnic minority consumers

Jinnie Jinyoung Yoo and Wei-Na Lee

Introduction

The United States has always been the embodiment of a multicultural society as seen from its diversity in race, ethnicity, religion and how someone identifies oneself and the lifestyle that a person adopts. The goal of this chapter is to offer a summary of our understanding of ethnic minority consumers in the US and point to knowledge gaps to be filled by future research.

Major segments of the ethnic minority population in the US include Hispanic, African and Asian Americans, those who do not identify themselves as non-Hispanic White. The U.S. Census Bureau further includes individuals who identify themselves as Black or Asian in combination with another race such as Native Hawaiian or Pacific Islander, American Indian, Alaska Native or some other race (U.S. Census Bureau 2010). Recent trends suggest that a growing number of ethnic minority consumers in the US are becoming increasingly proactive in expressing their unique cultural identities. This trend is reinforced by the changing demographic, technological, social, cultural and media environments. Ethnic minority consumers currently comprise nearly 30% of the U.S. population. They are estimated to reach 46.3% by 2050 (ibid.) Eventually, the so-called minorities will become the majority in the US. Specifically, the U.S. Census Bureau (2010) predicted that people who regard themselves as Hispanic American, African American, Asian American, American Indian, Native Hawaiian and Pacific Islander will become the majority by 2042, minorities accounting for 54% of the population and non-Census Bureau further reported that the population shares of Hispanics and Asians are set to double to 30% and 9% of the total population before 2050 (U.S. Census Bureau 2011). As the marketplace in the US becomes increasingly diversified and ethnic minority consumers' purchasing power and ethnic consciousness grow, marketing and advertising professionals have duly recognized the important role of multiculturalism. Significant efforts have been made to attend to cultural differences in marketing communication programs. Although there is little consensus on the definition of the term multicultural marketing, Friedman *et al.* (2007) succinctly pointed out that it is about 'targeting, communicating, and using differentiated marketing strategies with diverse cultures including ethnic groups, religious groups, nationalities, people living in particular geographic regions, or groups that share common beliefs, values, attitudes or a way of life' (p. 25). The goal of multicultural advertising is, therefore, to engage multiple target audiences who are distinguished by cultural characteristics. Put another way, multicultural advertising is a specific class of advertising that aims to simultaneously reach a culturally diverse target audience through the use of culturally relevant representations such as sources, symbols, traditions, beliefs, values and/or objects from multiple cultural backgrounds in persuasive messages (Johnson et al. 2010). The following sections first summarize research insights on ethnic minority consumers and their responses toward multicultural advertising. Subsequently, future research agenda are provided to offer directions for empirical work that fills the current knowledge gaps.

An evolving understanding of ethnic minority consumers' cultural identity is the core

People generally live within their cultural boundaries. Cultural values and norms influence the way individuals think, feel and act. People in the same ethnic groups tend to share similar language, customs, values and social views. These shared values influence people's cognition (beliefs and motives), affect (emotion and attitude) and behaviour (purchase and consumption). Based on the notion that 'advertising acts as a mirror of the society', cultural values and standards are to be presented in adverts in such a way that consumers can 'see themselves' and identify with the characters in the adverts and feel affinity toward the brands (Hong et al. 1987). Central to this culturally based approach to communication is the idea that communication is most effective when the message content, the characters and symbols used, and values portrayed are congruent with the target audience's cultural identity.

Ethnic minority consumers have been known to exhibit different marketplace responses in product use, shopping orientation, response to promotion, brand loyalty, media usage, attitude toward advertising, purchase decision, etc. (Hernandez and Kaufman 1991). They tend to be more responsive to messages that are reflective of their cultural values and assets than those that are not (Pitts et al. 1989; Green 1995; Hernandez 1988). Findings from a number of empirical studies on ethnicity in an advertising context generally suggest that ethnic minority consumers are likely to be aware of and thus respond more favourably to adverts with ethnic cues. Specifically, some of the early studies have found that ethnic minority consumers are more likely to deem their ethnicity important and trust spokespersons of similar ethnicity more than those who are not, which in turn leads to more favourable response the adverts using same-ethnicity actors (e.g. Deshpandé and Stayman 1994; Koslow et al. 1994). Furthermore, other early research has found that ethnic minority consumers tend to be influenced by adverts using ethnic language and show favourable responses to such adverts and associated brands (e.g. Deshpandé et al. 1986; Roslow and Nicholls 1996). In addition, subsequent work has found that relative to weak ethnic identifiers, strong ethnic identifiers evaluate adverts that feature same-ethnicity spokespersons more positively and have stronger purchase intentions for brands with them in the adverts than those who do not (e.g. Green 1999). In summary, clear ethnic cues in an advert encourage ethnically sensitive consumers to develop more positive attitudes about that advert, which in turn should induce more favourable attitudes toward and stronger purchase intentions for the featured brand (Appiah 2001a; Elliott and Wattanasuwan 1998; Forehand and Deshpandé 2001).

More recent literature has focused on the influence of ethnic identification on ethnic minority consumers' response to adverts. For example, Appiah (2001a) found that strong ethnic identifiers saw themselves as more similar to and identified more strongly with the same-ethnicity characters in adverts than weak identifiers did. Another study, introducing the idea of ethnic primes and its influence on consumers' advertising response, found that ethnic minorities responded more favourably to the same-ethnicity spokesperson and adverts targeted to that ethnic group when they were both primed and socially distinctive (Forehand *et al.* 2002).

Research examining ethnic salience and self-reference should be helpful in explaining the influence of ethnic culture identification on consumer response. Lee *et al.* (2002) found that ethnic minority consumers exposed to adverts consistent with their ethnicity were likely to spontaneously self-reference the advert, which in turn led to more positive responses to both the advert and the associated brand. Martin *et al.* (2004) found that unusual voice-over/subtitling increased ethnic self-awareness as well as advert recall, demonstrating that advert schema congruity moderated the effect of target market affiliation on attitudes toward the advert and the spokesperson.

As can be seen, research examining the influence of ethnic identity on advert response has evolved, and scholars have begun to pay attention to the complexity of ***cultural identity*** among ethnic minority consumers. Unlike majority consumers, most ethnic minorities must deal with two central issues: (1) the extent to which they are motivated or allowed to retain identification with the culture of origin, the non-majority or minority culture and (2) the extent to which they are motivated or allowed to identify with the dominant or majority culture (Berry 1990). The process of negotiating this dual or even multiple cultural identities is complex, multifaceted, and is at the core of how ethnic consumers behave. Some ethnic minorities perceive the two cultural identities to be compatible, whereas others see them as oppositional. How this identity negotiation process influences ethnic minorities' response to marketing communication efforts requires an in-depth understanding.

The consumer acculturation process

One of the key theoretical constructs that scholars have delved into when discussing cultural identity negotiation among ethnic minority consumers is acculturation. Although there have been many competing views about the meaning of the term acculturation, early views about its nature offer a useful foundation:

> Acculturation comprehends those phenomena which result when groups of individuals having different cultures come into continuous first-hand contact, with subsequent changes in the original culture patterns of either or both groups.
>
> *(Redfield* et al. *1936, pp. 149–50)*

A recent definition of acculturation by Berry (2005) focused on the notion of 'either or both groups'. Berry defined acculturation as:

> The dual process of cultural and psychological change that takes place as a result of contact between two or more cultural groups and their individual members . . . Acculturation is a process of cultural and psychological changes that involve various forms of mutual accommodation, leading to some longer-term psychological and sociocultural adaptations between both groups.
>
> *(Berry 2005, pp. 698–99)*

Berry went on to suggest that there are a number of alternative courses and goals to the process of acculturation. In other words, one key feature of all acculturation phenomena is the variability with which they take place. In this light, ethnic minorities enter into the acculturation process in different ways and to different degrees (Jun *et al.* 1993; Lee and Um 1992). The levels of acculturation have been reported to be critical in understanding the unique experiences of ethnic minorities living in a multicultural society (Berry 2005).

Consumer acculturation is that part of acculturation specific to the consumption process. Peñaloza (1994) defined consumer acculturation as 'the general process of movement and adaptation to the consumer cultural environment in one country by persons from another country' (p. 33). Acculturation can be seen as a socialization process in which an immigrant consumer learns the behaviours, attitudes and values of a culture that are different from their culture of origin (Lee 1988). Different levels of acculturation among ethnic minority consumers may result in differences in shopping orientation, use of language and media, perceptions of product attributes and attitudes toward advertising (Wallendorf and Reilly 1983). Some immigrants, when they first arrive in a new country may desire to maintain significant aspects of their home culture and to stay informed about events in their home country. On the other hand, newcomers who are faced with role conflicts in the new culture may also be highly motivated to learn its basic consumption-related attitudes, knowledge and skills to function as consumers in that new culture.

Many scholars have recommended that ethnic minority consumers be studied from the acculturative perspective. They argue that the level of acculturation can be a potent segmentation variable since it has been linked to differences in attitudes toward advertising, media use, coupon use, print advertising, direct marketing advertising and even consumer purchase decision and information search behaviour (Deshpandé et al. 1986; Donthu and Cherian 1992; Korgaonkar et al. 2000; Ueltschy and Krampf 1997; Webster 1991).

A number of studies have noted significant differences in media preferences and advertising effectiveness between ethnic minorities who were high versus those low in acculturation (Deshpandé et al. 1986; O'Guinn and Faber 1985). These differences have been found in many different types of media such as print advertisements (Adelson 1989), store signs (Hayes-Bautista et al. 1984), radio (Valenzuela 1973; Dunn 1975), and general media advertising (Deshpandé et al. 1986). Ueltschy and Krampf (1997; 2011) found that highly acculturated Hispanics showed significantly more positive attitudes toward the adverts when the advert copy was in English while Hispanics low in acculturation showed more positive attitudes toward the advert when the copy was in Spanish. Lee and Um (1992) found that mixed acculturation patterns contributed to differences between Korean immigrants and Anglo-Americans in consumer product evaluations. Specifically, highly acculturated Koreans, compared to less acculturated Koreans and to Americans, tended to actively adopt dominant American cultural styles by observing what their American friends buy, taking friends' advice on purchase recommendations and listening to what advertising says. Rajagopalan and Heitmeyer (2005) found a negative relationship between the level of acculturation and involvement in Indian ethnic apparel among Asian Indian consumers, suggesting that acculturation may be negatively related to ethnic consumption and positively related to mainstream consumption.

Theoretical conceptualization of acculturation has evolved from the earlier one-dimensional model to bi-dimensional models. While the one-dimensional model assumes that non-dominant groups and individuals would move from some 'traditional' way of living to a way resembling that of the dominant society (Berry 2005), bi-dimensional models consider diverse ranges of cultural identities with particular focus on the way that identity formation expresses minority and dominant cultures. Study by Peñaloza (1994) marked the beginning of the new phase of consumer acculturation studies. Her study on Mexican immigrants in the US focused on specific acculturation processes and conditions. It offered four practices of consumer acculturation: *resistance* (favouring Mexican practices over American practices), *acculturation* (adoption of American practices while maintaining Mexican practices), *assimilation* (adoption of American practices while deserting Mexican practices) and physical segregation (a spatial form of separation). It suggested that immigrant consumers commingle these practices in different ways to form identities.

Oswald's subsequent work (1999) added another interesting aspect to the study of consumer acculturation, focusing more on identity formation among ethnic minority consumers. Oswald's research of Haitian migrants in the USA introduced the notion of culture swapping, showing that a Haitian immigrant family unconsciously switched codes between the tastes of the Haitian elite and the American middle class depending upon the situation. This study provided rich insights to how consumer identities result from the dynamic interplay between the minority and the dominant culture. Many post-1999 acculturation studies have adopted Oswald's dualistic home/host notation. Askegaard *et al.* (2005) conducted a study regarding hybrid identities. Their study found that Greenlanders in Denmark moved between positions of hyperculture, assimilation, integration and pendulism. Importantly, Askegaard *et al.*'s study provided confirming evidence of the integrative cultural identities suggested by both Peñaloza (1994) and Oswald (1999). Collectively, these recent acculturation studies offer the possibility that ethnic minority consumers tend to individually pursue various 'integrative (or hybrid)' identities, thus the particulars of which vary across individuals and situations.

Recently, a few advertising studies have considered how different stages of acculturation affects consumers' advertising responses. For example, Khairullah (2011) examined whether the perceptions of Asian Indian Americans towards Indian print versus American print adverts vary within and across stages of acculturation. Their findings indicated that low and moderate acculturated participants had a greater preference for adverts with Indian cues while high acculturated Asian Indians had a greater preference for adverts with American cues. More recent work by Tsai and Li (2012) examined the the moderating effects of acculturation modes (assimilated, integrated and separated) on Hispanic consumers' responses to three advertising targeting strategies (Caucasian-targeted, bi-cultural and Hispanic targeted). They found a significant interaction effect between acculturation and message targeting on attitudes toward the advert. Specifically, Caucasian-targeted adverts generated the most favourable responses to the advert from assimilated Hispanic consumers, bi-cultural adverts generated the most favourable responses to the advert from integrated Hispanic consumers, and Hispanic-targeted adverts generated the most favourable responses to the advert from separated Hispanic consumers. Overall, findings of these studies suggest that an understanding of the effect of acculturation could aid in planning and executing appropriate advertising programs in order to effectively cater to specific segments of ethnic minority markets. However, research that adopts the concept of 'hybrid' identities or 'culture swaping' is still limited in the field of advertising.

Explanations of ethnic consumer responses

Ethnic affiliation, often called the strength of ethnic identification (Webster 1994), is a person's knowledge of his or her membership in a social group and the value and emotional significance attached to that membership (Phinney 1992). While one member of an ethnic minority group may have a strong ethnic identification with his or her culture and to a lesser degree identify with the majority culture, another member within the same ethnic group may have a weak identification with his or her culture and a high degree of affinity to the majority culture. Much research has shown ethnic identification to be a contributing cultural variable in consumer purchase behaviour (Donthu and Cherian 1992; Hirschman 1981; Webster 1994), media use (Deshpandé *et al.* 1986; Donthu and Cherian 1992; Appiah 2004; Becerra and Korgaonkar 2010) and evaluation of advertisements (Whittler 1989; Green 1999; Forehand and Deshpandé 2001; Wittler and Spira 2002; Appiah 2001a; 2001b; 2004).

An extended stream of studies has suggested that strong ethnic identifiers should display attitudes and behaviours that are consistent with the core cultural values of their ethnic group such as customs, language, foods, religion, product use and media use, etc. This, in turn, leads to a preference for advertisements that are congruent with their attitudes and behaviours. In contrast, consumers who have weak ethnic identities would display attitudes and behaviours that are less consistent with traditional cultural values and closer to those of the dominant culture (e.g. Appiah 2001b). Strong ethnic identifiers may see the ethnicity of the model in adverts as a positive cue confirming similarity and thereby pay more attention to and show more favourable attitudes toward the model and the media (Forehand and Deshpandé 2001; Whittler 1989). In other words, the ethnicity of the model may be particularly instrumental in inducing individuals with strong ethnic identities to infer similarity or dissimilarity, whereas the model's ethnicity may not function as a similarity cue for those with weak ethnic identities.

An important theoretical perspective that explains this racial similarity effect is the identification theory (Kelman 1961). The theory contends that people automatically assess their level of similarity with a source during an interaction and make similarity judgements. This process explains how individuals connect with spokespersons/models in adverts based on perceived similarities between them. Researchers have found evidence to suggest that when the symbols, characters and values depicted in the messages are drawn from the intended audience's cultural background, the audience is likely to better identify with the message and the source of the message (Appiah 2001a; 2001b; McGuire 1984; Pitts *et al.* 1989). Furthermore, individuals who are more likely to identify with the characters (Huesmann *et al.* 1983) and think of themselves as similar to the characters (Brock 1965; Burnstein *et al.* 1961) are more influenced by such message content.

Appiah (2001b) and Whittler and Spira (2002) found that strong Black ethnic identifiers perceived themselves to be more similar to and identified more strongly with Black characters in media and expressed greater liking for Black characters in adverts than Blacks with weak ethnic identities do. Furthermore, Whittler and Spira (2002) showed that Blacks with weak ethnic identities evaluated products and adverts similarly irrespective of whether the adverts were targeting Whites or Blacks. In contrast, strong Black identifiers evaluated products and adverts more favourably and showed a greater comprehension of message content after seeing a Black-targeted advert vis-à-vis a White-targeted advert. While much of the work examining the effects of racially targeted messages on ethnic minorities has focused specifically on print and television advertising, Appiah (2004) examined Blacks' differential responses to race-targeted websites and found that Blacks with a strong ethnic identity spent more time browsing a site and viewing each story when the site was targeted to Blacks. Additionally, Blacks with strong ethnic identity also rated the site and the stories more favourably when browsing the Black-targeted sites compared to White-targeted sites. In contrast, Blacks with weak ethnic identity displayed no difference in their browsing time on websites and stories or their ratings of the sites and stories with different racial targeting efforts (ibid.).

The other stream of research development in consumer acculturation focused on situational ethnicity or felt ethnicity (Stayman and Deshpandé 1989). Situational ethnicity is based on the notion that the acculturation process may vary depending on the context in which the behaviour occurs. The underlying premise here is that people take on different roles in their daily lives and these roles may involve different levels of acculturation or ethnicity (O'Guinn and Faber 1985). Consequently, a consumer's consumption behaviour can exhibit a considerable degree of situational variability depending on which personal meanings are salient in a given consumption context (Stayman and Deshpandé 1989; Zmud and Arce 1992).

A theoretical perspective that has been employed to help interpret the impact of situational ethnicity in the advertising context is the distinctiveness theory. The central idea here is that a person's distinctive traits in relation to the other people in their environment will be more salient to that person than other traits that are more common to everyone (McGuire 1984; McGuire and McGuire 1982). Put another way, this theory suggests that individuals who belong to a distinctive or numerically rare group tend to be highly aware and mindful of the characteristics shared by that group and are more likely to incorporate that group identity into their self-concept than individuals who do not belong to such a group (Grier and Brumbaugh 2004). Hence, for example, ethnicity will be more salient for members of the minority than the majority group. This might be because when one feels he/she belongs to a numerical minority group – and, hence, distinctive – the feeling is more likely to spontaneously evoke ethnic-based identification as a way to define oneself in social contexts (Deshpandé and Stayman 1994).

The distinctiveness theory has provided a wealth of insights into how social contexts and individual characteristics jointly influence consumer response to marketing communication efforts. Specifically, the theory supports the notion that numerical minorities are more likely to respond favourably to advertising messages designed to resonate with their distinctive characteristics (Grier and Deshpandé 2001). For example, Grier and Brumbaugh (1999) found that unlike Whites, Blacks as ethnic minorities appreciated the acknowledgement associated with being a target market and were more likely to use targeting cues based on their racial distinctive trait in evaluating messages than White majority members were based on their 'non-distinctive trait'. Further, due to their increased awareness of the trait that made them unique, Blacks were more likely to connect targeted messages with themselves. Several studies have shown that this leads Blacks to develop more favourable attitudes toward Black-targeted messages than toward White-targeted messages (Aaker *et al.* 2000; Appiah 2001a; 2001b; 2002).

Many empirical studies have found that consumer distinctiveness results in a heightened sensitivity to targeting efforts, more identification with and trust of a similar source, and increased favourability toward the advertisement and the brand (Aaker *et al.* 2000; Deshpandé and Stayman 1994; Forehand and Deshpandé 2001; Grier and Brumbaugh 1999). Among the findings, Deshpandé and Stayman (1994) showed that Hispanic Americans living in Austin, Texas (where they are ethnic minorities) were more likely than Hispanic Americans living in San Antonio (where they are ethnic majority) to consider their ethnicity salient. Furthermore, they found that members of the ethnic minority group (versus majority group) were more likely to believe that an advert spokesperson from their own ethnic group (i.e. Hispanic spokesperson) was more trustworthy and therefore hold a positive attitude toward the advertised brand. Grier and Brumbaugh (2004) further explained that ethnic similarity between the viewer and a source enhances advert responses among targeted ethnic minorities because similarity judgements are more readily made among these numerically distinctive individuals and impact the effectiveness of targeting efforts. These findings are consistent with the larger body of consumer research focused on spokesperson ethnicity effects, which has demonstrated that more favourable attitudes toward ethnically congruent stimuli exist among ethnic minorities (e.g. Whittler 1991).

Appiah (2004) cautioned that this notion should be qualified by the degree of ethnic identity maintained by the ethnic minority consumers. For instance, some Blacks may be a numerical minority yet not feel distinctive because they lack a strong connection to the Black culture. Blacks with weak cultural identity may not consider 'Blackness' an attribute that defines their self-concept and may use targeting cues based on their non-distinctive traits, focusing instead on similarities between themselves and the source that are less race-specific (e.g. dress, lifestyle, social class). In other words, weak Black identifiers may be less aware of their ethnicity and minority status and may, therefore, feel less distinctive (Appiah 2004). Thus, despite their numerical minority status within an environment, it is also important to consider ethnic identi-fication in consumer response to racially targeted messages.

The effect of ethnicity on consumers' evaluation of advertising messages can be further explained by the concept of in-group favouritism (Fiske and Taylor 1991), which suggests that individuals have a tendency to evaluate people who are members of their own group (i.e. in-group) more favourably than those who belong to other groups (i.e. out-group). The in-group bias theory (Brewer 1979) posits that people generally tend to show attitudinal and perceptual biases toward members of one's in-group, rather than toward members of the out-group. The basic premise of the theory is that people categorize other people on the status of their member-ship in in- or out-group. In-group membership is represented by identifying with other people who are similar in some way to the person doing the comparison, and out-group membership refers to people who are dissimilar in some way to the person doing the comparison (Qualls and Moore 1990).

The theory argues that there is a greater social distance between an individual and members of the out-group and that, in the absence of other information, individuals will rely on their knowledge of members of their own group and on preconceived assumptions and biases regard-ing out-group members in making comparisons and/or evaluations (Green 1999; Qualls and Moore 1990). Furthermore, minority group status makes in-group membership much more salient than does membership in a majority group (Gerard and Hoyt 1974). Research findings that show that Black consumers were more sensitive to racial cues and preferred Black models in comparison to White models (e.g. Green 1999; Qualls and Moore 1990) could be explained by in-group bias. Black consumers were likely to evaluate adverts featuring Black models more favourably than adverts featuring White models, while White consumers tended to be some-what indifferent.

However, Spira and Whittler (2004) later pointed out that the manifestation of in-group favouritism relies on the perceiver classifying others into in- and out-groups. With respect to a spokesperson's race, this suggests that the viewer of an advert must use race as a basis for categorizing the spokesperson. A number of variables that influence the salience or importance of race may determine whether and when it is used as a basis for categorization. For example, a spokesperson's race may be more meaningful to individuals who feel a strong affiliation with their own racial group. Using the strength of ethnic identification as an important explanatory variable, Spira and Whittler suggested that the Black spokesperson's race might have positively biased the advert perception of Blacks who strongly identified with their own racial group.

One other useful theoretical framework for understanding why individuals from different ethnic minority groups react differently to advertising messages is the theory of accommoda-tion. The underlying assumption here is that more accommodation results in more favourable responses: the greater the ethnic accommodation shown by advertisers, the more favourable the response by ethnic group members. Applying this theory to advertising efforts, it is possible that advertisers can improve marketing communication by making themselves more similar to con-sumers (Cho et al. 2004). Since ethnic audiences feel more affinity toward culturally congruent messages, they tend to appreciate efforts in providing culturally accommodating advert messages (e.g. featuring ethnic spokespersons, culturally sensitive messages, placed in culturally congruent media, etc.) and will then respond favourably.

A few researchers have applied the accommodation theory in the advertising context (e.g. Holland and Gentry 1997; Koslow et al. 1994). For example, Holland and Gentry (1999) introduced the concept of intercultural accommodation in evaluating the impact of cultural symbols (i.e. language, music, art, attire, spokesperson of a similar ethnic background) on advertising effectiveness. The term intercultural here refers to the notion that communication occurs between two different cultural groups (e.g. the advertiser, representing the dominant culture; and the audience, representing the ethnic minority culture), and the targeted group is expected to react most favourably to advertisements that are culturally accommodating (i.e. featuring models of similar ethnic background or placed in culturally congruent media; Green 1999). Holland and Gentry (1999) argued that advertisers can accommodate ethnic minority consumers by not only using ethnic languages but also applying many cultural symbols including ethnic spokespeople and models. Karande (2005) applied accommodation theory to explain the effects of using ethnically similar models on the minority consumer response to adverts. He argued that a consumer's response varies due to the extent to which the consumer believes that the advertiser is culturally sensitive or perceived to be so. If ethnic consumers feel that the use of an ethnically similar spokesperson is an indicator that the advertiser is sensitive to their culture, they will respond more favourably than if they feel this is not the case. The study found that the use of an Asian model in an advert influenced Asian American consumers' attitudes toward the company and intention to use the service when the advertiser was perceived as culturally sensitive, and negatively when the advertiser was not perceived as culturally sensitive (Karande 2005).

This concept can also be applied to media placement. Green (1999) suggested that the greater the accommodation by the advertiser in terms of culturally congruent media placement, the more favourable the evaluation of the adverts among the target audience. For example, placing adverts with Black models in minor or background roles in racially targeted media would be perceived as less accommodating than placing these adverts in non-targeted media by Black consumers, resulting in less favourable evaluations. By the same token, placing adverts that feature Black models in positions of dominance in racially targeted media should result in more favourable evaluations as they are perceived more accommodating (ibid.).

As a cognitive-based theory of stereotyping, polarized appraisal theory – also called the complexity–extremity theory, (Linville 1982; Linville and Jones 1980) – further explains how ethnic consumers respond to an ethnically similar in-group model versus an out-group model. The theory states that because in-group members are evaluated on the basis of a greater number of dimensions than out-group members, out-group members would be evaluated more extremely than in-group members (Linville and Jones 1980). A rationale for this perspective lies in the nature of prior knowledge structures (i.e. cognitive schema) concerning in-groups and out-groups. In particular, Linville and Jones argued that people have more complex schemas regarding their own groups than other groups. For example, they found that White subjects were more likely to show greater cognitive complexity regarding Whites than they did regarding Blacks, which, in turn, led to more moderate evaluations of their own group (i.e. Whites). This might be because perceivers must come to terms with a larger collection of diverse instances involving in-group members. This rich background of experience with the in-group generates a larger number of dimensions along which individual members may be characterized, and, thus, in-group members will be less likely to be perceived as being consistent with those categories or matching the set of dimensions used by the observer. In contrast, for out-group members, the cognitive structure held by the perceiver is less complex, therefore consisting of fewer dimensions, and the likelihood is that out-group members would match the set of evaluative dimensions. The lower cognitive complexity for out-group members increases the extremity of evaluation (ibid.). Put another way, evaluations tend to be more extreme, either positive or negative, with regard to out-group members as a result of having relatively less information and experience (Qualls and Moore 1990).

Applying this theory to the advertising context, Qualls and Moore (1990) postulated that people evaluated ethnically dissimilar models more extremely than ethnically similar models because of lower cognitive complexity or knowledge about dissimilar cultures. Unfortunately their findings were mixed. Qualls and Moore explained that while cognitive complexity might in fact be a key moderating variable in the process of racial stereotyping, its importance could not be validated in their study. This suggests that, although a single theory may hold promise by itself, race or ethnicity effects in advertising are complex and may require the application of multiple theories simultaneously to understand their relative impact (Williams *et al.* 2007).

Future research agenda

Understand identity negotiation involving multiple cultures

Ethnic minorities consistently experience challenges in dealing with multiple cultural identities. While scholars have acknowledged the importance of examining dual cultural identity among ethnic minority consumers (e.g. Berry 1990; Phinney 1996), little is known about how these individuals manage and negotiate their dual or multicultural identity in the acculturation process.

In order to describe how ethnic minority consumers negotiate and move between dual-cultural identities, researchers have used concepts such as 'culture swapping', 'context-shifting' (Oswald 1999) and 'frame switching' (Hong *et al.* 2000). Oswald (1999) suggested that the identity of ethnic minority consumers is an unstable construct that necessitates the process of 'context-shifting' or 'culture swapping'. That is, consumers move between multiple cultural identities rather than blending them into a single homogeneous identity; and situational demands influence consumers' need to switch cultural codes and 'negotiate day-to-day border crossings between home and host culture' (Oswald 1999, p. 307).

In a similar fashion, introducing the concept of 'cultural frame switching' among bi-cultural individuals, Hong *et al.* (2000) argued that individuals shift between interpretive frames rooted in different cultures in response to cues in the social environment. To capture how bi-cultural individuals switch between cultural lenses, Hong and colleagues conceptualized internalized culture 'as a network of discrete, specific constructs that guide cognition only when they come to the fore in an individual's mind' (Hong *et al.* 2000, p. 709).

Drawing from an extensive review of empirical and qualitative acculturation and bi-culturalism literature, Benet-Martínez *et al.* (2002) proposed the conceptualization of Bi-cultural Identity Integration (BII) as a framework for investigating individual differences in bi-cultural identity organization. BII focuses on bi-cultural individuals' perceptions of how much their two different cultural identities intersect or overlap and captures the degree to which 'bi-culturals perceive their mainstream and ethnic cultural identities as compatible and integrated vs. oppositional and difficult to integrate' (Benet-Martínez *et al.* 2002, p. 9). According to Benet-Martínez *et al.*, individuals high on BII are likely to easily integrate both cultures and develop a compatible bi-cultural identity, regarding themselves as part of a 'hyphenated culture'. These individuals do not perceive the two cultures to be mutually exclusive, oppositional or conflicting. On the other hand, individuals low on BII experience difficulty in incorporating both cultures into a cohesive sense of identity (Phinney and Devich-Navarro 1997; Vivero and Jenkins 1999). Although they also identify with both cultures, they are particularly sensitive to tensions between the two cultural orientations and see this incompatibility as a source of internal conflict.

Another approach regarding acculturation and dual cultural identity proposed by Roccas and Brewer (2002) identifies four alternative representations of multiple-group identity. They proposed that individuals cope with the demands of competing cultural identities by adopting different forms of identity management. The first form of this is called *hyphenated identities*. This locates one's cultural identity at the intersection of the ethnic and societal levels and thus forms a blended bi-cultural identity (Birman 1994; Phinney and Devich-Navarro 1997). With this representation, terms such as African American, Latino American, and Korean American represent unique cultural configurations derived from the specific experiences of enacting a particular ethnic cultural identity. Another mode of coping with alternative cultural identities involves subordinating one identity to the other. This is called *cultural dominance*. Assimilation to the host culture at the expense of ethnic cultural identity is one form of cultural dominance (Berry 1990).

Another form is the exclusive investment in one's ethnic cultural identity with alienation from the culture of the host society – the separation strategy (Berry 1990; Phinney and Devich-Navarro 1997). The third mode of adapting to the perceived conflict between alternative cultural group identification is *compartmentalization*, in which an individual consciously activates different cultural identities in different contexts or social settings – a pattern referred to as 'alternating bi-culturalism' (LaFromboise *et al.* 1993; Phinney and Devich-Navarro 1997). This type of identity structure is best illustrated by children of immigrant parents who alternate between the language used at home and the one used in the community. It can also be seen in other cultural practices, norms and values. Individuals who adopt this strategy have a sense of competence in both cultures (LaFromboise *et al.* 1993) but also an awareness of conflict between cultures that renders bi-culturalism sometimes problematic (Phinney and Devich-Navarro 1997).

The last form of dual cultural identity is termed *integrated bi-culturalism*. Unlike compartmentalization, in which different cultures are considered incompatible and situation specific, this form of bi-culturalism acknowledges multiple cultural identity simultaneously – where membership, values and norms of both groups are combined and integrated (Oyserman *et al.* 1998). This conceptualization clearly equates multiculturalism with the acquisition of a more inclusive complex group identity than that represented by any component cultural identity alone (Roccas and Brewer 2002).

Likewise, several social psychologists have suggested that ethnic minorities are likely to develop their own unique cultural styles through a blending of their old culture and the host culture (e.g. Benet-Martínez *et al.* 2002; Roccas and Brewer 2002). The blending of cultural styles suggests that these consumers may respond differently to advertising messages than other members of the host country. For instance, ethnic minority consumers high on BII or who possess hyphenated identity may easily move between their two cultural orientations by shifting between different cultures based interpretative lenses in response to cultural cues. Applying this to the advertising context, it may be that responses to cultural cues in advertising among ethnic minority consumers high on BII are more flexible than those of ethnic minorities low on BII.

Consumer acculturation helps us understand how and why ethnic minority consumers respond differently to various cultural cues in advertising. However, there have only been few studies that examine how the diverse identity negotiation process and the complex identity structures of ethnic minority consumers affect their response in the marketplace. Researchers in advertising and marketing will need to go beyond the traditional acculturation research to fill the gaps in our understanding.

Apply existing theories to multicultural advertising

A number of researchers have made an effort to incorporate diverse models or theories drawn from the broader fields of consumer behaviour and psychology to studies of ethnic minority consumers. For example, the *Elaboration Likelihood Model* (ELM) has been applied in multicultural advertising research in order to study the effect of a source's race or ethnicity in consumer response. Researchers have long argued that the role a particular spokesperson plays tends to be different for different groups. Because of differences in source perception being driven by the racial or ethnic background of the recipient or the source (or the interaction of a variety of factors), a source can be an additional argument, an inducement to process, a biasing factor or a cue (Williams *et al.* 2008). Specifically, based on the ELM, Spira and Whittler (2004) suggested that the race of the source might function as a biasing factor or a peripheral cue. A cue in a persuasion setting may activate a simple decision rule that forms the basis of an evaluation. For example, source attractiveness or likability has been shown to influence attitudes by functioning as a simple persuasion cue. Spira and Whittler reasoned that, like those other source characteristics, race might function as a peripheral cue. The findings of their study indicate that both White and Black consumers responded more favourably to the product endorsed by the same- versus different-race spokesperson in the adverts.

Other research has applied the *Persuasion Knowledge Model* (PKM) in examining the vulnerability of subsistence consumers in the US to marketing communication messages (Williams *et al.* 2007). According to Friestad and Wright (1994), people's knowledge about persuasion attempts influences their response to the attempts. Incorporating this concept to their study, Williams *et al.* (2007) proposed that the PKM framework offers one approach to assess the ability of 'cognitively vulnerable' consumers, especially racial/ethnic minority consumers who live at a subsistence level, to cope with persuasive marketing communications. As such, they attempted to identify whether low-literate consumers were more vulnerable in the marketplace because their cognitive capacity is significantly low to preclude the use of persuasion knowledge and to draw higher-order inferences about ulterior motives of salespeople or to correct invalid inferences. By incorporating the PKM with constructs such as self-esteem, locus of control, and powerlessness, Williams *et al.* (2007) provided insights into the coping process of these consumers and further suggested that future research should explore other ways in which there may be racial differences with respect to the PKM.

More recently, Oyserman (2009) provided a model that fits well with existing theories on self-concept and cultural differences, namely, the *Identity-Based Motivation* (IBM) model. The IBM model integrates several theoretical perspectives, including social identity theory (Tajfel and Turner 1986), self-categorization theory (Turner *et al.* 1987) and symbolic self-completion theory (Wicklund and Gollwitzer 1981). The model proposes that making a social identity salient activates relevant meanings associated with the in-group identity, which then results in actions that increase one's perceived similarity to the in-group and enhance one's positive social identity (Oyserman 2009). The IBM model helps explain why ethnic minority consumers' responses to culturally congruent cues are not always favourable. For example, ethnic minority consumers' responses toward adverts with an ethnic spokesperson may depend on whether the ethnic identity of those consumers is likely to be salient at that moment in time in the given context.

In a similar vein, several studies have demonstrated the consequence of identity salience by incorporating theoretical concepts such as self- and social-identity and self- and social-schemata. For example, Newman *et al.* (1997) showed that Black females who had their ethnic identity made salient had more favourable perceptions of O.J. Simpson's innocence. Similarly, Shih *et al.* (1999) found that Asian American females' maths test scores improved when their ethnic identity was activated, but worsened when their gender identity was activated. Built upon this research stream, Forehand *et al.* (2002) examined the underlying factors that heighten identity salience in the context of advertising. They proposed that identity primes and social distinctiveness would influence identity salience (i.e. the activation of a social identity within an individual's social self-schema) and subsequent response to targeted advertising. Findings of their study indicate that Asian American participants of the study responded most positively to Asian spokespeople and Asian-targeted advertising when the participants were both primed and socially distinctive (ibid.).

Although researchers have made an attempt to incorporate diverse theoretical perspectives to help us understand multicultural advertising aimed at ethnic minority consumers, the scope of their research is still somewhat limited. Importantly, ethnic consumers' identity structure is becoming complex as they may not need or be willing to be subordinated to the mainstream culture. In order to better understand ethnic minority consumers' needs, desires, interests, attitudes and behavioural patterns, it is critical for researchers to expand the scope of research by incorporating various theoretical approaches drawn from fields such as marketing, social psychology, sociology and many others. This will help better explain ethnic consumers' cognitive, emotional and behavioural processes in response to multicultural advertising.

Consider the new media landscape

From the standpoint of practice, some of the obstacles in reaching the ethnic minority markets can be attributed to differences in media use patterns (La Ferle and Lee 2005). It has long been acknowledged that careful media considerations are called for when communicating with ethnic minority consumers. Given the sizes, growth rate, purchasing power and the differential affinity toward various media platforms (Williams and Tharp 2001), it is obvious that media should be included as a key variable in future research on consumer response toward persuasive messages.

A number of studies have examined the media consumption habits of ethnic minorities (Korzenny 2008; La Ferle and Lee 2008; Villareal and Peterson 2008). These studies suggest that ethnic minorities are more likely to use certain type of media, different from that of non-Hispanic Whites. For example, ethnic minorities spend more hours per day reading newspapers and talking on their cell phones than non-Hispanic Whites, and they are also more likely to have their own blog. African Americans engage in television viewing and radio listening activities for longer periods of time than Hispanics and non-Hispanic Whites. About one-third of Hispanics do not read English newspapers or magazines (La Ferle and Lee 2005). They may prefer reading Spanish language print media over English language options (Koslow *et al.* 1994). Other than industry statistics, few academic studies have delved into ethnic consumers' media behaviour in the age of digital media.

With the fast proliferation of technologies, it is imperative to document the ways in which ethnic minorities use new media. How persuasive messages are delivered vary in different digital forms (Internet and mobile media), which would no doubt influence consumer information processing and response. Likewise, a consumer's proficiency with various media platforms is an important moderating factor to consider. Although online marketing and advertising has moved to the core of the business-consumer interaction (Plummer *et al.* 2007) and is poised to become the dominant marketing channel, how ethnic minorities react to and become involved with the online marketing communications is still one of the least understood areas. Only a few researchers have investigated the internet usage among ethnic minority population in the US. For example, the 2006 AOL Latino Hispanic cyber study (Business Wire 2006) revealed acculturation differences among online Hispanics that led to differences in preferences for Spanish-language content, the types of websites visited and watching television online. Singh *et al.* (2008) found that Hispanics with low levels of acculturation preferred websites that included some content in Spanish. Becerra and Kraognakar (2010) found that Hispanics had more positive attitudes than the general population towards online advertising in the form of pop-ups, banner adverts and emails.

A recent Nielsen Report also briefed:

- African Americans are the heaviest TV consumers, watching 6 hours and 54 minutes a day versus the 5 hour and 11 minute average for all U.S. households. More than 30 percent of African American households have four or more televisions, and they over-index in subscription to premium cable services.
- Hispanics are very active on their smartphones, texting the most out of all races/ethnicities (943 texts per month) and employing a wide range of mobile activities, including mobile banking. Smartphone penetration has reached 45 percent, matching only Asian American usage levels in popularity.
- Asians/Pacific Islanders are the most active PC and Internet users, spending nearly 80 hours on PCs in February 2011 versus the national average of about 55 hours. They also consume more internet content than any other group, visiting 3,600 web pages in February – about 1,000 more than their counterparts. While Asian American consumers watch less television, they do more watching online, streaming the most video.

(Pearson-McNeil and Hale 2011)

A clear understanding of media habits and behavioural patterns across ethnic groups not only helps make better media decisions but also facilitates our understanding of consumer response to advertising messages. Furthermore, although key disparities do remain (Pew Internet & American Life Project 2010), the increasing proliferation of new technologies adds to the complexity of the role of media delivery platform in influencing ethnic minority consumer response toward persuasive content.

Regarding the recent technological trend among ethnic minorities, researchers emphasize the emergence of a 'new digital divide' in how the internet is incorporated into people's everyday life. A Pew Internet & American Life Project's Report, *Asian-Americans and the Internet* (Spooner 2010), suggests that Asian Americans engage in their online activities at a much higher rate on a typical day than other ethnic groups, indicating that Asian American users have made the internet an integral part of their daily lives. This pattern cuts across all major internet activities, whether it is for fun, to transact commerce or to search for information related to major life activities. Asian Americans are proportionally much more likely than others to obtain information about financial matters, travel and political information from the internet. According to the report, just over a third (34%) of Asian Americans gets their news online on a typical day. In comparison, 22% of Whites, along with 15% of African Americans and 20% of Hispanics do so. Asian American users are also more likely to use the internet as a resource at school or at work.

For Hispanic Americans, language is a powerful factor as internet use is much higher among Hispanics who speak and read English fluently than among those who have limited English abilities or who only speak Spanish. While use of the internet among Hispanics is increasing, there is a large difference in internet use among English speaking and bilingual Hispanics compared to Spanish-dominant Hispanics (Pew Research Hispanic Center 2009). The Pew Internet Project's report suggests that online Hispanics were more likely than online Whites to search for information about books, movies and other activities, to download and listen to music, and to go online just for fun. In addition, Hispanics, once online, are as broadly and intensely connected to the internet as Whites. Phillips (2008) found that Hispanics use the internet for interactive purposes, with 46% using instant messages, 32% visiting social networking sites and 22% participating in chat rooms.

Like Hispanics, African Americans also use the internet to connect with others. African Americans are just as likely to participate in instant messaging, visit social networking sites and participate in chat rooms as Hispanics (Phillips 2008). According to the Pew Internet & American Life Project's Report (2010), African Americans are much less likely to use the internet for school or work compared to other ethnic groups. They are also less likely to use the internet to obtain information on products, make purchases, seek information about news/ sports/weather or use email. Instead, African Americans engage in online activities for entertainment at a much higher rate, such as playing games, downloading music.

Given the proliferation of new technology and media vehicles, fundamental changes are taking place in how advertising messages are delivered and consumed. The new media technology and devices offer consumers growing access to an infinite number of information sources, varying in content forms and length, at virtually no cost. Questions such as 'How does this access change the search strategies?' and 'How does the platform of message delivery influence consumer information processing?' are beginning to be answered for the general public but not ethnic minority consumers. This is an important information gap because ethnic minority consumers clearly have different levels of access to the new media, possess varying degrees of proficiency and exhibit vastly different patterns in receiving consumption-related information. Researchers have an important mission in uncovering how ethnicity plays a role in ethnic consumers' motivations, habits and patterns of using new media as well as their attitudinal and behavioural responses toward advertising messages received through the new media.

Furthermore, as discussed previously, today's ethnic minorities do not want to be merely lumped together with other American consumer segments. Therefore, marketers and advertisers should be reminded that not all ethnic minority consumers are gradually assimilating into mainstream culture. Instead, they should view the population as containing differing segments of consumers with varying degrees of acculturation. This understanding can be used to adapt online marketing messages, including developing culturally customized web content tailored to the cultural and language expectations of ethnic minority consumers online (Singh and Pereira 2005).

Concluding remarks

Increasing ethnic diversity in the population is a significant aspect of today's U.S. market environment. Moving away from the 'melting pot' ideal and into the 'salad bowl' notion, minorities of various cultures desire to develop a U.S. lifestyle while maintaining their language and values, thus creating their unique mixes of cultures. Today, it is not necessary for ethnic minorities to rid themselves of their mother culture before they can find a job, watch TV or succeed in school. A new path for becoming a successful American is to celebrate ethnicity, instead of hiding it, and assimilating into the majority culture. Research has shown that in a multicultural America, group identity, especially racial or ethnic, is the social base camp from which ethnic minorities make forays into the American culture.

In the U.S. multicultural market, marketing and advertising academicians and professionals need to understand each group of ethnic consumers well and use appropriate marketing communication strategies to engage them. These tasks are complicated further when cultural identity is influx. In order to successfully communicate with ethnic minority consumers, it is necessary for advertisers to (1) realize differences in communication patterns, values, behaviour, etc. across ethnic groups; (2) recognize individual differences in the process of identity negotiation and the structure of multiple cultural identity among ethnic consumers; (3) explore culturally acceptable/ unacceptable, sensitive/insensitive advertising messages; and (4) develop effective and efficient advertising messages targeted at the specific group of ethnic consumers and deliver them via appropriate channels. While past research has provided explanations of how ethnic minority consumers respond to multicultural advertising, there are still significant gaps in our understanding. Nuanced research that expands or seeks alternative conceptualizations is very much needed.

References

Aaker, J., Brumbaugh, A. and Grier, S. A. (2000) 'Non-target market effects and viewer distinctiveness: The impact of target marketing on attitudes'. *Journal of Consumer Psychology*, 9(3): 127–40.

Adelson, A. (1989). 'English role in Hispanic marketing'. *New York Times*, Jan 26, D19, col 1.

Appiah, O. (2001a) 'Black, White, Hispanic, and Asian American adolescents' responses to culturally embedded ads'. *Howard Journal of Communication*, 12(1): 29–48.

Appiah, O. (2001b) 'The effects of ethnic identification on black and white adolescents' evaluation of ads'. *Journal of Advertising Research*, 41(5): 1–16.

Appiah, O. (2002) 'Black and white viewers' perception and recall of occupational characters on television'. *Journal of Communication*, 52(4): 776–93.

Appiah, O. (2004) 'Effects of ethnic identification on web browsers' attitudes toward and navigational patterns on race-targeted sites'. *Communication Research*, 31(3): 312–37.

Askegaard, S., Arnould, E. J. and Kjeldgaard, D. (2005) 'Postassimilationist ethnic consumer research: Qualifications and extensions'. *Journal of Consumer Research*, 32: 160–70.

Becerra, E. P. and Korgaonkar, P. K. (2010) 'The influence of ethnic identification in digital advertising: How Hispanic Americans' respond to pop-up, e-mail, and banner advertising affect online purchase intentions'. *Journal of Advertising Research*, 50(3): 279–91.

Benet-Martínez, V., Leu, J., Lee, F. and Morris, M. W. (2002) 'Negotiating biculturalism cultural frame switching in biculturals with oppositional versus compatible cultural identities'. *Journal of Cross-Cultural Psychology*, 33(5): 492–516.

Berry, J. W. (1990) 'Acculturation and adaptation: A general framework'. In *Mental Health of Immigrants and Refugees*, edited by W. H. Holtzman and T. H. Bornemann. Austin: Hogg Foundation for Mental Health: 90–102.

Berry, J. W. (2005) 'Acculturation: Living successfully in two cultures'. *International Journal of Intercultural Relations*, 29(6): 697–712.

Brewer, M. B. (1979) 'In-group bias in the minimal intergroup situation: A cognitive-motivational analysis'. *Psychological Bulletin*, 86(2): 307–24.

Birman, D. (1994) 'Acculturation and human diversity in a multicultural society'. In *Human Diversity: Perspectives on People in Context*, edited by J. Edison, R. J. Watts, D. Birman. San Francisco: Jossey-Bass.

Brock, T. C. (1965) 'Communicator-recipient similarity and decision change'. *Journal of Personality and Social Psychology*, 1: 650–53.

Burnstein, E., Stotland, E. and Zander, A. (1961) 'Similarity to a model and self-evaluation'. *Journal of Abnormal and Social Psychology*, 62: 257–264.

Business Wire (2006) 'The AOL Latino 2006 Hispanic cyberstudy breaks new ground by analyzing internet usage across acculturation segments'. Available from: http://www.businesswire.com/news/home/20060918005614/en/AOL-Latino-2006-Hispanic-Cyberstudy-Breaks-Ground#.U5_u3pR_t1U.

Cho, C. H., Holcombe, J. and Murphy, D. (2004) *Multicultural Marketing*. Available from: http://insights-marketing.com/Documents/Multicultural+Marketing+in+ Contemporary+US+Markets.pdf.

Deshpandé, R., Hoyer, W. D. and Donthu, N. (1986) 'The intensity of ethnic affiliation: A study of the sociology of hispanic consumption'. *Journal of Consumer Research*, 13: 214–20.

Deshpandé, R. and Stayman, D. M. (1994) 'A tale of two cities: Distinctiveness theory and advertising effectiveness'. *Journal of Marketing Research*, 31(1): 57–64.

Donthu, N. and Cherian, J. (1992) 'Hispanic coupon usage: The impact of strong and weak ethnic identification'. *Psychology & Marketing*, 9(6): 501–10.

Dunn, E. W. (1975). 'Mexican-American media behavior: A factor analysis'. *Journal of Broadcasting*, 19(3): 3–10.

Elliott, R. and Wattanasuwan, K. (1998) 'Brands as symbolic resources for the construction of identity'. *International Journal of Advertising*, 17(2): 131–44.

Fiske, S. T. and Taylor, S. E. (1991). *Social Cognition*. NY: McGraw-Hill.

Forehand, M. R. and Deshpandé, R. (2001) 'What we see makes us who we are: Priming ethnic self-awareness and advertising response'. *Journal of Marketing Research*, 38(3): 336–48.

Forehand, M. R., Deshpandé, R. and Reed, A. (2002) 'Identity salience and the influence of differential activation of the social self-schema on advertising response'. *Journal of Applied Psychology*, 87(6): 1086–99.

Friedman, H. H., Lopez-Pumarejo, T. and Friedman, L. W. (2007) 'Frontiers in multicultural marketing: The disabilities market'. *Journal of International Marketing and Marketing Research*, 32(1): 25–39.

Friestad, M. and Wright, P. (1994) 'The persuasion knowledge model: How people cope with persuasion attempts'. *Journal of consumer research*, 21(1): 1–31.

Gerard, H. B. and Hoyt, M. F. (1974) 'Distinctiveness of social categorization and attitude toward in-group members'. *Journal of Personality and Social Psychology*, 29: 836–42.

Gould, J. W., Sigband, N. B. and Zoerner Jr., C. E. (1970) 'Black consumers reactions to integrated advertising: An exploratory study'. *Journal of Marketing*, 34(3): 20–26.

Green, C. L. (1995) 'Media exposure's impact on perceived availability and redemption of coupons by ethnic consumers'. *Journal of Advertising Research*, 35(2): 56–64.

Green, C. L. (1999) 'Ethnic evaluations of advertising: Interaction effects of strength of ethnic identification, media placement, and degree of racial composition'. *Journal of Advertising*, 28(1): 49–64.

Grier, S. A. and Brumbaugh, A. M. (1999) 'Noticing cultural differences: Ad meanings created by target and non-target markets'. *Journal of Advertising*, 28(1): 79–93.

Grier, S. A. and Brumbaugh, A. M. (2004) 'Consumer distinctiveness and advertising persuasion'. In *Diversity in Advertising*, edited by J. D. Williams, W. Lee, and C. P. Haugtvedt. NJ: Erlbaum.

Grier, S. A. and Deshpandé, R. (2001) 'Social dimensions of consumer distinctiveness: The influence of social status on group identity and advertising persuasion'. *Journal of Marketing Research*, 38(2): 216–24.

Hayes-Bautista, D. E., Schink, W. O. and Chapa, J. (1984). 'Young Latinos in an aging American society'. *Social Policy*, 49–52.

Hernandez, S. A. (1988) 'An exploratory study of coupon use in Puerto Rico: Cultural vs. institutional barriers'. *Journal of Advertising Research*, 28(5): 44–60.

Hernandez, S. A. and Kaufman, C. J. (1991) 'Measuring consumer acculturation: Coupon usage among "Barrio" Hispanics'. *Research in Consumer Behavior*, 5: 61–82.

Hirschman, E. C. (1981) 'American Jewish ethnicity: Its relationship to some selected aspects of consumer behavior'. *The Journal of Marketing*, 45(3): 102–10.

Holland, J. L. and Gentry, J. W. (1997) 'The impact of cultural symbols on advertising effectiveness: A theory of intercultural accommodation'. *Advances in Consumer Research*, 24: 483–89.

Holland, J. and Gentry, J. W. (1999) 'Ethnic consumer reaction to targeted marketing: A theory of intercultural accommodation'. *Journal of Advertising*, 28(1): 65–77.

Hong, J. W., Muderrisoglu, A. and Zinkhan, G. M. (1987) 'Cultural differences and advertising expression: A comparative content analysis of Japanese and U.S. magazine advertising'. *Journal of Advertising*, 16(1): 55–62.

Hong, Y. Y., Morris, M. W., Chiu, C. Y. and Benet-Martínez, V. (2000) 'Multicultural minds: A dynamic constructivist approach to culture and cognition'. *American psychologist*, 55(7): 709.

Huesmann, L. R., Eron, L. D., Klein, R., Brice, P. and Fischer, P. (1983) 'Mitigating the imitation of aggressive behaviors by changing children's attitudes about media violence'. *Journal of Personality and Social Psychology*, 44(5): 899–910.

Johnson, G. D., Elliott, R. M. and Grier, S. A. (2010) 'Conceptualizing multicultural advertising effects in the "new" South Africa'. *Journal of Global Marketing*, 23(3): 189–207.

Jun, S., Ball, A. D. and Gentry, J. W. (1993) 'Modes of consumer acculturation'. In *Advances in Consumer Research*, 20, edited by L. McAlister and M. Rothschild. Provo, UT: Association for Consumer Research: 76–82.

Karande, K. (2005) 'Minority response to ethnically similar models in advertisements: An application of accommodation theory'. *Journal of Business Research*, 58(11): 1573–1580.

Kelman, H. C. (1961) 'Processes of Opinion Change'. *Public Opinion Quarterly*, 25(1): 57–78.

Khairullah, D. Z. (2011) 'Acculturation and its relation to Asian-Indian immigrants' perceptions of advertisements'. *Journal of Applied Business Research*, 11(2): 55–66.

Korzenny, F. (2008) 'Multicultural marketing and the reasons why'. *Journal of Advertising Research*, 48(2): 173–6.

Korgaonkar, P. K., Karson, E. J. and Lund, D. (2000) 'Hispanics and direct marketing advertising'. *Journal of Consumer Marketing*, 17(2): 137–57.

Koslow, S., Shamdasani, P. N. and Touchstone, E. E. (1994) 'Exploring language effects in ethnic advertising: A sociolinguistic perspective'. *Journal of Consumer Research*, 20: 575–85.

la Ferle, C. and Lee, W.-N. (2005) 'Can English language media connect with ethnic audiences? Ethnic minorities' media use and representation perceptions'. *Journal of Advertising Research*, 45(1): 140–53.

LaFromboise, T., Coleman, H. L. and Gerton, J. (1993) 'Psychological impact of biculturalism: Evidence and theory'. *Psychological Bulletin*, 114(3): 395–412.

Lee, C. K., Fernandez, N. and Martin, B. A. S. (2002) 'Using self-referencing to explain the effectiveness of ethnic minority models in advertising'. *International Journal of Advertising*, 21(3): 367–379.

Lee, W.-N. (1988) 'Becoming an American consumer: A cross-cultural study of consumer acculturation among Taiwanese, Taiwanese in the United States and Americans'. *Doctoral Dissertation*, University of Illinois at Urbana-Champaign.

Lee, W.-N. and Um, K.-H. R. (1992) 'Ethnicity and consumer product evaluation: A cross-cultural comparison of Korean immigrants and Americans'. In *Advances in Consumer Research*, Vol. 19, edited by J. F. Sherry, Jr. and B. Sternthal. Provo, UT: Association for Consumer Research: 429–36.

Linville, P. W. (1982) 'The complexity–extremity effect and age-based stereotyping'. *Journal of Personality and Social Psychology*, 42(2): 193–211.

Linville, P. W. and Jones, E. E. (1980) 'Polarized appraisals of out-group members'. *Journal of Personality and Social Psychology*, 38(5): 689–703.

Martin, B. A. S., Lee, C. K.-C. and Yang, F. (2004) 'The influence of ad model ethnicity and self-referencing on attitudes'. *Journal of Advertising*, 33(4): 27–37.

McGuire, W. J. (1984) 'Search for the Self: Going beyond self-esteem and the reactive self'. In *Personality and the Prediction of Behavior,* edited by R. A. Zucker, J. Aronoff and A. I. Rabin. New York: Academic Press: 73–120.

McGuire, W. J. and McGuire, C. V. (1982) 'Significant others in self-space: Sex differences and developmental trends in the social self'. *Psychological Perspectives on the Self*, 1: 71–96.

Newman, L. S., Duff, K., Schnopp-Wyatt, N., Brock, B. and Hoffman, Y. (1997) 'Reactions to the OJ Simpson verdict: "Mindless tribalism" or motivated inference processes?' *Journal of Social Issues*, 53(3): 547–62.

Oakenfull, G. K., McCarthy, M. S. and Greenlee, T. B. (2008) 'Targeting a minority without alienating the majority: Advertising to gays and lesbians in mainstream media'. *Journal of Advertising Research*, 48(2): 191–198.

O'Guinn, T. C. and Faber, R. J. (1985) 'New perspectives on acculturation: The relationship of general and role specific acculturation with Hispanics' consumer attitudes.' *Advances in Consumer Research*, 12(1): 113–17.

Oswald, R. L. (1999) 'Culture swapping: Consumption and the ethnogenesis of middle-class Haitian immigrants'. *Journal of Consumer Research,* 25: 303–18.

Oyserman, D. (2009) 'Identity-based motivation: Implications for action-readiness, procedural-readiness, and consumer behavior'. *Journal of Consumer Psychology*, 19(3): 250–60.

Oyserman, D., Sakamoto, I. and Lauffer, A. (1998) 'Cultural accommodation: hybridity and the framing of social obligation'. *Journal of Personality and Social Psychology*, 74: 1606–1618.

Pearson-McNeil, C. and Hale, T. (2011) 'Dissecting diversity understanding the ethnic consumer'. *Nielsen*. Available from: http://www.nielsen.com/us/en/newswire/2011/dissecting-diversity-understanding-the-ethnic-consumer.html.

Peñaloza, L. N. (1994) 'Atravesando fronteras/border crossing: A critical ethnographic exploration of the consumer acculturation of Mexican immigrants'. *Journal of Consumer Research*, 21(1): 32–54.

Peñaloza, L. (1995) 'Immigrant consumers: Marketing and public policy considerations in the global economy'. *Journal of Public Policy & Marketing*, 14(1): 83–94.

Pew Hispanic Center (2009 December 22) 'Latinos Online, 2006–2008: Narrowing the Gap'. *Pew Research Center*. Retrieved from http://www.pewhispanic.org/2009/12/22/latinos-online-2006-2008-narrowing-the-gap/.

Phillips, L. E. (2008) 'US Hispanics online', *eMarketer*. Available from: http://www.grupofortunainc.net/wp-content/uploads/2012/01/U.S.-Hispanic-Online-Demographics.pdf.

Phinney, J. S. (1992) 'The multigroup ethnic identity measure: A new scale for use with diverse groups'. *Journal of Adolescent Research*, 7(2): 156–76.

Phinney, J. S. (1996) 'When we talk about American ethnic groups, what do we mean?' *American Psychologist*, 51: 918–27.

Phinney, J. S. and Devich-Navarro, M. (1997) 'Variations in bicultural identification among African American and Mexican American adolescents'. *Journal of Research on Adolescence*, 7(1): 3–32.

Pitts, R. E., Whalen, D. J., O'Keefe, R. and Murray, V. (1989) 'Black and white response to culturally targeted television commercials: A value-based approach'. *Psychology and Marketing*, 6(4): 311–28.

Plummer, J., Rappaport, S., Hall, T. and Barocci, R. (2007) *The Online Advertising Playbook*. NJ: John Wiley & Sons.

Qualls, W. J. and Moore, D. J. (1990) 'Stereotyping effects on consumers' evaluation of advertising: Impact of racial differences between actors and viewers'. *Psychology & Marketing*, 7(2): 135–51.

Rajagopalan, R. and Heitmeyer, J. (2005) 'Ethnicity and consumer choice: A study of consumer levels of involvement in Indian ethnic apparel and contemporary American clothing'. *Journal of Fashion Marketing and Management*, 9(1): 83–105.

Roccas, S. and Brewer, M. B. (2002) 'Social identity complexity'. *Personality and Social Psychology Review*, 6(2): 88–106.

Roslow, P. and Nicholls, J. A. F. (1996) 'Targeting the hispanic market: comparative persuasion of tv commercials in Spanish and English'. *Journal of Advertising Research*, 36(3): 67–77.

Shih, M., Pittinsky, T. L. and Ambady, N. (1999) 'Stereotype susceptibility: Identity salience and shifts in quantitative performance'. *Psychological science*, 10(1): 80–3.

Singh, N. and Pereira, A. (2005) *The Culturally Customized Website*. Oxford: Elsevier.

Singh, N., Baack, D. W., Pereira, A. and Baack, D. (2008) 'Culturally customizing websites for Hispanic online consumers'. *Journal of Advertising Research*, 48(2): 224–34.

Spira, J. S. and Whittler, T. E. (2004) 'Style or substance? Viewers' reactions to spokesperson's race in advertising'. In *Diversity in Advertising*, edited by J. D. Williams, W. Lee, and C. P. Haugtvedt. NJ: Erlbaum.

Spooner, T. (2010) 'Asian-Americans and the internet'. *Pew Internet & American Life Project*. Available from: http://www.pewinternet.org/Reports/2001/AsianAmericans-and-the-Internet/Summary-of-findings.aspx.

Stayman, D. M. and Deshpandé, R. (1989) 'Situational Ethnicity and Consumer Behavior'. *Journal of Consumer Research*, 16(3): 361–71.

Tajfel, H. and Turner, J. (1986) 'The social identity theory of intergroup behavior'. In *Psychology of Intergroup Relations*, edited by S. Worchel and W. Austin. Chicago: Nelson-Hall: 7–24.

Tsai, W. H. S. and Li, C. (2012) 'Bicultural advertising and Hispanic acculturation'. *Hispanic Journal of Behavioral Sciences*, 34(2): 305–22.

Turner, J., Hogg, M. A., Oakes, P. J., Reicher, S. D. and Wetherell, M. S. (1987) *Rediscovering The Social Group: A Social Categorization Theory*. Oxford: B. Blackwell.

Ueltschy, L. C. and Krampf, R. F. (1997) 'The influence of acculturation on advertising effectiveness to the Hispanic market'. *Journal of Applied Business Research*, 13(2): 87–101.

Ueltschy, L. C. and Krampf, R. F. (2011) 'The influence of acculturation on advertising effectiveness to the Hispanic market'. *Journal of Applied Business Research*, 13(2): 87–102.

U.S. Census Bureau (2010) 'Overview of race and Hispanic origin'. *United States Census Bureau*. Available from: http://www.census.gov/prod/cen2010/briefs/c2010br-02.pdf.

U.S. Census Bureau (2011) 'Demographics in the U.S'. United States Census Bureau. Available from: http://www.census.gov/compendia/statab/cats/population.html>.

Valenzuela, N. (1973) *Media Habits and Attitudes: Surveys in Austin and San Antonio*. Center for Communication Research, University of Texas.

Villareal, R. and Peterson, R. A. (2008) 'Hispanic ethnicity and media behavior'. *Journal of Advertising Research*, 48(2): 179–90.

Vivero, V. N. and Jenkins, S. R. (1999) 'Existential hazards of the multicultural individual: Defining and understanding cultural homelessness'. *Cultural Diversity and Ethnic Minority Psychology*, 5(1): 6–26.

Wallendorf, M. and Reilly, M. D. (1983) 'Ethnic migration, assimilation and consumption'. *Journal of Consumer Research*, 10(3): 292–302.

Webster, C. (1991) 'Attitudes toward marketing practices: The effects of ethnic identification'. *Journal of Applied Business Research*, 7(2): 107–16.

Webster, C. (1994) 'Effects of Hispanic ethnic identification on marital roles in the purchase decision process'. *Journal of Consumer Research*, 21(2): 319–31.

Whittler, T. E. (1989) 'Viewers' processing of actors race and message claims in advertising stimuli'. *Psychology and Marketing*, 6: 287–309.

Whittler, T. E. (1991) 'The effects of actors' race in commercial advertising: Review and extension'. *Journal of Advertising*, 20(1): 54–60.

Whittler, T. E. and Spira, J. S. (2002) 'Model's race: A peripheral cue in advertising messages?' *Journal of Consumer Psychology*, 12(4): 291–301.

Wicklund, R. A. and Gollwitzer, P. M. (1981) 'Symbolic self-completion, attempted influence, and self-deprecation'. *Basic and Applied Social Psychology*, 2(2): 89–114.

Williams, J. D. and Tharp, M. C. (2001) *African Americans: Ethnic Roots, Cultural Diversity. Marketing and Consumer Identity in Multicultural America*. CA: Sage Publications.

Williams, J. D., Lee, W. and Henderson, G. (2008) 'Diversity issues in consumer psychology'. In *Handbook of Consumer Psychology*, edited by C. Haugtvedt, F. Kardes, and P. Herr Mahwah. NJ: Erlbaum.

Williams, J. D., Qualls, W. J. and Ferguson, N. (2007) 'Potential vulnerabilities of US subsistence consumers to persuasive marketing communications'. *Advances in International Management*, 20: 89–110.

Zmud, J. and Arce, C. (1992) 'The ethnicity and consumption relationship'. *Advances in Consumer Research*, 19(1): 443–50.

17

Rethinking the Hispanic market

A call for reflexivity in advertising practice

Christopher A. Chávez

Introduction

About ten years ago I worked as an advertising executive at a reputable, creative agency in San Francisco. At the time, my client was an automotive manufacturer who had recently 'discovered' the Hispanic[1] market and was eager to reap the benefits of targeted advertising. In an effort to keep those advertising dollars from leaving the agency, the principals at this agency had convinced their client that they could manage such a campaign by setting up an ad-hoc Hispanic team. As the only account manager at my agency who was Latino, I was of course recruited to lead the effort.

One of the first projects to come out of this experiment was a radio spot intended to run in Spanish-language media. As is customary, the client was presented with three different scripts of which they would choose at least one to produce. The creative presentation was attended by Marco, a Mexican-born copywriter, his creative director Rob and me. Our client, based in Detroit, joined us via conference call.

Marco began his presentation by reading his scripts (called a 'creative') in Spanish, as intended for Spanish-dominant ears. The scripts were then re-presented in English, for the sake of the client, using what is commonly referred to as a 'back translation'.[2] During the middle of the presentation, however, it became clear that our client was having difficulty with the scripts. Perhaps it was a poor back-translation or perhaps he simply wasn't impressed by the quality of the creative. In any case, the client interrupted Marco's presentation and asked Rob what he thought of the scripts. After thinking for a moment, Rob admitted that he really couldn't evaluate the creative because he didn't speak Spanish and wasn't familiar with 'Latino culture'. Ultimately, he had to place his trust in his copywriter that the script was good. To the client, this seemed like a perfectly acceptable answer and so he approved the scripts.

It was at this moment when it first truly occurred to me that there is something fundamentally problematic about how we produce Hispanic advertising in the US. Here was an agency whose professional reputation depended on its exceptional creative. During my time at that agency, nothing ever left the doors without a thorough vetting. Every detail of every piece of communication was discussed completely and decisions about words, images and ideas frequently involved intense negotiations between creatives, account folks, clients and legal counsel. By the time the consumer ever saw or heard an advert, that concept had been talked about six ways to Sunday.

Why had this vetting process been utterly abandoned when it came to Marco's radio script? Furthermore, why did marketing professionals, who had built their careers on developing relevant messaging for various kinds of audiences, suddenly feel incapable of understanding the Latino consumer? Research on Hispanic advertising practices suggests that Marco's experience is not unique and the inclination for White practitioners to abdicate their role as 'cultural intermediaries' (Cronin 2004) has become standard industry practice. Consequently, a robust Hispanic industry has emerged enabling primarily Anglo clients to capitalize on Hispanic consumers without ever having to address them directly.

In this chapter, I examine how knowledge about the Latino consumer is generated and circulated within the advertising profession. As part of this question, I examine what forms of knowledge have been privileged but also who is presumed to have access to such knowledge. I begin the chapter by placing Hispanic advertising practices within their larger historical and cultural context. In doing so, I draw from the argument that like other social institutions, advertising practices may be seen as developmental rather than static phenomena. Here, I argue that marketing discourses have traditionally drawn from scientific discourses, which have ultimately rendered the Latino consumer foreign and remote. This has lead to a clear division of labour in which Latino practitioners are perceived as having proprietary access to Latino consumer insight while Anglo practitioners divest themselves of this responsibility. In the second part of this chapter, I reflect on how such challenges might be resolved through more reflexive practices. By drawing on insights from the field of social anthropology, I argue that by accounting for one's biases and by incorporating multiple perspectives into the advertising process, marketers may begin to develop more relevant and meaningful advertising for Latino consumers.

The producer–consumer gap

There are two conflicting realities that contribute to the problematic nature of Hispanic advertising. First, the consumer landscape is increasingly becoming more ethnically diverse. Largely as a result of globalizing forces, there has been a greater influx of immigrants from non-European countries. At the same time, the rate of growth for non-Latino Whites has decreased, leading to what Hsu Hua of *The Atlantic Monthly* (2009, p. 46) has provocatively described as the 'end of White America'. This trend is expected to continue in future years. Demographic projections indicate that by the year 2023, groups traditionally categorized as minorities will outnumber account for a majority of the country's population.

U.S. Latinos have figured prominently in this demographic shift. Because significant portions of the country were once part of Mexico, Latinos have historically had a significant presence, particularly in the western United States. But our numbers have increased in recent years due to a prolific diaspora. Today, U.S. Latinos account for more than 16% of the population and by 2050 this number is expected to grow to 30% (Ennis *et al.* 2012). According to the 2010 Census Brief (p. 11), Latinos are already a dominant presence in several large metropolitan areas including San Antonio (63%), Phoenix (41%) and Los Angles (48%).

While the growing Latino presence in the US has been met with some resistance, marketers have demonstrated a willingness to embrace Latinos in their role as consumers. While the average Latino household income of $39,000 is lower than the general population at $50,000 (PEW 2012), their relative youth makes them an ideal consumer segment. Current data indicates that **the U.S. Latino population is twenty-seven years old, nearly ten years** younger than that of non-Latino Whites (Nielsen 2012). Given the size and relative youth of the growing Latino market, several commercial sectors are expected to benefit from the Latino surge including residential buying, food and beverage, retail, financial services, transportation and media (IBIS World 2011).

Despite the changing complexion of the consumer audience, advertising agencies have remained primarily White, which leads us to our second reality: the advertising industry is, by and large, ill-equipped to accommodate ethnically diverse consumers. Chambers (2008) has pointed out that inequalities within the advertising industry have long been recognized as problematic. As early as 1964, the New York State Commission for Human Rights conducted an audit of the largest advertising agencies only to find that the industry had small percentages of people of colour, most of whom occupied clerical positions. There is little to indicate that much has changed. In 2006, the New York City Commission on Human Rights issued a scathing criticism of the New York advertising industry for what it found to be unfair hiring practices leading to an under-representation of ethnic minorities (Elliott 2006).

Aside from the lack of ethnic representation within the industry, the production of Hispanic advertising is also complicated by the issue of language. Today, 38% of U.S. Latinos identify as Spanish dominant, while another 24% identify as English dominant. Roughly 38% consider themselves to be bilingual (Taylor *et al.* 2012). For many U.S. Latinos, bilingualism is a simple fact of everyday life, but the diversity of Latino speech is at odds with Anglo-American sensibilities which Venuti (1995) describes as 'aggressively monolingual'. Because Hispanic advertising has largely been conflated with Spanish-language advertising, advertising practices involve various language ideologies (Woolard and Scheiffelin 1994; Scheiffelin *et al.* 1998) in which English monolingual clients maintain strict control over Spanish-language copy. In doing so, they are approving advertising concepts that they literally do not understand.

Collectively, the fundamental differences between advertising and the consumers they wish to target have sometimes led to various forms of advertising mischief ranging from literal (and sometimes poor) translations of English language work to fractious campaigns that represent Latino consumers as foreign and remote, wholly disconnected from the general population. In the following section, I examine how the Latino consumer has been imagined is largely a function of how a very insular community has employed 'objective' research to gain understanding about the outside world.

Epistemology, methodology and consumer insight

A historical perspective

Advertising professionals have often been described as a homogenous, like-minded community whose lived experiences are disconnected from most consumers with whom they are speaking. For example, Featherstone (1991) refers to advertising professionals as 'new cultural intermediaries', who actively promote and transmit the lifestyle of the elite to a mass audience and who collude with the elite to legitimate new fields such as fashion, music and advertising. According to Featherstone, their ability to act in this capacity is largely a function of their class position. As members of the 'petit bourgeoisie' (Bourdieu 1984), they are not quite members of the high class, but they have more social and cultural capital than the average consumer. Their exposure to and appreciation for both forms of high and popular culture is essential for creating interest in the commercial arts.

The chasm that exists between advertising producers and consumers appears to be a legacy of the early days of the profession. Like today, advertising professionals at the turn of the century were typically young, affluent and urban centred (Marchand 1985; Pope 1983). This was widely different from many of their consumers who generally had less formal education and lived in rural areas. Gender differences, however, appear to have been particularly problematic. Marchand (1985) points out that several industry measures indicate that the male–female ratio within the industry was ten-to-one.

With the emergence of general weeklies such as *Good Housekeeping, Ladies' Home Journal* and *McCall's*, middle-class women emerged as a lucrative opportunity worthy of the attention of marketers. Rather than attempt to comprehend the lived experiences of female subscribers, however, advert executives are said to have held a general contempt for the targeted consumer who they saw as increasingly tasteless, foolish and feminine. When writing for this audience, copywriters were advised to aim low and assume an 'unintelligent public' (Marchand 1985, p. 67). Furthermore, generating insight about the target audience was only semi-systematic, generally limited to methods such as reading the targeted media or getting reactions to creative concepts from a neighbour's wife (Marchand 1985).

Aside from gender and class differences, historians have also highlighted the cultural and ethnical homogeneity of the early advertising community. According to Pope (1983), half of the men who worked in advertising had been born in small towns located in the Midwest. Pope also points out that many of these professionals were the sons of ministers. Given their similar backgrounds, religious affiliation was strictly Mainline Protestant and there appears to have been little opportunity for Catholics or Jews. Furthermore, advertising professionals in the early twentieth century were largely of European descent, although there were very few agents from Eastern or Southern Europe or any of the other 'new immigration' countries that sent workers to America after 1880 (ibid.). The ethnic purity of the advertising industry did not go unnoticed by professional leaders of the time. The editors of *Who's Who in Advertising* proudly announced in 1931 that 'adherents to the theory of Nordic supremacy might relish the fact that blue-eyed advertising men are the majority' (Rogers 1931, p. xiv).

The disparity between advertising producers and consumers would become more problematic as more subcultural groups were identified as lucrative marketing opportunities. Turow (1997) indicates that as early as 1915, different periodicals actively catered to various populations including children, farmers, college students and religious communities, but Cohen (2003) argues that after the Second World War, a proliferation of empirical market research led marketers to increasingly recognize the fallacy of a unified mass market and embrace market segmentation as a commonplace strategy. Given the narrow experience of the advertising community, however, developing relevant messaging for subcultural groups proved to be problematic. Consequently, mechanisms for generating knowledge about consumers were necessary to help advertising professionals understand the experiences of consumers who they believed to be foreign and allusive.

Advertising practice and the presumption of rationality

In her discussion of the construction of the LGBT market, Katherine Sender (2004) discusses the false distinction that marketers make between business and politics. According to Sender, business implies a rational system in which economic action is separated from its cultural and social implications. Conversely, politics invokes an image of activities that are irrational, biased toward the interests of one group and incompatible with the needs of the economy. Sender argues that while marketing decisions are based on the rationality of the marketplace, they are always inherently political.

Sender's argument connects to an ongoing debate about knowledge production and the privileging of particular forms of knowledge within the advertising industry. Put another way, it is a discussion of the relationship between epistemology, the philosophy of how we come to know, and methodology, the specific practices we use to find out about the world in which we live. Historically, advertising discourses have favoured more positivist sensibilities that evolved out of the Reformation, the Scientific Revolution and other intellectual movements that are said to have led to a split between science and literature as different ways of understanding human experience.

The advertising industry's relatively early adoption of scientific thinking may be seen as a reaction to early advertising practices that were only semi-legitimate. At the turn of the century, the industry had not yet been regulated. As a result, sales techniques were suspect and advertising agents had little regard for the quality of the products they were promoting. By the early 1900s, however the profession sought to move past the hucksterism that characterized its early days and an effort was made to legitimize the profession. In 1914, the Audit Bureau of Circulations was formed, standardizing auditing procedures for paid circulations. In 1917, the American Association of Advertising Agencies (AAAA) was founded and continues to act as one of the industry's primary trade organizations (Pope 1983).

While industry leaders were calling for more disciplined practices, there is also evidence that advertising professionals sought to endow the profession with the prestige afforded other vocations. In *Modern Advertising*, Ernest Calkins and Ralph Holden (1905, p. 6) expressed their desire that the advertising profession be comparable to the three 'black graces': medicine, divinity and law. In an effort to achieve this, early industry leaders sought to certify practitioners through specialized exams or by requiring credentials of higher education not unlike the legal and accounting professions. At the time, Calkins also called for advertisers to embrace the scientific method. In his book, *The Business of Advertising*, Calkins (1915, p. 8) writes that:

> [T]he so-called advertising expert then is the man who studies the causes of great successes with the idea of applying them to other articles and other markets. It is for him to eliminate as far as possible the uncertainty, the waste, the non-essentials; to change advertising from an art to a science – or at least to a profession worthy of the ambition of trained minds.

Calkins' call for a more scientific approach to advertising reflects the privileging of scientific discourses, which limits knowledge to what can be observed and measured. This epistemological orientation is based on the assumption that the world operates according to cause and effect and that there is a single and correct set of procedures for investigating social phenomena. By 1923, industry leader Claude Hopkins believed that this goal had been achieved. Hopkins (1923, p. 2) wrote:

> The time has come when advertising has in some hands reached the status of a science. It is based on fixed principles and is reasonably exact. The causes and effects have been analyzed until they are well understood. The correct method of procedure have been proved and established. We know what is most effective, and we act on basic laws.

While the industry's call for a systematic approach to advertising may have been genuinely motivated by an interest in holding advertising agencies more accountable for their claims, infusing scientific thinking into advertising practice has also served a political purpose. Scientific discourses created the perception that advertising can be made controllable, measureable and predictable. This claim, in turn, invested advertising professionals with a degree of authority that is reassuring to clients who are investing significant amounts of economic capital into advertising. Furthermore, scientific approaches help provide the legitimization for the industry that Calkins so urgently sought. Today, a positivist outlook is evident in the preferred methodological choices that advertisers make to generate knowledge about the consumer world including tracking studies, user surveys, pre- and post-testing and other methods which have become mainstays of consumer research (Arens *et al.* 2010).

The inextricable link between scientific and advertising discourses may be useful for understanding how various ethnic and cultural groups have been re-constituted as market segments. Systematic attempts to classify and legitimize people of colour can be found as early as the 1930s, during which time, Fisk University Professor Paul K. Edwards provided the first empirical studies of African American consumers. Intended primarily for the U.S. business community, Edwards' studies of the 'Negro market' were designed to convince marketers that African Americans should be taken seriously as a source of potential corporate profits (Chambers 2008). After World War II, similar segmentation studies were designed to encourage mainstream marketers to reach out to African American consumers, with varying degrees of success. According to Cohen (2003), the unintended consequence of these efforts was an influx of mass-produced goods into Black communities, often at the expense of Black-owned business or products specifically designed for African Americans.

In a similar way, scientific research has been used for making Latino consumers intelligible and comprehendible to the mainstream advertisers. According to Rodriguez (1999), the development of a unified, pan-national audience called the 'Hispanic market' is a relatively modern phenomenon often associated with the establishment of the Spanish International Network (SIN), which would later evolve into Univision. The emergence of a national, Spanish-language network required that collective identity to be re-configured in ways that could constitute a broader, more profitable audience. In an effort to construct a cohesive and identifiable consumer market, industry professionals actively suppressed differences among Mexicans, Cubans, Puerto Ricans and other distinct groups, while promoting the ideal of linguistic and cultural unity Dávila (2012). These efforts were then legitimized through empirical, market research. In 1981, Yankelovich *et al.* (1981) published the first scientific study of the Hispanic market, titled 'Spanish USA'. Commissioned on behalf of SIN, Yankelovich concluded that the best way to reach the Hispanic market is in Spanish, stating that as 'la lengua de nuestra alma', Spanish is superior for conveying the emotional messages of advertising (Rodriguez 1999).

But as Silverman (2000, p. 825) points out, 'a way of seeing is also a way of not seeing' and the advertising industry's infatuation with quantitative, objective data has the potential to obscure the very phenomenon it purports to reveal (Hackley 2002). Like other pan-ethnic constructs, Hispanic/Latino is a construct that accounts for individuals from quite differing cultural traditions, linguistic backgrounds and racial groups. The diversity that naturally occurs within groups, however does not lend itself to scientific discourses, which start with the assumption of order and uniformity and where variety is either ruled insignificant or put aside as an exception to the rule (Duranti 1997). Thus, determining group membership has been inconsistent and has relied on such differing factors as surname, country of origin, paternal ancestry and language usage (Deshpandé *et al.* 1986).

Reacting to the industry's gravitational pull toward homogeneity, writer Junot Díaz (as cited in Flores 2003) has stated 'I'd rather have us start out as fractured so we don't commit the bullshit and erasures that trying to live under the banner of sameness entails'. Díaz's reaction casts light on the problems associated with promoting a view of culture as an ideational unity, which has become standard in marketing practice (Moisander and Valtonen 2006). Defined in this way, the construct obscures the social and cultural diversity that exists within any group. This is the fallacy of consumer markets. They purport to represent social relations as they exist in the real world, but as Ohman (1996) argues, marketers do not mine pre-existing niches.

Instead, they consciously and unconsciously shape the contours of those groups in order to present a credible, desirable and viable target market.

In recent years there has been a questioning of the degree to which scientific knowledge can be truly objective. An alternative line of thinking has emerged arguing that scientific discourses are themselves cultural texts that favour particular ways of thinking about the world and that the categories used to ground scientific research are ultimately based on cultural assumptions. In response to growing critiques of positivist approaches, scholars began to take an alternative approach to knowledge production, which assumes that we make sense of reality through our cultures and that different cultures can have very different experiences of reality. Furthermore, it is assumed that no single representation of reality can be the only true one because other cultures will always have alternative, equally valid ways of representing reality. To account for this perspective, there has been a growing appreciation for research methodologies that better capture the lived experiences of individuals such as ethnographies, in-depth interviews and focus groups.

Advertising practices have followed suit and professional practices have evolved to account for consumers in their cultural contexts. At the same time, there has been a growing awareness that national culture is not a homogenous collective of people who all make sense of the world in exactly the same way. Rather, it consists of a mixture of many overlapping subcultures who make sense of the world in their own ways (McKee 2003) and whose cultural life is organized around lifestyle and consumption choices. By adopting a social-anthropological approach to consumer research (Leiss *et al.* 2004), advertisers have attempted to understand how brands and products fit into the lived experiences of consumers.

This new way of thinking became embodied in the role of the account planner, a role that was first developed in the UK in 1965, but which later became established practice in the United States during the late 1980s and early '90s. Originally developed by Stanley Pollitt of Boase Massimi Pollitt, the account planning position was designed as a reaction to 'back-room gurus' who provided technical views on advertising without regard or considering its socio-cultural context (Barry *et al.* 1987). Today, account planning is a mainstay in many agencies and professional practices ensure that the voice of the consumer is adequately reflected in advertising (Dickinson 2009).

The advertising industry's evolution toward a more cultural approach to consumer research, however, does not appear to have fully extended to Hispanic advertising. This may be partially attributed to economic resources. As an auxiliary effort, clients are less inclined to invest in account planning services for Hispanic agencies. Consequently, cultural insight into Latino consumers has relied heavily on anecdotal information. In the same way that early advertising men informed their advertising by gaining insight from their neighbours' wives, it is not uncommon for Anglo clients to gain insight about Hispanic advertising from their nanny, their custodian or anyone Latino in their organization regardless of their marketing expertise (Chávez 2013).

Rather than attempting to better understand the lived experiences of the Latino consumer, Anglo clients and general market practitioners have invested authority in Latino practitioners, designating them as 'authentic' members of the targeted community. But Rotfeld (2003) argues that the decision for practitioners to abdicate their role as cultural arbiters is a fundamental break from good advertising practice. Rotfeld (2003, p. 87) writes:

> The people making day-to-day decisions at advertising agencies are usually well-paid, highly educated executives, often aged 25 to 40 and living in urban areas. Rarely is it seen as a source of concern that they often are selling to people who are less affluent, not as well

educated, older or younger than themselves, and who live outside the cities in which the agency is located. Yet when the target audience consists of African Americans or Hispanic/Latino consumers, advertising people often turn the work over to an advertising agency whose owners and employees are members of that minority group. Even worse, with an implicit assumption that women and members of minority groups are incapable of applying a marketing orientation to different customers, these advertising people are seen as being only able to prepare advertising for people physically like themselves.

Here, Rotfeld (2003) cautions advertising professionals to avoid essentialist sensibilities, but he also questions epistemological assumptions about who has access to cultural knowledge. White clients presume that ethnicity is reserved only for people of colour (Peñaloza 2006) and permit themselves the opportunity to disengage from Hispanic advertising. Exacerbating this issue, Hispanic agencies have been complicit in promoting the idea that they embody cultural knowledge, which gives them proprietary understanding of Latino consumers. Yet this is also a half-truth. Today, the Hispanic advertising industry is populated by 'Latin American elites', professionals who immigrated to the United States from relatively privileged backgrounds (Chávez 2012, Dávila 2012). At the same time, the Hispanic market is overwhelmingly of Mexican origin, a majority of who are located in the working classes (Borjas 1999). Thus, there are significant national, historical and class differences that separate Latino advert executives from Latino consumers.

Certainly, the normative presumption that 'it takes a Latino to know a Latino' has provided unique opportunities for Latino advertising professionals who have positioned themselves as linguistic and cultural gatekeepers for the Hispanic market, but as Rotfeld points out, these misguided attitudes about culture are ultimately career-limiting for professionals of colour and has inadvertently relegated them to the 'ad ghetto'. Here, there is little opportunity to produce Hispanic advertising that is thoughtful and meaningful (Rotfeld 2003).

Inserting reflexivity into advertising practice

In his discussion of advertising research, Kemper (2003) argues that advertising professionals are anthropologists at heart. In different ways, both advertising professionals and anthropologists are trained and get paid for making claims about how others think and they are interested in the same society, pictured in different terms. In the process of creating niche advertising, marketing professionals have similarly had to struggle with the challenge of understanding communities that are different from their own.

Still, advertising professionals can learn more from the field of anthropology. Anthropologists have also had to wrestle with the inherent contradiction involved with ascertaining and reporting on the lived experiences of others. Agar (1996, p. 91) aptly describes this form of research as quite an 'arrogant exercise' in which researchers ingratiate themselves into a group of strangers, document their social lives, describe their beliefs and report on their rituals, all within a relatively short period of time. To complicate this process, social anthropologists confront a legacy of colonialism within their profession, which limits their perspective.

Given these deficiencies, knowledge production can only be partial, but to account for these shortcomings, anthropologists have advocated for the wider practice of 'reflexive sociology' (Rosaldo 1993), which is an attempt to break from the conventional knowledge that the researcher is an impartial and neutral observer who remains an emotional blank slate. Scholars working in this tradition have argued that researchers are inclined to cling to a 'myth of detachment', in which they are presumed to be innocent from their complicity with colonialism and in perpetuating social inequalities and hierarchical relations of power. Instead, it is understood that researchers carry their own implicit assumptions about the nature of reality. These biases are a result of their personal backgrounds. Furthermore, as they later underwent some form of professional training, they learned yet another set of biases, about which determine which aspects of human experience are worthy of attention.

Reflexive anthropology assumes that social researchers can rarely, if ever, become detached observers. Rather their own lived experience both enables and inhibits particular kinds of insight. Thus, the question is not whether the researcher is biased but rather what kinds of biases exist and how might they account for them in their research. One such strategy is to approach knowledge construction as an inter-subjective process that incorporates various subjectivities, or particular angles of vision. Rather than being locked into any particular one perspective, a better understanding of social phenomenon can be achieved by studying it from a number of positions. These perspectives may include those of researchers, armed with the theoretical perspectives of their discipline, collaborators as well as the perspectives of study participants.

Kemper (2003) has further pointed out that advertisers play the role of ethnographer with disadvantages. Unlike the ethnographer's solitary work, advertising is a collaboration involving many stakeholders with competing interests who influence the produce in surprising ways. Consequently, marketing professionals must recognize that, like other social institutions, advertising agencies are sites of ideological negotiation. Given the racial disparities that pervade the modern advertising industry, practitioners must be conscious of the role that advertising agencies play in reproducing White privilege. Peñaloza (2006) has argued that by reserving ethnicity solely for people of colour, Whites position themselves as the standard against whom all others are measured. Consequently, ethnic consumer groups inherently considered deviant with respect to the wider group that is being resisted or negotiated. Within industry practice, Latinos are labelled as 'minorities', a 'subculture', or simply 'niche'; designations, which presuppose that Latinos are not only different, but inferior.

To account for these concerns, advertising professionals need to openly bring as many of their biases to consciousness as possible and to deal with them as part of their methods and to acknowledge them when drawing conclusions about consumer research. In this sense, advertising practice becomes both a professional and a personal process. Being reflexive enables researchers to critically consider their own cultural biases and negotiate various ways of seeing while investigating other cultures (Moisander and Valtonen 2006).

In this tradition, advertising practices would benefit by incorporating perspectives from those most intimately involved with the production of advertising: respectively the client, the Hispanic agency and the general market agency as well as those of the consumer. To illustrate this point, let us look at how the brand T Mobile has produced advertising for the Latino consumer. In line with common industry practice, T Mobile has elected to partner with Saatchi, their agency of record, for their general market advertising. At the same time, they have enlisted the expertise of Conill, a Hispanic agency, to assume responsibility for creating advertising for the Latino consumer. Under this model, Conill will attempt to understand how Latinos employ telecommunications in ways that are distinct from other consumers. Working somewhat independently, each agency arrives at its own truth about the consumer, but these separate truths are always bound within a larger 'truth' that Latinos and general market consumers are mutually exclusive.

This logic of practice then informs the strategic and creative decisions that will follow. For example, industry-supported data may indicate that Latinos speak Spanish, watch novelas and like fútbol (Nielsen 2012). These insights will, in turn, drive the specific facets of T Mobile's Hispanic effort. For example, it explains the decision to be the primary sponsor of the Telemundo novela 'Los Herederos Del Monte' and to integrate a T Mobile cell phone into the storyline of 'Eva Luna', a Univision produced novella. Finally, it explains the decision to launch a campaign called 'El llamado del futbol' that specifically targets Latino soccer fans.

While such decisions can be validated by 'objective' research, they reduce Latino experience to a handful of verifiable insights. That is why they have become such tired tropes within Hispanic advertising. But how might advertising look differently if clients, general market agencies and Hispanic agencies were in closer dialogue? Armed with a different set of data, might Hispanic agencies point out that Latinos are proficient in emerging technologies and, compared to non-Latino Whites, spend 68% more time watching video online and 20% more time watching video on their mobile phones (Nielsen 2012). How might these insights overlap with clients' own understanding of how consumers use telecommunications services? Informed with this knowledge, would the client begin to have a different picture of their 'general market' that is more reflective of a changing America? Might the boundaries that separate general market from Hispanic market be disrupted?

More collaboration between various communications partners seems commonsense but while clients preach the practice of integrated marketing, their efforts to include Hispanic agencies in planning processes has largely been nominal. Instead, Hispanic agencies are more likely to be drawn into planning conversations once the creative and strategic direction has already been set. In this position, they can either fall in line with the general market campaign or create something different altogether. They are rarely in the position, however, to shape the larger campaign, which leads to a sense of fractiousness – what one Latino practitioner I interviewed described as 'brand schizophrenia'. This requires that Hispanic agencies have a seat at the table early in the process, but it also requires that clients and general market agencies insert themselves into the process of Hispanic advertising. Different perspectives provide a more complete picture of any given social phenomenon, and reveal contradictions. Rather than being viewed as threatening, such collaboration should be seen as the beginning of a better understanding of Latino, social life.

Reflexivity and the Latino practitioner

Hackley (2002) argues that advertising agencies offer their clients creative and strategic services, but they have proven to be indispensible to clients because they generate a basic vocabulary of consumer cultural meanings from which advertising is crafted. Cultural knowledge is acquired by agencies formally through semi-systematic means, but it also resides in the judgement of advertising professionals and manifests itself in the form of conventional wisdom.

The idea that agencies serve as repositories of cultural knowledge is particularly relevant for Hispanic agencies, which position themselves as experts on how Latinos think. Thus, Latino practitioners are not exempt from practicing reflexivity and must similarly take stock of their own inherent biases. In *The Natives are Gazing and Talking Back*, Jacobs-Huey (2002) argues that researchers face particular challenges when they are studying communities that they consider their own. In the course of generating knowledge about their communities for professional purposes, multiple identities intersect and inform one's perspective. For example, my own understanding of the Latino community is shaped by my experiences growing up a pocho[3] in Southern California, a part of the country which has a decidedly Mexican skew. Furthermore, my professional and academic training have encouraged me to think pan-ethnically: 'Hispanic' in the advertising industry and 'Latina/o' in the academy. Finally, I am well aware of the relatively privileged position that I occupy in society, which puts me at odds with many of my Latino sisters and brothers throughout the country who are much more marginalized than I and who have much less social and physical mobility. The narrowness of my limited experiences cannot possibly enable me to account for the meanings that an Oaxaqueña, new to the country, faces when discerning between various financial products, or the ways in which a young, second-generation Dominicana living in New York uses her smart phone to engage with the world around her.

The shrewd researcher is aware of these limitations, but this is not to say that Latino practitioners bring no cultural insight. Strauss and Corbin (1990) argue that researchers investigating their own communities possess theoretical sensitivity, a personal trait that provides them with an awareness of the subtleties and meaning of data and the capacity to separate the relevant from the non-relevant. But McCracken (1988) also argues that familiarity with one's community may dull one's senses and that researchers must maintain analytical distance while at the same time drawing upon past experience and theoretical knowledge to interpret what is seen. My background may have provided me with theoretical sensitivity on the topic, but I am aware that this in no way entitles me to proprietary knowledge of Latino culture.

Jacobs-Huey (2002) further argues that there are added political considerations for native researchers. Decisions about representation – including whose voices to incorporate in published reports – entail a form of 'cultural brokering', in which researchers present the intricacies of everyday life to a community to a community of outsiders. Likewise, market researchers exercise power over the communities they observe (Moisander and Valtonen 2006). When they produce particular interpretations for their clients, they are putting forth one version of reality. Unlike anthropologists, however, the influence of advertising extends beyond mere knowledge generation (Peñaloza 2006). Advertising is inherently persuasive in nature and is disseminated to a mass audience. This has important implications for Latino communities.

Critical scholars have argued that advertising does not present reality as it is, but rather a distorted reality. As a site of ideological negotiation, particular segments of society are privileged while others are rendered invisible. In my own academic research on the Hispanic advert industry, Latino practitioners saw themselves as advocates for the Latino consumer by ensuring that they are included in marketplace dynamics. Certainly, this argument is not without merit. Competition for economic capital is highly competitive and general market agencies are not inclined to see advertising dollars diverted to efforts that are not their own. By fighting for even those limited dollars, Hispanic agencies ensure that Latinos are included in what Gross refers to as 'the republic of consumerism' (2001, p. 233).

But there is a fine line between representing the interests of the consumer and representing the interests of the agency, and it is essential that Latino advertising executives be more reflective about the work they do and its impact. Yes, it is important for Latinos be represented in advertising, but Latino advertisers must also attend to *how* Latinos are represented in advertising. Kemper rightly points out (2003) that advertising creates consumer segments by inventing or perpetuating existing tropes of gender, ethnicity and class. As a cultural system (Sherry 1987), advertising becomes part of the many ways in which Latinos acquire a sense of their own collective identity.

The influence of advertising is not solely symbolic, but also material. By design, advertising is intended to influence behaviours and to drive uniformed patterns of consumption. Thus, practitioners, Latino and otherwise, must be conscious about how predatory practices are aimed at Latino communities. Current research indicates that 10.5% of Latinos twenty years and older have been diagnosed with diabetes and in 2005 the death rate of diabetic for Latinos was 60% higher than the death rate of non-Hispanic Whites (Center for Minority Health 2009). Latinos are also said to live in residential communities in which there is a greater presence of fast food restaurants compared to communities that are primarily Anglo. Despite the propensity for health related problems in the Latino community, large, fast food corporations spend prolifically in Hispanic media. In 2013, McDonald's Corporation, Burger King Worldwide and Yum Brands (which includes KFC, Pizza Hut and Taco Bell) were among the top fifty spenders in Hispanic media (*Advertising Age* 2013).

Similarly, alcohol companies have been prolific Hispanic marketers, directing significant resources toward growing the Latino market, efforts that go back to the onset of a formal Hispanic advertising industry (Rodriguez 1999). Currently, both Anheuser Busch and SABMiller are among the top fifty spenders in Hispanic media (*Advertising Age* 2013), yet Big Alcohol's efforts are not limited to traditional advertising. Alcohol companies employ a range of promotional strategies including bilingual labelling, sponsorship of cultural events, the promotion of Latino artists and a heavy outdoor presence in Latino neighbourhoods (Kesmodel 2011; Lipschutz 2011). These efforts are coordinated by dedicated Latino/Ethnic marketing managers who work closely with Hispanic advertising practitioners to cultivate a heavy Latino drinker.

I appreciate why Hispanic agencies may be reluctant to challenge their clients. Agencies in general are under constant pressure to demonstrate their value and Hispanic agencies are particularly sensitive to client demands. Because many Hispanic agencies are small agencies, they are particularly vulnerable to external or market forces, causing them to be conservative in nature. However, silence breeds concession and there is a responsibility for Latino practitioners to directly challenge their clients on any number of decisions including how Latino characters are represented in commercials or the types of products they are actively selling to Latinos. I have argued in this chapter that the inclusion of more voices within advertising practices is needed to provide a more complete picture of Latino consumer practices. At the same time, Latino practitioners also have a responsibility to make their voices heard. If Hispanic agencies do not take a more active role in shaping advertising decisions, they risk becoming modern day Malinches,[4] merely serving as translators who serve up the populace to much more powerful forces.

Notes

1 This project follows in the tradition of other scholarship that utilizes dual terms: 'Latina/o' and 'Hispanic'. While both labels are pan-ethnic and have contested histories, scholars have been particularly critical of the term 'Hispanic' for its privileging of Spanish over indigenous origins. The term 'Hispanic', however, is the label of preference for U.S. advertisers. For the purposes of this study, I limit the use of 'Hispanic' to terms that are specific to the profession.
2 Early Hispanic advertising consisted of dubbing English language spots into Spanish. In order to sync up image with sound, it was often necessary to change English language dialogue. However, scripts then had to be re-translated back into English, in their literal form, for final client approval. Today, that particular process has become less common, but it is still standard practice to translate Spanish language copy into English for client approval. Today, practitioners still referred to this practice by its original designation of 'back-translation'.
3 Sanchez (1993) defines a pocho as the American offspring of Mexican parents, but the term has generally been used to describe Mexican Americans who have lost their culture by assimilating into the dominant culture.
4 Doña Marina, also known as 'La Malinche' occupies an ambivalent place in Mexican popular imagination. It is widely believe that her role as translator to Cortez expedited the colonization of the Americas. Her supporters argue that linguistic competencies enabled her to advocate on behalf of the native population.

References

Advertising Age (2013) *10th Hispanic Fact Pack: Annual Guide to Hispanic Marketing and Media* (Supplement), July 22.
Agar, M. (1996) *The Professional Stranger: An Informal Introduction to Ethnography.* San Diego, CA: Academic Press.

Arens, W., Weigold, M. and Arens, C. (2010) *Contemporary Advertising*, 13th edn. New York: McGraw-Hill.

Barry, T. E., Peterson, R. L. and Todd, W. B. (1987) 'The role of account planning in the future of advertising agency research'. *Journal of Advertising Research*, 27(1): 15–21.

Borjas, G. (1999) *Heaven's Door: Immigration Policy and the American Economy*. Princeton, NJ: Princeton University Press.

Bourdieu, P. (1984) *Distinction. A Social Critique of the Judgment of Taste*. Cambridge: Harvard University Press.

Calkins, E. (1915) *The Business of Advertising*. New York: D. Appleton and Company.

Calkins, E. and Holden, R. (1905) *Modern Advertising*. New York: D. Appleton and Company.

Center for Minority Health (2009, May 20) *Diabetes Data/Statistics*. Available from: http://www.omhrc.gov/templates/browse.aspx?lvl=3&lvlid=5 [accessed 1 February 2012].

Chambers, J. (2008) *Madison Avenue and the Color Line: African Americans in the Advertising Industry*. Philadelphia: University of Pennsylvania Press.

Chávez, C. (2012) 'Hispanic agencies and profits of distinction: An examination of the advertising industry as a field of cultural production'. *Consumption, Markets and Culture*, 15(3): 307–25.

Chávez, C. (2013) 'The ties that bind: Hispanic advertising and the tension between local and global forces'. In *The Routledge Companion to Advertising and Promotional Culture*, edited by M. McCallister and E. West. New York: Routledge.

Cohen, L. (2003) *The Consumers' Republic: The Politics of Mass Consumption in Postwar America*. New York: Vintage Books.

Cronin, A. M. (2004) 'Regimes of mediation: Advertising practitioners as cultural intermediaries?' *Consumption Markets and Culture* 7(4): 349–69.

Dávila, A. (2012) *Latinos, Inc. – the Marketing and Making of a People*, 2nd edn. Berkeley: University of California Press.

Deshpandé, R., Hoyer, W. D. and Donthu, N. (1986) 'The intensity of ethnic affiliation: A study of the sociology of hispanic consumption'. *Journal of Consumer Research*, 13: 214–20.

Dickinson, D. (2009) *The New Account Manager: Redefining the Crucial Role of Account Service in the Changing Business of Advertising*, 2nd edn. Chicago, IL: The Copy Workshop.

Duranti, A. (1997) *Linguistic Anthropology*. Cambridge, MA: Cambridge University Press.

Elliott, S. (2006) 'Human rights commission to study advertising industry's hiring practices'. *New York Times*. Available from: http://www.nytimes.com/2006/06/13/business/media/13addes.html.

Ennis, S. R., Ríos-Vargas, M. and Albert, N. G. (2010) 'The Hispanic population: 2010'. *2010 Census Briefs*. Available from: http://www.census.gov/prod/cen2010/briefs/c2010br-04.pdf [accessed 1 October 2013].

Featherstone, M. (1991) *Consumer Culture and Postmodernism*. London: Sage.

Flores, J. (2003) 'Nueva York, diaspora city: Latinos between and beyond'. In *Bilingual Games: Some Literary Investigations*, edited by D. Sommer. New York: Palgrave Macmillan.

Gross, L. (2001) *Up from Invisibility: Lesbians, Gay Men and the Media in America*. New York: Columbia University Press.

Hackley, C. (2002) 'The panoptic role of advertising agencies in the production of consumer culture'. *Consumption, Markets and Culture*, 5(3): 211–29.

Hopkins, C. (1923) *Scientific Advertising*. New York: Cosmo Classics.

Hsu, H. (2009) 'The end of white America?' *The Atlantic Monthly*, Jan/Feb, 2009: 45.

IBIS World, 'The growing Hispanic population means big business for these 7 sectors', Special Report, August 2011. *IBIS World*. Available from: http://www.ibisworld.com/Common/MediaCenter/Growing%20Hispanic%20Population%20(2).pdf [accessed 28 October 2013].

Jacobs-Huey, L. (2002) 'The natives are gazing and talking back: Reviewing the problematics of positionality, voice and accountability among "native", anthropologists'. *American Anthropologist* 104(3): 791–804.

Kemper, S. (2003). 'How advertising makes its object'. In *Advertising Cultures*, edited by B. Moeran and T. Malefyt. London: Berg and Co.

Kesmodel, D. (2011 July 11) 'Brewers go courting hispanics'. *Wall Street Journal*. Available from: http://online.wsj.com/news/articles/SB10001424052702303499204576389933372634042.

Leiss, W., Kline, S., Jhally, S. and Botterill, J. (2004) *Social Communication in Advertising: Consumption in the Mediated Marketplace*, 3rd edn. New York: Routledge.

Lipschutz, K. (2011 July 12) 'Brewers Tap Hispanic Consumers'. *Adweek*. Available from: http://www.adweek.com/news/advertising-branding/brewers-tap-hispanic-consumers-133331.

McCracken, G. (1988) *The Long Interview: Qualitative Research Methods*, Series 13. Newbury Park, CA: Sage Publications.

McKee, A. (2003) *Textual Analysis: A Beginner's Guide*. London: Sage Publications.

Marchand, R. (1985) *Advertising the American Dream: Making Way for Modernity, 1920–1940*. Berkeley: University of California Press.

Moisander, J. and Valtonen, A. (2006) *Qualitative Market Research: A Cultural Approach*. London, UK: Sage Publications.

Nielsen (2012) 'State of the Hispanic consumer: The Hispanic Market imperative'. *Nielsen*. Available from: http://www.nielsen.com/content/dam/corporate/us/en/reports-downloads/2012-Reports/State-of-the-Hispanic-Consumer.pdf [accessed 25 March 2013].

Ohmann, R. (1996) *Selling Culture: Magazines, Markets and Class at the Turn of the Century*. New York: Verso.

Peñaloza, L. (2006) 'Researching ethnicity and consumption'. In *Handbook of Qualitative Research Methods in Marketing*, edited by R. W. Belk. Northampton, MA: Edward Elgar Publishing, Inc.

PEW Hispanic Center (2012) 'Latinos express growing confidence in personal finances, nation's direction'. *PEW Hispanic Center*. Available from: http://www.pewhispanic.org/files/2012/11/Latinos_and_the_economy_final_11_2.pdf [accessed 21 September 2013].

Taylor, P., Lopez, M. H., Martínez, J. H. and Velasco, G. (2012) 'When labels don't fit: Hispanics and their views of identity'. Pew Hispanic Center. Available at: http://www.pewhispanic.org/2012/04/04/when-labels-dont-fit-hispanics-and-their-views-of-identity/.

Pope, D. (1983) *The Making of Modern Advertising*. New York: Basic Books, Inc.

Rodriguez, A. (1999) *Making Latino News: Race, Language, Class*. Thousand Oaks, CA: Sage.

Rogers, J. L. (1931) *Who's Who in Advertising, 1931*. New York: Harper and Brothers.

Rosaldo, R. (1993) *Culture & Truth: The Remaking of Social Analysis*. Boston, MA: Beacon Press.

Rotfeld, H. (2003) 'Misplaced marketing: Who Do You Hire When the Advertising Audience Isn't You?' *The Journal of Consumer Marketing, 20*(2): 87–9.

Sánchez, G. (1993) *Becoming Mexican American: Ethnicity, Culture and Identity in Chicano Los Angeles 1900–1945*. New York: Oxford University Press.

Sender, K. (2004) *Business Not Politics: The Making of the Gay Market*. New York: Columbia University Press.

Scheiffelin, B., Woolard, K. and Kroskrity, P. (1998) *Language Ideologies: Practice and Theory*. New York: Oxford University Press.

Sherry, J. F. (1987) 'Advertising as a cultural system'. In *Marketing and Semiotics* edited by J. Umiker-Sibeok. New York: Mouton de Gruyter: 441–61.

Silverman, D. (2000) 'Analyzing talk and text'. In *Handbook of Qualitative Research*, 2nd edn, edited by N. Denzin and Y. Lincoln. London: Sage Publications.

Strauss, A. and Corbin, J. (1990) *Basics of Qualitative Research: Grounded Theory Procedure and Techniques*. Newberry Park, CA: Sage Publications.

Turow, J. (1997) 'Breaking up America: The dark side of target marketing'. *American Demographics, 19*(11): 51–4.

Venuti, L. (1995) *The Translator's Invisibility: A History of Translation*. New York: Routledge.

Woolard, K. and Schieffelin, B. (1994) 'Language ideology'. *Annual Review of Anthropology* 23: 55–82.

Yankelovich, Skelly and White (1981) *Spanish USA: A Study of the Hispanic Market in the US*. New York: Yankelovich, Skelly and White, Inc.

18

Print advertising and Asian Indian consumers

Durriya H. Z. Khairullah and Zahid Y. Khairullah

Introduction

Advertising is a key component of marketing and print media is an important mode for communicating advertising messages. Magazine advertisements of products and services are widespread in countries across the world. Research within the field of marketing has looked at advertising, its effects and responses to different media and advertising aimed at different ethnic groups. This chapter reviews the results of our research in advertising related to ethnic minority consumers and the impact of acculturation on responses towards advertising. In particular the focus is on perceptions and effects of acculturation at different levels among Asian Indian immigrants especially in the United States (US). The chapter includes: conceptual background; description of our research studies and findings; followed by a discussion of theoretical and practical implications of our research.

Conceptual background

Ethnicity

Ethnic origin or ethnicity is defined as a group having common national or religious backgrounds (Cohen 1978; Hirschman 1981; Minor 1992); country of origin and surname (Hirschman 1981; Laroche *et al.* 1998); racial, language or national backgrounds (Hawkins and Mothersbaugh 2013). Ethnicity also means a group sharing common customs, language, religion, values, morality and etiquette (Webster 1994). Most contemporary researchers are of the view that ethnicity arises from the notion that certain individuals belong to or identify with certain cultural groups (Cleveland and Laroche 2007). 'Culture is the sum total of learned beliefs, values, and customs that serve to direct the consumer behaviour of members of a particular society' (Schiffman *et al.* 2010, p. 348). These factors encompass such elements as food, dress, religious beliefs and people with whom they associate with (Kara and Kara 1996). Ethnic groups do not just differ in the languages they speak or their skin colour. They differ in cultural values, attitudes, experiences, where they shop and what advertising appeals they pay attention to. Such factors intertwine to shape differences in buying behaviour (Perreault *et al.* 2011). Ethnicity affects consumer behaviour through choices related to clothes, music, leisure pursuits, food and drink consumption (Bocock 1993). Individuals originating from a particular nation normally share cultural values that are often different from cultural values of other nations (Hofstede 1983).

In the last three decades the US has become a more ethnically diverse society. The number of ethnic minority consumers is growing at a much faster rate than the overall White population in the US and their purchasing power is also increasing rapidly. This surge in ethnic minority populations has provided growth opportunities for U.S. marketers. In order to boost sales among ethnic minority groups some U.S. marketers have been designing marketing strategies that are reflective of specific cultural values (Cho *et al.* 2013; Dunne *et al.* 2014; Hawkins and Mothersbaugh 2013; Jamal 2003; Peñaloza and Gilly 1999; Perreault *et al.* 2011; Schiffman *et al.* 2010). In doing so, marketers often adopt a market segmentation strategy to cater to ethnic consumers in a multicultural marketplace. Much of the growth in ethnic minority populations has resulted from immigration (Perreault *et al.* 2011). According to Jamal (2003) the multicultural marketplace also provides an opportunity for ethnic entrepreneurs and retailers to tailor their marketing mix for their respective ethnic groups. According to several researchers, notions of ethnicity and culture are also linked to the phenomenon of acculturation, which is discussed in the next section.

Acculturation

When discussing culture, anthropologists often distinguish between the learning of one's own, or native, culture and the learning of some 'new' (other) culture. The learning of one's own culture is known as *enculturation* and the learning of a new or a foreign culture is called *acculturation* (Schiffman *et al.* 2010). Acculturation is a general term that incorporates intercultural interaction and adaptation and includes assimilation of a new culture, preservation of the old culture, and resistance to both new and old cultures (Peñaloza and Gilly 1999). Prior research considers acculturation from uni-directional, bi-directional and multi-dimensional viewpoints. Uni-directional acculturation is the acceptance of values of a host society by members of a minority or immigrant group (Garcia and Lega 1979; Gordon 1978; Phinney 1990). This view is consistent with an assimilation perspective that suggests that immigrants' adaption to the host culture invariably leads to a loss of one's original culture (Hraba 1979; Wallendorf and Reilly 1983). The bi-directional view proposes two dimensions of acculturation, the extent to which one identifies with the culture of origin and the degree to which one identifies with the host culture (Berry 1990). The multi-dimensional view incorporates ethnic identity into the adaptation process with the assumption that immigrants in the process of adapting some aspects of host culture may also independently retain certain aspects of their original culture (Berry 1997; Cleveland and Laroche 2007; Laroche *et al.* 1997; Padilla 1980; Mendoza 1989). According to this viewpoint, the process through which immigrants adapt to the host culture is called acculturation, and the process of retaining the home country's culture by the immigrants is called ethnic identity (Felix-Ortiz *et al.* 1995; Phinney 1990). The bi-directional and multi-dimensional views are consistent with the basic premise of 'multiculturalism', which postulates that a variety of cultures can, and do, co-exist in the same geographical region and show a part or whole of their ethnic identity (Cleveland and Laroche 2007; Hraba 1979; Jamal and Chapman 2000; Jamal 2003).

Consumer acculturation and marketer acculturation

In the consumer behaviour literature, culture and ethnicity are linked to the study of two concepts – consumer acculturation and marketer acculturation. When consumers come in contact with a new culture the resulting change due to intercultural contact in consumer behaviour is referred to as consumer acculturation (Peñaloza 1989; 1994). Marketer Acculturation is used to refer to the resulting change for marketers in contact with a new culture of consumers (Peñaloza and Gilly 1999; Peñaloza 1994). Several researchers have advocated that ethnic minority subcultures are growing in Europe, United Kingdom and the US and the globalization of world markets makes both consumer acculturation and marketer acculturation important agents in facilitating marketing strategies (e.g. Berry 2005; Cleveland and Laroche 2007; Jamal 2003; Peñaloza and Gilly 1999; Peñaloza 1994).

Acculturation and marketing studies

Some ethnic consumers retain a great many of their own culture's attitudes, values and behaviours, while others more readily adopt values, attitudes and behaviours of the dominant host culture. These differences are reflected in market related behaviours, including:

(i) The importance of product attributes (Barbosa and Villarreal 2008; Faber *et al.* 1987; Kara and Kara 1996; O'Guinn and Faber 1985a; 1986);

(ii) Product evaluation (Lee and Um 1992);

(iii) Consumption factors e.g. food, price, shopping/purchasing behaviour (Choe 1987; Gupta 1975; Hair and Anderson 1973; Hair *et al.* 1975; Hernandez and Kaufman 1991; Laroche *et al.* 1997; Nyer and Gopinath 2002; O'Guinn and Meyer 1983/84; O'Guinn *et al.* 1985b; Ownbey and Horridge 1997; Segal and Sosa 1983; Seitz 1998; Suri and Manchanda 2002; Wallendorf and Reilly 1983; Weinstock 1964);

(iv) Media usage (Cervantes 1980; Choe 1987; Cui and Powell 1993; Deshpandé *et al.* 1986; Kim 1978; O'Guinn and Meyer 1983/84; O'Guinn *et al.* 1985b; Shoemaker *et al.* 1985);

(v) Perception of time usage for work and leisure activities (Manrai and Manrai 1995);

(vi) Marital roles in purchase decisions (Ownbey and Horridge 1997; Stafford *et al.* 1996; Webster 1994);

(vii) Brand loyalty, language preference (Deshpandé *et al.* 1986);

(viii) Perceptions of advertisements (Green 1999; Khairullah 1995; Khairullah *et al.* 1996; Khairullah and Khairullah 1999a; Ueltschy and Krampf 1997);

(ix) Religious affiliation (Schiffman *et al.* 1981).

The two common findings of these studies are: (i) that ethnic consumers are not homogeneous groups and (ii) that there is a positive relationship between marketing related behaviours studied and the extent of acculturation. Based on the results of their studies, these authors conclude that marketers should study ethnic consumers from an acculturation perspective. Using acculturation provides ethnic marketers a means of refinement of an ethnic segmentation strategy. This in turn helps to develop improved ethnic marketing strategies to meet the needs of specific sub-segments of ethnic populations. This leads to our discussion of the development of some relevant conceptual models of acculturation.

Models of acculturation

According to Berry (1997), and in the context of two cultures meeting, migrant consumers adopt specific acculturation strategies. His conceptualization generates four acculturation strategies:

(i) *An Assimilation Strategy* when individuals do not wish to maintain their cultural identity and interact on a daily basis with others; (ii) *A Separation Strategy* when individuals hold on to their culture and at the same time wish to avoid interactions with others; (iii) *An Integration Strategy* when individuals maintain an interest in both maintaining one's original culture, while at the same time seek to participate as an integral part of the dominant groups and (iv) *A Marginalization Strategy* when there is little interest in cultural maintenance and in having relations with others.

Models of immigrant consumer acculturation (Peñaloza 1989; 1994) postulate that the immigrant enters the new consumer environment with consumption knowledge acquired from his/her culture of origin comes in direct contact with members of the new consumer culture. Several factors including demographics and socialization agents lead to three possible consumer acculturation outcomes: (i) Assimilate culture of origin, where immigrants mingle or assimilate into the dominant culture; (ii) Maintain culture of immigration, when immigrants maintain their original culture; and (iii) Express Hybrid Culture where immigrants adopt a combination of two cultures.

Peñaloza and Gilly (1999) propose a *Marketer Acculturation Process* when a marketer wishes to cater to a culturally distinct group of consumers. It consists of the learning and adaptation processes employed by marketers.

A model based on identification of microcultures (Ogden *et al.* 2004) postulates that the purchase outcomes of microcultures is influenced by two variables: (i) the degree or the level of consumer acculturation sub-groups within the microculture and (ii) the type of product under consideration – value expressive versus utilitarian products. The outcome sought is the purchase of the product.

Stages of acculturation

Similar to the descriptions of acculturation outcomes provided by the models discussed above, prior research has identified either three levels (e.g. Barbosa and Villarreal 2008; Berry 1980; Gupta 1975; Khairullah 1995; Segal and Sosa 1983) or four levels (e.g. Cervantes 1980; Sodowsky and Carey 1988) of acculturation. Our studies focused on the three levels: (i) low acculturation when ethnic consumers retain their original cultural values and do not yet accept cultural values of the host country; (ii) moderate acculturation when ethnic consumers retain not only their original cultural values but at the same time also accept cultural values of the host country; and (iii) high acculturation where ethnic consumers give up most of their original values and adopt cultural values of the host country.

Rational for our study on print advertising and Asian Indian consumers

The initial interest in our research was developed from a review of the literature on ethnic minority consumers in marketing journals and trade publications. These articles discuss the phenomenal growth of ethnic consumers in the US and also advocate the development of culturally attuned ethnic advertisements to reach ethnic groups effectively. Advertising is considered as a mirror reflecting cultural values of a given society (McCracken 1986). Based on this notion, cultural values are embedded in such a way that consumers can see the similarity between themselves and the content of advertisements (Hong *et al.* 1987; McCracken 1986). Thus the cultural diversity in the US affects how ethnic consumers perceive and accept advertisements. Studies on acculturation mentioned earlier, demonstrate the importance of acculturation on immigrants' consumption, buying and media usage patterns. However, there is little empirical evidence in marketing literature actually offering insights and information indicating how Asian Indian immigrants, originally coming from India, perceive Indian advertisements versus American advertisements of the same product class, and whether these perceptions were considered from an acculturative perspective. Our studies attempt to fill this gap. The result of such a comparison could help marketers evaluate the feasibility of developing culturally appropriate advertisements to reach Asian Indians effectively, an ethnic segmentation advertising strategy. The findings would also enable marketers to consider whether acculturation could help in refinement of ethnic segmentation strategy. It could allow development of improved advertisement campaigns to meet the needs of specific sub-segments of Asian Indian immigrants. The following sections provide background information on Asian Indian immigrants in the US. This is followed by a discussion of our studies regarding perceptions of advertising.

Asian Indian immigrants in the US

In the last twenty years, one of the fastest growing ethnic subcultures in the US is the Asian Indians who are coming from the sub-continent of India. There were approximately 2.8 million Asian Indians in the US in 2012 (Macioge 2012). Asian Indians have surpassed Filipinos as the second-largest Asian population after Chinese (El Nasser and Overberg 2011). The Asian Indian segment is growing rapidly as a result of fewer immigration restrictions applied to Indians under the U.S. Immigration Laws of 1965 (Gitlin 2005; Hawkins and Mothersbaugh 2011; Joseph 2006; Macioge 2012). This growing ethnic segment has strong purchasing power. They are the wealthiest ethnic group in the US with a median household income that ranges between $60,000–80,000 compared to the national median household income of under $50,000 nationwide (Macioge 2012; Sohrabji 2012). Asian Indians are also well-educated and fluent in English (Gitlin 2005; Mogelonsky 1995). Several studies have reported that most of the Indian immigrants in the US sampled in their research are married, younger, highly educated, well-to-do individuals coming from urban areas of India (e.g. Dasgupta 1989; Khairullah and Khairullah 1999b; Leonhard-Spark et al. 1980; Sodowsky and Carey 1988; Mehta and Belk 1991) and come from different religious, caste and regional backgrounds (e.g. Dasgupta 1989; Gandhi 1970; Gupta 1975; Khairullah and Khairullah 1999b; 2011) reflecting the regional, language and religious diversity of India's population. In spite of these differences they share a large number of common Indian traditional values that they retain and follow.

Studies regarding Asian Indians in the US

Dasgupta (1989) found that Indian immigrants see Americans as extroverts, practical, honest, technology oriented, self-confident, self-sufficient, hard working, assertive, lonely, self-centred and less attached to their families. Asian Indians consider themselves as introverts, emotional, knowledgeable but not practical, less confident and very much oriented towards family and society.

According to Ganesh (1997), among the Asian Indian families, the husband domination in the family is declining and that the wife domination is increasing perhaps, due to the influence of American culture and as a part of the acculturation process in the US. Although parents make joint-decisions and shop together, fathers usually dominate major purchase decisions (Jain 1995, cited in Mogelonsky 1995). Dasgupta (1998) found that first generation and older subjects are not in favour of dating and have more traditional attitudes towards women while the younger and second-generation subjects have more liberal views. Higher levels of anxiety are experienced by individuals who are more acculturated and assimilated in the host culture. Respect and value of age, religious beliefs and beliefs in simplicity and fatalism are important to Asian Indian Americans (Rossman 1994).

Indian cultural identity in terms of arts and crafts, furniture, heirlooms, movies, songs and religious objects of India are found in the homes of the Indian immigrants in the US (Desai and Coelho 1980; Gandhi 1970; Mehta and Belk 1991; Saran and Leonard-Spark 1980). Mathur *et al.* (2008) examined the consumption of cultural goods among the first and second generations in the US and in India. They concluded that the first-generation adults in the US have a lower level of culture-specific consumption than the second-generation youth in the US and in India. The second-generation youth in the US have a higher level of culture-specific consumption than the first-generation adults in India but a lower level of culture-specific consumption than the youth in India.

Asian Indian respondents sampled by researchers are found to follow and practise their religious beliefs (e.g. Gandhi 1970; Mehta and Belk 1991; Sodowsky and Carey 1987). A majority of Asian-Indian Americans eat Indian foods using herbs and spices rooted in Indian traditions, women wear traditional Indian dresses at their social functions (Pavri 2011). Studies have shown that compared to many other ethnic groups in the US, Asian Indians are conservative in their investment decisions and tend to save more rather than spend (e.g. Cheng 2003; Delpechitre and DeVaney 2007; Hussein and Thirwall 1999) especially for education and retirement (Jain 1995, cited in Mogelonsky 1995). Against the backdrop of Asian Indian immigrants discussed in the preceding sections, we now turn our attention in discussing our studies on Asian Indians' perceptions of advertising. The aim is to provide a richer understanding of cultural mechanisms in play that can explain Asian Indian consumers' responses to advertisements.

Khairullahs' studies of Asian Indian immigrant perceptions of print advertisements

Study I

Khairullah (1995) investigated whether the perceptions of first-generation Asian Indian immigrants' in the US towards Indian print advertisements versus American print advertisements of the same product class vary within and across the three levels of acculturation. Several tests find no significant differences ($p < .05$) in order of presentation of advertisements effects and gender effects. The results of product effect and ethnicity effect for male and female subgroups are mixed when these tests are performed without using the degree of acculturation as a variable; however, when it is introduced as a variable, a statistically significant effect of advertisements' ethnicity is found. The findings indicate: (i) Asian Indian immigrants sampled are not a homogenous group and (ii) the perceptions of Asian Indian immigrants for the Indian versus the American advertisements vary within and across different levels of acculturation. Low and moderate acculturated Asian Indian immigrants prefer Indian advertisements more than American advertisements while high acculturated respondents prefer American advertisements more than Indian advertisements.

Study II

Khairullah *et al.* (1996) examined whether Asian Indian immigrants would have a more favourable affective attitude toward an advertisement (Aad) for Indian magazine advertisements than toward American magazine advertisements. When the respondents are treated as a homogeneous group, without considering their degree of acculturation, the results are mixed. No clear preference by Asian Indians sampled for Indian advertisements is found. However, when acculturation is introduced as a variable, the results indicate that Asian Indian consumers with higher-acculturation scores have a more favourable Aad towards American advertisements than Asian Indian with lower acculturation scores. It is also found that as the degree of acculturation increases, Asian Indians' preferences for the American advertisements increases and their preference for Indian advertisements decreases.

Study III

In their 1999a study, Khairullah and Khairullah found that there was a strong positive relationship with Aad and purchase intention of the advertised products. The results indicate that: (i) if Asian Indian immigrants like the print advertisements, they are more likely to buy that advertised product and (ii) Aad is an important measure of advertising effectiveness. These results support the proposition and findings of earlier studies (e.g. Batra and Ray 1986; Lutz et al. 1983; Mitchell and Olson 1981) that the 'likeability' of advertisements could give that brand a competitive edge in the long run.

Study IV

Khairullah and Khairullah (2003) propose a conceptual model that postulates that the acculturation process of ethnic consumers is influenced by those consumers' demographic characteristics. The authors suggest that marketers of U.S. and ethnic goods should develop culturally loaded advertising messages based on immigrant consumers' levels of acculturation. Several studies have found that demographic characteristics influence the extent of acculturation of immigrants in the US (e.g. Baldassini and Flaherty 1982; Clark et al. 1976; Ghaffarian 1987; Goldlust and Richmond 1974; Gupta 1975; Khairullah and Khairullah 1999b; Mehta and Belk 1991; Olmedo and Padilla 1978; Padilla 1980; Peñaloza 1994; Sodowsky and Carey 1988; Szapocznik et al. 1978). These studies indicate that males tend to acculturate more rapidly than females. Younger immigrants acculturate much faster than older immigrants. Those immigrants married to spouses other than their own ethnicity acculturate more quickly than those who married spouses of their own ethnicity. Immigrants who stay longer in the US are more acculturated than those who are in the country for a shorter period. More acculturated individuals have a higher level of education, occupational status and income than their lower acculturated counterparts. High acculturated immigrants are more likely to come from urban areas of their original countries.

Study V

In 2005, Khairullah and Khairullah conducted an exploratory research to examine the cultural perceptions of second-generation Asian Indians in the US for Indian magazine advertisements versus American magazine advertisements of the same product class. The results show that second-generation Asian Indians prefer Indian advertisements more than corresponding American advertisements for the majority of products used in the study. The second-generation respondents used stronger language in describing the extent of sex portrayed in the American man's suit advertisement and the shampoo advertisement that they were shown.

Study VI

Khairullah and Khairullah (2011) conducted a study using one of the qualitative research methods, a projective technique, to obtain interpersonal interpretations of Asian Indian participants. The study had three objectives: (i) to gain insights regarding cultural differences that the Asian Indian immigrants' subjects see in terms of the general appearance, lifestyle and personality of the models appearing in selected Indian magazine advertisements versus American magazine advertisements of the same product class; (ii) to find out if the religious, caste and regional differences among the Indian respondents in the US would have an impact on how they feel towards Indian advertisements; and (iii) to ask respondents whether they prefer Indian advertisements or American advertisements. This research supports the contention of studies mentioned earlier in the chapter that Asian Indian immigrants through their cultural values, rituals, clothing, furnishings, religion, etc. see themselves as a unique group in the US. Religion, caste and regional diversity among those sampled did not have an impact on their perceptions toward Indian advertisements. Sign tests indicated statistically significant differences between male and female respondents in their preferences for Indian advertisements over American advertisements.

Having discussed our substantial work in relation to Asian Indian consumers' responses to advertising, we now turn our attention to discussing important implications for both theory and practice based on the results of our research.

Implications

Implications for theory

The results of our studies indicate that ethnic consumers in the US are not a homogenous group. They go through an acculturation process. While some ethnic consumers retain a great many of their traditional attitudes, values and behaviours, others more readily adopt the cultural attitudes, values and behaviours of the dominant host culture. These differences are reflected in their perceptions of advertisements.

There is a relationship between ethnic consumers' perceptions of advertising and their levels of acculturation. As ethnic consumers become more acculturated, their preference for American advertisements increases (positive relationship) and their preference for ethnic advertisements decreases (negative relationship). The rate of change in ethnic consumers' perceptions of advertisements with respect to acculturation differs with the nature of advertisements, i.e. whether the advertisements are 'ethnic' or 'American'. Low and moderate acculturated ethnic consumers prefer ethnic advertisements to American advertisements, while the highly acculturated prefer American advertisements to ethnic advertisements. Hence, if advertising messages are insensitive to the cultural values of a significant portion of low and moderate acculturated ethnic consumers, the advertising could prove to be ineffective in reaching them. Similar relationships have also been found in other studies on acculturation and marketing-related behaviours. Research results imply marketers should consider developing advertising campaigns and marketing strategies from a multi-dimensional perspective of acculturation. These observations lend support to the propositions of consumer acculturation process; marketer acculturation process; acculturation strategies; and also the work of researchers who conclude that intercultural contact and adaptation is an important feature of the contemporary global, multicultural marketplace.

Practical implications

Our results imply that just as marketers tailor their marketing mixes to suit the unique needs of their dominant target market, so should they consider the levels of acculturation as a basis for segmenting ethnic groups. By treating immigrant consumers as a homogeneous group, marketers could overlook the underlying differences in their behaviours. These differences may be quite significant and better allocation of resources, and appropriate media selection, can be made by marketers who take into account acculturation as a segmentation variable. Segmentation is said to be a useful strategy when the target market is (i) different in attitudes and behaviours from other segments; (ii) reachable by available media and (iii) large enough in size to be cost effective (Perreault *et al.* 2011). The results of our research together with the evidence available in the literature indicate that the Asian Indian immigrants considered in our research meet criteria for a segmentation strategy.

Our research has implications for U.S. and ethnic marketers who can effectively reach low and moderate acculturated Asian Indian immigrants by using appropriate visual stimuli in their advertising. These include using Asian Indian models, showing female models in the traditional Indian dress of sari and jewellery. Females can be shown as young conservative housewives and male Indian models can be portrayed as young, educated, well-to-do individuals where appropriate. Indian cultural and moral values can be portrayed through the acts of models; for instance focus on family bonds, respect for elders, husband/wife relationships and religious rituals can be depicted. Indian art and artifacts in the backgrounds can also be included in the advertisements. In order to avoid pitfalls in reflecting cultural values, marketers must make sure that Indian advertisements are either prepared or screened by those individuals who are familiar with Asian Indian cultural values.

Our research was conducted entirely in English. Language and media are important considerations in planning an advertising campaign for any ethnic group. Most of the Asian Indian immigrants coming to the US are proficient in both spoken and written English (Mogelonsky 1995). In terms of acculturation and the subsequent cultural change processes, the multi-lingual ability of Asian Indians makes them a distinct group. Further research should examine multi-lingual capabilities across different ethnic consumer groups and the impact of multi-lingual abilities on acculturation outcomes.

According to Gitlin (2005), it is a language-form of the spoken English language that is more formal and more precise than standard American usage that unifies diverse groups of Asian Indians immigrants in the US. Hence caution must be exercised in using English words and phrases that may be offensive to Indian immigrants' cultural values. Marketers can reach Asian Indians through various English language print media that is used by Asian Indian immigrants, such as: *India Abroad*, *India News*, *Little India* and *Masala*. Asian Indians are also heavy users of broadcast media in metropolitan cities such as Chicago, Los Angeles and New York, where Indian programs in Indian languages as well as in English are aired on a regular basis. The Internet should also be considered. There are a number of Indian organizations and associations that organize religious and cultural events (Pavri 2011). U.S. and ethnic marketers could participate in these events to familiarize their products and get recognized for their initiatives in reaching out to Asian Indians. Our results also reinforce that religion, caste and regional diversity are not important considerations for purchase decisions to Asian Indian immigrants once in the US. This is good news for marketers, as it means that they do not have to incur added costs of developing separate Indian advertisements based on Asian Indian immigrants' diverse religious, language, regional and social backgrounds. According to the established literature, the Asian Indian population has a favourable growth rate and is an affluent group.

Relatively few Asian Indian subjects in our studies were high acculturated. A plausible explanation may be that these subjects could have been Westernized in their upbringing in India before migrating to the US. India had been under the British rule for more than 200 years and British influence is still prevalent in many parts of India, more specifically in urban areas. In Sodowsky and Carey's (1988) study, a small percentage of Asian Indians who consider themselves to be 'mostly or very American' consistently choose not to maintain their original national identity. This can be been true of high acculturated Asian Indians in our studies. Earlier studies on other ethnic groups and Asian Indian immigrants found that the bi-cultural Asian Indians eat American food when they socialize with Americans and female Indians wear American dress at work. Like other immigrant groups, they celebrate traditional American holidays such as Thanksgiving and Christmas. It is likely that moderately acculturated Asian Indians sampled in our studies may not feel it necessary to comply with American ways and thus are more receptive to Indian advertisements than to American advertisements. Positive relationships between acculturation, Aad and purchase intention found in our study can provide marketers an added incentive for measuring the effectiveness of their culturally attuned advertising campaigns prepared for Asian Indians.

The results indicate the importance of advertising as a form of social communication that is particularly reflective of a society's culture. Consumers are exposed and overwhelmed by numerous advertisements, but ethnocentred advertisements catch their attention more easily. There was a time when Westerners would consider Asian subculture as one people, but now they have recognized that the Chinese, Japanese, Indians and others are all very different and these differences have been recognized in advertising media (Schmit 1977, cited in Krishna 1997). The effectiveness of ethnic marketing has inspired some U.S. marketers to develop culturally sensitive campaigns to reach Asian Indian immigrants residing in the US. These include long-distance telephone companies, airlines, insurance, Indian restaurants, match-making/dating services (Mogelonsky 1995; Krishna 1997). These authors note that Asian Indians tend to patronize those marketers who develop culturally sensitive advertising campaigns to reach them. Recently a few U.S. companies advertising such products as clothing (e.g. Guess, Gap); computer (e.g. IBM); cosmetics (e.g. Olay, L'Oreal); insurance (e.g. New York Life, Metlife); telephone (e.g. AT&T, Verizon) have included Asian Indian models in their advertisements.

Research also lends support to the characteristics of culture of being natural, shared, dynamic and learned, satisfying needs and wants, and being handed down from generation-to-generation (Schiffman, et al. 2010). The second-generation Asian Indians sampled in our study appear to have learned the cultural values from their parents and other social institutions to which they are exposed and perceive clearly the cultural differences between India and the US. They too prefer Indian advertisements over American advertisements sampled.

Conclusion

This chapter discusses literature on ethnicity, acculturation and Asian Indian immigrants in the US, which provide the conceptual background for our studies comparing Asian Indian immigrants' perceptions of Indian versus American print advertisements. Our results indicate that when Asian Indian immigrants are treated as a homogeneous group without considering their level of acculturation, the preferences for Indian versus American advertisements are mixed. However, when examined from an acculturative perspective, low acculturated subjects prefer Indian advertisements to American advertisements and the preferences change as acculturation level increases. While some Asian Indians retain a great many of their traditional cultural values others adapt to cultural values of the dominant U.S. society, showing that the Asian Indians sampled are therefore not homogeneous. Our findings confirm that the more the target audience like the advertisements, the more inclined they are to purchase the advertised products. Our research also indicates that Asian Indians coming to the US have favourable socio-economic characteristics in terms of education, occupation and income.

In summary, the results of the studies presented in this chapter lead us to conclude that marketers should evaluate the feasibility of developing appropriate advertisements to reach successfully the growing affluent Asian Indians in the US, who in spite of favourable demographics and socio-economic characteristics, have so far been ignored by U.S. marketers (Bell 2006; Gitlin 2005; Krishna 1997; Raju 1995; Robey 1988). Marketers should not only undertake an ethnic segmentation strategy, but also consider acculturation as a segmentation variable to meet the needs of specific sub-segments of this ethnic group.

The insights provided by our research and several other studies will help both U.S. and ethnic marketers to acknowledge, appreciate and understand that it is in the interest of marketers to develop culturally attuned advertising and other marketing strategies to be successful in the diverse multicultural market of the US. Furthermore, in today's competitive, global and multicultural marketplace, one of the important growth strategies for marketers is market development, where they look for new consumers. The surge in the growth and purchasing power of ethnic groups provides a lucrative opportunity for marketers to sell their goods and services to these groups.

References

Baldassini, J. G. and Flaherty, V. F. (1982) 'Acculturation processing of Colombia immigrants into American culture in Bergen County, New Jersey'. *International Journal of Intercultural Relations*, 6: 127–35.

Barbosa, L. and Villarreal, A. (2008) 'Acculturation levels play role in marketing strategy'. *Marketing News.* February 15, pp. 26–9.

Batra, R. and Ray, M. L. (1986) 'Affective responses mediating acceptance of advertising'. *Journal of Consumer Research*, 13(February): 234–9.

Bell, A. (2006) 'Indian-Americans: The secret market'. *National Underwriter/Life & Health Financial Services*, January 16, 110(3): 21–2.

Berry, W. J. (1980) 'Acculturation as varieties of adaptation'. In *Acculturation: Theory, Models and Some New Findings*, edited by A. M. Padilla Boulder. Colorado: Westview Press, pp. 9–46.

Berry, J. W. (1990) 'Psychology of acculturation'. In *Cross-Cultural Perspectives: Proceedings of the Nebraska Symposium on Motivation*, edited by J. J. Berman. Lincoln, NE: University of Nebraska Press, pp. 201–34.

Berry, J. W. (1997) 'Immigration, acculturation, and adaptation'. *Applied Psychology: An International Review*, 46(1): 5–68.

Berry, J. W. (2005) 'Acculturation: Living successfully in two cultures'. *International Journal of Intercultural Relations*, 29(6): 697–712.

Bocock, R. (1993) *Consumption*. London: Routledge.

Cervantes, F. J. (1980) 'The forgotten consumer: The Mexican-Americans'. In *AMA Educators' Conference Proceedings: Marketing in the 1980s*, edited by R. P. Bagozzi, K. L. Bernhardt, P. S. Busch, D. W. Craverns and J. F. Hair Jr. Chicago: IL, American Marketing Association, pp. 180–83.

Cheng, A. T. (2003) 'Native intelligence'. *Journal of Institutional Investor*, 3(3): 66–70.

Cho, C.-H., Holcombe, J. and Murphy, D. (2013) 'Multicultural marketing in contemporary U.S. markets'. *Insights Marketing Group. Inc.* [online]. Available from: http://www.greenbook.org/marketing-research.cfm/multicultural-marketing [accessed 21 March 2013].

Choe, S. T. (1987) 'The relationship between the level of acculturation and ethnic consumer behavior'. In *Proceedings of the Atlantic Marketing Association: Marketing Issues and Trends*, edited by R. C. Coulter and S. G. Green New Orleans: LO, pp. 43–9.

Clark, M. M., Kaufman, S. and Pierce, R. C. (1976) 'Explorations of acculturation: Toward a model of ethnic identity'. *Human Organization*, 35(3): 231–38.

Cleveland, M. and Laroche, M. (2007) 'Acculturation to the global consumer culture: Scale development and research paradigm'. *Journal of Business Research,* 60(3): 249–59.

Cohen, R. (1978) 'Ethnicity: Problem and focus in anthropology'. *Annual Review of Anthropology,* 7: 379–403.

Cui, G. and Powell, K. (1993) 'Segmenting the Asian American consumer market: An acculturation approach'. In *Minority Marketing: Research Perspectives for the 1990s,* 1–7, edited by R. L. King. Coral Gables, FL: The Academy of Marketing Science, pp. 1–7.

Dasgupta, S. D. (1998) 'Gender roles and cultural continuity in the Asian Indian immigrant community in the U.S'. *Sex Roles: A Journal of Research,* 38(11–12): 953–74.

Dasgupta, S. S. (1989) *On the Trail of an Uncertain Dream: Indian Immigrant Experience in America.* New York, NY: AMS Press, Inc.

Delpechitre, D. and DeVaney, S. A. (2007) 'Understanding the savings behavior and risk tolerance of Asian Indians in the U.S'. *Journal of Personal Finance,* 6(1): 60–80.

Desai, P. N. and Coelho, G. V. (1980) 'Indian immigrants in America: Some cultural aspects of psychological adaptation'. In *The New Ethnics: Asian Indians in the United States,* edited by P. Saran and E. Eames. New York, NY: Praeger Publisher, pp. 363–8.

Deshpandé, R., Hoyer, W. D. and Donthu, N. (1986) 'The intensity of ethnic affiliation: A study of the sociology of hispanic consumption'. *Journal of Consumer Research,* 13: 214–20.

Dunne, P. M., Lusch, R. F. and Carver, J. R. (2014) *Retailing,* 8th edn. Mason, OH: Cengage Learning.

El Nasser, H. and Overberg, P. (2011, May17) 'Census shows growth among Asian Indians'. *USA Today* [online]. Available from: http://usatoday30.usatoday.com/news/nation/census/2011-05-12-asian-indian-population-Census_n.htm [accessed on 27 March 2013].

Faber, R. J., O'Guinn, T. C. and McCarthy, J. A. (1987) 'Ethnicity, acculturation, and the importance of product attributes'. *Psychology & Marketing,* 4: 121–34.

Felix-Ortiz, M., Newcomb, M. D. and Myers, H. F. (1995) 'A multidimensional measure of cultural identity for Latino and Latino adolescents'. In *Hispanic Psychology: Critical Issues in Theory and Research,* edited by A. M. Padilla. Thousand Oaks, CA: Sage Publications, pp. 26–42.

Gandhi, R. S. (1970) 'Conflict and cohesion in an Indian student community'. *Human Organization,* 29 (2, Summer): 95–102.

Ganesh, A. (1997) 'Strategy: Why do professional leave?' *Data Quest,* December 15: 148–51.

Garcia, M. and Lega, L. (1979) 'Development of a Cuban identity questionnaire'. *Hispanic Journal of Behavioral Sciences,* 1: 247–61.

Ghaffarian, S. (1987) 'The acculturation of Iranians in the United States'. *The Journal of Social Psychology,* 127(b): 565–71.

Green, C. L. (1999) 'Ethnic evaluations of advertising: Interaction effects of strength of ethnic identification, media placement, and degree of racial composition'. *Journal of Advertising,* 28(1): 49–64.

Gupta, S. P. (1975) 'Changes in food habits of Asian Indians in the United States: A case study'. *Sociology and Social Research,* 60(1): 87–99.

Gitlin, S. (2005, September 27) 'Marketing to Asian-Indian Americans'. *Direct Magazine* [online]. Available from: http://license.icopyright.net/user/viewFreeuse.act?fuid=MTI2ODkynjY%3D [accessed 5 May 2011].

Goldlust, J. and Richmond, A. H. (1974) 'A multivariate model of immigration adaptation'. *International Migration Review,* 8(2): 193–225.

Gordon, M. M. (1978) *Human Nature, Class and Ethnicity.* New York, NY: Oxford University Press.

Hair Jr., F. J. and Anderson, R. E. (1973, Series, #34) 'Culture, acculturation, and consumer behavior: An empirical study'. In *Combined Proceedings: Marketing Education and the Real World and Dynamic Marketing in a Changing World,* edited by B. Becker and H. Becker. Chicago: IL, American Marketing Association, pp. 423–28.

Hair Jr., F. J., Bush, R. F. and Busch, P. S. (1975) 'Acculturation and black buyer behavior'. In *AMA 1975 Combined Proceedings,* edited by E. M. Mazze. Chicago: IL. American Marketing Association, pp. 253–256.

Hawkins, D. I. and Mothersbaugh, D. L. (2013) *Consumer Behavior: Building Strategy,* 12th edn. New York, NY: McGraw-Hill Irwin.

Hernandez, S. A. and Kaufman, C. J. (1991) 'Measuring consumer acculturation: Coupon usage among "Barrio" Hispanics'. *Research in Consumer Behavior,* 5: 61–82.

Hirschman, E. C. (1981) 'American Jewish ethnicity: Its relationship to some selected aspects of consumer behavior'. *The Journal of Marketing,* 45(3): 102–10.

Hofstede, G. (1983) 'National culture in four dimensions'. *International Studies of Management and Organization*, 13(2): 46–74.

Hong, J. W., Muderrisoglu, A. and Zinkhan, G. M. (1987) 'Cultural differences and advertising expression: A comparative content analysis of Japanese and US Magazine advertising'. *Journal of Advertising*, 16(1): 55–62, 68.

Hraba, J. (1979) *American Ethnicity*. Itasca, IL: F. E. Peacock.

Hussein, K. and Thirwall, A. P. (1999) 'Explaining differences in the domestic saving ratio across countries: A panel data study'. *The Journal of Development Studies*, 36(1): 31–52.

Jamal, A. and Chapman, M. (2000) 'Acculturation and inter-ethnic consumer perceptions: Can you feel what we feel?' *Journal of Marketing Management*, 16(4): 365–91.

Jamal, A. (2003) 'Marketing in a multicultural world: The interplay of marketing, ethnicity and consumption'. *European Journal of Marketing*, 37(11/12): 1599–620.

Joseph, G. (2006) 'The Indian-American Population Boom'. *Rediff News*. Available from: http://specials.rediff.com/news/2006/sep/01sld1.htm [accessed 18 March 2015].

Kara, A. and Kara, N. R. (1996) 'Ethnicity and consumer choice: A study of hispanic decision processes across different acculturation levels'. *Journal of Applied Business Research*, 12(2, Spring): 22–34.

Khairullah, D. Z. (1995) 'Acculturation and its relation to Asian-Indian immigrants' perception of advertisements'. *Journal of Applied Business Research*, 11(2): 55–66.

Khairullah, D. Z., Tucker, F. G. and Tankersley, C. B. (1996) 'Acculturation and immigrant consumer's perception of advertisements: A study involving Asian-Indians'. *International Journal of Commerce and Management*, 6(3&4): 81–104.

Khairullah, D. Z. and Khairullah, Z. Y. (1999a) 'Relationships between acculturation, attitude toward the advertisement, and purchase intention of Asian-Indian immigrants'. *International Journal of Commerce and Management*, 9(3&4): 46–65.

Khairullah, D. Z. and Khairullah, Z. Y. (1999b) 'Behavioral acculturation and demographic characteristics of Asian-Indian immigrants in the United States of America'. *International Journal of Sociology and Social Policy*, 19(1/2): 57–80.

Khairullah, D. Z. and Khairullah, Z. Y. (2003) 'A model for acculturation, demographics and advertising'. In *Proceedings of the 2003 International Business Research Conference*. Sponsored by the Clute Institute for Academic Research, Littleton. CO.

Khairullah, D. Z. and Khairullah, Z. Y. (2005) 'Second generation Asian-Indian reactions to Asian-Indian and American magazine advertisements'. *International Business & Economics Research Journal*, 4(9): 37–43.

Khairullah, D. Z. and Khairullah, Z. Y. (2011) 'Preferences expressed by Asian-Indian subjects for American versus Asian Indian print advertisements'. *International Journal of Business and Social Science*, 2(17, Special Issue-September): 38–45.

Kim, Y. (1978) 'A communication approach to the acculturation process: A study of Korean in Chicago'. *International Journal of Intercultural Relations*, Summer: 187–223.

Krishna, B. M. (1997) 'Culturally sensitive ad campaign by NY Life'. *India Abroad*, April 25: 24.

Laroche, M., Kim, C., Hui, M. and Tomiuk, M. A. (1997) 'A mutidimensional perspective on and its relative impact on consumption of convenience foods'. *Journal of International Consumer Marketing*, 10: 33–56.

Laroche, M., Kim, C. and Tomiuk, M. A. (1998) 'Italian ethnic identity and its relative impact on the consumption of convenience and traditional foods'. *Journal of Consumer Marketing*, 15(2): 125–51.

Lee, W.-N. and Um, K.-H. R. (1992) 'Ethnicity and consumer product evaluation: A cross-cultural comparison of Korean immigrants and Americans'. In *Advances in Consumer Research*, Vol. 19, edited by J. F. Sherry, Jr. and B. Sternthal. Provo, UT: Association for Consumer Research, pp. 429–36.

Leonhard-Spark, P. J., Saran, P. and Ginsberg, K. (1980) 'The Indian immigrants in America: A demographic profile'. In *The New Ethnics: Asian Indians in the United States*, edited by P. Saran and E. Eames. New York: Praeger Publisher, pp. 136–62.

Lutz, R. MacKenzie, S. and Belch, G. (1983) 'Attitude toward ad as a mediator of advertising effectiveness: Determinants and consequences'. In *Advances in Consumer Research*, 10, edited by R. P. Bagozzi & A. M. Tybout. Ann Arbor, MI: Association of Consumer Research, pp. 532–39.

Macioge, C. (2012, October 2) 'Asian-Indian demographics'. *US Census Bureau* [online]. Available from: http://ww.census.gov/econ/sbo/02asiansof_asianindian.html [accessed 15 March 2013].

Manrai, L. A. and Manrai, A. K. (1995) 'Effects of cultural-context, gender and acculturation on perceptions of work versus social/leisure time usage'. *Journal of Business Research*, 32: 115–28.

Mathur, S., Guiry, M. and Tikoo, S. (2008) 'Intergenerational culture-specific consumption differences between Asian Indian immigrants in the U.S. and Indians residing in an Indian Metropolis'. *Journal of International Consumer Marketing*, 20(3): 69–80.

McCracken, G. (1986) 'Culture and consumption: A theoretical account of the structure and movement of cultural meaning of consumer goods'. *Journal of Consumer Research*, 13(June): 71–84.

Mehta, R. and Belk, R. W. (1991) 'Artifacts, identity, and transition: Favorite possessions of Indians and Indian immigrants to the United States'. *Journal of Consumer Research*, 17(4): 398–411.

Mendoza, R. H. (1989) 'An empirical scale to measure type and degree of acculturation in Mexican-American adolescents and adults'. *Journal of Cross-Cultural Psychology*, 20(4): 372–85.

Minor, M. (1992) 'Comparing the Hispanic and Non-Hispanic markets: How different are they?' *Journal of Services Marketing*, 6(2): 29–32.

Mitchell, A. A. and Olson, J. C. (1981) 'Are product attribute beliefs the only mediator of advertising effects on brand attitude?' *Journal of Marketing Research*, XVIII(August): 318–332.

Mogelonsky, M. (1995) 'Asian-Indian Americans'. *American Demographics*, August: 33–9.

Nyer, P. U. and Gopinath, M. (2002) 'Bargaining behavior and acculturation: A cross-cultural investigation'. *Journal of International Consumer Marketing*, 14(2/3): 101–22.

Ogden, D. T., Ogden, J. and Schau, H. J. (2004) 'Exploring the impact of culture and acculturation on consumer purchase decisions: Toward a microcultural perspective'. *Academy of Marketing Science Review*, 8: 1–26.

O'Guinn, T. C. and Meyer, T. P. (1983/84) 'Segmenting the Hispanic market: The use of Spanish-language radio'. *Journal of Advertising Research*, 23(6, December–January): 8–14.

O'Guinn, T. C. and Faber, R. J. (1985a) 'New perspective on acculturation: The relationship of general role specific acculturation with Hispanics' consumer attitudes'. In *Advances in Consumer Research*, XII, edited by E. C. Hirschman and M. Holbrook. Provo: UT: Association for Consumer Research, pp. 113–17.

O'Guinn, T. C., Faber, R. J and Meyer, T. P. (1985b) 'Ethnic segmentation and Spanish-language television'. *Journal of Advertising*, 14(3): 63–65.

O'Guinn, T. C. and Faber, R. J. (1986) 'Advertising and subculture: The role of ethnicity and acculturation in market segmentation'. *Current Issues and Research in Advertising*, 9(1/2): 133–147.

Olmedo, E. L. and Padilla, A. M. (1978) 'Empirical and construct validation of measure of acculturation for Mexican-Americans'. *The Journal of Social Psychology*, 105: 179–87.

Ownbey, S. F. and Horridge, P. E. (1997) 'Acculturation levels and shopping orientations of Asian American consumers'. *Psychology & Marketing*, 14: 1–18.

Padilla, A. M. (1980) 'The role of cultural awareness and ethnic loyalty'. In *Acculturation: Theory, Models and Some New Findings*, edited by A. M. Padilla. Boulder, Colorado: Westview Press, pp. 47–83.

Pavri, T. (2011) 'Asian Indian Americans'. [online]. Available from: http://www.everyculture.com/muti/A-Br/Asian-Indian-Americans.html [accessed 6 May 2011].

Peñaloza, L. N. (1989) 'Immigrant consumer acculturation'. In *Advances in Consumer Research,* Vol. 16, edited by T. K. Srull. Provo, UT: Association for Consumer Research, pp. 110–18.

Peñaloza, L. N. (1994) 'Atravesando fronteras/border crossing: A critical ethnographic exploration of the consumer acculturation of Mexican immigrants'. *Journal of Consumer Research*, 21(1): 32–54.

Peñaloza, L. and Gilly, M. C. (1999) 'Marketer acculturation: The changer and the changed'. *Journal of Marketing*, 63: 84–104.

Perreault Jr., W. D., Cannon, J. P., and McCarthy, E. J. (2011). *Basic Marketing: A Marketing Strategy Planning Approach,* 18th edn. New York, NY: McGraw-Hill Irwin.

Phinney, J. S. (1990) 'Ethnic identity in adolescents and adults: Review of research'. *Psychological Bulletin*, 108(3): 499–514.

Raju, G. (1995) *Advertising Age*, 66(13, March 27): 14–15.

Robey, B. (1988) 'The spending power of Asian-Indians Americans'. *Adweek's Marketing Week*, July 4: 12.

Rossman, M. L. (1994) *Multicultural Marketing: Selling to a Diverse America*. New York, NY: AMACOM.

Saran, P. and Leonhard-Spark, P. J. (1980) 'Attitudinal and behavioral profile'. In *The New Ethnics: Asian Indians in the United States*, edited by P. Saran and E. Eames. New York, NY: Praeger Publisher, pp. 163–76.

Schiffman, L. G., Dillon, W. R. and Ngumah, F. E. (1981) 'The influence of subcultural and personality factors in consumer acculturation'. *Journal of International Business Studies*, (Fall): 137–43.

Schiffman, L. G., Kanuk, L. L. and Wisenblit, J. (2010) *Consumer Behavior,* 10th edn. Upper Saddle River, NJ: Prentice Hall.

Segal, M. N. and Sosa, L. (1983) 'Hispanic market segmentation for effective marketing'. *California Management Review*, XXVI: 130–4.

Seitz, V. (1998) 'Acculturation and direct purchasing behavior among ethnic groups in the U.S.: Implications for business practitioners'. *Journal of Consumer Marketing*, 15(1): 23–31.

Shoemaker, P. J., Reese, S. D. and Danielson, W. A. (1985) 'Spanish-language print media use as an indicator of acculturation'. *Journalism Quarterly*, Winter: 734–44.

Sodowsky, G. R. and Carey, J. C. (1987) 'Asian Indian immigrants in America: factors related to adjustment'. *Journal of Multicultural Counseling and Development,* 15(3): 129–41.

Sodowsky, G. R. and Carey, J. C. (1988) 'Relationships between acculturation-related demographic and cultural attitudes of an Asian-Indian immigrant group'. *Journal on Multicultural Counseling and Development*, 16: 117–35.

Sohrabji, S. (2012, July 2) 'Indian Americans most educated, richest, says Pew Report'. *New America Media* [online]. Available from: http://newamericamedia.org/2012/07/indian-americans-most-educated-richest-says-pew-report.php [accessed 27 March 2013].

Stafford, M. R., Ganesh, G. and Luckett, M. G. (1996) 'Perceived spousal influence in the service decision-making process'. *Journal of Applied Business Research*, 12(4): 53–69.

Suri, R. and Manchanda, R. V. (2001) 'The effects of acculturation on consumers' sensitivity to prices'. *Journal of International Consumer Marketing*, 13(1): 35–56.

Szapocznik, J., Scopetta, M. A., Kurtiness, W. and Arnalde, M. A. (1978) 'Theory and measurement of acculturation'. *Interamerican Journal of Psychology*, 12: 113–20.

Ueltschy, L. C. and Krampf, R. F. (1997) 'The influence of acculturation on advertising effectiveness to the Hispanic market'. *Journal of Applied Business Research*, 13(2, Spring): 87–101.

Wallendorf, M. and Reilly, M. (1983) 'Ethnic, migration, assimilation and consumption'. *Journal of Consumer Research*, 10: 293–302.

Webster, C. (1994) 'Effects of Hispanic ethnic identification on marital roles in the purchase decision process'. *Journal of Consumer Research*, 21(September): 319–31.

Weinstock, A. (1964) 'Some factors that retard or accelerate the rate of acculturation with specific reference to Hungarian immigrants'. *Human Relations*, 17: 321–42.

Part VII

Ethical and public policy issues in ethnic marketing

19

Revisiting ethnic
marketing ethics

Guilherme D. Pires and John Stanton

Introduction

Ethnically diverse populations are growing in many advanced economies (OECD 2013, Statistical Annex). In the US, minority ethnic communities have also gained in perceived importance, such that they are now commonly referred to as the new majority (Armstrong 2013; Dougherty and Jordan 2012) or the majority minority (Cui and Choudhury 2002). In Canada, where day-to-day living experiences are taken as evidence of the cultural diversity that underpins its population, ethnic communities are recognized as the 'the visible majority' (Daniels 2012). It is, therefore, unsurprising that the practitioner literature in the US reports on a growing number of businesses that are seeking to take advantage of the potential opportunities afforded by the growth of ethnic communities (Carrasco 2013; Burgos and Mobolade 2011), such as the Latinos, the Hispanics and the Asian American, and some more narrowly defined minority ethnic groups such as the Mexican and the Chinese.

As cultural and ethnic diversity are linked to ethical diversity (Segal and Giacobbe 1995), whether a business decides to focus on the mainstream, on a narrowly defined minority ethnic group or on some aggregate of minority ethnic groups, has implications for which notions of business ethics, 'what is good' related to business practice (Seelye and Wasilewski 1996), are present. This may create ethical dilemmas that provide a motivation for businesses to assess and make decisions about which standards and rules of conduct relating to marketing decisions and marketing situations will need to be applied (Vitell *et al.* 1993), or ethnic marketing ethics in the present context.

Purpose

This chapter provides an overview of ethical concerns linked to ethnic marketing covered in the specialist marketing literature, and identifies gaps that warrant attention by practitioners and researchers alike. Drawing extensively on the work of Pires and Stanton (2014; 2002) and Cui (1998), possible ethical related consequences from target marketing ethnic minority consumers with marketing programs designed for mainstream consumers, from unethical target marketing of ethnic minority consumers, and from marketing communications related to ethnic groups are discussed.

The extant literature provides substantial coverage of a variety of aspects pertaining to ethnic marketing ethics. Indeed, the review of the literature presented in this paper highlights a degree of maturity, reflected in the organization of issues by type and classification, hence amenable to systematic consideration. However, prompted by some paucity of scholarly commentary in recent years, our purpose is to uncover and to initiate discussion of apparent omissions in the literature with respect to the potential ethical implications associated with important and wide reaching new ways of doing business that have arguably transformed the way many business exchanges are conducted today and, predictively, into the future. The particular focus of this paper is on consumer socialization challenges involving ethnic minority consumers, which are fostered by structural changes in marketing practices triggered by continued advances in Information and Communication Technologies (ICT), such as consumers' changing access to market knowledge.

It is argued that information technology facilitates electronic markets that may offer advantages for ethnic minority consumers, such as greater consumer socialization and ICT-driven consumer empowerment (Pires et al. 2006), as well as additional ethics concerns ensuing from involuntary restricted participation in electronic exchanges. These concerns justify consideration by government, practitioners and researchers when making marketing decisions and considering marketing situations involving business exchanges and the targeting of minority ethnic groups or some related aggregate. Recommendations for further research conclude the paper.

Overview of ethics issues in ethnic marketing

Market segmentation and targeting have been identified as the quintessence of the marketing concept, the cornerstone of marketing (Gray et al. 1998; GrÖnroos 1989), while alerting for potential ethical concerns, such as those involving the targeting of vulnerable consumers with harmful products (Smith and Cooper-Martin 1997). At the turn of the twenty-first century, growing business recognition and support of cultural diversity within countries such as Australia, Canada and the US prompted both an interest in marketing to diverse minority ethnic groups or to some aggregate of these groups, as well as a consideration of the ethical issues that could arise intertwined with the design and implementation of related target marketing activities (Cui and Choudhury 2003; 2002; Cui 1998).

Particularly relevant to this paper, some analysts consider that ethnic marketing is inherently unethical, because it recurrently distinguishes people by criteria such as their race and culture, invariably leading to allocations of people to cultures and to subcultures, with minorities (the subcultures) being relegated to second class status (Petty et al. 2003). But the consideration of ethics issues in the ethnic marketing literature is much less radical, concentrating primarily on matters related to unethical marketing practices in targeting ethnic minority consumers and to the targeting of ethnic minorities with marketing programs designed for the mainstream (Pires and Stanton 2002). The underlying premise is that marketing strategies ought not to discriminate against minority ethnic groups based on their hypothetical inferiority, vulnerability or some other ethnic related weakness that may impair the consumers being targeted.

With a continuing growth of foreign-born populations in many OECD economies (OECD 2013) combined with changing marketing practices related to the growing use of electronic technologies (OECD 2012) capable of boosting or impairing consumer socialization processes, a reconsideration of the ethics implications of ethnic marketing is amply justified, particularly as a recent analysis of shifting perspectives and emerging trends covering over half a century of marketing literature (Schlegelmilch and Oberseder 2010) fails to acknowledge enquiry into ethnicity related ethics issues.

Examination of ethics issues related to ethnic marketing requires distinguishing general considerations of business ethics from poor business practices (as contrasted with unethical behaviour). With the primary function of businesses as providers of service to their customers (GrÖnroos 2011; 2008; Buchholz and Rosenthal 2000) for background, the distinction between poor business practices and unethical behaviour is not easy to operationalize even when only a mainstream culture is considered, because a business needs to define a level of 'what is good' that balances its own goals, customers' needs, and those of society in general (Pires and Stanton 2002). It is well known that operationalization is even more complex in the international environment because distinct cultures can lead to a lack of alignment of the notion of 'what is good' across countries (Kotler *et al.* 1998, p. 833). It is crucial to understand that this complexity is not exclusive to the international environment. It extends to domestic markets characterized by cultural diversity, because culture and ethnicity are relevant causal constructs for both seller–buyer and consumer behaviour (Sarwono and Armstrong 1998; Hui *et al.* 1992). The review of the literature conducted in this study sought to omit instances of poor business practices, but acknowledges that unethical behaviour may be inextricably intertwined with poor business practices.

Drawing from a recent critical review of the relevant literature by Pires and Stanton (2014), Table 19.1 reports ethics issues associated with ethnic marketing – that is, marketing activities within a host country targeted to minority consumers identified based on ethnicity criteria. Often noted in the literature for their vulnerability, inferiority and disadvantaged status, it is posited that immigrants and other racial/ethnic minorities may suffer from inequalities in the marketplace relative to other consumers (Wolburg 2005; Brenkert 1998). Particularly early in their settlement within a host country, ethnic minority consumers may be impaired by poor consumer socialization, reflective of limited market knowledge about what is available, where and for how much, as well as about how to behave as consumers. This is a matter of concern for ethnic marketing ethics because poor consumer socialization may justify that newcomers

Table 19.1 Ethical issues in marketing targeted to ethnic minority consumers

---

Failure to provide for basic needs may mean that some ethnic minority consumers will have to do without needed products, causing harm to their physical or psychological well-being (Kotler *et al.* 1998).

Failure to accommodate ethnic minority consumers' wants due to cultural sensitivity limitations may cause loss of self-esteem and contribute to cultural shock (Usunier and Lee 2009; Oberg 1960). There is a potential for ethnic minority consumers to take offense (Stages of Innovation 2000).

Discrimination against ethnic minority consumers by presuming alignment to a minority ethnic group with low substantiality. This may involve a deliberate distortion of a firm's primary function of providing a service (Buchholz and Rosenthal 2000).

Perpetuation of minority status by promoting continued invisibility of ethnic minority consumers and groups within official statistics, such as censuses of the population (Pires and Stanton 2002; Pires 1999).

Breach of ethnic sensitivity through undesired targeting as a separate minority ethnic group. Arguably this is the case of German minorities in Hungary (Sas and Kozma 2009).

Discrimination against ethnic minority consumers and minority ethnic groups by providing inadequate, insufficient, misdirected and/or misinterpretable information. Similar to principle of consumer education and information (Kotler *et al.* 1998) and a recurring issue in healthcare (Grier and Kumanyika 2008).

Unfair use of fine print in contracts and use of legalese to take opportunistic advantage of ethnic minority consumers' market inexperience (Fair Trading NSW 2013).

Adoption of an *etic* approach towards ethnic minorities' need for culturally sensitive therapies when an *emic* approach is justified (Hall 2001).

---

be perceived as vulnerable consumers, to be taken advantage of through deceptive practices (Moore-Shay 1996).

New arrivals in the host country often rely on referral or recommendation by similar immigrants that they trust (Frable *et al.* 1998) – eventually their minority ethnic group of affiliation or a group of similar others, particularly when market inexperience and communication difficulties limit the number and range of accessible secondary sources – as a means to enhance consumer socialization and reduce vulnerability to deceptive practices (Pires and Stanton 2000) and to lessen cultural shock effects (Oberg 1960). A current illustration of this situation is the case of the (relatively small at approximately 3,000 group members) Brazilian community opting to adopt the much more numerous Portuguese community in Sydney, Australia, and its ethnic resources (Pires and Stanton 2005), until such time as there is a critical mass of Brazilian consumers capable to generate their own ethnic resources (Pires *et al.* 2011).

A focus on group substantiality may lead to unrealistic assessment of group importance and eventual failure to focus on the affiliated consumer's needs and wants. Where ethnic minorities exhibit visible ethnic elements or features, consumer disadvantage may ensue from racial discrimination (Grier *et al.* 1996). Even if exposure to a multicultural experience may have ameliorative effects through epistemic unfreezing involving the questioning of a previously accepted view (Tadmor *et al.* 2012), deception and discrimination remain important ethics issues relating to ethnic minority consumers, although not exclusive to ethnic marketing.

When the focus of marketers is on finding commonalities across groups so as to build market substantiality, differences across narrowly defined minority ethnic groups may be tactically overlooked. Hence, the use of etic approaches when emic ones may be justified is a cause for concern (Hall 2001). One approach to avoiding over-estimation may be to emically presume differences before an etic approach is adopted.

Although we seek to omit situations of poor business practices, some of the potential ethical consequences listed in Table 19.1 may still result from or involve poor business practices. An example is the eventual failure to accommodate ethnic minority consumers' wants due to cultural sensitivity limitations. In such cases, the resulting ethics issue is present, although it may not be deliberate. Nevertheless, the targeting of minority ethnic groups may involve unethical deliberate actions, as well as actions intrinsically unethical. Illustrating the earlier referred degree of maturity in the literature, with issues able to be systematically discussed by type and classification, Cui (1998) identifies areas of eventual ethnic segmentation and targeted marketing failure, noting the possible incidence of associated ethical failure: inadvertent stereotypes, biology and genetics, nature of the product, redlining and ethnocentric bias. These are briefly discussed below, reflecting the breakthrough that Cui's work represents in the area of ethnic marketing ethics:

1. *Inadvertent stereotypes* refer to situations where recognition of the importance of a minority ethnic group leads to increased participation by members of that group in advertising to other ethnic minority consumers (similar others), although the actual messages are stereotypical and do not reflect the diversity of the minority ethnic group (Stevenson 1991), as is the case of many communications involving African Americans in the US (Craemer 2011);
2. *Biology and genetics* refer to the use of superficial or exaggerated physical or biological attributes of a minority ethnic group that may suggest that ethnic minority consumers are inferior to other consumer groups;
3. *Nature of the product* refers to the target marketing of ethnic markets with negative, inferior or harmful products (Smith and Cooper-Martin 1997);

4. *Redlining* refers to the selection or exclusion of markets based on racial lines and can be perceived as extending to the symbolic racism of Whites versus Blacks (McConahay and Hough Jr. 1976). It is also similar to *consumer racism*, a measure of consumer judgements of, and willingness to buy, domestic products that are perceived as being made by other ethnic minorities, with significant negative effects for minority-owned business performance (Ouellet 2007);

5. *Ethnocentric bias* questions whether fundamental principles of marketing based on research of the mainstream population can be generalized to minority ethnic groups. Here, the ethical question both focuses on the consequences of non-differentiation of ethnic minority groups from the mainstream population (hence, the denial of ethnic marketing practice) and on the consequences from targeting minority ethnic groups with mainstream marketing programs.

Table 19.2 reports ethics issues that may arise from unethical targeting of ethnic minority consumers. These involve the use of stereotyping, incorrect ascriptions to communities, racial discrimination, privacy concerns, dumping of products, alienation of trusted sources, price discrimination, behaviours that are opportunistic and/or discriminatory, and exclusion. Exclusion of an individual from affiliation to a minority ethnic group when an affiliation in fact exists may sometimes be in the interest of a service provider given the scarcity of its resources (Smith and Quelch 1993). As an example, while it is open to anyone to claim Australian aboriginality, in

Table 19.2 Unethical targeting of ethnic minority consumers

Emotional damage to ethnic minority consumers due to *stereotyping, incorrect ascription, discrimination,* etc., when appearance, country of birth, neighborhood of residence, etc. wrongly suggest affiliation to a minority ethnic group (Cocchiara and Quick 2004). Similar to *inadvertent bias* (Cui 1998) and *implicit bias* (Greenwald and Krieger 2006) or prejudice (Rudman *et al.*), an *ethnic stereotype* exists when ethnic minority consumers are perceived and treated by others in terms of a generalized notion of the minority ethnic group they are perceived to affiliate with, rather than in terms of specific information concerning individual consumers (Hamilton 1979).

Exclusion of ethnic minority consumers from affiliation to a minority ethnic group when an affiliation in fact exists (Pires and Stanton 2002).

Racial discrimination of ethnic minority consumers, similar to *redlining* (Cui 1998) and extensive to *symbolic racism* (McConahay and Hough Jr. 1976).

Infringing consumers' privacy since the right to be left alone includes consumers' right to be free from unwanted marketing solicitations. For example, personal data ethically collected by a marketer into a database – respecting ethnic minority consumers' autonomy, informed consent and freedom to withdraw – may not be passed to other marketers (Fisher *et al.* 1999).

Dumping of lower quality, unsuccessful, defective, untried products. There may be an element of danger (Cui 1998).

Alienation of trusted sources, potential gatekeepers to the minority ethnic group and affiliated ethnic minority consumers, through bribes or similar (Varner and Beamer 1995).

Deception by deliberate omission of information or use of small print in contracts (Fair Trading 2013). Also related to **bad faith**, which involves intentionally misleading someone or undertaking an agreement without any intention of fulfilling its provisions (Borgerson and Schroeder 2002).

Price discrimination in relation to prices set for the mainstream or for other ethnic communities (Rosenbaum and Montoya 2007).

Opportunistic behavior due to deliberate overpricing or limiting access to services in order to capitalize on lack of market experience and communication difficulties.

---

obtaining access to resources provided by both public and private (e.g. scholarships to private schools) providers, self-ascription alone is usually insufficient; the ability to show descent and acceptance by the minority group are also necessary (Australian Institute of Aboriginal and Torres Strait Islander Studies n.d.)). Since an ethnic group has the power to recognize who are its members, persons seeking to affiliate may be rejected, advantaging accepted members of the group and aiding the rationing problem of the service provider.

The literature also attends to complex ethical issues arising from misrepresentation of minority ethnic groups within (mainstream or global) marketing communications, reported in Table 19.3. For example, *typified representations* of particular ethnic groups in the media being recurrently associated with particular activities in stereotypical roles (such as the Portuguese immigrants in France and the Filipino in Hong Kong being domestic servants) may contribute to epistemic freezing, a juncture at which the need for cognitive closure (with respect to knowledge on a particular matter) locks a particular representation into a firm fact (Kruglanski and Webster 1996). *Exoticized representations* can undermine identities and reputations as in the case of Hawaiians, Polynesians and other Pacific Islanders (Costa 1998), although both inclusion (as in the case of Benetton's cultural inclusion) and exclusion (from brand identity by BMW) may lead to misrepresentation. Subliminal messages may involve unfair and unwanted manipulation of consumers' behaviour and the use of social paradigms may impinge on ethnic sensitivities.

The entries reported in all three tables should be seen as indicative of the issues that may eventuate rather than give a complete and detailed account of those issues. Nevertheless, augmenting the tables with anecdotal instances of apparent ethical infringements involving ethnic minority consumers should take into account the alternative benefits of conforming to apt

Table 19.3 Ethical issues in ethnic marketing communications

Typified representations influence how consumers and groups are viewed by others and may undermine a group's dignity and historical integrity, casting a demeaning light upon the members' ontological status as human beings (Borgerson and Schroeder 2005). Some marketing campaigns which cast particular groups in *stereotypical* roles (Sandilands 2013) may contribute to *epistemic freezing*, and may involve *inadvertent stereotyping* (Stevenson 1991). It is apparent that typified representations are applicable to many diverse consumer groups (such as gay and lesbian, aged, challenged, those determined by religion, bikers, and many others).

Exoticized representations are a type of typified representation involving stereotyping that calls attention to selected identity characteristics (e.g. skin color, appearance, etc.) and can undermine identities and reputations (Borgerson and Schroeder 2005).

Misrepresentation by exclusion refers to particular ethnic minority consumers and minority ethnic groups being left out of marketing communications, possibly undermining the importance and even existence of a group (Borgerson and Schroeder 2005), and creating image and identity problems among those who are excluded (Sandilands 2013). Also related to group invisibility issues. Inclusion often leads to *exoticized representations.*

Misrepresentation by inclusion refers to particular ethnic minority consumers and minority ethnic groups being included in marketing communications (e.g. Benetton's multi-cultural advertising) hence perpetuating stereotypes of difference (Borgerson and Schroeder 2005).

Subliminal messaging conveys hidden *messages* of which viewers are not consciously aware. Insertions in marketing material may be used to manipulate the thinking of the consumer about minority groups (Gratz 1984).

Exploiting social paradigms in advertising may impinge on cultural and ethnic sensitivities (Sandilands 2013), as in the case of differences between Whites and Blacks, Hispanics and Asian Americans, or Hongkongers or Hong Kongnese and the mainland Chinese.

existing classifications. An area omitted in the literature where this conforming approach may be difficult to apply relates to whether structural changes related to consumer based communication and accessibility issues are creating/diminishing/or compounding ethics issues arising from marketing activity. Notably, the strength of globalization and ICT convergence processes within ethnic (and other) markets may be difficult to dismiss, given that ethnic minority consumers and their minority ethnic groups of affiliation may well have the means to satisfy their unique 'ethnic' needs in their 'ethnic' preferred way, to take advantage of the benefits of globalization, at least for some types of goods and services.

Moreover, common concepts of connected and interactive consumers combine with significant real world evidence to suggest that communications are no longer exclusive to, or even mostly between consumers and businesses (B2C). Real world evidence suggests that consumption-related communications of consumers with others consumers (C2C, also often referred to as 'peer to peer') via electronic word-of mouth ('eWom'; Hennig-Thurau *et al.* 2004), cannot be discounted for their potential influence on exchanges within the B2C environment and on the power relationship between businesses and consumers. These are themes discussed in the next section, in order to provide a more complete picture of ethics issues in ethnic marketing.

Ethnic marketing ethics, ICT innovation and globalization

Rapid growth is transforming ICT into a ubiquitous, general purpose technology with ongoing economic impacts in many different areas at various levels. This evolution is 'increasing uncertainty in certain sectors due to the lack of new business models, the uncertain returns from switching to new technologies . . . and competing technologies in a fast changing technological environment' (OECD 2012, p. 13). The key characteristics of this ubiquitous and innovative technology include globalization, technological convergence and, in theory, access for everyone (Vagadia 2012; Collste 2008). The ethics implications of these new business models, however, remain elusive for both businesses and for consumers. Indeed, there is no special e-commerce ethics, deemed to be the same as the ethics applying to brick and mortar businesses and to their customers (Kracher and Corritore 2004).

Changes in marketing activity inherent to the new business models are justified, on one hand, because businesses arguably have gained in their ability to reach further and wider with standardized, internally efficient value propositions, potentially targeting the global market. Nevertheless, global reach is constrained by the digital divide or inequality (involving differences in people's online skills; Hargittai 2002) and, broadly, in personal computer and internet penetration (Chinn and Fairlie 2007; DiMaggio *et al.* 2004). On the other hand, changes in marketing activity are justified because consumers arguably have gained in market knowledge, in heightened access to larger numbers of competing suppliers, and in their ability to switch suppliers in search of better value propositions (Pires *et al.* 2006).

Changes in consumer based communication and accessibility raise potential conflicts with businesses' continuing strategic globalization perspectives powered by technological convergence assumptions. For example, if ethnic minority consumers benefit from improved accessibility and socialization, and this allows them to more easily switch suppliers in search of value propositions they perceive to more closely match their needs and wants, 'then their zone of tolerance is likely to be smaller than if they don't feel they have this flexibility' (Parasuraman *et al.* 1991, p. 43). This implies consumers with rising expectation thresholds, who are more demanding, assertive and less likely to accept poorer than expected service quality and/or unethical behaviour from their suppliers. To the extent that all consumers in a market are able to successfully raise their expectation thresholds and increasing demand assertiveness, any differences between ethnic minority consumers and mainstream consumers may actually increase.

Hence, rather than globalizing, differences across groups might actually increase and strengthen. Rather than targeting global consumers with global goods and services, business may need to target consumer groups more closely. Ultimately, one potential outcome from changing consumer communications is a shift in power from suppliers to consumers and markets that may become more diverse (Pires *et al.* 2010). One question that needs to be asked here is whether a shift in power from suppliers to consumers (APC 2011, Ch. 4) applies equally to all ethnic minority consumers and just as much as it applies to mainstream consumers, as this will influence approaches to ethnic marketing and the ethical implications of particular approaches.

A first observation is that the digital divide is also likely to divide ethnic minorities with distinct ethnicities. For example, the rates of internet usage early this century were assessed as higher for Asian Americans and non-Hispanic Whites (approximately 60%) than for non-Hispanic Blacks (40%) and for persons of Hispanic origin (less than 32%; NTIA 2002, p. 21). Internet usage was lower for African Americans than for Whites (Lenhart *et al.* 2003). But technological advances primarily in communications and transport, both domestically and globally, can reduce differences between consumer communities, including those defined by ethnicity, leading to convergence of ethnic minority consumers' tastes and preferences with those of other groups. These advances can also reduce existing ethnic minorities' and newer arrivals' reliance on the media and social capital available within the host country, potentially fostering transnationalism, the growth of social networks beyond the host-country border (Sanders 2002).

Matsaganis *et al.* (2010) extend several potential outcomes from a strong globalization process. In one scenario, ethnic minorities become more global, accessing home country and other cultures and becoming more socialized in different cultural environments. In another scenario, the same opportunities may take a minority ethnic group on a path of separation from the mainstream in their home country, heightening consumer differences with globalization from the perspective of ethnic consumer wants, potentially providing the ethnic consumer more resources to meet those wants. The ethical implications for business strategies under these alternative scenarios require consideration.

To presume that all ethnic minority consumers benefit from the same accessibility and become equally proficient in communicating within a single prescribed communication structure using a specified language does not appear a sensible presumption, given all the known vulnerabilities related to the cultural and digital divides (Pires and Aisbett 2003). For example, technological convergence clearly remains an aspiration because ICT carries embedded sets of cultural assumptions and is culturally dominated by English language content on the internet (Andrade and Urquhart 2009). Even if more computers could interact with other computers, user proficiency and levels in ICT usage, including for reasons related to proficiency in the language of the internet, are likely to be variable. Here, the suggestion is that gains in information accessibility are unlikely to be the same for all consumer groups. Moreover, there is the possibility that assumptions of generalized and equitable ICT-driven accessibility gains do not hold, contributing to both deepening and concealing consumption-related inequalities. These inequalities may arise from the decisions of governments and/or businesses in their approach to ICT policy and IT applications.

Wright (2011) called for the development of an ethical assessment framework to be used in the planning and implementation of ICT and its associated applications because of the need to consider how changes will impact on particular groups within that society. There are potentially widespread ethical implications impinging on such areas as the dissemination and use of information, privacy, the control and influence of power and social contact patterns, gender, minorities and justice. A recent illustration arising from a change in government is a decision by the Australian government to change from a nationwide, high speed broadband implementation policy of directly connecting to a very high percentage of Australian businesses and households, to a more restricted policy of high speed connection to nodes and use of a wider mix of technologies. This can be seen to have ethical implications because it can result in lower speed and less reliable access particularly in remote or regional locations, potentially disadvantaging some groups such as many of the indigenous minority population who reside in remote locations from the potential social, economic and health benefits that can flow from direct, high speed internet connection (Gerrand 2012). However, businesses and service providers, both for profit and not for profit, are also potentially exposed to ethical consequences in that their ICT and application decisions can disadvantage and or discriminate against particular groups. The following section examines the possible ethical issues from an empowerment perspective.

Ethics issues in ethnic minority consumers' empowerment

Consumer empowerment refers to the process of providing consumers, including those more vulnerable, with the best possible tools to take effective control of their consumption decisions (Brennan and Ritters 2004). Good decision making and informed choice require that consumers are well advised, informed and educated (Brennan and Coppack 2008). ICT-driven consumer empowerment emerges as an unanticipated consequence of businesses' endeavor to take advantage of opportunities afforded by the internet, often by increasing their information and interactivity presence (Deighton and Kornfeld 2009). The extent of ICT-driven consumer empowerment will depend on consumers' ability to discern potentially useful information for evaluating competing service-products on offer, and to satisfy their needs with the least waste of time and effort (Pires et al. 2006). The issue here is whether vulnerable ethnic minority consumers can be expected to form the same market knowledge that empowers the less vulnerable ones.

Consumers' ability to access, search, gather, comprehend and use quality information appears to be at the core of ICT-driven consumer empowerment. Following Andreasen and Manning (1990) in their definition of vulnerable consumers as 'those who are at a disadvantage in exchange relationships where that disadvantage is attributable to characteristics that are largely not controllable by them at the time of the transaction' (p. 13), the question arises whether ethnic minority consumers may fall into this vulnerable classification with respect to their access and ability to use sites available to the mainstream. Mueller (2008, Table 6.16) shows wide differences in online use for different search purposes between broadly defined ethnic groups with 'Asians' leading 'Whites' and 'Hispanics' in usage but 'Blacks' lagging behind all other groups.

For a similar time period Hacker and Steiner (2002) confirmed differences between Anglo-Americans and Hispanic Americans in internet skills and opportunities for using the internet with Anglo-Americans having the advantage. For both groups, usage frequency was correlated significantly with skills, opportunities and comfort. Usage frequency was also significantly related to obtaining job, financial, interpersonal communication and political communication benefits. Although the causes for the gaps could not be confirmed or disconfirmed as related to ethnicity, comfort and opportunity were associated with how well applications were designed to suit groups from different cultural backgrounds. However, more direct evidence that cultural adaptation of communications, including both the medium and the message, is relevant to removing differences between ethnic groups can be found in health related communications (Nierkens et al. 2013).

Consumer empowerment effects are likely to influence all exchanges, not only the online ones. But the access, searching, gathering and comprehension of information about the product (and information about the provider, for that matter) are increasingly likely to take place in an online, intangible environment (Pereira 1998; Peterson *et al.* 1997). Tangibility refers to the physical nature of the core product, the basic, generic central thing that is exchanged (Levitt 1973). It is well known that product intangibility makes it difficult for all consumers, but particularly for those with communication difficulties in sites they may need to use, to understand what is being offered, to identify potential providers, and to evaluate alternatives (Pires and Stanton 2000; Legg and Baker 1987).

While more languages are now used in accessing the internet, English is still the top language of the internet (Shea *et al.* 2006; Lund and McGuire 2005) and in the vast majority of links to pages on secure servers, albeit now closely followed by Chinese. Indeed, 51% of the world population are estimated to use either English or Chinese when accessing the internet (2011 estimate, IWS 2013). Hence, while Spanish, French and Japanese were reported at the turn of this century as the only languages with close to or more than 1% of the links on secure servers (OECD 2000), the situation may be less extreme today. By itself, this may make it difficult for ethnic minority consumers whose first or preferred language is neither English nor Chinese to use computers and computer networks and may complicate their online consumption ability from the outset with questions of accessibility, depending on their proficiency in those two languages (NCLIS 2001).

This also has clear consequences for their ICT-driven empowerment status. Even in a globalized environment characterized by technological convergence, different markets will have distinct levels of internet penetration and usage; hence consumer empowerment may vary from market to market. Similarly, within a specific domestic market, the ICT empowerment process cannot be generalized to all consumers. In fact, reflection on the recurring themes suggests that different consumer groups can be empowered to differing extents, possibly requiring tailored targeting. While not all ethnic minority consumers may be at a greater disadvantage in exchange relationships via the internet compared with their mainstream counterparts, and can therefore be classed as vulnerable (Andreasen and Manning 1990), evidence points to some groups where the samples appear to be less empowered than their mainstream counterparts (Mueller 2008; Hacker and Steiner 2002) and where the ethics of the access provided requires consideration.

Even if accessibility issues can be overcome, intangibility is a major issue for ethnic minority consumers with communication difficulties because of their restricted ability to read product literature, discomfort in consulting with service staff online, and possible difficulty in locating and comprehending information provided by institutions or consumption communities. Inexperience within the marketplace and differences in meanings and contexts can lead to further difficulties whether making a decision, negotiating a sales agreement, or signing a contract.

In its use of ICT, business communication may lack understanding of the fundamental cultural values involved, of the meanings that are not put into words, of the importance of the words that are used, of the way messages are received and transmitted and, ultimately, of what to expect when a stakeholder engages in a particular communication behaviour across cultures. Studies of the importance of cultural sensitivity in website design and other IT applications focus on the importance of cultural values in terms of how users react to particular elements of design or use of an application. Zakaria *et al.* (2003) focus on Arab cultural values and the requirements for web design and applications that do not hamper acceptance or take up stemming from a high-context culture (Hall 1976). If the importance of cultural congruence is that it can improve users' perceptions of websites in terms of their positive attitudes and intentions, usefulness and ease of use (Vyncke and Brengman 2010) then the opposite effects are likely if such sites are not available to different cultural groups, most likely reducing ICT use and those groups' empowerment.

Vyncke and Brengman (2010) called attention for the website features apparently needed in certain cultures, essentially what is likely to be important to the localization process. While focused on country cultural differences and how this might hinder users, the argument can be extended to ethnic minorities within a country. Their difficulties in website use and IT applications may be exacerbated by increased perceived risk due to limited access to sources of information, more subjective assessment of value and quality, and difficulty in participating in service encounters (Pires and Stanton 2000). Communication difficulties arising from language choices may only be one element contributing to lower participation compared with the mainstream.

Notwithstanding, it is clear that not everything arising from ICT and globalized markets is a threat to ethnic minority consumers. As noted by Matsaganis et al. (2010), these technologies increasingly allow ethnic minority consumers access to the global diaspora's ethnic communication network as well as potential access to products and providers irrespective of location, in many cases, including the consumers' home country.

Arguably, the web provides a 'safe' virtual space in which cultural and linguistic conflict between the place of origin and place of adoption can be resolved (Mitra 2005) and has the potential to socially empower consumers to connect with others – whether family, friends and business in the home country, or similar others and culturally aware businesses where they have settled. On the negative side, it is also argued that the internet can become a hindrance rather than a facilitator when minority consumers rely on absent friends and family to the exclusion of peers, and when involvement in the local market environment is replaced with electronic communications with the home country. As explained by Pascoe (2006), cultural learning won't happen and individuals can get stuck in the crisis stage of culture shock. Notwithstanding, it is apparent that by strengthening eWom communications, an effective use of the internet for C2C communications can empower ethnic minority consumers in their lives and in their consumption.

Critical for business is to understand that reaching these consumers require specific targeted strategies. As argued by Mummert (2007), Hispanic consumers feel overwhelmed by all the sources of information available today, as well as language barriers involved. If marketers offered more guidance and step-by-step instructions in Spanish, they would buy more products online, such steps including how to use the internet or a site, and firm advice rather than multiple opinions.

Ultimately, dependence on the cultural dominance of the English language as the lingua franca may be abating (Alam 2009), with Chinese catching up quickly (IWS 2013), but inequalities across groups remain. Other elements beyond language, touching on how cultural values such as context are incorporated into website design and applications, may take longer to overcome.

Conclusion

Scrutiny of potential ethical issues arising from either a neglect of ethnic marketing, or approaches that may be based on unwarranted assumptions about group preferences and behaviours, still appear a neglected research area. This paper has sought to categorize the main forms of ethical issues linked to the targeting of ethnic minority consumers, the consequences from unethical targeting and issues arising from misrepresentation of ethnic groups within marketing communications.

Rather than seeking to identify some set of ethical concerns brought about by the use of the internet for business related activities, this paper sought to draw attention to the lack of research considering the ethical issues involving ethnic minorities, arising from changes in marketing practices associated with the growth of ICT innovation and its effect on consumer socialization outcomes, namely in terms of access to market knowledge, social media and C2C marketing communications. Can the lack of research be an indicator that ethics concerns are independent of the environment where marketers and consumers meet for business? One way to consider this question is to carefully peruse the tables in this paper in order to identify entries that clearly do not apply in the online environment, an endeavour that supports the suggestion that most entries do apply, with more or less adaptation. The other way is for future research to focus on identifying potential ethical breaches exclusive to the online environment. For example, anecdotal evidence often promotes the scenario of marketers attempting to influence the free and unbiased operation of social networks and C2C communications by possible alienation of gatekeepers to minority ethnic groups. This, however, is neither separate from the issues in the tables of reference (see alienation, deception and bad faith in Table 19.2) nor is it exclusive to ethnic marketing practice.

Enhanced globalization capabilities by business invite the targeting of global consumers with standardized value offerings – exactly the opposite of the raison d'être of ethnic marketing. But the conclusion derived from the conceptual discussion of the impact of globalization and ICT convergence on minority ethnic communities does not question the tenet that these communities are socially determined. Consequently, not only do ethical and socially responsible behaviour concerns remain relevant, but appear justified to account for a possible ICT-driven vulnerability of minority ethnic groups that may not be attributable to any one business, or efficiently resolvable by market forces. It is, therefore, a matter of social justice for consideration in a social responsibility perspective.

The possible existence of a language-based segregation of the cultural and digital divides within multi-ethnic markets suggests the need for in-depth empirical research on the specific impact of language as a source of vulnerability arising from globalized perspectives about ethnic markets. From a business point of view, businesses considering the targeting of ethnic markets may need to develop flexible, tactical capabilities in a way that duly takes into account ethics. Flexibility encompasses the skills to take advantage of the sameness across groups while focusing when justified, on real differences. Focusing on ethnic differences if these differences do not exist is neither socially responsible nor does it contribute to positive outcomes for the business. The potential for the operationalization and implementation of glocalized marketing programs, both within multi-ethnic domestic markets and for minority ethnic communities with multi-locations globally, enhances the need for businesses to develop flexible capabilities but also justifies ongoing examination of the ethical and social implications arising from such strategies.

References

Alam, S. (2009) 'Adoption of internet in Malaysian SMEs'. *Journal of Small Business and Enterprise Development*, 16(2): 240–55.

Andrade, A. and Urquhart, C. (2009) 'ICTs as a tool for cultural dominance: Prospects for a two-way street'. *The Electronic Journal of Information Systems in Developing Countries*, 37(2): 1–12.

Andreasen, A. and Manning J. (1990) 'The dissatisfaction and complaining behavior of vulnerable consumers'. *Journal of Consumer Satisfaction, Dissatisfaction and Complaining Behavior*, 3: 12–20.

APC (Australian Government Productivity Commission) (2011) *Economic Structure and Performance of the Australian Retail Industry*. Canberra: Productivity Commission Inquiry Report No. 56, November.

Armstrong, M. (2013) 'Minorities – the new majority'. *Armstrong Economics* [online]. Available from: http://armstrongeconomics.com/2013/06/14/minorities-the-new-majority/ [accessed 17 September 2014].

Australian Institute of Aboriginal and Torres Strait Islander Studies (n.d.) *Confirmation of Aboriginal and Torres Strait Islander heritage* [Online]. Available from: http://www.aiatsis.gov.au/fhu/aboriginality.html [accessed 12 September 2014].

Báji-Bácheur, A and Özçaglar-Toulouse N. (2012) *L'ethnicité, fabrique marketing?* Cormelles-le-Royal, France: Editions Management et Société.

Borgerson, J. and Schroeder, J. (2002) 'Ethical issues of global marketing: Avoiding bad faith in visual representation'. *European Journal of Marketing.* 36(5/6): 570–594.

Borgerson, J. and Schroeder, J. (2005) 'Identity in marketing communications: An ethics of visual representation'. In *Marketing Communication: New Approaches, Technologies, and Styles,* edited by A. Kimmel. Oxford: Oxford University Press.

Brenkert, G. (1998) 'Marketing and the vulnerable'. *Business Ethics Quarterly* 1: 7–21.

Brennan, C. and Ritters, K. (2004) 'Consumer education in the UK: New developments in policy, strategy and implementation'. *International Journal of Consumer Studies,* 28(2): 97–107.

Brennan, C. and Coppack, M. (2008) 'Consumer empowerment: Global context, UK strategies and vulnerable consumers'. *International Journal of Consumer Studies,* 32(4): 306–13.

Buchholz, R. and Rosenthal, S. (2000) 'Ethics, economics, and service: Changing cultural perspectives'. In *Proceedings,* Seventh Annual International Conference Promoting Business Ethics (St John's University, New York), pp. 9–16.

Burgos, D. and Mobolade, O. (2011) *Marketing to the New Majority: Strategies for a Diverse World.* New York: Palgrave Macmillan.

Carrasco, M. (2013) 'Hispanic marketing: 5 facts about the U.S. Hispanic population every entrepreneur should know'. *YFS Magazine,* May 17th [online]. Available from: http://yfsentrepreneur.com/author/yfs-small-business-contributors/ [accessed 17 September 2014].

Chinn, M. D. and Fairlie, R. W. (2007) 'The determinants of the global digital divide: A cross-country analysis of computer and internet penetration'. *Oxford Economic Papers,* 59(1): 16–44.

Cocchiara, F. and Quick, J. (2004) 'The negative effects of positive stereotypes: Ethnicity-related stressors and implications on organizational health'. *Journal of Organizational Behavior,* 25(6): 781–785.

Collste, G. (2008) 'Global ICT-ethics: The case of privacy'. *Journal of Information, Communication and Ethics in Society,* 6(1): 76–87.

Costa, J. (1998) 'Paradisal discourse: A critical analysis of marketing and consuming Hawaii'. *Consumption Markets & Culture,* 1: 303–346.

Craemer, T. (2011) 'Preventing inadvertent stereotyping in the racial gap literature'. *APSA 2011 Annual Meeting Paper* [online]. Available from: http://papers.ssrn.com/sol3/papers.cfm?abstract_id=1901764 [accessed 17 September 2014].

Cui, G. (1998) 'Ethical issues in ethnic segmentation and target marketing'. In *Proceedings,* edited by J.-C. Chebat and A. B. Oumlil, *1998 Multicultural Marketing* Conference (Academy of Marketing Science, Montreal), pp. 87–91.

Cui, G. and Choudhury, P. (2002) 'Marketplace diversity and cost-effective marketing strategies'. *Journal of Consumer Marketing,* 19(1): 54–73.

Cui, G. and Choudhury, P. (2003) 'Consumer interests and the ethical implications of marketing: A contingency framework'. *The Journal of Consumer Affairs,* 37(2): 364–87.

Daniels, C. (2012) 'Multicultural marketing: The visible majority'. Marketing – Advertising, Media & PR in Canada, *Marketing* [online]. Available from: http://www.marketingmag.ca/brands/multicultural-marketing-the-visible-majority-48428 [accessed 17 September 2014].

Deighton, J. and Kornfeld, L. (2009) 'Interactivity's unanticipated consequences for marketers and marketing'. *Journal of Interactive Marketing,* 23(1): 4–10.

DiMaggio, P., Hargittai, E., Celeste, C. and Shafer, S. (2004) 'Digital inequality: From unequal access to differentiated use'. In *Social Inequality,* edited by K. Neckerman. New York: Russell Sage Foundation, pp. 355–400.

Dougherty, C. and Jordan, M. (2012) 'Minority births are new majority in demographic watershed for U.S., newborns among Non-Hispanic whites are surpassed by others'. *Wall Street Journal* [online]. Available from: http://online.wsj.com/news/articles/SB10001424052702303879604577408363003351818 [accessed 3 July 2014].

Fair Trading, NSW Government (2013) 'Unfair contract terms'. *Fair Trading* [online]. Available from: http://www.fairtrading.nsw.gov.au/Consumers/Contracts/Unfair_contract_terms.html [accessed 17 September 2014].

Fisher, J., Garrett, D., Cannon, J. and Beggs, J. (1999) 'Problem businesses: Consumer complaints, the better business bureau, and ethical business practices'. In *Proceedings*, edited by G. Gunlach, W. Wilkie and P. Murphy. *Marketing and Public Policy Conference*, University of Notre Dame, American Marketing Association, pp. 69–72.

Frable, D., Platt, L. and Hoey, S. (1998) 'Concealable stigmas and positive self-perceptions: Feeling better around similar others'. *Journal of Personality and Social Psychology*, 74(4): 909–22.

Gerrand, P. (2012) 'Implications of national broadband for Australia contrasting the current government and opposition broadband policies'. *AQ - Australian Quarterly*, 83(1), Jan/Mar: 20–8.

Gratz, J. (1984) 'The ethics of subliminal communication'. *Journal of Business Ethics*, 3(3): 181–4.

Gray, B., Matear, S., Boshoff, C. and Matheson, P. (1998) 'Developing a better measure of market orientation'. *European Journal of Marketing*, 32(9/10): 884–903.

Greenwald, A. and Krieger, L. (2006) 'Implicit bias: Scientific foundations'. *California Law Review*, 94(4): 945–67.

Grier, S. and Kumanyika, S. (2008) 'The context of choice: Health implications of targeted food and beverage marketing to African Americans'. *American Journal of Public Health*, 98(9): 1616–29.

Grier, S., Williams, J. and Crockett, D. (1996) 'Racial discrimination as a consumer disadvantage? The marketplace experiences of black men'. In *Proceedings*, edited by R. P. Hill and C. R. Taylor, *Marketing and Public Policy Conference*, 6, AMA, p. 131.

Grönroos, C. (1989) 'Defining marketing: A market-oriented approach'. *European Journal of Marketing*, 23(1): 52–60.

Grönroos, C. (2008) 'Service logic revisited: Who creates value? And who co-creates?' *European Business Review*, 20(4): 298–314.

Grönroos, C. (2011) 'A service perspective on business relationships: The value creation, interaction and marketing interface'. *Industrial Marketing Management*, 40(2): 240–47.

Hacker, K and Steiner, R. (2002) 'The digital divide for Hispanic Americans'. *Howard Journal of Communications*, 13(4): 267–83.

Hall, E. T. (1976) *Beyond Culture*. New York: Anchor Press/Doubleday.

Hall, G. (2001) 'Psychotherapy research with ethnic minorities: Empirical, ethical, and conceptual issues'. *Journal of Consulting and Clinical Psychology*, 69(3): 502–10.

Hamilton, D. (1979) 'A cognitive attribution analysis of stereotyping'. In *Advances in Experimental Social Psychology*, Vol 12, edited by L. Berkowitz. New York: Academic Press.

Hargittai, E. (2002) 'Second-level digital divide: Differences in people's online skills'. *First Monday*, 7(4): 1–19.

Hennig-Thurau, T., Gwinner, K., Walsh, G. and Gremler, D. (2004) 'Electronic word-of-mouth via consumer-opinion platforms: What motivates consumers to articulate themselves on the internet?' *Journal of Interactive Marketing*, 18(1): 38–52.

Hui, M. K., Joy, A., Kim, C. and Laroche, M. (1992) 'Acculturation as a determinant of consumer behavior: Conceptual and methodological issues'. In *AMA Winter Educators' Conference Proceedings*. Vol. 3, edited by C. T. Allen and T. J. Madden. Chicago, IL: American Marketing Association, pp. 466–73.

IWS (2013) 'Internet world users by language'. *Internet World Stats* [online]. Available from: http://www.internetworldstats.com/stats7.htm [accessed 17 September 2014].

Kotler, P., Armstrong, G., Brown, L. and Adam, S. (1998) *Marketing*. Sydney: Prentice-Hall.

Kracher, B. and Corritore, C. (2004) 'Is there a special e-commerce ethics?' *Business Ethics Quarterly*, 14(1): 71–94.

Kruglanski, A. and Webster, D. (1996) 'Motivated closing of the mind: "Seizing" and "freezing"'. *Psychological Review*, 10: 263–83.

Legg, D. and Baker, J. (1987) 'Advertising strategies for service firms'. In *Add Value to Your Service*, edited by C. Surprenant, AMA, pp. 163–68.

Lenhart, A., Horrigan, J., Rainie, L., Allen, K., Boyce, A., Madden, M. and O'Grady, E. (2003) 'The ever-shifting internet population: A new look at internet access and the digital divide'. *Pew Internet and American Life Project*. Washington, D.C.

Levitt, T. (1973) 'What's your product and what's your business?' In *Marketing for Business Growth*. New York: McGraw-Hill.

Lund, M. and McGuire, S. (2005) 'Institutions and development: Electronic commerce and economic growth'. *Organization Studies*, 26(12): 1743–763.

Matsaganis, M., Katz, V. and Ball-Rokeach, S. (2010) *Understanding Ethnic Media: Producers, Consumers, and Societies*. Thousand Oaks, CA: Sage.

McConahay, J. and Hough Jr, J. (1976) 'Symbolic racism'. *Journal of Social Issues*, 32(2): 23–45.

Mitra, A. (2005) 'Creating immigrant identities in cybernetic space: Examples from a non-resident Indian website'. *Media, Culture and Society*, 27(3): 371–90.

Moore-Shay, E. (1996) 'The lens of economic circumstance: How do economically disadvantaged children view the marketplace?' In *Proceedings*, edited by R. P. Hill and C. R. Taylor. *Marketing and Public Policy Conference*, 6, AMA, pp. 132.

Mueller, B. (2008) *Communicating With the Multicultural Consumer*. New York: Peter Lang.

Mummert, H. (2007) 'Culture: More than a language'. *Target Marketing*, 30(5): 54–5.

NCLIS (2001) 'A comprehensive assessment of public information dissemination'. *US National Commission on Libraries and Information Science* [online]. Available from: http://www.nclis.gov/govt/assess/assess.execsum.pdf.

Nierkens, V., Hartman, M. A., Nicolaou, M., Vissenberg, C., Beune, E. J., Hosper, K., van Valkengoed, I. and Stronks, K. (2013) 'Effectiveness of cultural adaptations of interventions aimed at smoking cessation, diet, and/or physical activity in ethnic minorities: A systematic review'. *PloS one*, 8(10): e73373. doi:10.1371/journal.pone.0073373. Available from: http://www.plosone.org [accessed 5 November 2014].

NTIA (National Telecommunications and Information Administration) (2002) *A Nation Online: How Americans Are Expanding Their Use Of The Internet*. February. Washington, D.C., U.S. Department of Commerce.

Oberg, K. (1960) 'Cultural shock: Adjustment to new cultural environments'. *Practical Anthropology*, 7: 177–82.

OECD (2000) *The Economic and Social Impacts of Electronic Commerce: Preliminary Findings and Research Agenda*. OECD Online Bookshop.

OECD (2012) 'The impact of internet in OECD countries'. *OECD Digital Economy Papers No. 200*. OECD Publishing.

OECD (2013) *International Migration Outlook 2013*. OECD Publishing, http://dx.doi.org/10.1787/migr_outlook-2013-en.

Ouellet, J. (2007) 'Consumer racism and its effects on domestic cross-ethnic product purchase: An empirical test in the United States, Canada, and France'. *Journal of Marketing*, 71(1): 113–28.

Parasuraman, A., Berry, L. and Zeithaml, V. (1991) 'Understanding Customer Expectations of Service'. *Sloan Management Review*, 32(3): 39–48.

Pascoe, R. (2006) 'Culture shock in a digital world: Tips for parents'. *Tales From A Small Planet* [online]. Available from: http://www.talesmag.com/tales/practical/culture_shock_in_digital_world [accessed 21 September 2014].

Pereira, R. (1998) 'Cross-cultural influences on global electronic commerce'. *AMCIS 1998 Proceedings*. Paper 109. Available from: http://aisel.aisnet.org/amcis1998/109 [accessed 5 November 2014].

Peterson, R., Balasubramanian, S. and Bronnenberg, B. (1997) 'Exploring the implications of the internet for consumer marketing'. *Journal of the Academy of Marketing Science*, 25: 329–346.

Petty, R., Harris, A., Broaddus, T. and Boyd III, W. (2003) 'Regulating target marketing and other race-based advertising practices'. *Michigan Journal of Race & Law*, 8: 335–529.

Pires, G. (1999) 'Domestic cross-cultural marketing in Australia: A critique of the segmentation rationale'. *Journal of Marketing Theory and Practice*, 7(4): 33–44.

Pires, G. and Aisbett, J. (2003) 'Macro issues in electronic commerce: The cultural divide'. *Global Business & Economics Review*, 5(2): 369–90.

Pires, G. and Stanton, J. (2000) 'Marketing services to ethnic consumers in culturally diverse markets: Issues and implications'. *Journal of Services Marketing*, 14(7): 607–18.

Pires, G. and Stanton, J. (2002) 'Ethnic marketing ethics'. *Journal of Business Ethics*, 36(1–2): 111–18.

Pires, G. and Stanton, J. (2005) *Ethnic Marketing, Accepting The Challenge Of Cultural Diversity*. London: Thomson Learning.

Pires, G. and Stanton, J. (2015) *Ethnic Marketing – Culturally Sensitive Theory and Practice*. London: Routledge.

Pires, G. Stanton, J. and Rita, P. (2006) 'The internet, consumer empowerment and marketing strategies'. *European Journal of Marketing*, 40(9/10): 936–49.

Pires, G. Stanton, J. and Rita, P. (2010) 'Assessing relevancy of ICT driven consumer empowerment for business'. *Global Business & Economics Anthology*, 2(1): 293–302.

Pires, G., Stanton, J. and Stanton, P. (2011) 'Revisiting the substantiality criterion: From ethnic marketing to market segmentation'. *Journal of Business Research*, 64(9): 988–96.

Rosenbaum, M. and Montoya, D. (2007) 'Am I welcome here? Exploring how ethnic consumers assess their place identity'. *Journal of Business Research*, 60(3): 206–214.

Rudman, L., Greenwald, A., Mellott, D. and Schwartz, J. (1999) 'Measuring the automatic components of prejudice: Flexibility and generality of the implicit association test'. *Social Cognition*, 17(4): 437–65.

Sanders, J. (2002) 'Ethnic boundaries and identity in plural societies'. *Annual Review of Sociology*, 28: 327–57.

Sandilands, T. (2013) 'Marketing issues that have ethical implications'. *Chron Demand Media* [online]. Available from: http://smallbusiness.chron.com/marketing-issues-ethical-implications-24089.html [accessed 17 September 2014].

Sarwono, S. and Armstrong, R. (1998) 'Cross-microcultural business ethics: Ethical perceptions differences in marketing among ethnic microcultural groups in Indonesia'. In *Proceedings*, edited by J.-C. Chebat and A. B. Oumlil, *Multicultural Marketing Conference*, AMS, Montreal, pp. 80–6.

Sas, A. and Kozma, A. (2009) 'Ethnic marketing possibilities and its ethics issues'. *Perspectives of Innovations in Economics & Business*, 3: 95–7.

Schlegelmilch, B. and Oberseder, M. (2010) 'Half a century of marketing ethics: Shifting perspectives and emerging trends'. *Journal of Business Ethics*, 93: 1–19.

Seelye, H. and Wasilewski, J. (1996) *Between Cultures: Developing Self-Identity in a World of Diversity*. Chicago: NTC Publishing Group.

Segal, M. and Giacobbe, R. (1995) 'An empirical investigation of ethical issues in marketing research: Asian perspectives'. In *Proceedings*, edited by J. R. Evans, B. Berman and B. Barak. *Research Conference on Ethics and Social Responsibility in Marketing* (Hofstra University), pp. 110–116.

Shea, T., Ariguzo, G. and White, D. (2006) 'Putting the world in the world wide web: The globalization of the internet'. *International Journal of Business Information Systems*, 2(1): 75–98.

Smith, N. and Cooper-Martin, E. (1997) 'Ethics and target marketing: The role of product harm and consumer vulnerability'. *The Journal of Marketing*, 61: 1–20.

Smith N. C. and Quelch, J. A. eds. (1993) 'Ethical issues in research and targeting consumers'. *Ethics in Marketing, Academy of Marketing*. Homewood, IL: Irwin, pp. 145–95.

Stages of Innovation (2000) 'Best practices in marketing to African-, Hispanic-, and Asian-Americans'. *Stages of Innovation* [online]. Briarcliff Manor, NY 10510. Available from: http://www.stagesofinnovation.com/ [accessed 21 September 2014].

Stevenson, T. (1991) 'How are blacks portrayed in business ads?' *Industrial Marketing Management* 20: 193–99.

Tadmor, C., Hong, Y., Chao, M., Wiruchnipawan, F. and Wang, W. (2012) 'Multicultural experiences reduce intergroup bias through epistemic unfreezing'. *Journal of Personality and Social Psychology*, 103(5): 750–72.

Usunier, J. and Lee, J. (2009) *Marketing Across Cultures*, 5th edn. Sydney: Prentice-Hall.

Varner, I. and L. Beamer (1995) *Intercultural Communication in the Global Workplace*. Boston: Irwin.

Vagadia, B. (2012) 'Globalization and convergence: Drivers and strategic outsourcing'. In *Strategic Outsourcing – The Alchemy to Business Transformation in a Globally Converged World*, edited by B. Vagadia. Berlin Heidelberg: Springer-Verlag. XXIII, pp. 1–19.

Visconti, L. M., Jafari, A., Batat, W., Broeckerhoff, A., Dedeoglu, A. Ö, Demangeot, C., Kipnis, E., Lindridge, A., Peñaloza, L., Pullig, C., Regany, F., Ustundagli, E. and Weinberger, M. F. (2014) 'Consumer ethnicity three decades after: A TCR agenda'. *Journal of Marketing Management*, 30(17–18): 1882–922.

Vitell, S., Rallapalli, J. and Singhapakdi, A. (1993) 'Marketing norms: The influences of personal moral philosophies and organizational ethical culture'. *Journal of the Academy of Marketing Science*, 21: 331–37.

Vyncke, F. and Brengman, M. (2010) 'Are culturally congruent websites more effective? An overview of a decade of empirical evidence'. *Journal of Electronic Commerce Research*, 11(1): 14–29.

Wolburg, J. (2005) 'Drawing the line between targeting and patronizing: How "vulnerable" are the vulnerable?' *Journal of Consumer Marketing*, 22(5): 287–8.

Wright, D. (2011) 'A framework for the ethical impact assessment of information technology'. *Ethics and Information Technology*, 13(3): 199–226.

Zakaria, N., Stanton, J. M. and Sarkar-Barney, S. T. (2003) 'Designing and implementing culturally sensitive it applications: The interaction of culture values and privacy issues in the Middle East'. *Information Technology & People*, 16(1): 49–75.

20

Ethnic marketing

Public policy issues

Lisa Peñaloza

Introduction

Ethnicity is a global phenomenon, augmented by births, identity- and religious-based social movements, immigration and acculturation. We have chosen ethnic marketing as the topic for this book because it is a major source of social and economic dynamism and conflict in nations, cities, neighbourhoods, work spaces and marketplaces across the planet. In this volume the authors write from diverse perspectives and use distinct methodological orientations in directing attention to the dimensions and processes characterizing the complex, interwoven relations between ethnicity and marketing. In this concluding essay I continue the discussion in focusing on public policy. I begin by highlighting key differences between business and government because it is important to maintain a sense of their different mission and activities, and then turn to key topics in marketing and organizational ethics forming the backbone for public policy. While my focus is on the US, I also direct some attention to global public policy concerns.

These are tough times to work in public policy. Contemporary political debates, talk shows, online postings, editorial columns and journalist reports are polarized and highly charged, with battles played out on the terrain of public policy. On one side critics charge 'Starve the beast', depicting bloated bureaucracy and striving to cut taxes and to have citizens think of the government spending less of '*my* money', to the point that former candidate Sarah Palin could say with conviction during her 2008 U.S. Vice-Presidential campaign, 'Paying taxes is unpatriotic'. In his opinion-editorial column, Friedman (2008) responded, provocatively querying Ms. Palin as to how she imagined paying for her preferred policies. On the other side, critics charge that public policy doesn't go far enough in addressing such social problems and injustices as unequal opportunity and treatment of racial/ethnic groups, unemployment and under-employment, and skewed distribution of wealth. Here political solutions are promised for what economists term 'externalities'. What the two political platforms share are concerted attempts to satisfy diverse constituents' demands for services to be provided at lower cost and greater efficiency.

It was not always this way. January 20, 1961 President John F. Kennedy put forth a challenge in his inaugural address to the nation, daring citizens to 'Ask not what your country can do for you; ask what you can do for your country'. It is difficult to imagine any sitting President or candidate saying this today. Kennedy's words resonated deeply with the American public of his time, invoking an *esprit de corps*, a unity and a desire to contribute to a greater good that ran

343

counter to the increasingly individualist, stratified, materialist trends that gained momentum with the affluence that swept the nation in the period after the Second World War. Relatively less damaged than the other industrial powers of Europe and Japan, the US had attained exemplary status and unprecedented popularity for its way of life, optimism and social mobility. Its chief cultural export at the time was consumer culture – music, film and consumer products (Kroen 2006) – that manifest in fairly general forms in comparison to their diversity today. During the 1970s 'runaway' inflation, the oil embargo and the international relocation of manufacturing jobs tempered U.S. economic growth. Offering a diagnosis, the Grace Commission formed under the Reagan Administration in 1980 compared government services to those of business and found the former lacking. The focus then on business as a model for government only recognized part of the picture, neglecting to mention that most new products fail, as do many companies. Nor did this influential report acknowledge their very different mandates and changing constituents. Public policy is grounded in general public enfranchisement and held to serve all citizens and to oversee business and social conduct, while business serves those who can pay and readily distinguish their consumers by demographic characteristics, identity and tastes, including those related to ethnicity, in order to serve them better. Yet as we will see, these strict bifurcations belie much more complex, diverse and nuanced realities.

While business is increasingly service oriented, and thus converges with the service dimensions of government, there are key differences between the two domains in policy. Matters of sovereignty, representation and justness in public policy are not equivalent to the profit goal of business, although the two spheres share cost and accountability controls, and somewhat similar notions of fairness and equal treatment. Their overlap is likely to increase in the future with pressing consumer demands for social and environmental responsibility. Furthermore, there is much interplay and cross-fertilization between the two social domains (Bevir and Trentmann 2004) as government attempts to serve and regulate business activity across the globe, as much for monetary and political support for candidates and policies as to stimulate jobs while guarding public health and attending to overall well-being.

In the field of marketing, ethnic marketing traditionally has meant the targeting of ethnic minority consumers by people outside the group, often in large firms, with ethnic marketing public policy charged with monitoring and overseeing such targeting (Pires and Stanton 2015). This chapter broadens the scope of discussion in taking into account developments in ethnic theory recognizing that everyone has ethnicity (Peñaloza 2007), and in recognizing the importance of ethnic entrepreneurs in developing ethnic communities and in contributing to the national economy (Peñaloza 2005). Thus, in this essay ethnic marketing deals with marketing activity that relates to ethnic groups. In turn, ethnic marketing public policy deals with the monitoring and oversight of ethnic marketing activity, to include the reception of marketing campaigns as well as their impact on ethnic identity, community and social relations among groups. What matters in ethnic marketing is who targets whom, who is targeted by whom, with what symbolic and material content and forms, and what social and economic interests, agenda and effects. For ethnic marketing public policy, added considerations are who formulates policy, who participates in the policy process, for what benefits, for whom and on behalf of whom, and with what resulting social, economic and community impacts. These broad characterizations are useful to keep in mind in appreciating the complex interests and diverse stakes that come into play in the development and implementation of ethnic marketing public policy.

In concluding this introduction, I offer a few personal acknowledgements. First, I want to acknowledge my respect and appreciation for public policy workers. My father, a career civil servant, retired from the U.S Veterans Administration where he worked in its hospitals in Kerrville and Waco, Texas, as a social worker. Like many government agencies, the VA system has undergone many changes over the years; key among them are cuts in resources for the medical benefits of armed forces personnel that parallel the budget cuts impacting the provision of health care for non-military residents in the US. As Harvey (2007) noted, pay-as-you-go market solutions are but part of the privatization characterizing the contemporary neoliberal turn worldwide. Distinct mandates and priorities, together with budget challenges, must be taken into account in considerations of ethnic marketing public policy.

Ethnic marketing

In addressing ethnic marketing public policy, it is important to situate ethnic and ethnic marketing phenomena in their social as well as market contexts. While the marketplace has been the main focus in this book, all of its essays necessarily touch upon the social sites of the nation, as well as neighbourhoods, cities and business organizations where ethnic people of multiple cultural orientations and experiences and marketing activities converge.

Immigration has been a touch point for ethnicity, yet the latter is much broader in scope, to include mainstream as well as minority peoples. Attention to the mainstream pushes the bounds of ethnic marketing public policy, in directing attention to the inherent inter-relations between mainstream and minority cultural genealogies, sensibilities and experiences, and in noting privilege as well as subordination and deprivation (Peñaloza 2007; Delgado and Stefancic 1997). Importantly, because wealth is diffused unevenly among racial/ethnic groups in U.S. society (Lui *et al.* 2006), a major concern in public policy is to ensure equal and just treatment. Furthermore, when we recognize the increasing heterogeneity in societies globally, it is necessary to broaden considerations of ethnic marketing phenomena beyond domestic relations between minority and mainstream groups to feature in policy important quality of life issues as people of multiple, mixed, pan, transnational and cosmopolitan ethnicities and experiences come together and apart in families, education, religion and neighbourhoods, as well as in the marketplace (Visconti *et al.* 2014).

As Williams (1975) and more recently Jenkins (1997) have noted, the term ethnicity historically referred to non-Christians. It was brought into the field of marketing in the 1970s in reference to the increasing trends of firms segmenting markets and targeting minority groups (Bouchet 1995). Today, largely due to the legacy of Civil Rights social movements, greater government inclusion and more common business targeting, the trend of multiculturalism has brought greater awareness and sensitivity of ethnicity as a valid part of society and not just a matter of private life. This change has not been without tension, both within and between ethnic groups, in the form of contested identity and cultural expressions.

In ethnic marketing public policy it is important to recognize the way marketing activity draws from and reconfigures ethnicity (Bouchet 1995; Peñaloza and Gilly 1999). Bécheur and Toulouse (2012) build upon this work in emphasizing the role of marketing activity in producing ethnicity. Indeed, the reproduction of ethnic identity and culture in the marketplace is but a particular form of the more general social accommodation of different people etching their lives in terms of what is important to them (Slater and Tonkiss 2002). Marketing, thus, is a central part of social life and not apart from it. The scholarship in marketing that takes the perspective of marketers most often consider ethnic people as consumers, and yet, as Mehmood *et al.* (this volume), Light and Gold (2000) and Peñaloza (2005) remind us in their work on ethnic entrepreneurship, ethnic people are also producers who support and enable ethnic communities.

At the same time, it is important to recognize a simultaneous trend blurring the conventional divisions between producers and consumers, as 'working consumers' animate brands and integrate them in daily life (Cova and Dalli 2009). Ethnic consumers are thus not only the targets of marketing efforts, the subjects of marketing research (Bjerrisgaard and Kjeldgaard 2012) and even the 'products' in data mining operations (Zwick and Dholakia 2012); they also are active product/service collaborators (Abela and Murphy 2008) who re/produce culture, community and nation.

Gibson-Graham (1996) advocate specific, empirically grounded and socially situated formulations of marketplace activities and circumstances to replace the abstract, generalized and uncritical studies that mystify and reify markets. These methodological and analytic maneuvers are just as vital to the purpose of this essay in deriving public policy insights.

To illustrate the interweaving of social and market dynamics in public policy, I revisit earlier work documenting how Mexican immigrants adapt to the consumption environment in the US (Peñaloza 1994), and conversely, how their presence is welcomed, even competed for by marketers (Peñaloza and Gilly 1999). As part of this project I reviewed the long, convoluted history of immigration in the U.S. Southwest, beginning with immigrants fleeing U.S. recession to live Mexico in 1820 and continuing in counter waves of recruitment, deportation and legalization of Mexican immigrant workers in the US from the 1940s to the present (Peñaloza 1995). I noted that the contributions of Mexican immigrants to U.S. society and economy are obscured in negative, stereotypical depictions of taking jobs from U.S. workers and illegally using social services. Notably, while market targeting legitimizes Mexican immigrants as consumers, such market inclusion does not necessarily extend to social inclusion and enfranchisement. Recommendations encouraged public policy workers to sift through conflicting information, hyperbole and scapegoating, and acknowledge consumption and community contributions as well as those of labour to better comprehend the impact of Mexican immigration in U.S. society. I further encouraged the use of humanistic terms and the development of literacy programs attuned to legal requirements in policy and in marketing, the provision of multilingual sales staff and the translation of business and credit terms. Much has changed since then; people are much more conscious of the political dimensions of consumption and organize for group interests and viability, putting pressure on public policy to balance group treatment. In the next section I turn to organizational and marketing ethics in setting a foundation for ethnic marketing public policy.

Marketing ethics

Carter et al. (2007) identify organizations as important sites constituting ethical judgements and practices. In marketing, Ferrell (2005) emphasizes individual ethical decision making, highlighting the importance of individual moral development and of individual responsibility for ethical transgressions, while acknowledging organizational responsibilities and accountability. He further emphasizes the powerful influence of monetary incentives and pressures stemming from people's dependence on work in earning their livelihood. This view applies to all marketing activities, including advertising, pricing, product development, research, selling and distribution channels in developing an ethical marketing organization (Murphy et al. 2004).

Individual and organizational contexts are important in ethnic marketing public policy. Yet we must go further to consider cultural differences and group interests as well as individual moral judgements and codes of behaviour regarding what is right and wrong in business organizations and to weigh the financial and political pressures impinging upon public policy. Pires and Stanton, this volume, converge with more general studies of marketing ethics in asserting fairness and equal opportunity for all – regardless of ethnicity. Such guidelines provide an important baseline for ethnic marketing public policy. Of particular relevance is monitoring market activity for discriminatory pricing and other unequal treatment. Cultural sensitivity is required to distinguish negative from positive stereotypes, as their more positive uses convey valuable cultural meanings, albeit in somewhat exaggerated forms. These authors are particularly concerned with online ethnic marketing ethics, noting how firms' use of social media impacts ethnic groups in offering members greater abilities as consumers to self-select in and out of markets. While working to promote online technologies that enable access to family and other social and business networks globally, public policy efforts can help bridge digital divisions between mainstream and marginalized ethnic peoples.

Increasing cultural heterogeneity and the accompanying demands for inclusion and acknowledgement by interest groups are dramatically altering the complex terrain of marketing ethics in contemporary societies (Peñaloza 2012). Gustaffson (2005) draws upon the work of gender scholars Benhabib and Young in bringing to the fore the power asymmetries that pertain to the social categories that come into play in organizations. Specifically, Benhabib (1992) directs attention to the limited ability of universal conceptions of the individual to encompass pluralized communicative activities, and suggests dialogic, diverse forms address and exchange to update the social contract to better apply in heterogeneous societies.

Young (1997) stresses that empathizing with others on the basis that they be like oneself has supported humanistic, universalized conceptualizations of ethical judgements and conduct, and that such complementarity often is undermined in multicultural social domains. In adapting organizational ethics to these insights, Gustaffson emphasizes the need to acknowledge social difference and related asymmetries of position and power. Indeed, many studies have documented that social differences are hierarchically organized, such that some differences matter more than others, and that power is detectable in the specific ways in which these differences matter (Delgado and Stefancic 1997; Peñaloza 2007).

In order to acknowledge cultural and power differences Gustaffson counsels organization members to suspend seemingly well-intended presumptions of being capable of ever truly 'knowing' others within and external to the organization. Without these presumptions, organizational members are obliged to interact with others via more open dialogue, presence, and active listening and learning, rather than striving to minimize or erase extant social difference in carrying out idealized forms of 'equal' treatment. Taken together, Gustaffson's (2005) application of Benhabib's (1992) and Young's (1997) work on social plurality and difference offers valuable insights relevant in more adeptly developing public policy regarding ethnic marketing. Explicitly dealing with differences of power related to race/ethnicity, nationality, language, religion, social class and gender in this way allows for different forms of address and communication styles in delivering public services.

In building upon this work, I provide additional philosophical bases for more inclusive and agile ethnic marketing public policy. Among the relevant philosophical insights is Taylor's (1991) work on authenticity. He traces its historical roots to the modernist tendency for individual self-fulfillment. Yet, rather than join the chorus lamenting the disruptive aspects of individuals' search for meaning and the coterminous forms of liberal economy and consumption for destroying common values and communal social forms, Taylor emphasizes the potentially positive implications of relational determinants of authenticity. In order to be authentic, he explains, one must be successfully recognized in this quest by others.

Such mutual recognition is vital in effectively carrying out policy, and yet it is thwarted by reductive characterizations of ethnic/racial peoples. Rhodes and Westwood (2007) assert that the 'foreign' is misrepresented when reduced to Western terms, and they thus challenge the essentialized, exoticized and denigrated representation of foreign others that reduces whole cultures to their 'typical' characteristic(s). While the authors give national examples such as the

Chinese reduced to Confucianism, Germans to authoritarians, British as aristocrats and African managers as primitive, such reductive treatment also occurs for ethnic groups.

Rhodes and Westwood draw upon the work of Lithuanian philosopher Emmanuel Levinas in re-conceptualizing self-other relations as fundamental to advancing our understandings of ethics. Levinas, who lived from 1906 to 1995, was a student of Edmund Husserl and drew upon his work and that of Martin Heidegger to explain how the self exists in relation to others. For Levinas (1998), the self is fundamentally misunderstood as a 'knower' of another because this act of knowing reduces the other to a creation of the self. Such creation is philosophically and practically untenable, because it tends to produce the other as an inferior projection, while constituting the authoring self as an eminently evident, superior being. Extending from Levinas (1998), Rhodes and Westwood (2007) assail historical misrepresentations that justified slavery. Their formula for more ethical treatment of others is based on the mutual recognition and inter-determinacy of social agents. For the self, then, to exist is to be recognized by others. In turn, this existence, as a social manner of being, demands an ethical response to the others who make it possible via their recognition. The self is thus inherently and inexorably connected to others; and because of these interconnections, the self is ethically responsible to others.

By extension, in multicultural society, marketing activity is not limited to economic transactions, nor is it narrowly bound to one ethnic group, but rather necessarily includes the ongoing social exchanges among multiple ethnic groups that precede and follow discrete, quid pro quo economic transactions among people who are increasingly mobile (Bauman 2012). The relational underpinnings of authenticity can be used to strengthen and enrich ethnic marketing public policy regarding the incorporation and reproduction of ethnic difference in ethnic marketing campaigns and, in turn, in the use of – and even reliance on – products and advertising representations by ethnic groups and consumers in forging identity and social relations can be used to strengthen and enrich ethnic marketing public policy. When explicitly recognized in firms, the relationality between a company and its consumers raises the stakes of attaining 'accurate' ethnic representations and practices; just as recognizing the authenticity and legitimacy that such campaigns provide ethnic groups and consumers for identity and community projects raises their stakes in appropriating market-based artifacts and activities. In the remainder of this essay I bring these insights to bear in specific aspects of public policy.

Identity

The incorporation of ethnic identity into consumption and market activity presents challenges and opportunities for public policy. Of particular interest in the market incorporation of ethnic identity is an intricate interweaving of social and market dynamics emphasizing individual choice and cultural freedom of expression (Baudrillard 1988; Bouchet 1995). Scholars have criticized market activity for commoditizing and aestheticizing cultural forms (Gabriel 1994), and for advocating ethnic and racial tolerance and inclusion, while enhancing and institutionalizing cultural divisions and inequalities in opportunity and access to resources (San Juan Jr. 2002).

A major point of contention is that marketing campaigns privilege some forms of identity at the expense of others, and that the forms of identity that marketers incorporate into these campaigns obtain some validation and legitimacy for the group (Bécheur and Toulouse 2012; Comaroff and Comaroff 2009; Peñaloza 2004). It is this social validation of minority ethnic identity as an artifact of market incorporation that some mainstream agents contest, because it challenges their central position within the respective shared social domain, as in the case of the nation. An example in the US is the backlash against Spanish speakers that followed a 2014 Coca-Cola advertisement aired during the Super Bowl football game that featured the

U.S. national anthem sung in multiple languages. An example in France is the mobilization of the National Front political party against the Quick hamburger chain for providing halal burgers (Crumley 2010). Ethnic group members contest target marketing campaigns as well. Congresswoman Lucille Roybal-Allard and the Congressional Hispanic Caucus protested the Tecate beer campaign, 'Finally a Cold Latina', for using humour that depended upon negative stereotyping of Latina women as sexy (Roybal-Allard 2004). As Weibe (1975) noted, the cohesion of separate sub-groups is one of the strengths of the US as a nation. In public policy, acknowledging of ethnic differences in dialogic forms of communication can foster national unity, provided the respective groups are addressed conjointly in mutual recognition.

Chávez, this volume, explains some of the potentially troubling aspects of ethnic identity in advertising agencies. In interrogating the market incorporation of *Latindad*, Latino/a identity, his work builds upon that of Dávila (2001), whose work in advertising agencies highlighted the cultural distance and misrecognition on the part of Cubans working to target advert campaigns to a predominantly Mexican American clientele. Chávez explains further how media specialization and industry concentration drove the formation of Latindad through the 1990s. He emphasizes how a few large organizations consolidated advertising globally by buying out 'specialty' firms targeting ethnic segments and by merging with global partners, and how they together leveraged the growth rate and numbers of Latinos/as in the US and beyond in Central and South America into an ever larger market. He notes with some irony how Latino/a executives in the agencies tend to discount their value added (i.e. cultural knowledge of clients) in seeking more general work with the larger mainstream to avoid being relegated to the 'margin' of the Latino/a market; while clients whose advertising instincts align with the general population contribute to the devaluation of Latino/a executives' cultural knowledge by holding onto myopic dreams that Latinos/as aspire to the mainstream and eventually will assimilate.

The trend over the past three decades in ethnic scholarship has been to challenge and move beyond essentialized treatments of ethnic identity to recognize its performative and situational qualities (Deshpandé and Hoyer 1986; Visconti *et al.* forthcoming). And yet such performative and situational advances in the study of ethnic identity should not eclipse persistent asymmetries. Asymmetrical relations between mainstream and Latino/a consumers and advertising executives are present in the advertising scenario Chávez describes. Implications for ethnic marketing public policy in applying Gustaffson's (2005) work are to acknowledge rather than erase these asymmetries, and from there recognize and validate the distinct, yet interrelational cultural skills and knowledge of Latino/a advert executives and their mainstream minded clients as distinct contributions to the advert agency in their own right, thus validating the integrity and place of Latino/a consumers in U.S. society.

Community

Internal, within-group notions of similarity, bounded by external, out-group distinctions are key markers of community (Barth 1969). There is much work to be done to advance understandings of the collective ethnic community forged in consumption and in markets in processes of internal identity and cohesion and of boundary distinction and maintenance. Regarding the study of ethnic community in marketing, some marketing scholarship remains focused on distinguishing and comparing ethnic group characteristics. Nakata (2009) provides a rich review and critique of the characteristic-based approaches that build upon the work of Geert Hofstede (2001; 1980). While useful in mapping and comparing ethnic communities, the characteristic approach must be supplemented with concerted attention to social relations in carrying out adept ethnic marketing public policy.

In his consideration of space, Visconti, this volume, demonstrates how ethnic groups come together and apart in the city. By applying insights from Taylor (1991) and Rhodes and Westwood (2007), we can develop public policy insights that facilitate the mutual recognition and co-creation of multiple cultural selves in specific places. Harboring the presence of multiple ethnic communities is vital in developing an overall sense of civic society. As Visconti notes, dissecting the workings of space – physically, socio-culturally, ideologically and commercially – enables deeper and more tangible appreciation of social relations. By extending beyond the narrow terms of economic transactions, spatial considerations offer great potential to invigorate ethnic marketing public policy.

Elliot, Cherian and Casakin, this volume, discuss how cultural groups support each other at a localized community festival in Chicago. Here artists bring forth cultural symbols and motifs to consumers who welcome the art and who are increasingly attuned to their role in recognizing and fostering a dynamic and diverse city. The production and exchange of cultural artifacts and processes offer a sound base for the economic advancement of ethnic communities, as Canclini (1995) noted, in providing rich, valuable consumption content for non-members that contributes to positive civic development.

There are potential drawbacks to community in the marketization of ethnicity, however, which Comaroff and Comaroff (2009) address using the terms *ethnicity, incorporated*. Drawing from decades of in-depth ethnographic work, these scholars direct attention to differences of power within cultural groups as well as the pressures and capital extractions from market consultants and others external to the group. Whose culture is represented, how such production and marketing activities are organized and carried out, who consume, and for whose benefit are key considerations in ethnic marketing public policy.

Legacies of colonization

While perhaps seldom thought of as such, market activities retain remnants of former colonial relations in language, customs and trade patterns between former colonizers and colonies (Tigar and Levy 1977), as well as flows of people in both directions. Early forms of market development entailed the extraction of resources and the development of industry by leveraging labour and materials that cost less than at home. At present these forms of market activity are compounded by transnational flows of people, capital and material in the form of products and services, including remittances sent to families by members working in other nations (Peñaloza and Cavazos Arroyo 2011) and energetic international brand communities (Cova 1997; Cova *et al.* 2007) that converge in markets (Peñaloza and Venkatesh 2006).

Ethnicity represents the simultaneous trends of cultural consolidation and differentiation in society and in the marketplace, as ethnic and racial diaspora disseminate and settle across regions and nations with specific multicultural histories and political relations. Public policies may benefit from the integration of Young's (1997) insights that universal conceptualizations of the citizen may be undermined in multicultural society, by acknowledging ethnic difference, not as an end in itself, but rather as a timely and expedient route to uniting peoples within the domain of interest, be it nation, city, neighbourhood or private/public organization.

Ruvalcaba and Venkatesh, this volume, begin with income and education disparities between Whites and Latinos/as, and then discuss how Latino/a entrepreneurs advance their businesses by incorporating social media technologies. There is much to be done in public policy to create wider access and cultural integration of technology by stimulating jobs by and for ethnic community members. And yet such policy may be crippled by cultural misrepresentations similar to those critiqued by Rhodes and Westwood (2007). Cultural misrepresentations that follow from the legacy of colonization may be seen in ethnic mainstream views of their superiority and a corresponding view among ethnic minorities of their inferiority and of business as something done to them by community outsiders and by insider *vendidas* who have 'sold-out', seeking private gain over community benefit (Peñaloza 2005). In policy, this post-colonial view can manifest in paternalistic mainstream posturing, un/conscious attempts to maintain their supe-riority, and well intentioned but short-sighted policies to aid 'vulnerable' minorities that stem from unquestioned and un-self-reflexive mainstream cultural sensibilities and practices. The view among ethnic minority community members that business is the purview of the eth-nic mainstream is just as limiting, and while somewhat grounded in historical experience, this myopic view contributes to the misguided notion that business is apart from the community, privileges labouring members of community and ostracizes ethnic entrepreneurs.

Public policy can foster greater understanding that business is a key aspect of community development, and thus help encourage ethnic/racial group members to make a place for ethnic entrepreneurs within their community. However, those promoting business in policy must be able to distinguish community enabling activities, and extend such evaluations to financial activities as well, including micro-lending. As community members, ethnic entrepreneurs have a responsibility to contribute to those they do business with, by providing jobs and market offerings at reasonable prices, as consistent with contemporary consumers' demands for social responsibility and ethics globally. Indeed, there is a long, sordid history of high prices charged by firms doing business in 'higher risk' ethnic communities (Andreasen 1975), including ethnic communities (Peñaloza and Gilly 1999), which is only partly due to higher insurance costs and lower volume. With growing recognition that business is vital to community development, non-government and non-profit agencies and sustainably oriented firms have stepped in with financial education, counselling and low-cost services. This growth sector in many nations, including developing one's merits both increased validation and scrutiny in policy.

Additional possibilities exist in building upon current public policies that attempt to rec-tify persistent socio-economic differences in income and opportunity by including 'minority' owned businesses in government bids. By considering consumption, policies may be better integrated to value the efforts of firms that hire ethnic workers in proportions greater than their representation in the population overall and those that encourage production of products and services that advance ethnic cultural development. Critics charging ethnic favouritism are parried somewhat by emphasizing in policy the redress for disproportional unemployment or other income and educational disparities affecting all members of ethnic/racial community/ies, and not just racial/ethnic minorities as those with lower income and education in ethnic/racial mainstream groups merit inclusion and advancement as well.

Social movements

Social movements have made and continue to make important contributions towards the growth and development of contemporary ethnic formations. Their mix of spontaneous activ-ity and formal organization is evident in demonstrations and meetings, some of which later become national and regional holidays celebrated within the larger social domain. Key histori-cal incidents and events in the Black, Chicano, women's and Gay/Lesbian movements – to name a few, etched in the writings, speeches, and pop cultural products of activists, artists, scholars and educational, religious and political leaders become internalized in the collec-tive memory of the community (Hampton 1985; Scagliotti 1985). The widespread activism through the 1960s and '70s across the globe challenged ethnic as well as racial and gender hierarchies and lopsided participation in socio-economic activity and distributions of wealth.

Indeed, the Civil Rights legislation that followed also must be credited to host of activists, organizations and public policy.

For Latinos/as in the US specifically, the GI Forum initially mobilized to bury Mexican American soldiers killed during WWII yet denied access to White-only cemeteries (Acuña 1988), while the League of United Latin American Citizens (LULAC) strove to register voters and desegregate public swimming pools through the 1950s among its other social functions including balls and dances. The 1980 U.S. Census inclusion is another landmark event for the Latino/a community in the US. In it we can see the tremendous impact of ethnic marketing public policy and how it is situated at the nexus of social and economic development. This official count of the number of Latinos/as in the US provided credible support for what later would become advertisers' and marketers' 'discovery' of the U.S. Latino/a market (Chávez, this volume), consolidating and legitimizing a common identity and community from a heterogeneous social group totalling over 500 million persons worldwide, roughly ten times greater than the colonizing nation, Spain, with just under 50 million people.

Social movements formed in the 1960s and '70s privileged labour and often denigrated consumption through the 1980s and '90s (Peñaloza 2004). While labour is still important, contemporary movement leaders are realizing the benefits of incorporating consumption dynamics in ways that foster its impact, as consumption is the site of much contemporary ethnic group activity. Indeed, how to channel the energy in ethnic group consumption, such that it translates to cultural awareness, skill building and jobs, is a valuable path to the continued viability of the movement and the larger communities within which they reside.

Izberk-Bilgin (this volume) examines ethnic and religious social movements in people's consumption and connections to brands, with attention to the simultaneous trends towards and away from religion in consumption and markets. Her findings are particularly significant in public policy, given the ever-larger numbers of migrant workers, tourists, expatriates, refugees and students who cross borders and, in the process of doing so, encounter and mobilize against what they perceive to be cultural threats from the 'religiously other'. More specifically, her insights at the intersection of religion, identity and social relations are potentially valuable to policy makers in better understanding how consumption, markets and governments come into play in people's pursuit of personal meaning and spiritual transcendence.

Contemporary social movements play an important role in the lives of ethnic peoples and communities in challenging and reinforcing social, political and economic traditions and institutions, with important public policy implications. The Arab Spring is one of the most dramatic in a long line of movement activity, giving hope to many even as others use its accompanying developments to inculcate fear, with implications affecting ethnic peoples and intergroup relations worldwide. Sadly, the prevalence of guns and violence in media and in popular cultural representations of ethnic groups have normalized these means of addressing cultural differences while contributing to the misguided equation of ethnic groups with terrorism, exacerbating stereotypes and accelerating conflict.

Public policy can help provide solutions. How a movement forms often reflects a crystallization of group identity and interests (Toch 1965), and so movement leaders are challenged to unite the group while addressing particular issues affecting its substrata. For public policy workers, social movement leaders represent access to the ethnic community, and yet addressing their concerns must be undertaken with a concerted eye towards external group differences within the relevant social domain. It is important that public policies reinforce human rights and principles of freedom, and safeguard those rights and freedoms up to the point when they impinge upon the rights and freedom of others. The integrating aspects of policy are of the utmost concern in helping channel movement activity towards appreciation and cohabitation with others and away from divisiveness and destruction.

Acculturation

It is rare today in social discourse, except among the most conservative groups, to see the sole focus on assimilation. Much more common is discussion of the retention of cultural values and traditions and awareness of multicultural, hybrid cultural expressions. Academic scholarship parallels these social developments. Begun as studies of assimilation, latter developments focus on adaptation (Peñaloza 1994), culture swapping (Oswald 1999), identity (Askegaard et al. 2005) and social relations (Luedicke 2011). Much more work is needed to better understand how people living in multicultural societies interact and change, and how consumption serves as the terrain for cultural adaption, identity development, community formation and the forging of social relationships. Further work is also called for examining how consumption and market actors find opportunity in all aspects of acculturation, including cultural assimilation, retention, the hybrid display of cultural traditions, and the consolidation, integration and separation of ethnic cultural groups.

Acculturation poses tremendous opportunities and challenges for public policy. On one hand people are increasingly obliged to express a unique and authentic identity in consumption (Campbell 2004), and one of the areas where acculturation is visible and measured is in market and consumption activity. On the other hand, distinction from the cultural mainstream is increasingly commoditized by marketers and expressed by people in consumption (Heath and Potter 2010). Such obligations and expressions converge in the reduction of ethnicity to a personal choice (Roosens 1989) and an economic expedient that can eclipse the complexities of acculturation and slight the support of identity and community in ethnic entrepreneurship (Mehmood, this volume; Light and Gold 2000).

Increasing mobility has become a valid topic for ethnic marketing public policy, as the mobility of ethnic groups colludes with and impinges upon their assimilation, resistance and hybrid negotiations, raising internal challenges of co-existence and cohesion and affecting external, between-group relations. Immigration particularly continues to test public policy, as evident in ongoing and heated debates and even posses that assemble at the U.S.–Mexican border to control immigration, most recently including youth from Latin America unaccompanied by their parents or adult guardians (Navarette Jr. 2014). Balancing constituents' concerns for border security, family unification and labour demands on one hand with concerns for humane treatment, domestic jobs and group fairness is vital in contemporary ethnic marketing public policy.

Segmentation

In the introductory essay to their classic work, *Marketing in a Multicultural World*, Janeen Costa and Gary Bamossey (1995) pondered the growing prevalence and impact of cultural groups in markets as impacted by the dramatic growth of emerging nations, trade blocks, tribal and national conflicts, migratory movements, and remittance payments, together with global corporate diffusion and product, service and capital flows. In various ways a host of scholars in the field of marketing build upon this work in acknowledging two general, simultaneous, and seemingly contradictory trends, homogeneity and heterogeneity, as cultural subjects and groups engage with, and resist marketization. The attention to the lived experiences of consumers and markers in consumer cultural studies (Belk et al. 2013; Ekstrom and Brembeck 2004; Joy and Li 2012) and in transformative consumer research (Visconti et al. 2014), specifically, provides valuable insights into ethnic marketing public policy.

Lindridge, this volume, situates market segmentation as an artifact of its time, following the ethnic, racial and gender social movements of the 1960s and 1970s mobilizing for recognition and fair and equal treatment before the law and in public policy. Indeed, market segmentation offers advantages to firms; in mapping micro-segments, they are able to better understand and develop markets. However, because it divides people into groups based on different characteristics and customs, market segmentation works in ways quite distinct and even somewhat opposed to the unifying concerns of public policy. The attention to lived experiences of market activity characterizing consumer cultural studies (Belk *et al.* 2013; Ekström and Brembeck 2004; Joy and Li 2012) and transformative consumer research (Visconti *et al.* 2014) provides valuable insights. Public policy development and implementation can benefit from mapping cultural group differences in sensibilities and traditions and incorporating them in manners of address that accomplish greater social inclusion and representation. Further, by operating at the level of shared values and experiences enabling convergence among distinct ethnic groups, policy makers can facilitate the reconstitution and reaffirmation of the shared, cohabited multi-ethnic social domain, be it neighbourhood, city, or nation.

Targeting

Developing distinct products and services, advertising/promotions, prices and distribution tailored specifically to group differences, including ethnic differences, has been one of the hallmarks of modern marketing. Indeed, as corporate efforts target ethnic/racial groups, their market incorporation can work with or against the interests and internal workings of ethnic/racial subcultures.

Regarding ethnic marketing public policy, one area that consistently receives criticism is the targeting of alcohol and cigarettes to Latino/a and Black minority consumers and their communities (Maxwell and Jacobson 1989; Moore *et al.* 1996). And yet, only while less controversial, as problematic is the targeting of high sugar, salt and fat content foods, such as soft drinks, candy and fried foods to Latinos/as and Blacks, given their higher rates of obesity and diabetes. Public policy warnings that feature dialogic forms of address on labels and announcements for moderation in consumption are welcome in all of these areas.

As importantly, public policy can help realign social divisions by incorporating cultural group differences in sensibilities and traditions in service delivery in order to accomplish the goals of more equal economic opportunity and participation. Nationalist cultural identities and ideals housed in an ethnic/racial mainstream can pose a challenge when not welcoming ethnic/racial minorities in specific social domains. Thus, reaffirming the mainstream while explicitly recognizing the value and importance of ethnic/racial minorities is essential in carrying out unifying public policy that serves the national mandates of fair and equal treatment.

A pedagogy of ethnic consumption

In public policy, ethnic/racial differences are but one of many axes of relevant social difference to monitor and address, together with religion, age, gender, education and income. Public policies positioning ethnic groups, and not just individual members, as valuable entities in their own right, worthy of recognition, address and treatment as equal participants in society and in the marketplace, offer much potential to advance citizen discourses and practices rejuvenating national unity and sovereignty.

However, we have a long way to go to get there. Market discourses tend to emphasize the economic gains of a few over those of the many, and thus it is important to sift through their overlaps with, and divergences from, the concerns of public policy. Indeed, the democratic ideals of inclusion, equal representation and opportunity, and fraternity have served as key ideological constraints on the social hierarchies fostered in capitalist market systems, especially capital over labour and the privilege determined by socio-economic endowment rather than merit, even as people hold market organizations to ever higher standards of social responsibility and environmental sustainability.

The future of nations depends on the vitality of their people and their natural resources. Still, many nations are characterized by uneven economic development and political difference set against the backdrop of post-colonial social relations, the continued struggles for the enfranchisement of indigenous and minority peoples, and the nationalistic demands of the ethnic/racial mainstream (Figueiredo *et al.* forthcoming). In both public policy and research, ethnicity presents valuable opportunities and challenges to advance and document novel forms of market and consumer culture that accomplish multicultural, collective, democratic ideals.

A key obstacle limiting public policy workers' and marketing researchers' ability to comprehend the social implications of ethnic consumption is its bifurcation from labour. And yet public policy workers and marketing academics join educators as border crossers (Giroux 1992) who can help realign their separate treatment in policy and research. With further research and policy development and implementation it is possible to recognize ethnic consumer buying power as a national resource to foster in addition to capital and labour. Indeed, consumption is a powerful socio-economic force that validates and legitimizes ethnic groups, and yet it can be divisive as the means of expressing and structuring status distinctions and cultural difference and in eclipsing labour and production considerations. Adept ethnic marketing public policy that reunites consumption, labour, and capital can help translate market inclusion into social inclusion that will benefit our nations, cities and neighborhoods.

References

Abela, A. and Murphy, P. (2008) 'Marketing with integrity: Ethics and the service-dominant logic for marketing'. *Academy of Marketing Science Journal*, 36: 39–53.

Acuña, R. (1988) *Occupied America: The Conquest and Colonization of the U.S. Southwest.* New York: Harper Collins.

Andreasen, Alan (1975) *The Disadvantaged Consumer.* Washington, DC: Free Press.

Askegaard, S., Arnould, E. J. and Kjeldgaard, D. (2005) 'Postassimilationist ethnic consumer research: Qualifications and extensions'. *Journal of Consumer Research*, 32: 160–70.

Barth, F. (1969) *Ethnic Groups and Boundaries. The Social Organization of Culture.* New York: Little Brown and Co.

Baudrillard, J. (1988) 'Consumer society', in *Jean Baudrillard, Selected Writings,* edited by Mark Poster. Stanford, CA: Stanford University Press, pp. 29–57.

Bauman, Z. (2012) *Liquid Modernity.* Cambridge: Polity Press, pp. 53–90.

Belk, R., W., Price, L. and Peñaloza, L. eds. (2013) *Consumer Culture Theory.* London: Emerald.

Benhabib, S. (1992) *Situating the Self: Gender, Community, and Postmodernism in Contemporary Ethics.* NY: Routledge.

Bevir, M. and Trentmann, F. eds. (2004) *Markets in Historical Context: Ideas and Politics in the Modern World.* Cambridge: Cambridge University Press.

Bouchet, D. (1995) 'Marketing and the redefinition of ethnicity'. In *Marketing in a Multicultural World,* edited by J. A. Costa and G. J. Bamossy. London: Sage Publications, pp. 68–104.

Bjerrisgaard, S. and Kjeldgaard, D. (2012) 'The way you see is what you get: Market research as modes of knowledge production'. In *Marketing Management: A Cultural Approach,* edited by Lisa Peñaloza, Nil Toulouse, and Luca Visconti. London: Routledge, pp. 231–45.

Campbell, C. (2004) 'I shop therefore I know that I am: The metaphysical basis of modern consumption'. In *Elusive Consumption,* edited by Karin Ekström and Helene Brembeck. Oxford: Berg, pp. 27–44.

Canclini, N. G. (1995) *Culturas híbridas: Estrategias para entrar y salir de la modernidad.* Buenos Aires: Sudamericana.

Carter, C., Stewart C., Kornberger, M., Laske, S. and Messner, M. eds. (2007) *Business Ethics As Practice.* Cheltenham, UK: Edward Elgar, pp. 68–83.

Lisa Peñaloza

Comaroff, J. and Comaroff, J. (2009) *Ethnicity, Inc.* Chicago: University of Chicago Press.

Costa, J. and Bamossy, G. (1995) 'Perspectives on ethnicity, nationalism, and cultural identity'. *Marketing in a Multicultural World: Ethnicity, Nationalism, and Cultural Identity*, edited by J. Costa and G. Bamossy. Newbury Park: Sage, pp. 1–25.

Cova, B. (1997) 'Community and consumption: towards a definition of the linking value of products and services'. *European Journal of Marketing*, 31(3/4): 297–316.

Cova, B. and Dalli, D. (2009) 'Working consumers: The next step in marketing theory?' *Marketing Theory*, 9(3): 315–39.

Cova, B., Kozinets, R. and Shankar, A. (2007) *Consumer Tribes.* Amsterdam: Butterworth-Heinemann.

Crumley, B. (2010) 'Halal burgers? Another French brouhaha over Islam'. *Time Magazine* [online]. Available from: http://content.time.com/time/world/article/0,8599,1967299,00.html [accessed February 24, 2015].

Dávila, A. (2001) *Latinos Inc.: The Marketing and Making of a People.* Berkeley, CA: University of California Press.

Delgado, R. and Stefancic, J. (1997) *Critical White Studies: Looking Behind the Mirror.* Philadelphia, PA: Temple University Press.

Deshpandé, R., Hoyer, W. D. and Donthu, N. (1986) 'The intensity of ethnic affiliation: A study of the sociology of hispanic consumption'. *Journal of Consumer Research*, 13: 214–20.

Ekström, K. and Brembeck, H. (2004) *Elusive Consumption.* Oxford: Berg.

Ferrell, O. C. (2005) 'A framework for understanding organizational ethics'. In *Business Ethics: New Challenges for Business Schools and Corporate Leaders*, edited by R. A. Peterson and O. C. Ferrell. Armonk, NY: N. E. Sharpe, pp. 3–17.

Figueiredo, B., Chelekis, J., DeBerry-Spence, B., Fırat, F., Ger, G., Nuttavuthisit, K., Tadajewski, M., Godefroit-Winkel D. (forthcoming) 'Development and markets: The good, the bad and the ugly'. *Journal of MacroMarketing.*

Friedman, T. (2008) 'Palin's kind of patriotism'. *New York Times*, October 7.

Gabriel, J. (1994) *Racism, Culture, Markets.* London: Routledge.

Gibson-Graham, J. K. (1996) *The End of Capitalism (as we knew it).* Oxford: Blackwell.

Giroux, H. (1992) *Border Crossings: Cultural Workers and the Politics of Education.* New York: Sage.

Gustaffson, C. (2005) 'Trust as an instance of asymmetrical reciprocity: An ethics perspective on corporate brand management'. *Business Ethics: A European Review*, 14(2): 142–50.

Hampton, Henry (1985) *Eyes on the Prize.* Documentary film. Boston: Blackside Productions.

Harvey, D. (2007) *A Brief History of Neoliberalism.* Oxford: Oxford University Press.

Heath, J. and Potter, A. (2010) *Nation of Rebels.* New York: Harper Collins.

Hofstede, G. (1980) *Culture's Consequences: International Differences in Work Related Values.* Newbury Park: Sage.

Hofstede, G. (2001) *Culture's Consequences: Comparing Values, Behaviors, Institutions, and Organization across Nations.* Thousand Oaks: Sage.

Jenkins, R. (1997) *Rethinking Ethnicity: Arguments and Explorations.* London: Sage.

Joy, A. and Li, E. (2012) 'Studying consumption behavior through multiple lenses: An overview of consumer culture theory'. *Journal of Business Anthropology*, 1(1): 141–73.

Kroen, S. (2006) 'Negotiations with the American way: The consumer and the social contract in post-war Europe'. In *Consuming Cultures, Global Perspectives: Historical Trajectories, Transnational Exchanges.* Oxford: Berg, pp. 251–277.

Levinas, E. (1998) *Otherwise Than Being: Or Beyond Essence.* Pittsburg, PA: Duquesne University Press.

Light, I. and Gold, S. (2000) *Ethnic Economies.* San Diego, CA: Academic Press.

Luedicke, M. (2011) 'Consumer acculturation theory: (Crossing) Conceptual boundaries'. *Consumption Markets & Culture*, 14(3): 223–44.

Lui, M., Robles, B., Leondar-Wright, B., Brewer, R. and Adamson, R. with United for a Fair Economy (2006) *The Color of Wealth: The Story Behind the U.S. Racial Wealth Divide.* New York: The New Press.

Maxwell, B. and Jacobson, M. (1989) *Marketing Disease to Hispanics.* Washington, D.C.: Center for Science in the Public Interest.

Moore, D., Williams, J. and Qualls, W. (1996) 'Target marketing of tobacco and alcohol-related products to ethnic minority groups in the U.S'. *Ethnicity and Disease*, 6: 83–98.

Murphy, P., Laczniak, G., Bowie, N. and Klein, T. (2004) *Ethical Marketing.* NY: Pearson.

Nakata, C. (2009) *Beyond Hofstede: Culture Frameworks for Global Marketing and Management.* Chicago, IL: Palgrave Macmillan.

Navarette Jr., R. (2014) 'Cruz doesn't get it: Senator's interpretation of immigrant crisis is wrong and will hurt his 2016 run'. *The Monitor* [online]. Available from: http://m.themonitor.com/opinion/commentary-cruz-doesn-t-get-it------senator/article_ff23b71e-1840-11e4-af2f-0017a43b2370.html?mode=jqm.

Oswald, R. L. (1999) 'Culture swapping: Consumption and the ethnogenesis of middle-class Haitian immigrants'. *Journal of Consumer Research*, 25: 303–18.

Peñaloza, L. N. (1994) 'Atravesando fronteras/border crossing: A critical ethnographic exploration of the consumer acculturation of Mexican immigrants'. *Journal of Consumer Research*, 21(1): 32–54.

Peñaloza, L. (1995) 'Immigrant consumers: Marketing and public policy considerations in the global economy'. *Journal of Public Policy & Marketing*, 14(1): 83–94.

Peñaloza, L. (2004) 'Multiculturalism in the new world order: Implications for the study of consumer behaviour'. In *Elusive Consumption: Tracking New Research Perspectives*, edited by K. Ekström and H. Brembeck. Oxford: Berg Publishers, pp. 87–109.

Peñaloza, L. (2005) *Generaciones/Generations: Cultural Identity, Memory, and the Market*. Documentary film, 48 min. Minidv.

Peñaloza, L. (2007) 'Research with ethnic communities'. In *The Handbook of Qualitative Research in Marketing*, edited by R. Belk. Cheltenham, UK: Edward Elgar, pp. 547–59.

Peñaloza, L. (2012) 'Ethics'. In *Marketing Management: A Cultural Approach*, edited by N. Toulouse and L. Visconti. London: Routledge, pp. 505–26.

Peñaloza, L. and Gilly, M. (1999) 'Marketers' acculturation: The changer and the changed'. *Journal of Marketing*, 63(3): 84–104.

Peñaloza, L. and Cavazos Arroyo, J. (2011) 'Here, there, and beyond: Remittances in transnational family consumption'. *Theoría y Praxis*, 10(December): 131–61.

Peñaloza, L. and Venkatesh, A. (2006) 'Further evolving the new dominant logic of marketing: From services to the social construction of markets'. *Marketing Theory*, 6(3): 299–316.

Rhodes, C. and Westwood, B. (2007) 'Letting knowledge go: Ethics and representation of the other in international and cross-cultural management'. In *Business Ethics as Practice*, edited by C. Carter, S. Clegg, M. Kornberger, S. Laske and M. Messner. Cheltenham, UK: Edward Elgar, pp. 68–83.

Roosens, A. (1989) *Creating Ethnicity: The Process of Ethnogenesis*. Thousand Oaks: Sage.

Roybal-Allard, L. (2004) 'Congresswoman Lucille Roybal-Allard and members of the Congressional Hispanic Caucus protest "racist and sexist" Tecate beer ad'. Available from: http://roybal-allard.house.gov/news/documentsingle.aspx?DocumentID=129762. Press release, May 14.

San Juan Jr. E. (2002) *Racism and Cultural Studies*. Durham, North Carolina: Duke University Press.

Scagliotti, J. (1985) *Before Stonewall*. Documentary film. New York: Robert Rosenberg, John Scagliotti, and Greta Schiller.

Slater, D. and Tonkiss F. (2001) *Market Society: Markets and Modern Social Theory*. Cambridge, UK: Polity.

Taylor, C. (1991) *The Ethics of Authenticity*. Cambridge MA: Harvard University Press.

Tigar, M. and Levy, M. (1977) *Law and the Rise of Capitalism*. New York: Monthly Review Press.

Toch, H. (1965) *The Social Psychology of Social Movements*. Indianapolis: Bobbs-Merrill.

Visconti, L. M., Jafari, A., Batat, W., Broeckerhoffd, A., Dedeoglue, A. O., Demangeotf, C., Kipnis, E., Lindridge, A., Peñaloza, L., Pullig, C., Regany, F., Ustundaglik, E. and Weinberger, M. F. (2014) 'Consumer ethnicity three decades after: A TCR agenda'. *Journal of Marketing Management*, 30(17–18): 1882–922; Published Online 08 Sep.

Weibe, R. (1975) *The Segmented Society: An Introduction to the Meaning of America*. Oxford: Oxford University Press.

Williams, R. (1975) *Keywords*. London: Fontana.

Young, I. M. (1997) *Intersecting Voices: Dilemmas of Gender, Political Philosophy and Policy*. Princeton, NJ: Princeton University Press.

Zwick, D. and Dholakia, N. (2012) 'Strategic database marketing: Customer profiling as new product development'. In *Marketing Management: A Cultural Approach*, edited by L. Peñaloza, N. Toulouse and L. Visconti. London: Routledge, pp. 443–58.

Index

For Product Safety Concerns and Information please contact our EU
representative GPSR@taylorandfrancis.com Taylor & Francis Verlag GmbH,
Kaufingerstraße 24, 80331 München, Germany

Printed and bound by CPI Group (UK) Ltd, Croydon, CR0 4YY
08/05/2025
01864358-0008